Three Bhakti Voices

'Among all the contemporary Western scholars of Hindi language and literature, John Stratton Hawley occupies a special place as the pre-eminent *bhakta* of the bhakti poets, both as a fine and lively translator and as an acute and sympathetic interpreter. I value him even more, however, for his extensive competence in both the Indian and the Western modes of approaching an Indian literature, and for his candid problematization of the great gap between the two modes. This is the concern writ large in this book, and this is what makes it an especially worthwhile contribution to Indian literary studies.'

—Harish Trivedi,
Professor of English, University of Delhi

'This carefully sequenced series of essays shows what can be achieved when expertise in textual history is paired with a sympathetic reading of primary texts themselves. Jack Hawley's forensic analysis of the processes through which devotional works are transmitted seeks not to undermine their status by showing how they have "grown in the telling", but rather to explain the phenomenon of their popular appeal...; the result is a thoroughly engaging study of Sur, Mira, Kabir, and many other stars of the devotional firmament. This book will rapidly earn a place alongside Hawley's *Songs of the Saints of India* as an authoritative history of devotional literature of the late medieval period.'

—Rupert Snell,
Director of the Hindi Urdu Flagship and Professor,
University of Texas, Austin

'Hawley's style has a flair of its own. Involved yet objective, nuanced yet lucid, he writes with a rare mix of emotion and detachment. His very fine sense of humour makes reading this book a pleasure.'

—Purushottam Agrawal,
:e Commission

'Hawley's arguments are well substantiated by references to both poetry and hagiography...[He] ventures into contemporary times and studies how the popular Amar Chitra Katha comic book series reconstructs the lives of the Bhakti poets...*Three Bhakti Voices* is a fine work of scholarship and an important addition to the corpus of literature on Bhakti.'

—*The Telegraph*

'His lively style and many beautiful translations (his own and others') throughout make the volume immensely readable for both specialists and non specialists...'

—*International Journal of Hindu Studies*

Three Bhakti Voices

Mirabai, Surdas, and Kabir in Their Time and Ours

JOHN STRATTON HAWLEY

OXFORD
UNIVERSITY PRESS

OXFORD
UNIVERSITY PRESS

Oxford University Press is a department of the University of Oxford.
It furthers the University's objective of excellence in research, scholarship,
and education by publishing worldwide. Oxford is a registered trademark of
Oxford University Press in the UK and in certain other countries

Published in India by
Oxford University Press
YMCA Library Building, 1 Jai Singh Road, New Delhi 110 001, India

First Edition published in 2005
Oxford India Paperbacks 2012

ISBN-13: 978-0-19-808539-3
ISBN-10: 0-19-808539-7

Typeset in Naurang 10.5/12.6
by Excellent Laser Typesetters, Pitampura, Delhi 110 034
Printed in India by Replika Press Pvt. Ltd., Haryana 131028

For Nell,
who decided to come along

Contents

SURDAS

KABIR

Preface to the Paperback Edition

In the seven years that have transpired since *Three Bhakti Voices* was first published, some important developments in scholarship have made Mirabai, Surdas, and Kabir live in a new way, both as creatures of their own time and of ours. Their own time, of course, was the fifteenth–sixteenth century, the early modern period. But the very use of the term 'early modern' points the way to one of these arresting new areas of research. A vibrant group of international scholars, Sheldon Pollock and Sanjay Subrahmanyam prominent among them, have urged with gathering force that we give true credit to global flows that connected sixteenth-century India to what was happening elsewhere in the world. Would it not be better, as in the European case, to see this period in Indian history as continuous with what was to come—modernity—rather than relegating it to the dusty closet called 'medieval'? For our 'three bhakti voices', no one has pursued this argument more vigorously than Purushottam Agrawal in his much-discussed *Akath Kahānī Prem Kī: Kabīr kī Kavitā aur unkā Samay* (Delhi: Rājkamal Prakāśan, 2009). Agrawal makes the case that Kabir participated in the new power that was experienced by mercantile and artisan groups of his time; this makes full sense of the fact that his poetry travelled in the same networks of circulation that they did.

Kabir's modernity—the indigenous *ādhuniktā* to which Agrawal addresses himself—has also advanced in other ways since 2005. Consider, for example, the 'Kabir Project' spearheaded by Shabnam Virmani, where we find several musical recordings, four new films, and a myriad of consciousness-raising events all indexed in a single web site (http://www.kabirproject.org). Or in another vein, consider the freshly contemporary translations that Arvind Krishna Mehrotra provides in his *Songs of Kabir* (Delhi: Permanent Black and New York: New York Review of Books, 2011). Here Kabir is able to say that

Those who are not
Devotees of Rama
Should be in Sing Sing
Or still unborn.

Finally, let us note the appearance of Linda Hess's *Singing Emptiness: Kumar Gandharva Performs the Poetry of Kabir* (London, New York, Kolkata: Seagull Books, 2009), where a book shares its jacket with a compact disc. In each of these recent expressions, Kabir is not just early modern but late modern and postmodern at the same time.

With Surdas other kinds of developments have transpired since the first edition of *Three Bhakti Voices*. Most dramatic of all, perhaps, is the publication of Kishori Lal Gupta's *Sampūrṇ Sūrsāgar* in five volumes (Allahabad: Lokbhāratī, 2005). In launching this immense project, Gupta daringly tries to distribute the entire corpus of poetry attributed to Surdas between two distinct poets of that name—the one who was initiated by Vallabhācārya and became a founding member of the 'eight seals' (*aṣṭachāp*) and the one who appears in Abu'l Fazl's records as a musician in the court of Akbar. Readers of *Three Bhakti Voices* will rightly conclude that I do not think Gupta's arguments for bifurcating the Sur corpus in this way can be sustained, but the effort is spectacular and the commentary this venerable scholar provides for poems of the *Sūrsāgar* itself is exceedingly valuable.

A very different image of Surdas—the Sur who can be inferred if we separate the poems that circulated in his name in the sixteenth century from those that were added to the *Sūrsāgar* later on—will soon be brought to light by the publication of *Surdas: Poems from the Early Tradition.* There Kenneth Bryant's critical reconstructions of Brajbhāṣā texts for 433 poems found in early manuscripts will be paired with my English translations in a facing-page edition to be published by Harvard University Press (Cambridge, 2013) in its new Murty Classical Library of India. An exciting feature of this project is that it aims simultaneously to restore the poet's sixteenth-century voice insofar as is possible—his early modernity, so to speak—while making that voice available at a reasonable price to readers who live five centuries later, both in India and abroad. For this visionary project, which involves many more classics than the *Sūrsāgar,* we are indebted to the general editorship of Sheldon Pollock and the generous subvention provided by N. R. Narayana Murthy, the Founder-Chairman of Infosys, and his family.

Finally, there is Mirabai. Ever the most elusive of our 'three bhakti voices'—the poet for whom there is no independent textual corpus, the poet whose distinct voice and historical presence are hardest to ascertain—Mirabai has remained as elusive in the years that have followed the original publication of this book as she was before. Luckily, we can anticipate the release of Nancy Martin's comprehensive study *Mirabai* from Oxford University Press of New York, and there has been a steady stream of conferences, recordings, and films that provide testimony to the fact that Mira's inspiration continues to be felt just as broadly as that of Kabir or Surdas. More than either of the male poets, she seems to invite people of our own time to inhabit her received persona and merge their lives with hers. It makes one think of how Krishna is said to have merged her life with his when she arrived at his great temple in Dvaraka after many years of searching, but it also makes us aware of how we ourselves are apt always to be searching for anything that might resemble a historical Mirabai.

Three Bhakti Voices, then: they continue to be heard.

Preface to the First Edition

This book gathers the work of many years. Some chapters are making their first appearance here, but others have long since seen the light of printed day. This has presented two problems as I have tried to knead them into a coherent whole. First, there have been occasions when the progress of scholarship—even my own scholarship—since the original date of publication has caused me to want to update as I edited, and I have felt free to do so. Chapter 9 provides a dramatic example. When I framed 'The Early *Sūrsāgar* and the Growth of the Sur Tradition' for print in 1979, the contents of the earliest Surdas manuscript had not yet been fully revealed. Now they have, and it's been not only possible but essential to revise the chapter's content accordingly. I have tried to make those emendations without changing the spirit of the original essay, which fortunately (I think) can still stand. Sometimes I have also thought it important to augment a chapter's notes to reflect developments that have affected a given area of scholarship since the time when an essay was first published, but largely I have relied on annotations included in the book as a whole to do this job.

A second issue concerns these essays' individual integrity as they don color-coordinated uniforms and line themselves up as chapters in a book. I have tried to strike a balance between the old and the new, making it still possible for a reader to approach an individual essay in its own terms, while at the same time pointing to the interconnectedness of the whole. For this reason there is a bit more repetition than might be expected in a book exclusively intended to be read cover to cover. Individual chapters typically state the bases for the claims they make—the editions I am using, the poems I accept as relevant, the early narratives I feature—and there is some overlap from one chapter to the next as I try to spare selective readers the necessity of searching through prior chapters for the information they need to understand the one at hand. I have also sometimes wanted to preserve the mood or circumstance that gave rise to a particular essay, which means that readers will occasionally find themselves present after the fact at events they missed the first time around. The study of Sur's Sudāmā in Chapter 11, for instance, emerged from a conference honoring John Carman on the occasion of his retirement and was written to honor not just a scholarly but a personal connection, like Sudāmā in relation to Krishna. I hope this will add spice to the book, not distraction.

In pulling the volume together, I have been struck by the variety of settings in which these chapters first emerged. In the headnotes that begin each chapter, I have tried to record my gratitude to the friends, colleagues, and students who were involved as all of that transpired. I am also grateful to persons associated with the presses and journals where earlier versions of certain chapters initially appeared, for permission to reprint them here: *The Journal of Asian Studies,* the University of California Press, the State University of New York Press, Oxford University Press of New York, the University of Pennsylvania Press, Beacon Press, Oneworld Press, the *Journal of the American Oriental Society,* the *Journal of Vaiṣṇava Studies,* Cambridge University Press, the University of Washington Press, and the Indian Council for Cultural Relations.

I am deeply indebted to the institutions where I have worked as various parts of this book developed: the University of Washington, Columbia University, and especially Barnard College. For the financial and personal support that grants, fellowships, and academic leaves have provided through the years, I owe thanks to the American Institute of Indian Studies, the Andrew Mellon Foundation, Barnard College, the John Simon Guggenheim Foundation, the Smithsonian Institution, the National Endowment for the Humanities, and the donors of the Ann Whitney Olin Chair at Barnard. Nitasha Devasar and the editorial team at Oxford University Press, Delhi, have been wonderfully helpful in the final publication process. James Hare and Tynisha Rue enabled me to overcome the difficulties inevitably posed by being far from my New York office during most of the time when the book was in preparation.

Countless people have contributed cheer, good sense, and a generous dose of humanity as I worked in India in the academic year 2003–2004. I would particularly like to mention the devoted staff of the Landour Language School in Mussoorie, the Sri Caitanya Prema Sansthana in Brindavan, and the India International Centre in Delhi, and to recognize the stimulating friendship of Mukund Lath, Sunil Kumar, Suman and Purushottam Agrawal, and Subhag and B. P. Singh. The Singhs transformed the environment in which the book took shape by offering me the chance to set up shop in their remarkable Landour retreat. Day by day, just beyond the computer screen I watched the intimate comforts of the monsoon give way to the vast, inspiring clarity of autumn.

Finally, let me express my thanks to the handful of people whose contribution to this book has been so profound that it goes well beyond a single chapter or even several: Ken Bryant and Vidyut Aklujkar, for their masterful handling of editorial problems connected with early manuscripts of the *Sūrsāgar*; Mark Juergensmeyer for help in translating many of the poems that appear here, especially in the early stages; Krishna Chaitanya Bhatt and Shrivatsa Goswami for deep and illuminating discussions of compositions attributed to Surdas; and Laura Shapiro for a quality of perception that often brought my thoughts into an otherwise elusive alignment. To be married to such an editor is an amazing thing.

The book is dedicated with great love to our daughter Nell, who defied every expectation by suddenly deciding to take her own sabbatical from the whirl of New York life in fall, 2003. She found the other side of the world so pleasurable and challenging—and somehow, so much her own—that she quickly determined to stay the whole year. I wonder what comes next.

Transliteration and Abbreviation

The task of transliterating various forms of Hindi from their Devanagari original into the Roman alphabet is a dangerous, delicate job, akin to tight-rope walking. Indological purists will expect true consistency and perhaps fealty to the system of transliteration that has become normative for Sanskrit; speakers of Hindi will find this hopelessly arcane and ill-suited to the rhythms of their language; and readers of English will find it a bit much if words long familiar there are gussied up unnecessarily with dots and macrons. What to do?

This book has several layers and a range of possible readers. One of its aims is to present text from manuscripts many centuries old in a way that will enable readers to reconstruct the original. Fortunately this will not be necessary when entire poems are quoted: these appear in Devanagari. If they are derived from a single manuscript, that manuscript is conveyed verbatim, except that word boundaries have been introduced to make reading easier and indicate the basis for choices affecting translation and interpretation. If I am working from a critical edition—principally the *Sūrsāgar* edition of Kenneth E. Bryant—I make that clear.

When I introduce Hindi or Sanskrit words into the main text, however, transliteration comes into play, bringing with it a series of challenges. For instance, a particular feature of sixteenth- and seventeenth-century manuscripts of Brajbhāṣā and related streams of Hindi is that they almost always represent the gutteral aspirant *kh* as *ṣ*, which in other contexts can represent the lingual sibilant, as in Modern Standard Hindi. When quoting directly from manuscripts or the Bryant edition, I have followed this system so as to allow readers to reconstruct exactly the critical edition or one of the manuscripts upon which it is based (e.g., *muṣa*, meaning 'face' or 'mouth'). If I use this word while commenting on a poem, however, I will revert to the more familiar Hindi form *mukh*. Similarly, I retain the neutral *a* that appears at the end of words (e.g., *badana)* when I am discussing poetry, since it would be pronounced in singing or reciting the poem in question and is necessary for its metrical structure. Yet when I depart from direct quotation, I hope to move to a level of discussion that would seem natural to speakers of Modern Standard Hindi, where the final vowel is unpronounced except after consonant clusters that demand it. Thus I present the name of Mathura's usurper king as Kaṃs, not Kaṃsa. Often this shift from direct quotation to general reference will appear on the page as a shift from words that are contained between parentheses and words that take their place in the diction of the commentary itself. At a third level, finally, I present the name of Kaṃs's slayer as Krishna (not Kṛṣṇa or Kṛṣṇ) both because that form has become so familiar in English and because when the cluster *ṣṇ* is pronounced in Hindi or Brajbhāṣā, it takes a subsequent *a* to render it audible. The same is often true when the retroflex *ṇ* appears by itself in the final position; hence, for example, I allow *nirguṇa* and *saguṇa* to alternate with *nirguṇ* and *saguṇ*.

Nasalization is normally indicated in early manuscripts by the simple practice of positioning of a dot above the vowel in question. In transliteration this is notoriously hard to reproduce. I have settled for the standard Sanskritized possibilities (*ṃ, m, ṅ, ñ, ṇ, n*) when the nasalized vowel precedes an interior consonant, but I give *ṅ* uniformly when nasalization occurs at the end of a word.

I have also tried to follow an appropriately layered approach when transliterating words that are not necessarily drawn from the manuscripts themselves. With place names that have come into common usage, I accept the English spellings that are usually assigned: e.g., Agra, Mathura, Dvaraka, Varanasi/Banaras. If such names are sufficiently unfamiliar that readers may not know the correct pronunciation, however, I do supply diacritics. In giving references, I spell the place of publication in a fashion that was standard at the time the work was published (e.g., Benares during British rule; Varanasi thereafter). I confess that I find the official spelling of the place hallowed by Krishna's youth (Vrindaban) to be sufficiently far from its usual spoken sound (Brindāvan) that I have preferred an anglicized rendering which has largely gone out of fashion—Brindavan—except when repeating others' usage.

Similar patterns appear in other realms—for example, the naming of languages. If a language or dialect has achieved a standard English form, I leave aside diacritics (Hindi, Avadhi); otherwise I retain them (Hindavī, Brajbhāṣā). With persons, the scale moves from more or less standard English usages (Krishna, Shiva, Vishnu, Ganges) toward a realm that represents normal Hindi speech (Rām, Jīv Gosvāmī), even if the name in question occurs in a context that suggests Sanskrit conventions would also be appropriate (Rāma, Jīva Gosvāmī). If the name is a title of a work written in Sanskrit, however, Sanskrit conventions apply (*Bhāgavata Purāṇa, Rāmāyaṇa*), as they do when Sanskrit is being quoted or the context of discussion clearly concerns works composed in Sanskrit. Writers of Hindi or Brajbhāṣā are represented with diacritics (Pārasnāth Tivārī) unless they also write frequently in English and have established conventional spellings for their names in that milieu (Braj Vallabh Mishra). I have generally avoided *w* as a means of transliteration even when it has often been used by others (Vishva—not Vishwa—Hindu Parishad). English words adopted into Indic titles are spelled in the English way (Saṅgīt Nāṭak Academy). The neutral vowel is dropped in compounds where it is generally inaudible in normal speech (Braj+bhāṣā>Brajbhāṣā), unless that omission might lead to a confused reconstruction of the Hindi original. Certain names appear so frequently in these pages that they are given without diacritics, starting with our 'three bhakti voices'—Mīrābāī (Mīrā), Sūrdās (Sūr), and Kabīr—and extending to others connected with them: Ravidās, Nābhādās, and the Kāśī Nāgarīpracāriṇī Sabhā. The diacritical marks visible in the previous sentence will not appear in the main text of the book, but will be retained for reference purposes in the notes.

Obviously we are dealing here with an awkward series of compromises. I hope readers will quickly become accustomed to any conventions that seem strange at first, and will forgive me for any decisions that seem ill-advised.

The following abbreviations have been adopted for frequently used terms:

§ Designates a poem (*pad*) as numbered in the Bryant edition of the *Sūrsāgar*

<	Introduces a more usually known form of a word, or a form from which it can be said to be derived
AH	After the Hijra (622 CE)
BhP	*Bhāgavata Purāṇa*
Brj.	Brajbhāṣā
CE	Common Era (equivalent to AD)
crit. ed.	Critical edition
HV	*Harivaṃśa*
KJV	King James Version of the Bible
KV	*Kabīr Vāṅmay*, ed. Jayadev Siṃh and Vāsudev Siṃh, vol. 3 (1981)
MSH	Modern Standard Hindi
MSS	Manuscripts
NPS	Nāgarīpracāriṇī Sabhā (i.e., Kāśī Nāgarīpracāriṇī Sabhā). NPS may designate either the Nāgarīpracāriṇī Sabhā version of a poem that also appears in the Bryant edition of the *Sūrsāgar* or a poem that is absent there.
PC	Paraśurām Caturvedī's edition of poems attributed to Mirabai: *Mīrāṅbāī kī Padāvalī* (1932)
Skt.	Sanskrit
Vārtā	*Caurāsī Vaiṣṇavan kī Vārtā*, ed. Dvārikādās Parīkh (1970)
vārtā	The account of an individual person featured in the *Vārtā*
VP	*Viṣṇu Purāṇa*
VS	*Vikram Saṃvat*, a lunar calendrical system that provides a date usually corresponding to CE+57

Poems Translated, by English Title

Note: This list is limited to poems of Mirabai, Surdas, and Kabir that are translated in their entirety, and to those with which I myself have been involved as a translator. In Chapter 16, in addition, I quote several *sākhīs* of Kabir as translated by Charlotte Vaudeville. If it is known, the date of the manuscript in which the poem makes its earliest appearance is listed in the middle column. All dates are given in their CE (AD) equivalent. Dates are not known for many of the Mirabai poems listed here: these derive from the widely used edition of Paraśurām Caturvedī [PC], *Mīrāṅbāī kī Padāvalī*.

Title	*Date*	*Page*
Mirabai		
After making me fall for you so hard	PC 49	122
Dark One, listen compassionately	PC 94	123
Don't go, yogi, don't go, don't go	PC 46	120
Go to where my loved one lives	PC 153	125
He's bound my heart with the powers he owns, Mother	1604	105, 168
How many cowherd girls have gathered, my friend?	1685(+)?	110
I have talked to you, talked, dark Lifter of Mountains	PC 51	126
I'm colored with the color of dusk, oh *rāṇā*	PC 37	36
Last night a creature of darkness spoke	1656	114
Let us go to a realm beyond going	PC 193	333
Listen with care, consider my petition	1769	108

Poems Translated, by Hindi Title

Note: This list is limited to poems of Mirabai, Surdas, and Kabir that are translated in their entirety, and to those with which I myself have been involved as a translator. The date of the manuscript in which the poem makes its first appearance is given in the list of *Poems Translated, by English Title*.

Surdas

Kabir

Illustrations

Introduction

For twenty-five years it has been my privilege and challenge to think about the best known devotional poets of North India—the great bhakti voices who emerged on the stage of history in the course of the fifteenth and sixteenth centuries. This book focuses on three of these: Mirabai, Surdas, and Kabir. The trio has pride of place in my own mental altar-room, with Surdas, a poet's poet and legendarily blind, standing at the center of the group. Known primarily and justly for his Krishna lyrics, Surdas is a poet of unusually wide range, flanked on one side by Mirabai, with her ecstatic devotion to Krishna expressed in a woman's voice, and on the other by Kabir, whose gripping first-person persona picks up where Sur's leaves off. 'Sur is the sun,' as we hear at the beginning of a familiar Hindi couplet, and he is the sun in this collection. But Mira and Kabir are a good bit more than 'the moon and fireflies' that come along to fill out the verse. They are famous in their own right; indeed, they have often generated a greater popular appeal than Sur.

For five hundred years the lives and words of North India's key bhakti poets—including these three and more—have served as major points of reference in religious celebrations and cultural debates that transpire in India itself. As the twentieth century yields to the twenty-first, this orbit is expanding to global proportions. Take my own city as an example: New York. Every year the Indian-American community sponsors numerous expositions of the *Rāmcaritmānas* of Tulsidas and week-long *bhāgavat kathās* in which the songs of Surdas are apt to figure prominently. Every year on Baisakhi day the city's Sikhs carry high the banner of Guru Nanak. As for Kabir, Philip Glass's Fifth

Symphony, a choral work that came to Carnegie Hall from its Salzburg Festival debut in 1999, includes the poet's verses just after translations from Rumi and St Paul. And the composer Douglas Cuomo, well known for the scores he contributed to the TV series 'Sex and the City,' enlists Kabir as a commentator on the immortal conflict portrayed in the *Bhagavad Gītā*. In his oratorio 'Arjuna's Dilemma,' which is yet to premier, Cuomo has the tenor intone Kabir on Krishna's behalf, as Krishna tries to persuade Arjuna to do his bidding.

Meanwhile uptown at Barnard College and Columbia University there was until recently the custom that every year campus women would take a banner made of sheets sewn end to end and use it to obscure the eminent males whose names are carved into the outer walls of Butler Library. For a day, at least, these literary and philosophical founding fathers turn to mothers. Sappho takes the place of Sophocles as a paragon of ancient Greek poetry, and the list proceeds from there to a carefully selected galaxy of notable women. Mirabai joined the galaxy in 1994.

Textual and Historical Criticism

India's classic bhakti poet-saints are fast becoming global personalities. Part of the reason is that scholarship on them is now also a global affair, with English serving increasingly as its primary medium among languages of European origin. This has had at least two important effects in the scholarly domain *per se*—especially in the realms of historical and literary criticism. I'll consider these in turn.

Scholars writing in English and other European languages—many of them Westerners—have insisted that to understand a text one must know as much as possible about the historical circumstances that produced it. If the text in question does not provide direct information about those circumstances, then one must devise other ways to discover them—not just in what people have always said and assumed, but on the basis of evidence as 'hard' as can be found. In regard to the bhakti literature of North India, this means a relentless search for dated or datable manuscripts that will reveal the evolution of the text in question. Almost invariably this process shows that the text is actually a series of texts, not just because the poetry of Mira or Sur or Kabir is constituted by a collection of individual, episodic lyrics and epigrams, but because these were collected over a considerable period of time. Many compositions were added to the corpus long after the century when each of the poets is remembered to have flourished. The implications of this fact are revolutionary. When one speaks of Mira or Sur or Kabir with this historical background at hand, one has to ask just who one means: the poet as known in the sixteenth century or the eighteenth century or the present? They simply are not the same.

I emphasize this point because it contrasts sharply with the general direction and widely-held assumptions of scholarship on the bhakti saints that one typically finds in books written in Hindi. There has been immensely important manuscript and text-critical work in Hindi, but on the whole it has failed to condition the tenor of what is written subsequently. Early editions such as those that emerged from the Kashi Nagaripracarini Sabha in 1920s and 1930s tend still to be taken as gospel unless an even more ample corpus of poems—whatever people sing—is assumed to be a valid starting-point for speaking about the poet in question. Relatively little effort goes into understanding how the currently remembered form of these poets emerges as the end-point of a long and sometimes convoluted historical stream.

Of course, there are important exceptions to this rule. Pārasnāth Tivārī's critical assessment of Kabir manuscripts found in the Dādū-Panthī recension, published as *Kabīr Granthāvalī* in 1961, revolutionized European scholarship in the field when Charlotte Vaudeville took it as the starting-point for future studies. But it failed to make a very deep impression in India itself. Rather, the Nagaripracarini Sabha's *Kabīr Granthāvalī* (1928) tends still to be the fulcrum for what Hindi critics say about Kabir.

Similarly, C. L. Prabhāt (1965) and Kalyāṇsiṃh Śekhāvat (1974, 1975) are responsible for overhauling the study of poems attributed to Mirabai by searching out the full range of manuscripts that need to be brought to bear when one attempts to understand who 'Mira' was and is. Yet if one takes Prabhāt's recently published magnum opus as an example—*Mīrā: Jīvan aur Kāvya* (1999)—one sees that he stops short of accepting some of the most deeply significant implications of his own work. When it comes time to choose the poems that deserve to be associated with the historical Mirabai, Prabhāt is willing to accept any poem emerging over time from 'various traditions' that correspond closely to one another. He does so irrespective of the dates when such poems entered the stream of manuscripts that contain poems attributed to Mirabai, believing that a linguistic criterion will be adequate to filter out later 'interpolations' (*prakṣipt aṃś*) from the real thing. What language would have been possible in 'Mira's period?' he asks.[1] Yet the real thing is actually very sparse. We have only a precious few old manuscripts that contain any poems of Mirabai at all. Prabhāt knows this full well—his own work demonstrates it—but when he pursues the literary-critical portion of his fine book, he seems to ignore that fact. To me, at least, this is a radically truncated historicity.

We meet something of the same pattern in studies of Surdas. As with Kabir, the Nagaripracarini Sabha edition of poems attributed to Surdas (*Sūrsāgar*, 1936, 1948) remains the standard point of reference, the one that most scholars writing in Hindi assume as their basis when they launch into works of commentary and criticism. As in the case of both Kabir and Mirabai, however, there has been more recent work.

The most significant example is the partially published critical edition undertaken by the eminent Mātāprasād Gupta (1968–74, 1979), which was based on a renewed search for manuscripts. His team amassed 120—a very impressive number—and forty of these became the basis of his edition.[2] Of these forty, however, only four can claim a place among manuscripts dating to the sixteenth and seventeenth centuries, and despite the large number of manuscripts they consulted, Gupta's team never located another nine extant manuscripts belonging to that early period. Like Prabhāt, moreover, Gupta does nothing in the way of prioritizing early manuscripts when he makes editorial decisions. Rather, he groups his forty manuscripts into twelve families according to the textual 'defects' (*vikṛti*) they share in common, then proposes that when manuscripts vary, the reading supported by a majority of families—say, two out of three—will usually be given preference. In other cases he acknowledges the familiar editorial principle that a more difficult reading (*lectio difficilior*) must often be preferred to a simpler one, but generally he reverts to his own judgment about which readings from any competing set are to be regarded as the most probable.[3] There can be no doubt about the value of Mātāprasād Gupta's seasoned expertise, but his approach plainly fails to take into account either the genealogical relationship between clusters of manuscripts or their relative dates.[4] Once again, we come only halfway down the road toward a view of our celebrated bhakti trio that would be based in the sources that emerge from or near their own times.

A keynote of the essays appearing in this book is that when I refer to Mira or Sur or Kabir, I try hard to separate out the historical layers—or at least to state that this is impossible when it is. Often I attempt to get as close as I can to the headwaters of the historical stream that constitutes the Mira or Sur or Kabir we remember. Not that I think we can arrive at any true source, a definite historical person, in any of the three cases. But out of respect for them and their times, I think we should not shirk the effort of trying. Confucius spoke of the importance of the rectification of names. I may not believe there is any truly right 'name' for any of these poets, but I am convinced we need at least to be aware of our limitations as name-givers. And, by the way, our strengths. We do possess dated manuscripts that can help guide us through this terrain—both for the poems themselves and for the lives of the poets—and we are able to ask what later poets meant when they spoke in the name of Sur, Kabir, or Mira. Evidently they felt completely comfortable in doing so, but as historians and critics we need to take a more complicated view.

I am sure that many readers—Indian readers in particular—will find this approach deeply unsatisfying, and I agree that it does impose constraints. Take Surdas, for example. It turns out that his most widely celebrated poem, *mayā mai nahiṅ mākhan khāyau* ('I didn't eat the butter, Ma'), is nowhere to be found in manuscripts of the *Sūrsāgar* that date to the sixteenth or seventeenth century. This is especially significant for Sur, since his situation, unlike that of Mirabai, gives us quite a number of early manuscripts to draw upon. Therefore when I speak of Surdas in this book in a context that refers to the poet who was active in the sixteenth century—*the* Surdas, so to say—I cannot mean the poet who framed the beloved words *mayā mai nahiṅ mākhan khāyau*. That poet, that 'Surdas,' evidently lived centuries later.

This doesn't mean that he or any other latter-day Surdas is irrelevant to the study of 'the Sur tradition' as it emerged over time.[5] To the contrary, he becomes important as one studies the contrasts that separate early collections of poetry attributed to Surdas and later, larger *Sūrsāgars* where poems of Krishna as butter-thief mushroomed.[6] That is an instructive and exciting exercise, and several of the essays included in this collection pursue such contrasts. The chapters on Mirabai, for example, begin with questions of history and move increasingly toward analyses of the 'vulgate' Mirabai who is well known to people alive today: the Mira of one chapter is not necessarily the Mira of another, and I try to keep them straight. Being careful about history in this way is a critical aspect of understanding how the Sur, Mira, and Kabir traditions grew and flourished through the years, and it opens us to the possibility of recognizing ourselves as part of their flow. After all, we too participate in keeping these traditions alive—as conservators, yes, but also because even in that very act we ourselves necessarily add to these traditions. This is true not only for performers and poets, but for scholars as well.

Not all readers will accept this fact with equanimity. They will want a poem like 'I didn't steal the butter' to belong to the real Sur. Unfortunately, I can't make that come to pass—not until I find a relatively old, reliably dated manuscript where the poem occurs. The recognition that this is so has led to some notorious twentieth-century instances in which certain scholars tried to produce manuscripts that would get around the problem, bearing early dates but containing all the poems modern-day readers would want to find. These can only be called forgeries. The Dakor manuscript of poems attributed to Mirabai, which I discuss in Chapter 4, is a case in point.

In the fall of 2003, Purushottam Agrawal, the well-known authority on Kabir, discussed the *Mahābhārata* before a knowledgable but largely non-scholarly audience.[7] He began by noting just the sort of thing I have been stressing: the scholarly consensus that this text is the product of a considerable evolution. Its versions range from 8000 verses (apparently the oldest) to 100,000 (the most recent), with important regional variations. Agrawal then went on to make a very important point. He said he had no wish to search for the 'authentic' *Mahābhārata* in the intention of any supposed author—presumably the creator of the earliest, leanest text. Rather, he preferred to locate its authority in the basic concern of the document as a whole. To make his point, he took Kabir as a means of comparison, quoting a verse in which the poet says,

> Hari has built a railway like this—
> Take your seat, brother, let's ride.[8]

Obviously the historical Kabir, whoever he was, can't have said any such thing—we know when railbeds were first laid in India. Yet the Kabir sensibility is surely there, and the Kabir performer from Malwa who sang these lines in Agrawal's hearing is perfectly aware of the difference.[9]

I want to side with Agrawal when he says that the *sensibilities* associated with the names Kabir, Mira, and Sur—sensibilities that have developed over time, but probably did not emerge out of thin air in the fifteenth and sixteenth centuries—sustain and give focus to their respective traditions. But I doubt that in most cases performers are aware of changes in that sensibility over time. Their job, after all, is the performance of poetry, not of history. That's where scholars come in, with a performative task that many people think of as dirty work. Dirtier perhaps in India, since the performance traditions strictly and legitimately associated with our 'three bhakti voices' are overwhelmingly concentrated there and continue to thrive: who needs carping scholars? Hence the Indian scholarly tradition, to maintain its *bona fides* with the public and to feel authentic to the scholars concerned, has been reluctant to float too free of the moods and canons that govern performance itself.

One could argue that there is no reason it should. Postmodern critiques have raised doubts about whether a true division between text and interpretation or between performance and reflection is really possible anywhere. In this respect Indian bhakti scholarship is well ahead of the game. Postmodern criticism is sometimes written in such a way as to render the distinction between scholarship and performance a blurry one, but scholarship of the pre-postmodern type makes the distinction much easier to defend. This is what one might call 'classical Western-style scholarship,' remembering of course that some of its most distinguished practitioners, like V. S. Sukthankar for the *Mahābhārata*, have been Indians. Such scholars regard themselves as being spared the weight of performativity. They do not see themselves, for instance, as textbook writers, and therefore can disregard any expectation that the texts they treat will match the texts that people hear. If it's Kabir, as it was for Pārasnāth Tivārī, there's no need for the fifteenth-century figure (remembered in the seventeenth) to correspond to the Kabir performed all over North India today.

When Purushottam Agrawal located authority in 'the central concern of the text,' he was speaking to an audience that expected some wisdom from him about what light the *Mahābhārata* might shed on social and religious conflicts raging in India today. Believe me, they got all they hoped for and more. But with a characteristic twist. Agrawal insisted that the central concern of the *Mahābhārata*, as it has been appreciated through the centuries, works against the sort of unilinear connections that would provide direct answers to questions like 'What does the Epic say we should do today?' Rather, it emphasizes the responsibility of all actors—individual and social, and representing different lived positions—to consider the conflicting demands of *dharma* as they present themselves. That, he urged, was the distinctive sensibility of this particular text, and a great deal of the reason it has been cherished for millennia.

The bhakti poets we have before us now are also associated with certain distinctive sensibilities, which explains how the railroad got into Kabir. But I would argue that railroad or no, these bhakti sensibilities open more directly onto questions of historical authorship than do those of the *Mahābhārata*. The perceived personality of a Kabir matters more to the reception of 'his' poetry than Vyās's does in the parallel case. People care whether Kabir was really a weaver and they care about whether the *Mahābhārata* war really occurred, but the image of Kabir sitting at his loom in Banaras or walking its streets is more important to the reception of his poetry than the image of Vyās dictating the epic to Ganesh. These poses appear in the poetry itself, and the very name of Kabir is expected as an element in countless poems, inviting the hearer to form and maintain a mental image of the poet. Vyās appears in his text too, but less centrally and more rarely.

The subject also makes a difference. Bhakti is not *dharma*, and its literature often expects a certain individuality—even idiosyncrasy—of attitude and practice that defies the common body of problems and dicta that give orientation to the massive literature that comprises the *Mahābhārata*. In this respect too, the core concerns that give authority to the bhakti poetry attributed to Mira, Sur, and Kabir lend themselves to a historical and therefore text-critical perspective in a way that goes well beyond what the Epic demands.

Finally, these texts come to us from a period of time that is much easier to bring into historical and text-critical view than the *Mahābhārata*. It's simply much more recent. Not that the task of historical and text-critical reconstruction is easy, but it's certainly easier than it would be if we were approaching the Great Indian Epic. To my mind, this places a different kind of responsibility on us as critics. It increases the demand that we take history seriously.

Hence I would accept Agrawal's argument that the 'central concern of the text' articulates a certain kind of authority—the kind that perdures and develops as the traditions of Mira, Sur, and Kabir grow through time. But I would insist, as he himself would, that this sort of authority or authenticity ought to be held in balance with the authority exerted by historical and text-critical research, in part because of the nature of these same 'central concerns.' And there is more. We really *can* know something about what separates Kabir as performed in the sixteenth century—and in particular 'locales' in the sixteenth century—from the Kabir we hear performed today (again, in different locales and circumstances). We may not arrive at the voice of the historical Kabir himself. We may think we hear it as we root around in the oldest available manuscripts, but it is not possible to be absolutely sure just when. Nonetheless, we owe it to Kabir to respond to the magnetism of his fifteenth-century presence by pursuing our historical and text-critical search as far as it will take us.[10]

Literary Criticism

The literary aspect of text criticism moves in a surprisingly parallel direction. Here too the Western, European-language embarrassment of standing at some remove from the performative traditions of India lends a special something—a particular *masālā,* or spice—to Western scholarship on North India's great bhakti poets. And part of the peculiar accent of this *masālā* is that such studies often urge us to play closer attention to specific performative circumstances than does much of the bhakti scholarship that emerges from India.

Back in 1978, for instance, Kenneth E. Bryant published a book called *Poems to the Child-God: Structures and Strategies in the Poetry of Sūrdās*. One of his main purposes was to overturn a good bit of accepted wisdom about how Surdas should be read—all in the service of getting us closer to the 'Surdas' who seemed to emerge from poems attributed to him. To my mind Bryant demonstrated conclusively that for an impressive number of poems in the *Sūrsāgar*—often poems that have received critical acclaim—it required acts of omission or even misperception to read them as giving expression to a single dominant *rasa* (mood, taste, sentiment), as would be expected according to the reigning canons of Hindi-language criticism.[11]

What Bryant proposed instead was a broadly rhetorical approach—one that would expect a poem not to *be* in any stative sense, as the practice of *rasa* theory so often implied, but to develop, to *become*. The conditions of a poem's becoming were evidently set by the performative circumstances in which it was composed—whether for the first time, as one might ideally want to hypothesize, or in some subsequent moment, say, the moment at which a text achieved a more or less standard form or at which it was committed to print in a given edition of the *Sūrsāgar*. Whichever case one chose, Bryant was insistent that a poem should be understood as an event.[12] In this he followed the lead of a host of twentieth-century critics writing in English: Northrop Frye, Daniel H. H. Ingalls, Stanley Fish, Barbara Herrnstein Smith, and Edward Said. If one looked closely, said Bryant, one could see a Sur poem develop as it moved from word to word and phrase to phrase, and one could infer from that process the intentions of the author/performer as stimulated by his own expectations of what a 'knowing audience' would and would not expect.

In this picture of how poetic compositions come to be, individual authorial intention was conditioned fundamentally by the genre into which a poem was 'thrown'—in this case, the *pad*. Knowledge of that genre was shared between poet/performer and audience, and radically shared in their common singing of the poem's refrain. But such sharing of expectation did not necessarily serve to dampen a poet's creativity. Instead it sometimes inspired subversions directed against what the audience might reasonably expect—or could be made to expect by a poet's skillful handling of the poem itself. Bryant depicted Surdas as a master of all these things: sometimes gifted in irony, sometimes guilty of 'intentionally misleading' his audience, sometimes adept at spreading 'distraction' for the sake of 'revelation.'[13]

I have been deeply influenced by this way of reading many Surdas poems, and I have found it often works for Mira and Kabir as well, though occasionally with rather different results. This sort of approach runs parallel to the text-critical canons I laid out earlier, in that it expects to find in an adequate reading of any poem a certain tension—a tension not unlike the tension in text-critical practice between what can be known historically about a poem's earliest performance and the way in which it came to be performed later on. In regard to purely literary questions, one wants to get at the tension between the intention of the poet and the expectations and experiences of the audience (if one can separate these two for analytical purposes), and one wants to observe the dynamics to which that tension might lead. In both these cases, the text-critical and the interpretive, both author and audience are involved, but in neither do we meet them in pure form. Rather, they are guiding principles for critical perception—postulates, one might say. And in both cases manuscript variants and different performance practices may well come into play.

This moves us in a different direction from what *rasa* theory has often produced, but I do not wish to give the impression that this sort of commentary is entirely foreign to canons of criticism that have developed in India itself. Consider, for example, the general analysis of sustained verbal utterance (*vākya*) that was articulated in the Mīmāṃsā school well over a millennium ago. The Mīmāṃsakas demanded meaningful correspondence between an annunciatory beginning (*upakrama*) and a summary conclusion (*upasaṃhāra*), giving special attention to structures of expectation (*ākāṃkṣā*) created by the former, fulfilled by the latter, and without which neither would make full sense. Along the way they also emphasized the roles played by novelty (*apūrvatā*), repetition (*abhyāsa*), and an economy of challenge and response. In my view such features, though they are broadly rhetorical and not specifically poetic, bear significantly on the ways in which the bhakti poems of Mira, Kabir, and especially Sur can best be understood. They also help reveal the presuppositions according to which they were constructed.[14]

Once the spotlight of rhetorical criticism is directed toward the important fact of how a poem will be received by its audience, still more questions emerge. After all, this hypothetical first reception is only the first of many; otherwise these poems could never have survived in memory. Several chapters in this book are devoted to exploring the longer history of the way in which these poems and the poets whose names they bear have been received. Generally speaking, I focus less on the literary domain than on the larger cultural and even political 'use' to which our three bhakti poets have been put, and I often suggest that current uses stand at quite some distance from the performative worlds in which the poetry first developed. The same is true for the life stories associated with Mira, Sur, and Kabir, and these two elements—poem and life—often move in tandem. But even in the period of the bhakti poet-saints themselves, it is important to address the question of how life and word interact, from the point of view both of the poets themselves and of those who prize them. Two essays on Surdas (Chapters 10 and 12) get at some of the details of what might be involved.

Plan of the Book

In forecasting the basic dimensions of this work I spoke of an altar-room, and sure enough, it is largely organized according to the individual images of the poet-saints who are under worship here. Yet as the metaphor would imply, these images stand on a certain shared surface, and the essays that appear in the first part of the book attempt to describe just what that surface is—or ought to be. Each of the chapters in this section ranges over the literature of North Indian bhakti as a whole. In different ways each of them draws attention to the fact that when we consider the figure of 'the bhakti poet-saint', we always need to keep an eye on both poetry and hagiography—economies of word and life.

The first chapter, 'Author and Authority,' focuses on the 'word' side of the coin but keeps fingering it to see how the 'life' side, inscribed on the back, works its way through to 'word'—and vice versa. The basic question this essay addresses is: What can one mean when one speaks of figures such as Mira, Sur, and Kabir as the authors of the poems attributed to them? The question has force not just because these poets' life stories are told with such obvious performative intent—that is the subject of the chapter that follows—but because the poems themselves share in the same game. The literary genre called *pad* is at the core of the bhakti traditions of North India, and before each *pad* comes to its conclusion, we listeners expect to learn the name of the poet who composed that *pad*. Normally, in fact, it is the very mention of that name that signals to the audience that a *pad* is about to conclude: the poet is giving it his or her oral signature.

But what's in a name, as Shakespeare asked? The argument of this chapter is that such a question can best be answered not by thinking about an author in the way that has become conventional in modern Europe—Foucault has famously laid bare its culturally confined presuppositions—but by thinking of authority instead. The authors of bhakti poems such as the *pad* are authors in the sense that they give a poem authority before its audience.

To what uses might such authority be put? That is the issue animating the second chapter, 'Morality beyond Morality.' Here the literary genre is quite different; it's the other side of the coin. We are speaking of hagiography now—hagiography written as poetry but not primarily celebrated for that fact, unlike the *pad*—and the text I explore is the most influential hagiography of its type. This is the *Bhaktamāl* of

Nabhadas (ca. 1600 CE) as interpreted in the *Bhaktirasabodhinī* commentary of Priyadas (1712 CE). As for the three Hindu saints featured in this chapter, only one of them appears among the 'three bhakti voices' that structure the book as a whole: Mirabai. The other two poet-saints whom I choose for this chapter are Narasī Mehtā, the foremost exemplar of Gujarati bhakti poetry, and the Rajasthani royal pair Pīpādās and his wife Sītā.

'Morality beyond Morality' was written for a comparative volume dealing with saintly exemplitude, and my purpose was to show how the *Bhaktamāl* and its commentary depict bhakti as a moral economy that contrasts to and exceeds the demands of 'ordinary' *dharma.* No doubt people turn to the precepts of the *dharmaśāstras* for moral advice, but it is likely that narrative genres are even more important for this purpose, including those that tell the lives of the bhakti saints. So one must deal with the special problem of what *dharma* looks like in a bhakti mode. It is certainly more extravagant than any quotidian analogue, and the definition of the community that gives *bhakti dharma* its contextual meaning is quite different from what one encounters in a text like *The Laws of Manu.* As Nabhadas and Priyadas tell it, the lives of individual bhakti saints—each of them poets—adumbrate individual lessons, yet there is a common thread: the ethical extravagance of bhakti. This gives bhakti its special authority.

The third and final chapter in this opening section of the book also takes up the issue of how the bhakti poet-saints of North India hang together as a group. This time, however, the issue is not authorship or authority, but taxonomy—how one ought to understand the group as a group. Ever since Rāmcandra Śukla published his enduringly influential *Hindī Sāhitya kā Itihās* ('History of Hindi Literature') in 1929, it has been customary to refer to a 'bhakti period' near the beginning of that history—Śukla dated it from VS 1395–1700 (1338–1643 CE)—and to divide authors identified with that period into two 'currents' *(dhārā): nirguṇ* and *saguṇ.*[15] *Nirguṇ* poets cultivate a style of speech to and about the Deity that stresses its 'qualitylessness,' insisting that every human formulation of what counts as divinity misses the mark, particularly those that depict God in the form of an image. They match this talk about God with an analysis of human existence that sticks to the plain facts rather than embroidering them with fancy. *Saguṇ* poets do just the opposite, addressing themselves to a Deity who stoops to devotees' needs, taking on symbolic and visual forms molded to suit the perceptual and emotional capacities of human beings. Such a Being has real attributes—attributes that are self-imposed. It—or more likely, he or she—is 'qualified.' Personal in form, deities of this type inhabit narrative worlds that draw on but add something distinctive to the quotidian round of ordinary life, and *saguṇ* poets like nothing better than to adumbrate such narratives. They often do so by taking on voices that belong to those divine realms.

The *nirguṇ/saguṇ* taxonomy goes far back in the history of Indian philosophy, figuring with special importance in the writings of the philosopher-theologian Śaṃkara (ca. 800 CE). Śukla gave this formulation quite a different twist, however, by using it as a literary-historical tool. His purpose was to distinguish between someone like Kabir on the one hand (exemplarily *nirguṇ*) from someone like Mirabai on the other (incurably *saguṇ*). And he was also quite comfortable placing Surdas on Mira's side of the ledger.

In 'The *Nirguṇ/Saguṇ* Distinction,' I address myself to the question of just how adequate this taxonomy is. Obviously the question could be raised in strictly conceptual or stylistic terms, but I address it historically instead. If one moved back from Śukla's time and approached the period in which the bhakti poets were first grouped as a single, more or less coherent unit, would one find this same classification? If not, would Śukla's latter-day effort still work, or would it make sense to adopt another taxonomy instead? I look at a certain range of hagiographies and anthologies (*sphuṭkar pads*) and observe that the *nirguṇ/saguṇ* taxonomy describes them less well than its propounders might have hoped.

The textual record is very mixed. Rather than grouping the *nirguṇ* and *saguṇ* poets in separate anthologies—a practice that belonged rather to major sectarian communities—these more generic and often humbler anthologies typically jumble them together. Recently, for instance, I was looking at an eighteenth-century manuscript that began as a collection of poems bearing the name of the Marathi poet-saint Tukārām—clearly a *saguṇ* figure in Śukla's terms. But after a score of Tukārām poems have been recorded, the manuscript turns into an anthology that spans the *nirguṇ/saguṇ* divide: Kabir, Mira, Ravidas, Sur, Nāmdev, Tulsidas, Mālukdās, Rāmdās—they all stand cheek by jowl. In later chapters of this book I will argue that it took quite some sectarian effort on the part of the Vallabha Sampradāy to divide the life and poetry of Surdas so that his *nirguṇ* and *saguṇ* sides would stand in clear opposition to one another, the *saguṇ* superseding the *nirguṇ*. The 'real' Surdas—the poet we meet in the old manuscripts—is much more of a mix, and I believe this was also true of Kabir and even Mirabai. When one looks at our trio as a whole, then, it makes good sense to remove the *nirguṇ/saguṇ* spectacles and take a fresh look at how they might be understood in relation to one another. Manuscripts of different types can be expected to give different answers, and they don't always correspond to what later classifications allow. They encourage us to think of the spectrum of bhakti poet-saints as a single, complex, variegated spectrum.

With this prolegomenon at hand we are ready to proceed to the heart of the book. Here we will find ourselves in a landscape organized around particular poets—Mira, Sur, and Kabir—but I hope the moods and motifs that connect them will still be visible on a cumulative reading. To set these poets parallel, I have included in each subsequent section of the book a chapter that deals with the question of how they appear in their oldest manuscript traditions. The essays in question are 'Mirabai in Manuscript' (Chapter 4), 'The Early *Sūrsāgar* and the Growth of the Sur Tradition' (Chapter 9), and 'Kabir in His Oldest Dated Manuscript' (Chapter 15). In highlighting these old manuscripts, I hope to show that the written traditions associated with our bhakti trio actually vary considerably and in interesting ways. No cookie-cutter will do. Yet however different the results may be, I am convinced that the common exercise of searching out early sources is necessary in each case.

For each of our 'three voices,' I also translate a number of poems that emerge from the earliest manuscript strata. Readers will sometimes be meeting these poems for the first time, since they have not previously been published. I offer more translations of early, datable poems attributed to Surdas than to Mira or Kabir. In Mira's case this has to do with the fact that very few poems associated with her name are extant in sixteenth- and seventeenth-century manuscripts. I translate the full range available—a measly six—in 'Mirabai in Manuscript' and 'Krishna and the Gender of Longing' (Chapters 4 and 7). As explained in 'Mirabai in Manuscript,' an additional store of seventeenth-century poems attributed to Mirabai apparently exists somewhere in the Gujarāt Vidyā Sabhā Library in Ahmedabed, but the manuscripts containing them cannot be located at present. One hopes they—and perhaps others—will come to light soon.

For Kabir too, I provide a list of translations that falls short of those belonging to Sur. This time, however, the reason is not that only those poems exist in old manuscripts. To the contrary, it's that much of the early poetry attributed to Kabir has already been translated into English. Therefore I give special attention to the Kabir poems that appear in the Fatehpur manuscript dated VS 1639 (1582 CE), which have not yet appeared in translation. This is in 'Kabir in his Oldest Dated Manuscript' (Chapter 15). Several further translations also appear in '*Vinaya* Crossovers: Kabir and Sur' (Chapter 16).

But let's be frank. An additional reason that Surdas gets star billing here is that Sur has stood closer to the center of my work over the years than Mira or Kabir. Translations from poems of Surdas that were known in the sixteenth century, to which he belonged, appear in 'The Verbal Icon—How Literal?,' 'Creative Enumeration in Sur's *Vinaya* Poetry,' and the chapter that deals with the portrait of Sudāmā that emerges from the early strata of the *Sūrsāgar* (Chapters 10–12). These are the chapters where my approach to the analysis of individual poems is most clearly on display. A few additional translations and analyses show up in 'Last Seen with Akbar' and 'Why Surdas Went Blind' (Chapters 8 and 13). Hindi and English first-line lists of all poems translated in this book can be found in the front matter.

As a complement to my focus on the earliest discoverable strata of poetry and hagiography relating to our 'three bhakti voices,' the second, third, and fourth sections of the book also contain essays on the development of poetic and hagiographical traditions since that time. 'Mirabai as Wife and Yogi' and 'The Saints Subdued in *Amar Chitra Katha*' (Chapters 5–6) investigate major transformations in the Mirabai tradition over time. They draw a contrast between the picture of Mira that emerges in early traditions and what one finds in more recent, even contemporary representations. 'Why Surdas Went Blind' (Chapter 13) is a similar essay, focusing on transformations of the poet's life that seem to have been engineered chiefly in response to the needs and desires of the major sectarian community that has claimed Surdas as its own, the Vallabha Sampradāy. Here, as the title would suggest, the history or legend of Sur's blindness is my primary subject. 'Last Seen with Akbar' (Chapter 8) focuses on a closely related aspect of Vallabhite hagiography: the specific effort to make Sur appear to have been a pupil of Vallabhācārya. I hope this essay also serves to present a more balanced perception of who the 'real' Surdas might have been.

A second concern of 'Last Seen with Akbar' is to evaluate this early Surdas against conflicting standards that are suggested by the religious politics of our own day. Was Surdas a person whose poetic perspectives align nicely with a specific and 'pure' form of Vaishnavism or was he someone more catholic—the sort of poet who could appear at the court of Akbar or Islam Shah and be celebrated not only by Hindus but by Muslims as well? In short, should he be seen through a sectarian lens or a syncretic one?

It turns out to be impossible to answer this question in the way it is posed, and this should come as no surprise: this is exactly the situation in which we find ourselves if we press the *saguṇ/nirguṇ* dichotomy into service. In both instances what we need instead is a dialectical approach, one that will help us get close to the poet as appreciated in the sixteenth century while simultaneously making us aware of the limitations of our own questions. The chapter on '*Vinaya* Crossovers: Kabir and Sur' (Chapter 16) bears on this *saguṇ/nirguṇ* issue by setting certain poems of Surdas, who is commonly viewed as *saguṇ*, alongside counterparts that are attributed to the famously *nirguṇ* Kabir.

Like the essays on Mirabai and Surdas that we have just reviewed, there are also chapters in which I consider some of the uses to which Kabir has been put. There are two chapters of this sort, and they frame the last section of the book. The first in this pair, 'The Received Kabir: Beginnings to Bly' (Chapter 14), begins early, then jumps forward to Robert Bly's adaptation of Kabir to the contemporary American scene. It's a very different Kabir from some others we have come to know, and he comes to Bly by the improbable route of earlier translations made by Rabindranath Tagore on the basis of a somewhat idiosyncratic Bengali transmission. Consider the catholicity!

The second chapter in the pair is quite different. Entitled 'Bhakti, Democracy, and the Study of Religion' (Chapter 17), it is particularly concerned with liberal or secularist uses of this great saint—Kabir as an apostle of 'national integration' by virtue of his supposed appeals to Hindu-Muslim unity. What difference would it make to such claims if we were to restrict our sense of Kabir to what can be learned about him from the oldest available manuscripts? A much more complicated picture would come into view, as it would in the case of other bhakti saints of his period. The chapter opens its lens to two other poet-saints as well—Mirabai and Ravidas—and raises the general question of how scholarship such as this book represents might matter when issues facing Indian democracy call for a reappropriation of North India's bhakti past.

The rigors of scholarship don't imply that we should abandon the effort to relate Kabir or any other great bhakti poet to questions and concerns that emerge in our own day. We cannot avoid that task. For one thing, it is being forced upon us by the Hindu right, whose use of historical bhakti, especially in the person of Tulsidas, is exactly opposite to the tolerant, accommodationist use that earlier administrations tried to make of Kabir. Another recent initiative comes from quite a different quarter: Dharmavīr's effort in *Kabīr ke Ālocak* (1997) to reclaim Kabir for the oppressed of Indian society, its lower strata, its Dalits.[16] But once scholarship comes into play, the purpose of such efforts cannot simply be to proof-text the past. Rather, it serves as an invitation to discover it—to use the bhakti past and its performative present as ways of contextualizing our own concerns. And why? So that we can see that ours are not the only concerns one could bring to these poet-saints and their times, and so that we can see that our present-day concerns, often seemingly at loggerheads, may fit together in a way that is more complementary than at first we might suppose.

In its largest dimension, then, this book is an appeal to historical reason—seeing ourselves in the many streams of history and accepting the humility this implies. It is also an appeal to the virtue of imaginative, critical engagement—the challenge of conceiving interactions between poet/performers and audiences that may be quite different from what we assume in the present day. Furthermore, it challenges the complacency of sectarian and nationalist claims: these often turn out to be products of histories of their own rather than of the worlds in which our three bhakti poet-saints actually lived. Finally, the book is an appeal to the importance of seeing family—the bhakti family—as family, with all the diversity and interconnectedness that implies: Muslim, Hindu, low caste and high caste, and both and none of the above.

These three bhakti poets—Mira, Sur, and Kabir—stand for a great deal in the self-perception of people living in North India today. Some of this perception, like the poets themselves, is deeply illuminating. Some of it, I think, could stand to change. And much reverberates beyond the borders of India itself, not just to Indians living abroad but to many of the deep concerns in any human life.

The Bhakti Poet-Saint

1

Author and Authority

This chapter originally appeared in *The Journal of Asian Studies* 47:2 (1988), pp. 269–90, as 'Author and Authority in the *Bhakti* Poetry of North India'. Thanks are owed to David Shulman for beckoning me to its subject by organizing a panel on concepts of authorship at the Wisconsin Conference on South Asia in 1983; and to Norman Cutler, Hew McLeod, Philip Lutgendorf, and Frances Pritchett for their illuminating criticism of various drafts.

In America we love to put our names on things. Everything from tree trunks to subway cars bears the evidence of our desire to announce what we are and own, and in the world of arts and letters the landscape is little changed. There the copyright expresses our instinct that even creativity has its property aspect: we claim what we have composed. There is a great tendency among us to be suspicious of anything unsigned, and pseudonymity is rare.

Not every culture is this way. To Americans it may seem a law of nature that books in libraries be catalogued by author's name first and only secondarily by title, but in India it is often done the other way around. Indians usually do acknowledge authors, yet the reality of many well-known Indian texts seems to overshadow their authors' identities, and even smaller, more personal works often betray the sense that an author's job is to transmit something that has been given—to give it again—rather than to create and in that act possess it.[1] Sometimes the author's name is omitted from a title page or dust jacket, and when it appears it often receives smaller billing than it would in the West.

Given the relatively understated role that is assigned to many Indian authors, it is intriguing to find a genre of Indian literature in which the author's signature plays a prominent role indeed. I refer to the *pad*, probably the most influential medium for the expression of devotion (bhakti) in North India. *Pads* are rhymed lyric compositions of about six or eight lines in length (although occasionally they can be much longer) that center on religious themes; each *pad* bears a refrain and is intended to be sung. *Pads* have been composed in most of the major literary dialects that contribute to what can broadly be called the Hindi language family, including Brajbhāṣā, Rajasthani, and *sādhukkarī bhāṣā* (a mixed argot of 'holy men's speech'), and some of the poet-saints who expressed themselves in *pads* in the fifteenth and following centuries did so in such compelling ways that their voices can still be heard today. What they said forms much of the foundation of Hindi literature.

One is not left to infer the names of authors of these *pads* on the basis of what they said. It is virtual requirement of the genre—and in this the *pad* is not alone[2]—that the poet's name appear in the last one or two lines as a sort of oral signature. But the question then confronts us: what do these signatures mean? For the closer we look, the plainer it becomes that such signatures register more—and at the same time rather less—than the name of a poem's author. Although many of these signatures express authorship in the familiar sense, others touch more on a meaning of 'author' that has lost its currency in modern English.[3] They say less about the authorship side of 'author' than about the author's authority, and they invite us to reconsider our preconceptions about the relation between art and life.

Poets Old and New

Let me report an experience I had as I attempted to locate a series of poems attributed to the bhakti poet Ravidas, who is traditionally said to have been a younger contemporary of the great iconoclast Kabir. Forty of Ravidas's compositions are included in the *Gurū Granth Sāhib* of the Sikhs,[4] which makes him the poet most frequently cited in the *Gurū Granth Sāhib* after Kabir and Nāmdev, if one leaves aside poems composed by the Sikh gurus themselves. Nor is his fame confined to the *Gurū Granth Sāhib*: other poems of Ravidas are anthologized in the *Sarvāṅgī* and *Pañcvāṇī*, which serve as the most important scriptures of the Dādū Panth.[5] Indeed, his is one of the 'five voices' that give the last named work its title. Yet he remains one of the less-sung heroes of North Indian bhakti.

For this reason I was most interested to learn that in present-day Punjab and in certain other localities across North India, Ravidas cuts quite a figure indeed. Temples are dedicated to him, cultural organizations and educational institutions bear his name, and a mission has been established in Delhi and the Punjab to discover more about his life and work in Banaras, his native city. The cause for all this stir in recent years is that Ravidas came from a caste that ranks below that of any of his compeers in the world of medieval North Indian bhakti. He was a *camār*, a leatherworker, and his castefellows, anxious to cancel the opprobrium that traditionally attends their social status, are the ones chiefly responsible for giving his name the luster it has attained of late.[6]

One of the most interesting activities of the Ravidas organizations falls into an area well known to many readers of this chapter. By means of a word borrowed into Hindi from English, this activity is called 'research,' and it involves a series of investigations into the exact circumstances surrounding Ravidas's life in Banaras. Most particularly, there has been a major effort to discover the place where he was born and grew up. B. R. Ghera, a vigorous man who had retired from a career as clerk in the Ministry of Labor and Works, managed to deduce that Ravidas must have been born in a little community called Sri Govardhanpur, where *camārs* still live. This village is located just beyond the southern wall of Banaras Hindu University. Other traditions about the poet's home are current in Banaras,[7] but Ghera reasoned that Sri Govardhanpur must have been the true site since it is the only *camār* settlement that lies between what is traditionally called the *camār ghāṭ* (in Assi) and the trade road to the south of the city that would have been used by the traveling merchants (*banjārās*) with whom Ravidas is said on occasion to have come in contact.

Furthermore, there is a tree in Sri Govardhanpur that is believed to possess remarkable properties and is associated in local legend with an unnamed Dalit (i.e., 'Untouchable') wonderworker (*caṇḍāl jādūgar*). Ghera deduced that this association must represent a vague memory of the incident, reported elsewhere, in which the famous ascetic Gorakhnāth came to hold discussions with Ravidas. Great yogi though he was, Goraknāth suffered from the heat, so Ravidas took a twig from a pile of sticks that had been gathered for firewood and plunged it into the ground near where Gorakhnāth sat. Miraculously, a shade tree sprang up to shelter the yogi; that tree, Ghera reasoned, is the tree still venerated today.[8]

When Ghera's research led to such positive conclusions, he proceeded to solicit funds from *camārs* who had attained a measure of wealth either in the Punjab or in England, and before long the foundation was laid for a temple to Ravidas on the site of his birth. In the years since 1967 that temple has slowly been constructed, and in it the poems of Ravidas are recited on a regular basis. It was to see this place and hear these poems that I traveled to Sri Govardhanpur. I expected that I would at last have the chance to hear how the poems of Ravidas sound when they are actually recited by members of the community that holds them in special esteem. I was ready with my tape recorder and eager to check them against printed versions of the same poems, particularly those included in the earliest known corpus, that of the *Gurū Granth Sāhib*.

How great was my naïveté. When the *Guru Ravidās Granth* was opened in the temple at Sri Govardhanpur and the old liturgist began to chant, I found a text totally at variance with anything I had been led to expect. As far as I was able to determine, it contained not one of the lyrics of Ravidas that appear in the *Gurū Granth Sāhib*. Instead, I was listening to a group of poems that are in a sense more about Ravidas than by him, even though he is their recorded author. These are poems about the greatness of the guru and the importance of one's fealty to him, of which the following may serve as a typically turgid example:

गुर की मूरती मन विखे धरो सो हर दम ध्यान
नाम दान असनान कर दुआरे पावे मान
मंत्र जप गुर हृदय में मिले सो निश्चल ज्ञान
भूख प्यास न उत्तरे नाम विना भगवान
सतगुर सो नहीं पावहि जो दिल माहे सुआन
मन सचा कित विध भयो कर है किया विजान
झूठा पालन पालते कहो कैसे कलियान
अज्ञा गुर की चित्त धर कहे रविदास विखाने

Project the guru's image in your mind,
    hold it ever steady in your thought.
Purity, charity, making yourself a name—
    these only bolster your pride,

But to mutter the name of the guru in your heart
will make you unshakably wise.
Hunger and thirst will never depart
except by the name of God;
No one will ever find the true guru
who is self-concerned at heart.
How shall the mind be set aright?
By telling what the guru has done.
Tell me then, what's the benefit
in nurturing hosts of lies?
Keep the guru's commands in mind—
so says Ravidas.[9]

Now in a certain way this is just the sort of poem I should have expected. The recitation of many sacred texts in North India begins with obeisance to the relevant guru, and in a theological tradition in which the *satguru*, the 'true guru,' is sometimes all but indistinguishable from God, this initial act of veneration becomes all the more important. But what is curious here is that the putative author and the subject of his praise are in an odd way one and the same.

At the first, most obvious level, Ravidas is presumably singing the praises of his own guru, and there has been some pointed discussion in the community about who that was, since these Untouchables are loathe to accept the traditional suggestion that it was the famous Brahmin Rāmānand.[10] At a second level, he is simultaneously singing the praises of another guru—the *satguru*, God himself—and the term *satguru* often appears in the first hymns listed in the *Guru Ravidās Granth*. Finally, a third guru is implied. He is implied in the very name of the book, which quite definitely echoes the title that has come to be applied to the Sikh scriptures and was certainly chosen in part because it was hoped that this *Granth* would be seen as parallel and equal in validity to the Sikh *Granth*.[11] The third guru implied in the opening poems of the *Guru Ravidās Granth* is, of course, Ravidas himself. It is his guru-ship at least as much as his authorship that gives the book the force it has for those who hear and recite it, and when they sing these lines, the guru they have most clearly in mind is none other than the author to whom the words are imputed: Ravidas. The tone, style, and form of the poetry have nothing whatever to do with the sort of poem that is attributed to Ravidas in the old anthologies, including the *Gurū Granth Sāhib*, but that bothers no one. His authorship is only secondarily relevant to his presence here; it is his authority that counts.

Since the 1980s the text read morning and evening at the temple of Ravidas has changed. Now Ravidas comes to the gathered worshipers from a little printed book in which are collected all the poems attributed to him in the *Gurū Granth Sāhib*. Ghera's handwritten book is a thing of the past. But the authority of the author celebrated in either collection remains immense, and is not only audible but visible. Enshrined at the heart of the temple is an image of the poet; and oleographs, paintings, and maps depicting incidents in his life are spread about its walls. These listeners are hearing the words of the figure who symbolizes their collective identity before God and the world. In a number of censuses undertaken by the British in the years prior to India's independence, many of the *camārs* of North India preferred to identify themselves as Raedāsīs (that is, Ravidasis) rather than use the more customary designation of their caste, with its derogatory connotations. When the name Ravidas appears in a poem, then, it is far more than a footnote indicating authorship: the life and status of poet and audience are intimately involved.

For Ravidas to urge veneration of the guru, as he did in Ghera's *Guru Ravidās Granth*, may seem more than a little tautological if one takes into account who the guru is for those who hear the poem, but that does not make the utterance meaningless—merely complex. In reciting the line, the community reaffirms its loyalty to its own ideals and consolidates its sense of identity by repeating words it understands as given to it rather than invented from within. The name Ravidas indicates that givenness. True, there has been a change from the time when the *camārs* who heard such poems would scarcely have questioned their authenticity. Now the leaders, at least, feel that Ghera produced these compositions himself. But what has mattered all along—both with Ghera's *Granth* and in the current substitute—is not so much the authenticity of these poems as their authority. If Ravidas is their author, they speak with the collective weight of the community's history before God. That shared history is made more explicit nowadays than ever before, in that the service ends with a recitation of the guru-lineage that links these present listeners to Ravidas himself.

Admittedly this case is a somewhat special one, involving as it does the authorial identity of a poet who is effectively the patron saint of a community, its guru. But it is by no means unique: a similar phenomenon is to be seen in the Sikh community. As is well known, the aniconic impetus of Sikh religion has prevented any of the Sikh gurus, even Nanak himself, from becoming the object of veneration in the form of an image; no statue of Nanak will be found in any Sikh *gurdvārā*. But if anything, this aniconic guard against the dangers of worshiping a human being has further increased the weight of Guru Nanak's words, which are so generously represented in the *Gurū Granth Sāhib*. Moreover, when his signature is recorded there, it is perfectly clear that more is at issue than his authorship of a given verse. As used by the Sikh community in reference to its scripture, the name Nanak refers not only to the first guru but to all those who had served as leaders of the community up to the time when the *Gurū Granth Sāhib* was assembled in its final form. One knows which guru was remembered to be the author of a given *pad* by means of the heading (*mahalā*) under which it is listed—these number from one to five—but in the poems themselves the only name one hears is that of Nanak.[12] Within the confines of a poem, then, Nanak's name clearly serves as a symbol of authority rather than of personal identity: when leaders subsequent to him in the history of the Panth composed poetry for the community, they did so in his name.

With Ravidas and Nanak, we are traveling in a sectarian world: these poets became gurus in a more or less well defined institutional sense. And one need not stop there. It is also possible to hear the poems of Kabir and Dādū recited with sectarian conviction, since *panths* ('paths') have been established to venerate their names, too.[13] In certain expressions of the Kabir Panth, indeed, Kabir is understood as a transtemporal figure, so his words have a resonance larger than life and his signature a force that goes beyond any single historical context. Particularly in the Dharmadāsī branch of the Kabir Panth, the term 'Kabir' signifies more than the name of a man.[14] But with other poets of the medieval period, this sectarian perspective, with its tendency to canonization and even apotheosis, is not so vividly present. Although Surdas, Mirabai, and Tulsidas have their special audiences, they are not primarily identified with a single sectarian community, nor is any of them revered as guru in an institutionalized way. Outside sectarian circles, however—and sometimes within as well—the names of these other bhakti poets are held in every bit as much esteem as is enjoyed by Ravidas, Nanak, and Kabir; hence it is worthwhile asking whether in poetry their names too point in the direction of authority rather than strictly of authorship.

The case of Surdas is especially instructive in this regard. Although Sur has been claimed by one community in particular—the Vallabha Sampradāy—his appeal is a catholic one.[15] People outside the sect do not usually dispute the claim that Sur received his teaching from Vallabha, but they tend to be much more interested in the poet than in his supposed teacher: Sur's hymns are sung far beyond the confines of the Vallabha Sampradāy. This seems to have been the case for a long time; only some of the manuscripts of the great anthology of poems attributed to him, the *Sūrsāgar* (Sur's Ocean), bespeak a Vallabhite provenance. And even within the Vallabhite community people hold him in special esteem. He is not the guru, of course—that role is reserved for Vallabha—but as a poet he has no peer. Just what is the weight and meaning of Sur's signature, then, when it is encountered in one of the poems attributed to him?

In brief, Sur's name (or any of its several variations) appears as much to guarantee authority as to indicate authorship. In a sense this is obvious if one contemplates the thousands of poems that have been added to the *Sūrsāgar* since Sur's own time. The currently standard Kashi Nagaripracarini Sabha edition of the *Sūrsāgar* contains upward of five thousand *pads*, and one mammoth nineteenth-century manuscript adds thousands more to that sum. Yet if one examines the oldest manuscripts of the *Sūrsāgar*, one finds collections comprising only a few hundred poems. The number grew in the course of time as other poems—some of them originally 'signed' by other poets—were added to the corpus; and over the course of time there was a general shift in the tenor of the poetry, too. All this makes clear that what we have in the *Sūrsāgar* is not the monumental work of a single poet that was early dispersed and had to be reassembled over the generations, but a sprawling, gradually evolving tradition that undoubtedly includes poems composed by several authors.[16] Yet each of these poems bears a single poet's name.

One factor to consider in attempting to understand how this is possible is the role played by middlemen in the process of transmitting an authorial tradition such as Sur's. These are the performers and editors of the *Sūrsāgar*, and in a certain number of cases they were doubtless responsible for altering the signatures of poems that came to them so that they conformed to the signature of the great figure in whose name a tradition of devotional poetry of Krishna was being amassed.[17] But it is also likely that the composers themselves (if for a moment we may consider them as distinct from performers) felt little obligation to make use of their natural names in 'signing' what they sang. Even in the relatively Westernized reaches of modern Hindi literature, it is very common for a person to make use of a pseudonym when assuming an authorial role, and Surdas's name must have presented itself as a natural choice to be the signature of many authors. In the first place, Sur is traditionally held to have been a blind poet, and the name Surdas is often used in a generic sense to address blind people; hence it would have been natural for blind singers, of whom there are many in India, to identify themselves in poetry as 'Surdas'.[18]

Second, I suspect that many of the singers who fashioned these poems wanted to be perceived as singing compositions of some importance and pedigree, and Sur, the greatest poet of the Brajbhāṣā dialect, could compose no other. Or to see the matter from still a third perspective, there was doubtless often an element of homage to Surdas in the singing of these other 'Surs,' an homage expressed by affixing to a poem the name of the poet who inspired it. Perhaps we should even consider that some of these poets composed poetry in roughly the way that music students like to sit down at the piano and compose a movement for a Mozart sonata.[19] Since the genre in which these poets wrote required a signature, it was natural for them to supply the name of the master of the form; in some circles the name Sur may have gone with the *pad* genre in the same way that Mozartian phrases go with the sonata.

Of course, Sur had no monopoly on the *pad*: other poets used it as well. It is quite possible that folk poets discriminated among possible pseudonyms (the word is not altogether apt) on the basis of the devotional mood being evoked in the poem at hand. The name of Mirabai, for instance, would go naturally with poems that emphasized the importance of ranking service to God above the callings of home and family. Ravidas was one of several names to which one could appeal if the poem had a strong vein of social protest. And if one were composing a poem that had to do with the childhood of Krishna or with the conflict between Krishna's lovesick milkmaids and the ascetic philosopher Ūdho, then at least after a certain point in the evolution of the *Sūrsāgar*, Sur's name would easily have come to mind.[20] When any of these names was adopted, much more was being added to a poem than a mere signature. The whole composition might well be tuned to such an authorial persona many verses before the name itself was uttered.

It is well to keep in mind that such apparently protean poetic identities are by no means anomalous when considered against the background of North Indian culture generally. It is perfectly common for a person to bear more than one name in the course of a lifetime. The assuming of a new identity, whether by reason of age, initiation, or sheer personal preference, will often mean the taking of a new name.

When one brings all these factors to bear, it comes as no surprise that in the course of the half millennium since Surdas sang, many people evidently became 'Surs' as they gave voice to poetic utterance. And this being the case, it is little wonder that modern editions of the *Sūrsāgar* such as the large one published by the Nagaripracarini Sabha contain as many mediocre poems as they do. Yet one should understand that from the point of view of the Sabha's editors—and certainly from the perspective of most readers, even most critics—these are *not* mediocre poems, since they bear Sur's signature. For how could a poem bearing his name lack an element of exaltation? How could Sur have composed a bad poem?

For all the effort that has gone into the creation of editions such as the Sabha's, there has been little willingness to cut away at the *Sūrsāgar* as if it were the product of multiple authors. The basic meaning of edition in this context is that individual poems are edited, not that the entire corpus has been refined and repaired. For there is a magic in the name Surdas that makes even modern editors who possess more than a passing acquaintance with the principles of Western textual criticism reluctant to set aside as inauthentic many poems that bear Sur's signature. Even for such scholars the poet's name seems to figure less as a piece of a historical puzzle than as a sort of imprimatur, and the tradition that Sur was vastly prolific is still quoted to justify this habit of mind.[21]

As I have implied, Sur was not the only poet to become the posthumous beneficiary of a large corpus of poetry of which he had no knowledge. The same is true of many poets and is particularly evident in regard to Mirabai, the famed Rajput poet-princess of Rajasthan. Indeed, Mira's case is even more extreme than Sur's. With Sur, we can certify on the basis of manuscript evidence that at least a certain proportion of the poems found in the present-day *Sūrsāgar*—upwards of 400, out of a total of about 5000 poems in the presently standard Nagaripracarini Sabha edition—had come into usage in or near the poet's own lifetime, but with Mira this is hardly the case. It is true that one poem attributed to her appears to have been recorded in the Kartārpur recension of the *Gurū Granth Sāhib*, dating to 1604 CE. Certain difficulties surround this poem, however, and we cannot be absolutely sure it was incorporated into the *Granth Sāhib* before VS 1699 (1642 CE).[22] A parallel set of circumstances attends another poem that may be datable to the sixteenth century—again, we cannot be sure—and as many as twenty more have been claimed for the century following.[23] Only in manuscripts belonging to the latter half of the eighteenth century—fully two centuries after the time Mira is universally supposed to have lived—do we have any substantial reference to the poet-princess of Rajasthan, and even there the sampling is remarkably sparse, considering her towering reputation in the present day.[24]

As with Sur, this means we must revise our impression of what Mira's signature means when it appears in the many poems that bear her name. It seems unlikely that all the poems attributed to her could have been composed by a single sixteenth–century princess. As in Sur's case, there is much about Mira that would have attracted later poets to the use of her name. Because she was a woman, her signature may well have served as an umbrella for a number of other female poets, and the force of her life story doubtless drew poets of both genders to her banner. It is possible, of course, that any poems composed by a historical Mirabai were retained purely in oral tradition until they began to be written down centuries later, but this seems improbable when one considers that we have substantial written collections for other poets with whom she is supposed to be roughly contemporary. Despite the uniform signature, what we have in present-day collections of Mira's poems is evidently not the work of a single author.

Signature and Syntax

In trying to arrive at a sense of what signatures such as those of Sur, Nanak, Mira, and Ravidas mean, we can learn a great deal by paying attention to the diction surrounding these names in the poems in which they appear. It is normal practice in the commentarial literature, both oral and written, to understand the poet's name as connected to the syntax of the rest of the line in which it figures by means of the verb 'to say' or some variant of it. This seems to imply in a straightforward way that the poet named is the author of the verse in question and of the poem that it concludes. When one looks at what is actually involved, however, one sees that the situation is more complicated. The discourse of these poems is telegraphic. One almost always has to supply a certain number of connections between words in order to render their meaning intelligible in prose, and the connecting element that has to be supplied more frequently than any other is the one tying the signature to the language of the rest of the poem. Only on rare occasions is such a signature accompanied by a second word that serves this function in an obvious, one-dimensional way.

To get some sense of what is involved in supplying such connections, let us consider two samples from the thousands of poems one could choose. The first is the concluding line of a poem bearing Nanak's name. The words of the poem itself provide only the following information:

> *nānaka / bhagatā / sadā / vigāsu /*
> Nanak / the devotees / always / happiness [or, happy] /
>
> *suṇiai / dukha pāpa kā nāsu /*
> on hearing / destruction of pain [and] sorrow /[25]

The commentator is therefore obliged to expand in providing a gloss in prose, and most commentators do so unflinchingly by supplying the verb 'to say' in tying the poet's name to the rest of his composition. Here is an example:

> Therefore the guru [i.e., Nanak] says that those who are devoted to the Name [of God] continually grow and prosper; on hearing the name all varieties of difficulty and sin are cut away.[26]

Or take, for comparison, a line from Sur. It too is a concluding line and it too is sparse in its diction:

> *sūradāsa / prabhu / yahai parekhau /*
> Surdas / Lord / this challenge /
>
> *gokula / kāhaiṅ / bisāre /*
> Gokul / why / forgot /[27]

In this case we can refer to the exposition of a very scrupulous commentator, one who places in parentheses any words that he feels are not directly given in the text. His comment reads as follows:

> Surdas says that this (is) the test of the Lord
> (Krishna): why has (he) forgotten Gokul?[28]

Even in so careful a rendering the commentator has not thought it necessary to place parentheses around the verb 'says.' Either he understands it as part of the plain structure of the line or he regards it as so constantly and apparently in need of being added that it would be tedious to draw attention to it each time.

For our purposes, however, what is noteworthy in all this is precisely the grammatical hiatus that exists between the signature and the remainder of the verse in which it occurs. Only rarely does a verb of 'authoring' appear in connection with the poet's name. Among the poets we have been considering, it is only Kabir who gives such a verb with any frequency, and that may have to do in part with euphony, for the commonest way to say 'to say' is with the verb *kah-*. Occasionally one finds the verb 'to say' in Ravidas too, but very rarely in the others.[29] And there are many times when clearly it is not even implied.

Such times are particularly frequent in the Mira corpus, for her name is often anchored to the rest of the signature line by means of a genitive postposition. The phrase that rings in memory, since it occurs so many times, is

> *mīrāṅ ke* [or *re*] *prabhu giridhara nāgara*
> Mira's Lord is the clever Mountain-Lifter

and the *Sūrsāgar* presents several instances of the same construction (*sūra ke prabhu* or *sūradāsa ke prabhu*). Much more numerous, however, especially in poems that can be dated to the earlier stages of the *Sūrsāgar*'s development, are equivalent phrases in which the explicit genitive marker is omitted. These implicit compounds, of which *sūra prabhu* and *sūradāsa prabhu* are the most common, all mean 'Sur's Lord' too, but the responsibility for forming the grammatical connection is left to the hearer. And there is often sufficient room for ambiguity even in such frequently occurring patterns. The line of Sur that we have most recently cited provides an instance. It will be recalled that the commentator chose to interpret the words *sūradāsa prabhu* by inserting the verb 'says' between them. He interprets the line as meaning 'Surdas says that this (is) the test of the Lord....' But one could equally well understand these two words as a compound meaning 'Surdas's Lord', in which case the line means 'This is the test of Surdas's Lord.'

Even apart from questions of text criticism and the growth of literary traditions, then, more than a simple claim to authorship is involved when a medieval Hindi poet's name appears in a poem. The relation between the signature and the line of which it is a part can be an intricate matter indeed—not at all so simple as the linear 'Surdas says' or 'Ravidas says' would suggest.

Poetry and Biography

At issue here is the relation between poetry and biography or, in the setting of North Indian bhakti, between hymnody and hagiography. In North India these two are very closely related.[30] It is probable that the first and greatest of the 'Lives of the Saints' to be composed in Hindi, the *Bhaktamāl* of Nabhadas, was drawn together at just about the same time that the first anthologies of devotional poetry were being fashioned, around the turn of the seventeenth century,[31] and many of the poets whose lives it highlights are also featured in these contemporary anthologies: the *Gurū Granth Sāhib*[32] and the Fatehpur collection containing poems by Sur and some thirty-five other poets.[33] As the poetic anthologies expanded and proliferated, so too did their hagiographical counterparts, and not merely as parallel genres. These hagiographies tend to be organized around poetic compositions attributed to the figures they describe, and substantial numbers of entries in the poetic anthologies take their inspiration from motifs associated with the lives of the poets who are said to have composed them.

Quite a number of poems attributed to Mirabai, for example, display this biographical emphasis prominently. The episode that most frequently makes its way into Mira's poetry is the one cited by Nabhadas when he introduces the devotee Mira to readers of his *Bhaktamāl*. It is the incident in which the king (*rāṇā*) of the family into which Mira married tries to poison her. Or apparently so: Nabhadas does not actually name the *rāṇā* or specify his relationship to Mira. Subsequent tradition clarifies things. It reports, as does Priyadas, who composed an influential commentary on the *Bhaktamāl* in 1712 CE, that the *rāṇā*'s anger was aroused by Mira's exclusive attention to Krishna and total neglect of the duties and affections that would have made her a good wife. As Priyadas tells us, however, the poison's effect was nil. Mira willingly drank, then continued to sing of her immortal Lord, and the poison merely improved the quality of her voice.[34]

If one compares Nabhadas's explicitly hagiographical poem about Mira with one of a number of poems said to have been composed by her, one sees that the distance between the two genres is not so great as one might expect. There is no denying that the poems are very different in mood, pace, and choice of words. But as one comes to the end of the contrasting compositions, one finds a common element. The story of the poison serves as the culminating episode for both, occurring in the penultimate verse, and it is followed in each poem by a concluding verse that makes reference to Mira's special attachment to Krishna in his role as the heroic lifter of Mount Govardhan. First let us hear Nabhadas's poem about Mira:

लोक लाज कुल-शृंखला तजि मीरा गिरिधर भजी
सदृश गोपिका प्रेम प्रगट, कलिजुगहिं दिखायौ
निरअंकुश अति निडर, रसिक जस रसना गायौ
दुष्टनि दोष बिचारि, मृत्यु को उद्दिम कीयौ
बार न बाँकौ भयौ, गरल अमृत ज्यों पीयौ
भक्ति निसान बजाय कै, कहू ते नाहिन लजी
लोक लाज कुल शृंखला तजि मीरा गिरिधर भजी

Modesty in public, the chains of family life—
    Mira shed both for the Lifter of Mountains.
Like a latter-day *gopī*, she showed what love can mean
    in this devastated, age-ending age.
No inhibitions. Totally fearless.
    Her tongue sang the fame of her tasteful Lord.
Villains thought it vile. They set out to kill her,
    but not a single hair on her head was harmed:
The poison she was brought turned elixir in her throat.
    She cringed before none. She beat bhakti's drum.
Modesty in public, the chains of family life—
    Mira shed both for the Lifter of Mountains.[35]

And here, for comparison, is a poem that the signature identifies as having been composed by Mira herself:

साँवरियो रंग राचाँ राणा, साँवरियो रंग राचाँ
लाल पखावजाँ मिरदंग बाजा, साधाँ आगे णाच्याँ
बूझ्या माणे मदण बावरी स्याँम प्रीतम्हाँ काचाँ
विख रो प्यालो राणा भेंज्याँ आरोग्याँ णाँ जाँचा
मीराँ रे प्रभु गिरधर नागर, जनम जनम रो साँचाँ

I'm colored with the color of dusk, oh *rāṇā*,
colored with the color of my Lord.
Drumming out the rhythm on the drums, I danced,
dancing in the presence of the saints,
colored with the color of my Lord.
They thought me mad for the Maddening One,
raw for my dear dark love,
colored with the color of my Lord.
The *rāṇā* sent me a poison cup:
I didn't look, I drank it up,
colored with the color of my Lord.
The clever Mountain-Lifter is the lord of Mira.
Life after life he's true—
colored with the color of my Lord.[36]

Obviously the latter poem has more than a bit of hagiography in it, and in other poems attributed to Mira the 'autobiographical' emphasis is even more pronounced.[37] Hence it is not surprising to find that the two genres are not always kept separate in the minds of those for whom Mira has meaning. On one trip to Rajasthan, for example, I happened to encounter a wandering *rāvaṇ-hattho* player in Jodhpur and took advantage of the occasion to ask him to sing me a song or two by Mira. I did receive two songs in response, and both of them included Mira's name quite prominently, but only the first contained her signature. The second, instead of being *by* her, was *about* her. Whether the performer himself would have been comfortable in making such a distinction, I do not know.

If it is possible for poems presumably 'by' an author to shape themselves around events in or aspects of the life of the poet, the opposite phenomenon can also occur, illustrating the proximity of poetry and biography from the other side.[38] For accounts of the lives of these poet-saints seem frequently to take their impetus from poems these poets are thought to have composed. To show how this could happen, we may take an example from the literature of Sur—in this case from literature about him rather than by him. I refer to the *Caurāsī Vaiṣṇavan kī Vārtā*, a work probably composed in about the middle of the seventeenth century, which provides the most extensive traditional biography of Sur that has come down to us. The entire structure of the *Vārtā*'s account of Sur's life appears to have been patterned after the arrangement used to organize certain collections of his poetry. Logically enough, it proceeds mainly in a sequence determined by the life story of the god to whom most of Sur's poetry is dedicated: Krishna. One moves from Krishna's birth through the episodes of his childhood and adolescence in the Braj country to the culminating event, his *rās* dance with the *gopīs*, and his departure from Braj. Poems with other emphases—compositions depicting Krishna's life as king of Dvaraka or his role in events recounted in the *Mahābhārata*, poems praising Rām or bemoaning the poet's own sorry biography—are fitted in around the edges.[39]

The *Vārtā* adapts the basic pattern of Krishna's life to Sur's. When Sur arrives near Braj, he meets Vallabha, the guru tradition ascribes to him, and there at Gaughāṭ on the banks of the Jamuna, Vallabha initiates him into the mysteries of Krishna. Initiation complete, Vallabha takes him off to Gokul, the site where Krishna is supposed by Vallabhites to have spent his early childhood. At both places Sur composes songs to Krishna. At Gaughāṭ he celebrates the god's birth on this earth, as if Sur were finding a language for Krishna's birth in his heart. At Gokul he sings of the charms of Krishna in his infancy. After that Sur's journey takes him to Govardhan, where he is introduced, in effect, to the heroic side of Krishna's adolescence, for when Krishna lifted Mount Govardhan to protect the residents of Braj from Indra's angry rainstorms, it signaled the conclusion of what was is many ways the culminating battle of his youth. Parāsaulī is the last stop on Sur's journey, and it too has a special significance in Krishna's life story. In the Vallabha Sampradāy it is thought to be the place where Krishna first danced his *rās* dance. Sur sings of these themes in Krishna's life as his own passes by.

One might think on the basis of the foregoing account that the *Vārtā*'s purpose is to cast Sur's life in the mold of Krishna's, but this is only secondarily so. The primary interest of the author of the *Vārtā* is to provide a framework within which the rough sequence that had come to be ascribed to Sur's poems about Krishna would make biographical sense. Because that sequence was determined by the order of events in Krishna's life, it appears that the poet's life follows the god's, but the *Vārtā*'s true preoccupation is not the tie between life and life but between art and life. Sur's life is retroactively fashioned to follow the order that was given to the poet's collected opus. In very short compass, the *sūrdās kī vārtā* mimics the *Sūrsāgar*. Once that bond is established, it cancels any suggestion that Sur's poems could have been composed on a purely random, occasional basis, each one appropriate to an event in which the poet participated or to a mood that welled up within him at a given time. Instead, we get a picture of Sur as the author of a whole, sequentially ordered corpus. He becomes the author of the *Sūrsāgar* in the form that it was known at the time the *Vārtā* was composed.[40] Indeed, on one curious occasion the *Vārtā* reports that the poet was actually called by the name of his work: Vallabha addresses Sur as none other than 'Sūrsāgar'.[41]

One of the most vivid of the vignettes in the *Vārtā* that seem calculated to demonstrate the intimate connection between Sur's art and his life is an episode in which Sur's poetry is put to the test. Sur was blind—this is his hagiographical hallmark, much as Mira's is the drinking of poison—so the great question was always how he could have produced poems that depend so formidably on visual detail. Was he cheating in some fashion? Did he just make it up on others' hearsay? Or was he endowed with a visual acumen of even greater sensitivity than that possessed by ordinary mortals?

To answer these questions the author of the *Vārtā* relates an incident involving the mischievous children of Vallabha's second son, Viṭṭhalnāth. Viṭṭhalnāth was in charge of the temple at Gokul and was punctilious in his efforts to provide fresh, decorous clothing for the image installed there, a tiny icon called Śrī Navanītapriyajī and depicting Krishna with a handful of newly churned butter. Seeing Sur in attendance among the spectators who had gathered to have a visual experience (*darśan*) of Śrī Navanītapriyajī in the hot season, Viṭṭhalnāth's children decided that they would exceed every norm and clothe the image in what amounted to no clothes at all. Pearls and flowers were to suffice as garments for the Lord on that devastatingly hot day. The urchins were sure that the blind poet would be unable to detect this daring departure, but as soon as the curtain was drawn back and the image revealed, Sur gave voice to a song that revealed his amazement at what he 'saw' and was clear evidence that he had passed the children's test. He spoke, as he customarily did, through the persona of the one of the *gopīs* in Krishna's world. She addresses a friend:

देखे री हरि नङ्गमनङ्गा
जलसुत भूषन अंग बिराजत वसन हीन उठत तरंगा
अंग अंग प्रति अमित माधुरी निरखि लज्जित रति कोटि अनङ्गा
किलकत दधिसुत भुख लेपन करि 'सूर' हसत ब्रज युवतिन सङ्गा

Hey, I've seen Hari naked, all naked!
A garland of lotuses glistens on his limbs
  which, lacking their garments, send out waves of charm.
Seeing the measureless sweetness of each limb,
  thousands of Passions and Limbless Ones feel shame.
He burbles with joy, smearing butter on his mouth,
  and Sur says the girls of Braj join him in his laugh.[42]

One of the effects of the *Vārtā*'s providing etiologies such as this for poems in the Sur corpus is to emphasize the poet's close involvement in what he sang. On the *Vārtā*'s telling, Sur is not merely producing exclamations of wonder that could have come from the lips of Krishna's milkmaid friends upon seeing their lover so scantily clad; he is reporting his own experience before an image of the Lord. In making this point, the *Vārtā* greatly reduces the potential distance between poetry and biography. After a certain number of such stories, the reader of the *Vārtā* should be able to hypothesize occasions on which Sur sang—and 'saw'—every poem in the *Sūrsāgar*, not just those discussed in the *Vārtā* itself. The poems of the *Sūrsāgar*, then, become testimonies to the experience of a saintly person, not disembodied compositions of literary or even devotional worth. And the blindness traditionally attributed to Sur becomes the guarantor not only of the accuracy of what he saw but of the force of what he said.

As in the case of Mira, moreover, things come full circle when Sur's poetry mimics his biography. It would have been possible for many poets to say 'how blind, how base, how blank' they have been in humbly lamenting their personal inadequacies before the Lord, but when Sur says it, as he does in these or similar words on more than a few occasions, it has a particular bite (NPS 198.3, cf. 135.6, 296.2). Not surprisingly, the references to Sur's blindness in poems attributed to him tend to become proportionately more numerous in relatively recent strata of a *Sūrsāgar* than they are in poems old enough to have come from the lips of the original Sur. As legends of the poet grew, they—and particularly their emphasis on his blindness—became more and more a part of what the poet himself was supposed to have said.

The Poet as Part of the Poem

It is not hard to see how such autobiographical allusions contribute to the force of the poems in which they occur. The sanctity of the speaker makes the poem worth listening to regardless of its literary quality, and if a poem conveys beauty as well as truth, so much the better. Yet this is not just a case of having a poem's reception potentially altered by the audience's knowledge of a poet's reputation and biography: the poem itself often changes at the moment that the identity of the author is revealed. So once again we see that more is involved in giving a signature to a poem than merely citing an author's name.

Let us turn to several poems of Ravidas for examples of the sort of shift that is apt to take place in a poem when the poet's signature is revealed. Frequently the realignment one feels in these bhakti poems is a subtle one, involving a slight shift of perspective such as one finds in the poem that follows. In this composition Ravidas speaks through a persona, as is customary for poets such as Sur and Mira, who often speak through the words of Krishna's *gopīs*. Here Ravidas assumes the identity of a young girl:

दूधु त बछरै थनहु बिटारिओ   फूलु भवरि जलु मीनि बिगारिओ
माई गेबिंद पूजा कहा लै चरावउ   अवरु न फूलु अनुपू न पावउ
मैलागर बर्हे है भुइअंगा   बिखु अंम्रितु बसहि इक संगा
धूप दीप नईबेदहि वासा   कैसे पूज करहि तेरी दासा
तनु मनु अरपउ पूज चरावउ   गुरपरसादि निरंजनु पावउ
पूजा अरचा आहि न तोरी   कहि रविदास कवन गति मोरी

Mother, she asks, with what can I worship?
    All the pure is impure. Can I offer milk?
The calf has dirtied it in sucking its mother's teat.
    Water, the fish have muddied; flowers, the bees—
No other flowers could be offered than these.
    The sandalwood, where the snake has coiled, is spoiled.

The same act formed both nectar and poison.
   Everything's tainted—candles, incense, rice—
But still I can worship with my body and my mind
   and I have the guru's grace to find the formless Lord.
Rituals and offerings—I can't do any of these.
   What, says Ravidas, will you do with me?[43]

This is one of the Ravidas poems in which a verb of speaking appears: the signature line begins *kahi ravidāsa*, 'says Ravidas.' That would seem to imply that one could simply subtract this phrase from the rest of the poem and end up with uninterrupted, unencumbered direct discourse comprising what the young girl said to her mother. Indeed, this is quite possible, as it is in so many poems—particularly the early ones—of the *Sūrsāgar*.[44] But more is involved, as is suggested by the fact that when a *pad* is given musical rendition, its intensity often builds to precisely the point at which the signature is announced. Far from engaging in an act of mental subtraction, many listeners experience a sense of heightened satisfaction when the performer reveals who it was that gave utterance to the sentiments expressed in the poem.

In the poem we have just heard, such a sense of expanded meaning is almost inevitable because of the theme on which the innocent girl chooses to question her elder. The issue is ritual purity, a matter close to the heart of Untouchables since it has been so commonly used to exclude them from Hindu worship, and the point of the poem is to ask whether even the purest substances used in Hindu rituals are not themselves 'untouchable', having been polluted by prior use.[45] With this question to the fore, when the poet's signature is disclosed one can scarcely help recalling more about him than his name. Ravidas is a man with an unusually high investment in whatever answer might be given to the girl's question. Hence after his name has been mentioned, one hears in the first-person utterance of the last line not only the girl's question but that of the poet himself. 'What will you do with me?' refers not just to her but to him. Like bifocals, the last line takes on a different focus depending on how far back one stands from the colloquy of mother and child, and the presence of the signature indicates that both distances are possible.[46]

In other poems the signature verse makes such a reorientation in the direction of the author not only possible but necessary. Consider the following instance:

जल की भीति पवन का थंभा रकत बुंद का गारा
हाड मास नांड़ी को पिंजर पंखी बसै बिचारा
प्रानी किआ मेरा किआ तेरा जैसे तरवर पंखि बसेरा
राखहु कंध उसारहु नीवां साढे तीनि हाथ तेरी सीवां
बंके बाल पाग सिर डेरी इहु तनु होइगो भसम की ढेरी
ऊचे मंदर सुंदर नारी राम नाम बिनु बाजी हारी
मेरी जाति कमीनी पांति कमीनी ओछा जनमु हमारा
तुम सरनागति राजा रामचंद कहि रविदास चमारा

The walls are made of water, pillared by air,
  sealed together with the mortar of blood,
A cell of veins and meat and bones,
  a cage to hold this poor bird.
Who cares what's yours or mine?—
  for we nest in this tree only briefly.
As high as you can build, as low as you can dig,
  your size will never swell the dimensions of a grave;
Those lovely curls, that turban tied so rakishly—
  they'll soon be turned to ash.
If you've counted on the beauty of your wife and home
  without the name of Rām, you've already lost the game.
And me: even though my birth is mean,
  my ancestry by everyone despised,
I have always trusted in you, King Rām,
  says Ravidas, a tanner of hides.[47]

Here Ravidas begins with a diatribe of a general nature, the sort of speech that implies no particular persona. In the penultimate line, however, he introduces first-person adjectives, something appropriate to a particular speaker, and the subject that he addresses in that verse—lowness of birth—makes it plain well before one hears his signature in the following line that Ravidas is indeed referring to himself when he makes this seemingly personal statement. Here biography has an obvious impact on poetry—the poet announces his own caste—but the realignment this causes is not just one of subject matter. The tone changes, too. There is a confidence in the last two verses that implies that they provide an answer to the question that is implicitly raised in the rest of this poem: how to escape one's blind and futile reliance on the transient appurtenances of this world? Humility and trust are the antidote to misplaced pride, and Ravidas is a natural heir to these gifts of the spirit by virtue of what others regard as his unfortunate position in society. As in the previous poems, he knows whereof he speaks not really in spite of, but because of, his social rejection. Whether or not he is the author of both these poems, then, he is the authority that makes them possible.

A similar case can be found in another sort of poem, which provides a contrast with the foregoing two in that it is entirely taken up with what seems to be autobiographical utterance. In this poem Ravidas speaks as a *camār* from the very beginning: one of his caste occupations provides the subject for the entire poem.

चमरटा गांठि न जनई   लोगु गठावै पनही
आर नही जिह तोपउ   नही रांबी ठाउ रोपउ
लोगु गंठि गंठि खरा बिगूचा   हउ बिनु गांठे जाइ पहूचा
रविदास जपै राम नामा   मोहि जम सिउ नाही कामा

I've never known how to tan or sew,
   though people come to me for shoes.
I haven't the needle to make the holes
   or even the tool to cut the thread.
Others stitch and knot, and tie themselves in knots
   while I, who do not knot, break free.
I keep saying the name of Rām, says Ravidas,
   and Death keeps his business to himself.[48]

The signature verse introduces a change of mood even in this poem, which is dependent on the author's identity from the start. The first two verses tell us about an inept *camār*, while the last two describe an adept of a different sort. Here too, then, the poet's identity is a tool of transformation. Implicitly it encourages the hearer to change along with the poem, to consider what it would be like to be not a shoemaker but the Lord's-name-sayer.

In each of these poems the poet is doubly present—first as the general narrator (in various guises) and then with redoubled force as the giver of his own signature. And when the poet's name is announced, the poem takes notice. It would not be right to claim that this happens with quite such intensity in every poem attributed to the great singer-saints of North India, but it happens with sufficient frequency to give a new dimension to our consideration of how an author's presence in these poems is apt to convey not only authorship but a sense of authority.

What's in a Name?

If one thinks back over the many ways in which bhakti poems from North India register the author's authority—the perception that some poets ought to be venerated as gurus, the attraction of poems by multiple authors to a single poet's name, the close interrelation of poetry and biography, and the often-strong impingement of a poet's signature on the verse of which it is a part—one will not be surprised to learn that the Hindi language itself has a way of recognizing the authority of these bhakti authors. It concerns the manner in which a poet's signature can be designated. One means of doing so is quite straightforward and seems to correspond easily enough to modern Western understandings of what it means to be an author: a poet's signature can be called a *bhaṇitā*. This word means simply 'speaker' and evidently refers to the role that most commentators point to when they explain what a poet's name is doing in a poem by saying that this is what Surdas or Ravidas or Mira or Nanak 'says.' Here is authorship pure and simple.

But there is another way of referring to these signatures in Hindi, a way that is perhaps somewhat more frequently used in the language and suggests that more is involved than authorship in the banal sense. One can also refer to a poet's signature as a *mudrikā* or, more commonly, a *chāp*: a 'stamp' or 'seal.' The Vallabha Sampradāy, for instance, speaks of the eight poets it regards as the finest in its tradition as the 'eight seals' (*aṣṭachāp*); Sur, of course, is included among them. The implication of the word *chāp* is that the poet who attaches his or her name to a poem not only acknowledges being its author but testifies that the poem is valid and complete, much as a passport officer might stamp a seal on a travel document or a merchant might place a seal on a letter or parcel. To affix one's 'seal' is to perform an act of witness or good faith, not just to sign a signature, and for that reason the seal bears the authority which such seals implied before the advent of automatic franking machines. The poem is lent credibility by the name affixed to it, as is made clear in the *Vārtā*'s exposition of the situation that led to the composition of 'Hey, I've seen Hari naked, all naked!'[49] In the many bhakti poems that are devoted to describing a vision of Krishna or Radha or Rām or Sītā, we meet this act of witnessing in its simplest form, but testimonies of experience such as Ravidas provides are scarcely a step away. In both cases the presence of the 'seal' is meant to indicate authoritatively that what has been said is true and bears listening to.

These seals make their poems affidavits in verse, and for that reason it is natural that they are sometimes supplemented, explicitly or implicitly, by other elements that strengthen the force of the author's name. Sur's name is a case in point, in that the meaning of the word *sūr*—or, even more explicitly, *sūraj*—is 'sun.' This causes one to stop and think, for according to all the biographical traditions associated with Sur, this poet's source of light was an extraordinary one, an inner sun for which his blindness provided the seal. And something similar is at work in poems attributed to Ravidas. His name too means 'servant of the sun,' but it is a different feature of his biography that lends his poems their peculiar credibility. What sets him apart is his caste, and as we have seen, that it is often what gives his witness its particular force. So it is fitting to find that in quite a number of the poems collected in the *Gurū Granth Sāhib* he expands his signature with a second word and identifies himself as 'Ravidas the leatherworker' (*ravidāsa camārā*).[50] These phrases function as strengthened, compound seals.

Finally we should mention Mirabai, whose seal—her human name—is often expanded so that effectively it incorporates its divine counterpart. Time and again the first half of Mira's signature line is taken up with the phrase *mīrā ke* [*re*] *prabhu giridhara nāgara*: 'Mira's Lord is the clever Mountain-Lifter.' One gets the feeling that the whole clause belongs together as an indissoluble unit of devotion in which the emphasis is distributed between Mira and her Lord. Indeed, if one had to state which element of this expanded signature is more important, the human or the divine, one would have to concede that at least as much stress is given to Krishna's side of the relationship as to Mira's.

This kind of signature is unusual in medieval North India, but it is not without precedent in the history of bhakti. In the Kannada hymns to Shiva that were composed by the Vīraśaiva community of South India in the eleventh and twelfth centuries, one finds a literature in which the individual name chosen by the poet to designate God becomes, in effect, the poet's signature. The poet's own name does not appear, but if the 'lord of the meeting rivers' is addressed, one knows that Basavanna is speaking; and if the 'lord white as jasmine' is mentioned, one can be sure that Mahādēviyakka is the author of the poem.[51] Although Mira's poems hybridize this tradition by combining it with the standard North Indian practice of giving the poet's own name, the force of having a 'divine signature' along with a human one is by no means lost. And these compound signatures once again point away from any notion that a poet's name connotes authorship in a simple, reduced sense. To expand an author's name in this way makes it obvious that its significance is larger than what one might at first think. In the Kannada poems the use of an individual designation of Shiva as a sort of signature has the effect of anchoring the poem to something stable and trustworthy, and Mira's 'Mountain-Lifter' does substantially the same. He is her protection, as the image suggests, and at the same time the ultimate source of her authority: she witnesses to him.

The seal on a bhakti poem does far more than indicate that so-and-so says thus-and-so. There is a long tradition in India, and in many other cultures as well, that knowledge and truth are personal things. One doubts that they can be learned from books, at least if there is no teacher at hand to impart them.[52] In order genuinely to grow and learn, the hearer must believe in what is heard, and that sense of primal educability—of vulnerability, if you will—can only be evoked in the presence of a trusted person. To be in the presence of this kind of personal authority makes it possible really to hear, in something of the same way that examples often have a greater power to influence behavior than prescriptions and codes do. Not all truth is propositional, and in the realm of bhakti, where verbal utterances are apt to be full of surprises and great saints such as Nammāḻvār and Caitanya remained speechless for long periods of time, this is especially so.

To mention the name of a renowned poet-saint at the conclusion of a *pad*, when the injunction to faith is the strongest, is to make the poem an event in this intense circle of devotional learning. It transports both singers and hearers—and they may be the same—into a realm where change is possible, where faith can grow. Therefore it is appropriate that the occurrence of the poet's name often signals a slight reorientation of the *pad* itself. It provides an earnest of such transformation. As the poet brings his or her name into what is being sung, even the plainest narrative format is metamorphosed into something with personal relevance. These are, after all, poems of faith, and they become the more trustworthy for having been uttered by one of the faithful.

To many who composed poems that eventually took their place in the Mira, Sur, and Ravidas traditions it must have seemed improper that they should suggest that their own names possessed such authority. They found it easier to lodge such authority in their poetic preceptors, just as Mira (or the many who sang in her name) had bound her own name to that of the God she trusted. So it is not strange that the poems in praise of God, guru, and Ravidas that were used until recently at Sri Govardhanpur might have been 'authored' in the voice of the very guru about whom they were speaking. And it is no embarrassment that the *Sūrsāgar* and the Mira corpus have grown wildly through the accretion of numerous poems 'by' Sur and Mira that cannot have been composed by the sixteenth-century poets of that name.

To call such instances of latter-day 'sealing' pseudepigraphic is broadly to miss the point. Here nothing is being altered, nothing falsified. Nothing is being put over on the historical Surdas or the historical Ravidas any more than Jesus is being willfully misquoted when he is given the *ego eimi* ('I am') passages in the Gospel of John. It is just that the meaning of authorship in devotional India or the cultic Levant is not what we have come to expect in Europe and America since the Renaissance. In devotional Hindi poetry, to give an author's name is not so much to denote who said what as to indicate the proper force of an utterance and the context in which it is to be appreciated. The author's name is no mere footnote. It anchors a poem to a life, a personality, even a divinity that gives the poem its proper weight and tone; and it connects it to a network of associations that makes the poem not just a fleeting flash of truth—not just new and lovely—but something that has been heard before and respected, something familiar and beloved. By providing this tie, the signatures in bhakti poems communicate much more than authorship. They lend these poems authority and conviction, and they establish an aura in which the act of listening can be as intense as the speech.

2

Morality Beyond Morality

This chapter first appeared as 'Morality Beyond Morality in the Lives of Three Hindu Saints' in J. S. Hawley, ed., *Saints and Virtues* (Berkeley: University of California Press, 1987), pp. 52–72. *Saints and Virtues* is a comparative investigation of connections between saintliness and moral exemplitude, as conceived in various religious traditions. Although the Roman Catholic Church—principal patron for English-language uses of the term 'saint'—insists that a person must be a paragon of virtue to be canonized as a saint, many essays in *Saints and Virtues* explore slippages between saintly charisma and exemplary morality. Such slippages resonate to tensions between bhakti and *dharma*, but they don't necessarily render less exemplary the sort of bhakti that is trumpeted in the life stories of North Indian poet-saints.

Westerners in search of Hindu ethics often proceed by a direct and unswerving path to *The Laws of Manu*, a classical textbook of codes compiled some two millennia ago, which depicts the proper relations that obtain in a society structured by caste.[1] What it describes is called *varṇāśrama dharma*, a set of proper obligations (*dharma*) that apply differentially depending on one's status in society (*varṇa*) and one's stage in life (*āśrama*).

While it is true that the spirit, if not the letter, of *The Laws of Manu* has set the tone for much Hindu thinking about ethics, Manu is hardly the final word. Indeed if one were to listen for moral lessons in village conversations or to seek them out in the bookstalls that fill the towns and cities of modern North India, chances are slim that one would come up with anything very close to the system bearing Manu's name. Instead of codes and formal prescriptions, one might find oneself attending to legends and tales—accounts of the god Rām, for example, who abandoned his throne in order to serve the dictates of *dharma*, or of his dutiful wife Sītā, who sacrificed every desire of her own to serve her husband. Or perhaps one might hear the story of king Hariścandra, who gave up his wealth, his kingdom, and his very wife and family to honor the demands of his Brahmin teacher. Or perhaps it would be Sāvitrī, the woman whose determination to save her husband's life was so great that she managed to hound Death himself into submission.

These stories show how the rules of *dharma* are embodied in people's lives—what it means in the most extreme circumstances to carry out obligations to one's father, teacher, husband, or society. But by emphasizing the extreme circumstances, they do something more. They teach character in addition to precept; they praise personal resourcefulness and tenacity in a way that codes scarcely can.

Another genre of moral literature moves yet a step further from propositional *dharma*. It too advances from the realm of codes into narratives, but now the stories serve less to reinforce the conventional prescriptions enunciated by Manu and his ilk than to call them into question. Whether published as sober-looking religious tracts or as cheap paperbacks, even comic books, such tales record the life stories of the great bhakti saints, heroes of an important devotional strand in Indian religion that extends back at least as far as the sixth century CE. Bhakti means, broadly, love—love of God—and poses the most serious questions to the canons of *dharma*.

Yet even here *dharma* is not left entirely behind. One could argue that the stories of these enthusiastic bhakti saints are not told merely to test *dharma* but to supplement it. Taken as a whole, they present a *dharma* of their own, an ethic based on certain qualities of character and communal identification that are not quite ignored but certainly obscured in the teaching of traditional *varṇāśrama dharma*. In effect they present to their readers a new version of *dharma:* a *bhakti dharma*, an ethics of character that focuses on love.

In what follows, I would like to investigate several aspects of this *bhakti dharma* as it emerges in the work that is the grandfather and prototype for most of the hagiographical collections one finds in North India today. This is the *Bhaktamāl*, the most important such anthology in Hindi, four centuries old but still widely available and widely read. I will focus on the portraits of three sixteenth- and seventeenth-century saints—Mirabai, Narasī Mehtā, and Pīpādās (together with his wife Sītā)—whose lives are depicted in the *Bhaktamāl* and its accompanying commentary, the *Bhaktirasabodhinī* of Priyadas (1712 CE). Each of these saints serves to highlight a particular virtue: fearlessness in the case of Mira, generosity in the case of Narasī, and community service in the case of Pīpā and Sītā. Though these virtues emerge with special clarity in their life stories, they are shared in various measure by other saints described in the *Bhaktamāl*, and they work together to set out three aspects of a single notion of saintliness. It is a saintliness that cannot be compounded on the basis of the 'secular' or 'ordinary' virtues one might deduce from the prescriptions and presuppositions of *varṇāśrama dharma*. Indeed the *Bhaktamāl* sometimes begins its devotional sketches by noting how these saints left that sort of *dharma* behind. Yet the saintliness depicted in the *Bhaktamāl* does not do away with all *dharma* either. Rather, it describes a more fundamental morality, which, if manifested with the naturalness that these saints evince, would lead to right living in the absence of all code and precept.

The *Bhaktamāl*

The *Bhaktamāl* ('Garland of Devotees') is the best known 'Lives of the Saints' in North India today.[2] Among Hindi works, it may also be the oldest, though precedents can be found in other Indian vernacular languages;[3] certainly it is more catholic than sectarian hagiographical collections such as the *Caurāsī Vaiṣṇavan kī Vārtā* ('Accounts of Eighty-four Vaiṣṇavas'), a product of the Vallabha Sampradāy. The *Bhaktamāl* seems to have been composed near the beginning of the seventeenth century by one Nabhadas, or as he called himself, Nārāyandās. Little about him is definitely known, since his autobiographical comments are limited to indications of who his guru was. The commentator Priyadas, however, writing near the beginning of the eighteenth century, depicts Nabhadas as a devotee of Rām and associates him with the well known ashram at Galtā, near Jaipur in Rajasthan.[4] As for Priyadas, he identifies himself as a resident of Brindavan and devotee of the fifteenth-century Bengali ecstatic Caitanya. This makes him, presumably, a member of the Caitanya or Gauḍīya Sampradāy. Taking Nabhadas and Priyadas together, then, we already have a work of sectarian breadth; that breadth has had much to do with its wide readership over the centuries. Indeed the telegraphic Nabhadas is almost always read together with his commentator, and when I use the term *Bhaktamāl* in the present chapter, I mean to denote that composite hagiography.[5]

The first section of the *Bhaktamāl* presents a galaxy of mythological figures who can be considered devotees (*bhaktas*) of Krishna or Rām, the principal manifestations (*avatārs*) of the god Vishnu in the human sphere. Other gods in the pantheon, such as Shiva, Brahmā, and Lakṣmī, are drawn into this worshipful array. Thus the *Bhaktamāl* begins at the beginning, as any good Hindu *purāṇa* should. Its bulk, however—the second section—concerns historical personages, denizens of this degenerate age (*kali yug*). Nabhadas starts with the four theologians whose names had by his time and in his sectarian context come to symbolize the four main Vaishnava teaching traditions (*sampradāys*). His purpose, apparently, is to set the present world-age off on the right footing, but he dispenses rather quickly with these four venerable figures of the eleventh and following centuries and moves on toward saints who lived closer to his own times. When he relates some of their stories, he seems genuinely at home, and Priyadas elaborates at even greater length. Evidently they held great significance in Nabhadas's and Priyadas's day, and many of them continue to do so in the present as well. Among these are the portraits of Mira, Narasī, and Pīpā, which we will now consider one by one.

Mirabai: Fearlessness

Among all the singer-saints of medieval or early modern North India none is better known today than Mirabai. Songs attributed to her are sung from one end of the subcontinent to the other; the bards of her native Rajasthan keep alive an ample cycle of songs about her; and not one but several feature films have taken her as their heroine. Her story is a gripping one, and the *Bhaktamāl*'s version of it is the earliest to have come down to us.

Like all subsequent accounts, the *Bhaktamāl* presents Mira as a Rajput princess so absorbed in the love of Krishna from early childhood that she understood herself to be his bride and therefore regarded her earthly marriage as a matter of secondary importance at best. Depicted in this way, she vividly replicates the devotion of the cowherding women and girls (*gopīs*) who peopled the land of Braj, just south of Delhi, when Krishna dwelt there. They too had husbands. But even if they had dedicated themselves to the lifelong service of their mates—their 'husband-gods' (*patidev*), as the Hindu expression tellingly puts it—they instantly abandoned the demands of conventional morality at the sound of Krishna's flute. They dropped their brooms, churning sticks, and cooking implements, and even slipped away from the conjugal bed itself, to rush out into the forest to dance the dance of love, Krishna's circular *rās* dance. Mira's urge was the same: to seek out the company of quite a different 'family' from that to which *dharma* had assigned her—a family composed of those who sang the praises of her Lord. This put her constantly at loggerheads with that family's earthly rival.[6]

To present Mira, the *Bhaktamāl* begins with the poem in which Nabhadas sets forth the major themes that her life displays:

> Modesty in public, the chains of family life—
>   Mira shed both for the Lifter of Mountains.
> Like a latter-day *gopī*, she showed what love can mean
>   in this devastated, age-ending age.
> No inhibitions. Totally fearless.
>   Her tongue sang the fame of her tasteful Lord.
> Villains thought it vile. They set out to kill her,
>   but not a single hair on her head was harmed;
> The poison she was brought turned elixir in her throat.
>   She cringed before none. She beat bhakti's drum.
> Modesty in public, the chains of family life—
>   Mira shed both for the Lifter of Mountains.[7]

The very first line sets up an opposition between conventional modesty (as defined by family bonds) and singing of Krishna, and the second line confirms that Mira's life displays the tension that the *gopīs* experienced, but on an earthly plane, or rather, as the Hindu concept has it, in the degenerate world-age of which we are a part. Mention is then made of the fearless, shameless quality of Mira's personality, which is presented as if it emerged from her singing. The poem then cites the great example of Mira's fearlessness: the episode in which she gladly drank the poison her husband or in-laws served up to her. As if in consequence of her fearlessness, she had no reason to fear, for the poison turned to ambrosia in her throat. The poem concludes in the same vein, making reference to her outspoken bhakti musicianship again (she is said to have beaten the great annunciatory *nisān* drum) and drawing attention again to its effect: it broke asunder the chains of ordinary morality.

The rest of the account—the part added by Priyadas—fleshes out the details. We are told that as a child in her father's house in the princely state of Merta, in Rajasthan, Mira fell deeply in love with Giridhar—Krishna in his role as lifter of Mount Govardhan, a heroic image of the Lord and very much Mira's favorite. When she was betrothed to an unspecified *rāṇā* from another state and followed him around the marriage fire, the mantras she said in her heart were all directed to her other husband, the Mountain-Lifter.[8] Instead of a dowry to take with her to her new home, she asked only for Him, the image of Krishna to which she had become so attached. And when she arrived at her in-laws' house, she refused to bow her head to her mother-in-law, as Hindu custom prescribes, or to the goddess who was the chosen deity of the household into which she had married. Her mother-in-law was humiliated; the *rāṇā* was put to shame (the text does not specify whether the term *rāṇā* refers to her father-in-law or her husband, but it was probably the former since the text calls him 'the king');[9] and her behavior cast discredit on the honor of her own father's lineage as well. All family bonds were threatened by Mira's sense of having already offered herself totally to Krishna.

But that did not mean that Mira was left with no family at all. Though her earthly family would rather poison than nourish her, Mira retained another family in 'the company of the saints' (*sādhu saṅga*) who are, as the text says, 'attached to the will of Śyām'—that is, Krishna (*jinhaiṅ lāgī cāha syāma kī*).[10] Her sister-in-law tried to dissuade her from associating with such *sādhūs* but to no avail; the *rāṇā*, on hearing of the state of things, dispatched a cup of poison. The poison was sent in the guise of a liquid offering (*caraṇāmṛt*) to the feet of Krishna, Mira's deity, since the king knew well that Mira was bound to consume whatever was left over from the table of her divine Lord. The irony is that, as she drank it, the poison became exactly the 'immortal liquid from his feet' that the term *caraṇāmṛt* implies. It made her glow with an even greater health and happiness than before.

In the section that follows, the *Bhaktamāl* takes a closer look at the nature of Mira's chosen family—the *satsaṅg*.[11] First the *sādhūs* who customarily gathered around her eventually stopped coming, which saddened her but showed that not even those who pass their lives singing of God always possess the fearlessness that such a life requires and, if pursued in truth, generates naturally. Mira is left with only Krishna for her *satsaṅg*. But the departure of the *sādhūs* is providential, since at that time the *rāṇā* extends his murderous jealousy from Mira to any with whom she might speak. It has been rumored that she has liaisons with other men. Indeed someone overhears her cooing to a lover behind her door. The *rāṇā* is summoned, appears hastily with sword in hand, demands to be admitted to her chamber, and asks her to show him the man with whom she has been conversing so lovingly. Her response is that the one he seeks is standing directly in front of him—her image of Krishna—and that he is not one to shy away from an encounter. The *rāṇā*, flustered and angry, freezes 'like a picture on the wall' and retreats.[12] Note that it is he, her 'true' husband, who fearfully flees, not the one who appears to worldly eyes her paramour, her illegitimate consort. And the way in which the *rāṇā* goes deepens the sense of irony that the *Bhaktamāl* takes pleasure in conveying: he, though flesh and blood, turns stonelike, a mere image of reality, when faced with the image who is much more than an image, 'real life' itself.

The next episode provides yet another instance of Mira's fearlessness, and again the battle is fought over the issue of marital fidelity and sexual propriety. This time Mira is truly faced with a vile and dissolute would-be lover, a man who comes to her in the guise of a *sādhū* and urges her to submit to his advances on the strength of the claim that Giridhar himself has commanded it. We learn nothing about sagacity or credulity from Mira's response; the lesson has to do, again, with absence of fear. She simply replies that she accepts Giridhar's orders in all humility, and with that she offers the man food and has a bed made. But she goes him one better. She lays out the bower in the presence of the *satsaṅg*, urging on him that same fearlessness that is by now her trademark, and in that open, communal context she urges him to have good fun as well—another Krishnaite virtue. The result is that it is he, not she, who fears and feels shame. He blanches, loses any desire for corporeal contact, and begs her to help him attain the godly devotion that she displays.

Thus Mira's place in the *satsaṅg* is tested from without (by the *rāṇā*) and within (by the false *sādhū*), and in both cases it is her absence of shame in the presence of Krishna that makes her defenselessness a true defence. By breathing the expansive magnanimity of her Lord, she shames the shameless.

By the same token she charms the great. The Mughal emperor Akbar—a frequent figure in the hagiographies of the time—is drawn from afar to hear her sing. Accompanied by his chief musician Tānsen, he comes into Mira's presence disguised as a commoner, which teaches that neither rank nor religious affiliation (Akbar is a Muslim) is relevant to *satsaṅg*, and before long Tānsen is moved to song.

Not everyone is so impervious to issues of status and boundary as Akbar, however, even within the bhakti movement itself. In the next episode Mira travels to Brindavan, the great center of Krishna worship in Braj, and is refused an audience with the important Vaishnava philosopher Jīv Gosvāmī. The reason is that Jīv has vowed never to have concourse with a woman. Mira sets him straight with a message in which she reminds him that in Brindavan there is really only one male, Krishna. All the rest are *gopīs* before him. The lesson, once again, is not only that *satsaṅg* is an open reality, devoid of the marks of hierarchy, but that fear and modesty have no place in it.

Mira's last journey takes her to Dvaraka, the great focus of Krishna worship in the west of India, in order that her service to Giridhar might be deepened one final measure. When she has been gone for some time, the *rāṇā* finally misses her and recognizes that she is the very personification of love (*bhakti kau sarūpa*).[13] The lesson, perhaps, is that even the world of profane morality cannot survive forever without the higher dimension that Mira represents.

The *rāṇā* sends a delegation of Brahmins to persuade her to return, but she refuses. Driven to extremes, they try to win her back with a hunger strike, which does indeed earn her sympathy, but Krishna himself prevents her departure. One day, as she worships, he draws her into his own image, and she is never seen again. The story ends, thus, on what from an ethical point of view is an ambiguous note. Mira may be willing to explore the possible coexistence of earthly propriety and heavenly devotion, but Krishna, the great hero of music and anti-structure, cannot bear to see her try.

Narasī Mehtā: Abundance and Generosity

Mira is a paragon of fearlessness; the word echoes over and over in the *Bhaktamāl*'s portrait of her. And she needs to be fearless if she is to sing God's songs, because the milieu in which she belongs, that of a traditional Rajasthani princess, has definite, almost inflexible expectations about women. But other lives face other barriers, and in the life of Narasī Mehtā, the great poet-saint of Gujarat, the barrier is not family but money. Hence the virtue to which his inveterate singing leads is not social but economic fearlessness.[14] It would be a great understatement to call him generous, though this virtue follows naturally from a life of song and divine service in the lives of a number of other saints. Narasī is generous even when he has nothing to give; he offers freely to others even when he has nothing to eat himself. He acts as if the Lord's economy is an endless abundance, and it always turns out that he is right. Just as Mira's fearlessness in the face of marital propriety turns the world's poison to divine nectar, so Narasī's sense of God's abundance spreads wealth in a world where the belief that all things are scarce leads to niggardliness and suspicion.

As in the *Bhaktamāl*'s chapter on Mira, the kernel poem in the section on Narasī—the one composed by Nabhadas—announces the main theme. It draws attention to a conflict between traditional, high-ranking Smārta Brahmins and devotional Bhāgavatas (that is *bhaktas*) of the time Narasī represents (though he too was born a Smārta). The poem reports that Narasī succeeded in turning the Brahmins' desert into a lake. His actions provide ample irrigation for a view of life and religion that was parched and dry.[15]

As the story proper begins—the part related by Priyadas—we learn just what it is that Narasī does: he wanders. Nothing explicit has yet been said about his musicianship, but the reader, knowing why Narasī's life is being reported at all, immediately understands that he wanders because he sings: he is preoccupied with songs of God.

The reader also understands why when Narasī returns to the home of his brother and his brother's wife, where he has stayed since he has been orphaned, his brother's wife rebukes him. She takes him for a wastrel and a drain on the family finances. When he asks for a drink, she accepts his request only grudgingly, taunting him with the remark that unless he is given water to drink, his work can scarcely be expected to proceed. The words she chooses have another resonance than the harsh one she intends, however, since the reader has already been introduced in the prefatory poem to the knowledge that Narasī's work is precisely one that depends on the availability of water: his songs irrigate the faithful.[16]

Nonetheless, it is to her harshness that Narasī responds. Deeply hurt, he turns away. He is content to let himself die, and goes off to a temple of Shiva to await the inevitable. But in this divine hospice earthly inevitabilities prove pliable. After seven days of waiting, Narasī is still alive. Indeed he is granted a vision of Shiva, who removes his thirst and hunger and agrees to supply him with whatever boon he might wish. The boy replies that he does not know how to ask for anything and merely suggests that Shiva give him whatever would make the god himself happy. Shiva does so, making known a desire that he cannot even acknowledge to his own consort—the desire to become a *gopī* before Krishna—and immediately Narasī is assumed into the circle of Krishna's *rās* dance. He never wants to leave, of course, but Krishna assures him that whenever Narasī remembers Krishna or meditates on his form, Krishna will be present. No wonder, then, that as Narasī returns to the world, marries, establishes his own household, and begins to sing of the Lord, many saints gather to sing those praises with him. And there more trouble begins, for Narasī's popularity arouses the jealousy of the Brahmins.

Note the logic of these events. Narasī is refused the most basic sustenance by his own family, the very unit that is bound by canons of earthly morality to give him succor. But in the presence of Shiva, not only is he given what he asks, he is given what he does not even know how to request. Boons are normally given in response to a prior action, but here there is not even a hint of a bargain. The wish Shiva grants to Narasī is purely an overflow of what he himself desires, and its content merely underscores this sense of plenty freely shared. In the *rās* dance Krishna multiplies himself many thousandfold so that he can become immediately available to the *gopīs* who join in the dance. The motif of abundance is expanded a step further when Krishna assures Narasī that he has access to the magic circle of the *rās* at the drop of a hat, even when he is 'gone' from it. In consequence, when Narasī begins to recall that circle in song, he is naturally joined by throngs of others who come to share the wealth of love.

Two economies have been described in the story of Narasī: that of the Brahmins, which is based on scarcity and exhibits on that account a begrudging niggardliness and angry jealousy, and that of God's musical fellowship (or rather sisterhood) in which there is infinitely much to give. The more is given, the more there is still to be dispensed.

The incidents that the *Bhaktamāl* reports from the remainder of Narasī's life underscore this contrast. The jealous Brahmins set themselves to scheming. Living as they do in Junagarh, on the road to the holy temple of Krishna at Dvaraka, they are often presented with requests from traveling pilgrims to hold their funds in safekeeping. Then the pilgrims can continue along the dangerous road to Dvaraka without fear of robbers. Upon arrival they can reclaim an amount equivalent to what they deposited at Junagarh by proceeding with an IOU to a relative or associate of one of the Junagarh Brahmins. Of course a commission is required for the service.

Now the Junagarh Brahmins know full well that Narasī is no moneylender like themselves. The thought of using family ties with Brahmins in distant places to extract interest from travelers had never occurred to him. But the Brahmins believe that by portraying him as someone like themselves, they may have a great deal to gain. Hence they send several pilgrims to his doors, claiming that Narasī is well known for his wealth. Their hope is at least to embarrass Narasī. If he accedes to these *sādhūs*' requests and writes them an IOU, he will have no way of reimbursing them and will have to suffer years in jail or worse in order to pay for his sins.

Sure enough, the pilgrims make their way to Narasī's ramshackle house, where he greets them cordially. He is a little surprised and suspects that someone is playing a practical joke on these folk, but he interprets their arrival nonetheless as a gesture from a high. His habit is simply to accept what is offered, as if the world were a reflex of God's abundance. He makes out an IOU, as the Brahmins had said he would, but it is of an unusual form. It reads, 'Śāh Sāṅval is very generous. Take this to him, get the money from him, and go about your business without a second thought.'[17]

When the travelers arrive in Dvaraka, they search assiduously for a merchant by the name of Śāh Sāṅval but to no avail. The money merchants in town have never heard of such a person. When the desperate pilgrims had just about given up, however, that very merchant appears to them, saying that he has been looking high and low for them. He has their money and is eager, in fact, to grant them 25 per cent interest in addition to the principal rather than extracting the customary reduction. As his letter of confirmation to Narasī, he writes that he has plenteous funds on hand and that Narasī is welcome on any occasion to write promissory notes in his name.

The mysterious financier, of course, is none other than Krishna, for Sāṅval is a variant on Śyām, one of his titles: 'the Dark One.' It is no surprise, on reflection, that the Brahmin merchants of Dvaraka, despite their physical proximity to Krishna's great temple and apparent call to his service, were ignorant of his true identity. He trades in a currency whose principles they do not understand. Its effortless abundance causes the Brahmins' joke on Narasī to backfire. As Joseph says to his brothers at the end of the biblical story, 'You meant evil against me; but God meant it for good.'[18]

Similar events follow. When Narasī's daughter is married and gives birth to a son, she notifies her father that custom requires he should present a substantial gift to her parents-in-law. Narasī sets off for her house in a broken-down cart. When his daughter sees his condition, she blanches with anger and shame and asks him why he came at all if he came empty-handed. He tells her not to worry and to have her mother-in-law make a list of things that will satisfy her on the occasion. The haughty mother-in-law complies, but in anger. She demands everything she can think of and brings her list to a conclusion by requesting two stones—a special insult intended to illuminate the actual extent of what Narasī has to give. Again, however, evil turns to good: as Narasī takes up his simple drone instrument and begins to sing, not only do all the desired items begin to crowd about him in the poor hut where he has been assigned to stay but the two stones in the assemblage turn to gold and silver. The mother-in-law is apparently satisfied, but a more important result is that Narasī's daughter is won away from her earthly values. She converts and accompanies her father back to Junagarh.

In the last episode that the *Bhaktamāl* reports, Narasī is so lost in song that he forgets to attend the marriage of his own son, despite the fact that it represents a great coup. His son has been paired with the daughter of the rich and respectable family with whom every Brahmin in town would like to achieve an alliance. Again Krishna intervenes—this time accompanied by his wife Rukmiṇī, as is appropriate for the nuptial occasion—and they lead the procession of the groom's family, spreading out before Narasī a display of incomparable pomp and plenty. The father of the bride, who had come to bemoan the betrothal when the local Brahmins informed him about Narasī's financial straits, reconsiders his qualms in an instant. The lesson is that even the richest, most proper Brahmin need not fear for his daughter's welfare in a family governed by the economic rules that seem to pertain to Narasī.

Time and again it is made plain that to sing of the Lord and not fear for want is to be the recipient of more than one could ever have imagined asking. To worldly vision, Narasī has nothing; yet, as events make clear, he has everything—provided he is giving it away.[19]

Pīpā and Sītā: Community Service

A third image of sainthood and its virtues is presented in the *Bhaktamāl*'s account of Pīpādās and his wife Sītā. Here too one finds the fearlessness of Mira and the unconscious, improbable generosity of Narasī, but these virtues are now bound up more closely than ever with a third: the service of *satsaṅg*, God's society, from within. Pīpā and Sītā epitomize a new view of householdership. Their marriage is presented as the very antithesis of most Indian marriages, which are cogs in the wheel of *dharma*, synapses in the vast and complex network of caste society. Pīpā and Sītā belong instead to the fellowship of the saints, the realm of devotion and song.

As the story begins, Pīpā and Sītā are king and queen, sitting at the apex of hierarchy: the place is Gāgaraun (or as Anantdās says, Gagraunī), in Rajasthan. But Pīpā defects, urged on by the secret wishes and obvious example of some visiting *sādhūs*, and looks for a new mode of worship: love (bhakti). People think him crazy, but he runs off to Banaras to be accepted as a pupil by Rāmānand, whom the *Bhaktamāl* depicts as the great guru of the *sants* and father of their spiritual family.[20] But Rāmānand does not ratify the simple bifurcation between *dharma* and bhakti that Pīpā's flight from the throne implies. In accepting Pīpā as one of his own, he commands him to go back where he came from and begin serving the saints right there.

Later Pīpā bolts again, desperate to loosen the ties that bind him to his twenty wives (this is householdership with a vengeance!), but the youngest among them, Sītā, refuses to let him go. She is willing to wear a humble torn blanket as clothing—she cares nothing for modesty and rank—if only she can be allowed to stay at her husband's side. Pīpā then orders her to go naked, so anxious is he to slip away from his domestic life, but again she consents, and at this point Rāmānand intervenes and orders his pupil to take her along. Earlier Rāmānand has said that it matters little whether one's station is that of householder or renunciant, and now he positively prevents Pīpā from lurching too greatly to one side. To do so would be merely to embrace a social role that the old, unregenerate order sanctions in any case: that of the outsider, the wanderer, the crazy enthusiast. What is wanted instead is a new understanding of what one already is, and a genuinely new society in which the roles of householder and renunciant are not polarized.[21]

In what follows we see that Pīpā and Sītā form the nucleus of that society precisely because they are both householders and renunciants, never one without the other. They remain married, but their marriage is a life devoted entirely to others. They are married in their mutual self-renunciation. Like Narasī, Pīpā finds unexpected treasure, but he shuns it as useless. Thieves, however, overhear his astonished discovery of a box filled with gold coins and seek it out for themselves, whereupon they find it filled with nothing but vipers. Enraged, they lay the box at Pīpā's door and there, at the touch of his hands, the contents turn to gold again. Pīpā spends the treasure immediately to feed the saints, offering to others what he has renounced himself.

Sītā too gives all. She learns 'true love of the family'[22]—God's family—from the example of a woman who, when she and her penniless husband are visited by Sītā and Pīpā, removes her very skirt so that her husband can sell it to provide something for the saints to eat. As they sit down to the meal, the poor wife is absent and Pīpā protests, explaining that in defiance of established hierarchical patterns of Indian hospitality, Bhāgavatas—the *satsaṅg*—eat together. It is then that Sītā goes to the kitchen to fetch her and finds her naked. Thus Sītā learns a convincing lesson in humility, generosity, and fearlessness. Sītā immediately tears her own sari in two and offers half to the poor woman, pulling her out into the full community of the *satsaṅg*. Indeed, so moved is she by the need of this poor man and woman that she rushes to the bazaar and presents herself as a prostitute to the lustful eye of every passerby in the hope of earning some money to feed her host and hostess. Miraculously, as in the case of Mira, her fearlessness changes the quality of her clients' vision, and soon she has a great heap of grain and cash before her, for which she has had to pay no corporal price.

On another occasion Pīpā and Sītā are visited by a group of saints—they are the hosts, not the guests, this time—and again nothing is in the house. Repeating her earlier foray, Sītā sets out to bargain her body for food, this time by going to a particularly lascivious merchant she knows. He is only too eager to strike such a deal, and she agrees to go to his house after serving her guests. It is the rainy season, however, and by the time the meal is done the roads have been deluged to the point of impassibility. Pīpā, who has already been delighted by his wife's willingness to put the welfare of the saints before any claims that their own marriage would make on her, insists on carrying her across the mud-soaked fields. When they arrive, he hides himself so that the merchant can satisfy his desires undisturbed. Such a scene is the sort of extreme situation that the Buddhist *jātaka* tales sometimes describe in recommending the virtue of selfless giving (*dāna*). But in this case divine providence prevents the sacrifice from being completed; when the merchant discovers Sītā at the door in spite of the miserable weather, he asks incredulously how she got there. As she tells him, his disbelief is transformed into shame, his eyes gush tears, and Pīpā, seeing his change of heart, initiates him into the fellowship of saints.[23]

The marriage of Pīpā and Sītā is a marriage for others, a marriage whose only rules of conduct are those that relate it to the *satsaṅg*, and a marriage that presupposes in that context both the fearlessness of convention that Mira evinces and the economy of abundance that Narasī Mehtā's life illustrates. As such, it makes a statement about a new kind of *dharma*—a *bhakti dharma*—and offers a paradigm of virtuous living that seems consciously intended to supplant the old. Surely it is no accident that Pīpā's faithful wife is called Sītā, for the story of their life together amounts to a new version of the Hindu marriage that is usually understood as the classic statement of virtue and self-sacrifice: the epic marriage of Rām and Sītā. Rām and Sītā too are willingly disenfranchised royalty; they too rely on the instruction of the husband's guru; they too shed the raiments of royalty and wander the forests. It is no wonder that the story of Pīpā and Sītā is full of references to animals, especially wild animals, as is the epic of Rām.[24] Once fear and false notions of society are dispelled, the very beasts are brought within the purview of human concerns. Once the passions have been domesticated, put to the service of saintly community, there is no reason to project their devouring presence onto the animal realm.[25]

The *Dharma* of Bhakti

One message that emerges clearly from each of these three hagiographies is that the life of bhakti has threatening consequences for ordinary morality. But this *bhajan sevā*, 'service through singing' as the commentator Sītārāmśaraṇ Bhagavānprasād Rūpakalā calls it in explaining the *Bhaktamāl*'s portrait of Ravidas, is not so amoral as it first appears.[26] Rather, these exemplary accounts show that bhakti has an ethical logic that demands more, rather than less, from those who come under its spell. And it creates an ethically significant community of its own, the *satsaṅg*. Whereas worldly *dharma* establishes its ethical community by means of social differentiation and complementary function, bhakti does so by reuniting socially disparate elements in a common cause: the praise of God. This seemingly external referent does not so much cancel recognizably *dharmic* virtues, as it liberates them from the social codes and contexts to which they are usually subordinated.

There is nothing new about any of the three virtues we have discussed. Each has its place in a broadly traditional, upper-caste Hindu view of life. Within the four-caste system, fearlessness (*abhaya*) is a virtue one expects of a warrior and therefore considers to apply by extension to the entire *kṣatriya* caste. But it also has a place outside the caste system, in the lives of ascetics who have renounced the strictures imposed by *varṇāśrama dharma* and wander at will. As with warriors, their fearlessness often makes them feared by others.

Generosity (*dāna*), by contrast, is one of the great virtues—perhaps the greatest—to which a householder should aspire. It too bears particular association with the *kṣatriya* caste but through the rules of kingship and governance as distinct from battle and protection. The virtue of generosity has a particular relation to the Brahmin caste as well, but it is an inverse one. Brahmins fulfill the role not of donors but of recipients; royal largesse, and that of all householders, is owed first and foremost to them.

Finally, in the *varṇāśrama dharma* view, community service (*sevā*) is a virtue especially incumbent upon those placed low in the caste hierarchy. It is their *dharma* to serve their betters. Thus each of these virtues has at least one particular niche in the *varṇāśrama dharma* system.[27]

When translated into the bhakti mode, however, the virtues look radically different. No one is more the object of protection in Hindu society than a woman, who is required by the *Laws of Manu* to be shielded all her life.[28] Yet in the *Bhaktamāl* it is none other than a woman who most directly incarnates the virtues of fearless independence. As for generosity, we have seen that Brahmins are paradigmatically its object, not its agent. Yet it is a Brahmin whose story most vividly describes what true generosity is. Finally, we expect service to emanate naturally from the low, but no one in the *Bhaktamāl* more clearly exemplifies the virtue of community service than a couple who are born king and queen.

Clearly bhakti inverts what is normally understood to be *dharma*, and the *Bhaktamāl* is very much aware that this is so. In introducing both Ravidas and Kabir, Nabhadas notes that these saints explicitly challenged the authenticity of *varṇāśrama dharma*. Ravidas, he says, 'left its conceits behind' (*varṇāśrama abhimāna taji*) and Kabir 'neglected to observe it' (*rākhī nahīṅ varṇāśrama*...), for he maintained that *dharma* was no *dharma* if it stood in opposition to bhakti (*bhakti bimukh jo dharma so adharama*).[29] Similarly, Hit Harivaṃś is portrayed by Priyadas as having cast aside rules and regulations (*bidhi au niṣeda cheda ḍāre*) in adhering to the bhakti path.[30]

And there are numerous incidents in which *dharma* is implicitly challenged: Ravidas neglects his parents; Bilvamaṅgal is infatuated with a woman of ill repute; Kabir travels in the company of a prostitute to keep the crowds away; Tulsidas welcomes a murderer into his presence and shares a meal with him; and on frequent occasions the sanctity of caste is ignored.[31]

Yet this challenge to conventional *dharma* is not the end of the matter. In bhakti, *dharma* is not ultimately abandoned but transformed. It is sublated, *aufgehoben*, taken to a different level. A hint of this is provided by the fact that the language of conventional *dharma* does make its way into the *Bhaktamāl*, particularly in regard to virtue as such. Gopāl Bhaṭṭ, for instance, is described among other things as *dharmaset*, 'righteous' (literally, one who grasps onto *dharma* as a bridge [through life]), and is said to be able to affirm people's virtues (*guna*) while casting aside their vices (*avaguna*).[32] Ravidas too is praised for his ability to articulate the bases for morality (*sadācāra śruti śāstra*) and distinguish between right and wrong (*nīra khīra bibarana*, literally 'discrimination between water and milk').[33] Though Nabhadas reports no action of Surdas other than his singing, even so he brings virtue into play. He claims that those who submit themselves to the virtues of Sur's singing (*gunaśravanani dharai*) strengthen their purity of mind and character (*bimala buddhi guna*).[34]

What happens in each case is that ordinary virtue is reshaped by being set in a new context. It is in the course of managing bhakti rituals in the temple of Rādhā Ramaṇ Jī in Brindavan, for example, that Gopāl Bhaṭṭ performs his role as arbiter of virtue. His power to do so, as context makes clear, comes from having 'tasted the unfathomable sweetness of Brindavan' (*bṛndābana mādhurī agādha hau savāda liyau*), and its effects are distributed by similar means.[35] Gopāl Bhaṭṭ is able to spread virtue through the smallest grain of rice (*sītha*) he may offer to a worshiper as a leftover from Krishna's table.[36]

Ravidas's moral sagacity is also set in an unexpected context. Though it is described in the most traditional Sanskritic, even brahmanical terms (*sadācāra śruti śāstra*) in the poem that introduces his character, Ravidas's command of ethics has nothing to do with his social station, as one would normally think. Quite the contrary, he is an outcaste. And in the poem eulogizing Sur, in which the word virtue (*guna*) appears three times in a relatively short space, the entire context is a devotional song.

We can see a similar process at work in the obverse case—when the starting point is not the seeming affirmation of ordinary *dharma* from a bhakti perspective but its abrogation. Here too bhakti and *dharma* prove unexpected partners, as bhakti accomplishes the ends of *dharma* by its own means. Consider an incident that Priyadas relates about Tulsidas, the poet who created a masterful vernacular *Ramāyaṇa.* Once, it seems, a funeral procession passed Tulsidas at a distance: a Brahmin had just died and his body was being taken to the cremation ground. Among others who accompanied the corpse walked the Brahmin's wife, whose own life was about to come to an end as she committed *satī* on her husband's pyre, thus fulfilling the highest calling of a woman according to a certain commonly accepted understanding of *dharma.* The Brahmin woman greeted Tulsidas from a distance, and he, looking up, answered with the common blessing, 'May fortune be yours' (*suhāgavatī*).[37] This, however, is a greeting reserved for women whose husbands are alive, since a woman's fortune is assumed to follow from the presence of her mate. Indeed one of its connotations is, 'May your husband have a long life.' The woman, who was forced into the position of having to acknowledge the inappropriateness of the greeting, explained that she was on her way to commit *satī.* As soon as she had done so, however, she was full of remorse, because in this circumstance to announce her intent was to vitiate the act before it took place. Through the inadvertent blessing of a *bhakta* she had been separated from her *dharma.*

Fortunately the story does not end at this unhappy impasse. Tulsi took matters into his own hands. He gathered the entire company and encouraged them to adopt genuine faith in Rām, as if to urge on them the literal truth of the dirge that familiarly accompanies a funeral cortege: *rām nām satya hai*, 'Rām's name is truth' or 'Rām's name is reality.' When he saw that their faith was real, he proceeded to restore the dead Brahmin to life, thus vindicating the blessing he had bestowed on the woman in the first place. Her *dharma* was restored, in that she could indeed be fortunate in serving her husband, yet the means by which this had taken place was bhakti. Both bhakti and *dharma* came to fruition through what to worldly eyes appeared a miracle, yet Tulsi was later to claim that he knew no miracles, only one Rām.[38]

As the story suggests, the demands of conventional *dharma* may be satisfied in the ethics of bhakti but rarely because bhakti has those ends in mind. If *dharma* comes true, it is as a reflex of bhakti, not as its aim. We have seen this to be true in the three biographies that have concerned us most. Mira's marriage finally promises to be set right as the *rāṇā* is won over to her ways. Narasī Mehtā meets his family obligations as his daughter's in-laws receive the gifts they demand and his son's marriage is properly observed. In the story of Pīpā and Sīta a lecherous merchant is won back from his sinful ways and converted to righteousness. But in none of these cases is the *dharmic* result accomplished by punctilious observance of *dharma*. Quite the reverse, these heroes and heroines of bhakti care very little for its prescriptions. Only unconsciously do they act on its behalf.

If one were to reconcile bhakti and *dharma* the other way around, beginning from the side of *dharma* rather than from that of bhakti, quite a different configuration would emerge. An amusing example of this approach can be observed in the modern comic-book version of the life of Mirabai, whose story must have been considered too flamboyant to be promulgated to the masses in the terms set forth by the *Bhaktamāl*. Doubtless this was particularly the case because of Mira's sex. In traditional Hindu society, broadly speaking, men may be allowed some moral latitude, especially in their youths, but never women.

If one has read the *Bhaktamāl*, one may be somewhat taken aback to find that in her comic-book incarnation Mira is represented as a paragon of wifely devotion. Indeed she is depicted as having been a dutiful wife before all else. Such a masterly metamorphosis is made possible by transforming the unidentified *rāṇā* in the *Bhaktamāl*'s version into two separate personages: Mira's husband—who dies while she is still relatively young—and her husband's brother, who succeeds him to the throne (but not, of course, to the conjugal bed). The first is a model of virtue who quickly repents any shortsightedness to which he may fall victim, so obedience to him poses no great problem. The second *rāṇā*, however, wields the poison cup and initiates all the other assaults on Mira. Thus, she presents no great affront to *dharma* when she leaves him, especially since he is only her guardian, not her husband. The intensity and musicality of Mira's devotion to Krishna are portrayed on almost every page, and the force of such devotion traditionally was seen as a challenge to her marriage. But, lest any ethical confusion be aroused, the comic-book assures its readers in no uncertain terms that Mira was 'an ideal Hindu wife.'[39] She is said to have been careful to complete her obligations to house and husband before she went off to serve Krishna. (In a booklet that might well reach the eyes of children, the matter of her abstinence from conjugal sex fortunately need not be broached.)

Dividing the *rāṇā* into two figures accomplishes a further objective from a *dharmic* point of view. It makes Mira a dutiful wife in just the years when active participation in family and household is required by Hinduism's classical four-stage conception of the life cycle (*caturāśrama dharma*) and conveniently assigns to her later years the moment when she decided of her own volition to leave her in-laws' house. At least for men, those later years are a time when it is considered entirely appropriate to shake off the obligations of one's home and hearth. When Mira does so, then, she conforms in another aspect to what conventional *dharma* would dictate. The tensions between a life of ecstatic devotion and wifely service have been all but wiped away, and with them the need for a resolution from the side of bhakti's own implicit *dharma* rather than in terms of what convention would dictate.[40]

One rarely finds in the *Bhaktamāl* a sense that the life of bhakti needs to be justified in the eyes of conventional *dharma*, but there is apparently an exception that proves the rule. On one occasion the *Bhaktamāl* registers a corrective to the extreme forms of behavior that bhakti can engender. The story concerns the culmination of Pīpādās's pilgrimage to Dvaraka, presumably the height of his devotional life.

We are told that when he arrived on the beautiful shores of the Arabian Sea, the musical fervor of his circle of *bhaktas* became so intense that he wanted nothing more than to jump into the sea and drown—presumably because he would then have had the sight of Krishna as his last earthly vision and the sounds of Krishna ringing in his ears for all eternity. Priyadas tells us, however, that Krishna saw things differently. He called the group back and sent them home, explaining that reports of religious drownings would not do much for his reputation in the world at large.[41]

At first blush this seems a minor victory for conventional *dharma*, but a closer look reveals that things are not so simple as they seem. No real compromise with worldly values is made, for if Pīpā bows in the direction of conventional morality, it is only at the behest of the object of bhakti itself: Krishna. Furthermore, the modification in Pīpā's behavior is such as to reinforce the bhakti virtue of which he himself is a paradigm: he is reminded of a better way to serve his flock and, by extension, the rest of the world. Indeed the exemplary function of the bhakti community is just what Pīpā has threatened to dissolve. Or to put the matter another way, when Pīpā's bhakti is in danger of becoming a simple rejection of every earthly convention, including the affirmation of life itself, he must be corrected. This redirection of Pīpā's impulse merely restates what he had learned at the outset of his devotional life. When Rāmānand accepted Pīpā into the bhakti fold, his first command was that Pīpā draw back from the life of a renunciant and accept the importance of householdership. To love God is not to leave the world but to transform it.

In the view of the *Bhaktamāl*, then, the life of bhakti is hardly a life without morality. Though saintliness is not constructed by any piling up of 'secular' virtues, it does not exclude them if they follow from a life of love and devotion. Even the codes of the *varṇāśrama dharma* can be accommodated on occasion—though often seemingly by accident. A much firmer place is set aside for the virtues that from time to time support these codes and infuse them with a meaning that is truly personal and social—virtues such as fearlessness, generosity, and service. The reality of the community created by bhakti welds them into patterns of complementarity that give them quite different locations from the ones to which they are assigned in traditional Hindu views of society. As we have seen, these virtues interlock in the lives of saintly individuals. They also serve to reinforce one another in that the *bhaktas* who especially manifest one virtue or another are linked in a single chain by means of the *Bhaktamāl* itself, 'A Garland of Devotees.'

Indeed, as John Carman has pointed out, the virtues these saints exhibit are aspects of the divine character itself.[42] According to the vision of God that is dominant in Vaishnava bhakti, God quells all fear, shows incalculable generosity, and serves his devotees at every turn. It is therefore no surprise that those who worship him should manifest these virtues, both individually and collectively, and that such qualities of life are genuinely fostered nowhere else but in the community of devotion.

3

The *Nirguṇ/Saguṇ* Distinction

This chapter was first published under the title 'The *Nirguṇ/Saguṇ* Distinction in Early Manuscript Anthologies of Hindi Devotion' in David N. Lorenzen, ed., *Bhakti Religion in North India: Community Identity and Political Action* (Albany: State University of New York Press, 1994), pp. 160–80. It was stimulated by David Lorenzen's conviction that *nirguṇ bhakti* functions largely as an independent tradition that contrasts to its *saguṇ* cousin. I am grateful for discussions of that and related matters that occurred at an international conference hosted by Lorenzen and his colleagues at the Colegio de México in 1991.

When we use the term *nirguṇ* to identify one of the great traditions of North Indian religion, one important point of departure is a basic discrimination that has been made between two types of voices emerging from the 'classical' period of bhakti literature in North India. In writing about this period—the so-called devotional period (*bhakti kāl*), extending from roughly the fifteenth through seventeenth centuries—historians of Hindi literature commonly make quite a sharp distinction between poets of the *nirguṇ* persuasion and those of the *saguṇ* camp. In the standard *Hindī Sāhitya kā Bṛhat Itihās*, for example, two volumes are devoted to the *bhakti kāl*, the first (volume 4) dealing with *nirguṇ bhakti* and the second (volume 5) taking up *saguṇ bhakti*. Poets included in the former volume include the iconoclasts: *sants* such as Kabir along with their Sufi counterparts. Poets discussed in the latter volume are the imagists: Sur, Tulsi, and company. These are categorized, for the most part, according to whether they are thought of as poets of Krishna or of Rām.[1] Table 3.1 presents a quick, schematic representation of this way of approaching the *bhakti kāl*, and contains a very short list of the major poet-saints involved:

TABLE 3.1: *Nirguṇ* and *Saguṇ* in *Bhakti-kāl* Hindi Poetry

School	'Without attributes' (*nirguṇ*)	'With attributes' (*saguṇ*)
Deity	(nameless), Rām	Krishna, Rām
Saints	*sants*	*bhaktas*
	Ravidas	Surdas, Tulsidas
	Kabir	Mirabai

Most scholars, including those who write in European languages, have accepted this fundamental distinction between *nirguṇ* and *saguṇ* orientations. Obviously I include myself in this number, since the diagram I have just produced is a very slightly altered version of the one that I prepared for another publication.[2] But I am hardly alone. Charlotte Vaudeville, W. H. McLeod, Shukdev Singh, and many other scholars consider that a coherent *nirguṇ* or *sant* tradition can be rather easily separated from the *saguṇ* persuasion that one otherwise finds in 'classical' Hindi bhakti literature,[3] and most contributors to the important collection of essays entitled *The Sants* take this discrimination as foundational and noncontroversial.[4]

Yet it is worth asking just how true-to-life this dichotomy is. How long has it actually been felt? As Karine Schomer observes in her introduction to *The Sants*,

> The concept of '*nirguṇa* bhakti' as a distinct devotional mode contrasting with '*saguṇa* bhakti', and of the Sants constituting a separate devotional tradition, is relatively new. The idea that there is a coherent body of Sant teachings (*sant mat*) and that individual Sants belong to a common spiritual line of descent (*sant paramparā*) distinct from that of sectarian Vaishnavas did not become fully crystallized until the mid-nineteenth century.[5]

In pointing to the mid-nineteenth century as a possibly crucial juncture, Schomer is apparently thinking of the origins of the Radhasoami movement, within which the concept *sant mat* came into prominent usage.[6] But Radhasoami thinkers took this term to be simply descriptive, nothing novel or of their own invention, and their publications in the early decades of the twentieth century suggest that they did not understand the word *sant* to designate an entirely exclusive *nirguṇ* category.[7] The idea that there was a true dichotomy between *nirguṇ* and *saguṇ* poet-saints may have come into strict usage as late as the 1930s, with the publication of a book that placed Radhasoami *sants* in a larger context: P. D. Barthwal's *The Nirguna School of Hindi Poetry*.[8] The writings of Rāmcandra Śukla at about the same time were probably even more important.

My purpose here is not to pursue this problem in the history of ideas from the nineteenth century backward, though that would be an important and fascinating exercise. Instead, I wish to approach the issue from the opposite end in time. In this chapter, I will ask to what degree we can see a clear distinction being made between *nirguṇ* and *saguṇ* paths in the *bhakti kāl* itself. Can one find it in writings that emerge from North India in the 'classical' period—fifteenth to seventeenth centuries—or must one assume that it was the result of sectarian definitions that grew strong as the centuries passed?[9] If the former, there is no reason to question the rubrics that we have come to accept in describing the religious poetics of the *bhakti kāl*. If the latter, we will need to learn to use a good deal more caution—and perhaps a good deal more imagination—than we have done in the past.

Internal Evidence

One way to investigate the point is to give closer attention than has normally been done to compositions of the *bhaktas* themselves—that is, to poems that can be shown to have existed in their own time, or not long thereafter. A growing arsenal of critical work begins to make this possible.[10] I know the terrain with Surdas far better than elsewhere, and can say that early poems bearing his name show less careful attention to the *nirguṇ/saguṇ* dichotomy than do those added to the Sur corpus later on. True, there are all those famous and eloquent *bhramargīt* poems ridiculing the *nirguṇ* persuasion. But on the other side of the issue, especially in the *vinaya* genre, there is a broad band of themes, tropes, and language that Sur shares not just with Tulsi and Mira but with Ravidas and Kabir.

I have written about this on an earlier occasion[11] and will be revisiting the theme in Chapter 16, so I will not belabor the point here. Rather, let a single poem suffice to show the sort of thing I mean. This composition (Bryant/Hawley §394, NPS 115) is first attested early in the seventeenth century, having almost certainly emerged in the sixteenth:

अपनै जान मैं बहुत करी
कौंन भांति हरि भगति तुम्हारी सु कछु न स्वामी समुझि परी
गए दूरि दरसन कै कारन ब्यापक की बिभुता बिसरी
मनसा वाचा कर्म अगोचर सो मूरति नहि ध्यान धरी
बिनु गुन गुन बिनु रूप रूप बिनु नाम नाम कहि राम हरी
कृपा सिंधु अपराध अपरमित छिमहु सूर पै सब बिगरी

Much I was able to grasp on my own,
But Hari, my master, the act of loving you
was something I could never understand.
I traveled great distances to have a glimpse of you,
forgetting that you reign everywhere
Inaccessible to thoughts, words, and deeds:
that was the image I never thought to see.
Its traits are no traits; its form, no form;
its no-name name they call Rām Hari.
Ocean of mercy, forgive the unbounded impertinence
that has made Sur spoil it all.[12]

The fourth and fifth lines are those that particularly bear remembering. There the renowned *saguṇ* poet, as if to contest that very designation, describes the search for images (*mūrati*) as misguided. He goes on to say that the true image has the trait of being traitless (*binu guna guna*) and the form of being formless (*binu rūpa rūpa*). As for a name, it has an unnamable name (*binu nāma nāma*). In the presence of lines such as this, it seems an understatement to observe that the *nirguṇ/saguṇ* distinction does not seem to work very well for Surdas. In fact, as I have tried to show, it took an invented conversion in his hagiography to make this notion plausible at all. Sur became a pupil of Vallabha, the sectarians said, and forswore this kind of poem, thereafter producing only poems in the approved *saguṇ* mold.[13]

Hagiography

That is indeed the next resource for tracing the history of the *nirguṇ/saguṇ* distinction: hagiography. But the problem with hagiography, as we see in the example I have just cited, is that the early hagiographies themselves seem to have been creations of writers with specific sectarian associations. They were often written precisely with the aim of establishing lines of affinity and affiliation that would give to received tradition a greater—or at least different—coherence than it formerly had. W. H. McLeod has certainly shown this to be the case in the Sikh *janam sākhīs*,[14] and Vallabhite texts such as the *Caurāsī Vaiṣṇavan kī Vārtā* and *Śrī Nāthjī ke Prākaṭya kī Vārtā* seem to evince the same pattern.[15] With Nabhadas and Priyadas, perhaps, one has a somewhat more catholic approach—we await a close analysis of the text of the *Bhaktamāl* on this point—but they too had their sectarian loyalities.[16] David Lorenzen would give considerable weight to the sectarian associations ascribed to Anantdās, though I myself am somewhat more skeptical about how accurately they reflect Anantdās's own historical position.[17]

Another means of approaching the *saguṇ/nirguṇ* question in a hagiographic vein would be to amass references to a sense of lineage in texts attributed to the poet-saints themselves, and there is a certain harvest to be reaped. The results are best on the *nirguṇ* side of the divide: Ravidas, for example, refers to Nāmdev, Kabir, Trilocan, Sādhanā, and Sen.[18] *Saguṇ* poets, by contrast, tend to refer themselves to a different sort of lineage, a mythological variety rather than a human one. Sur and Tulsi set themselves up as heirs to a tradition of divine grace that affected Gajendra, Ajāmil, Ahalyā, and the like. The strictly human connections—that Sur came to Tulsidas to ask his blessing on the *Sūrsāgar*, or that Tulsi carried on a sort of 'Dear Abby' correspondence with Mira (he was Abby)—are hagiographical inventions.[19]

Yet here too the lines are more blurred that the current *nirguṇ/saguṇ* taxonomy would lead one to expect. Consider the case of Sur—or rather, to be more precise, the corpus of poems attributed to Sur that would have been known in the sixteenth century. Within this corpus Sur does, on one occasion, cite another poet, and it is Nāmdev. He alludes to the story of Vishnu's appearing to cover Nāmdev's hut with thatch. Here is the poem (Bryant/Hawley §378, NPS 4):

करनी करुणासिंधु की कहत न बनि आवै
कपट हेत परसे बकी जननी गति पावै
बेद उपनिषद जसु कहै निर्गुनहि बतावै
सोइ सगुन है नंद कै दांवरी बंधावै

बरुन पास ते ब्रजपती छिन मैं छुटकावै
दुषित गजेंद्रहि जानि कै आपुन उठि धावै
उग्रसेन की दीनता सुनि सुनि दुष पावै
कंस मारि राजा कियौ आपुन सिर नावै
कलि मै नामा प्रगटियौ ता कि छानि छवावै
सूरदास की बीनती कोइ जाइ सुनावै

That ocean of mercy: the deeds he has done
  simply cannot be described.
Even for touching him with falsified love
  the bird-woman won a mother's prize.
The Vedas and Upanishads have sung his praise,
  calling him the Formless One,
Yet he's taken form as Nanda's boy
  and allowed himself to be roped down.
In an instant he rescued the master of Braj
  from being caught in Varuṇ's realm,
Just as he hurried to the elephant king
  when he learned what pain he bore.
When he heard of Ugrasen's sad state,
  he too felt the pain,
And made him king by killing Kaṃs.
  Then he himself bowed before him.
When Nāmdev appeared in the present world-age,
  he covered his hut with thatch,
But what of the appeal that Surdas makes?
  Who will make him listen to that?[20]

This alignment between Nāmdev and Surdas is an intriguing one, for of all the great Maharashtrian poets, Nāmdev is perhaps the hardest to situate firmly on one side or the other of the *saguṇ/nirguṇ* line. Furthermore, the way in which Nāmdev is introduced—namely, at the end of a list of figures we might call mythological—suggests that Sur may not have seen the sorts of distinctions that buttress our conception of the *saguṇ/nirguṇ* split. He may not have recognized our commonly observed distinctions between myth and history, and between gods and humans, although his reference to the *kali* age certainly goes some distance toward marking a separation between the divine and the human realms.

So far, then, we have looked at two resources for estimating the force of the *saguṇ/nirguṇ* distinction as felt in 'its own' time: the words of the poet-saints themselves and the hagiographies that soon developed around them. On both scores, the *nirguṇ/saguṇ* distinction survives with only mixed success.

Anthologies

Now it is time to introduce a third resource, one that to my knowledge has never been tapped in trying to deal with the question we have before us. This third resource is provided by early anthologies of the utterances of *sants* and *bhaktas*.[21] It is no surprise that this body of material has been neglected as a scholarly tool: of all the early texts, these are in many ways the most difficult to approach. They are the scrapbooks—and, indeed, the scraps—of the field. They are often the hardest genre to locate in catalogues and indexes of manuscript libraries, and once one finds them, the work has only begun. Often one actually has to go through them to see what poets these anthologies contain. For a catalogue is apt to give such amorphous descriptions as *Dādū jī ke pad*, *Kabīr jī ke kṛt*, *ādi* ('Dādū's poems, Kabir's poems, and so forth')[22] or simply to list the contents of such collections as *sphuṭkar pad* ('miscellaneous *pads*'). Because the more 'miscellaneous' sort in particular are not high-prestige documents—no name recognition, you know—their contents tend to be poorly catalogued, and for the same reason they are often in worse physical shape than the *Sūrsāgars* and *Vinayapātrikās* of this world. Frequently they are slimmer, smaller in physical size, and more haphazardly inscribed than the great named corpora. Finally, and for our purposes crucially, they are less apt to possess a dated colophon.

For all these reasons, many of the leading manuscript libraries of North India seem to have placed a low priority on collecting anthologies of *pads*, the genre that most commonly spans the *nirguṇ/saguṇ* gap. Remarkably, I have been able to find only one dated manuscript entitled *sphuṭkar pad* in the massive library of the Kashi Nagaripracarini Sabha in Banaras, to which, however, I would add two other collections noted among the manuscripts described below.[23] The Jaipur branch of the Rajasthan Oriental Research Institute also has only one *sphuṭkar pad*, and it too is late (VS 1953).[24] The Vrindaban Research Institute, a library located squarely in the middle of *pad* country, has only two (dating to VS 1825 and 1893). Even the Anup Sanskrit Library in Bikaner, a wonderfully rich collection, lists only ten dated manuscripts out of a total of sixty Hindi documents described as *phuṭkar kavitā* (miscellaneous poetry). Of these ten, seven predate VS 1800, the period with which we are concerned.[25]

It is a shame that early anthologies of *pads* have been so sparsely preserved; I find it hard to believe that there really were so few. It is much to be hoped that others will emerge from private collections in the future. For the nonce, however, we must deal with the early dated anthologies we have, and ask what they reveal. In these collections, who was put alongside whom? Does the *saguṇ/nirguṇ* distinction emerge?

We can get a sense of this by classifying the anthologies in question into three groups relevant to the subject at hand. In the first group let us place manuscripts that seem clearly to espouse a *nirguṇ* perspective. (Rām bhakti often abuts rather closely on this *nirguṇ* point of view, so we may have to admit poems of that sort to this list.) Into a second group let us put manuscripts that fall patently on the other side of the divide: *saguṇ* manuscripts containing the outpourings of Krishna *bhaktas*. These two groups should reinforce the *nirguṇ/saguṇ* classification. But what if still other manuscripts are left over? Then we will need a third group, to comprise manuscripts where *nirguṇ* and *saguṇ* voices are set side by side—or at any rate, allowed to nestle between the same two covers. Needless to say, it is this third group that we will watch with particularly strong interest.

Before listing the manuscripts I have found that can be grouped by means of this threefold categorization, I must point out how partial my sample is in relation to the territory that really ought to be covered. The field is vast. All I can report on are *pad* anthology manuscripts that I myself kept notes on—and in some cases, photographs. Not surprisingly, it was my doctoral dissertation (and its seemingly everlasting *Nachlaß*) that initially drove me to it. In the later stages of the project, happily, Kenneth Bryant and I did some of the work together, with Bryant gaining access to what is undoubtedly the most important early anthology of them all, the Fatehpur manuscript of 1582 (VS 1639) housed in the royal collection at Jaipur (see below and Chapter 15). As for myself, I tried to keep an eye out for anthologies as I went from library to library, and sometimes house to house, in Uttar Pradesh, Madhya Pradesh, and Rajasthan searching for early collections of the poetry of Surdas. For Sur's work, I took 1700 CE as my approximate cut-off date—VS 1763, to be precise—so what I have to report here will also fall more or less within that span. Specifically, I shall limit myself to manuscripts written or copied before VS 1800 (that is, 1743 CE).

The first limitation on my sample is therefore time. Obviously, later dated manuscripts are also relevant, and undated ones provide a particularly important additional challenge. But they are beyond the scope of what I can consider here.

A second limitation is geographical. I was primarily following leads about Sur manuscripts. These were rather extensive leads, to be sure, but they were specialized for Sur nonetheless.[26] I was looking for early dated *pad* anthologies in the hope that they would reveal poems of Sur that had hitherto been overlooked. (Luckily, they sometimes did.) This search led me to certain sections of North India rather than others. I tried to extend my list of the libraries to be visited as much as I sensibly could, but I can hardly claim to have been everywhere, even everywhere in northwest and north-central India. Moreover, my records for collections outside of India are particularly weak. Let me give a list of the libraries and institutions from which my survey of dated *pad* anthologies is drawn:

TABLE 3.2: Libraries Consulted

Agra Hindi Vidyapith
Allahabad Museum
Anup Sanskrit Library, Bikaner
Library of the Government Degree College, Datia
Hindi Sahitya Sammelan, Allahabad
Jiwaji University, Gwalior
K. M. Hindi Institute, Agra University
Maharaja Man Singh Pustak Prakash Research Centre, Jodhpur
Maharaja Sawai Man Singh II Museum, Jaipur
Mathuradhish Temple, Kota
Nagaripracarini Sabha, Banaras
Rajasthan Oriental Research Institute
Bikaner
Jaipur
Jodhpur
Kota
Udaipur
Rajasthani Shodh Sansthan, Chaupasini, Jodhpur
Library of the Tilakayat Maharaj Sri, Srinathji Temple, Nathdvara
Sarasvati Bhandar, Kankarauli
Vrindaban Research Institute

With the preliminaries now stated, we have before us the task of depositing the manuscripts I found into the receptacles we have created. As I have hinted, readers may be disappointed to see how few there are. Considering the size of the sample, we can only guess what contours ultimately will emerge from a more careful and extensive study. But that, I think, we can do.

In the list that follows, I give the manuscripts by accession number, prefixed by serial numbers where necessary. The numbers refer to the Hindi collections of the institutions named, except in cases where the collections are not subdivided by language and manuscripts. There, obviously, the number refers to the whole collection. I list documents by date, the oldest first. It is important to note—and this is yet another important caveat—that specifically sectarian collections such as the *Pañcvāṇī* and *Sarvāṅgī* of the Dādū Panth and the Sikhs' *Ādi Granth* are omitted from consideration. Otherwise the list would be much longer—and its first category, certainly, much larger, though Rajab's *Sarvāṅgī* strays a bit into Vaishnava terrain. Readers should set what they learn from the list that follows against the background of these better-known, better-published collections.

Here, then, is a description of early Hindi devotional anthologies that I have surveyed. Gaps in my knowledge will be quickly apparent, and there is no real defense for them. I can only plead that at the point I surveyed many of these manuscripts, I had in mind quite a different purpose from the present one, and that I have often not been able to consult these manuscripts since.

Group 1: Nirguṇ (and Rām Bhakti) Manuscripts

(a) No. 3322, Maharaja Sawai Man Singh II Museum, Jaipur, VS 1717. Regrettably, my data are not complete, so I cannot say at what point the various sections of this manuscript were conjoined or whether the colophon applies conclusively to all of them, as is implied by the catalogue of the Jaipur royal *pothīkhānā*.[27] I also do not know the size of the manuscript or its full contents. I can say with confidence, however, that *pads* attributed to Kabir, Gorakhnāth, Datta (presumably Dattātrey), Pīpā, Santāṅ, and Haraṇvant are included.

(b) Serial no. 2379, accession no. 1602/933, Nagaripracarini Sabha, Banaras, VS 1742. It contains *vāṇīs* and *sabadīs* of Gorakhnāth, Bharatharī, Dattātrey, Mahādev, Cirpaṭ, Hālīpāv, and others, in 101 folios. This collection seems to be a product of the Nāth Sampradāy.

(c) Serial no. 74, accession no. 773/48, Nagaripracarini Sabha, Banaras. Because this manuscript is a composite, of which only one part—the last and apparently latest—is dated, one may refer to its date as *terminus ad quem* VS 1757. It contains *pads* of Raidās (i.e., Ravidas), Kabir, and, as the catalogue says, 'so forth' (*ādi*).[28]

(d) No. 30587, Rajasthan Oriental Research Institute, Jodhpur, VS 1788. The manuscript contains *sākhīs* of Dādū and Kabir.

I wish I could say I have actually examined all these manuscripts. I have not. With this set, I am working from catalogues only, so I do not know, for example, whether on inspection the Jodhpur manuscript (d) would prove to be a standard *Pañcvāṇī*. It is not so called in the catalogue, and that may say something. This Jodhpur manuscript certainly seems the easiest to associate with a definite *sampradāy*. It, like quite a number of others in the Jodhpur collection of the Rajasthan Oriental Research Institute, is a product of the Dādū Panth. One of the Banaras manuscripts (b) seems similarly to have been compiled under the auspices of a particular community, in this case the Nāth Saṁpradāy. The remaining two (a, c), however, are not so easily assigned, and may not reflect the work of any sect as such.

Group 2: Saguṇ (and Krishna Bhakti) Manuscripts

This second group is somewhat larger than the first, but let us not forget that this may reflect the fact that I was searching especially for Sur, and that fixed, well-known sectarian anthologies have been excluded from the first group. The manuscripts in the second group are as follows:

(a) No. 1057, K. M. Hindi Institute, Agra University, dated VS 1713. Although the hand is uneven, the various sections of this manuscript are consecutively numbered, suggesting that the manuscript was assembled at a time at least approximately contemporary with the part that does bear a date. This colophon comes after the *daśamaskandh* (i.e., *rāspañcādhyāyī*) of Nandadās, the third section in the manuscript, and includes the date 1713. Preceding that are an incomplete *Hit Caurāsī* and some five hundred *pads* of Surdas. Following it is a brief *ṣaṭu rāg svarūp varṇan*, one folio in length, and thirty-five folios of *pad saṅgrah* enticingly entitled *mallā akhāḍo*. The poets represented are Nandadās, Surdas, Mānkavi, Govindasvāmī, Kiśordās, Caturbhujdās, Kṛṣṇdās, Mādhodās, Bakhatāvar, Jagannāth, Tursī [*sic*], Annadās, Hit Harivaṃś, Girathardās [*sic*], Narasiṃhdās, Rāmdās, and

Sundarkuṃvari. Although the words *śrī gorakh* have been inserted on what seems to have been a previously blank space just after the colophon, the whole collection is distinctively *saguṇ*. It is notable, however, that it crosses *sāmpradāyak* lines, beginning with Hit Harivaṃś and proceeding to many of the (Vallabhite) *aṣṭachāp* and beyond. If the parallel to manuscripts of the Dādū Panth could be trusted, this would seem to mean that the scribe or his patron held Hit Harivaṃś in special veneration, but the length of the Surdas section and the fact that the place of composition is given as Meḍtā make one wonder how this could have been so.

(b) No. 30346, Rajasthan Oriental Research Institute, Jodhpur, entitled *phuṭapadāḥ* (that is, *sphuṭkar pad*) and listed in the catalogue as bearing the dates VS 1713–14. These dates appear in notes of two financial transactions that were made on remaining pages of the manuscript, immediately after the *pads*. The manuscript is in two sections, of 110 and 91 folios respectively, and is written in at least two different hands. Agardās (elsewhere, Agradās), Kiśordās, Mādhodās, and Mira are among the signatures I saw, and I also noticed an enticing reference to the *vallabh kul*. The *pads* seem universally to be in the *saguṇ* mode.

(c) No. 2469, Rajasthan Oriental Research Institute, Udaipur, entitled *virah līlā*, dated VS 1731. This is a brief collection, comprising merely eleven folios.

(d) No enumeration, private collection of Dr Nareś Candra Bansal, Kasganj, *pad saṅgrah*, sections of which bear the dates VS 1740 and VS 1750. The main portions of the manuscript, which are numbered consecutively, are in the same hand and comprise chiefly the oldest dated *kīrtan praṇālī* (hymnbook) of the Vallabha Sampradāy that I have seen. The VS 1750 colophon comes at the end of this section, following *pads* arranged according to the seasonal (*varṣotsav*) and daily (*nitya sevā*) calendars, with a few additions at the end. Then follows a more casual Vallabhite *pad saṅgrah* in the same hand. A briefer *pad saṅgrah* in a different hand precedes the main section, and there are various short sections in Gujarati interspersed. Like *kīrtan praṇālīs* in current use, the *pads* that appear are largely of the *aṣṭachāp*, augmented by later sectarian poets, but one also finds the occasional verse from Narasī Mehtā in this manuscript of Gujarati provenance. This is definitely a *saguṇ*, Krishna bhakti collection. The few poems appropriate to Rām Navamī are also of a *saguṇ* nature.

(e) No. 2437, Maharaja Sawai Man Singh II Museum, Jaipur, a large manuscript written in different parts, with sections on the poetry of Priyadas and Nāgarīdās dated VS 1783 and that representing Sur dated VS 1784.

(f) Serial no. 3258, accession no. 3477, Rajasthan Oriental Research Institute, Kota, entitled *kīrtan janmāṣṭamī rādhāṣṭamī kīrtan caupaḍī*, with individual poems bearing dates ranging, in a puzzling fashion, from VS 1780 to VS 1810. Many are of Nagadhardās, but a substantial number of other poets are represented also, in a total of forty folios.[29]

(g) The next oldest sectarian collections of *pads* that I have seen bear dates later than VS 1800 and therefore fall 'off the map' from the point of view of this presentation. Yet I might mention that the Vrindaban Research Institute has a Rādhāvallabhī *varṣotsav ke pad* dated VS 1893 (serial no. 752, accession no. 4400). The library of the Tilakāyat Mahārāj Śrī at Nathdvara contains only three dated collections of *pads* used in daily worship (called in the catalogue *nitya kīrtan* and *nitya ke pad*), and these are more recent than the group under consideration here, since they bear the dates VS 1834, 1886, and 1890. Libraries of other Vallabhite *gaddīs*, such as those at Jatipura and Kamban, which I have not yet been able to survey, may of course provide earlier manuscripts, but if my somewhat schematic notes on the well-known collection at Kankarauli are an accurate forecast, one should not hold out too great a hope.

On the basis of the evidence at hand it is indeed surprising that a larger number of early, dated *kīrtan praṇālīs* have not appeared. One obvious explanation is that such volumes would have been in sufficiently frequent use that the oldest among them long ago deteriorated, to the point of needing to be replaced by more recent copies. One sees this preference for recently 'copied' versions even in the present day, at least in the Vallabha Sampradāy, for printed editions have quickly replaced manuscripts in temple use. Families known to have been singers (*kīrtaniyā*) in the *sampradāy* for many generations—at least the ones I have visited—do sometimes work from manuscripts, but these too look comparatively recent, certainly less than two centuries old.[30]

Group 3: Manuscripts Combining Saguṇ and Nirguṇ Poems

We now come to the group of manuscripts that is for our purposes the most interesting, namely those that span the gap between *saguṇ* and *nirguṇ bhakti* (if indeed the latter category makes sense, a question that Charlotte Vaudeville has forcefully raised).[31] The first entry in this group has a distinctly *saguṇ* bias—so much so that it has most often been referred to as a *Sūrsāgar*—but closer examination reveals that it belongs in this group of what would seem from a later point of view to be 'hybrid' manuscripts. It is:

(a) The manuscript written at Fatehpur, near Jaipur, and published in facsimile as *Pad Sūrdāsjī kā / The Padas of Surdas* by Gopāl Nārāyaṇ Bahurā, with an introductory essay by Kenneth E. Bryant. It is housed in the royal collection of the Maharaja of Jaipur.[32] The manuscript is complex in its organization. It is divided into three broad sections. The first and third are with but a single exception devoted entirely to Surdas, while the second section is an anthology. Two scribes are involved, and the sections are numbered independently, as if the scribes were copying from separate manuscripts. The second section—the anthology—contains 178 poems, beginning, actually, with Kabir. This middle section covers plenty of ground. One meets such *saguṇ* poets as Paramānandadās and Nāmdev (though there is some doubt about how he should be classified), but also, on the other hand, *nirguṇ* figures such as Kabir, Sundardās, Ravidas, Kīlhadās, and the *vinaya* poet Kānhāṅdās. After Sur, Kānhāṅdās is the poet who appears most frequently. The first section (106 poems) is exclusively Surdas and the third (127 poems) is tantamount to it: only a single poem bearing the signature Śyāmghan intervenes, and I wonder whether the scribe—one Rāmdās Ratan—understood it too to be a Surdas poem, since the poet's signature sometimes appears as Sūrsyām. This third section is organized by raga.

So looking at the manuscript as a whole, one has two 'book-end' sections—doubtless based on two independent earlier manuscripts (there is significant duplication)—and these are Surdas through and through. But they are separated by an anthology in which Sur appears along with a number of other poets. Clearly, then, this is a mixed *nirguṇ/saguṇ* manuscript, but not only on account of the fact that Sur is a *saguṇ* poet while Kabir and Ravidas are *nirguṇīs*. The poems attributed to Surdas also straddle the line. While most of his compositions fall easily in the *saguṇ* domain, there is an impressive sequence at the end of the first part (poems 96–114) that is given over entirely to *nirguṇ* poetry, including the lengthy *sūr pacīsī*. Perhaps in the mind of the first scribe these poems served as a natural introduction to the second section, which begins with Kabir before taking up a long sequence of Surdas poems and going on from there. For further detail, see Chapter 15.

(b) No. 209, Anup Sanskrit Library, Bikaner, dated VS 1668. The manuscript consists of assorted *dohās* and *savaiyās*—228 of the former, 132 of the latter. I have photographed the manuscript, but the prints, many of which are inadequate in their present version, remain to be closely examined. A quick survey, however, shows a considerable range of subjects and poets—all the way from cautionary *dohās* of the *nirguṇ* type to *pads* dedicated to Krishna.[33]

(c) An unnumbered manuscript from the collection of Harihar Nivās Dvivedī, now in the collection of Jiwaji University, Gwalior, where it is described as *bhajan ādi*. The portion bearing the colophon, dating it to VS 1727, contains thirty-nine folios. The collection begins with *dohās* and proceeds to *pads*. Both *nirguṇ* and *saguṇ* poems appear, but aside from Kabir no well-known poets are represented.

(d) No. 6992, Rajasthan Oriental Research Institute, Jodhpur, entitled *phuṭ pad saṅgrah sūr ādi* and containing at various places the dates VS 1736, 1742, and 1744. The poets represented are primarily Vaishnava—Nandadās, Tulsidas, Agardās, and Paramānand, and there is a *sūr pacīsī*—but Kabir is also included.[34]

(e) No. 992, K. M. Hindi Institute, Agra University, dated VS 1762, is a large (340 folios) Dādū-Panthī collection that begins with substantial collections of Dādū (with an internal colophon of VS 1660), Kabir, Nāmdev, Raidas, Har[i]dās, and Garībdās. It then proceeds to a *pad saṅgrah* before returning to Bakhnāṅ, whom one would expect in a Dādū-Panthī collection of this sort, and there is a final untitled *pad saṅgrah* section in which the colophon appears. In the *pad saṅgrahs*, *saguṇ* poets are represented. Six poems of Sur, for instance, appear on folios 260–1.

(f) No. 2062, Rajasthan Oriental Research Institute, Udaipur. This *pad saṅgrah* is undated, but it is bound together with a *prahelikā saṅgrah* (collection of riddles) bearing a colophon dating it to VS 1754. It seems a reasonable likelihood that both sections belong to the same period. In the *pad saṅgrah*, Krishna poets such as Sur are interspersed with others such as Raidās, Tulsidas, and less familiar figures such as Ahmad and Gaṅgā.

(g) No. 2511 (1), Rajasthan Oriental Research Institute, Udaipur, entitled *phuṭkar kavitā* and in sections bearing various dates extending from VS 1777 to VS 1791. The manuscript consists of seventy folios, numbered from 21 to 90, representing such poets as Kabir, Keśav, Navaraṅg, and Tursī (Nirañjanī?).

Conclusion

I set out by saying I wanted to find some means to assess how high the wall between the so-called *nirguṇ* poets and their *saguṇ* cousins was felt to be in their own time. That is, I wanted to find ways to determine how firm the *saguṇ/nirguṇ* divide might have seemed in the sixteenth and seventeenth centuries, up as far as VS 1800. I suggested there were various materials we could use to address the problem: internal references in the poetry of these *sants* and *bhaktas*; perspectives expressed in their hagiographies; and finally divisions—explicit or implicit—observed in early anthologies of their verse. The beginnings of an estimate can now be made.

It seems to me that each of these yardsticks teaches us to exercise caution when we speak of the great contrast between *nirguṇīs* and *saguṇīs* in the early or 'classical' period of North Indian *bhakti*, the *bhakti kāl*. The most influential sectarian anthologizers certainly saw the force of this distinction, but even there it sometimes took a while to sand down the rough edges, as in the case of the *Ādi Granth*. Mira and Sur, whom some put in, were cast out by others.[35] In addition one has to reckon with the fact that even among *nirguṇ* anthologies there was a range of personality. As Karine Schomer and Linda Hess have so nicely shown, there is a difference between the flinty Kabir of the *Bījak*; the hearty, domestic Kabir of the *Ādi Granth*; and the softer, more mystical Kabir of the *Pañcvāṇī*.[36] And then there is the fact that as the Kabir Panth itself branched out, Kabir branched with it.[37]

Even so, if one works from the great sectarian anthologies, the *nirguṇ/saguṇ* distinction largely works. From this vantage point the theological conclusions assumed by the editors of the *Hindī Sāhitya kā Bṛhat Itihās* and similar works—and the organizational strategies they pursued—make tolerably good sense. Yet there are other kinds of evidence, and other anthologies in particular, that need to be taken into consideration. The anthologies I have described here are only a part of the literature that deserves to be surveyed, but they do seem clearly to suggest that the *nirguṇ/saguṇ* distinction only reveals part of the truth about how poets of the *bhakti kāl* were viewed in documents that we can be sure were written within a century or so of the poets' own time.

It is true that, among the anthologies I have presented, there are some that bear a clear *nirguṇ* stamp—and some that bear a *saguṇ* stamp too. But there are also a considerable number of manuscripts that cannot be forced to either side of the *nirguṇ/saguṇ* divide. If my sample is any indication, this last group—the hybrids—is a substantial one, and as I have remarked, I suspect it may have been even more substantial in the sixteenth and seventeenth centuries than we might guess on the basis of the documents that have survived to our own time. Broadly speaking, then, we seem to be dealing with a period and a tradition that did see differences of theological slant, social perspective, and literary mood between *nirguṇ* and *saguṇ* poets. As we know, sectarian boundaries were early erected to enshrine those differences, though earlier in some instances (the Sikh Panth, for example) than in others. Yet at the same time there seem to have been many settings in which the sectarian divisions that later came to loom so large were not—or not yet—regarded as determinative. In such settings the *nirguṇ/saguṇ* division was often honored, if it was honored at all, in the breach.

MIRABAI

4

Mirabai in Manuscript

'Mirabai in Manuscript' is published here for the first time. A germ of the essay was delivered in oral form to the international conference on Mirabai hosted by the University of California at Los Angeles and the Los Angeles County Museum of Art in October, 2002. I am grateful to Nancy M. Martin, the principal organizer, for her invitation to attend and to other participants for vigorous discussion.

Conversations and written exchanges with a number of people have helped me formulate this chapter. I am grateful to Anne Murphy and Jaswinder Garg for help with the *Prem Abodh*; to Susham Bedi for a discussion of the proper interpretation of the fourth poem analyzed here; to Gurinder Singh Mann for a Devanagari text of the *Kartārpur* Mira poem; to Paul Arney, for his insightful study of the Dakor manuscript; to Nancy Martin for many helpful orientations to the field and for photographs of the three Jodhpuri poems discussed here; to Neelima Shukla-Bhatt for assistance in making contact with the Gujarāt Vidyā Sabhā; and to Vibhuti Shelat and her colleagues at the Sabhā itself. Heidi Pauwels' presentation to the Mirabai conference convened in Los Angeles was an inspiration. Last but not least, I am deeply indebted to Frances Taft, not only for her original framing of the problem addressed here, but for a helpful personal visit and several subsequent e-mail communications that have saved me from errors, altered my thinking, and revealed new horizons in the field of Rajasthani history.

History and Hagiography

Frances Taft has recently published a thoughtful and extremely helpful article entitled 'The Elusive Historical Mirabai: A Note,' in which she reviews the process by means of which we have arrived at the current consensus on who Mirabai was in 'a modern historical sense.' She lays it out in prose and chart, in part with the purpose of justifying a basic biographical framework for Mirabai that emerges from the work of the early historians who were making the transition to European-style history starting in the last two decades of the nineteenth century. Taft raises questions about certain details that have been fitted to this basic framework for Mira's life, and she points to areas where further research might provide a clearer picture, but through it all she remains confident about one basic distinction. She holds that records kept by earlier courts and genealogists may largely be trusted to provide the sort of information we would regard as history, while anything smacking of bhakti is suspect. The first sort of record leads back to 'the historical Mirabai,' while the second produces 'a myriad of traditional and/or popular Mirabais that have evolved [subsequently].' Although she concedes that Rajasthani traditions too are apt to be 'unreliable for historical purposes' in their raw form, Taft frames her essay as a clear binary. It's history on the one hand—as represented first by court professionals and later by Rajasthan's European-style historians—versus hagiography on the other.[1]

At the beginning of her essay, Taft explains why she went to the trouble of providing this genealogy of how the historical Mirabai took 'scholarly' shape in the course of the last century or so. She says she was startled to learn that other academics believed, in the words of one writer she quotes, that 'we lack a reliable historical frame to associate with Mira's life....' I am the writer in question, but Taft notes that Nancy Martin and Parita Mukta are guilty of saying similar things.[2] It may indeed be that I went too far, too fast in saying what I did, since at the time I wrote, I ignored a brief but important passage that appears in the mid-seventeenth-century Jodhpuri genealogy *(khyāt)* of Muṅhatā Naiṇsī. Naiṇsī is often cited—by Taft, for example—as saying that Bhojrāj was one of the sons of Rāṅā Sāṅgā of Chittor and that Mirabai Rāṭhor was married to him.[3] Actually it isn't quite that simple. Naiṇsī's *khyāt* says that 'people *say*' Mirabai was married to Bhojrāj. His words are these: 'Bhojrāj Sāṅgāvat: they say that Mirabai Rāṭhor was married to him' *(bhojarāja sāṅgāvata / iṇanuṅ kahe chai mīrāṅbāī rāṭhoḍa paraṇāī hutī).*

Of course, the fact that Naiṇsī should record this bit of popular knowledge about the Sisodiyā lineage as it was evidently accepted in mid-seventeenth century Jodhpur is itself quite significant, even if

Naiṇsī doesn't mention her when he comes to the Mertiyā aspect of his omnibus compilation. (After all, she was a girl and therefore not strictly speaking relevant to the Mertiyā lineage, though the man who came to be largely accepted as her father, Ratansiṃh Dūdāvat, had no sons.)[4] But I wish I understood the manuscript status of Naiṇsī's *khyāt*. The print version, published by the Rājasthān Prācyavidyā Pratiṣṭhān (Rajasthan Oriental Research Institute) from 1960–7, gives no information about the manuscript that it presumably reproduces. Probably it is one of the *Muṇhatā Naiṇsī rī Khyāts* in the Pratisthān's own collection, but its manuscript catalogue lists only a few of these as bearing a precise date—all within the last century or so. And for the manuscript most likely to have served as the basis for the Pratishān's edition (accession no. 3341), the 'date' column is simply left blank.[5]

I have no specific reason to doubt that a manuscript like the Jodhpur one has been faithfully copied since the time of its composition. But if there is any doubt, that question takes on more than nit-picking significance in view of what we know about how information about 'the historical Mirabai' did in fact expand expontentially—and on dubious authority—later on. On this point I would recognize the groundbreaking work of Nancy Martin, and call to witness the fine scholarship of Frances Taft herself. I would also mention the substantial literature in a similar vein on other major bhakti figures of the period—Ravidas, Kabir, Nāmdev, Guru Nanak, Surdas, and most pointedly Philip Lutgendorf's study on 'The Quest for the Legendary Tulsīdās.'[6]

Without meaning to doubt that there are genuine differences between the motives and canons that shaped texts on either side of the history/hagiography divide that Taft takes for granted, I would ask that the historical texts be subjected to the same level of manuscriptival scrutiny that we familiarly bring to bear when we smell the sweet-and-sour scent of hagiography. And I would ask that documents that did not originate at court—in this case, *bhaktamāls* and *pad-saṅgrahas*—not be thrown out of court for that reason alone. After all, just what is a 'court,' and why should we believe that they provide safe historiographical haven in all cases? Naiṇsī's way of mentioning Mirabai—'they say'—suggests that the boundaries were permeable; and his genealogical format shows that, as always, the questions asked cast a huge shadow over the answers received. Perhaps we'd know more if Mirabai had given birth to sons. But her whole mythology demands that she *not* give birth to sons. Who knows?—maybe it's not just mythology—but we are saddled with the limitations that the genre imposes. Historians have genres too; it's not just a 'literary' issue.

Frances Taft starts from the assumption that we can be sure about at least two things: that Mira came from Merta, and that she was married into the royal family of Mewar. Local knowledge about this point from the two cities in question does not take us very far back in time. For Mewar, Tod's famous statement in 1829 that Mirabai was married to Rāṇā Kumbhā is our earliest clearly datable reference—and vigorously disputed as to its accuracy, of course. The well known temple in Chittor popularly called the 'Mira temple' doesn't help. It is a venerable structure, but it bears no trace of her name or story in its sculptural program. At Merta lasting written records emerge only at the end of nineteenth century in Muṅśī Devī Prasād's *Mīrāṅbāī kā Jīvancaritra* (1898). He is the first, for example, to provide a date for Mira's marriage—1516. And there are problems. Frances Taft reports that an earlier document (*Meṛtīya Khāṃp Kulasā*) cited as evidence for this date by H. S. Bhāṭī does not in fact include it.[7] The reference to Mirabai in the Mertiyā genealogies attached as an annex to Naiṇsī's *Vigat* in the reign of Rājā Ajītsiṃh (1707–24) of Jodhpur may be more reliable.[8] There she appears in a note about Ratansiṃh, the third son of Rāv Dūdā, who is remembered to have been given Kuḍkī village and to have had no son, but rather 'a daughter, Mīrā, whom he married to the Rāṇā of Cittor' (*ratanasiṅghajī tiṇāṇ nai kuḍakī dīvī so kaṅvar to huvau nahīṅ nai bāī mīrāṅ parama bhagata huī nai cītoḍa rāṅṇājī nai paraṇāyā*).

Given the lateness and sparseness of this record, we are ironically thrown over to the bhakti side of the history/hagiography divide for anything further that would support Taft's conviction that Mira came from Merta and married into Mewar. And the principal evidence is this. Priyadas, who wrote his *Bhaktirasabodhinī* commentary on Nabhadas's *Bhaktamāl* in 1712, refers to the person Mira married and the person who tried to poison her as *rānā* (i.e., *rāṇā*). The reference to Mewar seems unmistakable: no other major lineage designates its kings in this way. Furthermore, he says she came from Merta. On the Mewar side of things a further shadow is cast by Priyadas's account of Ravidas, whom he depicts as having been patronized by an unnamed Jhālī queen from Chittor.[9] The Sisodiyā rulers did take wives from the Jhālā clan—Rāṇā Sāṅgā's mother was a Jhālī—and Priyadas may have had this queen in mind.[10] Other versions of the story apparently identify this or some other Jhālī queen with Mirabai herself, and it seems likely that Mirabai's presumed association with Ravidas—as his pupil—justified the inclusion of a poem attributed to her in early Sikh anthologies culminating in the *Gurū Granth Sāhib*, where Ravidas figures importantly.

Here then, with Priyadas, we find the great and substantive evidence for a connection between Mira and the courts of Mewar and Merta, but this evidence—somewhat hazy, as the Jhālī motif shows—takes us back only to the beginning of the eighteenth century. Nabhadas, writing sometime about 1600, gives us none of these specifics.[11] All we learn from him is that when Mira left aside the 'chains of family' (*kula-śṛṇkhalā*), certain 'evil ones' (*duṣṭani*) took it amiss and tried to poison her. The story is familiar, of course, and certainly tallies with Priyadas's exposition of it, but in its own terms, nothing forces or indeed urges us to locate this drama at the court of Mewar. Only when Priyadas speaks of the evildoer as *rāṇā* does the connection become plain, and it remains a general one: Priyadas names no names.[12]

A fascinating postscript to this tale is provided by the *Prem Abodh*, a hagiographical collection from the Punjab for which we have a manuscript dating to 1783 (VS 1840). This manuscript, now housed at Khalsa College, Amritsar, tells us that it in turn is a copy of a manuscript dated 1693 (VS 1750). In the *Prem Abodh*, like the *Bhaktirasabodhinī*, we find Mira arrayed against the *rāṇā*, though this Mira is devotionalized in what seems a distinctively 'Punjabi' way. We have multiple passages in which her pellucid inner spirituality, focused on Giridhar—the *aṇtarī* realm—is contrasted to the external deceptions of the world: *saṃsār*—the *bāharī* domain.[13]

But more interesting for our purposes is the plot against whose background this inner/outer dichotomy ultimately gets projected. This time the *rāṇā* in question—a principal protagonist of *saṃsāra*—turns out to be her own father rather than any of her in-laws. The *rāṇā* is neither her father-in-law nor Bhojrāj nor his evil brother Vikramājīt. This comes clear in a long exchange in which the king addresses Mira as a daughter (*putrī*), and he and his wife, in turn, are identified as her parents (*mātā-pitā*). Furthermore, there is no mention of Mira's ever getting married, so we apparently have a version of the story in which the connection between Mira and Mewar is understood to have been a natal one. In the brief portrait of Mira's devotee Karmābāī, which follows that of Mira herself, we are explicitly told that Mirabai lived in the city of Udaipur, which succeeded Chittor as the capital of Mewar after being founded in 1559.[14]

If this seems unfamiliar, other aspects of the story will not. The *rāṇā*, enraged by Mira's connections with a bunch of *sādhus* and by secret closed-door conversations with a man he assumes to be her lover, determines to poison her—not once but twice. When that fails, he goes to her at midnight with a sword. This time his weapon is met with another—the *sudarśan cakra* that Krishna holds in one of his four arms as he stands there listening to Mira sing—and the amazed *rāṇā* flees both its 'fine vision' (*sudarśan*) and its disc (*cakra*). After a long night of fearful trauma the *rāṇā* sees the light, and with that the story moves on to a happy ending. In an inversion of worldly values, the king and his wife go to Mirabai and become their daughter's devotees:

> Now you are no longer our daughter.
> You are Hari's servant, and Hari himself.[15]

What particularly intrigues me about this version of Mira's story is the generational element. I've always felt it was more natural to understand Priyadas's *rāṇā* as Mira's father-in-law than her husband,[16] and the *Prem Abodh* seems to confirm that I'm not the only one to have understood the story in that or a similar way. Harirāmvyās's line about Mira also stresses the father-daughter relationship rather than the conjugal one. His words are: *mīrāvāī vinu ko bhaktani pitā jāni ura lāvai* ('With Mīrābāī gone, who will embrace devotees like [a daughter] her father?')[17]

Heidi Pauwels interprets this line as referring to the absence of any improper, erotic component in Mira's interactions with the men who formed the greater part of her adoptive 'family' of Krishna devotees, and this may well be correct. But in light of the father-daughter dimension that appears in the *Bhaktirasabodhinī* and *Prem Abodh*, I wonder whether this motif may have had a wider, more complicated frame of reference by the time Vyās made it his keynote in lamenting the death of Mirabai. And when was this? The earliest manuscript attestation for the verse in question is 1737 CE, but Pauwels argues plausibly—from the convergence of existing manuscript recensions, from the apparent absence of updating in the service of sectarian aims, and from content *per se*—that it is probably to be traced to the hand of Harirāmvyās himself. This takes us to the mid-sixteenthth century or perhaps a little later.

Let it be noted, as we leave profiles of the daughterhood of Mira, that to feature this motif is to run at a definite tangent to the historicizing impetus that interpreted and shaped the story of Mirabai toward the end of the nineteenth century, when it was aligned in such a self-conscious way with the *Naiṇsī rī Khyāt*'s apparent focus on the Bhojrāj-Mirabai liaison. Fortunately the story has a happy ending, but otherwise the politics of bride-killing as a family affair have a truly modern ring.

So much for the Mewar side of Mira's story. As for the Merta aspect, I defer to Heidi Pauwels, whose discussion of evidence that Mira was understood to be associated with the Mertiyā branch of the Rāṭhor lineage will soon be in print.[18] Suffice it to say that the evidentiary road again requires that one make crucial use of bhakti sources, this time situating them in relation to royal chronicles written at Jodhpur and Agra.

Finally we should make mention of another seventeenth-century bhakti document that casts a different sort of light on Mirabai, one focused neither on Merta nor on Mewar. This is the *Caurāsī Vaiṣṇavan ki Vārtā* attributed to Gokulnāth, a grandson of Vallabhācārya to whom sectarian traditions attach the dates 1551–1640 (or sometimes 1647) CE. The date usually accepted as providing us with the earliest extant copy of the *Caurāsī Vaiṣṇavan kī Vārtā* is also 1640, which appears in the colophon of a manuscript archived in the Sarasvati Bhandar at Kankarauli.[19] Yet considering that this date coincides perfectly with the presumed date of Gokulnāth's death, that it is offered without any of the additional dating information manuscripts usually supply, and that the manuscript already contains portions of the commentary of Harirāy (1590–1715 CE according to sectarian traditions), certain doubts have been cast on its authenticity.[20] We can be sure, however, that the *Vārtā* was in circulation with its Harirāy commentary by 1695, when another dated manuscript appears.

The great interest of the *Vārtā*'s account of Mirabai is its adversarial tone. Kṛṣṇadās, one of the most important figures in the sect's early institutional formation, is said to have encountered her in her village (*gāma*), located somewhere on the road from Braj to Gujarat. He found her at home (*ghara*) surrounded by religious persons of various types (*santa mahanta aneka svāmī aura mārga ke*), who were waiting for donations. This scene paves the way for Kṛṣṇadās's reaction to Mirabai, which is exactly contrary on both accounts. For her part, Mira offers him a gift immediately, rather than making him wait. But Kṛṣṇadās refuses to accept this donation on the grounds that Mira is not an initiate of Vallabha and is surrounded by others of a similarly mongrel status.[21] That too has its irony, since Kṛṣṇadās was born *śūdra*, as the *Vārtā* freely tells us; but we are to understand that his initiation at the hands of Vallabha changed all that.

The art of the story is obviously to be found in its bold inversions, and the issue of its being trustworthy history scarcely arises. The *Vārtā*'s portrayal of Mira's 'village' and 'house' is interesting for its contrast to the way in which her legend usually features an opposition between life at court and life on the road, but this would surely reveal more about what one could say about Mira in the mid- to late-seventeenth century than about her own historical circumstances, strictly speaking. Yet the most riveting feature of the plot is clearly the enmity it describes between Kṛṣṇadās and Mirabai.

Christopher Chapple has recently proposed that this follows from a theological disagreement having to do with the Vallabha Sampradāy's presumed reception of the story that Mira died by being merged with Krishna at Dvaraka.[22] Perhaps, but there is no hint of that in the story itself. What stands out instead is the matter of money and the issue of whether Kṛṣṇadās will succeed on his fund-raising tour in Gujarat. There is every good reason to believe that Kṛṣṇadās did indeed go on several such tours, and this story is obviously dedicated to showing that the donations he received were 'clean money'—symbolic of a ritual and theological submission that had already been made on the part of their donors. Reflecting the high Brahmin caste and devotional compunctions of his initiating guru, Kṛṣṇadās didn't accept gifts from just anybody, or so the story says. Against this portrait of great financial punctiliousness, we have the figure of Mirabai, whose house plays host to a ragtag band of religious money-grubbers. Here the high theology of gift that is offered in Vallabha's vision of the *puṣṭimārg*—gift as reflex of what has been given—contrasts boldly to a more ordinary, even cynical view of religious philanthropy. But why should Mirabai be positioned as the focus of this sort of bhakti free-for-all?

Three explanations come to mind. First of all, she is a woman. She cannot live up to the patriarchal rigors of disciplic succession exemplified by the Vallabha Sampradāy and all other contemporary groups of which we have a record. The image of people gathering around a woman for spiritual and financial succor is the very antithesis of the institutional and ritual purity that the authors of the *Vārtā* wished to project.

Second, it is tempting to think that the image of Mira's royal lineage suggested her as a model of an older pattern of financial support for religious causes than the Sampradāy wished to project for itself. Its support, at least in the stories concerning Kṛṣṇadās, was to be found in the merchant communities instead—a cleaner, more principled kind of giving, according to the portrait being drawn. This interpretatation of the reason why Mira is portrayed as she is in the Kṛṣṇadās *vārtā*, however, would have to take account of the fact that she is represented as living in a house, not a palace—or at least, that its palatial quality is unmarked.

Third, and most important for our purposes, the telling of this vignette in the mid- to late-seventeenth century seems to show how widely Mira's story had come to be known by that time, and how firmly associated with patterns of devotional traffic connecting Braj and the Mughal heartland to Gujarat. Perhaps the sort of devotion that Mira stood for was indeed a financial opponent for the Vallabha Sampradāy, especially westward toward Gujarat. In that case, the best way the Sampradāy could carve out an independent financial base may have been to portray its version of *mādhurya bhakti* as ritually and financially correct, contrasting it to the 'vulgate' (and from a Vallabhite point of view, vulgar) bhakti that had evidently come to be associated with the name of Mirabai.

In the self-conception of the *puṣṭimārg*, as institutionalized by Vallabha's son Viṭṭhalnāth, this free-flowing bhakti was firmly channeled into a ritual setting focused on strict householdership. Each of the Sampradāy's 'temples'—for so they might appear from the outside—was reconceptualized as a shrine within the house of one of the lineal descendents of Vallabhācārya, and all other household shrines could be rationalized in relation to these by further ties of blood lineage or rites of initiation that drew other adherents into connection with these lineages. The story of Mira's rejecting her lineage evidently made a perfect constrast to this vision, as did any suggestions about the unprincipled, flabby, freely emoting sort of bhakti this style of religion might engender. Since the Vallabha sect wished to trade on substantially the same range of religious emotions, but in a rigorously centralized way, the figure of Mirabai evidently provided the perfect foil. Of course, this says little or nothing about the 'historical Mirabai,' but it may say a great deal about the way in which she had come to be seen by the middle of the seventeenth century. Not surprisingly, several of the motifs that emerge in Priyadas's account of Mirabai could well be understood as providing the background for this Vallabhite parody of them. The *Vārtā*'s parody would suggest they were well known at least some decades before Priyadas set them in verse in 1712.

Mira's Subjectivity: Two Roads Diverge

My object in guiding us once again through this contested and difficult terrain is not to assert that Mirabai didn't exist. If we hew to the letter of the law, I am simply agnostic in that regard. My point is rather that a close look at the sources of our knowledge, with a high level of demand for clarity about whether and when those sources can be dated, builds a sense of what really matters about Mirabai, which is the *memory* of her, not her historicity. But one of the most interesting features about that memory is its particular path of historical contingency: its history as a history of reception, perception, even production.

That is why I would argue that we find the truly meaningful Mirabai more in the performed, poetic bhakti vehicle where she is remembered, and less in the royal genealogies, where you really have to dig to ferret out her existence at all. Naiṇsī gives us a single line, but by the time he gave us that line we had two full bhakti portraits, one in the *Prem Abodh* (which also integrates Mira into its treatment of Ravidas) and the other in the *Bhaktirasabodhinī*. On top of that we have Nabhadas's earlier description of her and a passing reference by his possibly somewhat senior contemporary Anantdās, who mentions Mira's name alongside that of Trilocan, saying that both were deeply related to—or engaged with—Hari (*trilocana aru mīrāṅbāī tinakī hari sauṅ bahuta sagāī*). Interestingly, Anantdās speaks of Chittor in the course of introducing a *bhakta* named Cauhān Bhuvan in the verse just previous, but he allows another figure (Mādhavdās Jagannāthī) to intervene before coming to Trilocan and Mira, and there is nothing to show that Anantdās associates Mira with the royal lineages of Mewar or Merta.[23] Finally, we have two mentions of Mira on the part of Harirāmvyās, and these may be even earlier than those of Nabhadas and Anantdās. Writing in Brindavan sometime in the middle of the sixteenth century Vyās lamented that Mirabai had passed from the scene along with others in a charmed generation of *bhaktas* and *sādhūs* (his words) that he counted as members of his 'whole family' (*savu kuṭamu hamārau*, i.e., *saba kuṭumbha hamārau*).[24] Now this is a tradition—a corpus of memory—that really amounts to something!

But there is a catch on the bhakti side, as well—an internal barrier. This is the barrier between Mirabai as object and Mirabai as subject. So far we have been operating entirely on the 'object' side of that barrier. We have been considering what is said *about* Mira, rather than what she is supposed to have said herself. And when we look for utterances of that sort, again applying our rigorous standards about dating, the silence is deafening. Compared with male bhakti poets of her period, the sort that Nabhadas and Harirāmvyās and the *Prem Abodh* set alongside her, we have very little trace of poems attributed to Mirabai in early dated manuscripts. Our sources reveal Mira much more clearly as the object of attention than as its subject, the focus of a gaze rather than its eye.

Yet what subjectivity is displayed in these few early glimpses? If we bracket the large corpus of poems that we know have been sung in Mira's voice since the nineteenth century and admit that they may not tell us much about the Mira who was 'heard' earlier, what sort of persona do we find? What mood or moods?

To answer this question, we have to return to the manuscripts, and there we come to a major fork in the road. The general terrain, as I've suggested, reveals only a very faint trail leading toward Mirabai. At present scholars have located fewer than twenty-five poems bearing Mira's signature that appear in dated manuscripts belonging to the seventeenth century or can reliably be assigned to that century by indirect means.[25] The great bulk of these—sixteen poems (minus at least one that duplicates the poem that appears in the *Gurū Granth Sāhib*)—are said to exist in three mid-seventeenth-century manuscripts housed at the Gujarāt Vidyā Sabhā in Ahmedabad. Their dates are listed by both Prabhāt and the Vidyā Sabhā roster as 1638, 1644, and 1656 CE (i.e., VS 1695, 1701, and 1713), but when I visited the library in September, 2003, I found that all three manuscripts were either missing or misplaced.[26] Fortunately, Prabhāt published a photograph he had made of one Mira poem from the 1656 manuscript, so it can be added to the four poems that have been firmly located in manuscript collections in various parts of North India.[27] Compared with what we have for Surdas or any of the influential *nirguṇa* poets, this number is stunningly low. And of these, only one—the poem contained in manuscripts of what later would be called the *Gurū Granth Sāhib*—gives us unquestioned access to the century that was presumably Mira's own, since this poem appears in a manuscript dated to

1604, the *Kartārpur Pothī*. A good case can also be made for the poem that Heidi Pauwels has recently unearthed in Nabhadas's *Bhaktamāl* (see below). Once we have passed these poems, however—a total of six—the trail peters out altogether.

Yet right next to this faint trail, which is visible beneath the leaves only in the most scattered patches, we find another, remarkably different path. It has been claimed that there exists one manuscript that predates any of these fragments by almost two decades and is devoted entirely to Mirabai, containing 69 of her poems. We are told that its colophon places it at the well known temple of Raṇchorjī in Dakor, Gujarat, and assigns it the date VS 1642 (1585 CE). How amazing! This is not a path but a highway! Amazing—and alas, unlikely.

The claim that Mirabai could be found in a sixteenth-century manuscript written at Dakor is a very recent one—1949, to be precise. In a book called *Mīrāṅ Smṛti Granth* published in that year, Lalitprasād Sukul, head of the Hindi Department at Calcutta University, reported that he had been shown the 1585 manuscript by one Govardhandās Bhaṭṭ of Dakor, who said his forebears had been prominent officials in the Vallabhite temple of Dvārakādhīś.[28] This probably means the well known Dvārakādhīś temple at Dvaraka, but Paul Arney has rightly noted that there is another equally important Vallabhite temple of that name in Mathura and that the reference may even be to the temple of Raṇchorjī itself, in Dakor.[29] It is hard to know how many people, if any, had heard of the manuscript before Sukul published his findings, for the context and content of his revelation are suspicious.

The context is remarkable because the manuscript was said to have been preserved in the Vallabha Sampradāy. That sect serves as proprietor to the Raṇchorjī temple, but is also the very sect whose early records of itself most vividly disparage Mira, as we have seen.[30] As to content, the suspicion is cast from several directions. First, the poems claimed for this Dakor manuscript accord perfectly with 'Mira's greatest hits' as celebrated in the twentieth century, but very poorly with those that appear in the more reliably dated early manuscripts at our disposal. Second, there are serious linguistic and orthographic problems—initial *ṇ*, retroflex *ḍ*, and a frequent substitution of *ś* for *s*, as if these poems had come from the Bengal of Sukul's Marwari present, not the western provinces of his Marwari forebears.[31] Third, almost no other single-authored manuscripts of bhakti poems date to this period, and when they do there is a substantial group of other manuscripts to which they belong. Winand Callewaert likens this situation to thunder coming out of a clear blue sky.[32] Finally, as if all this were not enough, both the Dakor manuscript and its amplified copy, purportedly made in Kashi in 1670, have disappeared from sight.[33]

As a claim of manuscriptival fact, all this sounds exceedingly fishy, and the story of how the manuscript came to be preserved in Bhaṭṭ's family makes it even more so. Sukul says Bhaṭṭ told him that the copy he possessed had originally been copied from one that Mira's servant, friend, and amanuensis Lalitā (who doesn't appear in written versions of Mira's hagiography until much later) had left in Dakor as Mira's coterie of *bhaktas* traveled toward Brindavan.[34] In other words, the story surrounding the reception of this manuscript asserts a direct connection to Mirabai herself, as if to anticipate the fact that someone might be looking for just such a trail. It gives closure to the literary person of Mirabai, compensating for the spare open-endedness that would otherwise be there—the manuscript trail that peters out in the woods.

Not surprisingly, this story emerged precisely at the time when it was most needed, so while it may seem outlandish in its own terms, it makes perfect sense when seen against a broader background. At just this time Mira was becoming historicized and canonized in reference to evidentiary rules that would satisfy European and European-Indian standards. The discovery of the Dakor manuscript was published directly after Independence, when Hindi was being put forward as the national language and needed a firm, canonical authority it had never required before—classic authors, venerable dates, and all. The Dakor manuscript fit the bill perfectly, and perhaps it isn't accidental that knowledge of it was produced in Calcutta, in newly partitioned Bengal, in the very year that the image of Rām Lallā manifested itself in the Bābrī Mosque at Ayodhya. That too later emerged as a 'forgery'—this time, self-confessed. It's also interesting that the person promoting this manuscript, Lalitprasād Sukul, was institutionally situated in a major Hindi-teaching environment. When he published the Dakor manuscript, he laid claim to a deeper academic lineage. He reported that Govardhandās Bhaṭṭ told him he had also shown the manuscript to Śyāmsundar Dās, chief mover in the publication program of the Kashi Nagaripracarini Sabha in the early decades of the twentieth century.[35] No more important engine of Hindi/Hindu canon-making ever existed.

If a Dakor-Nagaripracarini Sabha connection was indeed made, it certainly was not anticipated in the earlier Nagaripracarini Sabha *Khoj Reports*, which reported on the Sabha's successes in locating vernacular manuscripts throughout North India. Furthermore it is hard to explain Sukul's success in finding sixteen other dated seventeenth- and eighteenth-century manuscripts at various sites, where other researchers have come up with nothing. Is it an accident that he gives no details beyond the cities' names?[36] And in the report that Sukul attributes to Bhaṭṭ, there is even a suspicious-sounding Bad Muslim/ Good Muslim motif: one unnamed Muslim ruler ransacked the Raṇchor temple and took the manuscript; another returned it minus its golden, jewel-inlaid cover.[37]

So the whole Dakor story fits perfectly into the cultural history of twentieth-century Hindi/Hindu nationalism, and fits very imperfectly into what is otherwise known about the manuscript history of Mirabai and other poets roughly contemporary to her. If Śyāmsundar Dās and Rāmcandra Śukla did indeed examine the Dakor manuscript at some point, as Sukul reports, it's no wonder they hesitated to print it as gospel, giving it the imprimatur of the Nagaripracarini Sabha. Or maybe, as Sukul claimed, they just intended to publish it and never got around to it.[38]

I've used the metaphor of a fork in the road to describe our situation as regards early manuscripts of poetry attributed to Mirabai. As you can see, I think we have to revise this picture. It's not that 'two roads diverged in a yellow wood' but that someone has tried to expropriate the land and pave a highway through the forest. So I think we need another metaphor to describe the terrain. Let's leave the woods and head for something more commmercial. How about an ice-cream cone? I mean, a sugar cone—the real conical variety, not the cake cup that you can actually set down on a flat surface. At the bottom end (on which everything else does *not* balance) we have the few poems attributed to Mira that can be found in reliably datable seventeenth-century manscripts, with one or two at the very bottom tip. Then we have the cone itself, which gets bulkier the farther up we go. In the nineteenth century it gets quite broad, apparently balanced on an oral tradition that has been accumulating all along. But the orality—the fact of textual invisibility—makes it almost impossible to know how full the cone is in its lower reaches.

Up on top, finally, someone has placed a well-defined scoop of the sweet, luscious Mirabai we know and love so well: the 'authentic' Mira that the Dakor manuscript claims to bring to light. This term, *prāmāṇik*, is used to typify the contents of the second book where the Dakor manuscript is published, a volume put out by Sukul's student Bhagavān Dās Tivārī under the title *Mīrāṅ kī Prāmāṇik Padāvalī* (Allahabad, 1974). Thereby the author suggests that its contents are 'all natural' in the way that the earlier classroom versions, such as Paraśurām Caturvedī's Hindī Sāhitya Sammelan edition published in the same city in 1932, were not. But what is 'natural'? I'm afraid you actually have to check the ingredients, and I don't think they turn out to be organic.

The Early Poems

In the space that remains, I invite you to sample what is found at the very bottom of the cone. We will consider the five poems attributed to Mirabai that have so far clearly emerged from manuscripts dating to the middle of the seventeenth century or earlier. A sixth poem from this period—and from very early within that span—will also be introduced, the one recently discovered by Heidi Pauwels.

The first of these poems is tolerably well known in scholarly circles. Nancy Martin treats it prominently in her forthcoming book *Mirabai*, and it is also the main focus of a 1990 article by Winand Callewaert and the jumping-off point for my essay on 'Krishna and the Gender of Longing,' which appears as Chapter 7 of this book.[39] We have three early manuscript versions for this poem, two of them coming from the collection of poetry that would later be called the *Gurū Granth Sāhib*. One occurs in the Kartārpur manuscript (1604) and the other appears in the so-called Banno recension (1642). The two are remarkably close, differing only in orthography and the inclusion (or not) of the feminine interjection *rī* at one point in the text. The third version is to be found in a manuscript primarily devoted to the *Ḍholā Mārū*, which is dated 1644 (VS 1701) and preserved in the Gujarāt Vidyā Sabhā in Ahmedabad.[40]

Let me lay out the Kartārpur original and three English translations, so as to give a sense of this poem from several angles. For the original I am indebted to the manuscript searches of Gurinder Singh Mann, who supplied me with the transcription I reproduce here and who discusses the poem in the context of its Sikh reception in *The Making of Sikh Scripture*.[41] The three translations include those of M. A. Macauliffe and Nancy Martin, in addition to my own.[42]

मनु हमारो बांधिउ माई कवल नैन आपने गुन
तीखण तीर बेधि सरीर दुरि गयो री माई
लागिउ तब जानिउ नही अब न सहिउ जाई री माई
तंत मंत अउखद करउ तउ पीर न जाडी
है कोउ उपकार करै कठिन दरदु माई
निकट हउ तुम दुरि नहि बेगि मिहु आई
मीरा गिरधर सुआमी देआल तन की तपत बुझाई री माई
कवल नैन आपने गुन अपने गुन बाधिउ माई

Macauliffe's Translation

God hath entwined my soul, O mother,
With His attributes, and I have sung of them.
The sharp arrow of His love hath pierced my body through and through,
O mother.
When it struck me I did not know it; now it cannot be endured,
O mother.
Though I use charms, incantations, and drugs, the pain will not depart.
Is there anyone who will treat me? Intense is the agony, O mother.
Thou, O God, are near; Thou art not distant; come quickly to meet me.
Saith Mîrâ, the Lord, the mountain-wielder, who is compassionate, hath
quenched the fire of my body, O mother.
The lotus-eyed hath entwined *my soul* with the twine of his attributes.

Martin's Translation

My body is bound tight, Mother,
in the ropes of the Lotus-eyed One.

The sharp arrow pierced me
clear through, Mother.
When it hit, I didn't know it;
now I cannot bear the pain.

I've tried spells, incantations, drugs—
even so, the pain won't go.
Can't anyone bring relief?
Such agony, Mother!

You are near, not far;
Come running now to meet me.
Mīrā's Mountain Bearer, the compassionate Lord,
has quenched her body's burning.

My heart is held fast, Mother,
in the bonds of the Lotus-eyed One.

Hawley's Translation

He's bound my heart with the powers he owns, Mother—
he with the lotus eyes.
Arrows like spears: this body is pierced,
and Mother, he's gone far away.
When did it happen, Mother? I don't know
but now it's too much to bear.
Talismans, spells, medicines—
I've tried, but the pain won't go.
Is there someone who can bring relief?
Mother, the hurt is cruel.
Here I am, near, and you're not far:
Hurry to me, to meet.
Mira's Montain-Lifter Lord, have mercy,
cool this body's fire!
Lotus-Eyes, with the powers you own, Mother,
with those powers you've bound.

To my ear, the poem projects a certain quality of indeterminacy that makes it pleasing. It evokes a mood of slight delirium. One moment it seems the subject is addressing her friend or even, if we take the word *māī* literally, her mother; the next it is Krishna. One moment she speaks of absence, the next of her/his being near. And this 'binding': is it a chain or a bandage? Of what does it consist? Is it *guna* (i.e., *guṇa*) in the sense of strands of a rope or is it *guna* in a rueful joking reference to Krishna's virtues or qualities, the powers that make him what he is? Nancy Martin translated by taking the first road, and I chose the second. Macauliffe, who translated the poem a century ago, was cleverer than either of us. He tried to have it both ways by translating the 'binding' verb (*bāṅdhiu*) as 'entwined' and the noun of agency (*guna*) as 'attributes.'

If any poem deserves to be canonical for Mirabai, this would surely be it, but I am not the first to notice that it does not appear very frequently in printed editions, or that it is absent in the Dakor manuscript.[43] I suppose its recent celebrity in scholarly circles is an effort to change all that, but it won't really happen until Bollywood catches on. And if our scholarly fascination with the Kartārpur poem seems a rearguard action, imagine how hopelessly arcane it may seem out there in the 'real world' to lift up for special attention the other poems I wish to put before you.

The first of these stands a chance of being as old as its Kartārpur cousin, and we owe its discovery to the gifted work of Heidi Pauwels. Its text is tucked away in the mid-eighteenth century *Pad-prasaṅg-mālā* ('Garland of tales about poems') of Nāgarīdās, where it forms a part of his description of a *bhakta* by the name of Nārāyandās. According to Nāgarīdās, Nārāyandās was celebrated as a dancer. It seems a certain *navāb* wanted to see him perform, and he obliged by dancing to a poem of Mirabai, which Nāgarīdās then quotes. Now obviously this only takes us back as far as the eighteenth century, and as Pauwels points out, there are certain manuscript questions to address even then. But the intriguing thing is that Nāgarīdās is not the only hagiographer to make reference to this *pad*. It is also cited by Nabhadas in his much earlier *Bhaktamāl*, which can have been written no later than the first quarter of the seventeenth century. Once again the context is the story of Nārāyandās, but this time only a single phrase in the poem is quoted: 'Kāma's Beguiler, drenched passion-red' (*madanamohana raṅga rāto*). Only when we have the later Nāgarīdās text at hand do we know that this is actually a poem of Mirabai—or at least, so he understood it.[44]

Skeptics may say that *pads* are sometimes attributed to more than one poet, and this is certainly true. Furthermore, Mira's own reputation as a dancer might well have had the effect of attracting the poem into her corpus by the eighteenth century. Nabhadas certainly knew of Mirabai—he reports on her life as well: why did he not mention her in relation to this poem? Perhaps because his style was so telegraphic? Whatever the reason, the trail of reception is sufficiently compelling that this poem deserves to be considered as the only Mira poem other than 'He's bound my heart' that can so far be claimed to have been known in Mira's own century, the sixteenth.

As we encounter this poem, it is worth noting that it shares with its apparent Kartārpur contemporary the connection between Krishna and Kāma (*madan*), although the Kartārpur poem refers to love's arrows without naming the archer. This time Krishna is called *mohan*, the Beguiler, which takes a chapter directly from Kāma's book: *mohan* is the name of one of his five arrows. Not only that, this poem, like the one that appears in the *Kartārpur Granth*, focuses on the binding power of love, so if it's just accidental that only these two poems survive from the repertoire connected with Mirabai in the sixteenth century, their links to one another are remarkable. Or was it that this was exactly the trope for which Mira's poetry was most celebrated at that point in time? Here is the Nāgarīdās text as edited by Pauwels, followed by my own translation:

साचौ प्रीति ही को नातौ
कै जानैं वृषभान नंदिनी कै मदनमोहन रंग रातौ
यहैं संखला अति बलवंती बांध्यो प्रेम गज मातौ
मीरां के प्रभु गिरधर नागर कुंज महल बसा तौ

What connects? True love.
Whether one thinks of Vṛṣabhānu's daughter
or Kāma's Beguiler, drenched passion-red,
Love it is that makes the strongest fetter,
binding down an elephant in rut.
Mira's Lord is the clever Mountain-Lifter,
even if his palace is a bower.

Another set of poems—these from the Gujarāt Vidyā Sabhā library in Ahmedabad—are somewhat later than this early duo, but they also deserve our attention. C. L. Prabhāt reported on seventeen Mirabai poems that were to be found in manuscripts dating to the seventeenth century; as we have seen, one of these is the same as the Kartārpur *pad*. Unfortunately, only one of the others remains to be consulted today—the one that he photographed and reproduced in his book *Mīrā: Jivan aur Kāvya*. The rest are at present unlocatable in the Vidyā Sabhā archives for unknown reasons. The poem published by Prabhāt is as follows, and it too has connections with the mood and language of its Kartārpur predecessor: the fever of love and the piercing (*bīdha*, 'shot through') that caused it.[45]

भाय री शाएबा पकनी जर जे हरों समें आसा करी
अब ता आंने जरी प्रीत जाई बीध नालजा संजोग री
जो मेरो एक लोक जाएगो हरी परलोक न जांए री
नंदनंद कु कबहु न छारु मीलूगी नीशान बजाए री
तनं मनं धनं यौवन पे वारू श्री वल्लभ भेज मुरार री
मीरां प्रभु गीरधर के उपर शरबस होऊगी वार री

My body is baked in the fever of feeling.
I spend my whole time hoping, friend.
Now that he's come, I'm burning with love—
shot through, shameless to couple with him, friend.

Suppose this world of mine vanishes, friend—
what does it matter if Hari's in the next?
Nanda's Delight—I'll never let him go, friend.
I'm telling you, I'm joining him. I'm sounding the drum.
Body, mind, wealth—they're offered to his youth.
Send me my beloved, my Murāri, friend.
Mira's Mountain-Lifting Lord—for him
I'm forfeiting everything, my friend.

Other Mira poems can also be found in the Vidyā Sabhā manuscript collection, but the earliest of them date fully a century later—to 1769 (VS 1826). The manuscript containing these poems, accession number 683 in Vidyā Sabhā's Gujarati/Hindi/Marathi collection, has only two of them, together with an intriguing mention of Mirabai in a *pad* attributed to Kabir. The Mira poems are as follows, and worth quoting to give a taste of the Mirabai who was remembered in this part of India as the eighteenth century got under way:

सुणह यानी ध्यांन अरजी रांम तारो तो तोरी मरजी
मात पीता कुटंब सुतहारा सब मतलब के गरजी
भव सागर मां वही जातहु बांहे पकडस्यो मोये हरज़ी
मीराँ के प्रभु गीरधर नागर मोहे मंह भाग्यण सरजी

Listen with care, consider my petition,
and Rām, if it please you, ferry me across.
Mother and father, a family with a son—
it's all such self-serving humbug,
Leaving me floating on the ocean of being:
Grab me by the arm! Ransom me!

And he answered, Mira's Lord,
the clever Mountain-Lifter.
He gave me good fortune:
he made me his wife.

नही रे वीसारु हरी अंतर मांथी नही रे वीसारू हरी
इत गोकुल उत मथुरां नगरी बीच मा जमुना बही
जल जमुना जल भर पाने गांतां श्रीर पर गगरी धरी
राणी रे राधाजी नां मोहोल तजी ने कुबजा सु प्रीत्यो करी
व्रंदा रे वन मां गौशन चारी मुख पर मोरली धरी
मीरांबई के हे प्रभु गीरधन नागर हरी चरण कमल चीत धरी

Never will I let myself let Hari be forgotten,
  never forget Hari inside.
Gokul's on this side, Mathura's on that side
  and in between the Jamuna flows—
The water of the Jamuna: I waded in,
  filling my water-pot, lifting it on my head,
And he: he abandoned the palace of Queen Radha
  to love that lovely hunchback instead!
Back in Brindavan he herded the cows
  and lifted Muralī to his mouth:
Mirabai's Lord is the clever Mountain-Lifter—
  Hari. I lift his lotus feet with my mind.

But with these poems, as I say, we have strayed into the eighteenth century. Let's try to return to the seventeenth by moving farther east—to Jaipur and Jodhpur, in present-day Rajasthan. The Sanjay Sharma Museum in Jaipur presents us with a manuscript (accession number 938/939/8) that promises to qualify for a place on our list of manuscripts containing Mirabai poems we know to have been performed in the seventeenth century. Its catalogue dates it to VS 1742 (1685 CE) and tells us that it includes a poem bearing Mira's signature. Not only that, the catalogue tells us that this collection of poetry was drawn together at Merta. What could be more logical than to see Mira represented there?[46]

Unfortunately it is not so simple. The information about Merta appears elsewhere than in the colophon, and while the colophon is very clear about the date, it refers itself only to the section where the *Virahamañjarī* of Nandadās is inscribed. Presumably it would also apply to everything that precedes it. But the Mirabai poem comes after the colophon, not before—and, to make matters worse, in a different hand—so its date remains unclear. It is certainly possible that it was added later, especially if at some point the manuscript moved from another location to Merta. Given these uncertainties, we cannot include this poem in our charmed seventeenth-century circle, but since it seems to come close in some way, it deserves quoting here nonetheless:

काती गोपी आयो हे सषी   लीला रास विलास
ब्रज नारी विहबल फिरैं
आज सषी मेरैं अंग ऊमाहों,   चौक चंदन गौंह लीए
कर मै अवला रंग राती   हरषि हरि मीली
नव रंग नारी चीर चोषी   पहरि कंठि मुक्तावली
दासे मीरां मीले माधो   काती कृष्ण र मोरली

How many cowherd girls have gathered, my friend,
to play in the sensuous circle dance?
Today in my house, on the floor, my friend,
I've drawn out a sandalwood square.
Women dye their hands with henna,
thrilled by the thought of meeting Hari,
Don clean clothes of all nine colors
and fit strings of pearls to their necks.
Mira the servant—if she can meet Mādhav,
how many Krishnas and Muralīs will be there?[47]

A somewhat different situation emerges in Jodhpur. There too we are dealing with a manuscript labelled 'miscellaneous poems' (*sphuṭa-padaḥ*)—this time by the Rājasthān Prācyavidyā Pratiṣṭhān, where it is housed—but in this case there is little reason to doubt that the three Mirabai poems it contains did actually belong to the seventeenth century. The manuscript in question is accession number 30346 in the Rajasthani/Hindi collection, and the Institute authorities date it to VS 1713–14 (1656–1657 CE). Both Winand Callewaert and I noticed this entry in the Institute's catalogue, but it was Nancy Martin who spent enough time with the manuscript to ascertain that it contained not one poem of Mira's on folios 50–51 but two, and an additional one on folio 43.[48]

This process of gradual discovery suggests, as Callewaert rightly says, that additional poems attributed to Mirabai might well emerge if a search of seventeenth-century anthologies such as this were pursued systematically.[49] But as we have seen, it would not always be an easy task to know just where one stood. Because such manuscripts are often composites, and because they are often in a poorer state of preservation than larger, more formal manuscripts, problems of dating frequently arise. Not in this case, however. The Institute cataloguers confidently established the date of VS 1713–14 on the basis of the fact that the manuscript in which the Mira poems are included was subsequently used to note down financial transactions—IOUs. These are the given dates VS 1713 and 1714, and they follow the anthology immediately, although, not surprisingly, in a different hand. Thus they serve as *termini ad quem.*[50]

The first poem that appears in this Jodhpur manuscript is associated with *rāg mārū*; the second with *rāg devagandhār;* and the third—appropriately enough, given its throat-clearing theme—is aligned to no raga at all. As far as I can tell, only the first of these has made its way into the collections that have latterly become standard.[51] Once again, I offer the originals in transcription, with word boundaries introduced. Let's begin with the first two in the set.

Folio 43B/44A: rāg mārū

नैना लोभी रे बहु री सके नही आय़
नीरषि सषी आगै आगै है ललची रहे ललचाई
हु ठाढ़ी सी अपनै द्वारै मोहन नीक से आय़ः
सारंगे ओट दीयै़ कुल अंकुस बदन दीय़ो मुकलाय़ा
सासु नणद द्यौ रजी गनीः सबही रही समझाय़
चंचल चपल अटक नहि मांनत पर हथि रहे विकाय़
कोऊ भली कहौ कोऊ बुरि कहौ सलइ सब लइ सिस चढाय़
मीरां प्रभु गिरधर जु कि प्यारी ऊन विन रह्यौ न जाय़

My eyes are greedy. They're beyond turning back.
They stare straight ahead, friend, straight ahead,
  coveting and coveting still more.
So here I am, standing at my door
  to get a good look at Mohan when he comes,
Abandoning my beautiful veil and the modesty
  that guards my family's honor, showing my face.
Mother-in-law, sister-in-law: day and night they monitor,
  lecturing me about it all and lecturing once again.
Yet my quick, giddy eyes will brook no hindrance.
  They're sold into someone else's hands.
Some will say I'm good, some will say I'm bad—
  whatever their opinion, I exalt it as a gift,
But Mira is the lover of her Lord, the Mountain-Lifter.
  Without him, I simply cannot live.

Folio 50B: rāg devagaṅdhār

घुमारे नयन जैसे काम भरे भाय सुं
सुरत रस रसीले त्रीया कै रंग रंगीले   मनमथ सज सुष ऊठे रंग भाय सुं
मुदीत ऊघरि जात सैन न कहत बात   निस के जागे कछु चितवत भाय़ सुं
गीरध्धर अंग ढीले मन हु मंत्र न कीलेः   मीरां प्रभु छाप दई त्रीया ऊर पाय़सु

These eyes: like clouds that gather
  filled with Love—
    with desire.

Drenched with the liquid pleasure of making love,
　　flushed with what makes a woman color—
Mind-Churning Love appears in such garb
　　that the joy of it makes eyes rise
　　　　with desire.

Drunken, exposed,
　　they send wordless signs,
Looking at something all night long,
　　awake
　　　　with desire.

Mantras cannot bind a mind
　　the Mountain-Lifter's limbs have loosed:
Mira's Lord has laid his stamp
　　on a woman's heart—
　　　　with his foot.

Interestingly, the first two poems from Jodhpur are more closely related by theme than the third, despite the fact that the first and second are separated by several pages in the manuscript, while the second and third appear consecutively. The first two are 'eye' poems, and as such take their place as members of a huge group in which Mira's signature occurs along with that of many other poets. The poem in *rāg mārū* echoes the defiance that Nabhadas singles out as being Mirabai's 'signature mood.' Here as there, the object of her defiance is the family into which she marries. Here it is the women of the family who attempt to restrain her—not the men, as in Nabhadas's poem about Mira. But this is no unusual feature: we find it in a number of other poems that end with her signature. What is noteworthy and delightful is that Mira's defiance of family propriety (*kula āṅkusa*), for which she takes full credit, also represents her eyes' defiance of her: 'they're sold into someone else's hands.' In poems of a similar date bearing Surdas's name, it would be usual for the *gopī* in question to lament this mutiny of her eyes, and we get a hint of this in the title line and in the formulaic description of their darting restlessness later on (*cañcala capala:* 'quick, giddy eyes).' Yet the defiant persona of Mira as a whole overrides this theme. As the penultimate line makes clear, she shares their brazenness, and in her it becomes a moral stance—or rather, as she says, an amoral one:

> Some will say I'm good, some will say I'm bad—
> 　whatever their opinion, I exalt it as a gift,

Nancy Martin's translation of this last phrase,

> I accept their words as a gift,
> raising them to my brow,

makes clear that it refers to a physical gesture, one that signals respect by touching the thing offered (opinions in this case) to one's forehead (*sira caḍhāya*) in the act of accepting it. But the effect, of course, is just the reverse. Mira's headstrongness is her trademark.

The second poem is also focused on Mira's eyes, but in a different way. The eyes are fixed once again—they stay awake all night long and cannot close—but they are 'drenched with the liquid pleasure of making love' (*surata rasa rasīle*), whether after the fact or in anticipation. Here it is not a confrontation with the boundaries of house (the door) and home (the in-law women) that matters, but a confrontation with Kāma himself. There is an interesting hint of memory. The word *surata* might mean 'remembering' rather than 'making love,' and one of Kāma's designations in general is 'memory' (*smara*), though that word is not used here. This reverie of desire is ultimately interrupted by Desire Himself, who materializes not as Kāma but as Krishna. He makes his way into the poem as it concludes, shedding the garb of Kāma (*manamatha*, 'Mind-Churning') and appearing as the Mountain-Lifter.

This epiphany—this transition from Kāma to Krishna—is sealed in the last words of the poem. All along the rhyming verses have ended 'with desire' (*bhāya su*), but now they end 'with his foot' (*pāya su*). Doubtless the touch of the divine foot can be placed in a devotional context—the moment when Trivikrama Vishnu placed his foot on the demon Bali, for example—but in this context it's hard to miss the phallic meaning, as well. The stamp (*chāpa*) of Krishna's foot on her heart—or more literally breast or chest (*ura)*—is simultaneously the stamp of his name upon the poem, for that term precisely is often used to designate the signature that signals a *pad*'s closure and conclusion. In the original, in fact, the word 'stamp' or 'seal' (*chāpa*) follows the name itself without the intervening verb that is natural to insert in an English translation. So one could also translate as follows:

> He's given the stamp 'Mira's Lord'
> on a woman's heart—
> with his foot.

The third poem in the set, and the last of our sixteenth- and seventeenth-century set, is in some ways the most charming of all. It is the one least affected by the dominant persona that has long been associated with Mirabai. Unfortunately, it is also the one that makes me worry most about the accuracy and adequacy of my translation. Here it is:

Folio 50B/51A (no rāg attribution)

नीसगत तमचर बोले
करत षंषार अंवाज़ जणावत अंगना मधी अवोले
चतुर सषियन सुंमन की ही लगनी सुदृढ बंधन कीत षोले
सरस बदन पर अलक बिथुरीया अलि गावत मधु टोले
अंग अंग पर नई नई [नस] बंदसि कहा दैहु ईन तोलै
मीरां प्रभु गीरधर जु की राजनी नील बस बबह मोले

Last night a creature of darkness spoke:
'Ahem, ahem,' the way you'd clear your throat,
    a voice announced wordless in the courtyard.
Worldly wise women like jasmine blossoms
    released the heavy locks that bound them;
Curls cascaded over elegant faces—
    swarms of bees buzzing after honey;
And on every part of the body, new nailmark bonds—
    how could you possibly assess them?
Mira's Mountain-Lifting Lord owns the night:
    the realm of the blue lotus,
        where the currency is a kiss.

The opening is wonderful, and wonderfully clear. First we have the evocation of those dark, threatening creatures that move about only at night (*tamacara*). Then we hear them speak: their half-human sounds make them sound as if they are clearing their throats (*karata ṣaṅṣāra* [i.e., *khaṅkhāra*]). And then we realize that these hoarse, whispered words-that-are-not-words belong to a human being after all. It is the lover, who has somehow sneaked into the house and says, 'Come into the courtyard!' (*aṅganā madhī avo le*). Or to read the line with word boundaries that give it a more neutral ring (...*avole*, i.e., *abole*), it is the lover announcing his presence 'wordless in the courtyard.'

Then comes the response, which is phrased in the most general way. A plural is used (*saṣiyana*) to describe what women experienced (*catura*) in love do in such circumstances. They respond with a total release of their hair: it spills from whatever binding it might have had like jasmine flowers, which are, not incidentally, fragrant at night. Indeed jasmine is often the flower chosen to decorate the hair as it is bound, so its blossoms are ready to be released when the bond is broken. Here the blossoms scatter everywhere before the half-human, 'unbound' onslaught of love. It's bees swarming over honey. But a riot of new constraints—bond-like (*baṅdasi*)—appear all over the lovers' bodies: a lilliputian network of scratch-marks. 'How can you measure a thing like that?' the poet asks.

In the final line Mira's Lord, Giridhar, either owns the night or is himself that very night (*ju kī rājanī*). In either case, we return to the theme of darkness with which the poem began, but now we recall the color of Krishna's skin and all it portends. Then we hear the phrase, 'in the control of the blue lotus' (*nīla basa*), and we ask: what is the measure of that control? I think the word *babaha*, which follows, may be a form of *babbā*, 'kiss.' Put that together with the final word in the poem and we have the familiar idea of being 'sold for a kiss'—that is, sold down the river—in the same way that one can be 'sold for a smile' in so many other poems of this sort. Or maybe it's not that but a case of haplography, a missing sibilant. If that's true, we should read *nīla basa saba bahu mole*. That would sound like a reference to the way in which all the women (those 'worldly-wise women') are sold into the power of the blue lotus, that is, Krishna. But I'll be frank: I hate to let go of the kiss.

Conclusion

We have located six poems that were evidently in circulation under Mira's name in various parts of northwest India in the seventeenth century or earlier. It would hardly be right to imply that they give us a portrait of the 'real Mira,' or even the 'early Mira.' After all, there are so few of them, and we know with fair probability, at least, that even now an additional cache of sixteen poems attributed to Mira exists somewhere at the Gujarāt Vidyā Sabhā library in Ahmedabad, just waiting to be unearthed. It is impossible to know what that cache will reveal, if ever it does, but we can be sure of this: poems recorded there would still give only a partial view of whatever body of song circulated orally in Mira's name at the time. Perhaps it was considerable. Thanks to Nabhadas, we know that by then poetry *about* Mirabai was also in existence. How could it have failed to be supported by a similar corpus of poetry attributed *to* her?

Yet for all these limitations, it is worth venturing several impressions about 'the early Mirabai' based on this small set of sixteenth- and seventeenth-century poems. After all, there are elements of consistency, and they are not exactly the same as those that would emerge from a study of the much more ample Mirabai corpus we tend to assume today.

First of all, there is the fact that these six poems 'by' Mira keep a sort of middle distance from songs sung 'about' her. Only the poem in *rāg mārū* breathes the defiance of *kula-śṛnkhalā* that is the keynote of much latter-day Mira poetry and forms the centerpiece of her hagiography as told by Nabhadas. 'The chains of family life' appear in several of the remaining five poems, but not with the same degree of explicit autobiographical grounding that we meet in 'My eyes are greedy.' I doubt it is accidental that that poem is the only one of the six that becomes a firm and vivid part of the canonical Mirabai who is known and taught in schools today. It fits just fine with so many others—both those recorded in a 'respectable' collection such as that of Paraśurām Caturvedī, so widely used in Indian classrooms, and those that form the backbone of the more confrontational oral repertoire performed by lower-caste musicians and studied by Parita Mukta. But even there the *rāṇā* is nowhere to be seen.

Second, when we take these six early poems as a group, it is hard not to be struck by their emphasis on love as such. It's a sickness, a burning, and it's not always referenced to Krishna. If he appears, it tends to be with some clear connection to Kāma. Of course, he is always there in the signature line as the Mountain-Lifter—the universality of that designation almost as a part of Mira's own name is significant (see Chapter 1)—but in the body of these poems he is the lover, nothing else. I particularly like the lover's tantalizing anonymity in the last poem we considered, as indicated already in its title line: 'Last night a creature of darkness spoke.'

Finally, in a rather different vein, let me say that I think these poems are cogent. They may not be as sophisticated as some of the poems attributed to Surdas in the same period, or as arresting as some of those attributed to Kabir, but to my ear, at least, they are good poems. They are appealing, musical, thought-provoking, and in the aggregate they seem a little denser than the average run of Mira poems that appear in Caturvedī's collection or that published by Sukul and Tivārī.

So in the end, I'd like to surprise Frances Taft by saying I think these poems could indeed have been composed by a Mertiyā princess. I'm not saying they *were*, you understand, but I am saying I don't think it's impossible. Do princesses a better poem make? We know it works that way for stories.

5

Mirabai as Wife and Yogi

'Mirabai as Wife and Yogi' was designed as a contribution to the international conference on 'The Ascetic Dimension in Religious Life and Culture' held at Union Theological Seminary, New York, in April, 1993. It was published in Vincent L. Wimbush and Richard Valantasis, eds., *Asceticism* (New York: Oxford University Press, 1995), pp. 301–19. Some of the thoughts—and some of the prose—were carried forward from the essay 'Asceticism Denounced and Embraced: Rhetoric and Reality in North Indian Bhakti,' in Austin Creel and Vasudha Narayanan, eds., *Monastic Life in the Christian and Hindu Traditions* (Lewiston, NY: Edwin Mellen Press, 1990), pp. 459–95. That volume emerged from the conference 'Ascetics and Asceticism in India: A Comparative Study,' held at the University of Florida in February, 1988. Both the New York and the Gainesville conference were comparative in nature, and I am grateful to the editor-organizers and other participants for the discussions they stimulated.

At first glance, Mirabai seems the most popular and accessible figure among the bhakti poet-saints of North India. In contrast to the poems of Tulsidas or Surdas, the compositions generally attributed to Mira are loose in construction, almost folkish; they lend themselves easily to song. This quality of directness and informality has something to do with gender. Mira is the only woman in the family of major North Indian bhakti poets, and Indian women are usually less well educated than their male counterparts. No wonder, then, that Mira's modes of speech seem on the whole closer to those of the mass than theirs. Some of the same circumstances may account for her box-office success, too. The Indian film industry has produced no fewer than ten movies about

Mira, while her nearest competitors among male saints have earned at most three or four.[1] And when the creators of the *Amar Chitra Katha* comic-book series crossed the shallow ford that separates myth and legend from hagiography, their first subject was Mirabai—book number 36. Kabir followed as number 55, Tulsi as number 62, and it was not until number 137 that they got around to Sur.[2]

Yet for all her accessibility, there is a dark, enigmatic side to Mira. To begin with, it is much harder in Mira's case than in that of her male rivals to have any confidence that she actually composed a substantial portion of the poetic corpus attributed to her. A poem in praise of Mira appears in the *Bhaktamāl* of Nabhadas, a hagiographical anthology composed in about 1600 CE, where she takes a natural place alongside the likes of Kabir, Tulsi, and Sur.[3] But when one searches among manuscripts of roughly the same period for poems bearing her oral signature, the disappointment is greater. Only twenty-two Mira poems have been found in manuscripts dating before the beginning of the eighteenth century, a far smaller number than one finds for any male saints of comparable stature. If one were to judge things solely by the manuscript evidence, in fact, Mira's efflorescence would seem best dated to the nineteenth century. It may not be accidental that the critical edition upon which most modern assessments of Mira are based—that of Paraśurām Caturvedī—contains only the scantiest scholarly apparatus and no reference at all to the manuscripts upon which it is based.[4] When Kalyāṇsiṃh Śekhāvat went in search of Mira's poetry in the manuscript libraries of her native Rajasthan, the earliest examples he was able to find dated to the latter half of the eighteenth century, and even these were notably sparse. There were plenty of poems—he was able to add a whole new volume to the *Mīra-Bṛhat-padāvali* published posthumously on the basis of the collection made by Harinārāyaṇ Śarmā—but only a handful predated 1800 CE. The rest were either more recent or, like those collected by Śarmā, bore no date at all.[5]

When one speaks of the poetry of Mirabai, then, there is always an element of enigma. In this chapter, by contrast to the last, we will take a Vulgate approach, using the collections mentioned above, but that means there must always remain a question about whether there is any real relation between the poems we cite—the Mira we construct—and Mira in any historical sense. In fact, we will compound the situation. Our aim here is to highlight an aspect of Mira's *œuvre* that is somewhat enigmatic in its own right: poems in which she departs from the received wisdom that is expressed in other bhakti compositions by depicting Krishna not as a debonair lover but as a yogi. Indeed, Mira sometimes pictures herself, though a married woman, as a yoginī ready to take her place at the side of her beloved yogi in a new form of marriage. Our purpose will be to see how the tradition of Mirabai elaborated this unusual vision of a female ascetic and then, as if thinking better of the matter, withdrew.

The Poetry of Mira

Some of the most haunting compositions in the Mirabai corpus are those in which she calls out to Krishna as a yogi. The basic experience is one of abandonment:

जोगिया जी निसदिन जोवाँ थारी बाट
पाँव न चालै पंथ दुहेली, आड़ा औघट घाट
नगर आइ जोगी रम गया रे, मो मन प्रीति न पाई
मैं भोली भोलापन कीन्हों राख्यौ नहि बिलमाई
जोगिया कूँ जोवत बोहो दिन बीता, अजहूँ आयो नाहिं
विरह बुझावन अन्तरि आवो, तपन लगी तन माहिं
कैं तो जोगि जग माँ नाहीं कैर बिसारी मोई
काँइ करूँ कित जाऊँरी सजनी नैण गुमायो रोइ
आरति तेरी अन्तरि मेरे, आलो अपनी जाणि
मीराँ व्याकुल बिरहिणी रे, तुम विनि तलफत प्राण

Yogi, day and night I watch the road,
That difficult path where feet refuse to go—
  so blocked, so steep, so overgrown.
A yogi came to town. He roamed around
  but didn't find the love in my mind,
And I was a girl of such simple ways
  that I had no way to make him stay.
Now it's been many days that I've watched
  for that yogi, and still he hasn't come:
The flame of loneliness is kindled inside me—
  inside my body, fire.
Either that yogi is no longer in this world
  or else he's gone and forgotten me,

So what am I to do, my friend? Where am I to go?
  I've lost my eyes to tears.
Yogi, the pain of you has burrowed inside me:
  see that I am yours and come
To Mira, a desperate, lonely woman.
  The life in me, without you, writhes.[6]

In this poem Mira is the *virahiṇī*, the desperate, lonely woman separated from her lover, and his absence is so painful that she imagines Krishna as a yogi, a wanderer entirely cut off from the settled life of home and town. Images of interiority punctuate the poem and cast the light of contrast on Krishna's elusiveness. In other poems the effects of Krishna's absence are even more vividly portrayed. In one poem addressed to her yogi, Mira explains that her suffering has made his absence seem a lifetime: it has caused her hair to turn white.[7] The shadow of death hangs over other poems, too. In perhaps the best known poem in the corpus, Mira represents herself not as old and wizened but as an incipient *satī*:

जोगी मत जा मत जा मत जा, पाँअ परूँ मैं तेरी चेरी हौ
प्रेम भगति को पैड़ों ही न्यारो हमकूँ गैल बता जा
अगर चँदण की चिता रचाऊँ, अपने हाथ जला जा
जल बल भई भस्म की ढेरी, अपने अंग लगा जा
मीराँ कै प्रभु गिरधर नागर जोत में जोत मिला जा

Don't go, yogi, don't go, don't go,
  I fall, a slave, at your feet.
The footpath of love is ever so strange,
  so please: show me the road.
I'll build myself a pyre of aloes and sandalwood—
  come: light it yourself,
And after the fire has turned to ash,
  cover yourself with the cinders.
To her clever Mountain-Lifter Lord, Mira says:
  merge my light with yours.[8]

A score of compositions ring further changes on the same theme, and in quite a few Mira defines her own response in the same way that she depicts Krishna's absence: if he is a yogi, she vows to be a yoginī. In one example that recalls the *satī* theme, we think we hear her say that she is adopting the signs of widowhood—she takes off her jewelry and shaves her head—but these turn out to be signs of a different life, a mendicant yoga in which she will search out her beloved:

सॉंवलिया म्हारो छाय रह्या परदेश
म्हारा बिछड़्या फेर न मिलया भेज्या णा एक सन्नेस
रतण आभरण भूखण छाँड्या, खोर कियाँ सिर केस
भगवाँ भेख धर्‌याँ थे कारण, ढूढ़्याँ चार्‌याँ देस
मीराँ रे प्रभु स्याम मिलण विण, जीवनि जनम अनेस

My dark one has gone to an alien land.
He's left me behind,
  he's never returned,
    he's never sent me a single word,
So I've stripped off my ornaments,
  jewels and adornments,
    cut the hair from my head,
And put on holy garments,
  all on his account,
    seeking him in all four directions.
Mira: unless she meets the Dark One, her Lord,
  she doesn't even want to live.[9]

There are times when Mira envisions her yoga as something sedentary, a life of isolation in a cave:

तेरो मरम नहिं पायो रे जोगी
आसण माँड़ि गुफा में बैठो, ध्यान हरी को लगायो
गल बिच सेली हाथ हाजरियो, अंग भभूति रमायो
मीराँ के प्रभु हरि अविनासी, भाग लिख्यो सो ही पायो

Your secret, yogi, I have still not found.
I've sat in a cave,
  taken a yogic pose,
    and trained my thoughts on Hari
With beads around my neck,
  a bag of beads in my hand,
    and body smeared with ash.
Mira's Lord is Hari, the indestructible.
  Fate is written on my forehead,
    and that is what I've found.[10]

Even in the meditative attitude Mira here describes, there is something restless. The last line is affirmative in form but opaque in content: what does she mean by her fate? And the first line, a refrain that is quoted at intervals as the poem is sung, is negative—an expression of continuous, unending search. It is no surprise, then, that Mira characteristically represents her yoga not as a static, meditative art but as a discipline of life that keeps her always on the move, wandering for Krishna's sake.

Two poems are translated here to illustrate such a mood. In the first Mira depicts her life of peregrination as the only possible alternative to death, which she also contemplates. In the second she sees it quite the other way around, as a sort of walking death that can only be ended by meeting her Mountain-Lifter. In both poems, and especially in the second, where she addresses not only Krishna but a companion, we meet the oscillation of focus that is so familiar in compositions attributed to Mira. The crisp voice of autobiography has been slurred, perhaps, by hagiography. Here are two poems of journeying:

ऐसी लगन लगाइ कहाँ तू जासी
तुम देख्याँ बिन कल न पड़त है, तलफ तलफ जिव जासी
तेरे खातिर जोगण हूँगी, करवत लूँगी कासी
मीराँ के प्रभु गिरधर नागर, चरण कँवल की दासी

After making me fall for you so hard,
        where are you going?
Until the day I see you, no repose:
    my life, like a fish washed on shore,
        flails in agony.
For your sake I'll make myself a yoginī.
    I'll hurl myself to death
        on the saw of Kashi.
Mira's Lord is the clever Mountain-Lifter
    and I am his,
        a slave to his lotus feet.[11]

करणाँ सुणि स्याम मेरी, मैं तो होइ रही चेरी तेरी
दरसण कारण भई बावरी, विरह विथा तन घेरी
तेरे कारण जोगण हूँगी, दूँगी नग बिच फेरी
                कुंज सब हेरी हरी

अंग भभूत गले म्रिगछाला यों तन भसम करूँ री
अजहूँ न मिल्या राम अविनासी, बन बन बिच फिरूँ री
रोऊँ नित टेरी टेरी
जन मीराँ कूँ गिरधर मिलिया, दुख मेटण सुख भेरी
रूम रूम साता भइ उर में, मिटि गई फेरा फेरी
रहूँ चरणनि तेरि चेरी

Dark One, listen compassionately
to me, for I am your slave.
The hope of seeing you has made me lose my mind
and my body is besieged by your absence.
For you, I'll make myself a yoginī,
wandering town to town looking for you,
looking in every grove.
Ash on my limbs and an antelope skin
pulled up to my neck, my friend:
that's how I'll burn my body to ash for him.
I've still not found the indestructible Rām, my friend,
so I'll wander forest to forest shrieking,
crying all the time.
But let that Mountain-Lifter come
and meet his servant Mira
and he'll wipe away her sadness,
he'll beat the drum of happiness.
The thrill of peace will fill her breast—
my breast—and this back and forth
will wipe itself away: I'll stay
at your feet, your slave.[12]

The note of hope on which the last poem ends is expanded in a group of poems in which the specter of a yogic life is merged with the happier vision of life in the presence of Krishna. Here Mira imagines herself not as a wanderer in search of Krishna but as a wanderer at his side. In doing so she concocts an unorthodox mixture of home and homelessness that has precedent only in a few extreme tantric groups and in the mythology of Pārvatī and Shiva. Thoughts of Shiva occupy her at least obliquely as she begins:

जोगिया ने कहज्यो जी आदेस
जोगिया चतुर सुजाण, सुजाणी, व्यावै संकर सेस
आऊँगी मैं नाह रहूँगी (रे म्हारा) पीव बिना परदेस

करि किरपा प्रतिपाल, मो परि, राखो ण आपण देस
माला मुदरा मेखला रे बाला, खप्पर लूँगी हाथ
जोगणि होइ जुग ढूँढसूँ रे, म्हारा रावलियारो साथ
सावन आवण कह गया बाला, कर गया कौल अनेक
गिणता-गिणता धँस गई रे म्हाराँ आँगलियारी रेख
पीव कारण पीली पड़ी बाला, जोवर वाली बेस
दास मीराँ स्याम मजिबै, तण मण कीन्ही पेस

Oh, the yogi—
  my friend, that clever one
  whose mind is on Shiva and the Snake,
  that all-knowing yogi—tell him this:

'I'm not staying here, not staying where
  the land's grown strange without you, my dear,
But coming home, coming to where your place is;
  take me, guard me with your guardian mercy,
    please.
I'll take up your yogic garb—
  your prayer beads,
    earrings,
      begging-bowl skull,
        tattered yogic cloth—
          I'll take them all
And search through the world as a yogi does
  with you—yogi and yoginī, side by side.

My loved one, the rains have come,
  and you promised that when they did, you'd come too.
And now the days are gone: I've counted them
  one by one on the folds of my fingers
    till the lines at the joints have blurred
And my love has left me pale.
  my youth grown yellow as with age.

Singing of Rām
  your servant Mira
    has offered you an offering:
      her body and her mind.'[13]

It is but a small step from here to poems in which yoga and marriage, those impossible bedfellows, meet in an explicit way. In the following composition, consider the alternation between the bride's red sari and pearl-parted hair on the one hand and the ascetic's saffron robe and dishevelled coiffure on the other. Is this merely ambivalence, or is Mira saying that with Krishna yoga and marriage are tantamount to the same thing?

चाँलाँ वाही देस प्रीतम पावाँ चालाँ वाही देस
कहो कसूमल साड़ी रँगावाँ, कहो तो भगवाँ भेस
कहो तो मोतियन माँग भरावाँ, कहो छिटकावाँ केस
मीराँ के प्रभु गिरधर नागर, सुणज्यो बिड़द नरेस

Go to where my loved one lives,
Go where he lives and tell him
if he says so, I'll color my sari red;
if he says so, I'll wear the godly yellow garb;
if he says so, I'll drape the part in my hair with pearls;
if he says so, I'll let my hair grow wild.
Mira's Lord is the clever Mountain-Lifter:
listen to the praises of that king.[14]

We have already explored one context for a poem such as this: Mira's visions of a life of yoga. There are others in which the marriage theme comes out explicitly—a second context for poems in which yoga and marriage are wed. Characteristically, however, Mira's visions of being married to Krishna have a certain subjective aspect, as will be evident in the following examples. In the first, Mira's marriage to Krishna is the stuff of dreams, and in the second, she approaches it not as realized fact but as something for which she longs:

भाई म्हाणे सुपणा माँ परण्याँ दीनानाथ
छप्पण कोटाँ जणाँ पधार्‍याँ दूल्हो सिरी ब्रजनाथ
सपणा माँ तोरण बँध्यारी सुपणामाँ गह्या हाथ
सुपणा माँ म्हारे परण गया पायाँ अचल सोहाग
मीराँ रो गिरधर मिल्यारी, पुरब जणम रो भाग

Sister, I had a dream that I wed
the Lord of those who live in need:
Five hundred sixty thousand people came
and the Lord of Braj was the groom.
In dream they set up a wedding arch;
in dream he grasped my hand;

in dream he led me around the wedding fire
and I became unshakably his bride.
Mira's been granted her mountain-lifting Lord:
from living past lives, a prize.[15]

थाँणे काँई काँई बोल सुणावा म्हाँरा साँवराँ गिरधारी
पूरब जणम री प्रीति पुराणी, जावा णाँ गिरधारी
सुन्दर बदन जोवताँ साजण, थारी छबि बलिहारी
म्हारे आँगण स्याम पधाराँ, मंगल गावाँ नारी
मोती चौक पुरावाँ णेणाँ, तण मण डाराँ वारी
चरण सरण री दासी मीराँ, जणम जणम री क्वाँरी

I have talked to you, talked,
dark Lifter of Mountains,
About this old love,
from birth after birth.
Don't go, don't.
Lifter of Mountains,
Let me offer a sacrifice—myself—
beloved,
to your beautiful face.

Come, here in the courtyard.
dark Lord,
The women are singing auspicious wedding songs;
My eyes have fashioned
an altar of pearl tears,
And here is my sacrifice:
the body and mind
Of Mira,
the servant who clings to your feet,
through life after life,
a virginal harvest for you to reap.[16]

Both yoga and marriage are striking visions of how a woman might establish a relation with Krishna, since both go beyond the orthodox view of what such a liaison ought to entail. This is the *parakīyā* pattern established by the *gopīs* of Braj, according to which women drawn to Krishna must abandon their husbands and all the familial solidarity to which their mates provide access if they answer the call of the divine.

Mira seems to reject the view that life with Krishna must be an illicit liaison and to posit marriage instead. Not only that, she often combines this deviant vision with another—the specter of a woman who is a yogi. On more than one occasion she says that she wears the forehead mark and necklace of a yogi as if they were bangles—the essential jewelry of a married woman[17]—and by doing so suggests that the love of Krishna is a force strong enough to fuse even logical opposites such as these. Her attraction to the company of other lovers of Krishna—*bhaktas* and yogis whose itinerancy meant that they were almost invariably men—is then also, by extension, a sort of marriage. When she answers for this unseemly behavior to her worldly husband, the *rāṇā* (king) of Mewar, she merely revels in the scandal:

राणो म्हाँने या बदनामी लगे मीठी
कोई निन्दो कोई बिन्दो मैं चलूँगी चाल अपूठी
साँकड़ली सेर्‌याँ जन मिलिया क्यूँ कर फिरूँ अपूठी
सतसंगति मा ज्ञान सुणै छी, दुरजन लोगाँ नै दीठी
मीराँ रो प्रभु गिरधर नागर, दुरजन जलो जा अँगीठी

This bad name of mine, oh king,
 is something sweet to me.
Let them blame me, let them praise:
 I'll stubbornly go my way.
I met the Lord's people in chainlike lanes—
 why leave my stubborn ways?
  Wisdom I learned in the gathering of the good—
 so the evil ones saw.
Mira's Lord is the clever Mountain-Lifter—
 evil ones: go roast in a stove![18]

Early Lives of Mira

Scandal such as this is certainly the keynote in the early hagiography of Mira, as we saw in Chapter 2. The point of departure in the hymn to Mira framed by Nabhadas in his *Bhaktamāl*, our earliest source, is her notorious disdain for the bonds that tie a woman to the family into which she marries. Nabhadas makes allusion to the well-known incident in which Mira survives an attempt on her life that is initiated by the *rāṇā*, a figure who could be interpreted as being either Mira's husband or her father-in-law. (Priyadas's commentary on the *Bhaktamāl* seems to suggest the latter.) Whoever he was, the *rāṇā*'s sense of jealousy and humiliation is easy to understand, for Mira had put the claims of Krishna ahead of the man whom Indian teaching regards as her *patidev* (husband-god). Here is Nabhadas:

> Modesty in public, the chains of family life—
> Mira shed both for the Lifter of Mountains.
> Like a latter-day *gopī*, she showed what love can mean
> in this devastated, age-ending age.
> No inhibitions. Totally fearless.
> Her tongue sang the fame of her tasteful Lord.
> Villains thought it vile. They set out to kill her,
> but not a single hair on her head was harmed:
> The poison she was brought turned elixir in her throat.
> She cringed before none. She beat bhakti's drum.
> Modesty in public, the chains of family life—
> Mira shed both for the Lifter of Mountains.[19]

A century after Nabhadas, in 1712 CE, Priyadas, a devotee of Caitanya living in Brindavan, composed an additional set of verses to explain the meaning of the *Bhaktamāl*. His *Bhaktirasabodhinī* draws out the theme of Mira's scandalous behavior even more clearly. Priyadas makes it plain that when Mira, princess of Merta, was married to the son of another royal Rajput family—later tradition said it was the house of Mewar—she mouthed the requisite marriage mantras but in her heart she dedicated them to Krishna, not her earthly groom. When young Mira came to live in her in-laws' house, similarly, she refused to bow to her mother-in-law and honor her in-laws' family goddess, believing that either act would compromise her loyalty to Krishna. Before long, says Priyadas, Mira was spending most of her time with wandering mendicants and religious enthusiasts—the *sādhu saṅg* (company of the saints) who were 'attached to the will of Śyām,' that is, Krishna.[20] It was this pattern of inattention to family mores as well as Mira's open flouting of the expectation that a Rajput woman's place is in the home that led to the incident in which her in-laws tried to poison her. It failed. Mira dutifully drank the poison, since it had been sent as an offering at Krishna's feet, but once the liquid reached her throat it actually became 'immortal nectar from his feet' (*caraṇāmṛt*). Not only did Mira survive, she found that she sang more beautifully than ever.[21]

Priyadas reports other episodes that also illustrate Mira's indifference to the conjugal duties ordained for a woman by Hindu standards set forth in codes such as *The Laws of Manu*. The conflict between love of Krishna and obedience to her husband is further elaborated in a story in which Mira is heard whispering sweet nothings to a strange man behind her bedroom door. The *rāṇā*—again it is unclear whether this is Mira's father-in-law or her husband—races forward to defend the family honor. Sword in hand, he demands to be admitted to her chamber, but when he is, he freezes like a picture on the wall, for he finds that she is merely conversing with Krishna, the image she worships.[22]

This time it is an imagined tryst, but other vignettes in the *Bhaktirasabodinī* show that Mira really does have more intimate contacts with her other family—the ragtag company of devotees—than she does with her own. There is, for instance, an account of how a lecherous man in their number develops a carnal attachment to Mira. Her response is to welcome his advances, provided that they be displayed in the company of all Krishna's followers, and this threat of ultimate sharing jolts the man into a change of heart: his misplaced ardor is transformed into true devotion.[23] Other stories in the *Bhaktirasabodhinī* tell how Mira ultimately left her family altogether and adopted the wandering life to which her poems say she aspired. Her first destination was Brindavan, where she visited Jīv Gosvāmī,[24] and her last was Dvaraka, where she merged her body with Krishna's. She died by entering the image enshrined in his temple there. Priyadas reports that before this event occurred, Brahmins sent by the *rāṇā* attempted to dissuade her from her extreme practices, calling her home. In this way he continues to highlight the tension between her life among those who wander for Krishna's sake and the life she would have led as a member of a noble Rajput family—right up to the end.[25]

In his account, then, the idea of Mira's marriage to Krishna appears explicitly, and something closely resembling a yogic pattern of life is often attributed to her, if not directly named. Both motifs serve to underscore the disparity between religious commitments and the demands of everyday *dharma* (caste duties and obligations)—the same sort of tension that emerges so strongly in poems attributed to Mira herself. In fact, the line separating poetry by Mira and poetry about her is a faint one at best. Many of the poems said to have been composed by Mira are in effect expositions of her life story. Though voiced in the first person, they function as additions to the corpus of her hagiography. Therefore it is not surprising that poems by Mira display an unusual ease of transition between first- and third-person utterances.[26] The poetry and hagiography of Mira, then, form a unified if somewhat unruly body of literature, and they agree in presenting her as a rebel, a woman who defied traditional patterns of womanhood to serve Krishna. She is his yoginī and his wife, eternally virgin, eternally ready to mate with him, ever separate from the life of home and family that keeps the world on its course.[27]

Modern Permutations

Both in poetry and in story, then, the 'canonical' figure of Mirabai presents us with a radical image of bhakti womanhood, an ideal that seems to challenge a woman's *dharma* at its most fundamental points.[28] In fact, this Mira evidently is too radical. As her fame increased, the offense implied in her *bhakti* asceticism must have been ever more pointedly felt, with the result that portrayals of Mira in the modern day yield a more complicated picture. As an impressionistic survey will show, Mira now comes in many more shades of gray than Nabhadas or Priyadas would have thought possible. There are settings—in the pilgrimage cities of Brindavan and Banaras, for example—where we get some semblance of the old Mira, but there are other contexts in which she seems to have changed almost beyond recognition.

Suppose we begin our survey by following Mira's footsteps to Brindavan. There we find a Mira temple that has become an important stopping point on the route of many pilgrims. It is said to mark the place where the Rajput princess stayed when she came to visit Jīv Gosvāmī, and indeed it lies only a small distance from the temple of Rādhā Dāmodar, where Jīv lived. The temple to Mira was constructed in the middle of the nineteenth century—not earlier, be it noted—by the chief minister of the state of Bikaner, in northwest Rajasthan, and its special claim to fame, aside from the location itself, is that it houses a *śālagrām* stone that is said to have been produced from a snake sent by Mira's in-laws to poison her.

The story of this snake was apparently not known to Priyadas, though it obviously echoes his own account of how the *rāṇā* tried to poison Mira. It may well have come into existence after Priyadas's lifetime and is a common feature of Mira's biography as told today.[29] The story states that the *rāṇā* of Mewar attempted to poison Mira not only with a glass of *caraṇāmṛt* but with a live snake, which he sent to her in a basket. The result was similar: the poison turned into its opposite when exposed to Mira's faith. As the initial *caraṇāmṛt* was transformed into *caraṇāmṛt* of quite a different kind, so the black cobra was transformed into a black *śālagrām* stone, an object universally revered in Vaishnava worship. In the temple of Mira at Brindavan, it is said, one has a chance to see that very stone.

So far there is nothing to challenge or qualify the traditional message of the Mira story, only a further variation on the theme of her opposition to ordinary conceptions of marital obligation. The arrangement of the deities displayed in the Mira temple also seems to accord with the teachings of the *Bhaktamāl* and the *Bhaktirasabodhinī*. Krishna is in center, with Radha at his left hand and Mira at his right. Radha's position is more or less dictated by Brindavan tradition: she is at Krishna's left because she is recognized to be *vāmāṅganī* (the left-hand side of his body), that is, his primary consort. Mira is exalted by being given a corresponding place at Krishna's right, and the symmetry is appropriate from the point of view of a theologian such as Nabhadas. Nabha, we recall, portrayed Mira as 'a latter-day *gopī*' who 'showed the meaning of devotion in our devastated age.'[30] Her role parallels that of Radha, who served as the paradigm for all the *gopīs* in Krishna's own time. Nothing is actually said about marriage here—in regard to either Radha or Mira—but similar sets of images, such as those that show Vishnu flanked by Bhūdevī and Nīlādevī, do imply a marital bond, which suggests the strength of the tie between Krishna and Radha and Mira. The arrangement of figures on the altar at Brindavan's Mira temple seems an appropriate way of acknowledging Mira's conception of herself as married to Krishna.

The other side of Mira—her identity as a *yoginī*—comes out in another pilgrimage city mentioned in the lore of Mira: Banaras. Several poems in the Caturvedī collection make reference to that city, and to a particular item within it: the *karavaṭ* (saw) that was embedded in a well near the famous temple of Viśvanāth. Pilgrims who wished to end their days in Banaras and reap the karmic benefits of dying in such a place would jump down the well and be cut in two as they fell—or perhaps they were pushed by greedy pilgrim guides who would then rob the corpses of any jewelry, as some aver.[31]

To judge by the sampling now available in printed editions of Mira's poetry, Banaras holds an ambivalent place in the Mira tradition. On the one hand it is criticized as a place where external practice, even suicide, is apt to obscure the importance of interior devotion.[32] On the other hand, as one sees in reference to the deadly saw, it is held up as the place that sets the standard for ascetic rigor.[33] In consonance with its rather distant and uncertain role in Mira's poetry, it is fitting that Banaras makes a good deal less of Mira than Brindavan does. What place she has, however, is an appropriate one, for she makes her entry in search of one of the *nirguṇa sants*. Of all the representatives of early Mughal bhakti, such *sants* come closest to living the life of renunciation (*vairāgya*) that yogis embrace.

The *sant* with whom Mirabai is associated is Ravidas, the leather-worker poet who lived in Banaras in the late fifteenth or early sixteenth century.[34] Mira is said by Ravidas's followers to have sought initiation from him, and sections from a number of poems attributed to her are quoted in support of that thesis.[35] Historically it may have been a story in the *Bhaktirasabodhinī* that gave rise to the tradition linking Mira with Ravidas, for we read in the section of the *Bhaktirasabodhinī* describing him that Ravidas was once visited by a certain Queen Jhālī—or Jhālī Queen—of Chittor, the former capital of Mewar in southwestern Rajasthan. Chittor is the city that represents the most extreme expression of Rajput heroic ideas, for both men and women, so it is not surprising that over the course of time the legendry of Mira, that paragon of courage, gravitated in the direction of Chittor. It came to be accepted that Chittor was the home of the family into which she married, and once that tradition was established it would be then but a small step to forgetting the identity of Queen Jhālī and putting Queen Mira in her place.[36]

As with Brindavan, there is nothing in Mira's connection with Banaras that challenges the traditional estimate of who she was. If Brindavan served as a natural locale for representing Mira's marriage to Krishna, Banaras was a logical place to associate with her peripatetic asceticism. Indeed, Ravidas himself is often pictured as someone who wandered the subcontinent, so Mira must have seemed an apt pupil. It is true that many people deny the validity of the connection between Mira and Ravidas. For a Rajput woman to adopt an Untouchable as a guru seems at least as bad to many Vaishnavas as Mira's dalliance with traveling *sādhus* seemed to her own much maligned in-laws, and one must grant that the purity of her devotion of Krishna makes the situation a little implausible. Ravidas speaks of Hari in his poetry—even Kabir does that (see Chapter 15)—but neither could rightly be classed as a Krishnaite poet in the normal sense. From Mira's side a better case could be made, yet there are strands in the poetry attributed to her that ought to make a place for a guru such as Ravidas: her reverence for the divine Name, for example, and her frequent praise for 'the company of the good.'[37] Whatever one may think of the likelihood of such a guru–pupil alliance, one can readily see how it serves to fill a hagiographical lacuna, one that relates particularly to the yogic side of Mira's personality. In someone's eyes, at least, the act of providing a guru for Mira must have been seen as giving credence to her own claim to be a yogi. There is nothing in the poems attributed to her that requires such an idea, but it is a commonplace assumption that every yogi (or yoginī) needs an initiating guru, someone to chart out the ascetic path at its outset. Whether Ravidas's fulfilling of that perceived need added more to Mira's stature or to his own depends upon the group with whom one is speaking.

In Rajasthan it would seem that Ravidas was the one to gain, and only among certain groups does the story have currency.[38] Lindsey Harlan's interviews with Rajput women of Mewar show that in their perception the ascetic streak in Mira can stand on its own. According to them, Mira was a one-of-a-kind phenomenon made possible by the ideals of bravery long cultivated in Rajput tradition. This is what made it possible for her to stand alone, defying social criticism and the cruelty of the family into which she had married. It was Rajput bravery, too, that gave Mira the courage to adopt an alternate family, the one defined by devotion to Krishna, even if its members consisted of *sādhus* and yogis, as Harlan's Rajput women affirm.[39] That Mira became functionally a yoginī is a matter of no great offense to these modern-day Rajput women, but an unusually vivid expression of Rajput courage.

What is problematic, however, is Mira's marriage, since marital obligations are at the core of what these women consider to be the meaning of a woman's life. Mira is so successful as an embodiment of one Rajput ideal—brave independence of action—that her slighting of another—*pativratā* (devotion to one's husband)—presents an even greater challenge than it otherwise would. The present generation of Rajput women cannot have been the first to face this problem, as is shown by the existence of a fundamental reorganization in the mythology of Mira that appears to have taken place around the end of the nineteenth century (see Chapter 4). Its results are assumed when these women speak about their bhakti heroine. It may well be that this shift in the story of Mira was necessitated by the fact that Mira had become such a widely revered figure in North India. The scandalous element in her legend could no longer be tolerated in the form in which it had been received: some way had to be found to lessen the shock of her disobedience to her husband.

At the beginning of the nineteenth century, when James Tod served the British crown in Rajasthan, the prevailing notion, at least in Mewar, seems to have been that Mirabai was married to Rāṇā Kumbhā, one of the greatest heroes of Mewari legend.[40] This had the virtue of confirming her heroism by coupling it with his, but it must have made her conjugal disloyalty seem all the harder to accept. Furthermore, and in part because of the existence of Tod's own work, it came to be realized that there was a chronological problem involved: Rāṇā Kumbhā's dates significantly preceded those of the man whom tradition had come to recognize as Mira's father. In consequence, apparently, the role of being Mira's husband was assigned to Kumbhā's grandson, the sixteenth-century prince Bhojrāj.[41] Elsewhere, at least—in Jodhpur—Bhojrāj seems to have been associated with Mira since the seventeenth century.

In any case, the historical problem was solved, but the moral dilemma remained: how could Mira be allowed to insult a figure so honored in the collective memory of Mewar with her unusual sense of marital priorities? The answer was found by proposing that after Bhojrāj died, at a relatively young age, Mira was set upon by his evil brother, a second *rāṇā* named Vikramājīt. This man could be held responsible for the cruelty shown to Mira, while both the honor and virtue of Bhojrāj remained unscathed. With her husband dead at an early age, furthermore, Mira's devotional version of widowhood made sense—or, as one might equally see it, her devotional substitution for *satī*. She certainly owed nothing to her husband's heinous brother, so her insistent marriage to Krishna was emptied of its scandal, at least once Bhojrāj had died.[42]

This is the form of the Mira story that is now accepted across Rajasthan, and it must help considerably in enabling modern Rajput women to emulate Mira obliquely, as Harlan says they do.[43] She is their heroine for bhakti though not for the conduct of their own marriages.

The device of shortening Mira's marriage goes some way toward muting her offense to conjugal *dharma*, though in traditional Rajasthani culture she herself would in some measure be regarded as responsible: a wife's auspicious power should keep her husband alive.[44] In elite Indian culture one need not worry about lingering superstitions of *satī*, but even so there remains a sense of unease about Mira's marital situation. One sees this particularly in instructional literature, where Mira now plays a standard role. Take, for example, the *Amar Chitra Katha* comic-book version of Mira's life, where the logic of justifying Mira's domestic behavior has been pushed yet a step further. There it is claimed that Mira was an ideal Hindu wife, as we will see Chapter 6. This seemingly impossible assertion is wonderfully worked out on the page (see Figure 3). In an initial frame, which is represented in full color, the reader sees Mira bowing at the feet of an enthroned Bhojrāj. This is the panel for which we have the caption, 'Mira was an ideal Hindu wife and was loved by her husband.' The next frame, however, reveals a different Mira. The caption at the top says, 'But as soon as her household duties were over, Mira would turn to her divine husband—her Gopala—whom she had brought with her [from Merta].' The figure we see just below is a silhouetted black-and-white Mira performing an *āratī* offering before a shadowed Krishna. (see Figure 3.) This way of representing the matter puts everything in good proportion: *dharma* comes first, then bhakti, and there is no hint of a contradiction between them. Fortunately nothing need be said to an underage readership about any uncomfortable dilemmas that may have arisen in the royal bedroom as Mira insisted on defending her virginity before Bhojrāj.

This is one extreme, then. In the *Amar Chitra Katha* version the *rāṇā* is split into a good and an evil half, with the result that in the first part of her married life Mira is construed as a paragon of family virtue—the episode in which she defies her mother-in-law at the threshold is forgotten—while in the second half she is placed in the position of being able to protest rightly against the advances of a wicked ruler and retreat to the kingdom of Krishna. Her virtue is doubly saved.

But that, after all, is a comic book, and one has a right to expect a certain fairy-tale touch. What happens when Mira is held up as a model for children in real life? This too is a genuine possibility, and the place in which it most obviously occurs is an educational complex in Pune: St. Mira's School for Girls and, for graduates of it and other schools,

St. Mira's College. Both institutions were established by a Sindhi visionary, T. L. Vaswani, who propounded what he called a 'Mira Movement in Education.'[45] Vaswani was celibate, but his interest in education and social reform marked him as a *sādhu* of the distinctly modern school, and he took the figure of Mira as his patron—or rather matron—saint. In fact, it was he himself who defined her status by adopting the English term saint, as in a book called simply *Saint Mira*.[46]

It was part of Vaswani's aim to adopt for Hindu society some of the standards that typically emerged in convent schools (most of which, needless to say, also had saints in their names) and the image of Mira seemed to provide a way to do so. To Sadhu Vaswani, she was the queen saint who exemplified the virtues of purity, prayer, simplicity, and service, and images of her that appear in his books and in the schools he founded bear a startling likeness to certain depictions of that other paragon of virtue, the Virgin Mary. One much reproduced portrait, for example, is clearly a Hindu adaptation of Fra Angelico's *Annunciation*. (See Figure 1.) The connection is a fascinating one, for Jesus' mother also caused a certain amount of marital embarrassment: the *Gospel of Matthew* reports that when Joseph first learned of Mary's pregnancy he was prepared (if in a nice way) to divorce her.[47] And Mary's example seems to have paved Mira's way in years since, too. It is possible nowadays to find images of Mira that represent her in a Madonna-like maternal pose. (See Figure 2.) The child, of course, is none other than Krishna, her erstwhile lover and yogi.

All this serves as an enthralling example of intercultural experimentation, and perhaps it was more than anything the simple domination of Mira in the female hagiography of North India that created the need for such bold innovations. The more important she became, the more she had to be able to encompass—not just the call of bhakti but the pull of familial and social responsibility. Oddly, the curriculum at St. Mira's College lays particular stress on the idea of being well-rounded. There is no question but that each of the graduates of St. Mira's College is expected to marry. Hence domestic science forms a required part of the curriculum and the whole thrust is to provide an education uniquely tailored to the life of a woman, including a woman's special charge to teach morals to her children. All this must sound like a travesty of the traditional Mira, but there is another side to the education at the institutions dedicated to St. Mira. The sense is also clearly conveyed that one's service as a human being ought to extend

FIGURE 1: Large painting of Mirabai on the wall of the 'sanctuary' (assembly) room at St. Mira's School for Girls, Pune.

beyond the bounds of one's family, even one's community. To the extent that Mira broke beyond the bounds of tradition, forging new meanings for marriage and appropriating for women aspects of a life that had been assumed to be the exclusive preserve of men, she really does serve as a surprisingly good exemplar for this sort of school. And when one must think of fending off the domestic strength of outsiders such as the Muslims and the British, what could be better than the example of Mira's defiant Rajput heroism?[48]

It appears that if a saint is great enough, and only loosely confined by the textual tradition with which she is associated, there is plenty of room for further growth. It is fascinating to see that even when the specifics of the case have changed to the point of reversal, the central message in Nabhadas's stanza on Mirabai continues to shine through. It is Mira's courage that matters most—her fearlessness. There are two ways to read events that have occurred in the hagiography of Mira over

FIGURE 2: Mirabai with the infant Krishna.
Poster produced by Brijbasi and Co., Delhi.
Photograph courtesy of Diane Coccari.

the last hundred years: either as a dilution of the strength that once was there or as a further complication of an already multifaceted and in some ways difficult image. The sober historian would probably have to choose the former, but for the hagiographer there is something attractive in the latter. It creates the possibility of seeing Mira as fearless even in the face of her own tradition.

6

The Saints Subdued in *Amar Chitra Katha*

This chapter was first published as 'The Saints Subdued: Domestic Virtue and National Integration in *Amar Chitra Katha*' in Lawrence A. Babb and Susan S. Wadley, eds., *Media and the Transformation of Religion in South Asia* (Philadelphia: University of Pennsylvania Press, 1995), pp. 107–34. It owes its origins to a paper called 'Saints for Kids,' which was prepared for a conference organized by the Joint Committee on South Asia of the Social Science Research Council and the American Council of Learned Societies, held at Carmel, California, in April 1989. At that conference my Columbia colleague Frances Pritchett also presented reflections on the *Amar Chitra Katha* comic book series. Her essay appears just before mine in *Media and the Transformation of Religion in South Asia*, and incorporates some introductory remarks about *Amar Chitra Katha* that we wrote together. Interested readers will find Fran's essay a helpful supplement to this one.

Amar Chitra Katha is an ungainly beast, including everything from stories of the Mughal jokester Birbal to portraits of great 'scientists and doctors' and 'the makers of modern India.' Yet one theme unifies the series in the eyes of its founder and editor, Anant Pai, and that is its moral resolve: the commitment to preparing today's Indian children, especially the urban and English-speaking among them, for a modern world. Almost every story is in some way intended to show how India's shared and for the most part premodern past can provide these children with guidelines for right living.

One of the major vehicles for achieving this objective is hagiography, the full-color portrayal of consistently, unerringly, and overwhelmingly exemplary lives. A good deal of this hagiography is implicit, as various figures from the life of Humayun or the plot of *Ānanda Maṭh* are brought forward and bathed in the light of exemplitude. But there is explicit hagiography too: the special issue devoted to Jesus Christ, the comic concerned with the Jain *tīrthankara* Mahavira, the issue depicting Vivekananda and subtitled 'The Patriot-Saint of Modern India,' and, of course, the many volumes that deal with *sants*, *bhaktas*, and *ācāryas* from the more distant Hindu past. In this chapter we will investigate a subset of these Hindu hagiographies that allows us to make comparisons between *Amar Chitra Katha*'s idea of what a sainted life was about and versions that were produced in earlier centuries. By studying the new against the background of the old, we hope to see more clearly the process of selection that makes an *Amar Chitra Katha* saint a saint.

At issue will be the six volumes of *Amar Chitra Katha* that deal with North Indian poet-saints of the so-called bhakti period, that is, the late fifteenth to early seventeenth centuries. We will begin with Mirabai, since Anant Pai and his staff did the same and since her life shows how an exemplar of religious ecstasy—her traditional role—could be transformed into a paragon of general female virtue, a good model for character-building for today's young middle-class Indians. Then we will turn to the five other saints in the group, devoting particular attention to the way in which they are made to serve the *Amar Chitra Katha* goal of encouraging 'national integration.' In all these lives, *Amar Chitra Katha* has developed its own perspective on Indian religion, and Pai's theological commitments, especially his vision of the inclusiveness of truth, have been worked out in a variety of ways. Finally, we will consider the extent to which this new understanding of Indian religion is forced on the comic-book series not just by the theology of its editor and his staff but by the distinctively new medium in which they work.

Mirabai Improved

The six poet-saints within our range are, in the order adopted by *Amar Chitra Katha*, Mirabai (36), Nanak (*Guru Nanak* [47]), Kabir (55), Tulsidas (62), Surdas (*Soordas* [137]), and Ravidas (*Guru Ravidas* [350]).[1] The order and spacing of this list may reflect the values of Pai and his associates, but they undoubtedly also provide a rough indication of their guess as to the relative importance of these saints in the national imagination. Unquestionably Mirabai comes first, a judgment that would be confirmed by the number of commercial films made about her since the inception of Indian sound cinematography.[2] In explaining Mira's widespread popularity not only in the north but in the south, the *Amar Chitra Katha* staff specifically cited the influence of these films, especially the one in which M. S. Subbalaxmi, a Tamil, played and sang the leading role.[3]

In Chapter 2 of this book I have described primary elements in the traditional hagiography of Mirabai, for which our earliest sources are the brief paean offered by Nabhadas in his *Bhaktamāl* of about 1600 CE and the more extended treatment of Priyadas, who in 1712 prepared a commentary on that work called the *Bhaktirasabodhinī*.[4] Numerous other versions of Mira's life have appeared in print during the three-and-a-half century span since the composition of the *Bhaktirasabodhinī*, and in them important departures from Priyadas's understanding of Mira are recorded. The most obvious of these concerns Mira's placement in history.

As we have seen in Chapter 4, James Tod's report near the beginning of the nineteenth century makes it appear that it was then conventional at least in Mewar to conceive of Mira as the wife of Rāṇā Kumbhā, the great king who was the outstanding builder of its first capital, Chittor. When it was observed, however, that this would ill accord with the dates ascribed to Mira's father in Merta, a husband later in the line of Mewari princes and kings was selected to fill the role of the unnamed *rāṇā* in Mira's poetry and early hagiography. This was Bhojrāj, whose sixteenth-century dates fit nicely with those of Mira's supposed father, and who may already have been cast in the role of Mirabai's husband in seventeenth-century Jodhpur, as we have seen. Bhojrāj had a further advantage—he died young, which meant that his own good name could remain unchallenged while the role of 'bad *rāṇā*,' so important in the legend and poetry of Mirabai, passed from him to his younger brother Vikramājīt. The latter became the one who tried to poison Mira and could be held largely responsible for driving her from her in-laws' house. This solution to the puzzle of accommodating the legend of Mira to Rajput history has remained intact even to the present. The national media, especially radio, have undoubtedly played a role in standardizing this version of the story, but whatever the cause, Rajput women living in Udaipur today accept it as truth and apparently know no other.[5]

Amar Chitra Katha also accepts this version of the story, but prefers to tell it without naming the evil prince as Vikramājīt. This obviates the need to insult any member of the heroic Mewari line directly and thereby damage the cause of 'national integration'—or, incidentally, the size of *Amar Chitra Katha*'s readership. It illustrates one of Pai's general principles of operation, the Sanskrit maxim *satyam bruvāt priyam bruyāt mā bruyāt satyam apriyam*. His translation is: 'You must tell the truth; you must tell what is pleasant. And that which is unpleasant—just because it is true, you need not say it.'

If *Amar Chitra Katha* leaves something out, it also puts something in, and that too in the apparent cause of domesticating Mira. Nabhadas placed great emphasis on Mira's fearlessness, and the object to be feared—though she does not—was the *rāṇā* into whose family she had married. Similarly for Priyadas, the linchpin in the entire tale of Mira's life was her defiance of codes of obedience and loyalty that govern the behavior of any Hindu wife, certainly a Rajput. Her rebelliousness was the measure of her conviction that she was married to a higher Lord, Krishna.

In the Mirabai comic book all this is changed: Mira's bhakti is made consonant with her fulfillment of a woman's *dharma*.[6] The text asserts forthrightly that 'Mira was an ideal Hindu wife' and that she 'was loved by her husband' (36:4), claiming that she would perform her 'household duties' fully before turning her attention to 'her divine husband—her Gopala—whom she had brought with her [to Chittor]' (36:4). The illustration makes the point even more emphatic by giving primary attention to a scene in which Mira bows at Bhojrāj's feet. The vignette, representing what the text describes as Mira's priorities, is rendered in color and is allotted the greater part of the band in which it appears. The remainder, a scene showing Mira seated in devotion before her icon of Krishna, is smaller and done in silhouette (36:4; see Figure 3).

In the pages that follow, the plot line further buttresses the reader's sense of Mira's fidelity to her *rāṇā*. The moment at which Mira crosses the threshold in Chittor and defiantly refuses her mother-in-law's command that she should embrace the tutelary goddess of the royal household (*kuladevī*) is transposed from the place it held in Priyadas's account to the scene that follows the one we have just seen. This means that Mira defies her mother-in-law (with tearful apologies) only after her devotion to her husband has been established; and lest this conflict between mother-in-law and daughter-in-law be too brilliantly apparent,

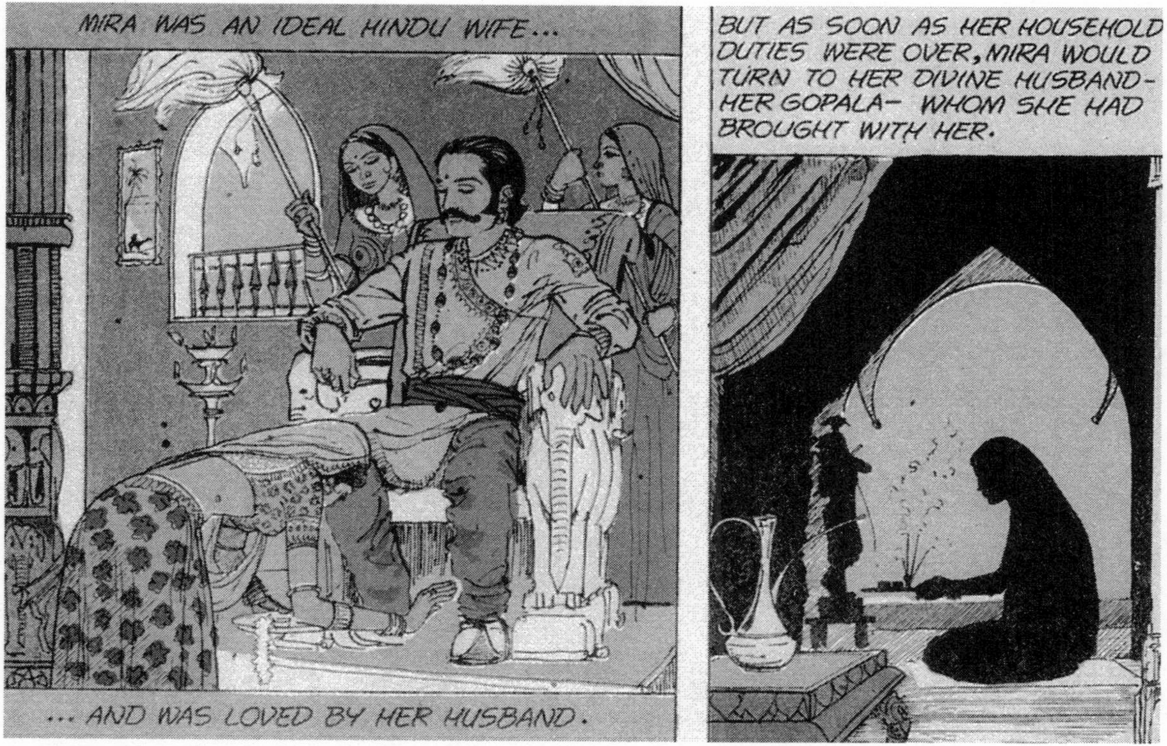

FIGURE 3: Mira in her household. *Amar Chitra Katha* issue number 36, p. 4.
Courtesy of India Book House Pvt. Ltd.

the plot at this point turns quickly away from Bhojrāj's mother. Priyadas goes on to tell how the older woman complained bitterly to her husband, the senior *rāṇā*, who determined at that point to kill Mira, but *Amar Chitra Katha* attributes no responsibility to the mother-in-law. It transfers the onus to Bhojrāj's sister Uḍā, whom Priyadas depicts in a more favorable light and does not mention by name. As in many a popular movie and pulp novel, this sister-in-law, now an evil force, connives to turn her brother against his new bride, and ultimately succeeds.

Two incidents are involved, and both introduce further alterations in the order given by Priyadas. The first vignette is the one in which the *rāṇā* hears Mira whispering sweet nothings to a lover behind closed doors. In Priyadas's version this episode follows the one involving poison, but here it precedes. The 'punch line' of the story is, of course, that the *rāṇā* discovers his would-be rival to be none other than Krishna himself, present to Mira in image form. That outcome persists here, too, but the evil Uḍā is made responsible for the fact that the king's suspicions are aroused in the first place. Since the *rāṇā* does no actual harm to Mira in this incident—the only cost is to himself, for he comes across as a fool—it is an appropriate one to associate with good prince Bhojrāj. Hence it is moved forward. The attempt to poison Mira is quite a different matter and must be reserved for his wicked brother.

The second incident inserted at this point is the story that Akbar once joined the throngs who gathered to hear Mira sing. This tale, too, is related in Priyadas's *Bhaktirasabodhinī*, but, again, later. When given its new position earlier in the story, it can be put to a clever use, for Akbar, after he hears Mira sing, asks permission to lay a garland at the feet of her lord. In a motif that echoes the traditional story of Mira's accepting the poison the *rāṇā* offered to her image of Krishna, Mira says she cannot refuse. Akbar makes the offering, but it is reported to Bhojrāj, presumably by Uḍā and her ilk, as if Akbar had touched not Krishna's feet but Mira's own. 'For the disgrace you have brought to the fair name of Rajputana'—by allowing 'a Muslim cur' to touch her feet—the angry Bhojrāj commands her to leave and drown herself. This provides an occasion to convert Mira's courage, the guiding leitmotif in older tellings of her story, into a display of wifely decorum. She remains silent through the entire tirade. As the final caption in this scene puts it, 'Mira, the true Hindu wife, did not protest' (36:11; see Figure 4).

FIGURE 4: Mira with her companions. *Amar Chitra Katha* issue number 36, p. 11. Courtesy of India Book House Pvt. Ltd.

At this point Mira goes off to Brindavan, where she is perceived as 'Radha reborn,' an artful adaptation of an evaluation made long ago by Nabhadas, that 'like a latter-day *gopī*, she showed what love can mean in this devastated, age-ending age' (see Chapters 1–2). The old story of her confrontation with Jīv Gosvāmī in Brindavan is omitted, an encounter in which she implicitly accuses him of theological stupidity. He refuses to see her because he is observing a vow that prevents him from having any contact with women so that he can avoid any temptation to compromise his total devotion to Krishna. Mira points out to him, through a messenger, that if one sees things aright there is really only one male in the world, Krishna himself, so the question of any other attraction between the sexes disappears.

In the story as Priyadas tells it, Jīv relents and all is well, but evidently the element of contest seems out of character for the Sītā-like Mira depicted by *Amar Chitra Katha*. Instead her presence in Brindavan is used as an occasion for Bhojrāj—a good-hearted man, after all—to see the error of his ways. He is delighted to learn that Mira is still alive and hastens off to beg her forgiveness and urge her to return to Chittor. She accepts and they depart together, quite over and above anything Nabhadas or Priyadas ever suspected; it is on that note of conjugal amity that Bhojrāj expires.

His death provides the occasion for another new twist: Bhojrāj's father orders Mira to prepare herself to become a *satī*, Mira resists on the grounds that she is not yet a widow—her true husband, Krishna, is still alive—and her refusal explains the animosity that is directed against her in the palace at Chittor ever after. The famous incident of ineffectual poisoning follows—not once but twice, for by the nineteenth century one story had been cloned into two. Even so, it is only a letter from Tulsidas, her brother in the family of *bhaktas*, that persuades Mirabai to leave Bhojrāj's family behind. The existence of such a letter is reported in the *Mūl Gosāīṅ Carit*, in all likelihood another nineteenth-century document, and its receipt is very convenient at this point in Mira's biography: she leaves for her natal family in Merta.[7]

There she is finally at peace, and though she leaves Chittor with the black hair of a woman no older than middle age, it is only 'a few more years' before her hair is shown as white. The text says 'Mira was growing old. She knew that her end was near' (36:29). At that point she sets out again for her old haunts in Mathura and Brindavan, and then moves on to Dvaraka, where she 'fell into a trance and fainted on her Lord' (36:31). In the final scene she is shown as an inset in Krishna's heart. The text says she 'became one with the Lord she had worshiped and yearned for, ever since she had taken him for her bridegroom, at the tender age of five!' (36:32).

Several elements are worth noting about the way the *Amar Chitra Katha* version of Mira's story ends. First, it happens in old age, a matter about which Priyadas has nothing to say. Old age is convenient because it adds further justification to Mira's decision to leave her husband's family behind, as a female ascetic, a *sanyāsinī* or *vairāginī*, might do. Though certain of the poems attributed to her do suggest that she yearned for such a life (see Chapter 5), this desire squares ill with the image of 'a perfect Hindu wife.' In old age, however, the offense is blunted, since that is the proper time for a person to choose a life of wandering—particularly a man, of course, but if at all the case arises, a woman as well.

Second, something like a *digvijaya*—the 'world victory tour' that is a frequent feature in the lives of philosophically minded saints—is introduced. While Priyadas knows only of a pilgrimage to Dvaraka at the end of Mira's life, it is here amplified to include a second trip to the Braj region. This serves also to underscore the romantic relation between Mira and Krishna that is so evident to any reader of the series.

Finally, a significant alteration has occurred in the image of how it was that Mira ultimately died. The traditional story states that she was absorbed into the image of Krishna at Dvaraka, but here we have not a word about such a event. Instead, Mira falls into a swoon and Krishna—the image, as it were—is shown bending over to receive her (see Figure 5). This does not exactly contradict the traditional story, but it also does not exactly repeat it: the element of miracle has been omitted. The text says that Mira 'becomes one with the Lord' (36:32), and the drawing represents this event by showing her as a medallion in the heart of the living Krishna (see Figure 6).

Despite the comic book idiom, in which it would be both possible and effective to show that miracles do happen, it is a general feature of *Amar Chitra Katha* policy to play down this element in volumes that are not explicitly mythological in nature. There are exceptions, particularly early in the series—several of the miracles of Jesus figure in 'Jesus Christ' and the cover of the issue on Kabir shows him walking on water—but when one compares the *Amar Chitra Katha* versions of these lives to traditional accounts, as in the case of Mirabai, the

FIGURE 5: Mira in a trance. *Amar Chitra Katha* issue number 36, p. 31.
Courtesy of India Book House Pvt. Ltd.

FIGURE 6: Mira as one with her Lord. *Amar Chitra Katha* issue number 36, p. 32. Courtesy of India Book House Pvt. Ltd.

element of moderation becomes clear.[8] An introductory disclaimer has appeared on the inside cover of reprints of the Mirabai comic at least since 1980, to the effect that 'the story of Mira, as narrated in this book, is based on legends about her and not on historical facts.' But even so, a restraining, rationalizing hand seems to have been at work bringing the saint within the purview of what modern children and their parents might construe as the realm of the possible. Here one sees shadows of the Protestant Reformation and the Enlightenment, as conveyed in the English language education that has shaped India's middle and upper classes since the nineteenth century.[9]

A somewhat parallel matter, one that intrudes into secular lives as well as religious ones, is the problem of what to do with violence. Here too the restraining hand prevails, and the staff at *Amar Chitra Katha* has a clear sense of its *satyam bruyāt priyam bruyāt* policy. They wish to keep too much blood and gore from the eyes of children, but are at pains to serve this 'pleasant' (*priyam*) desideratum while they stay as close to the truth (*satyam*) as they can.

For them, the famous case concerns Akbar's cruelty as a young king. The writer of the volume on Akbar had wanted to show how Akbar's increasing maturity meant that he put aside this aspect of his character, but to make the point some episode from his early years had to be told. His beheading of Hemu was chosen, but it was reported only in the text. The accompanying illustration shows not the beheading itself but the gallows where it occurred, and that, like Mira's late-in-the-day devotion to Krishna, only in silhouette. It is the illustration that makes the lasting impression, the staff observed, not the text. But lest children be aghast at what Akbar did, the text mitigates the blame: 'Poor Hemu's headless body was displayed on a gibbet. This was a cruel practice in those days' (200:7).

Violence and the emotion it engenders, fear, are downplayed in the religious realm, too. Pai rejected a proposal to do an issue on the snake goddess Mānasā because it might have stimulated too much fear in children, and for the same reason he several times fended off an *Amar Chitra Katha* entry on Santoṣī Mā.[10] The culminating episode in the story, in which this goddess goes on a rampage of destruction because someone had tampered with food offered to and blessed by her (*prasād*), was dismissed by Pai as being not only fearsome but unworthy and superstitious, a 'degradation of Hinduism.' Another version of the same motif would have had to figure in a proposed issue on Satyanārāyaṇan of Tirupati—another reject, despite the publisher's enthusiasm for the fact that it would have had guaranteed sales. There again, as Pai explained, a 'punitive god' demands restitution when a devotee forgets to eat *prasād*, and this he would not print. After all, 'there is no point in fostering faith in God for the wrong reasons'[11]

A final area in which restraint is thought to be called for is that of sex. Priyadas's account of Mirabai's life tells with relish of an incident in which a lecher makes his way into the company of Mira's devotees, then manages to force his attentions on her when she is alone. He tells her that her Giridhar—that is, Krishna—has commanded her to submit, and she is never one to challenge Krishna's word. All she requires is that whatever they do be done in the proper bhakti setting—before the eyes of all the other devotees. This amazes the evil man and brings him to his senses; her unquestioning submission to even a lecher's invoking of Krishna brings about his conversion.

The episode, which appears as well in the lives of other female saints memorialized by Priyadas and must have been a major motif in the Vaishnava hagiography of his time, is omitted in the *Amar Chitra Katha* retelling of Mira's life. And no wonder: Kamala Chandrakant, who was associate editor of the series for fifteen years, quipped that Pai often seemed to think it would strain the bonds of propriety to show a man and a woman sitting together on a couch having a normal conversation.[12] But if sex is out, romance of a certain sort is definitely in. The scenes of amorous devotion in which Mira encounters Krishna are lavishly, delicately depicted (Figure 7) (36:13). The Krishna to whom Mira referred in her poems may have been Giridhar Nāgar, the heroic 'clever Mountain-Lifter,' but the Krishna we see here is definitely the erotic Krishna, the one who bears the flute, not the mountain.[13]

The *Amar Chitra Katha* staff took a nonsectarian pride in the fact that the illustrator for this issue was Yusuf Lien (later Yusuf Bangalorewala), a Muslim. Pai recalled the special care that Bangalorewala lavished on this volume by telling how he once visited him at his house to urge him toward completion, only to find the artist in tears as he drew. Bangalorewala's explanation of how he could accomplish what for a Muslim ought to have been a feat of interreligious imagination was that he had the Muslim 'saint' Rābiā in the back of his mind much of the time. Here was a man who happily fulfilled the hope enunciated by V. Raghavan over All-India Radio in 1966, that the bhakti saints ought to serve and in fact do serve as 'The Great Integrators' of Indian

FIGURE 7: Mira with her Lord. *Amar Chitra Katha* issue number 36, p. 13. Courtesy of India Book House Pvt. Ltd.

culture: 'Emotional integration which helps to sustain territorial integration is an achievement on a different plane and is a matter of culture, personal, social and national.'[14]

Pieces in a Puzzle of National Integration

The motif of national integration is sounded at various levels in the comic book lives of the saints of North India—sometimes explicitly, sometimes not. Little could be more direct than what is said about Kabir on the cover of the English-language version of the volume describing him: he is billed as 'the mystic who tried to bring the Hindus and the Muslims together.'[15] The text reinforces the theme. One caption says 'It pained the good man to see religion, caste and creed keeping people apart' (Figure 8) (55:14), and in the scene that follows we see Kabir addressing the multitudes with these words: 'Let people worship God according to their convictions' (55:14). This live-and-let-live attitude is not without exception. In the following frame Kabir is shown challenging what is called, in the biblical phrase, 'idol-worship' (55:14), but this is used to introduce the enmity that Hindus felt in response, and the last scene in the sequence returns us to the integrationist perspective. Kabir prays, 'God, give me the strength to break the barriers of hate between men' (55:14). This message is reinforced on the inside front cover of the English-language version. As in the Hindi counterpart, five epigrams attributed to Kabir are quoted (in translation). Four of the five are the same, but the fifth—the clincher, as it were—appears to be an *Amar Chitra Katha* invention in English that puts together elements from various poems in Hindi: 'In the beginning, there was no Turk, nor Hindu—no race, nor caste.'

In fairness, it is well to observe that this synthetic ideology of sainthood is less clearly articulated in the case of Nanak than in the case of Kabir, perhaps in response to Sikhs' own sensitivity to a depiction of their faith as a simple amalgam of Hinduism and Islam. Nanak is shown as Kabir should be: a critic of malpractice on the part of both Hindus and Muslims, and a member of neither camp (47:19–20, 24–25). In other saints' lives, however, the theme reasserts itself. Tulsidas, for example, is portrayed as a peacemaker between two Hindu rulers, Rāṇā Pratāp of Mewar and Rājā Mānsingh of Amber, as he persuades Mānsingh to abandon an aggressive course of action pursued on behalf of Akbar. Remarkably, Akbar is pleased (62:27–30).

FIGURE 8: Kabir. *Amar Chitra Katha* issue number 55, p. 14. Courtesy of India Book House Pvt. Ltd.

In the volume on Surdas, which lays particular emphasis on Sur's childhood, this irenic motif is seemingly translated into the idiom of children themselves. In the hagiography presented in Hariray's commentary on the *Caurāsī Vaiṣṇavan kī Vārtā*, probably composed in the late seventeenth century, Sur's father despairs at the impact a blind child will have on the family's already meager finances, and in the *Amar Chitra Katha* version this motif is expanded into cruelty on the part of both Sur's parents. Again, there is some precedent in the *Vārtā*.[16] What is new is that Sur's brothers, who are nowhere mentioned in the *Vārtā*, are brought into the act. In a true-to-life motif, these children are depicted as having been even crueler than the adults.[17] They torment poor Sur mercilessly (137:2–5). The enmity between Sur and his brothers does not, however, go unmended. Years later—and again, in an episode I have not encountered elsewhere—two of Sur's brothers hear him sing, see him acclaimed, and are moved to beg forgiveness for the sins of their youth. The happy scene that ensues is a model of reconciliation. Sur says, 'Dear, dear brothers! Don't put me to shame by uttering such words. I have nothing but love for you' (137:22).

This story of reconciliation is a recent one, if not actually invented for *Amar Chitra Katha*. Another motif that buttresses the spirit of national integration is a genuinely traditional one, however, and is made to play a prominent role in the comic book classics. I refer to the notion that the saints of North India were in communication with one another or were related in other ways, either because they were approached with reverence by the same rulers or because they took initiation from one another or a common guru. *Amar Chitra Katha* seems eager to establish the existence of this far-reaching network of saints. As in seventeenth-century hagiography,[18] both Sur and Mira are made to receive visits from Akbar (36:7–9, 137:24–28), and—a more recent addition to legend—Akbar dispatches a message to Tulsidas as well (62:29–30). Other stories, apparently first attested in the nineteenth century,[19] tell of direct contacts between Tulsidas and the other two saints, and these are happily repeated as well (36:27, 137:29).

In instances where legend reports contacts between the various saints for the purpose of showing that one is superior to another, *Amar Chitra Katha* remains not unexpectedly silent. We hear nothing of the Sikh legend in which Kabir acknowledges the primacy of Nanak, for example,[20] and there is nothing to suggest that a rivalry exists between Kabir-Panthīs and Ravidasis, as one deduces from accounts of debates between the supposed founders of these two communities.[21] Caution is also observed in dealing with the numerous stories intended to show that most of these saints have a Brahmin connection; only Mira and Nanak escape. Sur and Tulsi are commonly assumed to have been Brahmins, but Kabir and Ravidas were not. So certain among Kabir's hagiographers tell a version of 'Moses in the bullrushes' to show how he, though brought up in a low-caste Muslim family, was really a Brahmin, and Priyadas portrays Ravidas as a Brahmin in the life immediately preceding his birth as an Untouchable.[22] Then when Priyadas tells how, in a confrontation with some Brahmin foes, Ravidas peeled back the layers of his chest to reveal a sacred thread inside, this inner Brahminhood already has its physical antetype.

To repeat such stories in the form in which they have been received would scarcely serve the cause of national integration, so they are either omitted or foreshortened. We see Kabir being discovered by his Muslim foster parents at the riverbank (not in the river, which might have seemed needlessly miraculous), but nothing is said of his true parentage (55:1–3). As for Ravidas, his comic book life makes no mention of his being a Brahmin at all, interior or otherwise. This is one of the best known episodes in traditional accounts of Ravidas's life, even as told by many Ravidasis,[23] so the omission is striking. Certain recent interpreters of Ravidas from among the *camār* community have wished to disown the story altogether, especially the influential Lucknow writer Candrikāprasād Jijñāsu, who desired so intensely to separate Ravidas from the Brahmin and even the larger Hindu tradition that he made him out to be a Buddhist.[24] *Amar Chitra Katha* did not go so far as to embrace that point of view, which is not accepted by most *camārs* in any event, but especially after the Vālmīki incident it wanted to be prudent about the whole affair. The result was silence.

On another matter, however, silence was not possible. Just as the Ravidasi community preferred that the incident of the thread be omitted, so did they insist that another incident be included. This was the episode in which it is asserted that Mirabai traveled to Banaras to be initiated by Ravidas. This story has a complicated history; if it is accepted as true by the public at large, that phenomenon is only recent.[25] The roots of the tradition are probably to be traced to a similar-sounding episode involving a Rajasthani queen of the Jhālā clan who is said by Priyadas to have come to Banaras in search of initiation and to have chosen Ravidas as her guru.[26] At some point the increasingly well-known Mira seems to have absorbed this Jhālī queen, and the story itself changed in response. Gone now is the tale of how the initiation was vindicated at a banquet from which Ravidas had been excluded by the Brahmins in Queen Jhālī's entourage: miraculously he took his place between each pair of them as they began to eat. Instead we have the simple story of Mirabai being initiated by Ravidas, and no one to challenge.

The staff of *Amar Chitra Katha* was faced with a delicate situation when urged by Dalit leaders to include Mira in its account of Ravidas. On the one hand, it wished to be as conciliatory as possible, but on the other hand it did not wish to raise the hackles of others in Mirabai's much broader and more loosely defined community of devotees. The result was a careful compromise. Mira would be included, but there would be no mention of initiation as such. Instead, she comes to Ravidas to be cured. She says, 'My love for my husband [Krishna, that is] has driven me mad' (350:30).

Even with this alteration, however, the tilt is toward the Ravidasis, who after all would figure largely in the readership of this particular issue. In the title itself Ravidas is called 'Guru Ravidas,' a fact that not only sets him parallel with the Sikh gurus, as Punjabi Ravidasis have for some time wished, but describes his relation to Mira. Moreover, he is shown with a halo, while Mira is not; and he is shown lecturing to her while she says nothing in response. Most pointedly, she is made to set down her image of Krishna at the conclusion of this one-sided colloquy. She faces Ravidas as he lifts his hand in what might be a gesture of blessing (350:31; Figure 9).

If one has closely followed the text, one would certainly interpret this as a response in which Mira subordinates her erstwhile *saguṇa* religiosity to the message of *nirguṇa* faith, for Ravidas has told her that with her and Krishna 'God and devotee have become one' (350:31). She needs her image no longer. But if one has been less than fully attentive to the text, things might look different, for there is an element of compromise. As Mira puts down her icon, she picks up her *tambūrā*, and, though the text makes no mention of the fact, readers would quickly assume that she is singing to Ravidas. This puts the shoe on the other foot—Mira gives, Ravidas receives—and it is well to recall in this connection what Pai's staff have to say about the relative impact of word and illustration: the latter, unquestionably, registers the stronger impression.

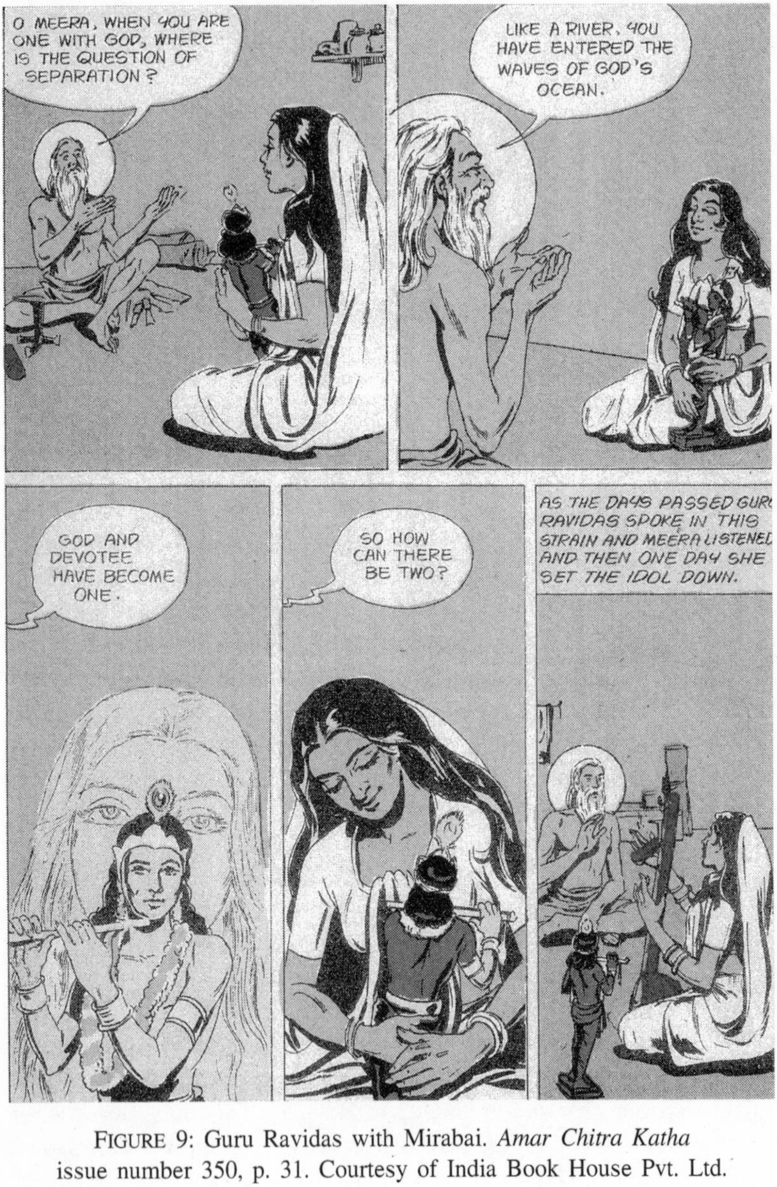

FIGURE 9: Guru Ravidas with Mirabai. *Amar Chitra Katha* issue number 350, p. 31. Courtesy of India Book House Pvt. Ltd.

Amar Chitra Katha's handling of Mira seems an adroit way of telling the truth in an inclusive fashion and making the saints serve the cause of 'national integration': a relation is established and, one hopes, neither party to the meeting is offended. And if this inspires admiration, one may also be impressed by the comic book treatment of the Ravidas story line as a whole. He is by no means made Brahmin—the now outdated vessel of 'national integration,' at least in its cultural mode—but he is made to enunciate a theology that sounds very much like the Vedantin position held in esteem by many of India's new elites. There are still many Brahmins among them, but the Brahmins are joined by merchant-caste groups such as the Birlas, whose charitable trust underwrote the publication of the script for Pai's videotape 'Ekam Sat' and one of whose family members is featured in a relatively recent volume of *Amar Chitra Katha.*[27]

The Ravidas comic begins with a long section showing how as a boy Ravidas became aware of the discrimination directed against his caste and refused to accept it. None of this is reported as such in the traditional hagiographies, which do not concern his childhood; the fact of prejudice is simply assumed. Because *Amar Chitra Katha* is aimed in large part at children, however, this is a logical place to amplify received tradition, and the Ravidas comic does so by describing a process of enlightenment in which Ravidas depends on the words of his guru, Sandan Svāmī. According to Priyadas this is incorrect—Rāmānand, a Vaishnava and a Brahmin, was Ravidas's guru—but because of the caste dimension this is one of the points that modern-day Ravidasis sternly disavow. They are not in total agreement as to who Ravidas's guru actually was, but the preponderance of opinion seems to favor Sandan Svāmī.

Little is usually said among Ravidasis about the explicit content of Sandan's teaching, so *Amar Chitra Katha* had room to invent. On the inner cover the staff claims to have done so on the basis mainly of Ravidas's own poems, and the canon consulted is named as many Ravidasis would like to see it named: *Ādi Prakāś*, 'The Primal Illumination' (350:32).[28] The essence that emerges has a distinctly Vedantin ring. Ravidas appeals to Sandan, 'I want to know about myself and about the God who created me' (350:9). He receives the answer that 'It is the same thing, Ravidas. When you know yourself, you will know God' (350:9). The solution Sandan offers to the problem of caste discrimination is: 'See yourself as you are. Do not see yourself by the label' (350:10). This is what causes a transformation in the young *camār* and ultimately enables others to see themselves in a new light too—as Ravidasis (350:27).

The comic book bears a definite social message. It shows that Brahmins—Brahmins who perform brahmanical rituals, that is—can be cruel to lower-caste people (350:28–29), and it shows that Ravidasis, armed with their new sense of self, can 'walk like a lion' and ignore them (350:27). But it does not preach overt resistance to social oppression. The emphasis is on transcendence instead (350:26, 29). In this respect, *Amar Chitra Katha* stops a good bit short of the Ambedkarite position Jijñāsu would tease out of the poetry of Ravidas and is therefore closer at least to the Ravidas whose poems are collected in the *Gurū Granth Sāhib* than is Jijñāsu. But it contravenes important elements in Ravidas's poetry and hagiography—the saint's suggestion, for instance, that bhakti made it hard for him to do a good day's work, or his emphasis on the value of his inferior position as a privileged point of access for bhakti: it attracts the attention of a merciful God.[29] *Amar Chitra Katha*'s Ravidas—along with its Rāmānand (55:12) and its Tulsidas (62:26)—imbibes and preaches the doctrine, if not of caste equality, at least of the common origin of all human beings (350:10).

All this amounts to the vision of bhakti propounded by that great modern Brahmin, V. Raghavan: bhakti is the 'democratic doctrine which consolidates all people without distinction of caste, community, nationality, or sex.'[30] Its result is envisioned as a social integration that follows from a common sense of relatedness to God or the One. Its behavioral manifestations are even-handedness in the social sphere, devoted labor in the economic, and a sense of individual dignity in the personal realm. This gentle amalgam contrasts markedly with the biting criticism and ecstatic extravagance one can find in the saints' own compositions.

The Message and the Medium

And now we must ask: to what extent are these saints of *Amar Chitra Katha* products of the medium in which they are presented?

Undoubtedly, the medium plays a role. First of all, these are comics. Although the staff is well aware that a portion of the *Amar Chitra Katha* readership is made up of adults, the adults concerned are primarily those who have children. Children define the ambience. On the whole they are middle-class children, with parents not in their twenties but, among women, in their mid-thirties and among men even somewhat older. The vast majority are Indian, although some readers are expatriate, and the most heavily subscribed languages are English—the language in which all issues of *Amar Chitra Katha* are first composed—and, interestingly, Malayalam. For in Kerala more than in any other state, literacy reaches well beyond the English-speaking classes.[31]

In the view of Anant Pai, at least, this readership places certain constraints on the series that are felt in the realm of religion. Children should not be exposed to violence, prejudice, sexual license, or superstition. And other constraints are imposed not just by the audience but by the medium itself. Except for comic books belonging to the increasingly florid mini-series genre, each story must be short, direct, and complete. Because it is illustrated—and because it must appeal to children—each must involve action. The plot must therefore be simple, coherent, and devoted to developing the 'core personality' of the lead personage.[32] Anything that would dilute that purpose must be omitted, so the medium creates its own justification for Pai's grandly articulated policy of selective omission in the service of truth.

While the comic book medium requires a fair amount of simplification, however, it does not entirely eliminate the possibility of subtlety. Because it combines text and illustration, and because it permits the existence of certain words outside the confines of the pictures, it affords the *Amar Chitra Katha* editors a margin of flexibility. We have seen several occasions on which they made use of the distance between print and picture to accommodate the expectations of more than one group of readers. The possibility of using black and white in addition to color creates another opportunity for nuance. Motifs that need to be included in the plot but seem best relegated to the background can be dealt with in just that way: they can be rendered in silhouette.

The Indian comic book medium does not exist in a vacuum. It owes an obvious debt to European cartooning, a genre that played an explicit role early in Pai's career—he worked on 'The Phantom'—and in the upbringing of Kamala Chandrakant, who for so long was his associate editor. As a child raised in an urban, English-speaking family, she devoured practically the whole of 'Classics Illustrated.' For other members of the staff, indigenous media have played a stronger role. Some of these genres are also influenced by contacts with Europe, as is the case with the poster-art industry that has defined so much of the aesthetic canon one sees in *Amar Chitra Katha*. But it is well to remember that the tradition of manuscript illustration is a venerable one in India, and there too one often sees that the verbal element does not strictly determine the visual.[33] In bhakti poetry, in fact, an implied icon can determine the shape of a poem.[34] Hence this series of 'illustrated classics,' as they are sometimes called when marketed in sets, has a right to be seen not just as an Indian adaptation of 'Classic Illustrated' but as an expression of an indigenous concept of what makes a classic—typically something at least as much visual as verbal.

Some Indian classics bear the unmistakable mark of individual inspiration—the plays of Kālīdās, the *Rāmcaritmānas* of Tulsidas, certain of the poems attributed to Kabir or Sur—but others, particularly the epics and large collections of poetry, owe their existence to a more complicated process, often one that developed over the course of several centuries and registered the contributions of groups with varying interests. The work of producing a composite classic—a canon—at *Amar Chitra Katha* involves a similar process of creation by the committee. While Pai's individual imprint is still strong, it has increasingly been registered in an editorial rather than an authorial capacity. *Amar Chitra Katha* comic books are group efforts. Although Pai is responsible for charting the relatively recent *Mahābhārata* mini-series, individual issues apart from that tend to come to him as the ideas of others, and often these are proposed not just by individuals but by representatives of whole communities. In such circumstances the term 'classic' comes to imply more a judgment about what ought to be included within a canon than a determination about what has intrinsic artistic worth. This reading of 'classic' is strengthened by market considerations, for each *Amar Chitra Katha* comic must be judged capable of selling a minimum number of copies before its printing can be justified.

So *Amar Chitra Katha* is a business, but it is also, increasingly, a quasi-public institution. Because of Pai's marketing efforts, schools have become important subscribers, and in part because so many copies must be sold to make production cost-effective, it has until recent years been hard for competitors to enter the market and challenge *Amar Chitra Katha*'s effective monopoly. This has meant that

Indians from the prime minister on down—particularly English-educated Indians—are aware of what *Amar Chitra Katha* does, and has meant that Pai himself has become a public figure, the subject of magazine articles and the recipient of public awards. It has also meant, as we have seen, that *Amar Chitra Katha* is exposed to pressure from various groups, political and otherwise. The Congress Party, for instance, urged Pai to create an issue commemorating its centennial in 1985; Pai had to find a means to accommodate that desire while not falling into the trap of taking political sides. The result is the mini-series called, with seeming neutrality, 'The March to Freedom'—but the first issue in the set concerns *The Birth of the Indian National Congress* (348).

Then too, there is the elaborate process of negotiation that has related *Amar Chitra Katha* to communities of low-caste people. As has been mentioned, Anant Pai's sensitivity to the subject was first stimulated by the reaction of Dalits in the Punjab to the way *Amar Chitra Katha* depicted Vālmīki. Pai made a substantial effort to meet their charges, traveling personally to Jalandar and Patiala, and later attempting to enlist Jagjivan Ram, the Dalit who had risen to the office of deputy prime minister under Indira Gandhi, as a mediator in his relations with lower-caste groups. As for the comic book on Ravidas, it was issued only at the end of a five-year process that also involved the careful editing of the issue on Cokhāmelā. At the time it emerged, there were again severe tensions between lower-caste and upper-caste communities: the city of Aurangabad was torn by riots. So Pai was careful to orchestrate an inaugural event at which Buta Singh, a Dalit leader who was the home minister in the national government, appeared as the guest of honor.

The members of the editorial staff at *Amar Chitra Katha* insist that they are creating a library of comic book classics on a body of history and mythology that is Indian, not Hindu. Looking back, they even hold this up as a way to justify their instinct for preferring to represent Mira's Krishna as Muralīdhar, a flute-playing lover accessible to all, rather than as Giridhar, a miraculously endowed lifter of a definitely Hindu mountain. But one cannot escape the fact that Pai's own Neovedantin, Hindu, or (as he would have it) Vedic theology helps greatly in guiding the emergence of such a canon. The line between 'Indian' and 'Hindu' has always been blurred: it can be argued that 'Hinduism,' as a distinct, internally consistent system running parallel with other 'religions,' is an invention of the nineteenth century.[35] For better or worse, readers of *Amar Chitra Katha* are not likely to be able to disentangle Hinduness from Indianness with any ease. And at least in one view, a view that is now being vocally espoused by such groups as the Vishva Hindu Parishad, the cause of 'national integration' forbids that they should.

7

Krishna and the Gender of Longing

'Krishna and the Gender of Longing' was first presented to a conference on 'Love and Gender in the World Religions,' organized by Nancy Martin and Joseph Runzo at Chapman University in April, 1998. They also edited the volume where it made its first appearance in print: *Love, Sex, and Gender in the World Religions* (Oxford: Oneworld Press, 2000), pp. 238–56. I am grateful to Cynthia Humes, who served as my respondent at the Chapman conference, for searching questions about the original draft. Interested readers may wish to consult a later essay in which I return to themes first broached here: 'The Damage of Separation: Krishna's Loves and Kali's Child,' *Journal of the American Academy of Religion* 72:2 (June 2004), pp. 369–93.

That love is an illness comes as news to no one. What language lacks a poet who has made this point? What person has never felt queasy and unable to eat in the presence of that particular someone else? And it's scattered like curry powder through the literature of religion. Take, for example, the early American composer William Billings, who turned to the Song of Songs to find his text:

> Stay me with flagons,
> comfort me with apples,
> for I am sick of love. (*Song of Songs* 2.5, KJV)

Billings' musical treatment of this verse and the passage in which it occurs is remarkable for several reasons. He arranges it as a dialogue between the 'sons' and the 'daughters.' In the written text, the weight of language falls easily to the bride who has been, as the Song says, 'brought...to the banqueting house,' but by often giving the vocal line to the men when the heroine describes her bridegroom, Billings shares the burden—well, the joy. He does the same with this verse too, which should by rights fall entirely to the bride. 'Stay me with flagons,' the women swoon. 'Comfort me with apples,' urge the men, as if they were ready to take a bite out of a big ripe McIntosh. And then both voices make a try at 'For I am sick,' before completing it in mixed-voice harmony: 'For I am sick of love.' Again there is the hint of swooning, but the overall line rises to a crest and settles into a great affirmative tonic. No hint of any minor key here. The Bible does recognize moments of deep estrangement between the allegorical Israel and her covenanted Lord (consider Hosea), but none of that intrudes as she waits for her Betrothed here—especially with all those delicious apples ripening on the branches just outside the church windows![1]

The story of divine lovesickness is not always told in this way. Where Krishna is the bridegroom—or rather, as almost always, the irresistible paramour—the mood is often quite different. Here too the poet-musicians tend to be male; at least these are the voices that predominate in the lyrics that survive from the great creative sixteenth and seventeenth centuries in the religious literature of Hindu North India. But when they speak of lovesickness, they project themselves almost exclusively into the voice of one of the women who wait for Krishna—before lovemaking or, even more likely, afterward. And although there is plenty of humor, there is a deep sense of longing and lament. This lament is echoed in the narrative line, for according to most versions, this love story has no happy ending: Krishna never really returns to the women he leaves behind. Whether one conceives it in the secular or religious sense (and these are not entirely separable), longing has a definite gender: it is feminine. And the metaphor of illness reigns supreme.

One can ask many questions here. Why should the paradigmatic lover, the image of God, be a man? Why should his mate, who shares much more in human limitation, be a woman? These things are hardly to be taken for granted, after all, even after one has intoned the word 'patriarchy.' For example, in the Islamic Mughal court that reigned throughout the region where Krishna was most intensely celebrated during this early-modern efflorescence of devotional literature, one met very different models, mostly Persian in origin. There the divine was seen in the form either of a beautiful woman or an elusive adolescent boy, and in both instances the human being was represented as male.

But certain members of the court also savored the Hindu, heterosexual construction of divine/human love, and there further questions remain. Why should the illness in love be shouldered so preponderantly by the woman? And why should it so often be male authors who luxuriate in her distress? Some of these questions could be asked of Billings and the Song of Songs too, but they assume particularly sharp outlines in the worship of Krishna.

The Gender of Longing

We'll come to the men in a moment, but for balance let us turn first to Mirabai: Mira, the upper-caste Rajput woman poet who is said to have been smitten with love for Krishna from earliest childhood, and who is arguably the best known of the great 'family' of Krishna poets who flourished in sixteenth-century North India. Famous as she is, only one poem bearing Mira's signature (encoded orally in the poem itself) can almost indisputably be said to have survived from her own century. As we saw in Chapter 4, it was preserved by being recorded in the Kartārpur manuscript of what was to become the Sikh *Gurū Granth Sāhib*, a manuscript dated 1604. The Mira poem appears in a hand different from that of the scribe who wrote the main manuscript and its colophon, so it's possible that it was appended some years later, but in any case it has to be dated before 1642, when it was copied as part of the regular text of *Gurū Granth Sāhib*—only to be cast out somewhat later, probably on theological grounds.[2] It is a poem of love and longing addressed to Krishna, and it's all about affliction.

मनु हमारो बांधिउ माइी कवल नैन आपने गुन
तीखण तीर बेधि सरीर दुरि गयो री माइी
लागिउ तब जानिउ नही अब न सहिउ जाझी री माझी
तंत मंत अउखद करउ तउ पीर न जाइी
है कौउ उपकार करै कठिन दरदु माइी
निकट हउ, तुम दुरि नहि बेगि मिलहु आइी
मीरा गिरधर सुआमी देआल तन की तपत बुझाइी री माइी
कवल नैन आपने गुन आपने गुन बाधिउ माइी

He's bound my heart with the powers he owns, Mother—
  he with the lotus eyes.
Arrows like spears: this body is pierced,
  and Mother, he's gone far away.
When did it happen, Mother? I don't know
  but now it's too much to bear.
Talismans, spells, medicines—
  I've tried, but the pain won't go.
Is there someone who can bring relief?
  Mother, the hurt is cruel.
Here I am, near, and you're not far:
  Hurry to me, to meet.
Mira's Mountain-Lifter Lord, have mercy,
  cool this body's fire!
Lotus-Eyes, with the powers you own, Mother,
  with those powers you've bound.

Like so many compositions attributed to Mira, the poem is relatively straightforward, a cry for help. The body is female, and love is a wound. The speaker appeals to a female friend, it seems, for she addresses her with the general and familiar expression 'mother' (*māī*). Yet as she continues, it becomes increasingly clear that at a deeper level she is appealing to Krishna. Her friend may stand near her, but Krishna is the person she really hopes is 'not far.' This is who she really wants to meet. At the end, when she repeats portions of the title line as a delirious refrain, she seems to be addressing more him than her.

This makes sense, since it is actually Krishna who is equipped to do the healing. His tools are his intrinsic powers, the qualities or virtues (*āpne guna*) that have caused this woman to fall in love with him. Or to change the metaphor slightly, as Mira does herself, love is a disease—the affliction of being absent from one's beloved. The wound itself is in the nature of a bond, a bondage: the verb *bāṅdhiu* is cognate to both these English words. But paradoxically, this wound also *needs* to be bound. It needs bandaging—and in saying that, we are still within the semantic realm of the word *bāṅdhiu*. This is just right, for the only true treatment is the lover's return. He is cause of the disease, he is also its cure and sole physician.

At a basic level, the gender realities here are stark and plain. It is the male who inflicts injury, whether that male be understood as love (the god Kāma) or the lover (Krishna); and the injured party is female.

Any gender confusions are ancillary, as when her friend's name lingers in her emergent appeal to Krishna. But matters become more complex when such confusions extend from the person being addressed to the person who is doing the speaking.

To demonstrate this, let us consider a parallel lyric attributed (through the signature, again) to the male poet Surdas—or Sur, for short. Like Mirabai, Sur is also a sixteenth-century poet, and he is the person regarded as the exemplar of poets composing in Brajbhāṣā, the language of the Braj region south of Delhi where Krishna is said to have spent his youth. In part for that reason, Brajbhāṣā was for many centuries the leading literary forum in the family of languages we nowadays call Hindi. Like the Mira poem, the composition we will hear can also be traced to the sixteenth century: it appears in a manuscript dated 1582. But far from being alone, like hers, it takes its place among some 400 roughly contemporaneous poems attributed to Sur. A remarkable number of these—about half—depict the struggles and longings of women in love.[3] So marked is the theme that it is given a distinct name: *viraha*, which can mean both the physical fact of separation between lovers and the various emotions that accompany it. And most often it is the *virahiṇī* herself, the woman afflicted by love, who speaks. Listen:

अति रस लंपट मेरे नैन
त्रिपति न मानत पिवत कमल मुष सुंदरता मधु बैन
दिन अरु रैणि द्रिस्टि रचना रचि निमषु न राषे चैन
सोभा सिंधु समाइ कहां लौं ह्दिै सांकरै ऐन
अब यह बिरह अजीरन है कै बमि लाग्यौ दुष दैन
सूर बैद ब्रजनाथ मधुपुरी काढि पठाउं लैन

My eyes have become so greedy—they lust for his juice;
They refuse to be satisfied, drinking in the beauty
    of his lotus face, the sweetness of his words.
Day and night they fashion their picture of him
    and never blink a moment for rest.
What an ocean of radiance! But where's it going to fit
    in this cramped little closet of a heart?
And now with raw estrangement its waters surge so high
    that the eyes vomit in pain:
Sur says, the Lord of Braj—the doctor—has gone.
    Who can I send to Mathura to fetch him here again?[4]

In a certain sense, not much has changed from Mira's poem. The voice is still female, its object male; though here it is more clear that the woman speaks not to Krishna but to a friend, or perhaps to herself. Once again we recognize the lotus in Krishna, but this time it is his entire face, not just his eyes. Once again the vision is refracted through longing—'raw estrangement' (*biraha ajīrana*)—and this time the separation is given narrative specificity: Krishna has departed for the city of Mathura, leaving his love-lost cowherder women (*gopīs*) to pine away in the countryside of Braj. Once again their experience of his absence is represented as illness—a nausea of tears—and once again the doctor is also the cause of the disease. The identity of these two makes particularly good sense when one considers the kind of doctor Krishna is said to be: an Ayurvedic *baid* (Skt. *vaidya*, v. 6). His homeopathic practices deploy elements in the disease itself to effect their cure.

But what about the signature? What about the fact that the person singing this song announces himself as male—a male taking the voice of a female? Does this change the poem in any way? What does it mean that a sort of verbal cross-dressing has occurred, and that this cross-dressing is actually the norm in poems of this kind? And then there is our old question. Looking beyond the obvious fact the sickness of love is here praised, romanticized, and emulated, what are we to make of a literature in which the normative condition of the female body is disease—a disease caused by and indeed consisting of the absence of the male?

The Female Body and the Body of Disease

Drawing on the resources of earlier centuries, North Indian aestheticians in the period we are considering elaborated a complete taxonomy of the stages and types of love. While the hero (*nāyaka*) received his due, it was the heroine (*nāyikā*) whose states and moods particularly fascinated these theorists, resulting at one point in a calculus of 384 types of love-heroines.[5] More to the point, one saw the emergence of influential independent texts such as Bhānudatta's *Rasamañjarī* (fifteenth century?) and Kṛpārām's *Hitataraṅganī* (1541) which focused entirely on the heroine. In a work like Rūp Gosvāmī's early sixteenth-century *Ujjvalanīlamaṇi*, these classifications were integrated with a theory of Krishna's 'plays' or *līlās*. And in the classic *Rasikapriyā* of Keśavdās

(1591), Krishna and Radha became themselves the hero and heroine, with Radha's moods receiving the great preponderance of attention.[6]

As this brief sketch suggests, it would be going too far to say that Indian love poetry, sacred or secular, always focuses on the longing of a woman for a man. In one lovely poem, for example, Surdas adopts the persona of a female go-between, a *sakhī*, who tries to persuade Radha to desist from her anger and rejoin Krishna. Here the wasted body is not hers but his:

जब तै श्रवन सुन्यौ तेरौ नाम
तब तै हा राधा राधा हरि इहै जु मंत्र जपत दुरि दाम
रहत निकुंज निसि कालिंद्री तट सुहृद सषा छाडे सुष धाम
बिरह बियोग महा जोगी लौं जागत ही बीतत जुग जाम
कबहुंक किसलय पीठ रुचिर रचि कबहुंक पाठ करत गुन ग्राम
कबहुंक लोचन मूदि मौन ह्वै चित चिंतत ये अंग अभिराम
तर्पण नैन हृदै होमत हवि बिप्र भोज बोलत बिश्राम
सूर स्याम कृस गात सकल बिधि दरसन दै पुरवहु पिय काम

Ever since your name has entered Hari's ear
It's been 'Radha, oh Radha,' only this mantra,
  a formula chanted to a secret string of beads.
Nightly he stays by the Jamuna, in a grove
  far from his friends and his happiness and home.
He yearns for you. Like a great yogi
  he is constantly wakeful through hours that are ages.
Sometimes he spreads himself a bed of tender leaves;
  sometimes he chants your treasurehouse of fames;
Sometimes he closes his eyes in utter silence
  and meditates on every pleasure of your frame—
His eyes the libation, his heart the fire-oblation,
  his mutterings and lapses, food for a Brahmin feast.
So has Śyām's whole body wasted away.
  Says Sur, let him see you. Fulfill his desire.[7]

It happens, then, that the male can also be a paradigm of longing—or at least, so it seems. Look closely. First, we do not actually know that Krishna is experiencing this mental torture. Yes, there is pleasure in contemplating it, but there is also pleasure in considering the possibility that this description of him may simply be an elaborate tactic on the part of the messenger girl; and Krishna himself may have given her the idea of saying what she says, with the purpose of drawing Radha to his side once again. I wouldn't put it past him, and neither would many in the audiences who revel in this Brajbhāṣā poetry. Then too, it may be significant that Krishna's longing is not here represented as disease. There is weakness, yes, but it shows itself more characteristically as a heightened measure of (male) self-control—as yoga, or as the ritual manipulations of a priest. A mantra there is, as in Mira's poem (we translated that word as 'spells'), but this is not a mantra of the sort that might be chanted over a body racked with disease.

Such things belong, rather, to women. And why? Because according to the pervasive views of Hindu males, at least, women are on the whole more vulnerable than men. There is also the competing view that in matters sexual, where men are in danger of losing control (particularly control of their preciously produced semen), women can be extraordinarily aggressive. But the preponderant emphasis is on a woman's vulnerability, her incompleteness—especially in relation to men—and this is what causes women often to be construed in the religious realm as natural devotees.[8] Obviously enough, this resonates to a structural imbalance in Indian society, where men are generally marked higher than women and the institutions of marriage by and large perpetuate the relative weakness and dependence of women. Such vulnerability may also be understood as a manifestation of female incompleteness. It's the absent Y-chromosome all over again, most famously encountered in texts asserting that women's *dharma* can only be achieved in dependence on men in this life,[9] or that women must become men in a subsequent life before they can be candidates for release (*mokṣa*) from the bonds of this world.[10] Of course, there is a full range of texts and practices that challenge such views, both openly and implicitly,[11] but one cannot gainsay their existence. And they have been influential.

Yet one of the interesting things about the poem in which Sur as a woman laments her greedy eyes is that, unlike a host of other poems, the woman involved is a victim of her own hyperactivity, not her lethargy. Her very agency does her in—the insatiably restless probing of her eyes. Let's take this as a symbol of the poet's awareness that no single stereotype of female longing suffices to represent the disease with which human beings are afflicted in relation to the divine.

We must recognize, moreover, that the *gopīs*' state of dissipation, dishevelment, and disease is lauded as being far superior to the supposed health of spirit that is personified by the man who emerges as their opposite number. This is the urbane courtier Ūdho (Skt. Uddhava), who comes to the *gopīs* as Krishna's messenger from Mathura with the advice that these distraught women can be cured by focusing on Krishna's invisible but nonetheless actual *presence* among them. They can do this by means of certain yogic techniques and a regimen of philosophical clarification. But this vision of divine pervasiveness comes across as just plain pallid, and the love-affliction of the female body shows just how vapid it is as a strategy of faith. The earlier *Bhāgavata Purāṇa*, in Sanskrit, may waffle on this point, but the sixteenth-century vernacular texts are very clear. Such male philosophizing stinks.[12]

All this gives a very positive conceptual spin to bodily, female affliction, but in real life one may wonder over whose dead body it gets spun. Does a woman contemplating this romantic paradigm of faith experience the same sense of amusement as might be expected in a man? Does she get the same sort of buzz that a man does from the idea that Krishna serves as a magnet for numberless, often rather faceless women?[13] The matter bears real research, and no one has yet quite done it, although Donna Wulff's current work on women's impressions of Radha comes close.[14]

In thinking about this point I have often been struck by the way in which poems attributed to Mirabai seem to differ from poems attributed to Surdas. The poems signed Sur positively revel in the gender disparity represented by this stand-off between Ūdho and the *gopīs*, while in poems attributed to Mira one finds quite a different mindset. Her poems seem often to build outward from 'women's roles' rather than reinforcing a male/female disparity, although you would never know it on the basis of the poem we quoted here.[15] Similarly, in a group of poems attributed to Mira by lower-caste, peasant, and itinerant singers of both genders we find a far more aggressive construction of her female embodiment, defined over against her upper-caste husband, than is typically found in the 'authoritative' schoolbook collections edited by upper-caste Brahmin males.[16]

So it is striking how many registers are provided for the language of female suffering in Mirabai poems, and how active these tend to be. Poems attributed to Surdas are by no means less varied—in fact, he is the greater virtuoso—but the persona of the *virahiṇī*, helpless victim of separation, is far more prominent. Why? Why is it that men revel in the weakness—and specifically the sickness—of women?

The Unspoken Mother

This is a big question, and I would not wish to answer it in general terms—not yet, anyway. Instead, let me make a suggestion about the specific milieu in which a number of these cross-dressed lyrics emerged. I would draw attention to the fact that the separation of lovers (*viraha*) is understood to have a special, archetypally appropriate season in the liturgical year of North Indian Hinduism. It is the rainy season, when the monsoon makes journeys hard and lovers are stranded far from one another. More than any other, this is the season for songs of estrangement. When women sing such songs, they often long for their brothers, hoping they'll come soon to take them back to spend some time with the families into which they were born and from which they have been separated by marriage. But in the mouths of men, the songs of the monsoon are typically addressed not to family but to lovers, and above all to Krishna.[17]

To understand why this is so, we might well look around and see what else is happening in the monsoon season, which serves as culmination and release for the hottest weather of the year. When the rains come, the earth turns green overnight. Waters rush dark with life, and thousands of microbes have their day. Whether from sheer heat or from microbe-mania, this is the season of disease, and the gendered language of religion is available to recognize that fact. The hot season and the monsoon are often felt to belong especially to the Goddess.[18] Diseases like cholera (Cetak) and smallpox (Śītalā) are goddesses whose visitation is experienced simultaneously as affliction and grace. These are real sufferings, but to contemplate them as divine holds a special promise. As Edward Dimock writes,

> By hearing of suffering, by realizing the extent of human frailty, one with the eyes to see may be spared the necessity of more particular pain. Śītalā allows us cognition of our position in the universe, and recognition of herself as Mother.[19]

I would stress two aspects. First, diseases such as smallpox bring bodily suffering in a real, obviously physical way. Second, their agency is understood as female, and not only female but maternal. And now the intriguing point: this massively present Mother—the Goddess with many names and forms—is eerily absent from the narrative world of Krishna. Her place has been taken by her shadow. The divine Woman who is massively, threateningly present is replaced by a human woman who suffers massive absence—the absence of Krishna.

The metaphor of disease shows the connection between these two, suggesting that we have a displacement here, a displacement whose purpose is to project the illusion of control. Men who stand in danger of being afflicted by the all-too-present Goddess generate a world in which women are afflicted by the absence of an irresistible God. These men project themselves into such a world through poetry, art, music, performance, and ritual, and thereby have the fantasy of experiencing themselves—that is, the male Krishna-self—as invincible. Faced with the danger of real suffering, they play in the suffering of imagination. Faced with the danger of real disease, they play at imagined disease. Their keyboard, their dress, their role is a woman in love.

But why is the Goddess experienced as so threatening that her image bifurcates in this way? Why is this sleight-of-hand so particularly successful with men? There is no way of providing a definitive answer to questions such as these, but my own urge is to venture into the realm of psychogenesis, guided by thinkers such as Dorothy Dinnerstein, Nancy Chodorow, and Karen McCarthy Brown; or in an Indian milieu, by Sudhir Kakar, Stanley Kurtz, and Jeffrey Kripal.[20] I would want to ask about the problem that boys face especially, the need to achieve a double separation from their mothers—separation by virtue of maturity and separation by virtue of sex. In a girl, I imagine, the power of mimesis holds out the prospect of healing that first tear of separation: in some sense, even if she must live in her in-laws' house, a daughter has the prospect of becoming her mother. But in a boy, the separation must be more fundamental if he is to climb into full adulthood. Hence the image of his mother is apt to remain at some level a threat of engulfment, and if he is a Hindu living in North India, that threat becomes aligned with the bodily realities of the season of heat and rains. No wonder he clings to his fascination with separation, while at the same time holding it at arm's length from his own ego.

He does this with a deft two-step that answers to both needs in his drama of psychic separation from his childhood and his mother (or mothers, as Stanley Kurtz has urged for extended families). As to the task of attaining a gender role that is contrary to his mother's, he reverses the genders in his own drama—his religious drama—so that the victim of separation becomes female, while the lover from whom she is parted is male. And to accomplish the task of attaining maturity, he imagines this male lover as omnipotent, eternally full of appetite and eternally fascinating to the women who surround him. Thus the young man disperses his mother everywhere, and he secures his victory by crippling the women who so desire him. He cripples them with the very desire he imagines them to have. By visiting upon these archetypes of womanly love a love that is disease, he controls the threatening Woman after all. For he represents himself—the ideal, projected self who is Krishna—as her only cure.[21]

Female Longing as Male Pregnancy

The Indologist Martha Selby has recently been developing an exposition of sections of the most basic Indian medical text, the *Caraka Saṃhitā* (ca. first century CE), in which she focuses especially on the passages having to do with obstetrics.[22] Her work brings to the fore a number of unsuspected parallels to major motifs we have been considering here, just as the study of Galen throws light on various metaphors of gender that emerged in early Christian thinking.[23]

The first set of surprising parallels between the Indian medical literature and its theological/amatory counterpart are a series of direct contrasts between the condition of a pregnant woman and that of a *virahiṇī*. The one is full, the other empty. The one grows day by day, the other diminishes. The one nurses life inside, the other has lost her life. The one experiences heat in the good sense—the heat of the internal hearth, the heat of cooking; the other is assaulted by bad heat—a fever she cannot control. The one looks forward to separation, the good separation of birth; the other laments a separation she does not wish.

Yet there is another set of parallels that are not in the nature of oppositions, and that seem in an almost excruciating way to show how closely the two archetypal women are bound together. Both are ultimately supine, for example. Both require medical help if they are to deliver or be delivered. And in both cases the chroniclers involved are primarily male, reporting on experiences that are understood to belong to women. True, a number of females hover about; in fact their presence is required. Caraka demands that in the advanced stages of pregnancy, 'suitable women' who have given birth gather round the mother-to-be and urge her on. In *viraha*, meanwhile, the heroine's good friends are expected to comfort her, sometimes acting as messengers to Krishna, sometimes using their own suasion to try to draw her out of her deep depression. But behind these many women, or perhaps through them, the authoritative, authorial voice almost always remains male.

So does the ultimate subject, the agent who witnesses from within. In the poetry of love, of course, this is Krishna. With Caraka, however, it is the fetus, who is inevitably imagined as a boy. In part this derives from the well-known Indian preference for male progeny. Yet in this setting, I believe, it also stems from the desire of the author of the text to locate himself within the body he describes. This has huge epistemological advantages. It gives Caraka access, as a man, to a set of experiences that otherwise would come to him only second-hand. But if we think, as Caraka does, that the fetus is the real author of a woman's pregnancy, carrying forward the dynamism of the father's seed, and if that fetus too is understood as male, then the mother's own experience of her pregnancy becomes in some way second-hand. Her gender separates her from the prime mover of the pregnancy, who is, like Caraka, male. So Caraka, the outer 'self' or author, can relish its desires and demands (sour food now, sweet food then) as cognate with his own. Even experiences so intrinsically female that Caraka can only have known them because women revealed this knowledge to men—for example, the sense of hot, vaguely itchy expansion that is said to feel like a bandage being peeled away from the skin[24]—are revalued through the agency of the male fetus.

Time and again, then, the woman is figured as the recipient of her own bodily experience, rather than as its true subject. The process is made male, and so is its *telos*, the much-desired birth of a son. Here too, in this quite unexpected place, we have *viraha* for the absent (or not yet present) male. It is he who will make her a real woman: a mother of sons.[25] Therefore her yearning is intense—both ideally, as in Caraka, and often in fact as well. It is widely reported that the most intense relationship in Indian societies, bar none, is felt to be the relationship between mother and son.

So far, so good. From a male point of view, it is the mother, the woman, who longs for the realization of that relationship. But it must be threatening when the son himself, the male, also longs for that same intimacy. Hence the literature of Krishna's childhood denies it. It drowns it out with the opposite fantasy: a host of would-be mothers, starting with Krishna's foster-mother and moving through all the other *gopīs*, who depend on him, who long for him to take their milk products or its distillate, their love.[26] God forbid that *he* should be emotionally dependent on *them*! So he steals their milk, rather than claiming or receiving it in a way that could imply any enduring connection.[27]

In a similar way much of the religious literature of estrangement and separation, though focused upon a woman's body, bears the mark of the male author. Here the agent who replaces the hidden male fetus is, of course, the absent male lover. Since he is the cause of her experience, he is its cure. He is, in fact, her deliverer—her delivery, just as the production of a male child at the moment of birth is for Caraka the true culmination of pregnancy. He, the lover, with his male presence, is her cure. Hence her love is best represented—retroactively, at least—as sickness.

Here in the world of erotic love, as in Krishna's childhood revels, the male author has a chance to play with an experience of separation that might be too threatening if experienced in 'real life.' As the doctor, the medical technician, Caraka can play with pregnancy and master it, without enduring its pain. As the poet, the verbal technician, Surdas can play with separation, feeling its threat but in a mediated, unthreatening way. His audience can do the same.[28]

And there is a final step. Much is gained by projecting this double fantasy of weakness and control, sickness and health—a fantasy that parallels pregnancy, the genesis of existence itself—onto the Big Screen. Much is gained by perceiving the primary actor as Krishna, that is, as God. We all come into the world as vulnerable babes, and we leave it for a future to which we are at least as vulnerable. But the power imbalance that men so anxiously establish between themselves and women is for men, at least, a major resource in this ultimate game of life. If one imagines God as male, then the threat of drowning that seems to be posed by women and by the sea of existence (*bhavasāgar*) that is life—these can in some measure be contained.

So *viraha* is a game. It is a man's game, a game of trying on women's clothes and women's feelings. It's a game of playing God, the way God (or Goddess!) plays with us men. This game gives a gender to longing.

SURDAS

8

Last Seen with Akbar

This chapter, published here for the first time, grew out of a presentation given to the South Asia Seminar at the University of Texas on 2 November 2000. The invitation came from Akbar Hyder, who was also responsible for the general rubric in which it is framed: discourses of syncretism and separatism as contrasting approaches to the religious politics of South Asia, past and present. I am grateful to Aditya Behl for expanding my ideas about the overall performative milieu that might have greeted a poet of Surdas's caliber in sixteenth-century North India.

Akbar, we know, was 'the Great Mogul.'[1] He was also the Great Syncretist, architect of the *dīn-i-illāhī*, and convenor of the famous interreligious salon at Fatehpur Sikri. I'm especially interested in a certain aspect of that: he was the great music lover, too. Everyone knows Akbar drew Tānsen to his side to establish in musical terms the most elegant court of his day, and the account that Abu'l Fazl provides of Akbar's musical entourage suggests that it didn't stop there. Half the Gwalior school of accomplished instrumentalists and *dhrupadiyās* apparently came with him when he joined Akbar's court. According to the *vārtās* ('accounts,' literally 'conversations') of the Vallabha Sampradāy, the sung lyrics of *bhaktas* such as Kumbhandās and Surdas also profoundly moved Akbar.[2] Priyadas's *Bhaktirasabodhinī*, written at Brindavan in 1712, says he was also quite taken with a *dohā* of Sūrdās Madanmohan, and Priyadas gives us a wonderful story of how Akbar was so smitten long-distance by the beauty of Mirabai that he grabbed Tānsen and set off to see for himself. Once there, he was so overwhelmed by Mira that he fell in love—not with the singer but with her song. He fell in love with her deity Krishna.[3] Truly an inspired syncretist!

In this chapter I want to look more closely at Surdas, and see how 'discourses of syncretism and separation' swirl around him in documents produced in the sixteenth and seventeenth centuries.[4] What we'll find is that syncretism and separatism are often two sides of a single coin, and that coin is not always negotiable in the currency of Hindu/Muslim relations. We'll discover this pattern in various ways, and we start seeing it as soon as Akbar decides he's got to meet the famous Surdas.

On Syncretism

Our source is the *Caurāsī Vaiṣṇavan kī Vārtā*, a document produced squarely within the Vallabha Sampradāy. The main text is attributed to one of Vallabha's grandsons, Gokulnāth, and comes to us in a form that dates to either 1640 (though the colophon of the manuscript in question has some oddities) or 1695.[5] The story involves Tānsen again: it was his singing of one of Sur's *pads* that made Akbar want to meet Sur immediately. The tale is told with a bit of humor. Akbar figured it was too bad for Sur to waste his poetic skills exclusively on the Lifter of Mount Govardhan, so he engineered a meeting in Mathura, which was on the way from Agra to Delhi in any case. After honoring the poet greatly, the Bādśāh said, *tumne viṣṇupad bahot kiye haiṅ, so tum mokoṅ kachu sunāvo*: 'You've composed plenty of poems for Vishnu. How about a little something for me?' The response was a *pad* entitled *manāre, tū kari mādhoṅ sauṅ prīti*—in other words, no. Sur instructed himself to love Mādhav alone.

The *vārtā* tells us that Akbar was pleased at this response, but thought he'd just test it a little further. 'God gave me this kingdom,' he said to Sur. 'All the worthies sing my praise, and I reward them handsomely. Come on, sing my praise a little, and ask what your heart desires.' To this the answer was a *pad* entitled *nahina rahyo mana meṅ thaura*, 'There's no room left in my heart,' and at this Akbar acceded, telling Sur he'd give him whatever he wanted anyway. Sur fires back that the best reward would be if the emperor would please excuse him and never make him come back. So this is definitely syncretism with a smile.

In fact, one might well that feel this story sounds less like a discourse of syncretism than of separation. After all, Sur gets to depart to the distinctly Hindu, or at least distinctly Vaishnava realm of Mt. Govardhan, where he is said to have been employed by his guru Vallabhācārya. He leaves Akbar behind. Yes, in a certain sense, one can see things in that separatist way, and I do think it's significant that this work is about Vaishnavas, as its title says, rather than about *bhaktas*, as in the title most frequently used for the broader genre to which it belongs: *bhaktamāl* ('garland of saints'). But it's equally important that the parting between Sur and Akbar was entirely amicable. We're seeing a version of the old narrative about the two-way relationship between spiritual and secular power—*vilāyat* and *duniyā,* Brahmin and *kṣatriya*—with the spiritual shown to be more powerful than the secular.[6] Not just more powerful, but truly independent, whatever the physical facts may seem to be.[7]

The establishing of Sur on Mount Govardhan with Akbar's explicit permission is indeed significant in a *vilāyatī* sort of way. It was probably only in the second half of the sixteenth century (1571? even later?) that the Vallabhites, working under Vallabha's son and successor Viṭṭhalnāth, managed to eject Bengali priests from the temple of Srī Govardhannāth, i.e., Śrī Nāthjī, claiming it exclusively as their own.[8] But whatever the actual date of that coup, the imperial *farmāns* do not recognize Govardhan as being basically Vallabhite turf until 1593.[9] Vallabha died long before, in 1530. Hence what we have here is a retrospective attempt to situate that temple—and therefore the Vallabha Sampradāy, which it anchors—in a *vilāyat*-like relationship to Akbar's *duniyā.* The geography is good: it's close, but not too close, to Agra. And after Śrīnāthjī's forced departure from Braj in 1669 for fear of Aurangzeb's iconoclasm, there may have been a special appeal in this remembered/projected golden age of concord and imperial legitimacy. Akbar's *farmāns* had indeed specified that Viṭṭhalnāth was to be a 'well-wisher' of Akbar's, a 'prayer-offerer,' a scholar who should 'daily engage himself in praying for the good of the eternity-allied Kingdom.'[10] But this *vārtā* account has the feel of taking things to a new level altogether.

On Separatism

If Sur's dialogue with Akbar was the obvious place to locate a 'discourse of syncretism' in his story, the obvious place to look for separatism is in his encounter with Vallabha. This, according to the

Vārtā, was what marked him off forever as a member of one particular Vaishnava *sampradāy* and not another.

The story of Sur's meeting with Vallabha is a very interesting one, and it signals the beginning of the Surdas *vārtā* proper—that is, the part said to have been composed by Gokulnāth, as distinct from the prologue added by the commentator Harirāy in the following generation. As Gokulnāth's *vārtā* opens, we see Surdas surrounded by disciples and ensconced at Gaughāṭ on the right bank of the River Jamuna, north of Agra but south of Mathura. Vallabha approaches from his home at Adel (Aḍail), across the river from Allahabad far downriver, and Sur is made aware of the great man's presence by his disciples. Sur asks to be informed when Vallabha has finished his meal and then goes to him, ultimately receiving, after his own ritual purification, the initiatory mantra of the *sampradāy*. At that point Vallabha reveals to him in short form (*anukramaṇikā*) the contents of his commentary on the tenth book of the *Bhāgavata Purāṇa*, which is called the *Subodhinī*, and the text tell us that the whole of the information conveyed in the *Subodhinī* was immediately established (*sthāpan bhaī*) in Sur's heart.

Thereafter the entire tone and content of Sur's singing changed. No longer is he preoccupied with what the *vārtā* calls 'simperings' (*ghighiyāt*) before the Lord. Rather, he invests himself totally in Krishna's *līlā*, singing dramatic lyrics that partake in that *līlā* discourse. And he is enabled to do so because Vallabha provides him the occasion. It is he who leads Sur into what the *vārtā* calls Braj, the charmed region to the north of Gaughāṭ that is the object of Vallabha's own pilgrimage. Sur sings of Krishna's childhood at Gokul because Vallabha leads him to the image of Krishna ensconced there—perhaps anachronistically, for this temple may actually have been established by Viṭṭhalnāth, Vallabha's son and eventual successor.[11] And Sur becomes the lead singer (*kīrtankār*) at the temple of Govardhannāthjī, atop Mount Govardhan, which becomes the *sampradāy*'s central shrine, as we have seen. From that vantage point he sings the rest of the corpus attributed to him—at least, the sections having to do with Krishna. Sur's corpus is so large and impressive that Vallabha on occasion actually calls Sur by the name that came to be attached to Sur's collected poetry: *Sūrsāgar*, 'Sur's Ocean.'

The point of the whole story is to locate Sur firmly within the sectarian orbit of the Vallabha Sampradāy. In that sense it is manifestly, almost paradigmatically a discourse of separatism. Here the word 'discourse' is just, because the events recorded in the *vārtā* are not, I believe, historical fact. You might already have raised an eyebrow of suspicion on hearing that Vallabha calls Sur 'Sūrsāgar,' since this would seem to indicate that the story's real aim was to incorporate an already well-known text. Not only that, the poems the *vārtā* chooses to exemplify what Sur sang as Vallabha opened each new stage of his life are apparently chosen from among the most celebrated compositions in the *Sūrsāgar*, as indicated by their prominence in early manuscripts and contemporary performance. At one level, the *vārtā* reads like a narrative constructed simply to give biographical context to these poems.

It's all true. Gokulnāth was writing in the wake of the great moment when his father Viṭṭhalnāth had managed to solidify the institutional base of the new *sampradāy* through major donations from the *baniyā* community, especially of Gujarat, and via the rigorous, even ruthless administrative practices of a man called Kṛṣṇadās. He also secured support from the Mughal throne, in a series of *farmāns* granting land and evidently solving legal disputes, perhaps notably with Bengalis, as we have seen. At this time, the ritual life of the sect was carefully regularized and theologically justified, and the poets whose hymns were to become its basis included Surdas. He became one of the *aṣṭachāp*, the 'eight seals' of the *sampradāy*, indeed the best known of the four founding members. The first datable occurrence of the designation *Sūrsāgar* comes in a Sur manuscript dated 1640, and perhaps the idea was in some circulation before then. But there is nothing in the earliest Sur manuscripts to indicate that it goes back to the time of the poet himself. So it looks as if the Vallabhites were attempting to annex the prestige of the *Sūrsāgar* after the fact, through a 'discourse of separation' that would set Sur apart from other contexts in which his poems must have been sung.

The story itself suggests that Sur was held in considerable esteem elsewhere than in the *sampradāy* itself: Sur already had devotees by the time Vallabha arrived on the scene. And our other early Vaishnava accounts of him—in Nabhadas's *Bhaktamāl* and in the poems of Harirāmvyās—make this plain. In both texts he is celebrated as the great poet of the language, its most celebrated *kavi*, the finest craftsman of the *pad*. Furthermore, the earliest extant collection of Brajbhāṣā poetry, the Fatehpur manuscript of 1582 (now preserved in the *khās mohar* collection by the House of Jaipur), focuses principally on him.

So when the *vārtā* gives Vallabha the honor of introducing Sur to Braj, something is radically amiss: Vallabha has been inserted between Sur and the audience of Brajbāsīs that had apparently gathered around his poems.

This is clearly a discourse intended to reshape Braj memories in such a way as to cordon the poet off behind a particular set of theological and institutional skirts—even at the cost of separating the poet from himself. In this discourse, his *vinaya* poems, the ones where he speaks in the persona of 'Sur' himself, without any dramatic interface from a member of Krishna's own *līlā* world, are made out to be less worthy than the others. They are pre-Vallabhite snivelings, the sort of thing Sur said before he got religious thanks to the *ācārya*'s giving him an instant, mystic infusion of the *Subodhinī*.

Some of the details by which this historical sleight-of-hand was achieved are quite wonderful, and it is worth taking a moment to describe at least one. As I said, some of the most celebrated poems of the early *Sūrsāgar* were marshaled by Gokulnāth, quoted in the *vārtā*, and made by implication to redound to the glory of Sur's guru, Vallabha. Let's look at how this happened in the case of one particularly important poem:[12]

चकई री चलि चरण सरोवर जहां न पेम वियोगु
जहं भ्रम निसा होत नहिं कबहू वह साइरु सुष जोगु
जहं सनक स हंस मीन सिव मुनि जन नष रवि प्रभा प्रकास
प्रफुलित कमल निमषु नहि ससि डरु गुंजित निगम सुवास
जिहि सर सुभग मुकति मुकता फल सुकृत विमल जल पीजै
सो सर छाडि कुबुद्धि विहंगम इहां कहा रहि कीजै
जहं श्री सहित सहज नित क्रीडा प्रणमत सूरिज दास
अब न सुहाइ विषै बन छीलर वा समुद्र की आस

O *cakaī* bird, flee to those feet, that lake
  where love never suffers separation
And the dark, aimless night never comes—
  that ocean of joy, of union.
There Sanak swims with swans,
  the fish are Shiva and sages,
    and sunlight glints from the nails on those toes.
Where the lotuses bloom,
  never shrinking from the moon,
    there comes a constant hum, a Vedic fragrance,

And everywhere are lovely pearls of freedom.
You should be drinking that pure water of good deeds.
You ignorant bird! Why are you here?
Why ever abandon that perfect lake,
That place where he forever plays, with Śrī,
his effortless game, while Surdas prays?
This puddle of existence, with its pleasures, seems so dry
when one could hope instead for the sea.

Consider the transcendent lake that is described in this poem,

Where Sanak swims with swans,
the fish are Shiva and sages,
and sunlight glints from the nails on [Vishnu's] toes....
That place where he forever plays, with Śrī,
his effortless game, while Surdas prays.

And consider particularly the line about playing with Śrī (verse 7): *jahaṅ śrī sahita sahaja nita krīḍā praṇamata sūrijadāsa.* Kenneth Bryant's critical apparatus is very useful at this point in organizing the information provided by the early Sur manuscripts I list at the outset of the next chapter. The apparatus quickly reveals that the most substantial variant is on the word *sahaj*, for which a group of relatively late manuscripts substitute *karat;* and we have the word *śrī* missing in a smaller but somewhat earlier group comprising B2, U1, and B4, which have something like *sara sākhā* (U1) instead of *śrī sahita.* Both these variants are rather pallid. The latter, with *sar*, is even somewhat repetitious of *sarovar* in the title line.

Now watch what happens when the *vārtā* quotes this line. It becomes *jahāṅ śrī sahasra sahita nita krīḍata sobhita sūrajadāsa*,

Where, says Surdas, he daily shines resplendent
and plays with thousands of Śrīs.[13]

This version of the line is out there in manuscript left field, considering that *sahasra* is attested in none of the earlier manuscripts, but one can understand how *sahaj* might have been heard and then sung that way somewhere along the line. *Sahasra* ('thousands') often becomes *sahas* in Brajbhāṣā, and from there it's not far to *sahaj* ('effortless').

So in the *vārtā* we have *sahasra*, and it's very interesting to see how the *vārtā* glosses it. Gokulnāth hears the phrase *śrī sahasra*, in its juxtaposition to the verb *krīḍat*, as an echo of an important line from

Vallabha, namely the first *kārikā* of the *maṅgalācaraṇ* of that part of the *Subodhinī* which explicates the tenth book of the *Bhāgavata*. That verse goes:

नमामि हृदये शेषे लीलाक्षीराब्धिशायिनं
लक्ष्मीसहस्रलीलाभिः सेव्यमानं कलानिधिम्

that is,

> I praise in my heart Him who reclines on Śeṣa on the milk-ocean of play—
> the moonlike one who is served by a thousand blandishments [*līlā*] of Śrī.

Now we have at hand the hard evidence that Vallabha's inaugural words for the *Bhāgavata*'s tenth book were what moved Sur to inaugurate his own poetry of Krishna in the way he did. This, Gokulnāth tells us, was the very first *bhagavallīlā* poem Sur composed, and the golden thread that made it possible was the connection between Vallabha's *lakṣmīsahasra* and Sur's *śrīsahasra*.

How awkward, then, that this latter phrase should be absent in all the old manuscripts! It almost begins to look as if the hearing of *sahaj* as *sahasra* might have been what we today would call 'prejudiced.' It makes the *sūrdās kī vārtā*, with its program of grounding Sur in Vallabha, look very 'separatist' indeed—consciously so.[14]

All this would be of only the slightest academic interest if the sectarian program of the Vallabhite community had not succeeded so admirably. Rare is the introduction to Surdas that does not remind the reader in the very first paragraph that Sur was a pupil of Vallabha. What if we were to release him from this sectarian, separatist bondage? He would be freed from the liturgy of the Vallabhite *puṣṭimārg*—to go where?

Other Separations and Joinings

Obviously, to a less rigidly sectarian realm, and we meet such a landscape in the *bhaktamāls* of Nabhadas and Harirāmvyās. Both these texts (nay authors!—let me say it) have their sectarian leanings for sure—Rāmānandī in the case of Nabhadas and Rādhāvallabhī (with an important nod to Haridās) in the case of Harirāmvyās. But their depiction of many figures in the world to which they belonged was not always determined by a sectarian purpose—at least, not obviously so. True, Nabhadas located figures like Kabir and Ravidas in the lineage of Rāmānand—an improbable claim at best.[15] But he also looked beyond his own *sāmpradāyik* household, and there he was less clinging. Nabha's *Bhaktamāl* places Sur just after the Caitanyites Nityānand and Raghunāth Gosvāmī, but this is only guilt by association.[16]

Harirāmvyās is even less definitive. In the poem where Vyās mentions Surdas, the verse devoted to him follows three others dedicated, respectively, to Mirabai, Jaimal, and Paramānandadās. This is quite an array. These greats are apparently presented without sectarian sorting, unlike those who appear earlier in the poem—first Hit Harivaṃś and Haridās, the *nikuñj līlā* group; then the Caitanyites Rūp and Sanātan Gosvāmī; and finally, to represent the Vallabhite camp, Kṛṣṇadās. The poem 'canonizes' a whole generation of sixteenth-century figures who composed poetry, both Sanskrit and *bhāṣā*, in Braj, and laments their passing.[17] They are hierarchically and institutionally sorted, but only to an extent, and in other poems we see that the whole group contrasts in his mind to an array of significant others—Śāktas notorious for their excess and so-called Vaishnavas who are actually religious hucksters. At one point Vyās singles out for blame Vallabhites and Gauḍīyas who abandon the holy soil of Braj to go on fund-raising tours in Gujarat and Bengal.[18] This reminds me vaguely of the way the Vārkarīs lifted Maharashtra above a pan-Indian other, as represented in the story of Nāmdev's journey with Jñāndev.[19] But the main point, perhaps, is that none of these 'others' is Muslim.

In these *Bhaktamāls*, then, we have somewhat contasting worldviews, but they share a desire to situate an inner circle against the background of a broader group of *bhaktas*. Degrees of distance and theological and practical correctness may separate them, but the relationship is hardly enmity. Enemies do appear in these stories—for instance, in the *bhaktamāls* of Nabhadas or the *parcaīs* of Anantdās—but they are far more apt to be stupid, self-serving Brahmin Pharisees than anyone outside the 'Hindu' realm. Rulers like Akbar and Sikandar Lodī were arbiters, not enemies.

Undoubtedly the *bhaktamāls* of Nabhadas and Harirāmvyās responded to categories, groupings, and institutional locations—actual temples and sources of livelihood—that already existed when they were being composed sometime around 1600. But more than sheer historical rapportage was involved. After all, Nabhadas included gods alongside humans in his 'garland of devotees.' The metaphor of the garland suggests broadly the syncretist side of things—or at least an urge toward parallel association—but lineage-building goes on there too, with its separatist valency. Sur may happen to escape, given the Rāmānandīs' priorities, but as Richard Burghart has shown, the sect-forming urge among Rāmānandīs deformed (or at least reshaped) history elsewhere.[20]

Now let's move one final step further. Let's consider non-Vaishnava sources—dynastic discourses, if you will.

It is well known that the name Surdas appears in Abu'l Fazl's *Akbar-nāmā*. Like Tānsen, he is depicted with a Gwaliori background, since he is said to be the son of Rāmdās, who came from there. But he is ranked far lower than either Tānsen or Rāmdās. Tānsen is celebrated as the best musician at court, and is listed first; Surdas comes in nineteenth. The radical contrast between this evaluation of his artistry and what appears elsewhere, and the somewhat confusing association with Rāmdās—who also appears in Badāūnī, but without Surdas—make one wonder if this Surdas can be the same as the Vaishnava poet of the same name. And the fact that he would have been raised at least substantially within the Mughal court makes one think twice about the very low incidence of words of Perso-Arabic origin found in early collections of poems attributed to Sur, as well as the fact that the Mughal archives are devoid of any of his poetry. The first extant Surdas manuscript written in *nāstālīq* appears in 1769, and no Devanagari manuscript has a colophon associating it with the imperial court. Moreover, even if one did want to make out that the Mughal Surdas is the same as the Vaishnava one, one would still be a long way from a 'discourse of syncretism' in surveying Abu'l Fazl. Religion doesn't seem to be an issue when he lists these musicians.

A far better candidate for a 'discourse of syncretism' comes to view in quite an unexpected place. This is the *Afsānah-i-Shāhān* of Muhammad Kabīr bin Ismā'īl, written during the reign of Jahāngīr—so in the early years of the seventeenth century—but by a man whose family associations were anything but Mughal. Muhammad Kabīr came from an Afghan family that had been displaced by Mughal successes. In his *Afsānah* he calls to mind the glories of the court of Islām Shāh, and they involve none other than Surdas. Muhammad Kabīr says that

दर ऐश व जश्न नशतन्द। वह हमः वक्त उलमा व फुजलः व शुअरः हमराह भी बूदन्द। व दरजाए कि खुद भी बूदन्द गिर्द व गिर्दआँ कोशखः बरपा साख्तः बूदन्द व दराँ कोशखः पान व गालिया हर किस्म निहादा बूदन्द। व आँजा वमिस्ल मीर सैयद मंझन मुसन्निफ

मधुमालती व शाह मुहम्मद फरमूली, व मूसन बिरादरे खुर्द शाह मुहम्मद व सूरदास वगैरह उलमा व फुजलः व शुअरः दराँ कोशखः भी बूदन्द। व शेरे अरबी व पारसी व हिन्दवी भी गुफ्तन्द। इसलाम शाह फरमूद कि चूँ मनइजा बेयायम कसे अज शुमायानताजिमे मन न खाहेद कर। अगर कसे निशस्त; बाशद उ हम चुना निशस्तः बाशद व अगर खुस्पीदा बाशद हम चुना बाशद।

Wherever he [Islam Shah] happened to be, he kept himself surrounded by accomplished scholars and poets. Kiosks [*khushak*] were set up, scented with '*ghalia*' (a compound of musk, ambergris, camphor, and oil of ben-nuts), and provided with betel leaves. Men like Mir Sayyid Manjhan, the author of *Madhumalati*, Shah Muhammad Farmuli and his younger brother Musan, Surdas, and many other learned scholars and poets assembled there and poems in Arabic, Persian, and Hindavi were recited. . . .[21]

In this brief characterization of the cultured life of the Afghan court, Muhammad Kabīr apparently understands Surdas as the Vaishnava 'poet of record' in an ambience otherwise dominated by poets bearing allegiance to Sufi *shaikhs*, as did Muhammad Kabīr's own ancestors. From another point of view, Surdas epitomizes the poetic achievements of Brajbhāṣā, while Manjhan represents the greatness of Avadhi. Shāh Muhammad Farmūlī and his brother Mūsan are more difficult to place linguistically, but they too apparently belonged to the 'Hindavī' (that is, Hindi) range.[22]

It is tempting to accept Muhammad Kabīr's account as a straightforward, historically trustworthy remembrance. Alas, things are not so simple. Nothing in the *Afsānah-i-Shāhān* suggests that Muhammad Kabīr was himself an eye-witness to the court of Islām Shāh, and there is a great deal in the text to raise historical eyebrows on other accounts. It is filled with episodes that feature genii as main characters, depict fabulous night journeys between Istanbul and India, serve a clearly panegyric rather than documentary purpose, and generally conflict with information that appears in other records of the time.[23] Of course, one might feel that the section where Surdas appears could reasonably be distinguished from the more problematic passages in the *Afsānah-i-Shāhān*, and Iqtidar Husain Siddiqi, a painstaking critic of other aspects of the *Afsānah*, takes just this position. He classes this passage with others that allow readers to 'pick up interesting information about the achievements of the nobles in cultural, political, and administrative fields during the Afghan period.'[24] The difficulty is that he fails to articulate a criterion that would clearly separate such passages from their more obviously problematic neighbors.

There's more to be said, but what's important from our point of view is that Muhammad Kabīr's writing emerges as being plainly in the nature of discourse—a discourse that could make use of Sur, whether he ever appeared at the court of Islām Shāh or not. Looking back from today's perspective, this sounds like a discourse of religious syncretism. A Brajbhāṣā-wielding Vaishnava poet is made to stand alongside Hindavī- and Persian-wielding Sufis. Yet we must remember that Muhammad Kabīr himself makes mention only of language, not religion. If this is syncretism, it is literary or cultural syncretism, forged in an explicitly political orbit. And it is far from being universal. If Gokulnāth's *Vārtā* was inclusivist in name—Sur is brought aboard the great ship of the *puṣṭimārg*—but separatist in aim, then the same is true for Muhammad Kabīr: syncretist in name but separatist in aim. By gathering Sur and others alongside representatives of his own *silsilā* at the court of Islām Shāh, he was implicitly debunking Mughal pretentions to cultural and perhaps even religious paramountcy. Things were better when the Afghans ruled. They had a poet like Sur at court. Did Akbar claim the glories of Brajbhāṣā patronage at Gwalior simply by virtue of having carted off a bunch of musicians to Agra? Islām Shāh's connection was far more organic: he actually held court at Gwalior—at least sometimes—where Muhammad Ghaus established his Shattārī *khānaqāh*. And when he welcomed scholars and poets, they were at ease. Unlike the self-promoting Akbar, implicitly, this old-aristocracy sultan made them feel they were equals with himself.[25]

So it all comes back to Akbar, once again, but this time from a perspective of resentment and exclusion. This is a far cry from Charlotte Vaudeville's effort in 1971 to build a bridge between the Sur of the Vallabhite *vārtās* and the Sur of the Mughal court. That volume was published with UNESCO funding and well served the Indian government's much-vaunted cause of 'national integration,' even if unintentionally so. We might well be sympathetic to such nonsectarian aims, but it turns out that the actual lay of the sixteenth-century land was more complex.

Conclusions

As we step back from our tour of sixteenth- and seventeenth-century 'discourses,' the lessons we learn are a little less ambitious than those

Vaudeville hoped we would. Contrary to her proposal, we cannot discover the 'author' of the *Sūrsāgar* to be a *sant*-ish poet of that name, by background a *ḍhāḍhī*, employed professionally at the court of Akbar in a capacity that made him a staff musician for the All India Radio of its time. Our sources also leave us several steps short of the picture of cosmopolitan performative amity that Aditya Behl and Simon Weightman wish to reflect when they take Muhammad Kabīr's historical romance as history. But the lessons we learn as we fall short of these cosmopolitan, perhaps even syncretist ideals are basic and important. Here is a summary list:

1. Religion as such is not always the issue in talk we might consider syncretist or separatist. In many narratives of the period we have been reviewing, Akbar emerges less as a Muslim than as a ruler, patron, classifier,[26] and paradigmatic aesthete.

2. The Hindu/Muslim divide is by no means paramount. We are dealing here with multiple 'others.' These are often perceived to inhabit the Vaishnava span itself, as we have seen to be implied by the boundary-creating efforts of Viṭṭhalnāth and Gokulnāth; and even within the Vaishnava span localized in Braj, as in the outlook of Harirāmvyās.

3. If we are to speak of syncretism and separatism, we must expect that there will typically be a dialectical relation between them. We have seen examples of this in the Vallabhite creation of the institution of the *aṣṭachāp* and in the latter-day Afghan project of depicting Islām Shāh as a ruler of singular breadth, by implicit contrast to the Mughals. Thus one person's syncretism is another's separation.

There is one great theme that draws together poets—many of them doubtless professional poets—who stand on both sides of the *nirguṇa*/*saguṇa* divide, just as it does *sants*, Sufis, and Vaishnavas; women and men; and members of the upper and lower classes. Exemplary in its 'synthetic' promise, this theme turns out to hide a surprise, for its name, precisely, is separation (*viraha*). If we learn anything from our travels among friends of Akbar, it is that syncretist-sounding discourses often conceal a separatist dimension, and that a separatist is apt to be, in his own way, a synthesizer—perhaps even a syncretizer.[27] Most of us would want tolerance, moderation, and a celebration of diversity to be the main names of this precolonial game, but irony is also in the running.

9

The Early *Sūrsāgar* and the Growth of the Sur Tradition

This chapter represents my first effort to report publicly on my searches among early dated manuscripts relating to the *Sūrsāgar*. It was published in the *Journal of the American Oriental Society* 99:1 (1979), pp. 64–72. I am grateful to Daniel H. H. Ingalls, a stalwart member of the American Oriental Society and my teacher of Sanskrit and Indian Studies at Harvard, for letting me know he thought the essay was ready to go. Like all his students, I had the privilege of meeting in him qualities of mind and attention that few mortals possess.

In the original version I referred to the manuscripts under discussion by means of the accession numbers they had been assigned in the various libraries where they are housed. These numbers still appear in the brief descriptions of manuscripts I give on pages 197–8, but I have revised the manuscripts' shorthand designations to accord with the system Kenneth Bryant and I adopted as we launched into the task of creating a critical edition of poems attributed to Surdas that can reasonably be said to have been in circulation in the sixteenth century. For instance, I now refer to the earliest known manuscript relevant to the *Sūrsāgar* as J1 rather than Jaipur 49, the term I adopted in the original printed text. The forthcoming book *Sūr's Ocean*, which includes Bryant's critically edited versions of 433 poems datable to the sixteenth century along with my translation and analysis of each poem, adopts the same system.

The greatest poets of medieval Hindi, Tulsidas and Surdas, traditionally are conceived as translators, conveying the sense if not the words of Sanskrit texts into the vernacular. Tulsi, one hears, brought the *Rāmāyaṇa* into Avadhi and Sur brought the *Bhāgavata Purāṇa* into Brajbhāṣā. In regard to Tulsidas this conception is substantially correct: he seems to have been working from fixed and written texts, if not from Vālmīki's alone.[1] In regard to Sur, however, it is not. The honor of 'translating' from the *Bhāgavata Purāṇa* into Brajbhāṣā belongs instead to Nandadās a generation later.[2] Sur knew the *Bhāgavata* in some form—that much seems clear—but his relationship to it was much more independent.

If one studies the early manuscripts of the *Sūrsāgar* one finds nothing either in the extent or in the organization of that work which would suggest that Sur was indebted to the *Bhāgavata* in any overarching way. Collections of his poetry have sometimes, it is true, been termed vernacular *Bhāgavatas*; but that is a relatively recent convention. The oldest surviving manuscript of the *Sūrsāgar* that was organized so as to approximate the twelve books (*skandhas*) of the *Bhāgavata Purāṇa* dates only to VS 1753 (1696 CE).[3] There is nothing in the ten earlier manuscripts of the *Sūrsāgar*—some of them a century or more older—to suggest such a connection.

In this regard, then, the twelve-*skandha* format of the *Sūrsāgar* which is currently standard, that of the second and subsequent editions published by the Kashi Nagaripracarini Sabha, is fundamentally misleading. The same can be said for the scholarship intended to support it—or rather, since this is closer to the historical fact, for the scholarship that took the assumptions of the Nagaripracarini Sabha editions as certainties and proceeded from there. Every attempt that has been made to show Sur translating the *Bhāgavata* on the basis of internal evidence in the poetry itself has relied fundamentally on poems which turn out on inspection not to belong to the ancient manuscripts.[4] In many cases such poems were themselves the attempts of later poets composing in the name of Sur to draw their namesake into a closer, simpler relation to the high tradition than he in fact stood.[5] One can make a much more nuanced case on the basis of the old manuscripts, showing how Sur took advantage of his and his audience's knowledge of certain key passages in the *Bhāgavata* and gave them a characteristic twist. The Sudāmā poems analyzed in Chapter 11 of this book provide several good examples. But this is a far more intermittent and creative relationship than is usually implied when people claim that Sur's project was to translate the *Bhāgavata* into the common, spoken tongue.

Early Manuscripts

Over the past century several efforts have been made to gather materials upon which a critical edition of the *Sūrsāgar* could be based.[7]

These have proved inadequate in the two respects. First, no complete search for manuscripts was undertaken. This meant that the early Nagaripracarini Sabha lists of manuscripts were never revised on the basis of subsequent scrutiny: once a manuscript was reported, its existence tended to be assumed. But if there was this superfluity of manuscripts reported, there was a paucity of manuscripts actually used. One never knew the full extent of the evidence from old manuscripts that could be marshaled in support of a particular critical reading. This went hand in hand with the second weakness in the critical editions which have been attempted to date, namely, that the old manuscripts were not given their proper weight. The readings they provided were regarded as no more valuable than those of more recent or undated manuscripts. Hence the value of these critical treatments of the *Sūrsāgar* was lessened and no accurate impression of the scope or character of the early *Sūrsāgar* emerged.

What follows is my attempt to improve this situation. As a preliminary to a more adequate critical edition of the *Sūrsāgar*, which has been undertaken by Kenneth E. Bryant in cooperation with several other scholars including myself, and as a basic orientation to the chapters that will follow, I would like to report briefly on the manuscript evidence for the *Sūrsāgar* and describe some aspects of the process according to which the earliest collections of Sur's poetry became amplified and modified in the course of time.

In 1975 and 1976 I undertook a search for early manuscripts of the *Sūrsāgar*. I attempted to locate all manuscripts which had been reported as bearing the date VS 1764 (1707 CE) or earlier. This was an arbitrary cutting off point, but convenient in that it permitted the inclusion of manuscripts from a variety of locations: earlier dates would have been geographically much more exclusive. I list below, in chronological order, the manuscripts whose existence I was able to verify.[8] There may be others, of course, whether unreported by their owners out of ignorance of their importance or intentionally withheld from public view. In regard to the former eventuality, however, we must remember that reports on the *Sūrsāgar* have been solicited for hundred years now and that there has been a tendency for more manuscripts to be reported than apparently exist. And in regard to the latter, one often has the evidence of catalogues, at least for the more prominent collections, which antedate the report that a certain *Sūrsāgar* is to be found there yet do not register such a volume. Still, particularly in the case of manuscripts said to be owned by isolated individuals, it is possible that a number of manuscripts exist which I have been unable to locate.

My method was simple. I visited every place and person mentioned in a published statement about a *Sūrsāgar* antedating VS 1764. In two cases I was only able to investigate by mail, but visits by Kenneth Bryant in 1977 confirmed that no manuscripts could be found.[9] In the royal library at Jaipur some manuscripts did emerge which had been previously unreported and they are included in the list which follows. In describing these manuscripts I have made note of the designations applied to some of them by Mātāprasād Gupta since the information given in the key which prefaces the posthumous publication of his critical edition is often too sparse to imply a correlation.[10] If no reference to Gupta is given it means that he did not take the manuscript into account. Here then are early manuscripts of the *Sūrsāgar* which I have been able to locate.

(1) J1. MS no. 49 in the Hindi collection of the Maharaja of Jaipur. VS 1639 (1582 CE); written at Fatehpur; 48 folios and 411 *pads*, of which, once 23 repetitions are subtracted, 239 belong to Sur; untitled. This manuscript has been published in a facsimile edition edited by Gopal Narayan Bahura and Kenneth E. Bryant: *Pad Sūrdās kā / The Padas of Surdas* (Jaipur: Maharaja Sawai Singh II Museum, 1982).[11]

(2) B1. Hindi MS no. 156, Anup Sanskrit Library, Bikaner. No date (ca. VS 1655–1685) or other colophon information.[12] 150 folios, 423 *pads*, untitled. Resembles Mātāprasād Gupta's 'Bi. 4.'

(3) B2. Hindi MS no. 157, Anup Sanskrit Library, Bikaner. VS 1681, copied at Burhānpur, in the Deccan, by a scribe in the entourage of the Maharaja of Bikaner, 161 folios pertaining to Sur, 492 *pads*, untitled. Gupta's 'Bi. 1.'

(4) B3. Hindi MS no. 149, Anup Sanskrit Library, Bikaner. VS 1695, no place given, 132 folios, 480 *pads* of Sur, untitled.

(5) U1. Hindi MS no. 575/2396, Rajasthan Oriental Research Institute, Udaipur. VS 1697, at Ghānorā (probably near Banswara), 202 folios, 793 *pads* of Sur, entitled *Sūrsāgar*.

(6) B4. Hindi MS no. 158, Anup Sanskrit Library, Bikaner. VS 1698, Mathura, 109 folios, 615 *pads* of Sur, untitled but with divisional headings. Gupta's 'Bi. 3.'[13]

(7) J2. Hindi MS no. 6732(2), 'Khās Mohar' collection, Maharaja of Jaipur. Before VS 1718 (the date of its acquisition by the House of

Jaipur), 150 folios, 503 *pads* of Sur, untitled and without divisional headings.

(8) J3. Hindi MS no. 3538, 'Khās Mohar' collection, Maharaja of Jaipur. Before AH 1059, the date of the first seal it bears (i.e., VS 1706), acquired by the House of Jaipur AH 1075 (VS 1722), 188 folios, 681 *pads* of Sur, untitled but with divisional headings.

(9) J4. Hindi MS no. 1979, 'Khās Mohar' collection, Maharaja of Jaipur. VS 1733, at Cātsu (near Jaipur), by a scribe of Gokul, 305 folios, 1472 *pads* of Sur, entitled *Sūrsāgar,* divisional headings.

(10) J5. Hindi MS no. 3387 (1), 'Khās Mohar' collection, Maharaja of Jaipur. VS 1734 (?)[14] at Ājavgaḍh (Alwar District).[15] 34 folios contain 95 *pads* of Sur under the general title *śrī sūrdās jī kā pad.*

(11) A1. MS no. 76/220, Allahabad Municipal Museum. VS 1743, no place given, 213 folios, 585 *pads* of Sur, entitled *Sūrsāgar*, sporadic divisional headings.

(12) K1. Hindi MS no. 3335, Rajasthan Oriental Research Institute, Kota. VS 1758, at Pachor, originally 64 folios, 209 *pads* of Sur, entitled *Sūrsāgar*, divisional headings. Gupta's 'Pa.'

(13) U2. Hindi MS no. 133/1954, Rajasthan Oriental Research Institute, Udaipur. VS 1763, at Udaipur, 30 folios, 170 *pads* of Sur, entitled *Sūrsāgar*, divisional headings. Gupta's 'Śrī'.

Of these manuscripts, J4 shows a clear connection with J3, U1 often reproduces the readings of B1, and U2 has a loose affinity with A1. Otherwise they seem to be independent.

Four additional manuscripts from this early period (VS 1688, 1740, 1745, and 1758) may exist in the so far inaccessible collection of the late Javāharlāl Caturvedī, in addition to a mysterious fragment dated VS 1644 which Caturvedī mentions in an article in 1953 but omits in his 1956 book. Greater doubt surrounds other manuscripts reported to have survived from this early period. I have made a search for, but have been unable to confirm the existence of, the manuscripts allegedly to be found at Nathdvara (VS 1958), Pārlau (1660), Kota (1670), Cīrghāṭ (1672), Kucāman (1675), Jhālrāpāṭan (1678), Bundi (1681), Śergaḍh (1682), Jodhpur (1688 and 1700), and Banaras (1745 and 1753).[16]

Shape and Emphasis

Two points about the early manuscripts of the *Sūrsāgar* emerge even on the basis of this summary information. First, the oldest extant collections of Sur's poems were very much smaller than what one finds in today's printed editions. Second, these collections grew gradually in size. In or near the lifetime of the poet himself 239 poems were collected in a single place (J1).[17] This number doubled in fifty years (492 *pads*, B2) and that number, in turn, tripled in the course of the next half century (1472 *pads*, J4).

It would be too simple to speak of this process as accretion around a common single core. A major contrast emerges between a western or Rajasthani group of manuscripts (B1, B2, U1) and another that we can think of as coming from farther east, since the two earliest manuscripts in this group (B4, J4) are associated with Braj. The others (B3, J2, J3, and A1), alas, give us no indication of their provenance, though two somewhat later manuscripts associated with the group are from Pachor, near Kota (K1), and Udaipur (U2), so obviously this 'eastern' group came to cover a considerable geographical span. J1, being the earliest of all, sometimes mediates between the two groups, but is much more closely aligned with the first.[18] Despite these broadly 'recensional' patterns, it remains significant that manuscripts of the same period tend to have at least as much in common with each other as they do with earlier or later manuscripts of the 'family' to which they belong: it will be noted that the Rajasthani group are almost all earlier than their eastern counterparts. Moreover, generally speaking, Surdas manuscripts tend to grow larger as time passes.

This general pattern is to be seen in regard to individual poems as well: the earlier poems tend to be shorter. Poems containing six verses are extremely common in the earliest manuscripts, proportionally much more so than the Nagaripracarini Sabha edition, and they have a tendency to expand with time. Long summary or didactic poems that make their way into narrative (as against *vinaya*) poetry are a great rarity. They first appear in B2 and B4, but their number is small and they are strictly confined to the function of introducing whole groups of poems. NPS 642 (Bryant § 3), for example, is the first poem recorded in B2 and serves to introduce the *bāl līlā* section. In B4, written seventeen years later, a similar poem is added (NPS 622) and performs the same role.

In regard to most poems from these early manuscripts it is impossible to say for sure whether they were composed by Sur himself or by other poets. The gradual increase in the number of poems collected could be explained either as the result of an enhanced sense of urgency about preserving in written form all the known poems of Sur, especially after his death, or as resulting from the fact that the poems of other 'Surs' became enshrined in the corpus as time passed. With the advent of these longer, didactic poems, however, the case seems much clearer. In style and intent such poems contrast boldly with the overwhelming majority of poems in these early collections, which are individual and episodic. Here one finds instead a programmatic intent, one that betrays an editorial purpose on the part of the creators of such poems and suggests that they stood at some remove from Surdas himself. Such poets were consciously shaping a *Sūrsāgar*, and indeed that title first appears in a manuscript of the same period, U1.

The organizational patterns of older manuscripts tend to be more informal than what one sees later on. In manuscripts such as B1 and U1, for example, some prominent phrase or idea seems to have suggested that one poem follows another. There are even cases in which the poems are arranged in roughly alphabetical groupings.[19] One can easily imagine a collection being amassed from memory in this rather *ad hoc* way. This sometimes seems to have happened in the first two sections of J1, which were written by one scribe and probably copied from earlier manuscripts; but by the time we come to the third section, in another's hand, there is a clear organization by raga.[20]

It was not long before a dominant order did appear. By about VS 1700 we begin to see something like a 'standard' *Sūrsāgar*. This happens in U1, B4, and J3. We do not know where the last manuscript in this trio came from, but it seems significant that the first two, written within a year of one another, are associated with places widely separated by geography: Ghānorā (probably the one near Banswara in southwestern Rajasthan) and Mathura. What ties them together is that all three contain divisional headings—the first manuscripts to do so—and although the headings vary, they all serve to arrange the poems in a sequence corresponding roughly to that of Krishna's life in Braj.

Where other materials are included, they are put at the end. Such is the position assigned to the significant number of poems about Rām which often appear, as for instance in U1, in direct contradiction to the order that the *Bhāgavata Puraṇa* establishes. When large numbers of *vinaya* poems are included, as in the case of J1, U2, and A1, they too are put at or near the end, except in manuscripts organized by raga (B2, J2) where they are interspersed throughout. This time the position at the end contradicts not the *Bhāgavata* but the traditional conception of Sur that was developed in the Puṣṭimārgīya Sampradāy. The followers of

Vallabhācārya hold that the poems of petition and praise which Sur raised in his own voice were composed prior to his encounter with Vallabha, who is thought to have taught Sur the *Bhāgavata* and weaned him away from poetry not based on it, as we saw in the previous chapter. Among old manuscripts of the *Sūrsāgar* only the Kota manuscript (K1) conforms to this pattern by listing its few *vinaya* poems first.

It is noteworthy that the liturgical and theological imprint of the Puṣṭimārgīya community is absent as well. The Puṣṭimārgīya ritual calendar follows the events in the life of Krishna with some regularity, but it also departs from that life story. The *dān līlā*, for instance, is celebrated on *bhādrapad śukla* 11, early in the ritual year which begins with *janmāṣṭamī* little more than a fortnight previously. Our manuscripts, however, register no such deviation. The liturgical calendar of the Vallabha Samparadāy seems not to have determined the shape of these early *Sūrsāgars*, even though many of the personages for whom they were copied should have had close ties with the Sampradāy.[21]

This is not to say that there was no relationship. The absence of *vinaya* poems in B1, J3, and J4 may be evidence of a Vallabhite point of view. Still it is true that the oldest *Sūrsāgar* I have seen preserved in a specifically Vallabhite library (that of Tilakāyat Mahārāj Śrī in Nathdvara, no. 12/3, to be dated sometime before VS 1830)[22] is organized in a way that only vaguely approximates that of the manuscripts from this early period to which it bears the closest resemblance, J3 and J4.

Moreover the specific marks of Vallabhite liturgy and theology are absent in these old *Sūrsāgars*. One looks in vain for the central terms of the theological vocabulary of Vallabhācārya, for concepts such as *puṣṭi*, *nirodha*, *tirobhāva*, and *āvirbhāva*, even *anugraha*. The one term that could be said to characterize vividly the language of both Sur and Vallabha is *antaryāmī* (*antarjāmī*), and even that can be shown to be more frequent in the more recent layers of the *Sūrsāgar* than in the earlier. What we learn from the study of the manuscripts is not just that the historical connection between Sur and Vallabha is tenuous—that was clear before[23]—but that subsequent generations of the Puṣṭimārgīya community as well seem to have had at best a limited impact on the formation of the *Sūrsāgar* in the first century (roughly) after the poet's death.[24]

What then was the central emphasis of the early *Sūrsāgar*, if its structure was determined neither by sectarian allegiance nor by the example of the *Bhāgavata Purāṇa*? Insofar as one can tell from these early collections, Sur seems first and foremost to have devoted himself to depicting the longing of the women of Braj when separated from Krishna: in a word, *viraha*. Other moods intrude, to be sure. Most significantly there are Sur's celebrated childhood poems and poems which offer their audience *darśan*, a vision of the beauty of Krishna is one posture or another. But the dominant note is *viraha*.

B4 seems to challenge this pattern. There a total of 615 poems are grouped in such a way that the dominant category is that of *siṅgār* (i.e., *śṛṅgār*), the mood of amorous love, which is taken to characterize 280 poems. By implication it refers to fulfilled love, *saṃyog*, since an alternative category is given to represent love in separation. The editor employs that label, however—*karunā* (i.e., *karuṇā*)—to characterize 112 of the *vinaya* poems as petitions addressed to the Lord in the hope of his mercy. Indeed they are pervaded with a sense of separation, and it is significant that the editor includes them under a heading that would be appropriate for great numbers of poems that fall within the confines of the Krishnaite narrative drama itself. These poems are as full of *viraha* as are many of the utterances of the *gopīs* themselves. When one inspects the poems in the *śṛṅgār* category, however, one finds there too a great number that are more expressive of love's pain than love's fulfillment. The same is true for poems grouped under the categories of *muralī* and *dhyān* (the latter term referring to the *gopīs*' infatuation with Krishna in the early stages of love). Even the poems of Krishna's childhood, the *bāl carita*, include a significant element of longing and complaint when they involve the butter thief, as we shall see.

The arrangement and distribution of poems in U1 and J3, by contrast, reflect much more clearly Sur's emphasis upon *viraha* in its many stages. In U1 the element of suffering involved in the 169 poems depicting the onset of love (*anurāg*)—in particular the way in which love causes the disintegration of personality and pits the eyes against the ego—is brought out clearly in the categories chosen to characterize the moods of love which follow. We have 47 poems of the *khaṇḍitā*, the woman who finds her lover (Krishna) absent from her bed on awakening; 187 of *viraha* as such; and an additional 122 giving voice to the *viraha* that finds expression in the *bhramargīt* once Krishna has left Braj for Mathura.

In J3 much finer discriminations are attempted, but taken together the element of *viraha* becomes if anything even more pronounced and the number of headings required to describe the various contexts in which it occurs similarly increases. The same pertains to the other manuscripts we have from this early period, including A1, which is not of the Rajasthani group and in which quite a number of poems are found which are not known there. Moreover there are manuscripts which focus almost exclusively on *viraha*, such as J2 and, in its high proportion of *vinaya* poems, J5.

The Later *Sūrsāgar* as Commentary

In later editions of the *Sūrsāgar* this element of poignancy was to be significantly muted, both quantitatively and qualitatively. Of course, the old poems survived, though sometimes in expanded, and therefore altered, form. But they were increasingly surrounded by poems of various other aims and impulses, with the result that the table of contents of the Nagaripracarini Sabha edition of the *Sūrsāgar* no longer reveals the pervasive force of *viraha*. Nor is it simply a question of numbers. There is quite an explicit irenic tendency in many of the poems that were added to the *Sūrsāgar* in its more recent forms: it serves to blunt, remove, or explain away the painful force of *viraha* which comes across so clearly in earlier collections.

One can see this process clearly in the case of the poems associated with the motif of Krishna as a thief of butter. Much of their impact in the early *Sūrsāgar* derives from the way in which the thievery they depict prefigures that state of loss which will become the common fate of the *gopīs* once Krishna steals their hearts and leaves Braj altogether. There is scandal here, though there is desire as well, and the poet gives it full voice in the genre of *urahan* (or *upālambha*) where the *gopīs* shout their complaints about Krishna to Yaśodā, his alternatively long-suffering or bristlingly defensive mother.[25]

On the basis of the poems themselves one is never able to decide who is at fault: whether the *gopīs* have lured Krishna willingly into their homes and fed him butter, as Yaśodā prefers to believe,[26] or whether he is the thief they claim him to be and they his hapless victims. The two sides simply state their cases, and the poet refuses to dissolve the drama which this tension generates. He does offer one dialogue poem in which they meet to accuse and defend, but the case goes undecided. The poem ends with a statement from the *gopī* which can be read either as the contrite apology it seems or as an expression of defiant irony:

बात एक बोलत सकुचित हौं कहा दिखाऊँ गात
है गुन बड सूर प्रभु के ह्या लरिका ह्वै जात

I shame myself to talk like this;
    I hate to show my face.
He may be just a boy, Sur's Lord,
    but what fine character![27]

What fine character indeed!

Later poems are not so. In them we find a number of devices for expressing a theological conclusion that was reached by later generations, namely, that the *gopīs*' complaint is only pretense. These girls, one understands, are responsible for the whole affair and register their complaints with Yaśodā only in the hope of catching another glimpse of their beloved Krishna. Either they are found out in the course of the poem itself, or, in a device still more heavyhanded, the neutral voice of a narrator intrudes and simply tells the audience that what they say is purest fabrication (*mis*).[28] Thus any anger their words might have communicated is undercut, leaving the contours of Krishna's idyllic Brindavan smooth and unruffled.

If a suspicion of Krishna's mischief survives, that too is subverted in these later poems. With a frequency far greater than in poems of the old *Sūrsāgar* Krishna himself, assuming his divine identity, justifies his actions. In the words of one of the most familiar poems from the later *Sūrsāgar* Krishna explains that he has become incarnate for the sake of those who love him and that his thievery is merely a part of that plan, fulfilling every *gopī*'s wish that he come and eat her butter.[29]

Such summary, interpretive comments are commonplace in more recent strata of the *Sūrsāgar*. Indeed, not just this but many of the roles that are normally reserved for the figure of the commentator in Sanskrit literature are absorbed into the poetic corpus itself in this vernacular tradition. In the absence of a formal commentary, many of the poems later added to the *Sūrsāgar* serve as commentary on earlier compositions. Often it is the commentator's task to supply a relationship between two apparently independent facets of his text. This function is served in the later *Sūrsāgar* by the supplying of poems that depict incidents in the *kṛṣṇacarita* about which Sur did not compose but which, according to the *purāṇas*, intervene between episodes that did interest him. The poems about the defeat of the crow and whirlwind demons, for example, fall into this category. Then there are poems which go beyond the *purāṇas* but answer this same need. In one poem, for example, the hunchback Kubjā, having been slandered by the *gopīs*, is given the chance to make the response to which the poet-commentator feels she must surely have been provoked.[30] Like Talmudic rabbis these poets of the later *Sūrsāgar* have the tendency to tie up loose ends left in the *textus receptus*.

Another purpose served in commentarial literature is the supplying of a systematic framework for a less than systematic text. One sees this especially in some of the long, didactic poems of the later *Sūrsāgar*, where individual pericopes are rendered part of a larger providential scheme.[31] A related tendency in the later *Sūrsāgar* is equally striking. Without wishing to impute a strictly pejorative connotation to the term, one might call it sloganeering. Here simple phrases frequently repeated perform some of the same functions that didactic poems do: they integrate the text and focus the audience's attention. To return to our example from the butter thief poems, the phrases *mākhan cor* and *mākhan corī* themselves ('butter thief,' 'butter thievery') occur with much greater frequency in the later poems than in the earlier ones because they have come to summarize an aspect of Krishna's personality which the emphases of the earlier poems made famous.[32]

A parallel example is provided by the use of the phrases which capitalize on the emphasis placed by Sur and whatever other poets contributed to the earlier *Sūrsāgar* on metaphors of liquidity, such as the term *sāgar* ('ocean') itself. Earlier poems offer a number of images and phrases to describe the emotional sea in which the *gopīs* and the poet dissolve as they contemplate Krishna. Later poems tend to reduce these to standard formulae, of which perhaps the most frequent is *sukh sāgar*, 'the ocean of happiness' in which Krishna immerses Braj. Other poets use this phrase as well, but it seems particularly widespread in the *Sūrsāgar*.[33] In fact the word *sāgar* or one of its synonyms often occurs in the final line of a *pad*, the line where the name of the poet will typically be recited, with the result that the name which came to be applied to the collection as a whole is echoed in individual poems: *Sūrsāgar*.[34]

Other familiar commentarial traits also appear in the later poems of the *Sūrsāgar*. A commentator often writes with the purpose of bringing a text into closer alignment with the positions espoused by his own community. In this way the later poets of the *Sūrsāgar* give more explicit attention to Radha than one finds in earlier poems. These poets underscore the non-duality of Radha and Krishna. For instance, they tell how Radha pretended she had lost her pearl necklace and persuaded her mother to let her out of the house in search of it, with the result that she was able to keep a tryst with Krishna.[36] Like the cycle relating how Radha claimed to be afflicted with a mysterious snakebite that only that extraordinary *gāruḍī* Krishna could cure,[37] the necklace story is told in large part with the intent of praising Radha for a cleverness commensurate with that for which Krishna is lauded in older poems.[38] The fact that these stories are told as connected narratives, though in a series of individual *pads*, is also a feature entirely strange to the early *Sūrsāgar* and consistent with the commentarial mentality we have been describing. They fill out and consolidate a narrative rather than exploring isolated moments.[39]

Finally we see the commentarial urge in the tendency to draw other materials into relation with the text at hand. In the case of the *Sūrsāgar* this was sometimes done in a radical way: whole poems which make their original appearance under the signature of another poet are brought within the Sur corpus. Apparently the size and prestige of the *Sūrsāgar* attracted other poems to it. But we must not conclude that this borrowing was conscious. The *pad* is an extremely fluid form and a given poem was often remembered in quite different versions. What is significant is that poems whose authorship was attributed to Sur and another poet turn out to have been drawn into the Sur corpus from elsewhere rather than dissipated from the *Sūrsāgar* into other collections.

This happened in several cases. I have noted a poem attributed both to Paramānandadās and to Sur, and Mātāprasād Gupta lists several others. The one I have in mind is NPS 949[40] or *Paramānand Sāgar* 147[41] and the pattern it reveals is typical in that the *Sūrsāgar* entry is late rather than early. This suggests that the poem was first registered among the works of Paramānandadās and later included in the *Sūrsāgar*. A full critical study of the *Paramānand Sāgar*, however, would have to be undertaken before one could be sure: Govardhannāth Śukla's edition is based on only a partial inspection of the ancient manuscripts. And there are several such double entries in which the *Sūrsāgar* version appears in relatively early manuscripts: the matter requires more detailed attention.

In cases where critical study has proceeded further, however, this pattern of increasing the size of the *Sūrsāgar* by borrowing from the works of other poets emerges more clearly. The *Hit Caurāsī* of Hit Harivaṃś shares six poems with the *Sūrsāgar*, and once again none of them are to be found in the earlier strata of the *Sūrsāgar*.[42] The same applies in regard to the seven poems in Tulsidas' *Śrīkṛṣṇagītāvalī* which are also attributed to Sur.[43] They too are absent in early Sur manuscripts and must have been added later.

Evidently the prestige of the *Sūrsāgar* attracted other poems to it, and its relative amorphousness made their inclusion easy. Then too there was its size. Impressive from the beginning, the great extent of the *Sūrsāgar* came to be almost a matter of doctrine by the time of the writing of the *Caurāsī Vaiṣṇavan kī Vārtā*: Sur was held to have composed more than a lakh of poems. No wonder poems from other sources were so readily accepted into the *Sūrsāgar* in a gesture that could be called, broadly, commentarial.

Conclusion

As one pares away later accretions to the *Sūrsāgar*, then, and studies the poems that formed its early core, one is met with a collection of short, lively, and sometimes even irreverent compositions which depend only rarely upon the formulations of the *Bhāgavata Purāṇa* and do not fit easily within the doctrinal framework of any particular *sampradāy*. Insofar as there is a central concern it is that of *viraha*. Later additions to the *Sūrsāgar* had the effect, as a group, of muting the scandals, surprises, and conflicts of this earlier poetry. Often they were longer, more didactic, and suggestive of an irenic theology reminiscent of that of the *Bhāgavata* itself. Vignettes were consolidated into narratives, phrases became formulae, Radha's role was elevated so as to keep pace with theological currents of the times, and poems of other poets were brought into the *Sūrsāgar* as if to consolidate it. All these tendencies remind one of the rationalizing role of the commentator. Indeed, in the absence of an independent commentarial tradition, these later poems do act as commentary on the earlier *Sūrsāgar*, setting Sur's poems in contexts intended to make them more palatable and more comprehensible for later generations.

10

The Verbal Icon—How Literal?

An oral version of this chapter was presented to the Ninth International Conference on Early Literature in New Indo-Aryan Languages, held at the Sudasien Institut óf the University of Heidelberg on 23–26 July 2003. It is being simultaneously published in the conference proceedings, under the editorship of Monika Horstmann: *Bhakti Literature in Current Research, 2001–2003* (Delhi: Manohar, forthcoming). I first formulated these ideas under the title 'Surdas: Iconreader/Iconmaker' for a panel organized by Dennis Hudson at the Wisconsin Conference on South Asia in October, 1996, and benefited from perspectives offered by Richard Davis, Richard Freeman, Steven Hopkins, and Dennis Hudson on that occasion. In coming to know about the temple of Veṇī Mādhav in Allahabad I have been greatly assisted by Purushottam Goswami, who was kind enough to visit it on my behalf in 1998, and by Satyanand Giri and Arun Kumar Agrawal, who welcomed me there in 2003–4. A helpful, pointed question from Monika Horstmann in Heidelberg spurred me on.

Let me begin with a story. It comes from the *Caurāsī Vaiṣṇavan kī Vārtā* ('Accounts of 84 Vaishnavas'), the major hagiographical collection created in the Vallabha Sampradāy as early as 1640,[1] and it concerns the great Brajbhāṣā poet whom many in the sect consider its leading literary light: Surdas.

The *Vārtā* tells us that Sur was already renowned in Braj before Vallabha (1479–1531) traveled there from his home in Arel (Aḍail), near the *saṅgam* where the Jamuna and Ganges meet at Allahabad. But when Sur met Vallabha and became his disciple, it was a whole new ballgame. Sur began to flower, and he did so in two temples where Vallabha held sway. That's where Vallabha took Sur for inspiration after adopting him as the first of eight poets (*aṣṭachāp*) who were to serve as the liturgical backbone of his fledgling community.

The more important of these two sites was the great temple of Krishna the Mountain-Lifter atop that very Mount Govardhan. Bengali, immigrants to Braj had apparently transformed this temple in the preceding century, but as early as the 1530s it would come wholly under Vallabhite control.[2] The *Vārtā* tells how Vallabha made Sur a key player in his program of liturgical renovation.[3] The other locale that served as Sur's inspiration, according to the *Vārtā*, was Gokul, a spot associated with Krishna's early childhood. When Sur first visited it with Vallabha, it was just a hallowed place on the riverbank, but in the 1570s, as we learn from other sources, Vallabha's second son Viṭṭhalnāth established a network of family temples there.[4]

As the *Vārtā* pictures it, Vallabha devoted his own main efforts to worshipping in the temple of Govardhannāth (i.e., Śrī Nāthjī) and Sur performed his musical role there to his guru's great satisfaction. But once the community was well established and others could share his musical burden, Sur liked to slip off to Gokul to worship before the tiny deity who reigned there, Śrī Navanītapriyajī, Krishna the child who loves fresh butter. There he encountered Vallabha's grandsons, the playful offspring of Viṭṭhalnāth. One of these boys, Gokulnāth, is remembered as the person who would later become the author of the *Vārtā*.

In the *Vārtā* Gokulnāth explains that Sur had a great talent for recording exactly the way Śrī Navanītapriyajī appeared in any given *darśan*. But how could this happen day after day? The boys wanted to know. After all, Sur was blind. They decided they would put him to the test. They conjured up a *darśan* so outlandish, so utterly beyond the canon, that it would test definitively whether Sur was actually responding to the appearance of Śrī Navanītapriyajī, or cheating by composing poems that were appropriate in a general way. It was the month of *āṣāḍh*, deep in the hot season, and what they determined to do was to dress the icon in nothing at all—no garments, that is, just pearls. Pearls on his forehead, pearls around his arms, pearls at his waist, ankles, and neck; then they affixed a *tilak*, a nose-ring, and earrings, and that was it.[5]

Needless to say, Sur passed the test with flying colors. Already as they worked behind closed doors, he felt something remarkable was about to be divulged, and when the *darśan* began and the icon appeared,

Sur sang a poem with the following refrain: *dekhe rī hari naṅgamanaṅgā*: 'Hey, I've seen Hari naked, all naked!' The body of the poem goes on to marvel at how the deity's limbs blaze all over with pearls and nothing else, as he shrieks for joy, smearing butter over his mouth, laughing amid the girls of Braj.[6] Thus we have a playful but utterly convincing vindication of the notion that for religious poetry, at least, the visual icon is the prototype of its verbal counterpart.[7] Even if the poet is blind, this is how it works, and even if the visual display is so extreme that it seems to transgress the limits of divine propriety.

The theological point is clear. A poem of true inspiration takes its pattern from a *mūrti*, a deity in iconic form, by a process so pure that the physical faculty of vision is of only secondary importance. Real poets see what they say—and do so by virtue of their initiation at the hands of a genuine guru. Hence it is entirely to be expected that, within the Vallabha Sampradāy at least, their poetry will align itself naturally with the seasons and times when the community witnesses the Lord's self-manifestations: eight times a day, with a change of mood each time; in the annual calendar of festivals; and in an independent sequence at the time of Holī. Such is the shape of Vallabhite worship, and the poems of Surdas feature prominently in almost all its aspects. True, the community honors as ancient a collection of Sur's poetry (the *Sūrsāgar*, 'Sur's Ocean') that is not organized in this way at all—in the main, it follows the life of Krishna—but a scholar such as Dharmanārāyaṇ Ojhā finds no difficulty working out the points of connection. That is the mission of his hefty book *Sūr-Sāhitya meṅ Puṣṭimārgīya Sevā Bhāvanā* ('The Vallabhite Spirit of Worship in the Literature of Sur').[8] It attempts to remove any doubt about Sur having been a liturgical poet, and in doing so aligns him with the iconic base and cultic form that make the Vallabhite community what it is.

It sounds great. But alas, there are difficulties—difficulties too numerous to explore fully here. For one thing, as we have seen in the previous chapter, if we turn to the oldest manuscripts of the *Sūrsāgar*, it turns out that Sur's theology answers poorly to Vallabha's: the key concepts are missing, the language is distant. Moreover, unlike certain others belonging to the inner circle of Vallabhite poets (*aṣṭachāp*), Sur doesn't ever refer to Vallabha. Most devastating of all for our present concern, there is not a single poem among those that can reasonably be shown to have been in circulation in the sixteenth century, in which we can see the peculiar features of either Śrī Govardhannāthjī or Śrī

Navanītapriyajī. Yes, there are poems on the Mountain-Lifter and the Butter Thief, but these are surprisingly rare—fewer than twenty in a corpus of more than 400—and none of them takes us directly to the distinguishing characteristics of the *mūrtis* in question. The diamond now embedded in Śrīnāthjī's chin may not go back to Sur's time,[9] so one can excuse its absence in Sur's poetry, but if Sur was taking his cues from this specific image of the Mountain-Lifter, how could he not refer to its one truly distinctive feature: the lotus stalk held in its right hand?[10] Nor is there mention of the places that house these icons, as we might expect from the Tamil analogue—no Elephant Hill at Kāñcī, no shrine of Ālavāy, no Lord of Kāṭkarai.[11] Yes, we have plenty of the mystery of epiphany, as Kenneth Bryant has so clearly shown,[12] but it is the epiphany of a universal Lord in the form of a village child—not the Lord who adopts a particular place as his own, making 'our place,' the place where this temple stands, a *divya deśa*.[13] The stark virtuosity of the Tamil verb *nil* ('to stand [here]'), which Ramanujan has so beautifully explained,[14] is simply not present.

But what about the poem we just discussed, the one about nakedness? It is quite absent from every *Sūrsāgar* dating to the sixteenth or seventeenth century, and you won't even find it in the large 'vulgate' edition of the *Sūrsāgar* published by the Kashi Nagaripracarini Sabha of Banaras in the middle years of this century.[15] The place-oriented sectarian claims for Sur are a meaningful tradition with roots in the seventeenth century, but they are evidently not the same tradition of transmission that gave us the ever-expanding *Sūrsāgar* we know by that name today.

When we go back to the poems of Sur that can be shown to have been in circulation by the end of his own century, the sixteenth, we also seem to leave behind any dependable relation between *Sūrsāgar* compositions and any specific moment of performance.[16] If Ojhā's project were really to be fulfilled, we would expect that poems attributed to Surdas would be clearly and reliably associated with a particular festival or time of day. But again there are problems. It's not just that we lack Vallabhite liturgical anthologies ('hymnbooks,' *sevā praṇālīs*) going back anywhere near that far. It's that what we would expect to find there—a stable association between a given poem and the raga in which it would have been performed—is absent in the manuscripts we do have, some of which are very old indeed. There a raga is indeed specified for each poem, but the problem is that a given poem is often linked to several ragas—one in one group of manuscripts, another in another. Even when the same poem is duplicated within in a given manuscript, it is apt to be assigned a different raga the second time around.[17] Hence it is not altogether surprising that the traditions of major Vallabhite temples vary as to when particular poems should be performed, even today when there is a common printed hymnbook to work from.[18] Either the original performance context for a given poem (if we may speak of such a thing) has been lost to the memory of at least some within the Sampradāy, or a musician had more latitude than we tend to think in choosing the raga with which a certain poem belonged—and by the same token, its cultic context, its liturgical hour or season.

This is discouraging, perhaps, but let's not fold our tents and walk away. There are plenty of poems in the sixteenth-century *Sūrsāgar* that really do translate an image into words—an image of exactly the sort one might see in a temple. In his book on Surdas, Kenneth Bryant has dealt beautifully with one of these, the triply bent image of Krishna as a flute-player (*tribhaṅgī veṇugopāl*), showing how it is the poet's purpose to bring that image to life before allowing it to return to bronze or stone.[19] I have tried to perform similar exegeses for poems that take, in fact, our friend *navanītapriya* Krishna as their inspiration.[20] And one could present many, many more examples. But in no case does the form of Krishna as seen in a particular temple emerge. Rather, these poems take as their basis such general iconographic canons as might be represented in a *śilpaśāstrī*'s book of archetypes—the sort of thing we find summarized in Gopinatha Rao's *Elements of Hindu Iconography* or Banerjea's *The Development of Hindu Iconography*.[21] This doesn't mean that a poet like Surdas 'enjoys' the Deity head to foot (*āpādacūḍanubhavam*) any less than a poet such as Vedāntadeśika, as Steven Hopkins shows in his book *Singing the Body of God*.[22] But it does seem that Sur's debt to a specific cultic environment is not so marked, no matter what the Vallabhite chroniclers of the seventeenth century and later may have wanted us to believe.

Ah, but perhaps you've been studying the list of poems that will comprise the critical edition and translation of the *Sūrsāgar* that Kenneth Bryant, Vidyut Aklujkar, and I—with help from many others—have been working on for so many years. Perhaps, on paging through it, you worked your way to the very last poem and found there a title line that promises to falsify all that I have said. The refrain reads *jai ho jai mādhau bainī*, and you are certain this must be a *stotra* addressed to

Vishnu as we see him in the temple of Veṇī Mādhav at Allahabad, that is, Prayāg. Here he is Mādhav of the Triveṇī, the triple confluence (*triveṇī saṅgam*) where the Ganges meets the Jamuna and the invisible Sarasvati. Not only that, you think, this little known poem may provide surprise confirmation that Sur really did venerate Vallabha, for here we have Sur praising the local deity of the place from which Vallabha came when he traveled to Braj. After all, Veṇī Mādhav is just across the Jamuna from Arel.

These are good instincts, for the Veṇī Mādhav temple has a substantial history. Located in Dārāganj just north of the road and railway bridges that now connect Allahabad with cities farther east, and on the last bit of high ground before one descends to the *saṅgam* itself, it is mentioned in the *Caitanya Caritāmṛta* (1615 CE?) as the very place where Caitanya met Vallabha.[23] Portions of the *Caitanya Caritāmṛta* that concern the Doab area seem much more accurate than those about more distant regions. No wonder: the author, Kṛṣṇadās Kavirāj, knew it well. But even if we doubt the historical veracity of the meeting between Vallabha and Caitanya and its provenance, it remains significant that Kṛṣṇadās thought the Allahabad meeting must have happened there. The Veṇī Mādhav temple was familiar enough to function as a stable bit of mental furniture.

Its antiquity, or at least that of some predecessor, is also confirmed by the fact that a replica was constructed across the river in Arel in the eighteenth century. That temple billed itself, of course, as the original (*ādi*) Veṇī Mādhav temple, and the 'original' in its title is a dead give-away that it was not. One may suspect here another example of Vallabhite attempts to reshape history after the fact, but I hasten to add that Mohanjī Śarmā, the *adhikārī* who presently looks after the historic place (*baiṭhak*) where Vallabha established his residence in Arel, tells the story of the meeting between Vallabha and Caitanya in the correct way: it happened not in the Veṇī Mādhav temple in Arel but on the Allahabad side of the confluence.[24] Similarly there is a temple of Veṇī Mādhav on Prayāg Ghāṭ in Mathura, whose purpose is to bring Prayāg to Mathura, making its benefits accessible to pilgrims traveling to Braj. As with Arel, it seems unlikely to me that this temple would have been in existence in Surdas's time, and Alan Entwistle apparently shared that view. He thought it might originally have been a Rāmānandī temple, although it has now passed into Śrī Vaishnava hands. Whatever the precise date of its founding, it too bears witness to the original in

Allahabad, confirming its prestige and suggesting its antiquity.[25] The Veṇī Mādhav Ghāṭ in Banaras does the same.

So much for the temple, but what about the Veṇī Mādhav image itself? Veṇī Mādhav is a black, standing, four-armed icon of Vishnu, and his consort is similar. Satyānand Giri, the person currently in charge, reports that Veṇī Mādhav's accoutrements, invisible to me because of his garments, include a disc in the (proper) back right hand, a conch in the back left, and a club and lotus in the front right and left. This does not exactly match the presumed copy in Arel, which arrays three of these differently and subsumes the fourth to the gesture of generosity (*varadā mudrā*). This mismatch need not detain us, however, since the main point is clear. Veṇī Mādhav is clearly understood on both sides of the river as a four-armed Vishnu accompanied by a four-armed Lakṣmī, and there is every indication that he would have been so understood in Sur's time, even if there is no precise way of attesting to the age of the image now installed in the temple in Allahabad.

Thereby hangs the tale. For if Sur did compose his Veṇī Mādhav poem on a visit to the *saṅgam* temple, he nonetheless found no reason to greet the deity in his iconic form. He did not copy the image into words. This is what we hear instead:

जै हो जै माधौ बैनी
जग हित प्रगट करी करुणामय अगतिनि कौं गति दैनी
जानि कठिन कलिकाल कुटिल नृप अंग सचे अघ सैनी
जनु ता लगि तरवारि त्रिबिक्रम कीनी कोपि उबैनी
मेरु मूठि बर बारि बालि छबि बहुत बित्त की लैनी
सोभित अंग तरंग त्रिसंगम धरी धार अति पैनी
दरसन ही जीते जम सेनक जमन कपालक जैनी
एक नांव कै लेत भजे तजि निरये भूमि सुचैनी
जा जल जुद्ध सुमुषि निरषत दिबि सुंदरि सरसिज नैनी
सूर परसपर करत कुलाहल कर सृक पहिरे नरैनी

Hail to Mādhav's Braid, the confluence of rivers
That he mercifully manifested in the world
    to give a way for those who'd lost the way.
It is as if Trivikram, the Triple-Victory Lord,
    knowing this Kali age to be a harsh, crooked king
Whose body is adorned with armies of evil,
    unsheathed his sword against him, in anger:

With Mount Meru for a hilt, glistening with great waters,
and purchased at enormous cost—
That Triple Confluence! How the waves of its body glint,
and the blade of its current is so very sharp
That the merest sight of it conquers Yama's soldiers—
Greeks, Kāpālikas, Jains.
They take its one name as their boat and flee,
leaving their hells for a fine peaceful realm.
Heavenly damsels observe that water war
with lovely faces and lotus eyes,
Raise a great uproar among themselves, says Sur,
and with their hands bear garlands
for the river of Nārāyaṇ.[26]

It's a wonderful poem and it is full of the celebration of a particular place, the *triveṇī saṅgam*, yet there is nothing besides the name itself to root that place in the temple of Veṇī Mādhav or its cults. Rather, Sur constructs a vast and vastly different icon in which the triune Ganges—'that Triple Confluence' (*trisaṅgama*), braided from the Ganges, the Jamuna, and the Sarasvati—becomes a great sword to Trivikram, 'the Triple Victory Lord.' So the triple nature of the *saṅgam* as sword actually seems to cause us to bypass Veṇī Mādhav, turning him into another form of Vishnu, Trivikram. Wielding the hilt of this massive weapon—the Himalayas ('Mount Meru,' *meru*, v. 5)—and using it to slash straight through the North Indian plains, he defeats the crookedness (*kuṭila*, v. 3) of the Kali age by drawing it back into a unity, as the metaphor of the braid suggests. In the process, Trivikram too is transfigured, for he comprehends not the three levels of the cosmos, as classically he should, but the three sorts of heretics who symbolize the confused dispersion of the Kali age. These are the divisions of Death's enemy army: Greeks (barbarians), Kāpālikas (scull-begging Shaivas), and the heterodox Jains (v. 7).[27]

In making the Ganges into Vishnu's scimitar, the poet takes advantage of the fact that *dhār* (v. 6, translated in v. 7) can mean both 'blade' and 'current,' so I include both meanings in the translation. He also puns on *nāv* (v. 8), which can mean either 'name' or 'boat,' and must here mean both. The desperate enemies seize on that as their lifeboat—the name of Veṇī Mādhav, that is, who is at once the confluence and Vishnu himself. Foreigners, apostates, and heretics, they have oriented themselves to other 'names,' but in truth there is only one name: the name of Vishnu. When these lost souls flee (*bhaje*, v. 8) to that 'one name' as their refuge, their lifeboat, at the same time they 'sing' (*bhaje*) of Veṇī Mādhav. For *bhaje* too is a pun.

The 'heavenly damsels' (*dibi sundari*) who appear in the penultimate verse to celebrate all this provide the poet a way of pointing even more unambiguously to the One about whose name he has been speaking. For when, in a gesture that has for millennia fallen to such beauties, they present their garlands to the Ganges, they do so in the name of Nārāyaṇ (*naraini*, v. 10). Nārāyaṇī is one of the names of the Ganges, which it earned by originating in the heavens at the toe of Vishnu. This name, with which Sur concludes his poem, is thus appropriate to the heavenly damsels with whom the poet associates it. As to their 'uproar' (*kulāhala*, v. 10) this may be the sound that is made when the Ganges and the Jamuna coalesce. But it is also the sounds we hear here—in this very composition. The first eight verses can be interpreted as the damsels' uproar—and, of course, it is also the poet's. And as we move on to the refrain, as in performance we must, this becomes our uproar as well, for we in the audience freely join in singing as the refrain comes around: *jai ho jai mādhav bainī*, 'Hail to Madhav's Braid!'

How self-referential: as the poet feeds the diction of the poem back into its refrain for a last time, causing the full composition to rest in its title, he seems to affirm that in his 'naming' he's been letting us discover how the Ganges' real name is Vishnu. She is Nārāyaṇī, and Nārāyaṇ (as we recall, moving on to the refrain) is Veṇī Mādhav, who braids her together from the three tributary strands that make her what she is.

Sur may well have sat in the temple at the *saṅgam* when he composed this hymn, and he may well have addressed it to the deity installed there. I like to believe he did. But the verbal offering he makes is far from being a copy of anything he sees. If this poem is a verbal icon, it is not an 'icon of an icon,' the sort of thing Steven Hopkins sometimes sees in the place-specific *stotras* of Vedāntadeśika. Instead it is its own icon, a fully transsubstantiated form; and for this reason, as Hopkins elsewhere reports of Deśika's language, it is as divine as any image.[28] By situating itself as divine speech, by identifying its own uproar with the uproar of the 'heavenly damsels' (*dibi sundari*), this poem begs us to recognize it as being no less holy than the stone image that may have served as its occasion. A verbal icon, indeed.

11

Sur's Sudāmā

'Sur's Sudāmā' was first published in the *Journal of Vaiṣṇava Studies* 10:2 (2002), pp. 19–37, as part of the issue presented to John Braisted Carman on the occasion of his retirement from the faculty of the Harvard Divinity School. That issue built upon papers presented to John and Ineke Carman at the annual meeting of the Conference on Religion in South India, held at Mt. Holyoke College on 15–17 June 2001 and organized by John Cort and Indira Viswanathan Peterson. In explaining the genesis of Chapter 9, I have had occasion to record my gratitude to Daniel H. H. Ingalls, who was one of my principal teachers at Harvard. This chapter gives me a chance to offer similar thanks to John Carman, and at the end I extend my list of mentors to include some very significant others.

This chapter began not as a text, but as a talk. It was offered to John Carman at a particular time of a particular day. The date was 17 June 2001; the day was Sunday; and the time was 11:00 a.m. At that hour Christians filed into churches across America in anticipation (perhaps in dread) of a sermon that would be appropriate to Father's Day. Anticipating the 'sermon' I myself had been scheduled to give at that time on that day—namely, a talk that would somehow honor John Carman's career by showing how it had touched my own—I thought I had better take cognizance of the particular moods implied by the instant itself.

It seemed plain that under almost any other conditions, John Carman would far rather have been in the pews himself, surrounded by members of his family. Perhaps the best I could do would be to recognize a shadow of that in the gathering we actually had: friends and students of John's assembled under the generous roof of the annual Conference on Religion in South India. So I began thinking in the direction of a Father's Day sermon that might be offered in this virtually Indian/ Hindu 'church,' if such a thing were ritually thinkable. For a text, the story of Sudāmā came quickly to mind. Here was a story about a husband and father. And not just about a father: it's also about a guru, about families of learning, about remembering old school days. Finally, it's a story about majesty and meekness, a central strand of John Carman's work and a central strand of his personality. So I raced to the relevant scripture, John's *Majesty and Meekness,* and began thumbing the index for references to Sudāmā.[1] He was absent, so I thought the time might truly be right for drawing Sudāmā's story into alignment with John's, thereby attesting to the strange *lagna* of the moment.

If you resist such evocations of a certain providentiality, please feel free to revert to the simple dictates of academic propriety. Just think of this as some poor student's footnote to a book his teacher wrote. But it will be another kind of footnote too, a debt to another teacher, the great sixteenth-century Brajbhāṣā poet Surdas, and you'll see him footnoting one of his own teachers, the author of the *Bhāgavata Purāṇa.* Indeed, the *guru paramparā* goes farther still, for the *Bhāgavata* itself can be seen as a footnote on an older tradition, as represented in the *Harivaṃśa* and the *Viṣṇu Purāṇa*. Ultimately, of course, 'footnote' is the wrong metaphor. Anthony Grafton has shown us that the footnote must be footnoted to Germany in the nineteenth century.[2] What we have here is much older than that. It's a tradition of teaching, story-telling, and performance that takes us back at least 2000 years and invites us to tour the Indian subcontinent as we retrace its steps.

In this chapter I will attempt to enter the performative world of Surdas in sixteenth-century North India, using the *Sūrsāgar*'s poems about Sudāmā (Figure 10) to suggest how Sur marshaled the tradition to which he was heir for the sake of those who listened to his poems. In that way, it is a local exercise, and time-specific. But if we accept that the *Bhāgavata* owes a significant debt to the Tamil South, then this is a North-South story, as well. And since the *Bhāgavata* locates Sudāmā first in Ujjain (i.e., Avantipurā), where he studied, and then near Dvaraka, where he settled, it is also a story of middle and west India. Thus our local, time-specific exercise opens onto a much wider and longer vista, one that spans at least a millennium and reaches to most corners of India.

Five Sudāmā compositions (*pads*) in the *Sūrsāgar* can be traced with fair certainty to the sixteenth century, when the poet to whom they are attributed must have lived. Hagiographical poems composed by Nabhadas and Harirāmvyās around the end of the sixteenth century make it clear that the memory of Surdas was fresh, and we have a manuscript from Fatehpur, in eastern Rajasthan, that dates to 1582 CE and is full of Surdas poems. Nothing like the 5000 or so that had come to be attributed to Sur by the time the Kashi Nagaripracarini Sabha published its widely-used edition of the *Sūrsāgar* in 1948, but still, a goodly number, some 239 in all; and the Fatehpur manuscript reveals itself as part of an editorial project that was already well begun. It apparently draws together three separate and sometimes disparate earlier anthologies where Surdas poems appear. Three of the five poems we will explore can be found in the Fatehpur manuscript, two of them more than once. The second and fourth do not appear there, but they can be found, respectively, in eight and six manuscripts written before 1700. Their spread is wide enough that we can be tolerably sure they were also in circulation in the sixteenth century, along with the trio recorded at Fatehpur.[3]

Does this mean that we are hearing the voice of a single poet? Not at all. We are merely tuning in on a performance tradition that can be given a certain date. But if these poems were not all composed by the master to whom they are attributed, then at least he was fortunate in having other poets listen carefully to the particular rhythms of his style. Therefore I will speak as if Surdas was the author of them all—'author' not in the twentieth-century sense, but still, in a manner that would do honor to a genre where the name of the poet mattered in a deeply significant way.[4]

The Story and Its Dispersion

To hear Sur's Sudāmā poems in anything like the way they would have been heard in the sixteenth century, we have to be at home with the basic story into which they tap. Clearly Sudāmā was a household name among speakers of Brajbhāṣā at the time. He appears in Nabhadas's *Bhaktamāl* (1600–1625 CE) and not one but three poets appear to have composed independent *Sudāmācaritas* late in the sixteenth century. We will return to that point in a moment, but for now let us focus on the fact that anyone with a Sanskrit education would have had access to the oldest extant form of Sudāmā story, which we find in chapters

80–81 of the tenth book of the *Bhāgavata Purāṇa*. The *Bhāgavata* appends Sudāmā's story to its account of the miraculously rapid course in Vedic learning that was undertaken by Krishna and Balarām at the feet of their guru Sāndīpani in Ujjain. This episode, which follows their defeat of the evil Kaṃs and initiates them into adult life, was a part of the standard Bhāgavata tradition, attested in the *Harivaṃśa* and the *Viṣṇu Purāṇa*. To it the *Bhāgavata* added a tale that bears all the marks of a popular yarn, probably giving a Sanskrit redaction of what was circulating in the words of vernacular story-tellers, purveyors of *hari kathā*. It's a classic story of rags to riches, and the subject of the great transformation is exactly the person one would expect from the *Bhāgavata*'s point of view: a good and faithful Brahmin. This, of course, is Sudāmā, who was also a pupil of Sāndīpani.

Rupert Snell has done us the service of summarizing the *Bhāgavata*'s version of the Sudāmā story in a valuable article published in 1992.[5] As Snell points out, the tale has not one climax but two, and the author of the *Bhāgavata* parcels them out in such a way that each serves as the culmination of a chapter. Chapter 80 follows Sudāmā to his remarkable meeting with Krishna, where his meekness encounters Krishna's majesty. Chapter 81 follows him on his equally miraculous journey home, where he is astonished to find that he has been visited with not a little majesty himself. The following is Snell's summary of the *Bhāgavata*'s tale.

> *Chapter 80*. Sudāmā, a brahmin friend of Kṛṣṇa and a penurious householder, lived an uncomplaining life of poverty with his wife, subsisting on whatever came his way; though clothed in rags and emaciated with hunger, he was free from desires and had complete control over his senses (*jitendriya*). His wife reminded him many times of his friendship with Kṛṣṇa, now ruling in Dvaraka, and suggested that he visit him in order to dispel his poverty: Kṛṣṇa is after all a friend to brahmins and compassionate to all his devotees. Enthused at the prospect of *darśana* of his friend, Sudāmā travelled to Dvaraka, taking with him a small gift of parched rice (*pṛthuka*) wrapped in a scrap of cloth. He crossed the three checkposts of guards and the ramparts which surrounded the city, and entered the most splendid of the palaces of Kṛṣṇa's sixteen thousand queens. He was warmly received by Kṛṣṇa, who personally washed his guest's feet and sprinkled the washing water on his own head. Rukmiṇī waved a chowrie over Sudāmā's head while Kṛṣṇa worshipped him with lamps and incense, offering him betel and the brahmin's prerogative of the gift of a cow. Kṛṣṇa's queens marvelled at this welcome, while he and Sudāmā reminisced about their childhood days.

> *Chapter 81.* His powers as *antaryāmin* enabling Kṛṣṇa to realise that Sudāmā had a gift for him, he reminded his friend that any offering, however mean, is valued if made with devotion. Kṛṣṇa realised that Sudāmā, who was too abashed to present his humble gift, did not himself desire material wealth but had made this visit at the wish of his virtuous wife: he resolved to reward this selflessness. Kṛṣṇa seized the parcel of rice and ate a handful with enthusiasm; but he was prevented from eating more by Rukmiṇī, who insisted that a single handful had already ensured Sudāmā's future prosperity. Royally feasted, Sudāmā returned home the following morning, full of grateful wonder at Kṛṣṇa's exhibition of grace (which he attributed to his caste status as a brahmin) and yet somewhat disconcerted at not having received any long-term improvement in his own economic circumstances. He consoled himself with the thought that Kṛṣṇa's withholding material reward had doubtless been inspired by a compassionate desire not to turn a pauper's head. Pondering this, Sudāmā reached his home, only to find it metamorphosed into a resplendent palace peopled by god-like attendants; his wife too was translated into a damsel of celestial beauty, and Sudāmā was quick to attribute this reversal of lifelong misfortune to the grace of his lord Kṛṣṇa, to whom he payed immediate homage. He was not, however, greatly attached to his new wealth, and was in any case soon granted the higher and more enduring reward of residence in Kṛṣṇa's paradise Vaikuṇṭha.

Clearly Sudāmā's story was much told in Sur's day, as the several surviving vernacular versions from that period attest. Perhaps its popularity had something to do with the rapid monetization that transformed the subcontinent's economy in the centuries just preceding Sur's. There seems to have been a new sense that wealth could be amassed quickly, and that it could happen in several social locations. Some Punjabi versions of the Sudāmā story, as if to reflect this view, promised an escape from poverty to anyone who read it.[6] The fact that the story was set in Gujarat probably attested to perceptions about a certain market savvy in that part of India. Françoise Mallison shows how this sensibility affected versions of the story that circulated in Gujarat itself, and Marco Polo's reference to the banking practices of Gujarati Brahmins make one wonder whether they might have been famous for their pecuniary talent throughout the subcontinent and perhaps beyond.[7] Not surprisingly, the earliest vernacular Sudāmā accounts to which I have seen reference are associated with Narasī Mehtā, whose traditional dates fall in the fifteenth century—and of course, in Gujarat. Some of these appear to reflect a time or ambiance that associated the Sudāmā story not with Krishna but with Shiva, for

Narasī Mehtā's poems about him can be called *Sudāmājina Kedāra.*[8] The temple in Porbandhar where he is venerated is indeed dedicated to Kedārnāth and dates to the thirteenth century.[9]

But by the time the story circulated widely in North India, it did so in a decidedly Vaishnavite milieu. We have not one but two *Sudāmā-caritas* that survive in Brajbhāṣā from the latter half of the sixteenth century, by Narottamdās and Haldhardās, and there is also a *Sudāmā-carita* in *caupāī* meter attributed to Nandadās.[10] There is some possibility that Nandadās was initiated into the Vallabhite community by Viṭṭhalnāth, the son of Vallabhācārya, and Viṭṭhalnāth largely oversaw the development of the community's major presence in Gujarat, so in those terms it might make sense that Nandadās was interested in telling Sudāmā's story.[11] But it clearly was known well beyond the Vallabha Sampradāy. Trade connections between Gujarat and Braj are longstanding—we see them reflected in the ancient story of Krishna's own westward migration after his defeat by Jarāsandh—so it is no surprise to find Sudāmā in the *Sūrsāgar,* even though, as I believe, he was not himself a Vallabhite initiate. And as we will see, whatever other forms of the story Sur knew, he almost certainly knew the *Bhāgavata*'s, and expected at least some members of his audience to do the same.

Sur's Sudāmā

I have promised to bring you five Sudāmā poems from the early strata of the *Sūrsāgar.* Commenting on them one by one, I hope to show how the poet (or poets) who fashioned these compositions brought 'Sur's Sudāmā' to life before the eyes—or ears—of those who heard these songs. It will emerge at several crucial points that the poet is well aware of swimming in a tradition he did not himself create, and that he expects at least some of his hearers to be able to swim with him. If they know the *Bhāgavata Purāṇa*, whether as readers or as frequent hearers, they will be borne along by a series of nuances of which others could not be aware. Doubtless the poems could be enjoyed without such knowledge, but their true deftness emerges only in that intertextual realm. Thus we have a situation in which the content of the poems appeals to a common heritage—both Krishna and Sudāmā emerged into maturity through their common education in Sāndīpani's ashram—and the way in which these *Sūrsāgar* poems address that subject also resonates to a fine awareness of what has gone before.

These poems owe their shape to the labors of Kenneth Bryant, who has been assisted by several other scholars working in Vancouver and Seattle. The poems will be published along with Bryant's critical apparatus as the second volume of *Sūr's Ocean*, which is forthcoming. I have written the first volume, which contains translation and commentary—again, with assistance from many others. I cite here the number (§) assigned to each poem in *Sūr's Ocean*, but as in Chapter 9, I amplify that with the number that was used by the creators of the standard Nagaripracarini Sabha edition (NPS). Of course, individual poems can be substantially different in their Bryant and NPS versions, but these five compositions do at least appear in both places, which is not always the case.

I will present the poems in narrative order, but I urge readers to remember that they are not, actually, a *Sudāmācarita* in the normally accepted sense. They form no connected narrative. Rather, they are incidental lyrics, and were probably intended to be performed independently of one another. Indeed part of the listeners' pleasure, especially early on in the performance of each, would have come from figuring out where each poem fits into the larger story. 'Where am I?', the hearer asks.

We begin with the poem that the Nagaripracarini Sabha editors placed first among the five (§337, NPS 4843):

कहि न सकति तुम सौं इक बात
इतनक दूरि द्वारिका है दुज तुम काहे न जदुपति पैं जात
जा कै सषा स्याम सुंदर से श्रीपति सकल सुषनि कै दात
तिन कै अछत आपनै आरस काहे कंत रहत क्रिस गात
कहियत परम उदार क्रिपानिधि अंतरजामी त्रिभुवन तात
सर्बसु द्रइ है देत भगत कहुं रीझत है तुलसी कै पात
छाडि सकुच बांधहु पट तंदुल सूरिज संग चलहु उठि प्रात
लोचन सफल करहु पिय अपने वह मुष कमल देषि मुसकात

There's still one thing I haven't been able to say
And it's this, oh Brahmin: Dvaraka's so close.
  Why don't you go to the Lord of the Yadus there?
Anyone who has a friend like handsome Śyām—
  Śrī's husband grants every happiness to him.
Considering he's there, why laze around here,
  my beloved, making your body weak and thin?
They say he's most compassionate, a treasury of mercy,
  father of all three worlds, knower of what's within,

Someone who provides for his devotees' every need,
  thrilled to have a *tulsī* leaf in exchange.
So leave your hesitation. Take some grains of rice,
  tie them in your garment, set off with the sun,
And let your eyes, my dear, reap the satisfaction
  of seeing his lotus face open to a smile.

Anyone who listens to this poem knows the answer to the question 'Where am I?' by the time the performer has arrived at the end of verse 2. By that time mention has been made of Dvaraka and a Brahmin, and the audience knows that this is Sudāmā's wife urging her husband to plead his poverty before Krishna, Lord of the Yadus. Later on—many verses later on—she notes his hesitation (v. 7), and Narottamdās's *Sudāmācarita* suggests that people loved to hear the details of how she'd been nagging him about it for years.[12] She does have a word for his laziness here (*ārasa*, i.e., *ālasya*, v. 4), but that's not really Sur's point. This is truly a devotional poem. There may be only a little about Sudāmā's meekness (v. 7), but there's plenty about Krishna's majesty (vv. 3–6).

In the last verse Sudāmā's wife urges her husband to let his eyes reap a satisfaction her own eyes cannot see. In the original, this is expressed in the language of attaining a goal or literally fruit (*locana saphala karahu*, v. 8), and the moment when it happens is almost classically a moment of *darśan*: Sudāmā will set eyes upon Krishna, and Krishna will return this visual recognition with a smile. That smile is the last word in the poem (*musukāta*, v. 8); it brings true closure.

There's a lot going on at the end of this poem. Sur gives Krishna's smile a modicum of poetic context by comparing it to the way a day-blooming lotus opens to the morning sun. Nothing could be more familiar than the comparison of Krishna's face to a lotus, but here Sur inverts the standard expression 'lotus face' (*kamal mukh*) to give us literally a 'face lotus' (*muṣa kamala*, v. 8), and this, in turn, he calibrates with the early morning departure that is urged on Sudāmā by his wife. Not only that, he encodes his own presence into this *darśan* scene. The term *sūrij* (v. 7) is a common designation for the sun, and that is its essential meaning here, but it is also a form of Sur's own name and functions simultaneously as his signature. The unusual position of the signature in the penultimate line, rather than the last, draws attention to this pun.

The poem is characterized by a precise use of Krishna's epithets. When Sudāmā's wife alludes to Krishna's role as king of Dvaraka, she uses his dynastic title 'Lord of the Yadus' (*jadupati*, v. 2). When she goes on to mention his generosity, however, she calls him a *pati* of a different sort: 'Śrī's husband' (*śrīpati*, v. 3). That title serves to locate Krishna in a web of domestic responsibilities that echoes her own situation and simultaneously connects him, as Vishnu, with the goddess who is often understood as the inspiration for all his blessings to his devotees (*bhagata*, v. 6), material ones most especially.[13] A string of other titles follows in verse 5, including the designation *antarjāmī* ('knower of what's within'), which promises that Krishna will have the sort of intuitive recognition of Sudāmā's plight upon which his wife relies, given her husband's reticence to ask anything for himself.[14] Finally, there is a nice juxtaposition of the epithets Śyām Sundar ('handsome Śyām,' v. 3) and Śrīpati, which serves implicitly to place Krishna's profligate, adolescent, man-about-town, Braj personality under the yoke of the more mature married man he has become at Dvaraka. Sudāmā's wife now depends upon that.

Given our 'meekness and majesty' theme, it's worth drawing attention to the *tulsī* leaf in verse 6. Did you notice it? Did you think it might be a reference to the leaf that appears in that celebrated verse, *Bhagavad Gītā* 9.26?

पत्रं पुष्पं फलं तोयं यो मे भक्त्या प्रयच्छति
तदहं भक्त्युपहृतमश्नामि प्रयतात्मनः

As translated by Barbara Stoler Miller,

The leaf or flower or fruit or water
that he offers with devotion,
I take from the man of self-restraint
in response to his devotion.[15]

How would we know if Sur was thinking of this verse, and what difference would it make?

The first thing to notice is that Sur was not the first to quote the *Bhagavad Gītā* in connection with the story of Sudāmā. The *Bhāgavata Purana* itself chooses this verse as its point of departure, quoting it in full (BhP 10.81.4). In the poem at hand Sudāmā's wife takes the leaf that opens the *Gītā*'s *śloka*, and then the *Bhāgavata*'s, and aligns it with the tiny leaf that Vishnu loves best. And she doesn't forget the rest of the *śloka*, either. There bhakti surfaces twice, and we find it here as well: those devotees in verse 6 are *bhagats* (i.e., *bhaktas*). And the *Gītā*'s echo continues: in the final verse Sudāmā's eyes are promised their 'fruit' and Krishna's face provides the flower. We have already highlighted one way in which the smile on Krishna's face grants the poem its closure. Here, intertextually, is another.

If one's standards for Sur as a 'translator' are exacting, one may object that the fourth potential offering mentioned by the *Gītā*—the water—is still absent from this scene. It's always hazardous to deal in arguments from silence, but here too there may be a way to justify Sur's practice. If in his mind he is following the *Bhāgavata*'s telling of the Sudāmā episode, his silence about the water offering might be attributed to the fact that by this point in the story, a water offering has already been made. Krishna makes it when he welcomes Sudāmā—both with the tears of joy he sheds on that occasion (BhP 10.80.19, cf. §338.4 below) and in the ceremony of washing his guest's feet and then sprinkling some of the water over his own head (BhP 10.80.20). Of course, nothing in the language of the poem at hand alludes to this moment, but Sur's characteristic precision leads one to wonder whether he might not have taken its existence into account—by his silence.

Are you satisfied that this poet knew what he was doing—or, to put it more cautiously, that a high standard could be expected of poems to which the signature 'Sūr' was affixed in the sixteenth century? If so, I believe the next poem will reconfirm your impression (§338, NPS 4846):

दूरि ही तैं देषे बलबीर
अपनौ बाल सषा श्रीदामा बिलष बदन अति षीन सरीर
बैठे हुते पर्यक परम रुचि रुषमिनि चवर डुलावति तीर
उठि धाए अकुलाइ अगमने मिलत नयन भरि आए नीर
तिहि आसन बैसारि परम सुष बूझत कुसल कहौ मति धीर
ल्याए कछू देहु हसि हम कौं अजहू कहा दुरावहु बीर
दरस परस अरु पैम समागम रही न उर कछु एकौ पीर
सूर सुरति चावर चबात ही करु पकर्यौ कमला भइ भीर

Balarām's brother saw him from afar—
His boyhood friend Śrīdāmā, but his face had grown sad
  and his body was wasted away.
Seated on his couch in supreme contentment,
  fanned with a chowry by Rukmiṇī at his side,

He jumped up and ran in a frenzy of welcome
and his eyes welled up with tears when they met.
Then, overjoyed, he sat him down on the throne
and asked, 'How are you? Relax, tell me all.
What have you brought me?' He laughed: 'Let me have it.
Why still hide it now, my friend?'
Seeing and touching and coming together in love—
it left his heart with not the slightest care.
Sur says, the moment he started chewing the rice
he remembered—
and Kamalā gripped his hand in fear.

Once again we encounter a poem that reveals Sur's detailed awareness of facets of the Sudāmā story that emerge in the *Bhāgavata Purāṇa*, some of which appear in the poem's own narrative and some of which are telling in their absence. This time Sudāmā is given the alternate name Śrīdāmā (v. 2), which appears in the colophon to *Bhāgavata Purāṇa* 10.80 but not in the text itself. Krishna too is given a distinctive name. He is designated Balabīr, that is, 'Balarām's brother' (v. 1).

As the poem develops, we come to understand that neither of these variants is accidental. The term *bīr*, which means 'brother' as it appears in the title Balabīr, can also mean 'friend,' and Sur gives it that usage when he repeats it in the emphatic rhyming position at the end of verse 6. Such a repetition is very unusual in the early *Sūrsāgar*, and would normally be avoided. Is it a flaw? I don't think so. First of all, it is not a flaw in the technical sense—that's critically important to Sur—since *bīr* is forged into a compound in verse 1, while it functions independently in verse 6. Furthermore, even if you regarded it as the same word, the meaning changes—from 'brother' to 'friend.' And I believe the poet is using this repetition consciously: to trigger his audience's awareness of an aspect of the *Bhāgavata*'s narrative that he prefers to omit, challenging them to see if they can supply the missing link.

The key is found in the way the *Bhāgavata* describes this moment, for it says that Krishna 'embraced him as if he were his elder brother' (*pariṣvakto 'grajo yathā'*, BhP 10.80.26). This displacement of the brother by the friend is what Sur achieves verbally by allowing a second occurrence of the word *bīr*—this time meaning 'friend' (v. 6)—to be overlaid on its initial usage as 'brother' (v. 1). And in fact the displacement is complete, since Sudāmā really *is* his brother. He's his guru-brother (*guru bhāī*)! I don't know whether the author of the *Bhāgavata* saw the fullness of this logic, but Sur clearly does. He names Krishna 'brother' at the outset, and even uses a term that in other contexts can refer to his brother (*balabīr* = 'Bala the hero'). Moreover, Balarām did actually accompany Krishna when he went to study in Sāndīpani's ashram in the first place. So when Surdas slots his name into the rhyming position at the end of the first line, he is precisely preparing the way for everything that is going to come: the incredible Esau and Jacob moment, or Rām and Bharat moment, that the whole poem celebrates.[16]

And did you think you'd arrived at the poem's climax by the time you got there? Did you think that was its full contract, and that the contract had been fulfilled once the faraway vision of the title line had been replaced by the embrace we witness in verse 7? If so, you were wrong. The poem does achieve that displacement of distance by presence and, as we have seen, of brother by 'brother,' but these are only two of the displacements it achieves. We must still deal with that troubling last line.

Here, once again, we meet the power of silence. We cannot appreciate the last line unless we remember that when Krishna seats Sudāmā on the couch, treating him as his long-lost brother, he dislodges not Balarām, who is only on the scene poetically, but Rukmiṇī. She is the one who was actually sitting in that place before this bedraggled visitor arrived. The author of the *Bhāgavata* makes an explicit point of telling us so in a phrase that precedes the one we quoted a bit earlier. 'He [Krishna] embraced him [Sudāmā] as if he were his elder brother [Balarām],' we heard, but that news is prefaced by another crucial bit of information: 'replacing Śrī [Rukmiṇī] who was seated on the bed' (*paryaṅkasthām śriyaṃ hitvā*, BhP 10.80.26). The *Bhāgavata* goes on to say that the women who were in attendance on the scene were scandalized by this behavior, or at least astonished. In fact, they are the ones who actually report what has happened and give us the words we just quoted from the *Bhāgavata*.

Of course, Sur doesn't come out and tell us all this—that would spoil the fun. Instead, he points. His first hint comes in the way he introduces Sudāmā. He chooses the rather unusual designation Śrīdāmā (v. 2). In doing so, he put us subliminally on guard: we should be watching for a connection between the long-lost Brahmin and *śrī*. The name Śrīdāmā means literally 'one whose allotment is auspicious' or 'one who has a share of wealth,' and as such it serves as a fine index to the story as a whole. But the term indicating the auspicious wealth in Śrīdāmā's name is *śrī*, and that, of course, is also a name for Vishnu's wife, who appears here as Rukmiṇī. When Krishna abandons her temporarily to embrace Śrīdāmā, then, the Brahmin becomes not only 'the one whose allotment is auspicious' but 'the one who has Śrī's share.' Thus the silent prophecy is fulfilled.

The language of the penultimate verse drives the point home. 'Seeing and touching' (*darasa parasa*, v. 7) are a standard enough way to speak of attaining an experience fully, but when Sur goes on to talk of 'coming together in love' (*aru paima samāgama*, v. 7), he uses a term (*prema* > *paima*) that poaches on amorous, even conjugal turf. And the same is true for *samāgama*, which is also 'coming together' in a sexual fashion. No wonder the attendants, who are invisible here but present in the *Bhāgavata*, raise their eyebrows!

But that is not the end of the story. As we know from the language of the poem itself, Krishna senses that his guest has brought something, and as we know from the *Bhāgavata,* Krishna proceeds at this point to reach into Sudāmā's garments and pull out the rice (BhP 10.81.8). Perhaps that movement is the precise embrace or 'coming together' to which Sur refers in verse 7, for when we emerge in the final verse, Krishna has started chewing the rice. This sets the stage for the final revelation, and here the drama climaxes. Something happens. Someone remembers something. But what is it? The original Brajbhāṣā simply gives us the noun 'remembrance' (*surati*, v. 8) without telling us who has this recollection, so again we have to piece things together ourselves.

The first and most obvious option is that Krishna remembers as he begins to chew the rice:

> Sur says, the moment he started chewing the rice
>   he remembered—
>   and Kamalā gripped his hand in fear.

This is how the story is most often told today. Krishna recalls how when he and Sudāmā went looking for fuel at the request of Sāndīpani's wife and were marooned in the jungle overnight by a thunderstorm, they had only a little bit of food with them. In the *sudāmā līlā* that forms a part of today's *rās līlās*, in fact, we sometimes hear that Sudāmā kept a little stash of rice secret from Krishna when the two of them were hungry that night. This moment of miserliness is offered as the cause of his life-long poverty, a karmatic drag that comes to an end only when Krishna accepts (in fact, insists on taking) rice from him in Dvaraka. Yet neither the *Bhāgavata* nor Narottamdās seems to know this interpretation, and I doubt that Sur does either. In his version of the story, Krishna is just savoring the remembrance of old times as he chews, and Sudāmā's hesitation about giving him the rice stems not from a sense of guilt but from a keen awareness of how paltry a gift it is, especially when it is being offered to a personage as splendid as Krishna has become.

A second possibility is that the act of remembering, which the poem merely denotes by means of the unvarnished, unpossessed noun *surati*, belongs not to Krishna but to his wife. After all, the verse goes on to concern her actions even more dramatically than his:

> Sur says, the moment he started chewing the rice
> she remembered—
> and Kamalā gripped his hand in fear.
> (*karu pakaryau bhai bhīra*, v. 8).

Kamalā, the 'lotus one,' is Śrī=Lakṣmī=Rukmiṇī. Could it be that *she* remembers something that makes her afraid?

Indeed she does, and again it is a knowledge of the *Bhāgavata*'s story line (if not necessarily the Sanskrit text itself) that supplies the key. Rukmiṇī is afraid because she remembers the rest of what Krishna said when he discovered Sudāmā's rice. In recognition of the power of devotion and of a Brahmin's humility, he affirmed that 'The beaten rice will satisfy not just me but the entire universe' (*tarpayantyaṅga mām viśvamete pṛthukataṇḍulāḥ*, BhP 10.81.9). With his first taste of rice, he satisfies himself. Rukmiṇī fears that if he were to take a second, he would fulfill his own pronouncement, satisfying the cosmos and inviting it to dissolve. Since Krishna actually is the entire cosmos, he has this power. So she grasps his hand: to restrain him and save the world—and at the same time, at least as important, to save him for herself.

Rupert Snell credits the 'fresh vivacity' of the Sudāmā story with its mushrooming importance in the late sixteenth century.[17] If so, this poem is an extreme example of the genre. One is struck by the way Sur gathers the carefully laid contours of a familiar, comfortable narrative and proceeds to herd them over a precipice. In retrospect, everything in the poem leads forward to its sudden, final moment of crisis. Only the audience's memory, by following the story beyond Rukmiṇī's moment of terror, can make this crisis pass. And that would be yet a third interpretation of the memory upon which the poet insists in his final verse. It would refer to—and appeal to—the memory of the audience itself.

Old House, New House, Guru's House

The poem we have just recited follows the *Bhāgavata* in poking fun at women. In fact, it searches for ways to make the joke funny again. But lest we come away thinking that Sur's men matter to him more than his women (Sudāmā displaces Śrī), or that the guru-lineage trumps flesh and blood (Sudāmā displaces Balarām), we must remind ourselves that the Sudāmā story has a second climax. Śrī does return—Sudāmā's Śrī—and she's very much the lady of the house. In the discourse that came to be collected under the title *Sūrsāgar*, this appears not as a subsequent stage of a single narrative but as an independent composition. We find it in the third poem in our set (§339, NPS 4854), as follows:

देषत भूलि रह्यौ द्विज दीन
मन सुधि परै न पूछै पावै अपनौ ग्रिह प्राचीन
चक्रित चित्त दूरि भयौ ठाढौ अद्भुत रचना रीति
उचे भवन मनोहर छाजै मनि कंचन की भीति
किधौ देव माया हौं मोह्यौ किधौ अनत ही आयौ
त्रिनहु की छाह गई निधि मांगत बहुत जतन हौं छायौ
पति पहिचानि धसी मंदिर ते सूर सु त्रिय अभिराम
चहलु कंत यह हित है हरि कौ पांउ धारिये धाम

He looked, the poor Brahmin, but it left him at a loss.
His memory was clear, but he didn't dare to ask
  what had happened to his old familiar home.
He stood at a distance, dizzy-headed
  at the wondrous creation ahead:
A lofty mansion with jeweled, gilded walls
  and charming balconies.
'Have I been duped by some divine illusion
  or have I simply come to the wrong place?

Searching for wealth has made me lose even the shade
    of the straw I labored so hard to thatch!'
Then his beautiful wife, says Sur, recognized her husband
    and descended from the house:
'Come, my dear, it's all from Hari's care.
    Come, set foot inside your home.'

This moment is also conjured up in the fourth poem of our sixteenth-century set (§340, NPS 4855):

भूल्यौ दुज देषत अपनौ घरु
औरै भांति और रचना कछु संकि संकोचि हिदै उपज्यौ डरु
कीधौ ठौर छिडाइ लियौ काहु रह्यौ आइ कोड समरथ नरु
कीधौ मैं औरै षंड आयौ यह कैलास जहां सुनियत हरु
बुधि जन कहत द्रुबल घातक बिधि सो हम आजु लह्यौ पटतर बरु
ज्यौ नलिनी बन छाडि दुरी जल दही हेम जहं हुतौ बिपन सरु
तच्छिन तै त्रिय उतरि कह्यौ पिय चलियै ग्रिह कर सौं पकर्‍यौ करु
सूरदास प्रभु स्याम क्रिपा तैं द्वारैं आनि रच्यौ जु कलपतरु

The Brahmin got confused as he looked at his house:
Its style was wrong and it was built all wrong.
    He wondered, he wavered, he felt fear:
'Either someone's come and snatched away my place—
    some powerful person who chose to live here—
Or else I've simply come to the wrong address.
    This must be Kailās, where they say Shiva lives!
There's a saying among the wise that fate attacks the weak—
    well, I'm the perfect example. I'm like the lotus
That left the wilderness to hide in open water
    and was burned by a golden sun, where once it had a jungle pond.'
At that very moment his wife descended:
    'Darling, enter the manse!' She lent him her hand.
'By the grace of Sur's Dark Lord,' she said,
    'a wishing tree's been planted at your door.'

I love this descent-of-the-staircase theme, like something from a 1940s movie. It's a little different from the moment when Krishna rushes out to meet Sudāmā—much more self-consciously decorous: these are the *nouveaux riches*, after all. But one can scarcely miss the analogy. And the poet has quite a time contrasting the plain old *ghar* (§340.1) that Sudāmā expects with the fancy new *grih* (§340.7) that he actually finds—the 'manse.' Or better yet, the lofty *dhām* that he steps into at the conclusion of §339! These wives—Krishna's Śrī and Sudāmā's Śrī—put up with a great deal, and they are handsomely rewarded for their pains.

One poem remains (§341, NPS 4859), and it takes us directly into Sudāmā's speech:

ऐसै मोहि औरु कौनु पहिचानै
सुनि सुंदरि वा दीनबंधु बिनु कौन मित्रइ मानै
कहं हौं क्रिपन कुचील कुदरसन कहं वै जादौराई
लियौ उठाइ अंक भरि भेट्यौ अरजुन की सी नाई
उठि आसन दीनौ आदर करि निज कर चरन पषारे
पूछी कुसल बात तब घर की सब संकोच निवारे
लीनै छोरि चीर तैं तंदुल कर करि मुष महि मेले
पूरब प्रीति बिचारि सूर प्रभु गुरु ग्रिह बसे अकेले

Who else is there that knows me as he does?
Who, my dear, but that kinsman to the wretched
  would even admit to being my friend?
Here I am lowly, ragged, ugly,
  and there he is the Yādav king,
Yet he raised me up as he did with Arjun
  and took me to his chest in an embrace.
He rose from his throne, sat me there in honor,
  washed my feet with his very own hands,
And asked how things are going for me at home,
  banishing any embarrassment.
Then he loosened the knot in the cloth,
  put the rice-grains in his palm,
    and tossed them all into his mouth
As he thought, Sur's Lord, of the love he had for me
  when we lived away from home in our teacher's house.

Rather than commenting on this poem in anything like its original context, even in the brief way I have done just above, I would prefer to let the trail of memory wander back to where I began. The last two verses of this poem do evoke a memory—the memory of the guru's house—and it is that memory I would recall: the memory of my own Sāndīpani. I remember with deep gratitude the house of my guru and his wife, John and Ineke Carman. I remember also their extended house, the Center for the Study of World Religions at Harvard, affectionately dubbed God's Motel. I call to mind, with gratitude, two other pairs of gurus who lived there: Wilfred and Muriel Smith, and Jarava Lal and Vimla Mehta. Each member of this quartet is illustrious, and in the latter pair Vimla Mehta was my teacher at least as much as her remarkable husband. Finally, in the spirit of Surdas, I call to mind the long and glorious lineage that John Carman represents, beginning with Rāmānuja and ending with Norvin Hein. It has been a precious privilege to be welcomed into this ample 'teacher's house,' and it was a special pleasure to celebrate it on Father's Day, 2001.

FIGURE 10: Krishna welcoming Sudāmā to Dvaraka.
Painted clay, Banaras.

12

Creative Enumeration in Sur's *Vinaya* Poetry

This chapter first took shape in a paper called 'Signing Up for Salvation,' which I presented at the International Conference on Indian Literatures hosted by the University of Chicago in April, 1986. 'Creative Enumeration in the *Vinaya* Poetry of Sūrdās,' its lineal descendent, was published among essays contributed to the Fourth International Conference on Early Literature in New Indo-Aryan Languages, held at the University of Cambridge in 1988. The citation is: Ronald Stuart McGregor, ed., *Devotional Literature in South Asia: Current Research, 1985–1988* (Cambridge: Cambridge University Press, 1992), pp. 225–36.

In one of the most compelling sections of Kenneth Bryant's *Poems to the Child-God: Structures and Strategies in the Poetry of Sūrdās*, he discusses what he calls 'frames for the icon'.[1] The icon is that of the child Krishna, which serves as the focus for his study, and he goes on to describe these frames as 'paratactic' and 'sequential'. By pairing the two adjectives, Bryant is pointing to the particular finesse with which Sur (using the name to refer to the collective author of poems in the Kashi Nagaripracarini Sabha edition of the *Sūrsāgar*) makes use of sheer enumeration in building his poems. It is not, Bryant says, that Sur merely lists instances of a phenomenon to create a median section—a body—for a poem whose structure is 'thesis; examples; summation', but that he shapes this list of instances to form a sequence that will create the possibility of a tighter summary contract than the hearer can envision when the poem begins.[2]

With observations such as these, Bryant, like A. K. Ramanujan, forces us to pull away from the notion that in the poetry of bhakti we have anything so simple and spontaneous as was thought to be the content of the Romantic *Erlebnislyrik*. First of all, it is clearly not raw experience that provides for a poem whatever structure it has.[3] And secondly, it is not necessarily the freshness or idiosyncracy of an experience that gives a poem its worth. The lists Sur spins out are often conventional ones, and if one did not look too closely one might feel that the individual creativity and 'folkishness' that have often been taken as the hallmarks of bhakti verse had been altogether lost. The Hindi *pad*, which had seemed so well suited for its role as a vehicle of personal devotion, would then have been perverted in its function by the poet who is often considered to have used it best. As programmed by him it might turn out to be as highly crafted, as impersonal, and in the end as precious a medium as any other in the span of Indian literature.

To Sur's enormous audience, for whom his verse has religious as well as literary import, such suppositions would seem to cut off the poetry from the poet's own experience, and in so doing fly in the face of a tradition that has always attempted to hold these two together. It has never taken long, in any language in which bhakti is expressed, for anthologies of devotional poems to be followed by anthologies of poets' lives: poetry and hagiography are twin garlands placed around the neck of the deity. Must we give up this close association?

In certain sense, yes: the 'life' itself is a constructed one. As I have tried to show on earlier occasions, Sur's biography reveals a craft less intricate than but fully as intentional as his poetry.[4] But in another sense, no. The carefully classified lists that shape a number of Sur's poems typically arrive at their point of summation just when the poet's signature—his 'own voice', in a sense we have yet to discover—enters his compositions. These lists and multiples, then, often turn out to have a personal reference that is distinctly appropriate to this genre, something more than the achievement of closure and the attainment of a successful poetic contract. Conventional lists that in some sense have first-person conclusions may seem strange beasts—telephone books that look you in the eye—but just such a phenomenon is part of the genius of Sur's *pads*.

The purpose of this chapter is to investigate several such lists as they occur in the *vinaya* sections of Sur's poetry, that is, in poems that display what would seem to be a personal, petitionary stance on the part of the poet. The *vinaya* label, which was first applied to Sur's poems a century after the poet's probable lifetime, is more than a little misleading, since the word means 'humility'. Many of these poems are anything but humble. Still, the *vinaya* categorization has served the useful function of distinguishing between those poems in the Sur corpus that involve the voice of a poetic 'I' and those in which the poet assumes the persona of one or another participant in the mythology of Krishna or Rām. *Vinaya* poems are especially interesting for anyone asking the question of whether there is such a thing as a 'poetics of bhakti' since they seem to involve the poet—the devotee, the *bhakta*—so directly.[5] The *vinaya* poems with which we will concern ourselves here are some of the oldest in the *Sūrsāgar*. In fact, they were drawn together in Sur manuscripts half a century before that title was applied to the collection as a whole. The sampling of 'lists' upon which we will draw takes us into the earliest strata of the *Sūrsāgar* to which we have access—all of them are attested in the Fatehpur anthology dated to the equivalent of 1582 CE (J1)—and on that account, perhaps as close as we can come to the poet himself.[6]

Let us begin with a list that seems almost as simple in its design as the proverbial telephone book (§399, NPS 135):

राम कहीयत है बड त्यागी दानि
चारि पदारथ दिये सुदामहि अरु गुरु को सुत आनि
भभीषन कों लंका दीन्ही पूरवली पहिचानि
रावन के दस मस्तक छेदे कर गहि सारंग पानि
प्रहलाद की प्रतिग्या पारे सुरपति कीन्हौ जानि
सूरदास कौं कहा निठुराई नैननि हू की हानि

They say you're so giving, so self-denying, Rām,
That you offered Sudāmā the four fruits of life
  and to your guru you granted a son.
Vibhīṣaṇ: you gave him the land of Laṅkā
  to honor his early devotion to you.
Rāvaṇ: his were the ten heads you severed
  simply by reaching for your bow.
Prahlād: you fulfilled the vow he made;
  Indra, leader of the gods, you made a sage...

The structure of the poem is quite obvious in its critically edited form, although there are variants in which that structure is seriously compromised.[7] Clearly we are hearing a paean to the glories of Rām.

The first or second word of the poem, depending on the manuscript, is *kahīyata*, 'They say', and the list that follows serves time and again to confirm that what people have always said is true. Rām is indeed *tyāgī dāni*, 'so giving, so self-denying': Sur's cascade of examples proves it. The poet does not restrict himself to recalling incidents connected with Rām in the sense of Rāmacandra, either. Vibhīṣaṇ, an ally of Rāmacandra's, is on his list, but so is Sudāmā, the boyhood friend of Krishna; so it is plain that Sur is using the name Rām in the generic sense so frequent in North Indian bhakti poetry. Here Rām means 'God' in a sense at least wide enough to embrace these two aspects of Vishnu. The guru who was granted a son is again on Krishna's side of the ledger: he restored to life the son of Krishna's teacher Sāndīpani.

The examples of divine mercy that the poet calls to mind suggest breadth in another way, too. This time it is far more dramatic, for the next name on the list is that of Rāvaṇ. When we first hear it, our reflex is to understand it as having been introduced merely so that Sur can explain how forceful was the Lord's intervention in worldly events on behalf of his devotee Vibhīṣaṇ: Rām took up his own bow to make Vibhīṣaṇ victorious over the brother from whom he had become estranged. Yet the positioning of Rāvaṇ's name at the beginning of the phrase it governs aligns it with the names of Vibhīṣaṇ and Krishna's guru, suggesting that Rāvaṇ too ought to be understood as a recipient of divine grace. For indeed it is an article of Vaishnava faith that the touch of the Lord, even a touch that brings death, is sufficient to redeem even the worst of his enemies.[8] This, then, is still more powerful evidence that what 'they say' is true: God saves both friend and foe.

In the next verse the poet makes this point yet again, as if to be sure we have understood. Here he lists two more targets of divine mercy, and they are again friend and foe. Prahlād is a willing devotee like Sudāmā, Sāndīpani, and Vibhīṣaṇ, while Indra resembles Rāvaṇ as one who struggled against the Lord. In the battle at Mount Govardhan, he acknowledged Krishna as Lord only after an arduous, furious combat ended in defeat. This division of verse 5 into two parts—two more names on the list—recalls more than the typological division between Vibhīṣaṇ and Rāvaṇ. It also brings echoes of the second verse, which likewise served to list two names, and makes one wonder if the poet is moving in the direction of symmetry. If he were, this would be the penultimate verse, and its quickening of pace with reference to two preceding verses suggests this may be so. It is a sort of stretto, and the experienced listener knows that in a *pad* this often serves as a clue that closure is at hand.[9]

Sure enough, the next word we hear—the poet's name, his oral signature—confirms that this is so. In a great number of *pads* the signature comes at just this point, announcing, even without a verb to connect it to the rest of the syntax, that every other word in the poem is what Surdas says. Indeed, commentators usually supply the verb 'says' without a second thought. Here, however, there is something unusual. The name Surdas is followed by the postposition *kauṅ*, forcing it into precisely the sort of grammatical connection with the rest of the phrase that is usually lacking. Sur becomes himself some sort of object. The full phrase is *sūradāsa kauṅ kahā niṭhurāī*, 'What is the cruelty pertaining to Surdas?' That is, 'Why this cruelty to Surdas?' And the final words of the poem explain what this cruelty is: *nainani hū kī hāni*, 'the lack of [his] very eyes', or to be more precise, 'an injury to the very eyes'.[10] The whole verse, then, can be translated:

Surdas: how could you be so harsh with him—
leaving him without his very eyes?

Suddenly we see that this is not at all the sort of poem we thought. The ever-expanding catalogue of names that demonstrates the appropriateness of the title *tyāgī dāni* has come to a screeching halt, and precisely with the last name on this list. It is more than convenience and convention that has caused the poet to place his name at the beginning of this line: he wants it there so that it will take its place on the roster, right at the beginning of the phrase it introduces, just like the names of Sudāmā, the guru, Vibhīṣaṇ, Prahlād, and Indra before it. And that introduces a performative dimension. This is not mere accusation: the poet hopes that by putting his own name on the list—right here, in the most intensely lit spot in the poem—he can shame his Lord into granting him salvation like all the rest. 'It is not too late', he implies. 'Take away my blindness and you can still keep your record clean.'

So in the end this poem is not just a list—or rather, it is certainly not the sort of list one finds in a telephone book. It is a gauntlet thrown down, a challenge to God to act. The alternation between 'good guys' and 'bad guys' that develops as the list lengthens leaves the Lord no excuse: regardless of whether Sur does or does not deserve salvation, there must be a place for him on the list. In fact, there is a certain peremptory sense in which, because the poem has now been constructed, he has already given himself such a place.

Here, then, is a variation of what Bryant calls a 'mythological sequence'.[11] Unlike the example he cites, one guided by the succession of Vishnu's avatars, it does not proceed according to a fixed pattern. The poet does not make use of a definite sequence known to his audience. But he does choose from a range of very familiar examples, incidents in which Vishnu-Rām-Krishna displayed mercy. The range is not broad enough, however. The poet avers that the net of rescue must be spread still wider if it is to catch him, and he manages such a suggestion merely by constructing a list—and not even a strictly sequential one at that.

A contrasting instance of the same type of poem is provided by §383 (NPS 37), which begins, 'If Mohan adopts'. Here too the composition appears to be built on the recalling, one by one, of several well-known examples in the vast array of *magnalia dei* that the poet could potentially adduce as proof of God's protective power. We have Prahlād again (v. 5), and Indra, who is again called Surapati ('captain of the gods', v. 7), but this time it is not Indra's own salvation that is celebrated but the salvation of those upon whom he unleashed his rainy wrath: the people of Gokul and their leader Nanda, Krishna's foster-father (v. 8). The new entries are Draupadī (vv. 3–4) and Dhruv (v. 6), both faithful devotees of Vishnu, as are all those featured in the list.

What is intriguing here is that, unlike the poem we have just considered, a scanning of the left-hand margin—or better, a recalling of the beginning of each phrase—would not enable one to construct the relevant list. It is woven into the syntax more delicately than that, and not merely because the position in which the names of the saved devotees are invoked has been changed from time to time. No, there is a definite principle of organization, and the title line proclaims it: these are devotees each of whom has been linked with God by a process of adoption (*aṅga karai*). The Lord is here referred to as Mohan, 'the Beguiler', a title of Krishna, and those he has saved are identified by means of the blood relationships that defined them before they were adopted into a new sort of family. Hence we meet Draupadī as 'Drupad's daughter' (v. 3); we hear of Dhruv as 'Uttānapād's son' (v. 6); and Hiraṇyakaśipu's name sets the stage for a mention of his son Prahlād (v. 5). Here is what happens as this list of adopted devotees grows:

जा कौ मोहन अंग करै
ता कौ केस षिसै नहिं सिर ते जो जग बैरु परै
राषी लाल द्रुपद तनया की को पट चीर हरै
दुरजोधन को मान भंग करि बसन प्रवाह भरै
हिरनकसिप पचिहारि थक्यौ प्रहलाद न रंच डरै
अजहूं लौ उत्तानपाद सुत राज करत न टरै
जो सुरपति कोप्यो गोकुल परि क्रोधें कहा सरै
राषि लियौ ब्रज नंद के ठाकुर गिरिधर बिरदु फिरै
जा कौ बिरद है गर्ब प्रहारी सो क्यौं हित बिसरै
सूरदास भगवंत भजन तै सरन गए उबरै।

If Mohan adopts someone as his own,
Not a single hair on the head can be harmed
even if the world is armed to oppose.
With him to guard the modesty of Drupad's daughter,
who could steal away her clothes?—
He broke the proud plans of Duryodhan
by covering her with streams of cloth.
Hiraṇyakaśipu went down in weary defeat
while Prahlād felt no shred of fear;
And Uttānapād's son reigns unflinching to this day,
shines with an unwavering light.
The captain of the gods aimed his rage at Gokul,
but what could his fury command?
For Nanda's master gave protection to Braj:
his Mountain-Lifter fame filled the land.
Since he earns his fame by shattering pride,
how could he fail to show the lowly his love?
Surdas says, by singing praises to that Lord
one finds a place of refuge and is saved.

The final incident in the list of 'adoptions', the Govardhan episode (vv. 7–8), is (not unexpectedly) the most complicated of the set. This time it is the protector, not the protected, who is introduced in terms of his family ties—'captain of the gods'—but, like the other guardian figures listed before him, he too attacks his charges. This happens when the cowherding people of Braj turn away from him who had formerly been their chosen deity, and begin to worship Krishna by means of the mountain that represents him. For the first time since the title line, Krishna is explicitly named as he comes on the scene—he is, of course, the Mountain-Lifter—but, like Indra, he is also designated by means of his relation to his wards. He is identified as Nanda's *ṭhākur*: 'Nanda's master' literally, but perhaps also Nanda's personal household god. In Brajbhāṣā this is a familiar, even affectionate, term of reference, since one tends one's family images, often called *ṭhākurs*, with a tenderness that frequently approximates the care that parents lavish on their children. And though Nanda's *ṭhākur* is his master, he is indeed also his son, since the Mountain-Lifter is Krishna. This incident, then, both fits the paradigm established earlier and goes beyond it. Krishna does intervene as a guardian when the old family relationships between gods and humans fall apart, but his intervention is from within: he is genuinely a member of the family he saves. Or so it appears. The truth is that the paradigm is fully apt and the list intact, since quite unknown to Nanda, Krishna is not his natural but his adopted son.

Once again, then, the list that Sur builds develops a density that goes much beyond parataxis. One associates the greatest extent of this density, as in the case of the stretto, with the penultimate line of the *pad*: the final line normally provides resolution and relaxation, as in music. But here we have not one line to go but two after this dense complication. The experienced listener will still expect a full couplet at the end of verse 8, since *pads* usually have an even number of verses even if, as here, the end-rhyme is constant throughout the poem. (When the rhyme varies from couplet to couplet, an even number of lines is absolutely required.) And if symmetry is again to prevail, as it did in the earlier poem, a two-verse 'summation' will be required to match the two-verse 'thesis' propounded at the beginning of the poem. The intervening verses are already well balanced, with two-line episodes occupying verses 3–4 and 7–8 and single verses inserted between them at the 'centre' of the poem (vv. 5–6), each relating a separate incident.

All this suggests that a couplet is still to come, but even so the poet keeps his listeners guessing. He first summarizes with the words 'Since he earns his fame by shattering pride', and then asks a question: 'How could he fail to show the lowly his love?' (v. 9). The verb that ends the line, *bisarai*, which means in general 'forget' and is here translated 'fail', is one that Sur frequently uses as the very last word in poems of this sort. It is the poet's eternal lament: 'how could he forget *me*?'[12] But a further verse is still to come: a disappointingly bland one, it seems, since it appears to dismiss the question that has just been raised as a merely rhetorical one. 'How could he fail to show the lowly his love?' He can't. Therefore the following affirmation:

> Surdas says, by singing praises to that Lord,
> one finds a place of refuge and is saved;

or alternatively,

> To sing the praises of Surdas' Lord
> is to find a place of refuge and be saved;

while there is still a third way of possibly understanding this verse:

> Surdas, singing praises to that Lord,
> has found a place of refuge and is saved.

The syntax of Brajbhāṣā poetry is sufficiently elastic to accommodate all three translations, and the last is perhaps most interesting. It raises the possibility, once again, that the poet himself is to be understood as the final cipher in the column, the last example on the list. The absence of definitive syntax governing the introduction of the poet's signature into his poem makes it possible to understand him not only as its narrator but as an important part of its subject-matter. And if there is performative utterance here, its effect is to bind the Lord into adopting the poet 'as his own' by declaring that the act of singing about him is what brings salvation. That, after all, is what Sur has been doing, so it is unthinkable that he should not be the beneficiary of divine love. His stance is not combative this time—quite the contrary—but the effect is much the same. He smuggles his way to salvation by means of the list he has constructed; he adopts himself into the field of events that his own poem describes.

This, then, is a list of devotees who were saved—'good guys'. Sur insinuates himself into their number by adopting the devotee's stance: he sings his obedient song. We have also seen a list that combines these worthy recipients of salvation with a sprinkling of enemies redeemed to salvation by their very contact with God, even if in combat. Now let us look at a third type, equally common, in which Sur builds a list exclusively constructed of 'bad guys'—reprobates who nonetheless became the recipients of divine attention.

The personalities involved in the next list are so well known in the literature of bhakti that there is no need for the poet to supply any narrative about them. Their names alone, even their occupational titles, are sufficient to establish their identities. This makes them the bane of a translator's existence, for they are as unfamiliar to most English speakers as they are familiar to speakers of Indian languages. They are the stuff of which glossaries are made:

Ajāmil: the Brahmin who deserted his family and ran off with a prostitute, but who happened to call out for help to his son Nārāyaṇ as he was dying and received instead the ministrations of his son's namesake, Vishnu (Nārāyaṇ) himself;

the hunter: Guha, who despite birth outside of caste and the nature of his livelihood, which required him to purchase his own survival at the expense of others, was drawn into the army that served Rām in his forest wanderings and became the recipient of his saving grace, even as an aboriginal;

the prostitute: Piṅgalā, who was accepted into Rām's fold when she reconsidered a life misspent, despite years of living in sin; or who, as another version has it, came to salvation only because she happened to teach her parrot the syllable 'Rām' (which meant that she pronounced the saving name frequently just to get the bird to speak); and

the vulture: Jaṭāyu, a member of the most heinous species of animals but a creature who was regarded by Rām as having leapt far above the deserts of his karma because he lost his life trying to save Sītā from being abducted by Rāvaṇ.

Note how these personalities are arrayed in the following poem:

जनु जिन के संग उर गायौ
तिन तुम पै गोबिंद गुसाई सबनि अपनपौ पायौ
सेवा इहै नाम सर औसर जा काहू कहि आयौ
कियौ न विलंब कबहु करुनामय सोइ सोइ निकट बुलायौ
अजामेल मुषि मित्र हमारौ सु मैं चलत समुझायौ
और कहां लौं कहौं गुसाई काहु कहत न आयौ
ब्याध गीध गनिका जिहि कागर हौं तिहि चिठी चढायौ
मरियत लाज पांच पतितनि में सूर समै बिसरायौ

Those others with whom my heart sang out for help
Have been redeemed by you, Govind Gosāiṅ.
    You've taken them on as your own.
And this is how they served you: at some uncharted moment
    your name chanced to pass across their lips

And that would send you scurrying, merciful one,
  to summon each of them to your side.
Ajāmil—he's great friend of mine.
  As he walked along, I talked with him,
And master, what can I say?
  He didn't whisper even a word of it to you.
Other names are also written on your list—
  hunter, harlot, vulture—and I've added another:
One more sinner to make a Council of Five,
  but when his time came, you forgot this Sūr.
    The shame of it—I could die!

This time the list is less constitutive of the structure of the poem than of its content, and even that is not entirely overt. We do not understand until the end—and with a surprise—that a list is being built, though the intriguing phrase with which the poem begins, 'Those others', suggests something is afoot. Another oddity is that the poet addresses himself to his Lord in the second line as Govind Gosāīṅ, an appellation that is infrequent in the *Sūrsāgar* and that increasingly suggests, as the poem proceeds, some landowner or petty monarch, someone who would customarily be known by a forename and surname, the latter indicating his station (Gosāīṅ = Master). At first the poet relates himself to 'those others' with whom he ought to stand as a general group: others who have received favor while he, as we suspect from the beginning, has been passed over. It is particularly Ajāmil, the worst of the lot, that he claims as his close associate, and we hear him bluster and despair as things pass from an oral to a written medium (*kāgara*, *ciṭhī*, v. 7) and still he is not counted within the charmed circle of sinners whom Govind Gosāīṅ has accepted. The penultimate line rises to a sudden stretto as three more names are added to the list.

In the last line the poet plays his final card. He says that he is dying of shame to have been excluded from the 'five sinners' (*pāñca patitani*, v. 8), and we see that the group with which he has associated himself since the beginning forms a *pañcāyat* of sorts. Four have already been listed, both in the poem and in the document that is placed before Govind Gosāīṅ (they are, in essence, the same) and as the poet reveals his own signature, we have the fifth. Thus in yet another way he seems to have forced his name into the magic ledger of salvation by enrolling himself in a poem of his own composition.

Of course, the person so enrolled is not a historical individual of the sort most easily conceived in the modern West. We are not talking about a 'personal' dimension that could be glossed as 'private'. We are not in the realm of individual autobiography here, perhaps not even in the poem that makes mention of blindness, Sur's trademark. For the blindness he describes seems more an admission of spiritual deformity than physical, and that he shares with many of the rest of us.[13] No, the poet is using a generalized 'himself' precisely as an example of what must be true in some dimension for everyone. The signature required by a *pad* provides Sur with a chance to inject into his poems an element of subjectivity or reflexivity—an 'I'—that is potentially inclusive of us all, all the people who are his audience. That is why he so often styles himself the worst of sinners: so that he, the speaker, may come to represent the limiting case that places all his hearers somewhere inside the pale of divine mercy at whose boundary he stands. The implication is that if Sur can be saved, so can anyone. And the method by which this salvation occurs is the very singing of the poem, as he sometimes explicitly says.[14] This is how Sur adds his name to the list of those who have experienced the divine presence, and it is the medium that he shares with his audience.

The function of the list in Sur's *vinaya* poetry is not just to establish some genus of which the poet wants to be included as a member. It is also a self-distancing device. Unpoetic, even: it creates the impression that the poet is merely a receiver of what is given, a transmitter of tradition. He is just reporting what 'they say' (*kahīyata*). The passivity he projects has the effect of moving him in the direction of his hearers, for this, after all, is the position they occupy in relation to him. As the lists roll on, he seems to join his audience. The sense is that he too is merely taking it all in; they know the content of these lists as much as he does.

Once this bond of receptivity has been established, Sur's exercise of the right to append his signature to a poem takes on a dramatic potential. When he speaks as 'Sur' he is speaking not just for himself but for his whole audience: for anyone who has been listening to this extended, patterned recital. When he jumps back into the poem with the 'right of signature', he has the possibility of taking the rest of us with him. As he does so, he is speaking for himself not in some narrowly autobiographical sense but in a more broadly reflexive sense—for all our selves, for anyone who participates with him in achieving, by understanding, the closure of the poem he has created. His self—

his reflexivity, the relentlessness with which he focuses the message on himself—becomes potentially the selfhood, reflexivity, and focus of every hearer.

Maybe this happens somehow in every poem, of whatever kind. Maybe poetry ultimately is religion. But it certainly makes sense in relation to that sort of engagement between self, others, and God that bhakti is said to describe. Like a poem—and really this is synecdoche more than simile—bhakti creates community as it emerges. One person's possession by God does not exclude others, it draws them in; yet the communality of devotion does not dilute it. The experience of bhakti is so intense as to seem more pointed than that of an individual ego, so although our experience of it has much to do with our sense of what it is to be an integer, a self, our language for it is appropriately displaced: we name it by the name of God. Insofar as the peculiarly intense interaction between list and signature in Sur's *vinaya* poems illuminates this dynamic, such a dialectic deserves to be seen as something that has especially to do with bhakti. I doubt that it has to do exclusively with bhakti, and it surely does not exhaust the field of bhakti poetics. But perhaps it highlights what must somehow be there for bhakti poetry to exist.

13

Why Surdas Went Blind

This chapter originally appeared in the *Journal of Vaiṣṇava Studies* 1:2 (1993), pp. 62–78, and grew out of an oral presentation I made to the conjoint Religion Departments of Barnard College and Columbia University in January, 1985. I offer more extended reflections on the meaning of blindness in the hagiography and poetry of Surdas in chapter 1 of *Sūr Dās: Poet, Singer, Saint* and in chapter 1 of the introduction to *Sūr's Ocean*.

A wonderful time to be in India is for the celebration of Krishna's birthday, which usually falls in late August or early September. Even Banaras, which is really Shiva's town, goes all out for Kṛṣṇajanmāṣṭamī, and in the bazaars you can find everything you need to celebrate this great day—dolls; little ferris wheels; they even sell miniature Banaras mailboxes, with the pin code carefully painted in.

But most of all, of course, there are religious objects. The most prominent, undoubtedly, is a simple image of Krishna himself holding up a ball of butter, his favorite food (Figure 11), but you may also find a companion piece of exactly the same style and dimension. This is Surdas, the poet whose songs of the child Krishna are the most celebrated in all of North India (Figure 12). Sur's hymns to Krishna were composed in Brajbhāṣā, the dialect spoken in the Braj region south of Delhi, where Krishna is said to have passed his youth, and they are absolutely legion. Tradition says that there are 125,000 of them, and the largest manuscript of the *Sūrsāgar* contains almost 10,000 poems, which is plenty to satisfy the average reader.[1] The size of the corpus, both real and reputed, attests to Sur's importance. He

FIGURE 11: Infant Krishna holding a ball of butter. Painted clay, Banaras.

FIGURE 12: Surdas with *ektār*. Painted clay, Banaras.

is held up as one of the two greatest poets in Hindi and his *Sūrsāgar* comes closer than any other work to serving as the vernacular Bible for Krishna worship in North India. People know these songs by heart. They sing them in temples, homes, and schools; in informal devotional gatherings; in fields and stores as they go about their work.

Take a look at our Banaras 'birthday' Surdas. Fancy he isn't, but then, he only costs a few rupees. He wears the sacred thread, signifying that he belongs to one of three upper-caste groupings: legend has it that he was a Brahmin. He has a cute little cap, an iconographic hint of the sectarian community to which he is said to have belonged—people who look to the sixteenth-century theologian Vallabhācārya as their guru and, indeed, as an incarnation of Krishna himself. The mark on Sur's forehead confirms his identification. Its shape is intended to show that Sur was a follower of Vallabha. In his right hand he carries a little clacker, for percussion, and with his left he plays the one-stringed *ektār*, simplest of instruments and the one traditionally ascribed to him. But most important of all is a feature that you might not notice if you didn't know to look. The eyes of any Hindu icon are arguably its most essential part; they are often painted or implanted on the image in a special ceremony designed to bring the icon to life. Yet if you look carefully at Surdas's eyes, you will see that he has none. For Sur is the great blind poet of North India, patron of every blind singer and indeed every blind person who followed after him.

Blindness is no sacrament in Indian society. On the contrary, it is distinctly inauspicious and is often regarded as the fruit of bad karma, a recompense for misdeeds in past lives. Some religious organizations go so far as to refuse initiation to the blind. So in encountering a blind person one may be at a loss to know what form of address to use. It would be cruel and impolite to refer to the deformity directly, but there is always a safe option. One can call such a person Surdas (or if it is a woman, Sūrdāsī) and know that the reference to blindness comes in the form of a compliment. For Sur is regarded not just as a poet and singer but as a saint as well. Often, in fact, he is depicted with a halo (Figure 13). People feel that his descriptions of Krishna's world were so inspired that he must have had direct access to the divine realm. The poster-art depiction of Sur that is most popular today shows him serenading the god himself (Figure 14).

Now Sur was supposed to have been blind from birth. Yet the best evidence available to us denies this. In fact, the evidence indicates

सूर पंचशती के अवसर पर श्री कृष्णलीला संस्थान की भेंट.

FIGURE 13: Surdas plucking a drone instrument (*tambūrā*). Chromolithograph created by 'Vallabha' (Braj Vallabh Mishra) in 1979 to honor the five-hundredth anniversary of the traditionally observed birth of Surdas.

FIGURE 14: Surdas sings for Krishna.
Poster illustration printed by S.S. Brajbasi & Sons, Bombay.
Photograph courtesy of the University of Washington Press.

that for most of his life, at least, he could see perfectly well. The earliest testimony to Sur that can be found outside the *Sūrsāgar* makes no mention of blindness. This is the citation in the *Bhaktamāl* of Nabhadas, which dates to about 1600 CE. As we know from Chapter 2, this 'Garland of Devotees' has a way of highlighting the most striking features of the saints it describes. The strident, forceful Kabir, for example, is portrayed as someone who had no tolerance for the hypocritical niceties of external religion, and the courageous Mirabai is praised for just that—her absence of fear.[2] But when Nabhadas speaks of Sur, what he brings front and center is the quality of Sur's poetry, not his blindness.[3] What seems to have set Sur apart was that other poets flocked to him, as they have for hundreds of years since. We do hear, in one tantalizing phrase, about a 'divine vision' (*dibi diṣṭi*) that Sur is supposed to have had, but that is a long way from saying he was blind.[4]

By contrast to this, the *Sūrsāgar* itself has many references to Sur's blindness, but the trick is that they have all been added fairly recently. If one picks up the currently standard Kashi Nagaripracarini Sabha edition, one will find a poem, for instance, in which Sur depicts himself as a depraved blind man—a beggar, presumably—who stands outside his Lord's door and sings, hoping to attract a gift of mercy from within.[5] In another poem he complains that his two eyes are no good and curses the Creator for his condition, since hearing Krishna's name can hardly compare with really seeing him.[6] And there are other poems in the broader Sur corpus that actually say he was blind from birth.[7]

But these, as I say, are relatively recent poems. When you ferret out old manuscripts of the *Sūrsāgar*, which usually contain far fewer poems than the Nagaripracarini Sabha's 5000, all of these clear and distinct references to Sur's blindness simply disappear. It turns out that these blind-man poems must have been added to the *Sūrsāgar* two hundred years or so after the oldest surviving manuscript was written, and many seem to be even more recent than that. No blind poet jumps out from the earliest levels of the *Sūrsāgar*—certainly no one blind from birth.[8]

This leaves us with a big, obvious question: Why was it that Sur went blind? Who blinded him? When? With what motive? In short, if Sur was not blind himself—or only very late in his life—then what does his blindness mean?

Physical Blindness

Before we leave the words of the poet, however—or the words he is supposed to have said—we had better be sure of our facts. Is there a possibility that he was partially blind, or that he became increasingly blind as he got older? Many people in India do suffer this fate, and in Sur's day the situation would have been even more extreme than it is now.

To most people, the idea that Sur was only sort of blind is anathema. To deny that this poet was blind from birth, and thereby to rob his depictions of Krishna of their absolutely unpolluted, ethereal quality, is for some people almost as shocking as it would be to many Christians to question the virgin birth of Jesus. Yet there is a small group of liberal Sur scholars who are willing to admit that Sur may only have gone blind late in life. This has the obvious advantage of explaining in secular terms how Sur could have had a knowledge of the massive visual detail that he habitually injects into his poems of Krishna, while holding onto the notion that he was in some sense blind. Several scholars of this inclination were delighted to learn of a heretofore unknown composition that I came across in my manuscript searches which had Sur's signature and bore the refrain or title line proclaiming *aja hoṅ andha*—'Now I am blind.' Now, and not before.

Unfortunately, the evidence is not as conclusive as all that. While the manuscript is more authentic than it might appear at first glance, the meaning of the poem raises a number of questions. Let us consider the manuscript in question.

I found this poem in a manuscript that was written at Ahipur, 'Snake City' literally—that is, Nagpur, near Jodhpur in Rajasthan. The date is VS 1793, or 1736 CE. That makes it 154 years more recent than the oldest extant manuscript containing Sur's poems. But its pedigree is somewhat better than one might think on the basis of that. In general it is true that the older a Sur manuscript is, the more trustworthy. Because the *Sūrsāgar* was an oral as well as a written tradition, and because it consisted of independent poems, its size and form were malleable. So it expanded at a regular rate over the years, as the manuscripts show, and the older, smaller manuscripts seem on a variety of indices to be closer to the source than their larger, later cousins. The situation is more like geological stratigraphy than what one might expect on the basis of classical Lachmannian principles of textual analysis.

But there are a few relatively late manuscripts that have a better claim to authenticity than most because they represent special lodes in the ore, so to speak, and the Ahipur manuscript is one of these. It was written and preserved by the Dādū Panth, a group that often kept pretty much to itself over the years, and that means this poem attributed to Sur might well come from an older stratum of Suriana than its date indicates. It would also explain why it was never absorbed into the mainstream of the *Sūrsāgar*—why it did not take a place, for instance, in the Nagaripracarini Sabha edition that everybody reads today.[9]

No, the real problem is not with the poem's pedigree—it may be quite old—but with what it says. Here is the poem:

अज हों अंध हरि नाम न लेत
माया मोह भ्रमि सूझत नहीं वूझत
आये नर सीस सिरारुह सेत
सकुचित अंग उतंग भंग दिज
द्रिग जल श्रवत उराहत हेत
करि सुतंत मंजार आष लौं
क्रीडत काल नहीं लषत अचेत
म्रिग बिझुन कै काज मन जैसैं
मानौं रचे बिझुका षेत
सूरदास स भगवंत भजन बिन
परै मुण्डि मुदगिर जम बेत

Now I am blind; I have shunned Hari's name.
My hair has turned white with illusions and delusions
    that have wrung me through till nothing makes sense.
Skin shriveled, posture bent, teeth gone;
    my eyes emit a stream of tears;
        my friends, a stream of blame.
Those eyes once ranged as free as a cat's,
    but failed to measure the play of Time
Like a false-eyed scarecrow failing to scatter
    the deer from the field of the mind.
Surdas says, to live without a song for the Lord
    is courting death; his sledge stands poised
        above your waiting head.[10]

Clearly this poem is about much more than physical blindness. In a way, the title line says it all. It is not just 'Now I am blind,' but 'I have shunned Hari's name.' The aging that the poem describes seems real enough, but it is firmly linked to a spiritual decrepitude, and it is the spiritual blindness that really matters. Even the physical blindness—if it is actually there—is just one of the general marks of aging. When Sur says, in a poem attested at a somewhat earlier date, that

The eyes have turned blind, the ears do not hear,
    and the feet become tired when they walk,[11]

he is just repeating an old formula found in Apabhraṁśa texts as many as eight centuries before: *naṇa suṇaṁti kaṇṇa ṇa ṇiyai ṇayaṇu ṇa calanti calaṇa ṇa karanti kara*, 'The ears do not hear, the eye does not see, the legs do not walk, and the hands will not work.'[12]

Does the Ahipur poem, then, refer to actual blindness, or is it just a stylized reference to aging? The fact that this poem belongs to a distinct genre, a subset of what is usually called *vinaya* or petitionary poetry, makes one suspect that the poet was actually using this convention to speak about spiritual blindness, for the eye failure he describes has to do with seeing Time—*kāl*, a word that also means Death. And the deer that his stony eyes fail to scare away are predators in a mental landscape, not a physical one. Perhaps this very clear reference to Sur's blindness doesn't concern physical blindness at all. Or if it does, the poet's interest goes well beyond the physical realm.

This is undoubtedly the perspective we must bring to a much earlier poem, which provides the single convincing bit of evidence from Surdas poems of the sixteenth century that the poet may indeed have gone blind at some point late in life. It is a poem we have already considered in another context—a rhetorical one—but its rhetoric does not necessary rob it of history. I am referring to the poem with which we began the last chapter, 'They say you're so giving, so self-denying, Rām' (§399, NPS 135), which appears in the very earliest manuscript to display Surdas *pads*, J1. As you will recall, the poem ends with the following striking lament:

> Surdas: how could you be so harsh with him—
> leaving him without his very eyes?

Clearly this is not disinterested autobiography. As we have seen, it is rhetorical and performative; it is *līlā*, like all the rest. And yet, there may be something more. One might indeed imagine a sighted poet asking for a gift of divine vision so that he could see the Lord with new eyes, but here something more basic may be implied. The poet apparently has no need to construct or explain the 'capital' of his failed eyesight: he seems to expect his audience to recognize it without being told. Maybe Sur is just begging for *darśan*, for revelation, asking to be relieved of the frustration of not being able to see his Lord, but the language in which he expresses his frustration sounds terribly down-to-earth. Maybe the poet who uttered these words—doubtless a celebrated figure in the temple and perhaps court culture of his time—was now physically blind, after all.

The Blindness Legends

If this indeed was what happened, it was hardly the end of the story. Rather, it was the beginning. For the most eloquent testimony to Sur's blindness comes not from his 'own' poetry, where the trace is very faint, but from the hagiographical literature that began to build around him. Not at the beginning—not with Nabhadas—but by the time we get to the *Caurāsī Vaiṣṇavan kī Vārtā* ('Accounts of Eighty-four Vaishnavas') in the mid- or late seventeenth century. There we meet a clear, dramatic treatment of Surdas's blindness, and it is given an entirely different meaning from the one that emerges in the poems we have just surveyed. As you will recall from Chapter 8, the *Caurāsī Vaiṣṇavan kī Vārtā* is said to have been compiled by Gokulnāth, who lived in the third generation after Vallabha, perhaps about the middle of the seventeenth century, and it was amplified with a commentary written by Gokulnāth's nephew Harirāy, probably several decades later. The work is clearly Vallabhite in perspective, and it is adamant about Sur's blindness. As in the case of the poem from Ahipur, a definite connection is made between the poet's blindness and his spiritual state, but this time the relationship is not direct but inverse. Sur's blindness is not a stigma here, but a mark of grace.

Let us consider the *Vārtā*'s life of Sur as we meet it in its pristine form, before Harirāy's commentary was added. As we begin, we find Sur on the banks of River Jamuna at a place south of Mathura called Gaughāṭ, when Vallabha, his guru-to-be, arrives from farther east and disembarks. Sur is told of Vallabha's arrival by one of his followers and resolves to meet the philosopher as soon as possible. After ascertaining the proper time through one of his disciples, he approaches Vallabha and prostrates himself before the master. Vallabha asks him to sing, which he does, and the song he chooses is one in that large series of laments and self-deprecations in which he throws himself upon Krishna's mercy. In short, it is a poem just like the one we just heard.

Vallabha is not pleased. 'Sur,' he says, 'what is the point of such simpering? You should describe God's playful story [*bhagavallīlā*] instead.[13] Sur is nonplussed. He says he does not know what Vallabha is talking about, at which point Vallabha tells him to go and bathe, and welcomes him back with a rite of initiation that makes him his pupil and a member of the Vallabhite community. Then he explains to Sur the whole of his *Subodhinī*, his commentary on the *Bhāgavata Puraṇa*, the standard Krishnaite scripture in Sanskrit. At that point Sur's eyes are opened, as it were, and he never gives voice to those pusillanimous complaints again. Instead he composes poems to explore various aspects of the life of Krishna, the sort that would be appropriate to sing during the worship services conducted at the temples Vallabha was just then establishing at several important places in the Braj country. Indeed, we are told that Vallabha commissioned Sur to be one of the senior members of the select company that would generate the music appropriate for such ritual occasions, especially at the great temple atop Mount Govardhan.

The story moves swiftly on from there, and a number of vignettes have to do with Sur's blindness. Early on, for instance, the great, syncretically inclined Mughal emperor Akbar is said to have sought to meet Sur—we explored facets of this encounter in Chapter 8—and Sur does indeed sing him a song. In its final line, the poet says that his eyes are dying with thirst for the sight of Krishna. Akbar, cast in the role of the straight man, the literalist, asks how this is possible, which gives Sur an occasion to reply that the sort of eye he is speaking about is no ordinary eye. It is an eye in God's possession, and it has the special property of being constantly flooded with the sight of God, yet always thirsting for more. Akbar withdraws in wonder.

Later on, Sur's special eye serves a function that relates not directly to Krishna but to his followers. The story concerns a merchant who owns a store at the base of Mount Govardhan and caters to the pilgrim trade, but only masquerades as a genuine devotee himself. Each day he is careful to ask the first worshipers who descend from the temple on top of the mountain how the image of Krishna has been dressed that day by the priests in attendance. In subsequent conversations, then, it will seem that he himself made the early morning pilgrimage, and that is good for business. Surdas, however, has an eye that is blind to such worldly shows and he sees through the ruse. He threatens the shopkeeper with public exposure and financial ruin unless he becomes in actuality as faithful as he has always pretended to be. After long and humorous shillyshallying on the part of the greasy merchant, this pious blackmail finally succeeds. Sur's perspicacious blindness earns Krishna another devotee, and the man's life is transformed.

When Harirāy adds his commentary to the *Vārtā*, he amplifies these tales of blindness with still others. In particular, like Matthew and Luke in relation to Mark, he fills in the poet's heretofore missing childhood. First we learn how Sur's parents despised him when he emerged from the womb. When told of his son's malady, his father, a poor Brahmin, openly wondered why God had sent him an affliction that would further deepen his poverty. We also hear how no one would speak to Sur as a child. But one day, after mice made off with two valuable gold coins that a local grandee had given Sur's father, the little boy demonstrated his strange capacity of vision. He said that he would reveal where the coins were if his parents would allow him to leave home. When they discovered this new talent, they were suddenly eager for him to stay, of course, but by then they had no choice. The coins were revealed and the son released.

As Sur wandered and sang, his miraculous power of insight became widely known, to the point that he had to hide it and flee its rewards.

Patrons grateful for his having located stolen cattle were busy building little palaces for the blind boy to live in. As he thought about it, Sur decided that this kind of vision, the kind that found its way to gold and cattle, was ultimately no truer than what ordinary people possessed. So he resolved to do no more miracles. He picked up stakes, and slipped off to Braj alone. It was at Gaughāṭ that he stopped, and there a purely musical, spiritual fame began to spread. Then he met Vallabha, and you know the rest.

What Blindness Means

By now we have the material we need to address head-on the question of why Sur went blind. The general picture, obviously enough, is that we live in the sort of world in which apparent blindness can be a disguise for real vision. By extension, what we think we see all about us is not really all that real at all. Indian philosophy and theology, including its Buddhist brand, have always had a component that takes illusion, sleep, dream, and mental projection more seriously than we in the West have tended to do, and the figure of a poet natively wise enough to discriminate between what seems to be and what is, is a particularly attractive one. And indeed, like most poets of his period and ilk, Sur was the author of a number of compositions that describe the ravages of Māyā—'illusion,' but not just illusion: the goddess of illusion, Krishna's own brand of magic show.[14]

So that is one dimension, but it is not everything, and in fact the writings of Vallabha are very critical of anyone who would take this insight too far. For Vallabha the 'real' world is a part, an aspect of Krishna himself—not intrinsically deluding, but partial, dark, and in need of further illumination. Hence it is not out of place for Sur to have a perspicacity that can lead one to wealth in the physical sense, as the childhood stories illustrate, and in the Vallabhite community in general the wealth and resources of the world are not thought to be bad things, provided that they are properly husbanded. What Sur's miraculous blindness does illustrate is that people tend to get out of touch with the real dynamics that make that wealth available. The greedy merchant, once set right with God, prospers all the more.

Another dimension of this general theme emerges when one looks at other hagiographies of the period, and it is this: the scarcity that attends the lives of many saints is really just scarcity to worldly eyes.

These saints have no need to gather wealth around them because they have access to wealth whenever they want it, and God is not the sort of being who keeps a ledger to control a flow of resources whose sum is fixed and changeless. To the devotional mentality, the world of faith is better described by Keynes than by Adam Smith, so a singer-saint such as Narasī Mehta has limitless wealth at his command, so long as he is giving it away.[15] It is the same for Sur. He too gives wealth away rather than gathering it for himself, and his blindness is a form of the apparent scarcity that so generally signals access to a different order of wealth in this type of hagiographical literature.

But there is more. Sur's scarcity is of a specific sort: he lacks sight. And the religious milieu in which his brand of scarcity exists is one in which seeing is just about everything. I mentioned earlier that there are religious communities in India—the Radhasoamis, for example—who are reluctant to initiate the blind into membership. The reason in the Radhasoami instance is that it is felt that the sight of one's living guru is so fundamental to faith that blind people simply do not have access to the tools of salvation—or, as it is sometimes put, the negative karmic load borne by blind people is so great that it is impossible for them to develop an intimate connection with a guru.[16] However the matter is articulated, it is clear that blindness is interpreted as a curse, and one must just wait for the next life to be out from under it.

This is scarcely less marked in popular Hinduism generally. Hinduism as most people know it is an iconic faith in which the sight of God, in image form, conveys unequalled benefits as God stoops to acknowledge the sensory vocabulary that most sharply structures our mental landscape—the visual. To the eyes of faith, Hindu images are alive; the most important are regarded as self-generated (*svayambhū*), not made; and to see them is just as important as to be seen by them. Eye contact is everything, the most fundamental thing that can shape the mind, and Hindus stand before their images—their gods—repeatedly and for long periods of time simply in order to see. If you wanted to ask someone if he or she had been to the temple that day, you might ask if that person had had *darśan*. Had she yet seen? Had she had a vision of the deity that day?

Now what does this mean if you are blind? At the mundane level, it means you will not find many blind people among the worshipers thronged around images in Hindu temples. But the story of Surdas shows, if you can forgive the expression, that there is more here than that meets the eye. It shows that true sight is subtler than our gross vision, as poetry is subtler than prose—and therefore, on occasion, more revealing. And it shows that what is to be seen in an image really has more to do with poetry than prose, or, in another Hindu way of putting it, more with feeling than with fact.

There is a story in the *Vārtā* that illustrates this precisely, and we have already had occasion to refer to it in other contexts (pages 38–9, 209–10). One day, it seems, Sur slipped away from his duties on Mount Govardhan to see the image of Krishna as Navanītapriyajī, the child who is fond of fresh butter, in the town where Krishna was brought up, Gokul. The image there was being tended by several of the grandsons of Vallabha that day, and they decided that they would put Sur's divine eye to the test. They knew that Sur always seemed to be able to describe the image before which he sang exactly as it had been adorned that particular day, so they clothed the deity in such an unusual manner that they were sure Sur's inner eye would falter. What they did was this: they decided not to clothe the image at all. They just draped him in pearl garlands and a few other ornaments.

Of course, you know the result. Sur was all but blind to their mischief. Unflustered, he described the exact regalia of the day in song, only pausing to remark that it was an especially wonderful display. The title line of the song he is supposed to have sung says 'Hey, I've seen Hari naked, all naked!,' and people speak of that song today with an awe that suggests that Sur not only saw the minimalist *darśan* he described—he actually saw Krishna naked, period.[17] That kind of totally stripped vision ordinary people cannot have. It belongs to the person whose form of sight puts nothing between him or her and God.

So this is the crucial test case for Sur's blindness. It certifies the accuracy of his vision and the attunement of his feeling in the arena where it counts. It makes one trust not only that Sur's descriptions of Krishna are visually accurate, but that he has access to the full range of behavior that Krishna could possibly display. The poems of the early *Sūrsāgar* were celebrated for their visual virtuosity, and as more and more were added, this reputation increased—if the quality of the poems did not. Furthermore, this visual acumen was touted for its naturalness (*svābhāviktā*).[18] Sur was the poet, more than any other, who saw Krishna in the things of this world and the things of this world in Krishna—who was able to bridge the gap between secular and sacred.

He was the one who excelled in reproducing the lisps and whimpers of a child's speech, and the child—Everychild—was Krishna. Sur was the one to report a dozen different games of jumping and playing ball. And, to take a particular example, it was he who noticed how little Indian boys feel about their hair, which is customarily left uncut until the age of three or four. In a favorite poem he has little Krishna remonstrating with his mother as follows:

जसौदा कब बाढैगी चोटी
किती बेर मोहि दूध पिवत भइ यह अजहू अति छोटी
तू जु कहति बल की बेणी तै ह्वैहै लांबी मोटी
काढत गुहत अन्हात नागिनि लौ फिरिहै भुइ मैं लोटी
तब तै धुपि धुपि दूध पिवावति देति न माषन रोटी
सूर बाल रस त्रिभुवन मोह्यौ हरि हलधर की जोटी

'Yaśodā, when will my topknot grow?
How many times have you made me drink my milk?—
    and still it's so little, so small.
You keep saying sometimes it will be thick and long—
    longer than brother Balarām's.
Comb it and braid it and wash it, you say,
    and it'll slither to the ground like a big black snake,
But all the while you're after me with milk, milk, milk.
    You never give me bread and butter.'
Sur says, a taste of the childhood of these two—
    Hari and his brother, the Bearer of the Plow,
        is enough to make the three worlds reel.[19]

If Sur could see that, together with all the other visual detail that surrounds Krishna's world, it had to be real—something more than merely phenomenal. The effect is not merely to certify the reality of that world from our perspective but to certify the reality of our world from the perspective of the divine. Sur's blindness serves as a sort of two-way mirror. If his vision is for real, our actions and feelings—those that are baptized by being a part of Krishna's vocabulary—are ultimately real too, just as Vallabha had insisted. Sur lacks the biased perspective that worldly vision implies, and for that reason his sightings of this world and of Krishna's world in it never go out of focus. Nor do they intrude. Hence of all the vernacular poets whose works were illustrated with miniature paintings, it was only Sur who appears in the painting himself. Tucked away in a pavilion in one of the bottom corners, the blind poet watches Krishna's world—even its most intimate aspects—without disturbing it.[20]

One final point, and this takes us back inside the Vallabhite fold. In addition to all the rest, there is a sectarian reason for Sur's blindness. You will recall that the *Vārtā*'s account of Sur is a tale of before and after. It shows how Sur was transformed by Vallabha's tutelage from being a poet of this world who lamented his condition and yearned for Krishna, to being a poet who celebrated Krishna's hidden but actual presence here. The *Vārtā* makes all his visions ultimately a poetic transcript of what Vallabha described. There is even a tortured attempt to show against all logic how a few words in one famous poem were directly inspired by something Vallabha once wrote in Sanskrit.[21] In short, the *Vārtā*'s depiction of how Vallabha made Sur see turns everything Sur ever said after his great conversion into a product of grace—specifically Vallabha's grace—rather than nature or works. If one believes what the *Vārtā* says, this is revealed poetry. It springs up *sola gratia*, for its verbal source is Vallabha's word, which is that of Krishna himself, since Vallabha is understood by his followers to be Krishna's 'full avatār' (*pūrṇāvatāra*). And its experiential analogue is Sur's blind vision.

For good historical reasons, however, not everyone always saw that Sur and Vallabha went so closely together. As I have argued in Chapters 8 and 9, I think there is ample reason to believe that the historical Surdas was never actually Vallabha's pupil, and one of the rubbing points was that, unlike some of the other poets with whom the sect was eager to group him, Sur never made reference to his supposed guru in anything he sang. The author of the *Vārtā* tries to meet this objection. He has some fall-guy ask Sur the obvious question, 'How come you never mention Vallabha?' Sur comes back with the surprising answer that everything he ever sang about Krishna is really about Vallabha, too. Others find it necessary to have Sur spell out this connection—which he does, to serve their needs, with a poem containing the word *vallabha*. The word means 'beloved,' and its plain reference is to Krishna; *vallabha* is one of his titles. But it might also be interpreted as referring to the other Vallabha—Sur's guru—who was known to his followers as the Krishna of the present age.[22]

The commentator Harirāy, however, is unwilling to leave it at that. He takes this poem and does even more with it. And to see what he does, we had better take a look at the poem itself:

भरोसो दृढ इन चरनन केरौ
श्रीवल्लभ-नखचन्द्र-छटा बिन सब जग मांझ अंधेरो
साधन और नहीं या जगमें जासों होत निवेरो
सूर कहा कहे द्विविध आंधरो बिना मोल को चेरो

With firmness of faith I cling to these feet.
But for the brilliance that shines from the moonlike
toes of the Beloved, all the world would be dark.
Those feet bring salvation; there is no other vessel
in this worst of all ages that is separate from him.
Any diverging, any doubleness, is darkness—
so says Sur, a worthless disciple.[23]

Harirāy argues that the doubleness (*dvividhi*, *dubidhi*) to which Sur refers is not the failure to give whole-hearted fealty to the beloved (*vallabha*), but the specific failure to recognize that the two possible references of *vallabha*—Krishna and Vallabha—are really one and the same. In paraphrasing, he supplies Sur a second time with what from the sectarian point of view is the ultimate meaning of his visual incapacity. He has him say, 'I am blind to any difference between Govardhannāth [that is, Krishna] and Vallabha.' The implication is that if Sur, with his ethereal eye, could see no such distinction, there must not be one. Vallabha and Krishna may seem two distinct personalities to ordinary eyes—the one a philosopher, the other a mischievous divine child—but to Sur's subtler vision they were one.

I am not suggesting that Sur's blindness was an invention of the Vallabha sect. On the contrary, I think it likely that stories of Sur's blindness predated the drawing together of the *Caurāsī Vaiṣṇavan kī Vārtā*. The sect wanted to draw Vallabha into the orbit of an already famous blind saint by making it appear that it was Sur who, by a contrary motion, was drawn into Vallabha's orbit. But once that move had been made, and once Sur had been fashioned into the kind of poet who would serve the theological and liturgical needs of the sect, there was one more drop to be squeezed from the juicy fruit of his blindness. Just as the wide prestige of Sur's name lent increased credibility to the community who adopted him, so his particular incapacity—or rather capacity—had something to contribute to the man supposedly responsible for the adoption. If Sur's vision was uniquely to be trusted in relation to Krishna, then why should it not be trusted for Vallabha himself? Vallabha had other prophets to herald him, to be sure, but Sur's testimony was so special it could not be ignored.

KABIR

14

The Received Kabir: Beginnings to Bly

This chapter was written as an afterword to the revised and expanded edition of Robert Bly's *The Kabir Book*, which was retitled *Kabir: Ecstatic Poems* (Boston: Beacon Press, 2004), pp. 77–102. I am grateful to Brian Halley of Beacon Press and to Robert Bly himself for their invitation to contribute to the new version of this remarkable and influential work, and to Linda Hess for an affectionate and challenging discussion of a draft.

The Transcendental Bly

Translations are rivers—their sources often hidden, their destinations potentially oceanic—but for all that, they have a true claim to history. The history I imagine for Robert Bly's immensely influential translations of Kabir connects them with the New England Transcendentalists, especially Emerson and Thoreau. Here were men whose sense of human dignity and personal possibility, like Bly's, led them to look beyond the shores of their own little Calvinist lake. They read the *Upanishads* and the *Bhagavad Gītā*. Thoreau took a copy of the *Gītā* with him when he retreated to Walden Pond. As winter came and workers broke Walden's ice into blocks, he indulged the thought that some of those blocks might end up before 'the sweltering inhabitants... of Madras and Bombay and Calcutta'—floating upstream, as it were, on the river that had brought him the transcendental wisdom of the *Gītā*. Or rather, they dipped from the same well.

The aquifer may have been the same, but the surface concourse between Calcutta and Walden was indirect. Thoreau read the *Gītā* not in Sanskrit but in Charles Wilkins' English translation of 1785. Bly's *Kabir* is not so different. It reworks the 'hopeless' Victorian English of Rabindranath Tagore and Evelyn Underhill, which benefited from an earlier English translation by Ajit Kumar Chakravarty and like it was based on the Bengali-script version of Kshitimohan Sen.[1] And that takes us back, finally, to the Hindi linguistic stream where Kabir himself swam as a weaver living in Banaras in the late fifteenth-century. Or almost. Actually a complex history of written and oral transmission fills the time that intervenes between Kabir's death in about 1518 and the publication of Tagore and Underhill's *Songs of Kabir* almost exactly four centuries later.

It's true, as Bly says, that most of what has been said about the historical Kabir is 'rumors.'[2] Yet since the time Tagore translated Kabir, we've come to know a good bit more about the conditions under which these rumors spread, and especially about the ways in which early anthologies of Kabir's poetry took shape. That doesn't get us back to 'the real Kabir.' Nothing ever will. But it does get us close enough that we can see how people saw him within a century of his own lifetime.

The Early Collections

Kabir had an enormous impact on the life of his times. As in the case of Ravidas, the leatherworker poet who was somewhat his junior, or Tulsidas, the liberal Brahmin whose Hindi version of the *Rāmāyaṇa* later became North India's single most important religious text, the fact that he lived in Banaras meant worlds. It meant that his utterances could spread with a speed and authority that would otherwise have been hard to envision. Then as now, Banaras was a major center of learning, trade, and pilgrimage. Words spoken there had built-in resonance as students, businessmen, performers, and religious travelers moved in and out of the city to locations all over India and even beyond. It was the perfect pulpit.

Evidently Kabir's words were quite unforgettable. Within a century of his death people were writing them down many hundreds of miles away, in Rajasthan and the Punjab. They came in three literary forms, each rhymed and possessing distinctive metrical arrangements:

1. *dohās* (two-liners) or *sākhīs* (witnessings), also called *śaloks* by the Sikhs—terse epigrammatic couplets that can be either recited or sung;

2. *ramainīs*—rhymed lyrics in *caupāī* meter that end in a couplet (*dohā*); and

3. *pads* (verses) or *śabdas* (words)—sung compositions whose length could vary from four verses to twelve or more. Each begins with a title verse that also serves as refrain.

Only the last of these made it into the Sen>Tagore>Bly corpus to any perceptible degree, and because the medium definitely conditions the message, that's important. What's said cannot always be sung, and vice versa. Bly's Kabir, moving with the dominant spirit of the *pad* or *śabda*, is intrinsically lyrical, though other Kabirs manage to subvert the form, making the singing sing against itself.

As this implies, medium and message are closely related but not the same, and in fact collections of Kabir's poetry that have survived from the early years tend to display quite distinct personalities, depending on how and where they were sung and who was doing the collecting. The great divide emerges between collections that were made in west-central India—in Rajasthan or the Punjab—and those that were made farther east, nearer to Kabir's own home in Banaras. The western Kabir is far more intimately, devotionally (*bhakti*) oriented than his eastern counterpart,[3] though it would be wrong to paint the contrast black and white. East or west, Kabir retains a certain bodily focus and critical edge that sets him apart from other poet-saints of his time.

Still, the regional difference is important, and within the western branch of the 'family' of remembered Kabirs one can discern an additional divide. Collections made by the Sikhs differ in their overall tone from those made by Vaishnavas, that is, worshipers of Krishna and Rām and their consorts.[4] The Sikhs' Kabir often sounds like a down-to-earth householder, while the Vaishnava Kabir is more easily swayed by love's intensity. 'Intensity,' in fact, is the term Bly uses to translate *bhakti*, and of all the poetry collected in the early stages, it is this western, Vaishnava Kabir who bears the closest relationship to his.

The Banarsi Kabir is quite different. This is the Kabir remembered and indeed worshiped in the Kabir Panth—'Kabir's Path,' a mixed community of ascetics and householders, mainly from humble backgrounds, who were responsible for assembling the poetry collected in a volume called the *Bījak* ('Inventory' of poems or 'Guide' to where treasure may be found). Here we find in much purer form the salty, confrontational Kabir, the man of 'rough rhetoric,' as Linda Hess has said. He goads, he berates, he challenges. Confident of his own oral capacities, he dismisses anything written on paper along with the self-important personages who present themselves as custodians of those dusty documents. Muslim or Hindu, Qazi or Brahmin, they're all cut from the same cloth, and yogis are no better—maybe even worse. This *Bījak* Kabir makes precious little reference to any deities. Rām comes in—but only as a name, a general designation for God—and Krishna, like Shiva, is absent except in jest or in denial. As for goddesses like Durgā or Shakti with their taste for blood-sacrifice, he treats them as enemies.[5]

Oddly enough, the eastern manuscripts, the ones called *Bījak*, are much younger than their western counterparts. One might have thought that since Kabir came from Banaras (no dispute about that) the local traditions would have produced a longer record, but they did not. The earliest extant *Bījak* manuscript dates only to 1805. Perhaps the poor, lower-caste social location of the Kabir Panth—these were his people—made such a record impossible. In the early centuries, at least, its members would have been far less likely to be literate than those who transmitted the more catholic 'western' bhakti strand. Linda Hess and Shukdev Singh estimate that the Kabir-Panthīs made their first structured, written collections of Kabir poetry—the earliest *Bījak*—in the late seventeenth century, but there is no record to prove it.[6]

The first Sikh collection of Kabir poems was apparently made in the early 1570s (the so-called *Goindvāl Pothīs*)—fifty poems that swelled to 220 by 1604, when they were inscribed in the Sikhs' *Kartārpur Granth*.[7] These manuscripts attest to the fact that poems attributed to Kabir were sung alongside compositions of other poets, especially the Sikh Gurus themselves, in congregational worship, as they still are today. The first Vaishnava collection was smaller—fifteen poems, which appear alongside those of other bhakti poets in a manuscript compiled in Fatehpur, near Jaipur (Rajasthan), in 1582.[8] As we have seen, the manuscript is constructed in such a way as to make it clear that these poems formed part of a still earlier manuscript that the scribe/editor was bringing into conversation with two others, the latter being much more consistently Vaishnava and oriented especially to Krishna. A subsequent western collection, assembled for the liturgical use of followers of the poet-saint Dādū, who was a cotton-carder, dates to 1614, and a number of other Dādū-Panthī manuscripts anthologizing

Kabir appear in the course of the seventeenth century.[9] So we see that early on, Kabir found himself in quite diverse company. He was a linchpin in all kinds of anthologies of bhakti verse intended to be sung.

It would be fair to ask how many poems included in *The Kabir Book* can be found in the early manuscripts we have just reviewed. This ought to give some sense of how well Bly's Kabir corresponds to the Kabir at least some people knew and loved in the sixteenth and seventeenth centuries—people who, like us, lived outside Banaras itself. Of the 44 poems published in the first edition of *The Kabir Book*, only a single one appears in the early, dated manuscripts that form the basis of Winand Callewaert's *The Millennium Kabīr Vāṇī*—all of them 'western' by that token. The golden poem is number 6, 'Why should we two ever want to part?,' which appears in the Rajasthani stream but not the Punjabi. This very low match is not Bly's fault, of course—if it's a fault at all. It just means that the Sen>Tagore>Bly lineage can't rightly be regarded as giving us 'the authentic songs' that Tagore and Underhill believed it did.[10] It makes us ask again what we might mean by 'authentic,' and how much that question really matters.

Who was Kabir?

There is no way of knowing who Kabir was apart from the history of his reception. As we have seen, that history is far from being just a fog, thank goodness, but it does encode a fundamental problem. Even if we grant that the *Bījak* owes its origins to an oral tradition that goes back much earlier than its manuscripts, how are we to deal with the fact that the western and eastern traditions don't converge on a single group of poems, a corpus we could then take as representing the 'real' Kabir? This will always present us with a puzzle, and a similar set of puzzles emerge when we look at the legends surrounding Kabir's life—legends that date back to the last years of the sixteenth century. Of course, there are those who say they know the sound of his voice. The great mid-twentieth-century scholar Hazārīprasād Dvivedī was a good example of this, and many people accepted his bhakti version of Kabir, a personality he believed to have been shaped by the teaching Kabir received from his guru, the Brahmin reformer Rāmānand.[11] Others also know the sound of the Master's voice. The blind Rajasthani performer Birjāpurī Mahārāj, celebrated for his renditions of Kabir, says, 'If a *vāṇī* (poem) has a deep meaning, then of course it is Kabīr's; if not it is only an imitation.'[12] Unfortunately, the Kabir who emerges from this act of determined listening turns out to be substantially different from Dvivedī's. So it won't do to say, as another scholar has, that we must 'take Kabīr at his word and in his context.'[13] Which word? Which context?

Let's start with Rāmānand, since he is so important to anchoring Kabir in a lineage that will serve to define him. The hilarious story of Kabir's initiation by Rāmānand—he arranged for the great man literally to stumble over him as he made his way to bathe in the Ganges at dawn—is one of the central motifs of his hagiography. 'Rām!' shouted Rāmānand, and Kabir took it as his initiatory mantra. Tagore found Rāmānand in one of the poems he translated from the set provided by Kshitimohan Sen, and it reassured him that this guru-pupil connection was a historical fact.[14] But alas, a study of the old manuscripts unearths this poem nowhere, nor is Rāmānand's name found in any of the other old poems, as one might have expected if he was so important for Kabir.[15]

Alhough the Kabir authority David Lorenzen disagrees, I find no way to resuscitate this connection from the hagiography, either. Rāmānand solves too many problems on too little evidence. He supplies the missing link that would relate Kabir's non-theist 'eastern' Banarsi side to the theist bhakti personality so prevalent in manuscripts that show up farther west. He locates Kabir in a specific monastic lineage—the Rāmānandīs'—while also providing the means for him to have come from a Muslim family, as his name suggests, and then later be aligned by conversion with a kind of bhakti that at least some Brahmins could call their own. It's all too neat, and too unechoed in the poems themselves. I have to side with lower-caste critics who think the connection between Rāmānand and Kabir was just a pious invention, a way to deny Kabir his roots.[16]

Much more reliable is the general portrait given of Kabir in about 1600 by Nabhadas in his *Bhaktamāl* ('Garland of Saints'), even though his commitments too are Vaishnava and even specifically Rāmānandī. It is true that Nabhadas locates Kabir among the pupils of Rāmānand in a general listing he provides, but when he speaks of him directly, any sectarian interest falls away. He says Kabir rejected the Brahmin formulations that defined caste distinctions, along with the six schools of 'proper' philosophy and the idea that a man's life ought to follow a certain sequence. These were the fundaments of a *dharma* of caste and station (*varṇāśrama dharma*) that had become central to classical Brahminical thinking. According to Nabhadas, Kabir begged to differ. He believed it to be the exact opposite of true *dharma* if bhakti wasn't present on the scene.[17] His trademark conviction was that organized religion was worthless. 'Intensity,' as Bly calls it, was all that mattered.

Given his social location, it's no surprise Kabir might take this position, and it's notable that according to Nabhadas, he had no use for caste. As we learn from not a few of his poems, he was a Muslim weaver (*julāhā*), low on the totem pole of status. No surprise, then, that he should be considered authoritative by communities who tended to share his humble position, and his admirers also included the Jats, Punjabi farmers who were the backbone of the Sikh community and evidently considered themselves outside the pale of *varṇāśrama dharma*.[18] But let's not forget that lots of other people evidently also heard the call—Vaishnavas, certainly, and even Brahmins.

One important strand that emerges in early collections of Kabir's poems tends to get somewhat obscured by the contexts in which they are typically performed, and we need to grant its due before leaving the 'historical' Kabir. This is the fundamental debt Kabir owed to a community of yogis called Nāths, whose teaching crystallized an approach to the technology of bodily transformation that appears in his poetry time and again.[19] It is *haṭha yoga*, the stringent yoga of intense bodily discipline. Bly admits candidly that he steers clear of this dimension, which he refers to as 'the whole matter of Sakti energy.'[20] Yet as a system of thought and practice (one that Kabir himself never associates with Shakti), it seems to have been a key element in providing the sense of religious and metaphorical security we always associate with his name.

To get a sense of it, let us turn again to the earliest dated manuscript. There we read about a certain upside-down well:

दुभर पनीआ भरनि न जाइ मेरी बहुत त्रिषा गोबिन्द बिना न बुझाइ
ऊपर कूवटा लेज तलैहारी कैसे नीर भरै पनीहारी
निघय्यै नीर भयौ घट भारी गई निरास पांच पनिहारी
गुर उपदेस भयौं है नीर राम सरनि होइ न पीवहि कबीर

That water, so rare, so beyond being carried—
one cannot get one's fill.
My thirst is great
and won't be slaked without Govind.

The well is above,
  the rope extends below:
  How can the watercarrier
  ever hope to draw?
The water level drops,
  the waterpot grows heavy.
  The five watercarriers
  despair.
The water is full
  of the teacher's exhortations.
  But one who seeks refuge in Rām
  won't drink—Kabir.[21]

The 'rare, unbearable water' with which the poem begins almost certainly refers to introjected semen, sent up to the roof of the skull by means of yogic—perhaps Tantric—discipline. Because this water defies gravity, one cannot draw it with the senses ('the five watercarriers'), and for the same reason, one cannot get one's fill. It is mysteriously heavy: it overtakes the body. Kabir seems to know the whole Nāth Yogī routine, the husbanding of *kuṇḍalinī* energies, and to be comfortable with it—at least verbally. Then comes the surprise. He says, in closing, that he won't drink this water. Is he refusing the fulfillment of orgasm and ejaculation, as Tantric practitioners do? No, that's not what the words say. They say instead that he refuses 'the teacher's exhortations.' He refuses to accept, as the Nāth Yogīs put it, that

In the circle of ether is an inverted well that is the place of nectar.
He who has a guru drinks his fill; he who has no guru goes thirsty.[22]

Kabir would rather drink of Rām or Govind (Krishna). Time and again in poems from early manuscripts we meet this Kabir—a stalwart who seems to be bodily adept, a *haṭha yogī*, yet who identifies instead with the subtle inner guru, the True Guru who is also Rām/Govind. It's a bhakti reading of a Nāth Yogī base: a form of ease, spontaneity, and honesty (*sahaj*) that's simpler than the product of bodily hydraulics that serves as its primary metaphor. That form of discipline, at least as an end in itself, is not for him.[23] No wonder he can speak as he does about the yogis that fill the streets of Banaras:

का नागैं का बांधे चांम   जौ नहिं चीन्हसि आतमरांम
नांगे फिरें जोग जौ होई   बन का मिरग मुकुति गया कोई
मूँड़ मुड़ाएं जौ सिधि होई   सरगहिं भेंड़ न पहुँची कोई

बिंदु राखि जौ तरिऐ भाई तौ खुसरै क्यूं न परम गति पाई
कहै कबीर सुनौं रे भाई रांम नांम बिन किन सिधि पाई

Go naked if you want,
Put on animal skins.
What does it matter till you see the inward Rām?

If the union yogis seek
Came from roaming about in the buff,
every deer in the forest would be saved.

If shaving your head
Spelled spiritual success,
heaven would be filled with sheep.

And brother, if holding back your seed
Earned you a place in paradise,
eunuchs would be the first to arrive.

Kabir says: Listen brother,
Without the name of Rām
who has ever won the spirit's prize?[24]

Kabir in the Stream of Translation

We've been appealing to the earliest manuscripts in an attempt to approach the Kabir of history, and that's all we can do. But we've also seen that these manuscripts fail to speak in unison. There is no single Kabir. For all the stubborn sure-footedness built into his persona, he floats along on diverse streams of performance and reception.

The range of communities who have embraced Kabir is immense—low-caste and high-caste, ascetics and householders, rickshaw drivers and CEOs, and famously the Muslims and Hindus who are said to have fought over the privilege of disposing of his bodily remains: 'We'll bury them.' 'No, we'll burn them.' As 'the apostle of Hindu-Muslim unity' Kabir became Exhibit A in the Indian government's effort to encourage 'national integration'—while simultaneously a place was being made for him in the canon of Urdu literature that officially Islamic Pakistan wanted to claim as its national heritage.[25] In 2003 these two streams converged in a cassette tape in which Gulzar, the creator of several important Bombay film scripts, presents 'Kabir by Abida,' the brightest new star among Sufi performing artists in

Pakistan.[26] And when human rights organizations staged a musical event in the cavernous sanctuary of the Riverside Church in New York to benefit Muslim victims of Hindu violence in Gujarat, whose verse do you think they sang?

If Kabir remains a signal presence along the Muslim-Hindu faultline, he is no less important in ongoing debates about social inequality, caste discrimination, and the overall coherence of Indian society. B. R. Ambedkar, the Columbia-educated Dalit (erstwhile 'Untouchable') who became the principal architect of India's constitution and served throughout his life as the leading force in struggles to abolish caste and untouchability, used to mention Kabir as one of his prominent forebearers.[27] By contrast Hazārīprasād Dvivedī, one of the country's leading literary critics, insisted that Kabir learned his bhakti from a forward-thinking Brahmin in a moment of ultimate self-transformation. Far from being a voice of dissent, he exemplified for Dvivedī the common humanity that could and ought to flower in a single broad stream of Indian culture that made social and religious differences irrelevant. In a moment that galvanized intellectual Delhi in the late 1990s, the Dalit critic Dharmavīr struck back. This Dvivedī thing, he said, turning Kabir into a Hindu and giving him good manners by subjugating him to a Brahmin, was all hogwash.[28]

So where do we put Bly in this controversial global-historical mishmash? Clearly his lineage binds him to Tagore, and that tends to make his Kabir hover at a safe distance above any sectarian or social fray. After all, Bly could strip away Tagore's upholstery, but he was still left to choose among the pieces of furniture that Tagore had first selected. He was evidently less than thrilled with some of these. Compositions that required too much background; that seemed too long-winded; that were constructed as insoluble puzzles; that savored too much of drinking, madness, cosmology, or servitude; that were polluted by verbal whiffs of Christianity such as 'salvation' or 'deliverance'—all these went out the window. Even the relatively few examples of poems in which Kabir challenged the relevance of social distinctions were consigned to the dustbin, along with poems that pointed to the importance of good company. What emerges is a Kabir who stands for self-reliance (remember Emerson?), principled disobedience (remember Thoreau?), and a set of practices that honors the meeting of mind and body and celebrates the intense emotions that connect them (Bly himself?).

Some of this instinctive editing on Bly's part takes us much farther than Tagore in getting a feel for the Kabir we meet in earlier collections of his poetry than the one Sen provided for Tagore. And that goes a long way toward explaining how Bly could play such a crucial role in making Kabir a global household name. But the rest was achieved by poetic genius and by taking a fair number of chances—as Kabir evidently did, himself.

A few newcomers mount the stage as Bly digs in and imagines what Kabir might have said to speakers of English living five hundred years after his death. The vocabulary of sadness and pain—that old Buddhist word *dukkha*—is distinctively Americanized as 'spiritual flatness' and 'constant depression.' Banaras and Mathura are transformed into places Americans might more likely have heard of—Calcutta and Tibet—and Tagore's 'bowers and groves,' still anchored in India, become 'canyons and pine mountains.' The Rockies? Almost every Indic word gets translated. Tagore's yogi (and Kabir's) becomes a 'spiritual athlete,' and 'the Supreme Brahmā' comes out as 'the Secret One inside us.' Sound matters a lot. *Purān kurān* may trip off the tongue in the original Hindi, but Tagore's literal rendering, 'the Purana and the Koran,' is far too flat for Bly. Better we should see them as 'the Sacred Books of the East'! Kabir, especially the Banarsi Kabir, had fun with his audiences, and Bly has fun with his.[29]

Sometimes you have to wonder if maybe he's gone too far. Because the discriminating *cakor* bird is said to survive only on moonbeams, Bly gives it a try as an owl. That works well in the West but Indians may rebel, since for them the owl is a symbol of blank-eyed stupidity. A diamond changes to a ruby. In a valiant effort to give the leaf of a lotus its due, Bly calls the flower itself a 'water rhubarb.' As for the Hindu forehead mark so ubiquitously familiar in India, it comes out looking like 'weird designs.' The drone instrument *tambūrā*, which Tagore couldn't resist calling a lyre (because it accompanies the voice? because of the way it's held?), goes a step further and emerges as a dulcimer. And the beautiful Guest who weaves in and out of *The Kabir Book* is even more elusive than Bly makes him seem. He's cobbled together from various sources in Tagore's translations and is nowhere to be found in originals—truly a guest![30]

In other instances, however, Bly hits the original nail squarely on the head. He takes a disembodied 'Lover' at the end of one Tagore poem and turns him (her?) into 'we.' And when he reverses Tagore's

'He is I' so that it comes out 'I am he,' it's at least as good a translation of the original *soham*, and it sounds a whole lot better. Still, the weight of change leans plainly toward invention.[31]

Let's not call these 'errors in translation,' though Bly himself suggests the phrase. Let's say instead that they mark a meeting of minds that Bly just couldn't resist. Our review of the very different ways Kabir has spoken over the centuries to other performers, other poets, shows that this is no anomaly. In the course of half a millennium many poets found themselves before audiences who were eager to hear the voice of Kabir, and they obliged by adding their own Kabirs to the common store. They must have felt they really spoke for him, like Bly.

In the end, I think, some of the Kabir-Panthīs had it right. They pictured Kabir as a force beyond time, the archetypal opponent of the demiurge Kāl, whose name means Time-and-Death.[32] It's Kabir versus Kāl in the world as we know it, and with Bly at his side, Kabir will be around for a good long time.

15

Kabir in his Oldest Dated Manuscript

'Kabir in His Oldest Dated Manuscript' is being published here for the first time. It owes its origin to a panel convened on 22 November 1998 at the annual meeting of the American Academy of Religion to celebrate the 600th anniversary of the year in which Kabir is traditionally considered to have been born. I am grateful to several persons in the audience, particularly John Carman, for their encouragement at that point, and to Gurinder Singh Mann, a fellow panelist, for enlightening discussions about several of the poems. Much later, in November 2003, Shukdeo Singh shared the fruits of his long experience reading manuscripts of Kabir and solved several intransigent problems of interpretation.

600 years of Kabir—that was the landmark we came to in 1998, and the number has real majesty. As a commemorative marker for the year of Kabir's birth, it carries none of the difficult associations that would have come with 500, taking us back to Vasco da Gama's arrival on the west coast of India. 600 is a fine multiple of 60, the age at which one can celebrate a life well spent. And it reminds us of another multiple of 60, too: the 120 years Kabir-Panthīs today traditionally claim as the length of their founder's life. If the memory of Kabir's death date (1518 CE) is in fact accurate—and David Lorenzen has given us several good reasons why this may be so[1]—then this magical 120-year unit would explain how we got back to 1398 in the first place. So 600 celebrates a great life, even if one doubts it stretched all 120 years back to 1398. To judge by the wide dispersion of manuscript evidence, it seems that by the end of the sixteenth century lots of people living in North India had heard of Kabir. His name means 'great,' and he *was* great.

Yet the early anthologies and biographies that display Kabir inevitably show that his greatness was perceived differently by different people.[2] Here I would like to present the view of Kabir's greatness that appears in the earliest reliably dated manuscript in which his name appears.

Kabir at Fatehpur

This is the anthology of poetry—mainly Brajbhāṣā poetry— that was prepared in the town of Fatehpur, located northwest of Jaipur in Shekhavati (now Sikar) district, in the year 1582 (VS 1639).[3] There is good reason to believe that another anthology, the *Goindvāl Pothīs* from the Punjab, may actually have been compiled a few years earlier, as Gurinder Singh Mann has endeavored to show.[4] This is quite possible, and in any case the Goindvāl and Fatehpur collections are close enough to being contemporaneous that we should see them in relation to one another, although in a moment I will try to show that the Fatehpur manuscript embeds an even earlier anthology containing Kabir. We should also note another claimant to this early date—a manuscript of the hagiographical text *Nirbhayajñān* that was evidently listed in the 1909–11 *Khoj Reports* issued by the Kashi Nagaripracarini Sabha and assigned the date 1576 (VS 1633). This manuscript, however, like quite a number of others claimed in the *Khoj Reports*, has never emerged, and David Lorenzen is quite right to observe that its format—a conversation between Kabir and his alleged pupil Dharmadās—strongly suggests it must have been written later, in the eighteenth century.[5]

Of course, we do have biographical works on Kabir from almost that period. It would seem that both Anantdās's *Kabīr Parcaī* and Nabhadas's *Bhaktamāl* were composed not long after 1600, and a real wealth of Kabir poetry is found in the Sikh *Kartārpur Bīr* of 1604 (VS 1661). But as far as firm dates are concerned, the Fatehpur manuscript stands as the first wave in the flood. It contains fifteen *pads* attributed to Kabir, and they have not yet figured very importantly in scholarly discussions about who Kabir was. The single exception to this rule is the helpful comparison Winand Callewaert has made between one of the best known poems that appears at Fatehpur (Poem 4) and its versions in other early manuscripts.[6]

I outlined the contents of the Fatehpur manuscript in Chapter 3, but it's worth refreshing our memories as we meet it in this new context. I have already mentioned its date and provenance. This is the most important information divulged in any colophon, and this one has every look of authenticity. It gives just the range of information we expect in a colophon of the period to which it belongs. It is written in the same hand as the third section of the manuscript itself—the other two, perhaps written (very likely copied) somewhat earlier, bear the handwriting of another scribe. Also present is the seal of Mahārājā Rām Singh, which attests to the fact that this manuscript was acquired by the House of Amber (later Jaipur) in 1661. This accords well with both the geography and the date of the original colophon. For all these reasons no one, to my knowledge, has challenged the early date of the Fatehpur manuscript or its colophon.

The colophon tells us that the manuscript—or rather, its third part, since the handwriting changes between the second and third sections—was inscribed by a man named Rāmdās Ratan, who wrote at the behest of one Chītarjī, who was in turn the son of Rājśrī Naraharidāsjī. There is little other information about this Chītar, apart from an eighteenth-century genealogy confirming that he was Naraharidās's son.[7] We know a bit more about Naraharidās. Gopal Narayan Bahura has unearthed in the *Kyām Khāṅ Rāsā* a reference to one Naraharidās who owned land in Fatehpur at that time.[8] This social location is just what we might expect: the Fatehpur epithet *rājśrī* probably refers to this *ṭhākur* status, associating him with the Kachavāhā clan. It is interesting that Rāmdās Ratan himself, however, situates his literary moment in relation to the imperial Mughal throne. He says he lived during the reign of *pātisāh śrī akabara* (Akbar).[9]

Some years later, the *Kyām Khāṅ Rāsā* tells us, Naraharidās and his family fled from Fatehpur when it came under the control of Daulat Khān, an agent of Jahāngīr. The family settled in Loharu, and it is unclear what happened to the manuscript. All we know is that by 1661 it was in the hands of the royal house of Amber, who were, as is well known, the most important Rajput (and by the way, Hindu) allies of the Mughal court. Thanks to them, the manuscript has been preserved to this day. It was old enough—and evidently regarded as precious enough—to be included in the *khās mohar* ('great seal') collection within the royal Jaipur library, its *pothīkhānā*, where it keeps company with some extremely valuable illustrated manuscripts. In 1980, on the occasion of a state visit from the Prince of Wales, the Fatehpur manuscript joined some of its illustrated cousins in being taken out for a brief period of public inspection—and photographed. That made possible the publication of a fascimile edition not long afterward. For all this, we are indebted to the devoted, timely, and yes, clever work of the *pothīkhānā*'s fine librarian and scholar, Gopal Narayan Bahura, and his associate Kenneth E. Bryant of the University of British Columbia.

After brief invocations to Krishna and Rām, the Fatehpur manuscript introduces itself as presenting *kṛṣṇpadam sūrdās ke* ('Krishna Poems of Surdas'). Indeed, Surdas dominates the collection. The manuscript contains 239 poems bearing his signature—actually 262, but 23 of these are duplicates. But what is interesting for our present purpose is that the manuscript also contains 149 compositions attributed to other poets, in the following order of frequency:

Kānhāṅ	52
Kabir	15
Paramānand	13
Nāmdev	11
Raidās	8
Brahmadās	7

and so forth. Given that the family of Naraharidās was obviously devoted to Vaishnava poetry, as represented by Surdas, Kānhāṅ, Paramānand, and Brahmadās, it is striking that Kabir, Nāmdev, and Ravidas, whom we usually think of as *sant* or *nirguṇa* poets, also 'made the cut.' These latter poets appear prominently in the Sikh and Dādū-Panthī anthologies, where they largely part company with their Vaishnava peers. The *Pañcvāṇī* of the Dādū-Panthī canon omits Vaishnavas altogether, and only Surdas is represented in the Dādūite *Sarvāṅgī* of Gopāldās.[10] In the Sikh scriptural tradition we find only the faintest trace of Surdas and Mirabai, and no mention at all of Vaishnava poets such as Paramānand and Kānhāṅ.

The internal organization of the Fatehpur manuscript gives us a hint about how these '*sants*' (to use a designation that became commonplace only much later[11]) came to be included. The Fatehpur manuscript's own enumeration of the poems it contains suggests that its scribes worked from three earlier collections of poetry. The manuscript returns twice to the number 1 and then proceeds,[12] and both times at points when it seems the scribe in question intends to start afresh. At the first transition point (after *pad* 106) the scribe's identity is anonymous but consistent: the handwriting does not change. But when the second renumbering from 1 occurs (after *pad* 284), so does the handwriting. This time Rāmdās Ratan is responsible.

The first and third groupings of poems are devoted exclusively to Surdas, but the intermediary one is different, as we have seen. It is an anthology comprising 178 poems—or by its own numbering, 183, since the lengthy *sūr pacīsī* is apparently assigned six consecutive numbers.[13] It includes a great many Sur poems, some of which are duplicate poems that appear elsewhere in the manuscript, another broad hint that the scribes of Fatehpur were copying not one but several earlier manuscripts—at least three. In this inner anthology, the Sur poems begin with number 2 and continue for 50 poems without a break; nine others straggle along later. This is a substantial number, so it's no wonder the first Fatehpur scribe thought it natural to include this anthology as one of his resources for surveying *kṛṣṇapadam sūrdās ke*. Luckily—and perhaps significantly (see Chapter 3)—he did not extract the Surdas poems recorded there, but apparently copied the whole anthology. Launched primarily by Sur, this hypothetical earlier collection of *pads* concluded with a set of fourteen compositions attributed to Kānhāṅ (158–81); and two other clusters of Kānhāṇ poems appear along the way (56–65, 132–44).[14]

As for poems attributed to Kabir, these are somewhat more evenly distributed throughout the anthology (see Table 15.1). They occur one or two at a time, except for a group of six which fall between numbers 145–51 (one poem of Pūrandās intervenes as number 150). But I would especially call attention to the fact that the very first poem in the anthology belongs to Kabir. It almost sounds as if one could scarcely think of having an anthology of vernacular devotional poetry at that time and not begin with Kabir. I am reminded of a much later manuscript, the wonder from Datia that qualifies as the world's largest *Sūrsāgar*, undated but perhaps belonging to the nineteenth century. It contains some 10,000 poems attributed to Sur (there is some internal repetition, to be sure)—and to introduce it all, someone has affixed a poem of Kabir on the front page.[15] Recall that in the Sikh scriptures as well, with the exception of the Sikh Gurus themselves, Kabir leads the pack.

Who is this Kabir, as reflected in the Fatehpur manuscript? Given the work's general orientation, it will come as little surprise that he feels a good bit more Vaishnava that some other Kabirs we know and love. To take an extreme example, if we look at the last poem of Kabir that appears in this anthology (15),[16] we find a composition addressed to a deity the poet calls variously Murāri, Mādhav, and, interestingly, Viṭṭhal (*bīṭhulā*). Furthermore, the language of address is governed by an expression that we meet many times in Vaishnava poetry: *bali jāu* ('I sacrifice myself,' or in the translation I will venture below, 'I give up').[17] The Vaishnava orientation is also visible at many other points in the Fatehpur hymns attributed to Kabir. We have poems addressed to Murāri (9), Govind (5), Krishna (6), Hari (1, 12, cf. 9), Bhagavān

TABLE 15.1: Kabir Poems in the Fatehpur Anthology

Poem	*Pad**	Page	Refrain (*tek*)	KV #	KV p.†
1	1	76	सरवर कै तति हंसनी तिसाई	311	395
2	73	134	कारनि कौन सवारै देही		
3	74	135	राम राम ए भनि राम चितावनि		
4	87	143	राम वान अनियारे तीर	262	333
5	88	144	दुभर पनाई भरनि न जाइ	150	188
6	106	155	अमर मेरी काया नरु जानै		
7	113	160	स्वाद पतंग परै जलि जाई		
8	124	165	जिहि नर राम भगति नहि साषा	124	154
9	125	166	जलि जाऊ ऐसौ जीवन		
10	145	186	मेरी मति भौंरी रामु बिसार्‍यौ	232	294
11	146	186	तूं गारुडी मै विष का माता	145	183
12	147	187	अब मरिबौ तब जइगो कहं		
13	148	187	रवि रह्यौ एकु अवरु नहि हुआ		
14	149	188	ना मनु रहै न घरु होइ मेरा		
15	151	189	कहा करौ कैसे तरौ भवजल निधि भारी	69	90

* The enumerations given here apply to the second sequence of poems found in the Fatehpur anthology. The *pad* number refers to that, using the numbers assigned by the original scribe. Page numbers have been assigned by Bahura and Bryant.

† KV refers to Jayadev Siṃh and Vāsudev Siṃh, *Kabīr Vāṅmay*, vol. 3: *Śabad* (Varanasi: Viśvavidyālay Prakāśan, 1981). The first KV listing gives the number assigned the *pad* (*śabad*) in question; the second gives the page on which it appears. I cite this only as a sort of reference-of-first-resort to printed editions. If no KV number is assigned, I do not believe the poem in question can be found in that volume, but in at least two additional cases it can be found elsewhere: for poem 2 see Vaudeville, *Weaver*, pp. 250–1; for poem 9 see note 30.

(13), and—again interestingly—Paramānand (14). In one poem, where an interlocutor is called for, the name Gopāl is chosen (9). And in many places, as we might expect, we find the broad designation Rām (3, 4, 5, 7, 8, 9, 10).

Although the manuscript's opening invocation, presumably offered by the scribe of the first two sections, is to Rāmacandra, this 'Rām' of the Kabir poems has a wider range. On one occasion, it is subsumed in 'the name of Rām' (7). On another, it occurs in conjunction with the verb 'mumble' or 'repeat' (*rāmu japata*, 10). On a third, it forms part of the phrase *rām bhakti* (*rāma bhagati*, 8). And on a fourth, it seems to be understood as synonymous with 'Hari' (9). Surely this is Vaishnavism, but in a far broader sense than you might mean, say, if you were describing collections of poetry designed to be sung in a temple associated with one of the major Braj *sampradāys*. Those Haridāsīs, Rādhāvallabhīs, Caitanyites, and Puṣṭimārgīs would count as Vaishnavas in a narrower sense; in their ritual personae they are specifically Krishnaite. Our scribe does indeed invoke Krishna and seems to title his work after him, but he invokes Rām as well, and the poems he includes in the middle section of his manuscript suggest that he understands Vaishnavism (if he would use the term) in quite a catholic way.[18]

At the same time, however, he stands at some remove from the '*sant* synthesis' we are accustomed to hearing so much about.[19] To take one indication, there is an almost complete absence of Islamic or otherwise Urdu or Persian vocabulary in the language of the Fatehpuri Kabir. This Kabir is hardly 'the apostle of Hindu-Muslim unity,' as he was called in the subtitle of an important book published in the late 1970s and portrayed in a serial that made its appearance on national Indian television a decade later.[20] He is not even the common *enemy* of Hindus and Muslims (or rather Turks), as we might expect on the basis of some of the best known utterances attributed to him, since he makes no reference to either group in the Fatehpur poems. We simply do not meet any *qāzīs* here, even as the butt of criticism, and when he does on one occasion summon a pundit to the bar (12.3), calling him 'brother' (12.2), the man's identity as a Hindu seems not to be at issue. Not once in these poems do we find the celebrated face-off that animates a number of famous Kabir compositions, with Hindus and Muslims arrayed on opposite sides of the caesura only to join common cause as Rām-Rahīm or Allah-Rām before the poem ends—or to be dismissed equally with a stroke of Kabir's sharp tongue.[21] This Hindu/Muslim program is one of the aspects of Kabir that Nabhadas most celebrates in his description of Kabir, probably written sometime between 1600 and 1625, so its absence in the Fatehpur collection is striking.[22] Here we simply do not find the Kabir who talked of yogis, *mahants*, and *śāktas*; of *miyāṅs*, *sultāns*, and *mullāhs*. The whole fabulous street-scene panoply of Banaras is absent, and if Kabir was a weaver, a *julāhā*, you would never know it from the Fatehpur collection.

Instead, we seem to find ourselves well within the boundaries of some sort of 'vulgate' Vaishnava milieu—and yet, with some interesting twists.[23] I'll attempt to portray this Kabir by presenting and translating all the poems included in our fifteen-poem corpus, but in two stages. First, I'll simply lay a third of the poems on the table, hoping to convey a sense of the general run of the collection. Then I'll double back and consider the remainder thematically. In doing so, I'll start at the most 'Vaishnava' end of the spectrum we've been considering and work my way across to the end that many scholars think of as being richly informed by Kabir's encounters with the Nāth Yogīs.[24] My hope is that this approach will give us a feel for the range of this early collection, but also a sense of its particular emphases.

Six Poems: A Sampler

Without comment or gloss, let me invite you to sample six of the poems that appear in the Fatehpur manuscript. I'll give them in the order they appear, skipping those we will consider in greater detail later.

Poem 2: rāg soraṭh

कारनि कौंन सवारे देही अंति भसम जरि हवैहै षेही
कोटि जतन करि दह मुड्डाई अग्नि दहै कै जंजु कषाइ
दूध दही घृत देहे मुड्डाई अंति कालि नाटी मै जाई
बहुत जतन करियो तन पाल्यौ सो तन देष्यौ बाहरि जाल्यौ
माथै रचि रचि बांधते पाग तिस सिर चिंचु सवारी काग
कहि कवीर जिन पांवै चूरी तिन सौ कहा अभै पदु दूरी

You've got yourself a body, and you're mounting it for a ride—
Big deal! When your time is up, it's only ash from the fire.
Thousands of times you've tried to stuff that yawning pit,
but once you reach the pyre, it's the flames that get to eat.[25]

Fatten yourself up with yogurt, milk, and ghee:
   Where does it go in the end? Down the drain.
So much effort you've lavished on that frame:
   One look and they'll take it out to burn.
That tasteful turban you've wound around your brow:
   You know who's going to mount your head
      and peck at it? Some crow.
Kabir says, ply yourself with nice dried cakes
   as holy food, but what will it do
      to set you free from fear?

Poem 3: rāg gauḍī

राम राम ए भनि राम चितावनि   भाग वडौ पायौ छाडौ जिनि
ह्रिदै कवल मै राषि लु काइसि   पैम गांठि दीजे छुटि न जाइसि
असंत बचन सुनि डति रे भुलाइसि   असंत मुष मै ते विसरी जाइसि
अष्ट महासिधि नव मडारी   कहि कबीर हू दै देखि विचारी

Rām, Rām—with those words,
   Rām—with that thought,
Your fortune will be great:
   Don't lose it!
Hide it away deep in your
   lotus of a heart,
Tie the knot of love
   and don't let go.
Suppose you hear some worthless talk—
   get it out of your head:
Let your inward-facing face
   forget to register.
The eight great accomplishments,
   the nine baskets of treasure—
Kabir says, sight them from afar
   and fasten there.[26]

Poem 4: rāg gauḍī

राम वान अनीयारे तीर   जिहि लागै सो जानै पार [पीर]
तन मन षोज चोठ न पाउ   वौषद मूरी धसि कहा लगाउे [लगाउ]
एक भाइ दीसै सब नारी   ना जानै कोई राम पिआरी
कहत कबीर जाकै माथै भाग   ना जानौ कोई लेइ सुहग [सुहाग]

Rām is an arrow, the strangest arrow:
   Whoever gets hit turns saint, feels pain,
But for all you might try to search body and soul,
   you still won't find the wound,
So how are you going to find the place
   where the poultice needs to go?
Women, you know—they all look the same,
   so how to determine which one Rām loves?
Kabir says: Fortune must be written on her brow,
   but I don't know who gets to be the bride.

Poem 7: rāg bilāval

स्वाद पतंग परै जलि जाई   अनहल चित्त उवी न रहाई
किते मूये मरहेगे केते   मूरिष लोग अजहु नहि चेते
माया कै रस चेत न देष्यौ   हूै नहि जात एक नहि पेष्यौ
तंत मंत वौषद सब माया   राम कै नाम कबीर हि गाया

That taste: for its sake
   the moth heads for the fire.
That fire: there's no way
   to stay conscious there.[27]
How many deaths died?
   How many yet to go?
People are so dumb. Their minds
   just can't get the point.
The mind cannot see it's tasting
   Māyā's fake flavor.
It just doesn't happen.
   The truth never dawns.
Tantras, mantras, medicines—
   fakes, one and all—
And only Kabir is left around
   to sing the name of Rām.

Poem 10: rāg āsāvarī

मेरी मति बौंरी रामु बिसार्‍यौ   हौं किहि बिधि रहनि रहौ रो
सासु का दुषी ससुर की प्यारी   जवे कै नाम डरौ रे
नणद सहेली गरब गहेली   देवर कै विरहि जरौ रो
   मेरी मति बौंरी रामु बिसार्‍यौ

बापु साव का करति लराई　　माया कै संगि रहौंगी
　तब हौ पियहि पिचारी रे
यह संसारु पंच कौ डगरा　　डगरति जनमु गवायौ
कहत कबीर सुनहु रे लोगौ　　मै रामु जपत सवु पायौ

My mind's gone mad
　forgetting Rām.
　　How can I manage to stay alive?
I'm my mother-in-law's torture,
　my father-in-law's beloved,
　　and I fear my husband's elder brother.
Sisters-in-law, girlfriends—a haughty, grabby lot
　and I'm burning with yearning
　　for my husband's younger brother.
　　　My mind's gone mad forgetting Rām.
I've set the father at war with his young buck son,
　sticking close by Māyā's side,
　　hoping to be my lover's bride.
This world we're in is a winnowing basket
　where they shake the five elements:
　　I've shaken away my life.
Kabir says: Hey you people, try to hear:
　Repeating Rām's name
　　I've found what's real.[28]

Poem 13: No rāg specified

रवि रह्यौ एकु अवरु नहि हुआ　बुडि गई अगिनि न निकसै धुंआ
जलि गई बाती तेल निषूटा　　बजै न मंदलु नदु पै सूता
टूटी तारन बजै रबाबु　　जानि बिगास्यौ अपनौ काजु
कहत कबीर छाडहु अभिमानु　　भगतहि दूरि नही भगवानु

The sun's still here,
　but everything else is gone.
The fire's burned out.
　There isn't even smoke.
The wick is at its end.
　There's nothing left of the oil.
The troupe is silent and the tightrope man
　has got himself tangled in the rope.

The strings are broken
  that it takes to play the *rabāb*:
Who did it? The player himself—
  ruined his own job.
Kabir says, the time's now come
  to set aside your pride.
The love of God's not far away
  and neither is God.

The 'Vulgate Vaishnava' Question

Much of what we hear in this chorus of poems is familiar to an ear attuned to Kabir: the bluntness, the preoccupation with body and death, the wiles of Māyā, the in-laws, the praising of Ram's name. But in the remainder of the collection we meet some features that are not so widely shared in the broader Kabir corpus. Since I have announced that a certain Vaishnavism figures importantly among these, let's proceed immediately to a poem that makes this hard to miss: *pad* 15. There we meet the theme of a life ill spent, the sort of thing we found in poems 2 and 7 and something one could also find in the *vinaya* poetry of the *Sūrsāgar* (e.g., *Sūr's Ocean* §389, 401 = NPS 77, 154) or the *Vinayapatrikā* of Tulsidas (e.g., VP 71, 81). It's *sant* poetry in all cases, but this time, like poems in the *Sūrsāgar* or the *Vinayapatrika*, the theme is given a distinctively Vaishnava inflection.

Since we are working from a single document in this chapter (and not a critically edited version of several, as with Surdas), I retain in translation whatever repetitions the manuscript itself presents. When the scribe gives us all or part of the title line as a refrain, I show that repetition with italics. In doing so I don't mean to suggest that the refrain would only have been sung at this particular point; I'm merely conveying the shape of the manuscript as it appears on the page. That, in turn, reminds us that this written source is conscious of its oral underpinnings. Either it anticipates performance by means of this cue to the singer ('Sing the refrain now'), or it recalls a performance that had transpired before it attained written form, or both. If by means of these repetitions the scribe is gesturing to a prior oral source, that source must have been at least one step removed from the Fatehpur manuscript itself. Two examples of dittography at the right margin—one in the following poem (the syllable *ja*, 15.4), one elsewhere (*ka*, 6.2)—strongly suggest that this scribe's immediate source was written. Here then is our 'most Vaishnava' poem:

Poem 15: rāg bilāval

कहा करौ कैसे तरौ भवजलनिधि भारी
राषि राषि मुहि बीठुला तोहि सरनि मुरारा [मुरारी]
कहा करौ कैसे तरौ भवजलनिधि भारी
बलि जाऊ घरु तजि बन षंडि जाइयौ षैयै चुनि लंदा
अजहूं बिकारू न छाडई पापी मनु मंदा
बलि जाऊ जीवत जनमु जोबनु गयौ कछु कीआ न नीका
यह जी निरमोल काकौं डालगि बीका
बलि जाऊ जीवत जनमु जोबनु गयौ कछू कीआ न नीका
यह जी रिमोल काकौं डालगि बीका
बलि जाऊ ज जन्म जन्म की बासना टूटी नहु जाई
अनक जतन करि राषीयै फिरि फिरि लपटाई
कहु कबीर मेरे माधवा तोहि सरब बिआपी
तोहि समान नहि को दयाल मोसा नहि जावी

What can I do?
How can I cross
this heavy sea of being?
Save me, save me, Viṭṭhal.
Shelter me,
Murāri.
What can I do?
How can I cross
this heavy sea of being?
I give up:
I've left my home,
gone to the forest,
chewed on roots—
All in vain.
I couldn't leave
my sinner's mindlessness.
I give up:
My life, my birth,
and youth are gone.
I've done nothing good.
This priceless life—
how have I spent it?
Poured it out for what?

I give up:
    The leftover cravings
        of birth after birth—
            I couldn't break free.
    How many many
        many times I tried,
            but they just kept sticking to me.
Says Kabir:
    Oh my Mādhav, everything
        there is, is shot through
            with you.
    None is your equal, merciful one—
        but as for me,
            I'm through.[29]

Several other Fatehpuri Kabir poems run in this same general vein. One is unusual and a little confusing because the poet addresses himself to someone named Gopāl, who apparently gets his name from a familiar designation for Krishna. Or does he mean Gopāl in a literal sense, someone who is 'guardian of the senses'? If so, this Gopāl has surely failed on guard duty: Kabir reprimands him for forsaking Rām. The last line in the poem, strangely abrupt, continues to identify the Vaishnava/Krishnaite title Murāri with Rām, so it doesn't seem that the poet is here setting the Rām and Krishna milieus in opposition. And his mention of Shiva's devotion (*bhagati* < *bhakti*) to Rām, as attested in the *Rāmāyaṇa*, makes it clear that Rām doesn't function here merely as a name. It's much more Vaishnava than that.[30]

Poem 9: rāg gauḍī

जलि जाउ अैसौ जीवना	जिहि राम परीति न होई
गुपाल करि करि झूठी कामना	पूजहु देव अनेका रे
एकु न सूजौ रामैया	जाकी काछी भगति महेसा रे
गुपाल जिउ माषामधा संचवै मधु	महा या हरि लै जाई रे
अध लै रामु न चेतियौ	पटि गुणि गोल सुनाई रे
गुपाल कहु कबीर चित चंचला	मन की वृथा निवारी रे
बहुरि न मिलै मुरारी रे	

Is there a life without the love of Rām?
    Go and throw it in the fire!
Gopāl, you whined and whined your desires,
    addressed your prayers to numberless gods,

But never managed to sulk your way to Rām.
    Shiva's love should have showed you how.
Gopāl, the bees go out and gather more honey
    but the beekeeper meanwhile spirits it away:
Idiot, you never gave a single thought to Rām,
    though decent people told you how to try.
Gopāl, says Kabir, the intellect is fickle—
    take away the stuff that jams the mind.
        Murāri doesn't wait for a second time.[31]

Then there is a poem like *pad* 14, which presents a different sort of challenge to a Vaishnava interpretation. This too is a lament. Kabir reports wistfully that neither mind (*manu*) nor house (*gharu*) remain to him, neither the life of the householder nor that of the hermit. He's homeless and he needs a home:

Poem 14: rāg gauḍī

ना मनु रहै न घरु होइ मेरा   इति मन घर जारे बहुतेरा
घरु तजि बनि षडली आबास   घरु बनु देषौ दोऊ है ऊदास
जरा मरण तन अधिक बिआपु   सो घर करहु रे न सोक संतापु
दास कबीर सरणि निजु बंदा   तूं घर महि घरु दे परमानंदा

My mind is gone
    My house gone too—
These minds, these houses: good for what?—
    To be charred and charred yet again.
I left my house, I built myself
    a place to live in the woods,
but look at them now—the house, the woods:
    both of them abandoned, lost.
Look who's living in this body now:
    feverishness and death.
Make me instead a house that's something more
    than the burn that comes from mourning the past.
Kabir the servant says:
    Give me shelter—I'm your slave—
A house housed in your house,
    Paramānand, Joy-That-Lasts.

The last word in this poem is slightly ambiguous. *Paramānand* may mean 'the highest joy' in a non-theistic sense—'the joy that lasts'—

or it may refer to the giver of that joy, the Person in whom it is possible. Because Paramānand is such a frequent designation for a personal God, and because other poems in the Fatehpur manuscript lean toward a theism of this type, I have followed that interpretation here too. But as one senses in the translation, the joy that pertains to the giver bleeds over into the gift.

Similar sentiments are expressed in poem 8, but not in such a clearly autobiographical fashion. Here Kabir gives voice to the common idea that anyone who neglects a life of devotion wastes a life—not just one life, in fact, but all the lives it took to earn this human birth. Here again, such devotion or love (bhakti) is especially tagged to Rām (*jihi nara rāma bhagati nahi sāṣī / janama te vasana mūvau aparādhī*). While this poem feels less like autobiography than some of the others we've discussed—certainly it is less in the nature of lament—it has a definite thematic parallel in poem 9, which we have already quoted. Poem 8 is shorter and simpler, however, and it has a special interest because it supplies a motive for Kabir's own chosen vocation as a poet:

Poem 8: rāg gauḍī

जिहि नर राम भगति नहि साषी   जनम ते कस न मूवौ अपराधी
जिहि कुल प्रतु न ग्यान बिचारी   विधवा कस न भई महतारी
बहुते गरभ पकै नहिं बांध्यो   सूकर जन्म जीव जगि साध्या [साध्यो]
छिन महि बितसै यहै सरीरा   तिहि कारन पदु रचै कवीरा

A person who fails to witness the love of Rām
    in the living of this life, dies a criminal.
A family with a son who pays no mind to this—
    doesn't he make his mother a widow?
So many wombs, and he never grasps that tie.
    His accomplishment: to wake to the life of a pig.
It passes in an instant, this body of ours.
    That's why Kabir makes poems.[32]

The word I have translated as 'poems' is *pad*, the broad name of the genre in which Kabir is represented in the Fatehpur manuscript. These are poems of elastic length, usually four to eight lines, usually possessing an even number of verses. They are marked by an opening line that also serves as a refrain, by rhyme at the end of the verse, and by the insertion of the poet's signature toward the end. *Pads* here attributed to Kabir tend to be four or five verses long, and the four-verse length admirably suits a poem for performance in the *dhrupad* style, though we have no way of knowing how these *pads* were actually sung. Clearly, however, they contrast to the other major genre in which Kabir is remembered—the terse epigrammatic couplet normally called *dohā* but designated *salok* in the *Guṛū Granth Sāhib* and *sākhī* in many other collections of Kabir, including the *Bījak*.[33]

The word *sākhī* actually means 'witness,' and it is noteworthy that this is exactly the word Kabir uses when he speaks of witnessing in the first line of poem 8. Retrospectively, at least, it verges on being a kind of pun, and the same can be said for the word *pad.* In the poem at hand there is no question but that Kabir is referring to the act of 'making poems,' since he uses the verb *racai*, 'to compose.' But elsewhere—in poem 12, whose signature is missing but which the anthologist places in the very middle of the set he attributes to Kabir—the poet takes advantage of the broader meaning of the word *pad.*[34] In that instance it means 'foot' not in the poetic sense, but as a footprint, hence a step, station, or position. When poem 12 concludes with a reference to *hari pad*, then, it speaks simultaneously about a hymn to Hari and the state of being located in reference to him. In this broad sense of Vaishnavism, a name like 'Hari' designates the place where the world of speech and the world of being converge. Unfortunately, I have found it impossible to convey this meaning in translation:

Poem 12: rāg śrī

अबि मरिबौ तब जाइगो कहां घरु आंगनु द्वारु नहि जहा
सिषरन रूष बिरषु नहि भाई काकी छाह वैसै गोजाई
तुम्ह पंडित मैं मूरिष सनहु रे लोई हरि पदु बिरला बूझै कोई

Now you're going to die, and where will you go?
Where there's no house, no courtyard, no door.
Brother, don't expect to see a tree of fine desserts.
If you want to reap barley and wheat, you have to sow.
You're the pundit, and listen, I'm the idiot,
but Hari's state is rare—that much I know.

We can observe this word/world feature of 'vulgate Vaishnavism' in other places too. In Fatehpur poems attributed to Surdas there are several examples in which the term Śyām, a name of Krishna meaning 'dark,' does double duty, referring to him personally and at the same time to a set of moods in nature, especially those that come with the darkening skies of the monsoon. The Fatehpuri Kabir also sees Krishna in places beyond his narrative, proper-name location: he's out there in the world at large. In the final verse of poem 6, Kabir transports the name Krishna, which means 'black,' into the subtle syntax of yoga. This he does without leaving behind the strong associations with lotuses for which Krishna is celebrated in the narrative, *saguṇa* realm so deeply explored by Mirabai and Surdas: his lotus-eyes, his lotus-hands. Instead he extends the realm where lotus-Krishna can be found, moving it out of Braj and into the body of every true yogi.

In rendering the poem I have taken the liberty of conveying both the denotative and connotative senses of the verb *jānai*, 'know.' In Hindi usage this and related verbs are much farther toward the subjective end of the objective/subjective scale than their English counterparts. To know is sometimes just to think one knows:

Poem 6: rāg gauḍī

अमर मेरी काया नरु जानै
  जैसा घरी घरी वात दुपहर की छाया
    नर जानै
कछू एक कायौ क कछू एक रनै
  मुगधु न चेतै सिर ऊपरि मरनौ [मरनै]
सुपना फिरि फिर टेषि गरवानी
  अयाति सहीं पुनि जानी
जल बुद बुद देषीय संसार
  उपन षपत नहि लागै बार
पांच पषे सू एक सरीरा
  कृष्ण कमल दल भवर कबीरा
    नरु जानै
      अमर मेरी काया नरु जाने

'My body is immortal.' That's what people know.
  Moment to moment:
  something like that,
  a shadow at noon.
    That's what people think they know.
Body to body:
  some debt to be repayed—
  engrossing! So they don't perceive
  death overhead.

One dream, the next dream:
  after a while you're proud—
  ignorance!—
  and then the truth dawns.
Water drop by drop:
  look how the world revolves—
  arises, demises,
  never once sticks.
Five sides there are,
  but only one body.
  On the black lotus petal, the bee—
  Kabir.
    That's what people know—'My body is immortal.'
    That's what people think they know.

In other poems signed 'Kabir' one can sometimes do a more or less systematic yogic analysis by interpreting the black bee (*bhramar*) as the uncoiling *kuṇḍalinī* that tastes the various lotus *cakras* as it rises.[35] Here, however, the *cakra* in question would have to be a five-petaled lotus, a strange number because it is odd, and one that seems to transport us from the level of practice to that of metaphor, since the number five suggests the general rubrics of elements and senses. In a similar way, the word *pakh* (*paṣa*, v. 5), which I have translated 'petal,' would naturally be associated with the number two, not five: two sides of the body, first and foremost, and then that whole set of dualities that cluster around in-and-out (in reference to breathing) and up-and-down (in reference to the principal *nāḍīs* of yogic physiology). In this poem Kabir seems to be doing battle with that self-confident technology of body and spirit. He invokes it only to puncture it. He begins by quoting its partisans—'My body is immortal'—then proceeds in every verse but the last to convert its language of systole and diastole into two-part repetitions that suggest how hopeless any reliance on a bodily technology must be. *Gharī gharī* (v. 1), *kachū eka…kachū eka* (v. 2), *phiri phira* (v. 3), *buda buda* (v. 4): moment to moment, body to body, dream after dream, drop by drop—look where it all leads. What remains but Krishna?

For this reason I do not think it is mistaken to judge that a poem like this might belong in a collection of Vaishnava verse. At first one might have thought the anthologist was fooled by the chance occurrence of the word *kṛṣṇa* (black) in the last line—fooled into thinking this yogic poem had anything fundamental to do with Vaishnava devotion. But I'm not so sure. True, Kabir's black bee (*bhramar* > *bhavara*, v. 5) is hardly the same *bhramar* we find in Surdas or Nandadās or the tenth canto of the *Bhāgavata Purāṇa*—the bee of the *bhramargīt*—but Kabir seems to be adopting it with a full knowledge of its intimate connection to Krishna. In 'strict Vaishnava' poetry the shared blackness makes Krishna and his messenger Ūdho overlap in the perception of the Braj *gopīs*, but that overlapping blackness works in a no less convincing way to connect Krishna with the adept/devotee Kabir. If we were listening to the original, we would have to hear that final line in two ways. First, there would be the general 'black' way our translation has already implied, with Kabir merely acting as the narrator (*bhavara*... *kabīrā*). Second, a more specific thrust would be felt, whereby Kabir himself becomes the bee in question (*bhavara kabīrā*). Let me set these options side by side:

Five sides there are, but only one body. On the black lotus petal, the bee— Kabir.	Five sides there are, but only one body. On Krishna's lotus petal, the bee Kabir.

A similar pattern emerges in relation to the familiar trope of the *gāruḍī*, the Garuḍa-man (see Chapter 7). In a series of Surdas poems, the woman who finds herself bereft at the loss of Krishna (*virahiṇī*) complains of being crippled by the bite of a snake. Her body is pervaded by the poison of separation (*viraha*), and the snakebite curer must be called to lower the fever. This is the *gāruḍī*, so called because he wields mantras associated with Garuḍa, the bird-vehicle of Vishnu who is the legendary enemy of snakes. Of course, Krishna is perfect for this role because absence from him is the very poison that needs to be extracted. If he comes to the aid of one of the women who writhes in pain because of her love for him, his presence automatically cures her illness.

It is interesting to see what the Fatehpuri Kabir does with this trope. As with the *bhramar* bee, the specifically erotic Vaishnava associations fall into the background. The poison to be extracted is no longer *viraha* but *saṃsāra* itself—the same entity that was translated (or perhaps masked) by the phrase 'how the world revolves' in the poem we just surveyed.[36] As for the snake, it is no longer patterned after the lover god, a deviant male, but is represented as a woman (*sāṃpini*, 11.3)—the delusionary, *sāṃsāric* force Māyā, who appears in this poem as the hallucinations associated with snakebite (*māyā*, 11.2):

Poem 11: rāg gauḍī

तूं गारुडी मै विष का माता   का दन मिलहु मेरौ अबृंत दाता
सैसार भुवंगम डसी मेरी काया   इक दुषु ब्यापै अरु दारुण माया
  तूं गारुडी मै विष का माता
सांपिनि अधिक पिटारै जागै   जो सोवै तिसहीं पुनि लागै
कहत कबीर जिनि बुधि न विचारी   वालक मरत मुई महतारी

You're the snakebite curer. I'm a pot of poison.
  What will you give me, elixir-giver?
The serpent of this world has bitten my body—
  one pain everywhere, fearsome delusions.
    You're the snakebite curer. I'm a pot of poison.
This snake—she awakens in many a basket.
  If you sleep, she strikes again.
Kabir says, unless you hold this thought in your head,
  the child dies, and the mother's already dead.[37]

In this poem, as in the one we just discussed, resonances of *haṭha yoga* again appear. We hear of snake charmers' baskets, implying a *gāruḍī* who is more a snake charmer than snakebite curer, and this role does indeed fall within the broad semantic domain of the term *gāruḍī*. Is this an appeal to someone capable of causing snakes to rise out of baskets—the *kuṇḍalinī* in every body—and channeling them to disciplined erectness as they do? Or is this the reverse: an appeal to someone capable of calming or removing serpents and their dire effects? One catches a hint of the same ambiguous, volatile mix we meet with Krishna, who afflicts with separation and cures by erasing it. In this way, as several impressive Surdas poems make plain,[38] it replicates Vishnu's cosmic power. Vishnu produces Māyā from himself, and is by the same token capable of removing that *māyā*.

So this poem makes us confront the same question in a different guise. Is the *gāruḍī* metaphor a frayed thread that the anthologist has mistakenly grasped to draw this poem into the Vaishnava milieu, or is it something more substantial? Again I would answer that the poem itself forces us beyond the specific orb of yogic practice. In Kabir's depiction these baskets are not just bodies where the *kuṇḍalinī* arises;

they are instead births, whole lives, and again the Vaishnava connection seems far from being haphazard. The axis that connects Vishnu/Krishna to Māyā/Mohinī is really important. Because of it the name *gāruḍī* carries deep significance when the poet uses it to address the person after whom all other *gāruḍīs* are named. Elsewhere in the Fatehpur collection, Kabir ridicules too detailed a preoccupation with 'tantras, mantras, medicines' (*tanta manta vauṣada*, 7.4)—the toolbox of a real-life *gāruḍī*. The *gāruḍī* he addresses here is at once grander and simpler than that. But by the same token, Kabir doesn't collapse the tent and remove the force of these Nāth Yogī resonances, as he is effectively made to do in later versions of the poem which reduce it to name mysticism. These convert the last line into a paean of praise for 'tasting the juice of Rām'—that is, reciting his name over and over again.[39] As we know, the name of Rām means something in this Fatehpuri collection. One poem begins with the affirmation,

> Say Rām, Rām; think of Rām;
> and you will find great fortune.[40]

But names are not the be-all and end-all. The body is still there.

I hope that by now I've made a plausible case for the appropriateness of a 'vulgate Vaishnava' interpretation of the Fatehpuri Kabir, but we have yet to deal with the two poems that pose the greatest challenge to such a view. On a first reading, at least, both of them seem to fit quite comfortably in the Nāth Yogī niche and require very little in the way of a Vaishnava awareness. Both seem to go a step further than anything we have yet heard in describing the antidote to the 'poison' of *saṃsāra*, giving us a more specific notion of what the 'elixir-giver' (*aṃbṛta dātā*, 11.1) might have to dispense. In one poem this elixir is called 'the water of Hari' (*hari jalu*, 1.1)—there's that Vaishnava word, but perhaps it means something more generic. In another that last cloud disappears: the elixir is simply 'water' (*panīā*, 5.1), the water brimming with the guru's teaching (*gura upadesa bharyauṅ hai nīra*, 5.4). In both poems we enter upon the 'reversal language' (*ulaṭbāṃsī*) that was for many, evidently, Kabir's hallmark. Again, this was nothing that required Vaishnavism to interpret, although we have seen in the 'puzzle poems' of Surdas that conundrums could also be at home on Vaishnava turf.

Perhaps it is no accident that this 'yogi' side of Kabir comes forward in the very first poem attributed to him in the Fatehpur collection. I hinted early on that I thought this poem might have special significance, since it stands so isolated at the head of half a hundred compositions assigned to Surdas. Both it and poem 5 have as their central image not just reversal but upending, the basic meaning of the word *ulaṭ* (*ulṭā*) in common parlance. Do we have here a graphic portrayal of the central meaning of *ulaṭbāṃsī* that ties it once and for all to exactly that Nāth Yogī spiritual physiology I have been so eager to recast in a Vaishnava light? Listen to what this poem and its mate have to say:

Poem 1: rāg soraṭh

सरवर कै तटि हंसिनी तिसाई　जुगति बिना हरि जलु पीयो न पाई
कुंभ लीये ठाढीयै पनिहारी　लेज बिनु नीर कौ भरहि कैसै नारी
कूवौ लो रैलै षक वारी　उडि न सकै दोऊ पर भारी
कहत कबीर इक बुधि विचारी　सहज सुभाइ मुहि मिले वनवारी

At the edge of the lake
　a thirsty *haṃs* bird:
　But how, without the wherewithal,
　can she drink Hari's water?
There stands the watercarrier.
　She's brought her waterpot.
　But the well has lost its rope:
　how can she draw it up?
The bird can make it
　down the well to the water,
　but how can she fly back
　when her wings get weighed down wet?
Kabir says, just one thought
　to keep in mind:
　In what's natural—what's your own—
　you'll find The Forest One.

Poem 5: rāg gauḍī

दुभर पनीआ भरनि न जाइ　मेरी बहुत त्रिषा गोबिन्द बिना न बुझाइ
ऊपर कूवटा लेज तलैहारी　कैसै नीर भरै पनीहारी
निघय्यै नीर भयौ घट भारी　गई निरास पांच पनिहारी
गुर उपदेस भयौं है नीर　राम सरलि होइ न पीवहि कबीर

That water, so rare, so beyond being carried—
 one cannot get one's fill.
 My thirst is great
 and won't be slaked without Govind.
The well is above,
 the rope extends below:
 How can the watercarrier
 ever hope to draw?
The water level drops,
 the waterpot grows heavy.
 The five watercarriers
 despair.
The water is full
 of the teacher's exhortations.
 But one who seeks refuge in Rām
 won't drink—Kabir.

With this upside-down well and its unspeakably precious, even divine water, we are clearly in the realm of gravitational reversal that we associate with *kuṇḍalinī yoga*. It is because this water defies gravity that one cannot draw it with the senses; for the same reason, one cannot get one's fill.[41] Words for water (Hindi offers many more than English) positively fill these poems—so much so that one wonders if it is water in any plain sense at all. It certainly sounds like introjected semen, the bread and butter of Nāth Yogī practice, but the poet calls it something else. It's Hari in the first case (1.1), and Govind in the second (5.1).

In both poems the final line, the punchline, seems to hold a secret. In the first, we expect the holy grail—the object of the search for truth—to be some interior field of experience. We hear of 'what's natural' (*sahaj*) and 'what's your own' (*subhāi* < *svabhāv*), and we expect the final word, which names that state, to be along the same lines. That word is *vanavārī*, which can indeed indicate a flower garden—some central, carefully tended space that makes sense of the welter of experience.[42] In another poem attributed to Kabir, this is associated with a cultivation of attention to the sixteen-petaled lotus, presumably the fifth *cakra*.[43] But in both this poem and that, there is no relinquishing the idea that to enter such a place is to encounter the *vanavārī* who is The Forest One, namely, Krishna. Later versions of the Fatehpuri *vanavārī* line 'Rāmacize' it, so if you look in the printed editions, you'd find the words *rām rāī* rather than *vanavārī*.[44]

And with that, the 'pun' between Nāth Yoga and Vaishnavism would be gone.

The conclusion of the second poem in our final two-poem set presents a somewhat different scene. Here the poet surprises us by jumping ship at the very end, disowning any *sādhanā* (the 'wherewithal' the *haṃsinī* lacks in poem 1) or any 'teacher's exhortations' (*gura upadesa*, 5.4) geared to help one slip by the incapacities of the senses or elements ('the five watercarriers,' *pāñca panihārī*, 5.3). In doing so, he seems explicitly to challenge the wisdom of the Gorakh *bānī* that David White calls 'perhaps his most renowned':

गगन मंदल मैं ऊंधा कूबा तहां अमृत का बासा
सगुरा होई सु भरि भरि पीवै निगुरा जाई पियासा

In the circle of ether is an inverted well that is the place of nectar.
He who has a guru drinks his fill; he who has no guru goes thirsty.[45]

Kabir needs no such *guru upades*. This is spontaneity—'what's natural, what's your own'—with a vengeance, and what makes it possible is 'refuge in Rām' (*rāma sarani*, 5.4). One may fairly ask whether this is Tantra hiding under the skirts of bhakti, with a subtle meaning for those who understand the language and a gross meaning for those who don't. It surely sounds that way. In poem 1 he takes us to 'the edge of the lake' (*saravara kai taṭi*, 1.1), but what is this lake? Is it not the head (*sar* < *sir*)—the lake of the head, that is, the uppermost *cakra*, the inverted lotus *sahasrāra*? And is that not the upside-down well so clearly described in poem 5.2, which drips the refined 'water' of sublimated, redirected semen?[46] As for the female watercarrier, is she not the *kuṇḍalinī* that coils around the central *suṣumna* well-shaft, impossibly ready to gather that virile water?

And let's go a step further. Isn't Kabir adjusting the mythology that goes with this spiritual physiology so that it comes out to be Vaishnavite rather than Shaivite? Isn't he precisely taking the white, male *haṃs* bird that we associate with the high flight to this interior, semen-snowy Kailāsa and transforming it into its female, Vaishnava alter-ego? Isn't this the real meaning of all that Vaishnava poetry that has *haṃsinīs* and other female birds drinking at Lake Mānsarovar?[47]

I want to say 'yes' to all this—and then, 'no.' 'Yes' in the sense that Kabir seems to assume a close knowledge of all this yogic, perhaps even Tantric teaching and practice. 'Yes' in the sense that he inveigles us into believing that he believes it all. He makes us see the force of all those connections between interior and exterior, microcosm and macrocosm, subtle and gross. But 'no' in the sense that he goes further. In one poem he says, finally, he won't drink that water—apparently the very same liquid he called 'the water of Hari' in the other. Anything that depends on a technology of the senses ultimately doesn't work. The bird gets washed into the well (1.3). The watercarriers despair (5.3). Real naturalness, real selfness (*sahaja subhāi*, 1.4) eludes the disciplines of yoga.

In the end, Kabir seems to battle the upside-down hydraulics of *kuṇḍalinī yoga*, however much he also loves to do this verbal plumbing. His point of orientation may often be this rarefied physiology, but at least in the Fatehpuri collection it yields to the language of Krishna and Rām—'vulgate Vaishnavism,' as I've been calling it. When you come to the bottom line, that is apparently the *pad*—the footprint, the position—upon which this Fatehpuri Kabir stands. That's why he makes poems: *pads* in the other sense of the word (8.4).

Toward the conclusion of her translation of the *Bījak*—in fact, when she has moved on to an appendix and is going head to head with Kabir's *ulaṭbāṃsī*—Linda Hess looks back on it all and says,

> As usual, we are working within the irony (some would say absurdity) of subjecting Kabir's verse to the pawing and pinching of the pandits—a *tamāśā* ('comic spectacle') starring ourselves. With each poem, we can construe the meaning as utterly simple; or we can pursue the meaning endlessly, hopping through commentaries, dictionaries, glossaries, recensions, and similar images in different contexts, sometimes enjoying wordplay like elegant wits, sometimes tripping over ourselves like the Three Stooges.[48]

In some of the poems collected at Fatehpur, Kabir does commit us to this contradictory process. But when all is said and done, he urges on us a measure of simplicity—a simplicity he seems to associate with words for Vishnu.

16

Vinaya Crossovers: Sur and Kabir

This chapter reworks a series of comparisons that were first laid out in chapter 5 of *Sūr Dās: Poet, Singer, Saint* (Seattle: University of Washington Press; and Delhi: Oxford University Press, 1984), pp. 130–41.

In introducing this book I predicted that Surdas would figure as its central icon, and I suppose the size of its third section has borne that out. Moreover, his influence has been felt in chapters other than those that by right belong to him. In Chapter 7, when we were considering what difference it makes for longing to have gender, we began with Mirabai and then set her alongside Sur. Now it's Kabir's turn to play host to Sur, but this time not so much by way of contrast. Their shared laments and petitions now take center stage, and sometimes the parallels are striking. On the face of it, one might think this is Sur poaching on Kabir's turf—a *saguṇī* among the *nirguṇīs*—but it turns out not to be so simple. Sur belongs here, it isn't borrowed turf; and as we saw in the previous chapter, it works the other way around as well. All of this continues to exemplify what we concluded about the provisional nature of the *nirguṇ/saguṇ* distinction in Chapter 3.

The most numerous, and in many ways the most impressive, of Sur's *vinaya* poems are those that can be strictly described as *vinaya*: compositions in which the poet calls upon the Lord of salvation. Yet to assume that they are in the same vein as the petitions of, say, Tulsidas's *Vinayapatrikā* is to miss the distinctive characteristic of many of them, for they bespeak anything but the humility (however measured and confident) of a Tulsidas. These are poems of bitter complaint and strenuous contest in which the poet demands that the Lord follow through on promise and precedent and save him, a sinner, or relinquish any claim to being known as savior of the fallen. We had a taste of this in Chapter 12. Other moods, represented in less numerous poems, array themselves around this theme. There are poems in which some of the protagonists of the *Mahābhārata* also call upon the Lord—particularly Draupadī, whose situation is the most extreme and the most scandalous. Her Pāṇḍava husbands bargained her away in a game of dice, leaving her defenseless before the appetites of their Kaurava cousins, one of whom attempted to disrobe her in public. At that she raised a helpless plea to Krishna, who supplied her with endless lengths of cloth. Such petitions as these are complemented by a number of others in which reassurance is given that the Lord is attentive to cries of distress. The Kashi Nagaripracarini Sabha editors label these *bhaktavatsaltā*— Krishna's solicitude for his devotees, like a parent's for a child—and facets of the Sudāmā poems bear the same stamp. In the opposite vein there are poems of deep remorse, in which the poet laments a life wasted in absorption with the things of this world, contemplates death, and finds that it is too late to change. These are poems of unusual sobriety, and unlike most later additions to the genre, they are not often relieved by a message of hope. The act of giving voice to one's condition before the Lord provides the only glimmer.[1] In a companion series the poet's reflections turn to self-accusation and he remonstrates with his own heart. Here some of the blindness poems come to mind (Chapter 13).

Among these outpourings are several motifs that place Sur firmly in the company of *sants* like Kabir. There is the frequent mention of death, particularly as the god Yama[2] or as the devouring 'snake of time' (*kāl-vyāl*),[3] accompanied in both cases by the plea to be released. And because death is so pressing a concern, those whom the Lord has saved from its noose and jaws, Ajāmil and Gajendra respectively, figure with special prominence when Sur is listing the recipients of the Lord's grace. Ajāmil, though born a Brahmin and properly married, deserted his family and caste obligations to elope with a low-caste prostitute and live a life of sin. Only once did he ever call upon the name of the Lord, and that was by accident. As the terrors of mortality assailed him on his deathbed, he shouted out for his son Nārāyaṇ—but it was Krishna (also called Nārāyaṇ) who answered by bringing Ajāmil the assurance of a totally unearned heavenly salvation. Gajendra the elephant was in similarly dire straits. As a crocodile had grabbed hold of his toe and was pulling him steadily beneath the water, he too bellowed out for

Krishna, who arrived in split-second haste and saved him at a stroke from death and his deadliest foe. Ajāmil and Gajendra figure frequently in *sant* poetry, providing object lessons not only about God's grace but specifically about his power over death, a pressing *sant* concern.

Other expressions of the struggle against death also tie Sur closely to the *sants*. A number of figures of speech common in *sant* poetry appear when Sur looks back—sometimes explicitly in the face of death—on a life that has gone to waste. In poems full of bitter remorse we find the dogs, jackals, and vultures that often symbolize the voracious world of the senses in *sant* compositions (e.g., NPS 150.6). There is also mention of the bird of the soul, who has been so callously entrapped in the snares of this world (e.g., §420=NPS 337). In the example that follows, it is the dog who comes to the poet's mind: he finds himself suspended between his canine soul and the master it has foolishly forsaken (§390=NPS 103).

मेरौ मन मतिहीन गुसाई
सब सुष निधि पद कमल बिसरि श्रम करत स्वान की नाई
फिरत ब्रथा भाजन अवलेहन सूनै सदन समसान
तिहि लालच कबहू कैसी बिधि त्रिपति न पावत प्रान
जहं जहं जात तहां तहं त्रासत असम लकुटि पद त्रान
कवल कवल कारन कुबुद्धि सठ सहत इतै अपमान
परम दयाल बिस्व पालक हरि अषिल हिदै निज नाथ
ताहि छाडि यह सूर महा सठ भ्रमत भ्रमनि कै साथ

Master, my mind is drained of thought.
It's left your lotus feet, treasury of all delight,
  and taken to toiling like a dog,
Endlessly wandering, licking pots
  in barren houses and on burning pyres.
Can one ever satiate such greed?
  No, the soul never slakes its thirst.
Wherever it goes, it's in constant fear
  of stones and sticks and shoes.
How many insults has it suffered, poor dumb fool?
  How many slurs for a mouthful here and there?
Hari, most merciful, you guard the whole world;
  you yourself take charge of every heart.
Only a grand fool, says Sur, a fool like me,
  would leave that home to scavenge with the lost.

Another familiar theriomorphic image for the misguided soul is that of the parrot who watches carefully over the ripening of the silk-cotton (*semar*) fruit. The parrot waits with anxious greed until the fruit appears juicy and full, and pecks it at last—only to have the inedible cottony substance inside fly away in the breeze. So do we nurture our affections in this world, and they, like the silk-cotton, are ultimately indigestible. Here are two poems among many that draw on this image, one by Sur (§387= NPS 59) and one by Kabir. Both orient themselves to Hari/Rām.

रे मन छाडि विषै कौ रचिबौ
कत तू सुवा होत सैवरि कौ अंतकि पासि न बचिबौ
अनंग तरंग कनक कामिनि ज्यौं हाथ रहैगौ पचिबौ
तजि अभिमानु राम कहि बवरे नतरकु ज्वाला तचिबौ
सतगुर कह्यौ कहत हौं तौ सौं राम रतन धन सचिबौ
सूरदास प्रभु हरि सुमिरन बिनु जोगी कपि ज्यौं नचिबौ

My soul, abandon the blandishments of flesh.
Why yearn like a parrot for some silk-cotton fruit?
  You won't escape the grasp of death.
Waves of elusive passion—for gold and women and such—
  leave only remorse in your hands.
Fool, dispense with pride and pretension
  and before you roast in the flames, say the name of Rām.
The True Guru said it, and I say it too:
  Rām is the jewel, the wealth you should amass.
Unless you reflect on Hari, the Lord of Sur,
  you'll be like those yogis—like monkeys they are—
    you'll wriggle on a leash, and dance.

बिखै बांचु हरि रांचु समझु मन बउरा रे
निरभै होइ न हरि भजै मन बउरा रे   गह्यौ न रांम जहाज
तन धन सौं का गर्बसी मन बउरा रे   भसम किरिम जाकौ साजु
कालबूत की हस्तिनी मन बउरा रे   चित्र रच्यौ जगदीस
कांम अंध गज बसि परै मन बउरा रे   अंकुस सहियौ सीस
मरकट मूंठी अनाज की मन बउरा रे   लीन्हीं हाथ पसारि
छूटन की संसै परी मन बरा रे   नाचेउ घर घर बारि
ज्यौं ललनीं सुअटा गह्यौ मन बउरा रे   माया यहु ब्यौहार
जैसा रंग कुसुंभ का मन बउरा रे   त्यौं पसर्‍यौ पासारु
नावनु (न्हांवन?) कौं तीरथ घने मन बउरा रे   पूजन कौं बहु देव
कहै कबीर छूटन नहीं मन बउरा रे   छूटनु हरि की सेव

Fool soul, jettison the flesh,
Save a second's thought for God.
Fearless fool, refusing Hari,
You've cast off the life raft of Rām.

This world, fool soul,
This elephant effigy
Is made by the Lord to lure
And lead on your elephant lusts:
  the goad
  to prod your dense head.

Fool soul, jettison the flesh,
Save a second's thought for God.

The monkey, fool soul,
Stuck in his hand,
Searching for grain in a narrow-necked pot,
And it stuck, and he couldn't get it out,
  he was caught,
  and ever after danced from house to house.

Fool soul, jettison the flesh,
Save a second's thought for God.

The parrot, fool soul,
Is lured to silk-cotton;
  likewise the lure of illusion:
It flies in the face,
A fistful of color,
Of safflower powder
  that spreads in the winds.

Fool soul, jettison the flesh,
Save a second's thought for God.

Fool soul,
There are rivers and rivers
In which to bathe
And gods and gods to praise,
But none will set you free,
  says Kabir:
  freedom comes in serving Hari Rām.

Fool soul, jettison the flesh,
Save a second's thought for God.[4]

Sur and the *sants* share not only images of dogs, jackals, and birds drawn from the great storehouse of common speech, but whole proverbs as well. Take, for instance, two widely known sayings having to do with human obduracy and heedlessness: 'You can't pierce a stone with an arrow,' and 'If you dye a blanket black, the color will never change.' Both formulae make their way into the rhetoric of Kabir and Sur, but the effect is not quite the same. Here are two *sākhīs* of Kabir, as translated by Charlotte Vaudeville:

तकत तकावत रहि गया, सका न बेझा मारि
सबै तीर खाली परे, चला कमांनहिं डारि

The Bowman kept aiming and aiming,
  but his shots never pierced:
All his arrows fell to the ground,
  so tossing away his quiver, he left.[5]

करिए तौ करि जादिए, सारीखा सौं संग
लीर लीर लोई भई, तऊ न छाड़ै रंग

If you keep company, then do so with discernment,
  associate with your own kind:
Even if the blanket be torn to pieces,
  still it will keep its own color![6]

And here is a *pad* of Sur, which concludes by incorporating both images (§419=NPS 332):

छांडि मन, हरि बिमुषनि कौ संग
कहा होत पय पान कराऐं, बिष नहिं तजत भुजंग
कागहिं कहा कपूर चुगाऐं, स्वान न्हवाऐं गंग
खर कौं कहा अरगजा लेपन, मरकट भूषन अंग
पाहन पतित बान नहिं बेधत, रीतौ करत निषंग
सूरदास कारी कामरि पै, चढ़त न दूजौ रंग

Turn away, mind, from those who turn from Hari.
What's the good in giving cobras milk?
  Snakes never lose their venom.
Why waste camphor feeding it to crows
  or squander Ganges water washing dogs?

Why go plastering perfume on an ass
  or covering a monkey with jewels?
Empty your quiver, but arrows cannot pierce
  a stone that's fallen to the ground.
Surdas says, once a blanket's dyed black
  it never takes on a different hue.

The motif of arrow and blanket are the same from poet to poet, but they are employed in characteristically different ways. When Kabir speaks of the bowman and the arrow, he has something quite specific in mind. The archer is the *satguru*, the divine interior teacher in whom the *sant* tradition placed such confidence, and his arrow is the *sabad* or *śabda*, the inner word through which he speaks to those who seek him out:

सतगुरु सांचा सूरिवां, सबद जु बाहा एक
लागत ही भुइं मिलि गया, परा करेजै छेक

The Satguru is the true Hero,
  who loosed off a single Śabda;
The moment it struck, I fell to the ground
  and a wound opened in my breast.[7]

Sur's use of this image is more general. He never explicitly identifies the arrow in question with the *sabad* and, as the passage above shows, the meaning would not necessarily be clear if one made that interpretation.

Where the blanket is concerned, it is Sur's world rather than Kabir's that gives an added specificity to the meaning: for black is Krishna's color, and the *gopīs* are hopelessly dyed. As they themselves say (§79=NPS 2276.5–6),

अब तौ जिय ऐसी बनि आई स्याम धाम मैं कियौ बसेरौ
इहि रंग सूर रंग्यौ मन मेरौ बहुरि न होइ सेत नहि पेरौ

Our lives, it seems, have immersed themselves
  in the sea of Śyām, the dark one;
And once they touch that color, says Sur,
  you'll not squeeze a drop of white from them again.[8]

Sur and the *sants*, then, share much, but he retains—as many of them also do, individually—a particular perspective.

A comparable difference emerges in regard to the issue of equality before God, with the closely associated criticism of social hierarchies that one finds in the utterances of *sants* like Kabir. Sur apparently has as little use for institutionalized inequality as Kabir, but his style of expressing himself on the point is different. Instead of lashing out at the meaninglessness of social distinctions and the hypocrisy of the great, Sur cites example after example in which the Lord, primarily as Krishna, has preferred the company of the lowly and outcaste to that of the pure and well-placed. In the following poem (§381=NPS 19), one of a great many similar poems, he alludes to four such vignettes: the time Krishna was out in the forest and accepted food at the hands of the wife of Vidur, who though wise was a half-breed; the time he came to the aid of the Pāṇḍava brothers when they had been exiled from their rightful throne and reduced to the status of wandering mendicants; the time he granted wealth to Sudāmā, the penurious Brahmin who had been his boyhood friend; and the time he had mercy on Kubjā, the hunchback of Mathura, and healed her deformity.

स्याम गरीबनि ही कौ गाहक
दीनानाथ हमारे ठाकुर साची प्रीति निबाहक
कहा सुदामा के घन ऐसौ कुबिजा कै गुन चाहक
का पंडव कुल की ठकुराई अरजुन कै रथ बाहक
कहा विदुर कै नाम जाति कुल हरि जी प्रीति कै लाहक
सूरदास प्रभु कौ सुभाव यौं संतन कै दुष दाहक

Śyām is solely the patron of the poor.
Our Lord is the one who fends for the wretched,
  brings fulfillment to those whose love is pure.
What storehouse of wealth did Sudāmā possess?
  Why was Hari drawn to a hunchback's charms?
What sort of lordliness did the Pāṇḍav clan claim?—
  Still he volunteered as Arjun's charioteer.
What were Vidur's name, birth, and clan?
  No matter to Hari—he was moved by love.
Surdas's Lord is this kind of lord:
  He burns away the trials of the true.

Kabir is remembered for his trenchant perceptions about human depravity. His perspective is tough and realistic, and the path to salvation that he describes is often regarded as more difficult than that presented by straightforwardly Vaishnava poets.[9] But there is a sense in which Sur's assessment of human need is even more radical than Kabir's—particularly in what he says about himself. In Kabir, especially as we meet him in the *Bījak*, there is a definite self-confidence. This is the man who takes it upon himself to address others in phrases such as the following, assembled from various poems in the *Bījak* and translated by Linda Hess:[10]

> Pandit, you've got it wrong.
> Monk, stop scattering your mind.
> Pandit, do some research...
> Morons and mindless fools—
> Enchanted madman—
> You simple-minded people...
> Saints, once you wake up don't doze off.

And last but not least, the following salvo:

> Son of a slut!
> There: I've insulted you.
> Think about getting on the good road.

This is hardly the language or attitude of Sur. In the old poems of the *Sūrsāgar* he never places himself in the position of criticizing others. It is only himself he ventures to call a fool, leaving his listeners to draw their own conclusions about themselves.[11] He is similarly diffident about according himself any sort of status in relation to the Lord, even the lowest sort, that of a servant or slave. Tulsidas, by contrast, does not hesitate to claim such status for himself (*Vinayapatrikā* 271.1):

> जैसो हौं तैसो राम! रावरो जन जानि परिहरिये
> कृपासिंधु कोसनधनी! सरनागत-पालक, ढरनि आपनी ढरिये

> Whatever I am, I am yours, O Rām,
>   your servant. Do not desert me.
> Ocean of mercy, Kośala's overlord,
>   guardian of those who come begging shelter,
> Shield me, I pray, with your shield.[12]

Only rarely is Sur confident enough to declare himself a servant of the Lord, and even then he does not speak as if such slavery were his hereditary right, making him a member of the Lord's household. This is often Tulsi's starting point, as in the example just quoted, but if Sur claims servitude it is on the basis of his bad character, which has caused him to be auctioned and bought. He reinforces his sense of lowly status by dwelling on its most obvious and distasteful manifestation: the requirement that his food should consist of another's leftovers (NPS 171, cf. B4, J4).

हमैं नँदनंदन मोल लिये।
जम के फंद काटि मुकराए, अभय अजाद किये
भाल तिलक स्रवनानि तुलसीदल, मेटे अंक बिये
मूँठ्यौ मूँड़ कंठ, बनमाला, मुद्रा-चक्र दिये
सब कोउ कहत गुलाम स्याम कौ, सुनत सिरात हिये
सूरदास कौं और बड़ौ सुख जूठनि खाई जिये

Nandanandan has bought me, redeemed me,
Cut me clean from the fetters of death
  and shown me what fearless freedom can mean,
Decked my forehead with a *tilak* mark,
  settled a sprig of *tulsī* in my ear,
    and wrapped my body in close embrace;
Shaved my hair, my initiate's head,
  draped fresh flowers around my neck,
    and branded me with his holy signs.
Everyone now calls me the Dark One's slave.
  Hearing it my heart breathes cool and free,
For what, says Sur, could measure the pleasure
  of living on leftovers,
    scraps from such a plate?

In a similar vein, the question of having attained an experience of plenitude (*pūrā*), a state Kabir is willing to claim for himself, simply does not arise for Sur in the *vinaya* context. One poem in which Kabir makes this affirmation, in fact, is quite revealing in the contrast it makes to its counterpart in the *Sūrsāgar*. In both poems the speaker takes on the role of a dancer who has performed so long that not another step is left in him. For Kabir this emptying of every human desire and versatility yields, paradoxically, the plenitude that is the presence of Rām. For Sur, however, there is no such release, and the poem ends in a devastated petition to the Lord to do away with this ignorant, misguided life (*avidyā*). Here is Kabir:

जउ मै रूप कीए बहुतेरे अब फुनि रूपु न होई
तागा तंतु साजु सभु थाका राम नाम बसि होई
अब मोहि नाचनो न आवै मेरा मनु मंदीराआ न बजावै
कामु क्रोधु माइआ लै जारी त्रिसना गागरि फूटी
काम चोलना भइआ है पुराना गइआ भरमु सभु छूटी
सरब भूत एकै करि जानिआ चूके बाद बिबादा
कहि कबीर मै पूरा पाइआ भए राम परसादा

Too many, many roles
  these parts I've played,
      and now
  I'll part from them.
Too tired of all pretense,
  tuning, tuning the strings,
  and now it's over, done—
      thanks to the name of Rām.
I haven't another dance to dance
  and my mind
  can no longer maneuver the drum.
Life's postures, love, hate—
  lost to the flames;
  the craving-filled kettle drum
      finally burst.
Lust's veil, this body,
  is tattered with age;
  every errant shuffle is stilled.
All that lives and dies—
  why, they're one,
  and the this and that
  and haggling
      are gone.
What I have found,
  says Kabir,
    is fullness itself,
  a finality granted
    by the mercy of Rām.[13]

Here, in the same vein, is Sur (§400=NPS 153):

अब हौं नाच्यौ बहुत गुपाल
काम क्रोध कौ पहिरि चोलनौ कंठि विषै की माल
डिंभ मोह के नूपुर बाजे निंदा सबद रसाल

माया कौ कटि फेटौ बाध्यौ लोभु तिलकु दियौ भाल
त्रिस्ना नाद करत घट भीतरि नाना बिधि कै ताल
भ्रंम भोयन मन भयौ पषावज असत संगति मैं चाल
जो बहु कला काछि दिषराई जलद थलद क्रित काल
सूरदास की सबै अविद्या दूरि करौ नंदलाल

Now I have danced too much, Gopāl,
Dressed in anger and lust, and garlanded
with a necklace of passions at the throat.
Girded with ankle-bells of sham and delusion—
how sweet their slanderous sound—
I am bound at the waist with a sash of illusion,
and the vermilion of greed is daubed on my brow.
Cravings roar inside my body
in a host of differing rhythms
And my mind, a drum pasted with the dough of confusion,
sets my movements to a dissonant pulse.
I've marshaled and flaunted so many artful steps
and filled my sinful net:
All this ignorance Surdas has learned—
take it far away, Nandalāl.

Kabir is extremely pessimistic about human nature, if left to its own devices. He trains on it a barrage of exhortations about the need for concentration and repentance. Sur's tone, if one reads the *Sūrsāgar* as a whole, seems less barbed, more relaxed. But in the *vinaya* poems it becomes obvious that on this point too Sur is among the most radical of the *sants*. Kabīr, after all, was at least willing to give open praise to the human capacity for love (*prem, prīti*);[14] whereas Sur is more guarded. Among the early poems in the *Sūrsāgar* there are only occasional instances in which love is singled out as the element in the human psyche to which God responds (§381.2–3)—

Our Lord is the one who fends for the wretched,
brings fulfillment to those whose love is pure.
What storehouse of wealth did Sudāmā possess?
Why was Hari drawn to a hunchback's charms?

—and even then the initiative rests on the divine side of the interaction. For Sur it is the fact of Krishna that equalizes all beings before him more than any quality inherent in people. In a similar way Sur places much less emphasis on the unique privilege of the human condition, namely the potential for ultimate salvation that it offers, than one would think from reading the Nagaripracarini Sabha edition. Poems that make a point of the countless births it takes to be born human, are rare in the earlier years of the Sur tradition.[15] On the contrary, Sur is likely to be found lamenting how many lives—human, presumably—he has wasted cursing others or otherwise misbehaving (e.g., §384.2). Sur is suspicious, evidently, of all status, even Darwinian hierarchies: what matters in life has nothing to do with one's position. When Sur talks of status there is irony in his voice, as when, paradigmatically, he styles himself the best of sinners. If one must have hierarchy, better to be low than high.

Perhaps this sounds like an upper-caste voice. For such a person the foregoing of status can be an act of will, not necessity, and touched with an element of *noblesse*. Ravidas too sings the praises of lowliness, but in a much less self-conscious sort of way. And for Kabir it would simply be unthinkable. Whatever *sant*-hood means for him, it can't be this.

Yet looking back over the array of poems we have studied in this chapter and the last, we find important analogies between Kabir and Sur. In general terms it is possible to argue that the identities *sant* and Vaishnava stand for two distinctive styles—the one expounding the perils of earth, the other revelling in heaven. But we also have to take into account the interesting moments when the borders blur. These make Sur and Kabir far more than quarreling cousins, and perhaps even render them brothers.

17

Bhakti, Democracy, and the Study of Religion

This chapter began as an essay written for the International Symposium on India Studies convened by the Indian Council on Cultural Relations of the Government of India at Kovalam Beach, Kerala, in November–December, 1994. The printed version appeared in K. Satchidananda Murty and Amit Dasgupta, eds, *The Perennial Tree* (New Delhi: Indian Council for Cultural Relations, 1996), pp. 213–16. I am grateful to Alan Babb, Ainslie Embree, Linda Hess, Mark Juergensmeyer, and Laura Shapiro for critical readings of an earlier draft.

In this final chapter we emerge from the particular currents and controversies surrounding each of our 'three bhakti voices' and step out onto a broader stage. We will be focusing on some of the great challenges of this or any day: the valuing of human equality and dignity, the acceptance of a variety of religious orientations, and a concern for how they might become resources for—rather than obstacles to—the consolidation of an open, democratic, truly interactive society. These are global issues, but they are specifically Indian ones as well, and it is here that the bhakti heritage counts. Kabir has often been close to the heart of debates about these matters in India, and he will be our primary inspiration, guide, and irritant. Yet as we have seen so clearly, Kabir does not float in gravity-free space. The Kabir we know is the Kabir we are taught to know. So it is important to think about who should do the teaching as we find ways to let him and other bhakti poet-saints speak to the question of what religion ought to be today, and it is important to think about how that teaching should proceed.

India and the Study of Religion

Public institutions in both India and the United States have been very cautious in dealing with the question of whether religion ought to be studied in a public setting, and there has been a reticence in both countries to study it in its own terms—as its own field—in a secular academic environment. At the university level, however, there is a clear and marked divergence between the two countries. In the United States there are hundreds of departments of Religion (or Religious Studies, Comparative Religion, The Study of Religion, etc.) at both private and public institutions; whereas in India's public universities, at least, there are no more than a handful.

One can well understand why things are as they are. Religion was a very sensitive topic at the time the Republic of India was fashioning its university system, and the British model that it mainly inherited had not yet managed to make the Copernican jump from faculties of divinity primarily dedicated to teaching Christianity, to faculties of religion in which the basic syllabus (the introductory course, in American parlance) was devoted to the even-handed, comparative study of a number of religious traditions, from as many perspectives as proved helpful. Yet the result is strange. Here you have the nation that is in many ways the world's most religiously sophisticated country—and scarcely a single scholar at the university level who identifies herself or himself by discipline as a student of religion. True, there have been very astute evaluations of religion on the part of Indian historians, sociologists, psychologists, and anthropologists, but there seems no place in most Indian universities where such studies from different disciplinary perspectives can come to focus; and no place for the comparative study of religion itself.

I realize that there are deep problems associated with the concept 'religion' as it is used in European languages (the word translates only awkwardly into any Indian language I know).[1] So I would hope that if the field were made a part of Indian curricula, we could avoid a new reification. Indeed, Indian scholars would help unreify 'religion' as it is studied in the West, by pointing regularly to the inadequacies of the concept—and I believe they would find droves of scholars out there waiting to listen to them. The process has already begun.[2]

For at least a quarter of a century, the basic paradigm for studying religion in America has been strictly comparative, rather than confessional. The increasing pluralism of our own society will make it ever more so. In American higher education, many students with a particular interest in India decide to base themselves in departments of religion. The idea that India's culture is extraordinarily or essentially religious may be the result of an unfortunate type-casting by Euro-Americans (one that in some ways goes as far back as the Greeks);[3] but there is enough truth in the stereotype that it deserves, at the very least, to be corrected by scholars from India itself.

This task is too important to leave to amateurs and foreigners. Marx, Freud, and perhaps even Nehru may have expected (indeed, wished) that in time religion would wither and die, but every indication we have from their generation to ours is that it is a permanent feature of human life—always changing in its forms, but persistent as a phenomenon. We need people in every educated culture who are trying to understand it. And who knows? There might even be some practical benefit.

There are signs that this need for serious, impartial education and scholarship about religion is being strongly felt in India today. Religiously, we live in difficult times, and it is to the credit of many Indian academics that they have chosen not to hide their heads in the sand, even if their own disciplinary training did not force them to engage in the study of religion. In this connection I might particularly mention the series called 'Tracts for the Times', edited by Neeladri Bhattacharya with help from Sarvepalli Gopal and Romila Thapar, which began to appear in 1994. The first volume, *Khaki Shorts and Saffron Flags*, was an attempt to provide a primer in the history of organizations connected with the drive to destroy the so-called Bābrī Mosque, and its subtitle identifies it clearly as 'A Critique of the Hindu Right'. Given the scholarly world in which the series was born, this comes as no surprise.

But the third volume, perhaps, does. This is Rustom Bharucha's sensitive essay, *The Question of Faith*, in which his purpose is twofold. On the one hand, Bharucha wishes to make religion intelligible to its 'cultured despisers', as the Protestant theologian Friedrich Schleiermacher called them when he faced a similar task in the Berlin of 1799.[4] In this regard, Bharucha especially hopes to break down Marxist stereotypes, although he has strong loyalties to Marxist forms of thought. On the other hand, Bharucha tries to move towards a language and research agenda that hold the promise of making religion intelligible, not just to the 'cultured despisers' but to anyone; and this he does by emphasizing the complexity of religious experience, particularly through what he calls 'the ambivalences of faith'. In concluding the book, he says,

> [I]t is heartening to acknowledge the increased scholarly and activist interest in the radical religious movements of our past history, most notably in studies of *bhakti*. . . . [F]or a 'secular theology' to exist in India, there would have to be a theory that could be adapted within the multireligious context of differing faiths. The basis for such a theory is less likely to be found in the existing political rhetoric of 'religious tolerance', than in the vision of saints like Kabir, Guru Nanak, and Chaitanya who, as Tagore understood so well, 'preached one God to all races in India', adapting different idioms of communication. Secularists have a lot to learn from the idioms of 'tolerance' embedded in every religious faith.[5]

When taken to its conclusion, Bharucha's appeal seems to me to be a call for new generation of Indian scholars and, indeed, a new field of study of Indian universities. Bharucha himself makes very creative use of the work of a number of his Indian contemporaries, from Ashis Nandy, to Kumkum Sangari and Sudesh Vaid, to D. P. Dubey, to Anuradha Kapur. But in dealing with the field as a whole, his single point of departure is Mircea Fliade, the grand old man—now gone—at the University of Chicago.[6] Bharucha states some basic reservations about the applicability of Fliade's dichotomizing of 'sacred' and 'profane', questioning the aptness of this approach for India. Yes indeed, and scholars in the field of comparative religion, especially younger ones, have many times questioned its aptness in *any* culture. A new generation of Indian specialists in the field would know that literature, and would be able to register in intricate and seminal ways just the sort of critique that Bharucha lodges. India teaches worlds to students of religion.

Kabir and International Bhakti Studies

Now let me shift gears, as promised, and comment on Bharucha's appeal in a different way. Since he mainly restricts himself to Indian scholars addressing 'studies of bhakti', it may be useful to open the lens and explore certain motifs in recent work on North Indian bhakti by scholars living both inside and outside India. The purpose: to see what light they shed on our developing understanding of what fascinates Bharucha, the 'vision' of such saints as Kabir, Guru Nanak, and

Caitanya. It has long been a conviction of many important Indian scholars that, as the great Sanskritist V. Raghavan put it, bhakti is the 'democratic doctrine which consolidates all people without distinction of caste, community, nationality, or sex.'[7] Or at least bhakti contains the resources for articulating and enacting such a view. Yet there is also the opposing camp: scholars who either deny that there ever was a genuinely anti-authoritarian urge in bhakti, or who say that it was always subverted in practice.[8]

In what follows, I will try to see what light is shed on this debate by current international scholarship on such luminaries as Kabir, Nanak, and Caitanya. What does it take to 'get at' the vision of this cohort of bhakti saints? And what does this mean for the view that bhakti supports the ideals of democracy and tolerance? As we move forward, I will be trying to disentangle the question of whether bhakti is intrinsically egalitarian from the issue of its being representative, that is, broadly popular. 'Democracy' can mean both things, but these two are not the same.

Current work suggest that we should consider at least three areas of study to see how such questions could be answered in relation to the great bhakti 'voices' of North India:

1. *Textual studies strictly speaking*: editions and translations of the fifteenth- to seventeenth-century bhakti poet-saints;

2. *Biographical or hagiographical studies*: the lives of these persons in relation to the poetry attributed to them; and

3. *Studies of context—historical, social, ritual, performative*: the communities in which bhakti is embedded, and their rules of operation, explicit or otherwise.

Let us consider these as they relate to just one of the bhakti heroes and heroines of North India—Kabir, the one Bharucha mentions first and the one who has figured as importantly as any in recent rhetoric in India. We will also make occasional nods to other bhakti saints, in particular Mirabai. So, then: if one looks closely, who is this Kabir upon whom Bharucha calls?

For many years there has been a strong desire to enlist the authoritative voice—and, indeed, the authoritative persona—of Kabir in the cause of Hindu-Muslim reconciliation. This, after all, is the saint whose bodily remains are said to have been fought over by Hindus and Muslims, only to reveal themselves as a heap of flowers accessible to both.[9] According to one version of the story, it was the existence of this single, transubstantiated pile that showed the futility of sectarian, communitarian claims to possessing the truth about God, here symbolized by the saint himself. According to another version, there were actually two piles of flowers, and a voice from heaven (Kabir's own?) told the two warring communities to deal with the flowers after their own customs—burial for Muslims, cremation for Hindus. Thus the two practices are set parallel and equally trivialized: both are ranked as clearly secondary in value to the veneration they symbolize.

As a sequel to this second version of the story of Kabir's death, two parallel shrines—a Muslim mausoleum and a Hindu temple—have now been erected on the supposed spot of Kabir's death in Magahar, near Gorakhpur.[10] This was further to render him, as the subtitle of a notable work in English put it, 'the apostle of Hindu-Muslim unity'.[11] And the subtitle of his comic-book in the *Amar Chitra Katha* series does the same, dubbing Kabir 'The Mystic Who Tried to Bring the Hindus and the Muslims Together.' Inside, in the English version, we read that 'It pained the good man to see religion, caste and creed keeping people apart', so he prayed, 'God, give me the strength to break the barriers of hate between men.'[12] Indeed, *Amar Chitra Katha* seems to have invented a new poem to underscore the point. Five exemplary poems of Kabir appear on the inside cover. Four translated poems appear in the Hindi version and can be found in various editions of Kabir, but the fifth—the clincher—seems to be a new amalgam: 'In the beginning, there was no Turk, nor Hindu—no race, nor caste.'[13]

One can certainly find lines such as these in the Kabir corpus as it has come down to the present day, but what is striking about poems that have the best textual pedigree is that they show Kabir as playing a peacemaker's role in only the most backhanded fashion. To the contrary, his style is often downright confrontational:

> Pundit, how can you be so dumb?
> You're going to drown, along with all your kin,
>   unless you start speaking of Rām.

Or:

> Hey Qazi,
>   What's that book you're preaching from?
> And reading, reading—how many days?
>   Still you haven't mastered one word.[14]

Writers such as Hedayetullah try to take the edge off this by balancing such passages with others in which Kabir seems to take a more conciliatory line—the verse, for example, that says:

> Kabir is a child of Rāma and Allah,
> and accepted all gurus and pirs.[15]

Actually, there is some difficulty with this translation, with its pronouncedly ecumenical ring. Hedayetullah is working from the version found in the standard edition of the *Gurū Granth Sāhib*, but P. N. Tivārī's critical edition favors a crucial alternate reading as being stronger. This produces the following meaning, as in the translation by Charlotte Vaudeville:

> Kabir is the child of *Allah-Rām*:
> He is my Guru and my Pir.[16]

This is much more in the spirit of a poem overwhelmingly occupied with pillorying the beliefs and practices of Brahmins and Qazis and their followers, in which the poet shucks off everything but the direct witness of his own heart. Sometimes Hedayetullah concedes this, saying that Kabir 'rejected the usefulness of the scriptures of both religions, precisely because they were misused and misrepresented by the so-called guardians of both religions, the Brahmins and the Mullas.'[17] But he goes on to say that Kabir also has a conciliatory side: 'Otherwise, there is evidence to show that Kabir regarded the essential validity and truth of religious scriptures.'[18] I can find no evidence for this sort of claim.

From what I have said here so far—and at greater length in the Introduction—it must be clear that to my mind it is essential to bring to bear the work of textual criticism if one wants to claim that a position was adopted or an orientation held by a major figure in the past. Recent thinking of the deconstructionist variety has challenged textual work that might be construed as trying to discover the *ipsissima verba* ('exact words') of a figure such as Kabir. And it is also possible to arrive at the same conclusion from other points of departure, as do critics who emphasize the importance of an audience's reception of a text in determining the nature of the text itself. For a poet whose words were originally remembered orally, insofar as we can tell, this is particularly important to keep in mind.[19]

Yet I think it is very mistaken to believe that every saying attributed to a figure such as Kabir has the same status as every other. Two of the most important discoveries of recent textual labors in the bhakti vineyard have been that different recensions of a given poet often display different personalities, and that in traditions of transmission where the oral element is fundamental, the age of a poem can be quite a good predictor of the range of stylistic and conceptual possibilities it may contain. In other words, poets' personalities change over time and from region to region. The traditions associated with them develop and, one could say, drift as commentators and performers focus on one set of poems rather than another, and amend—doubtless for the most part unconsciously—as they go.[20] This leads to the composition of more poems attributed to the same poet, with the effect that the overall personality of the poet in question steadily evolves. Often it evolves rather differently from one community of transmission to another.

Recent studies have suggested that in the case of Kabir, all this happened early on. As we have seen in Chapter 14, there are three quite distinct manuscript recensions, each reflecting his veneration in a separate community or in a set of related communities. One early set of manuscripts is associated with the Sikh *Gurū Granth Sāhib*, in that Kabir poems appear in its predecessors the *Kartārpur Bīr* (1604) and even earlier in the *Goindvāl Pothīs,* probably dating to the 1570s.[21] Another set was produced in Rajasthan, with the earliest example being the Fatehpur manuscript of 1582, which we studied in Chapter 15, followed by the collections gathered for the Dādū Panth: the *Sarvāṅgīs* of Rajab and Gopāldās (probably composed quite early in the seventeenth century, but manuscripts survive from 1714 and 1724 respectively[22]) and the *Pañcvāṇī*, which achieved liturgical use (1614, 1636, 1653, 1658, etc.).[23] The third oldest recension, belonging to the Kabir Panth, commands no manuscript earlier than 1805, but important scholars have argued from internal evidence that it be dated at least to the time of the *Pañcvāṇī*, if not before.[24] To a certain extent, as we have hinted in earlier chapters, each of these recensions presents us with a different Kabir.

The Kabir of the *Gurū Granth Sāhib* is a 'householder-saint', to use the term coined by Karine Schomer in her study 'Kabir in the *Gurū Granth Sāhib*: An Exploratory Essay'.[25] More than the Kabir of the Dādū Panth, this Kabir emphasizes the importance of keeping company with good people (*satsang*), the justice of fearing the consequences of sin as death approaches, and so forth. The Dādū-Panthī Kabir, by contrast, is more mystical, dwelling on the difficulty of the way of faith and speaking of the true teacher (*satguru*) in ways that make it clear he exceeds the limitations of any human embodiment. There is much about the virtue of asceticism, too, and not a few broadsides against women.[26] And by now we know well the 'vulgate Vaishnavism' of our other Rajasthani Kabir, the one who appears at Fatehpur (Chapter 15). Despite his theistic, devotional tendencies, he can hardly be aligned point by point with the Kabir whom the Dadū Panth wanted to embrace, even though both come to us from Rajasthan.

As for the Kabir of the Kabir Panth—headquartered at Banaras but with related organizations located at various places throughout the northeast (especially Bihar and Chattisgarh) and elsewhere—this is a figure who stands strikingly apart from the bhakti orientation of the Kabir we meet in western India, whether it be Punjab or Rajasthan. He is more caustic and self-confident (very little *viraha* or *vinaya* here), and by contrast to the other two, he is no worshiper of Krishna, whose name only once appears in the *Bījak*.[27] In the climate of present-day discussions of Kabir, this perhaps causes no amazement, but as Linda Hess has shown, in 17 per cent of Kabir *pads* recorded in the *Gurū Granth Sāhib* and in 15 per cent of those that appear in the *Pañcvāṇī*, the poet addresses himself to Krishna or has other occasion to mention him. Is Kabir then some sort of Vaishnava, of all things? (See Chapter 15.)

There are further complications, as well. While the *ramainī* sections of the *Pañcvāṇī* and *Bījak* agree with one another to a surprisingly high degree—they hold 50 per cent of their *ramainīs* in common—that number begins to dwindle when one moves to the *pads* and especially the *dohās* (or *sākhīs*, 'witnesses', as they are called in the *Bījak*; *saloku*—i.e., *ślokas*—in the *Gurū Granth Sāhib*). Here the correlation between the *Pañcvāṇī* and the *Bījak* is very meager: somewhere between 3 per cent and 9 per cent, depending on how you count.[28] Considering that this genre is probably the most frequently quoted in current appeals to Kabir, this is a fact worth pondering. And to make matters worse, this is the genre where the name of the poet least frequently appears in the poem itself.[29] One has the feeling that this was the place where it was easiest for new poems to be set alongside old ones, and all grouped under one authoritative name.[30] So there is plenty of room for various kinds of slippage when one performs the seemingly simple act of quoting Kabir.

Fortunately, however, it does not end at that. Linda Hess believes she can move forward in a search for the 'real' Kabir (wisely, she does not use the term herself) by giving special attention to the *Bījak*, despite the late date of its manuscripts, since in its narrower focus 'it contains what is universal and typical, what is present, even dominant, in all three collections.'[31] This is what Charlotte Vaudeville has called Kabir's 'extraordinary independence of character.'[32] Hess believes, furthermore, that we can be pretty confident in discounting the Krishnaite and generally Vaishnava component in the western Kabir because it is so easy to understand how that dimension might have been 'sung' into Kabir poems as they traveled westward from what all traditions and much internal evidence confirm must have been his home: the Banaras region. She shows that mentions of Krishna occur overwhelmingly in a *pad*'s first or last line—precisely the 'packaging' verses where you would expect it—and that they sometimes fit awkwardly with the language and message of the rest of the poem.[33] This moves us back to a poet who unselfconsciously designates the principle of ultimate reality by terms such as Hari, *satguru*, or, very often, Rām. Yet it is important to remember that early on, in two rather different western traditions, he was understood in some way as a Krishna *bhakta*, whatever else he was. As I have tried to show in considering the Fatehpur manuscript in Chapter 15, I do not believe the references to Krishna are always superficial even if they do cluster in the first and last verses. They can actually be climactic.

This moves us naturally enough into the realm of hagiography, for we recall how Kabir is understood to have come by his Vaishnavism. He is said to have sought initiation from the great teacher Rāmānand, who is in turn associated with the lineage of Rāmānuja. The story goes that Kabir tricked Rāmānand into shouting the name of Rām while Kabir touched his foot, thus imparting to Kabir an initiatory mantra in more or less the proper ritual circumstances. Kabir lay down on the steps of one of the Banaras *ghāṭs* where the great teacher would not see him in the early morning darkness—and the rest is, so to speak, history. It's a great story, whose outline first appeared in 1712 when Priyadas composed his commentary on the *Bhaktamāl* of Nabhadas and which came to be cited along the banks of the Ganges in the course of the following century. A manuscript dated 1814 provides our first attestation. If we press back before Priyadas, the association between Kabir and Rāmānand becomes much more vague, with Nabhadas and his contemporary Anantdās merely asserting in about 1600 that it existed. Then it disappears altogether. There˜ is nothing in the early recensions of Kabir's poetry to confirm it—not a single mention of Rāmānand's name.[34]

David Lorenzen, a very serious Western student of these matters, thinks the tie between Kabir and Rāmānand was a real one, but in my view, especially given certain problems with dating, the story of their liaison is all too neat a way for a particular kind of Brahmin liberal theology to incorporate (and perhaps co-opt) the charisma of Kabir.[35] The well-known story of his early infancy—that he was abandoned by Hindu parents and adopted by Muslims—reveals the same desire. Faced with a poet whose name clearly identifies him as Muslim, and whose poetry sometimes confirms that he was a weaver (*julāhā*), probably a Muslim one, the upper-caste Vaishnava tradition reinvented the earliest days of his life. Just as they awarded the *camār* Ravidas a former life as a Brahmin, so they supplied Kabir with a new and (from their point of view) purer infancy—something that could justify his later eminence in their eyes.

It is astonishing to see the power that these stories have—they are told and told again—unless one remembers that in religious traditions the world over, the narrative mode has at least as much force as the explicitly didactic (see Chapter 2). These tales have remained remarkably immune to critical analysis,[36] since to take them away would hold out the danger of leaving nothing in its place. We cannot live without stories. Hence a sophisticated critic like Hazārīprasād Dvivedī uses the Rāmānand connection to graft the Vaishnava Kabir onto his yogic, Kabir-Panthī counterpart. Dvivedī postulates a case of before and after, with Kabir learning his Vaishnava bhakti from Rāmānand.[37]

Muhammad Hedayetullah takes this a step further, in the service of rather different aims. He argues that the kind of bhakti Rāmānand was carrying to Banaras from his native South was already so informed by Islam, thanks to Sufi influences first felt on the southern shores of the Arabian Sea, that to be a Vaishnava of Rāmānand's type was to be, in effect, a kind of Muslim. Then he adds in the old story of how Kabir was also a pupil of Sheikh Taqī and presents Kabir as the architect of not one but two great fusions of Hinduism and Islam—first in embracing the synthesis for which Rāmānand stood, then by reinforcing it with an allegiance to Sheikh Taqī.[38]

Now it has long been in the nature of hagiographies to fuse—not just in India but worldwide, as the comparative study of religion so clearly teaches. Episodes travel easily from the life of one saint to another, or are accepted with equal facility into both, so that in actuality the force of any particular hagiography can usually be understood only by seeing it in relation to the lives of other saints. But we must not merely draw from this the lesson that hagiographies are notoriously unreliable as historical documents. We must go on to see what they do convey about the intentions of their authors. Like the collections of poetry attributed to the bhakti saints, they evolve over time and differ from place to place, and in each situation they tell us something about the community that shaped them. Still, we must be aware of their tendency to smooth the rough edges left by the sayings or tone of the saints themselves, and we must take account of the likelihood that the hagiographical narratives themselves may generate huge bodies of poetry attributed to the saint in question, as surely happened in the case of Mirabai. Much of the poetry attributed to her seems autobiographical, but really it is hagiographical.

Consider, for instance, that we possess only two poems in the entire Mirabai corpus for which a date in her century, the sixteenth, could be proposed on any compelling basis.[39] And her life is on no firmer historical ground than Kabir's. Although the movies, in particular, have had the effect of creating a unified 'master narrative', earlier versions sometimes diverge sharply from it and from one another. (See Chapter 4.) To deal with this legendary life at any level as if it had been history just cannot bear scrutiny. Even Kumkum Sangari, for all her carefully exposited awareness of the difficulties inherent in trying to disentangle legend and history, and of 'an oral corpus which cannot be reduced to a single author', ultimately proceeds as if there were a real, really knowable Mira. The reader forms an image of a person located at a real moment in the history of Mewar (despite the absence of any dynastic record from Mewar that mentions her) and producing poems that belong to that period.[40]

Yet given the status of our evidence for Mira, we have to conclude that these reflections, however nuanced, must be read as a new kind of meta-hagiography. Whenever we speak of Mira, we must do so in a way that makes it clear we know we are just using shorthand for one or another 'Mira tradition': our sources cannot support more. In this regard, it is the great merit of Parita Mukta's sociological work on the performance and veneration of Mira by lower-caste communities in present-day Saurashtra and western Rajasthan to have shown how markedly their Mira differs from the one projected in, say, Paraśurām Caturvedī's widely used edition.[41]

At a certain level it cannot be doubted that Mira is an integrating force in Indian national mythology: she is known throughout the country. But scratch the surface and you find that different communities of interpretation have actually made her what she 'is'—and she is no one thing.[42] With Mira we see pointedly what is ultimately true for all the bhakti saints: since we possess autographed manuscripts for none of them, we know the saints only through those who have loved (or perhaps occasionally despised) them. In the end, there is no breaking the hermeneutical circle.

At least from a literary point of view, that is perhaps as it should be, and this is the point at which hagiographical and historical studies merge with studies of ritual and performance. Philip Lutgendorf has drawn attention to the fact that the *Rāmcaritmānas* is structured internally as *kathā*: Tulsidas composed with more than a passing thought to how he expected the *Mānas* to be performed.[43] Similarly Kenneth Bryant has stressed the point that what makes so many *Sūrsāgar* poems great is their success in manipulating the expectations of the audiences they anticipate.[44] Linda Hess's rhetorical analysis of Kabir is a kindred exercise.[45] And David Lorenzen has shown how Kabir has been interpreted and 'used' in a variety of differing ways, depending on region, social location, and the period in question.[46]

When we look closely, then, we see in Kabir a poet-saint whose authority rests on a good deal more than the force of his own language: we see in him the authority of the communities who received and shaped those words. Wilfred Cantwell Smith has powerfully argued that this is exactly what we must expect when a body of words becomes scripture.[47] For the three communities (*panths*) that have preserved—and doubtless altered, augmented, and edited—Kabir's words over the past half millennium, 'Kabir' is clearly scripture. The desire to appeal to Kabir that we see in Rustom Bharucha and others—the broadside directed by the Dalit writer Dharmavīr against 'Kabir's critics' is the best-known recent example[48]—shows that he also has an authority that goes beyond these communities, and probably always has. In the same vein Bharucha's setting Kabir alongside others generally of his period and ilk reveals an implicit sense of canon. Like any other, this is a constructed canon, and if there is a single lesson to be drawn from observing current work on the bhakti poet-saints of North India, it is probably that.[49]

North Indian bhakti may not always satisfy the demand that it provide resources for strengthening democratic values and heightening respect for the validity of various religious traditions. Certainly Kabir is hard to line up as a dependable warrior on that battlefield: his way of respecting the truth was to denigrate the falsehoods surrounding it. He repeatedly belittled the cherished beliefs and practices of Hindus and Muslims alike. Even the good side of this—that he treated 'Hindu and Turk' evenhandedly—may have been motivated at least in part not by conceptual but by rhetorical or literary imperatives. The parallels they present to one another in a *pad* or *dohā* make good hearing when, as in both these genres, each verse is separated near the center by a caesura: the Hindus tend to go on one side, the Turks on the other. When the poet emerges with his own voice at the end of so many *pads*, he sometimes obliterates the caesura, thus dramatizing his triumph over these two literary straw men. This is reconciliation in only a limited sense. Both substantively and stylistically, it is not tolerance, but unsparingly evenhanded critique, a critique whose purpose is to make us, the audience, conspirators in the intolerance—we smile—and therefore capable of transcending our own worlds.

Or perhaps, on occasion, we can be made to weep. It was a stroke of genius when Anand Patwardhan, at the end of his documentary 'Rām ke Nām' ('In the Name of Rām'), quoted the following Kabir *pad*:

> Saints, I see the world is mad:
> Hindus claim Rām as the one,
> Muslims claim Rahīm.

In the aftermath of Ayodhya 1992, these words could be heard as a lament over religion on the part of a figure Patwardhan identifies as 'poet-saint of the working classes'. The implicit lesson seems to be that class consciousness ought to supersede religion, and the poem itself presents no bar since, unlike so many others in the Kabir corpus, it makes no appeal to the deity as it concludes. Patwardhan's, then, is a deft use of Kabir, for he draws on a poem whose pedigree is good and whose critical agenda is clear. It is the 'easier' Kabir poems, the ones where kindly tolerance flows right there on the surface, that turn out to come from much more recent strata of the Kabir tradition.

Yet in both instances we face a dilemma if we try to rescue from Kabir a respect for multiformity and religious pluralism. If these are to be found along with a respect for 'democratic values', we must discover them at another level. They must be located not in the poet himself, whoever he was, but in the different communities that have revered and remembered him, and we may say the same thing in greater or less measure for all his bhakti peers. These poets' intimate involvement with their audiences—in their own lifetimes, doubtless, but certainly down the generations as subsequent performers and their audiences have taken up these roles—is the real democracy of bhakti. What is striking about the communities who have made Kabir their own is not their homogeneity—their regionlessness or classlessness—but their variousness; sometimes they have openly conflicted with one another. To acknowledge that even a personality of such seemingly ineradicable definition as Kabir has in fact been interpreted in a hundred ways, both theoretically and socially, is to locate authority where so much of it is actually to be found: in dialogue and even dispute. Literary/textual, hagiographical, and social/historical studies of Kabir show that he is organic and complex, for he exists only in relation to those who remember him, from whatever angle.

I am not sure I find anything in Kabir to suggest guidelines for managing that dialogue, except an uncanny mix of raucous amusement and utter seriousness, but his fearlessly wide scope certainly suggests that everybody belongs in the game. The ways in which he has been revered show that all sorts of people felt they did belong in the game, and that has been Kabir's greatness. Among other things, it is the greatness of the variousness of his transmission—and that goes as far back in memory as scholarship will permit us to see.

Conclusion

It is surely true that the bhakti 'movement', experienced all over India, has constituted an interregional network that can be and has been useful to the cause of national integration and conflict mediation. This is true horizontally—many bhakti motifs seem to have passed from one linguistic region to another without being mediated through 'hegemonic' Sanskrit—and in some ways it is true vertically, as well. There is much in the multi-caste organization of bhakti (the well known regional 'families' of *bhaktas* and the contrasting *panths* that enshrine them) and in its explicit content that criticizes the inequities of caste. Consider, for example, these two visionary poems—one attributed to Mira, the other (since at least 1604) to Ravidas:[50]

चालाँ अगम वा देस, काल देख्याँ डराँ
भराँ प्रेम रा होज, हंस केल्याँ कराँ
सावा संत रो संग, ग्याण जुगताँ कराँ
घराँ साँवरो ध्यान चित्त उजलो कराँ
सील घूँघरा वाँध तोस निरताँ कराँ
साजाँ सोल सिंगार, सोणारो राखडाँ
साँवलिया सू प्रीत, मीराँ सूँ आखडाँ

Let us go to a realm beyond going,
  where death is afraid to go,
Where the high-flying birds alight and play,
  afloat in the full lake of love.
There they gather—the good, the true—
  to strengthen an inner regimen,
To focus on the dark form of the Lord
  and refine their minds like fire.
Garbed in goodness—their ankle bells—
  they dance the dance of contentment
And deck themselves with the sixteen signs
  of beauty, and a golden crown—
There where the love of the Dark One comes first
  and everything else is last.

बेगम पुरा सहर को नाउ   दुखु अंदोहु नही तिहि ठाउ
नां तसवीस खिराजु न मालु   खउफु न खता न तरसु जवालु
अब मोहि खूब बतन गह पाई   ऊहां खैरि सदा मेरे भाई
काइमु दाईमु सदा पातिसाही   दोम न सेम एक सो आही
आबादानु सदा मसहूर   ऊहां गनी बसहि मामूर
तिउ तिउ सैल करहि जिउ भावै   महरम महल न को अटकावै
कहि रविदास खलास चमारा   जो हम सहरी सु मीतु हमारा

The regal realm with the sorrowless name:
  they call it Queen City, a place with no pain,
No taxes or cares, none owns property there,
  no wrongdoing, worry, terror, or torture,
Oh my brother, I've come to take it as my own,
  my distant home, where everything is right.
That imperial kingdom is rich and secure,
  where none are third or second—all are one.

Its food and drink are famous, and those who live there
 dwell in satisfaction and in wealth.
They do this or that, they walk where they wish,
 they stroll through fabled palaces unchallenged.
Oh, says Ravidas, a tanner now set free,
 those who walk beside me are my friends.

Both these poems envision a happy social democratization before God, and it is hard to read the 'Queen City' poem, describing a 'place with no pain' (both phrases translate the word *begampurā*) without feeling the years and years of pain the *camār* poet must have known in the cities of this world. Does it help the cause of national integration that in other poems he seems to accept and even glory in his lowly social status, seeing it as a vehicle of grace? For Brahmins and Vaiśyas, maybe yes; for Dalits, no. Perhaps in that mix of response lies the hope of bhakti as a resource for democratization, social reform, and meaningful integration.

Jagjīvan Rām's temple to Ravidas in Banaras is designed so that four of its spires, one at each corner, will represent major religious traditions, and these serve effectively as *lokapālas* for a fifth: the central tower representing a universal 'people's religion', the faith Ravidas is held to have espoused.[51] Well and good, you may say, particularly if you have sympathies for the Congress Party to which Jagjīvan Rām belonged and which is also implicitly represented as holding that faith. But look at what many feel happened to the well-intended homogeneity that Rāmānand Sāgar wished to project in his TV vision of the *Rāmāyaṇa*. The various languages (including Urdu) that appeared on screen at the beginning of each episode were all too easily transmogrified into bricks for the Rāmjanmabhūmi temple at Ayodhya, drawn together from all parts of India and abroad. This is a sort of national integration that unifies some by excluding others. Exclusion—and therefore destruction—is at its symbolic core.

Bhakti has its antipluralist potential too, and nothing symbolizes it so clearly as the distance between Kabir's catholic, non-sectarian sense of Rām and the construction that has been put on that word (that deity!) by the Vishva Hindu Parishad. For many of us who care about the history and potential of bhakti, it has been chilling to see the ground troops of the VHP's Ayodhya agenda increasingly characterized by friend and foe as *rām bhaktas*. One has to say yes to this term in one sense—this is how the *kārsevaks* portray themselves—but one has to say no in many others.

So we must not romanticize. There are certainly occasions, as for instance in performances of *rās līlās* in Brindavan, when bhakti breaks down distinctions of class and caste that are observed in other contexts. But as Christopher Fuller's recent summary of various bhakti traditions in their social contexts shows, it is at least as easy to argue that bhakti has upheld the hierarchical *status quo* as that it has called it into fundamental question. Even when it seemed to be an instrument of social facilitation or amelioration, as Milton Singer perceived it to be in performances of the Radha-Krishna *bhajans* of Chennai, social hierarchies were actually in some ways being further reinforced.[52] Yet because bhakti poetry and sometimes bhakti sociology do typically pitch themselves at an angle to the *status quo* and *dharma* as commonly understood, the resources for social criticism and the appreciation of others who are silenced or neglected are always, in some sense, there.

David Pocock said about his experience of living in Gujarat that he 'never heard anybody suggest that the ritual and caste-transcending message of the *bhajan* should be put into practice.'[53] Perhaps not, but Parita Mukta's experience in the same general region was quite different. And even in the Pocock vein, the important point to grasp is that whether or not bhakti is always in some fundamental sense *about* democracy, it nonetheless *is* democracy.[54] Undoubtedly there are settings where bhakti has been carefully cordoned off from the rough-and tumble of everyday life, and represented as some splendid, polished pavilion.[55] The pavilion may take the shape of a temple or a theology (perhaps even with a commentarial literature in Sanskrit explaining the words of a poet who deplored that language—Kabir), or it may take the very different form of modern social scientese pressed into service for the advancement of a progressive agenda. But the great thing about bhakti as a resource for democracy and national integration is that it always eludes such airy pavilions. It is a people's literature, a people's religion, and its expressions vary across the social spectrum, with new infusions all the time. Here we have real people's reactions to the world, real people's imaginations and aspirations—and in ever so many voices. So bhakti is a resource for national integration in the same way that religion differs from philosophy. It is practices along with words, a whole multiform experiential complex, and both words and practices range from the most complex and arcane to the roughest, most down-to-earth.

By making a habit of looking at such things as bhakti from all sides, and insofar as possible without prejudice to any faith commitment, the modern academic study of religion tries to achieve clarity about what religion means in its many contexts. At its best, it does not romanticize. But neither does it rob the religious realm of the fascination—and sometimes the horror—that has drawn people to it for as long as our species can remember. As Rustom Bharucha suggests, some attempts to 'denude' religion of that central element have proved as dangerous and false (and as perversely 'religious') as the extreme forms of religion itself.[56] Only by looking at these facts, and taking the good with the bad—not that we always know which is which—can we hope to make real progress in a world from which religion is not about to disappear.

Might the institutionalization of secular learning about religion help along the way?

Notes

Introduction

1. C. L. Prabhāt, *Mīrā: Jīvan aur Kāvya* (Jodhpur: Rājasthān Granthāgār, 1999), vol. 2, p. 265.

2. Mātāprasād Gupta, 'Sūr Sāgar kī Bhūmikā,' ed. Udayśaṅkar Śāstrī *Bhāratīya Sāhitya* 13:1–2 (1968), pp. 43–5.

3. Gupta, 'Sūr Sāgar kī Bhūmikā,' p. 7.

4. Kenneth E. Bryant, 'Toward a Critical Edition of the *Sūrasāgar*,' in Winand M. Callewaert, ed., *Early Hindī Devotional Literature in Current Research* (Delhi: Impex India, 1980), p. 9.

5. Indeed, one could argue, as Rachel Dwyer has proposed, that 'the later versions of the *Sūrsāgar* have a greater validity because it is these versions which are read and loved today. . . . ' See Dwyer, *The Poetics of Devotion: The Gujarati Lyrics of Dayārām* (Richmond, Surrey: Curzon Press, 2001), p. 10. The phrase 'Sūr tradition' was coined by Kenneth E. Bryant, *Poems to the Child-God: Structures and Strategies in the Poetry of Sūrdās* (Berkeley: University of California Press, 1978), pp. xi–xii.

6. See Hawley, *Krishna, The Butter Thief* (Princeton: Princeton University Press, 1983), pp. 99–177.

7. Purushottam Agrawal, 'Crisis Points in the Mahabharata,' lecture given at the India Habitat Centre, New Delhi, 9 September 2003.

8. Other sections from this poem, *hari ne aisī rela banāī*, as heard from a different performer, are recorded and translated by Bahadur Singh in 'Problems of Authenticity in the Kabir Texts,' in Monika Horstmann, ed., *Images of Kabīr* (Delhi: Manohar, 2002), p. 195.

9. The performer is Prahlād Siṃh Tipāniā (1993), and a cassette recording is available from Sonotek Electronic Industries, 40 Saket Nagar, Jabalpur, M.P.

10. In a stimulating recent study, *Kabir: The Weaver's Songs* (New Delhi: Penguin, 2003), Vinay Dharwadker approaches this set of issues from a somewhat different angle. Surveying the range and diversity of sources in which we meet poetry attributed to Kabīr, he asks whether one can really speak

of a single Kabīr at all. Dharwadker argues one cannot—the Kabīr we have is a 'community of authors'—and suggests that only the ingrained preoccupations of 'colonial and post-colonial philologists' have prevented them from owning up to the implications of their own work in this regard (p. 60). Thus he holds a somewhat different group of scholars, including philologists writing in European languages, responsible for substantially the same failure of nerve that I have associated with the general drift of scholarship in Hindi. Dharwadker paints with a broad brush and has a view of the scholars he criticizes—'philologists'—that I do not always find sustainable (see Chapter 15). His general point is an important one, and runs closely parallel to what I have argued above, yet I wonder whether he ends up succumbing to the same malady he diagnoses in others. He finds at the core of the Kabīr corpus a 'remarkable thematic and imaginative consistency' that allows him, before he is through, to set forth a veritable systematic theology that belongs to 'the Kabir poets' (pp. 77–8), if not to a single, historical Kabīr. And I wonder if he has thrown out the baby with the bath water by largely resisting, in the name of collective authorship, the admittedly philological task of separating earlier textual strata from later ones. Philology or no, it would be a great mistake to think that the task of doing history, either within or outside the 'literary' domain, is somehow un-Indian. On this point, and specifically against 'the post-modernist attempt... to deny any distinction whatsoever between history and literature' on the grounds that 'all is discourse, internal to language itself,' see Velcheru Narayana Rao, David Shulman, and Sanjay Subrahmanyam, *Textures of Time: Writing History in South India 1600–1800* (New Delhi: Permanent Black, 2001), p. 18 and *passim*.

11. Bryant, *Poems to the Child-God*, pp. 21–42. A related line of thinking, though at a much more general level, is pursued by G. N. Devy in *After Amnesia: Tradition and Change in Indian Literary Criticism* (Bombay: Orient Longman, 1992), pp. 74–92.

12. *Ibid.*, p. 40.

13. *Ibid.*, pp. 37, 39.

14. These connections emerged in conversation with Shrivatsa Goswami (Brindavan, October, 1998), and I am grateful to him as well for subsequent correspondence on the matter. For a general discussion of the subject, focusing on *ākāṃkṣā* as syntactic mutual expectancy, see K. Kunjunni Raja, *Indian Theories of Meaning* (Madras: Vedanta Press, 1963), pp. 151–62; cf. K. Kunjunni Raja, 'Ākāṅkṣā: The Main Basis of Syntactic Unity,' *Adyar Library Bulletin* 21: 3–4 (1957), pp. 282–95.

15. Rāmcandra Śukla, *Hindī Sāhitya kā Itihās: Saṃśodhit evam Pravardhit Saṃskaraṇ* (Allahabad: A to Zed Publishing, 2001 [originally Benares, 1929]), pp. 39–155.

16. Dharmavīr, *Kabīr ke Ālocak* (New Delhi: Vāṇī Prakāśaṇ, 1997).

1. Author and Authority

1. David Shulman, 'From Author to Non-Author in Tamil Literary Legend,' *Journal of the Institute of Asian Studies* 10:2 (1993), 1–23; Mukund Lath, *Half a Tale: A Study in the Interrelationship between Autobiography and History* (Jaipur: Rajasthan Prakrit Bharati Sansthan, 1981), pp. x–xx.

2. In the second verse of a Hindi *dohā* (rhymed couplet), the author's name often occurs (an early example is translated in R. S. McGregor, *Hindi Literature from its Beginnings to the Nineteenth Century* [Wiesbaden: Otto Harrassowitz, 1984], p. 26), and one typically finds it near the conclusion of the early Bengali *caryā* poems and Marathi *abhaṅgas*, both of which are roughly analogous to the Hindi *pad.* See Dusan Zvabilel, *Bengali Literature* (Wiesbaden: Otto Harrassowitz, 1976), p. 131; Sukumar Sen, *A History of Bengali Literature* (New Delhi: Sahitya Academy, 1971), pp. 19, 24–30; and S. G. Tulpule, *Classical Marāṭhī Literature from the Beginning to A.D. 1818* (Wiesbaden: Otto Harrassowitz, 1979), pp. 336–7, 347, *passim.* Certain analogies are also to be found in the Urdu *ghazal*, the Kashmiri songs of Lālded, and in Dravidian lyrics: the *vacanas* and *padams* of Kannada and Telugu and the *patikams* of the Tamil *Tevāram.*

3. The *Oxford English Dictionary* gives as its third definition of the term author 'One who sets forth written statements....' The fourth and fifth options, however, are the ones I have in mind here. They are, respectively, 'The person on whose authority a statement is made...' and 'One who has authority over others...' (1970, p. 572).

4. Padam Gurcaran Siṃh, *Sant Ravidās: Vicārak aur Kavi* (Jalandhar: Nav-Cintan Prakāśan, 1977), pp. 191–204.

5. Rajab's *Sarvāṅgī* contains 22 *pads* and one *sākhī* of Ravidās, and its parent work, the *Pañcvāṇī*, contains a total ranging from 65 to 71 poems in various manuscript versions dating from 1636 to 1676 CE: Winand M. Callewaert, *The Sarvāṅgī of the Dādūpanthī Rajab* (Leuven: Katholieke Universiteit, 1978), p. 436, and private communication, 21 February 1987.

6. Mark Juergensmeyer, *Religion as Social Vision: The Movement against Untouchability in Twentieth-Century Punjab* (Berkeley: University of California Press, 1982), pp. 260–2; Julie Womack, 'Ravidas and the Chamars of Banaras,' undergraduate essay, University of Wisconsin, 1983, pp. 56–7; R. S. Khare, *The Untouchable as Himself* (Cambridge: Cambridge University Press, 1984), pp. 40–50, 97; J. S. Hawley and Mark Juergensmeyer, *Songs of the Saints of India* (Delhi: Oxford University Press, 2004), chapter 1.

7. K. N. Upadhyaya, *Guru Ravidas: Life and Teachings* (Beas, Punjab: Radha Soami Satsang Beas, 1982), p. 12.

8. Bantā Rām Gherā, *Śrī Guru Ravidās jī kā Saṃkṣipt Itihās* (n.p.: All India Adi Dharm Mission, n.d.). A very different sort of re-evaluation of traditional accounts of Ravidās's life—this one having a theological or ideological format

rather than a biographical one—has been assayed by Candrikāprasād Jijñāsu, *Santpravar Ravidās Sāheb* (Lucknow: Bahujan Kalyāṇ Prakāśan, 1984 [originally 1968]). The 1990s saw a thoroughgoing revision in understandings of what Gherā had accomplished. A struggle between Gherā's group and that of the Punjabi religious leader Sant Sarvan Dās was settled in court—in the latter's favor. Nowadays one hears in Sri Govardhanpur that, for instance, it was not Gherā but Sant Sarvan Dās who discovered the link between the *imlī* tree and Gorakhnāth (Prakāś Māhī, Interview, 11 November 2003).

9. Poem no. 2 in the *Guru Ravi Dās Granth* (handwritten in Devanagari script on the basis of a published original in Gurmukhi) as transcribed for Virendra Singh. I am grateful to Virendra Singh for permission to make use of this copy.

10. Gherā, *Itihās*, p. 1; Khare, *The Untouchable as Himself*, p. 47.

11. B. R. Gherā, Interview, New Delhi, 23 August 1983.

12. W. H. McLeod, *Early Sikh Tradition* (Oxford: Clarendon Press, 1980), pp. 287–8.

13. Monika Thiel-Horstmann, 'The *Bhajan* Repertore of the Present-day Dādūpanth,' in Horstmann, ed., *Bhakti in Current Research, 1979–1982* (Berlin: Dietrich Reimer Verlag, 1983), pp. 385–401, and *Nächtliches Wachen: Eine Form indischen Gottesdienstes* (Bonn: Indica et Tibetica Verlag, 1985).

14. Kabīr [attributed], *Anurāg Sāgar* (Allahabad: Belvedere Printing Works, 1975), pp. 44ff., translated by Raj Kumar Bhagge, Partap Singh, and Kent Bicknell as *The Ocean of Love* (Sanfornton, NH: Sant Bani Ashram, 1982), pp. 85ff.

15. J. S. Hawley, 'The Sectarian Logic of the *Sūr Dās kī Vārtā*' in Horstmann, ed., *Bhakti 1979–1982*, pp. 158–69.

16. J. S. Hawley, Chapter 9 *infra*, and *Sūr Dās: Poet, Singer, Saint* (Seattle: University of Washington Press; Delhi: Oxford University Press, 1984), pp. 35–63; Kenneth E. Bryant, 'The Manuscript Tradition of the Sursagar: The Fatehpur Manuscript,' in Gopal Narayan Bahura and K. E. Bryant, eds, *Pad Sūrdāsjī kā/ The Padas of Sūrdās* (Jaipur: Maharaja Sawai Man Singh II Museum, 1982 [actually appeared 1984]), pp. vii–xx.

17. We know that this happened in the case of several poems normally listed as part of the *Sūrsāgar*. They seem to have appeared earlier, with different signatures, in collections of verse attributed to Hit Harivaṃś, Paramānandadās, and Tulsīdās. See R. S. McGregor, 'Tulsīdās's Śrīkṛṣṇagītāvalī,' *Journal of the American Oriental Society* 96:4 (1976), pp. 520–6; and Chapter 9 of the present work. On the Mīrābāī question, compare Bhagavāndās Tivārī, ed., *Mīrāṅ kī Prāmāṇik Padāvalī* (Allahabad: Sāhitya Bhavan, 1974), p. 33, and McGregor, *Hindi Literature*, p. 82.

18. Hawley, *Sūr Dās*, pp. 3–33.

19. I am grateful to my musical wife for this comparison. Vinay Dharwadkar has put it another way by proposing that every poem in the Kabīr corpus is

'explicitly a palimpsest,' but his idea that 'each poem is [intended]...to be recomposed until all its particular poetic possibilities have been exhausted' goes beyond what I would claim (*Kabir: The Weaver's Songs*, p. 65).

20. Philip Lutgendorf, Private communication, 7 April 1987.

21. Cf. Gokulnāth [attributed], *Caurāsī Vaiṣṇavan kī Vārtā,* ed. Dvārikādās Parīkh (Mathura: Śrī Bajaraṅg Pustakālay, 1970 [originally 1948]), pp. 434–45.

22. W. H. McLeod, *The Evolution of the Sikh Tradition* (Delhi: Oxford University Press, 1975), pp. 72–5; Pritam Singh, 'Bhāī Banno's Copy of the Sikh Scripture,' in Horstmann, ed., *Bhakti 1979–1982,* pp. 325–7, 331–2.

23. Heidi R. M. Pauwels, 'Rāṭhauṛī Mīrā: Two Neglected Rāṭhauṛ Connections of Mīrā: Jaimal Meṛtīyo and Nāgrīdās,' in Nancy M. Martin, ed., *Mirabai: Hindu Saint for a Global World,* forthcoming. For further details, especially concerning the additional score of poems apparently discovered by C. L. Prabhāt in the Gujarāt Vidyā Sabhā Library, Ahmedabad, see Chapter 4.

24. In his *Mīrāṅ-Bṛhatpadāvalī*, a study of manuscripts in Rajasthani collections that contain poems of Mīrā, Kalyāṇsiṃh Śekhāvat has found poems bearing Mīrā's signature in manuscripts dating to VS 1826, 1834, and 1836 (= 1769, 1777, and 1779 CE). See Mīrābāī [attributed], *Mīrāṅ-Bṛhatpadāvalī,* vol. 2, ed. Kalyāṇsiṃh Śekhāvat (Jodhpur: Rajasthan Oriental Research Institute, 1975), pp. 4, 6. In the early 1950s, C. L. Prabhāt surveyed collections in Gujarat and Bombay and found 173 poems in seven eighteenth-century manuscripts: see his *Mīrā: Jīvan aur Kāvya* (Jodhpur: Rājasthānī Granthāgār, 1999), pp. 225–35. All but twelve were concentrated in a Dakor manuscript of VS 1805 (1748 CE) and a manuscript in the collection of Raman Desai of Bombay dating to VS 1851 (1798 CE); I do not know how many of these are duplicates. The sources underlying the first volume of the *Mīrāṅ-Bṛhatpadāvalī* (1968) and the methods used by its editor, Harinārāyaṇ Śarmā, to compile it are unknown, as are the sources and methods lying behind the edition that is most widely used today: Paraśurām Caturvedī's *Mīrābāī kī Padāvalī.*

Similar uncertainties attend many other editions. Of these, the one that most directly challenges the conclusions presented above is Lalitāprasād Sukul's *Mīrāṅ Smṛti Granth,* which purports to give the contents of two manuscripts of Mīrā's poetry that Sukul obtained in Dakor, Gujarat, in 1924. One, said to have been written in Dakor itself, is dated to VS 1642 (1585 CE), and the other, from Banaras, is dated to VS 1727 (1670 CE). The former contains sixty-nine poems, which the latter repeats in the same order before giving an additional thirty-four. These poems have been reproduced with a comparative apparatus in Bhagavāndās Tivārī's *Mīrāṅ kī Prāmāṇik Padāvalī.* I regret that I have not as yet been able to see the manuscripts upon which these editions are based, since the information published about them has caused me to doubt their authenticity. The very early dating of the Dakor manuscript, in particular, would make it remarkable, considering that the great manuscript libraries of North India (e.g., the Kāśī Nāgarīpracāriṇī Sabhā in Banaras, the royal Pothīkhānā in Jaipur, and the Vrindaban Research Institute) contain no early manuscripts exclusively devoted to Mīrā. With the rarest exceptions, as stated above, her poems are not even anthologized in early manuscripts. Further doubt is cast by the fact that these two manuscripts were obtained from a single source and that, despite the disparate provenances claimed for them, they contain a common store of poems with identical readings. Śekhāvat was bothered by the occurrence of *ḍ* in some of the poems: Kalyāṇsiṃh Śekhāvat, *Mīrāṅbāī kā Jīvanvṛtt evaṃ Kāvya* (Jodhpur: Hindī Sāhitya Mandir, 1974), p. 15. I am more struck by the frequent substitution of *ś* for *s*, a fact that would seem to suggest the place of publication (Calcutta) rather than the cities with which the manuscripts themselves are said to be associated, unless hypercorrection is involved. At the very least, such circumstances force us to question the authenticity of these two manuscripts until the originals can be examined. For further details, see Chapter 4.

25. *Japjī* 10.3.

26. Manmohan Sahgal, commentary on the *Japjī* in *Śrī Gurū Granth Sāhib* (Lucknow: Bhuvan Bāṇī Trust, 1978), p. 40.

27. Sūrdās [attributed], NPS 3854.6.

28. Dhīrendra Varmā, *Sūrsāgar-Sār Saṭīk* (Allahabad: Sāhitya Bhavan, 1972), p. 244.

29. E.g., Sūrdās, NPS 3847.14, 2376.5; *Mīrāṇ-Bṛhatpadāvalī,* vol. 1, ed., Harinārāyaṇ Śarmā (Jodhpur: Rajasthan Oriental Research Institute, 1968), *pads* 36.4, 173.4.

30. See, e.g., Friedhelm Hardy, 'The Tamil Veda of a *Śūdra* Saint: The Śrivaiṣṇava Interpretation of Nammāḻvār,' in G. Krishna, ed., *Contributions to South Asian Studies*, vol. 1 (Delhi: Oxford University Press, 1978), pp. 29–87; A. K. Ramanujan, *Hymns for the Drowning: Poems for Viṣṇu by Nammāḻvār* (Princeton: Princeton University Press, 1981), p. 165; Shulman, 'Author to Non-Author'; or Norman Cutler, 'Implied Poets in the Real World: A Study of Tamil Saints,' paper presented to the Wisconsin Conference on South Asia, Madison, 5 November 1983.

31. Narendra Jhā, ed., *Bhaktamāl: Pāṭhānuśīlan evam Vivecan* (Patna: Anupam Prakāśan, 1978), pp. 40–6; Gilbert Pollet, 'Early Evidence on Tulsīdās and his Epic,' *Orientalia Lovaniensia Periodica* 5 (1974), pp. 157–9.

32. Cf. McLeod, *Evolution*, pp. 60–2, 73–9.

33. Bryant, 'The Manuscript Tradition,' pp. 37–47.

34. Nābhādās, *Śrī Bhaktamāl*, with the *Bhaktirasabodhinī* commentary of Priyādās and ed. by Sītārāmśaraṇ Bhagavānprasād Rūpakalā (Lucknow: Tejkumār Press, 1969 [originally 1910], pp. 718–19.

35. *Bhaktamāl*, pp. 712–13.

36. Paraśurām Caturvedī, ed., *Mīrāṅbāī kī Padāvalī* (Allahabad: Hindī Sāhitya Sammelan, 1973 [originally 1932]), p. 111, *pad* 37. In translation, as in performance, the refrain is repeated at intervals throughout the poem.

37. Mīrābāī [attributed], *Mīrāṅ-Bṛhatpadāvalī*, vol. 2, ed. Śekhāvat, pp. 68, 72, 76—*pads* 140, 148, 167.

38. Hardy, 'Tamil Veda,' pp. 338–9.

39. Hawley, *Sūr Dās*, p. 48.

40. *Ibid.*, pp. 7, 19, 45.

41. *Vārtā*, p. 414.

42. *Ibid.*, p. 422. In verse 3, Passion is Rati, wife of the god Kāma, who is 'limbless' (*anaṅga*) in consequence of his famous encounter with Shiva, in which the ascetic god reduced him to ash with a blast of yogic heat stored in his third eye. The second half of the fourth line is capable of a second interpretation, which will become relevant to our discussion presently. It could be rendered 'and Sūr joins the girls of Braj in laughing at him.' The implications of this poem are reconsidered in Chapter 10.

43. Siṃh, *Sant Ravidas*, p. 195, *pad* 13. The reference to the act that 'formed both nectar and poison' is to the churning of the primordial milk ocean on the part of the gods and demons. They desired the liquid of immortality, but as they churned the ocean, they drew up not only the elixir but a deadly poison as well.

44. Hawley, *Krishna, The Butter Thief* (Princeton: Princeton University Press, 1983), pp. 171–6; *Sūr Dās*, pp. 54–86.

45. Cf. A. K. Ramanujan, *Speaking of Śiva* (Baltimore: Penguin Books, 1973), p. 90.

46. Hawley, *Butter Thief*, pp. 118–20 [Sūr], and 'Images of Gender in the Poetry of Krishna,' in Caroline Walker Bynum, Stevan Harrell, and Paula Richman, eds, *Gender and Religion: On the Complexity of Symbols* (Boston: Beacon Press, 1986), pp. 238–41 [Mīrā].

47. Siṃh, *Sant Ravidās*, p. 197, *pad* 19.

48. *Ibid.*, p. 198, *pad* 20. Similar sorts of poems, in which the central motif is the poet's caste occupation, can be found among compositions attributed to Kabīr, Nāmdev, and many others. For Nāmdev, the tailor, see Nāmdev [attributed] *rāg āsā*, no. 4 in the *Gurū Granth Sāhib* and as given in Rāmcandra Miśra, ed., *Sant Nāmdev aur Hindī Pad-Sāhitya* (Farukhabad: Śailendra Sāhitya Sadan, 1969), pp. 179, 209—*pads* 2145 and 2166. These are translated in Prabhakar Machwe, *Namdev: Life and Philosophy* (Patiala: Punjabi University, 1968), pp. 96, 101, 105. For Kabīr, the weaver, see Kabīr [attributed] *Kabīr Granthāvalī*, ed. Pārasnāth Tivārī (Allahabad: Allahabad University, 1961), vol. 2, p. 9, *pad* 12, translated in Hawley and Juergensmeyer, *Songs of the Saints of India*, p. 53, cf. p. 58.

49. A slightly different usage in South India is alluded to by Shulman, 'Author to Non-Author,' p. 2: *tirukka-ṭaikkāppu*, 'closing the gates,' in the *Tevāram patikams* (cf. Ramanujan, *Drowning*, p. 163). More directly apposite is the instance of the Hindi *dohā*, which is sometimes called a *sākhī*, as in the case of couplets attributed to Kabīr. This word means 'witness'—literally, 'one

who possesses an eye'—and suggests that the force of the utterance has something to do with the character of the person who makes it.

50. Siṃh, *Sant Ravidās*, pp. 192–4, 197—*pads* 3–5, 9, 19; cf. *ravidāsa dāsa, ravidāsa udāsa* in *pads* 6, 7, 16, 34, 38, 39.

51. Ramanujan, *Speaking of Śiva*, pp. 67–90, 115–42; cf. Ramanujan, *Drowning*, p. 163.

52. Wilfred Cantwell Smith, 'A Human View of Truth,' *SR: Sciences Religieuses/Studies in Religion*, 1 (1971), pp. 6–24; Werner Jaeger, *Paideia: The Ideals of Greek Culture*, trans. Gilbert Highet (New York: Oxford University Press, 1943–5); Peter Brown, 'The Saint as Exemplar in Late Antiquity,' *Representations* 1:2 (1983), pp. 1–25, and in J. S. Hawley, ed., *Saints and Virtues* (Berkeley: University of California Press, 1987), pp. 3–14.

2. Morality Beyond Morality

1. On *The Laws of Manu*, see P. V. Kane, *History of Dharmaśāstra*, 5 vols. (Poona: Bhandarkar Oriental Research Institute, 1930–46), and Robert Lingat, *The Classical Law of India*, trans. J. Duncan M. Derrett (Berkeley: University of California Press, 1973); in regard to its date, pp. 92–6, 123–32 of the latter.

2. I shall be referring to the following edition: Nābhādās, *Śrī Bhaktamāl* (Lucknow: Tejkumār Press, 1969). Critical work on the *Bhaktamāl* has been undertaken by Narendra Jhā in his *Bhaktamāl: Pāṭhānuśīlan evam Vivecan* (Patna: Anupam Prakāśan, 1978). The texts he offers differ insubstantially from those given in the Tejkumār Press edition. In addition, one may consult two articles of Gilbert Pollet: 'Eight Manuscripts of the Hindi *Bhaktamāla* in England,' *Orientalia Lovaniensia Periodica* 1 (1970), pp. 203–22, and 'The Mediaeval Vaiṣṇava Miracles as Recorded in the Hindi "Bhakta Māla,"' *Le Muséon* 80 (1976), pp. 475–87. An important recent contribution is that of William R. Pinch, 'History, Devotion, and the Search for Nabhadas of Galta,' in Daud Ali, ed., *Invoking the Past: The Uses of History in South Asia* (Delhi: Oxford University Press, 1999), pp. 367–99.

3. Lists of the Tamil Shaiva saints began to appear in the eighth century and were expanded into full-blown hagiographies in the eleventh and twelfth centuries. On the Vaishnava side, Tamil hagiographies begin to appear in the thirteenth century with the *Āṛāyirappaṭi Kuruparaparāprapāvam*, though the *Divya Sūri Carita* has sometimes been thought to be a century earlier. The *Śūnyasaṃpādane* of the Vīraśaiva community in Karnataka was produced in the fifteenth century. A century later the Maharashtrian saint Eknāth went on to compile a hagiographical collection in Marathi. On the Tamil materials, see Kamil Zvelebil, *Tamil Literature* (Wiesbaden: Otto Harrassowitz, 1974), pp. 91, 170, 173–5; in addition, I have benefited from a personal communication from Dennis Hudson (March 1983). On the *Śūnyasaṃpādane*, see R. Blake Michael, 'Aṣṭāvaraṇa in the *Śūnyasaṃpādane*' (PhD diss., Harvard University, 1979).

On Eknāth, see L. R. Pangarkar, *Marāṭhī Vāṇmayācā Itihās* (Pune: Vidarbh Marāṭhavāḍā Book Company, 1972 [originally 1935]), p. 242. In regard to the hagiographical tradition that followed Nābhādās, see Kailāś Candra Śarmā, *Bhaktamāl aur Hindī Kāvya meṅ unkī Paramparā* (Rohtak: Manthan Publication, 1983), pp. 65–159. One other work competes with Nābhādās's *Bhaktamāl* for the honor of being the oldest hagiographical collection in Hindi. These are the *parcaīs* of Anantdās, taken as a group (see note 20 below). Unlike the Nābhādās text, however, they do not always appear so grouped in their manuscript versions.

4. *Bhaktamāl*, pp. 41–6. In regard to the dating of Nābhādās's text, see Gilbert Pollet, 'Early Evidence on Tulsīdās and His Epic,' *Orientalia Lovaniensia Periodica* 5 (1974), pp. 157–8 (sec. 3.2). Corroborating evidence adduced in sections 3.3ff., however, seems problematic, especially insofar as it relies on biographies of Tulsīdās whose early date is doubtful. On this point, see Philip Lutgendorf, 'The Quest for the Legendary Tulsīdās,' *Journal of Vaiṣṇava Studies* 1:2 (1993), pp. 79–101, and—somewhat expanded—in Winand Callewaert and Rupert Snell, eds, *According to Tradition: Hagiographical Writing in India* (Wiesbaden: Otto Harrassowitz, 1994), pp. 65–85.

5. On Priyādās, see R. D. Gupta, 'Priyā Dās, Author of the *Bhaktirasabodhinī*,' *Bulletin of the School of Oriental and African Studies* 32:1 (1969), pp. 57–70; also Philip Lutgendorf, 'Kṛṣṇa Caitanya and His Companions as Presented in the *Bhaktamāla* of Nābhā Jī and the *Bhaktirasabodhinī* of Priyā Dāsa' (Master's essay, University of Chicago, 1981), pp. 24–9.

6. This is a fundamental tension in the life stories of many of India's best-known women saints, though it is not always worked out in the same terms as it is in Mīrā's case. Variations on the theme are explored by A. K. Ramanujan, 'On Women Saints,' in J. S. Hawley and Donna M. Wulff, eds, *The Divine Consort: Rādhā and the Goddesses of India* (Berkeley: Berkeley Religious Studies Series, 1982), pp. 316–24, and by Anne Feldhaus, 'Bahiṇā Bāī: Wife and Saint,' *Journal of the American Academy of Religion* 50:4 (1982), pp. 591–604. Further materials have been presented by R. Blake Michael in 'The Housewife as Saint: Tales from the *Śūnyasampādane*' (paper delivered to the American Academy of Religion, New York, 1979).

7. *Bhaktamāl*, pp. 712–13.

8. The term *rāṇā* refers to a male member of a royal or princely family and is in use in southwest Rajasthan.

9. *Bhaktamāl*, p. 718: *desapatī*.

10. *Ibid.*, p. 717. The term *sādhu* (or *sādhū*) has come to refer specifically to a religious mendicant in modern Hindi. I have translated it here, however, as 'saints' because the term had a wider range of meaning in older forms of the language, as the gloss offered by the text itself suggests.

11. *Satsaṅg* means 'the gathering of the good' or 'company of saints,' though the word 'saint' bears no etymological relation to *sant*. The term *sant*, deriving

ultimately from the Sanskrit participle of a verb that means both 'to be good' and 'to be real,' comes into vernacular North Indian usage with several meanings. In fifteenth- and sixteenth-century usage, it generally connotes 'the good,' almost invariably with the specific sense of those who are worshipping and singing of God. A somewhat different connotation has come to be attached to the term in intervening centuries. *Sant* is taken to refer to one of a group of holy men whose lineage can be traced back to the Nāth Yogīs and who espouse what has come to be referred to familiarly as *sant mat*, 'the point of view of the *sants*.' This is the usage given to the term by H. P. Dvivedi, Charlotte Vaudeville, W. H. McLeod, and others. Finally, in current Punjabi usage the term *sant* has come to refer to any holy man who lives apart from ordinary society. I shall use the term here in the first sense, the one that I believe is most directly in line with medieval usage. Further on this point, see J. S. Hawley, 'The *Sant* in Sūr Dās,' in *The Sants: Studies in a Devotional Traditional of India*, ed. Karine Schomer and W. H. McLeod (Berkeley: Berkeley Religious Studies Series; and Delhi: Motilal Banarsidass, 1987), p. 203.

The term *bhakta*, meaning 'loving devotee' and related to the Sanskrit root meaning 'to participate, to share,' is often distinguished from the term *sant* according to the second meaning of the latter term. The effect is to apply the term *bhakta* to those medieval poet-devotees who approved of the worship of God through image and drama (the *saguṇa*, 'with qualities,' approach) and *sant* to those who insist that such avenues are misleading (the *nirguṇa*, 'without qualities,' approach). In medieval usage, however, the two are much more closely synonymous than this distinction would suggest (cf. Chapter 3).

12. The phrase is *likhayau citra bhīta māno* (*Bhaktamāl*, p. 719).

13. *Bhaktamāl*, p. 722.

14. Indeed a term that might be translated 'fearlessness' (*niśaṃka*) is used to describe him, as it is various others of the saints of the *Bhaktamāl*—for instance, Sūrdās Madanmohan (*Bhaktamāl*, pp. 679, 748).

15. *Bhaktamāl*, pp. 673–4.

16. The imagery of irrigation and soaking is also used with reference to the lives of Pīpādās and his wife Sītā (*Bhaktamāl*, pp. 496–500), and liquid imagery is applied to Jīv Gosvāmī, Sūrdās Madanmohan, and Tulsīdās (*Bhaktamāl*, pp. 610, 749, 756).

17. *Bhaktamāl*, pp. 679–80.

18. *Genesis* 50:20 (Revised Standard Version). The *Bhaktamāl* tells a somewhat similar story about the disinterested stewardship of another's wealth on the part of Ravidās. In gratitude for the simple hospitality the saint has offered him, a visitor decides to entrust his *pāras* stone to Ravidās for safe-keeping. The *pāras* is no ordinary stone. It is capable of transforming base metals into gold, but this is a matter of no concern to Ravidās since he already has the stone he needs—namely, the image he worships. Because of the *pāras* hidden away in the thatch of his hut, however, Ravidās's assets begin to

multiply whether he wills it or not, but this is all due to the desire of Hari himself, who wants the money used to construct a splendid new temple where many can come to sing his praises under the guidance of the diffident saint (*Bhaktamāl*, pp. 474–5).

19. The motif of 'unconscious wealth' is an especially common one in the *Bhaktamāl*. Haridās squanders great amounts of a donor's precious perfume by pouring it on the banks of the River Jamuna, but the odor miraculously reappears in the temple for which the donor had intended it (*Bhaktamāl*, p. 602). Rāmdās is unjustly accused of stealing a valuable image and is required to pay for it. He says he has no gold whatever, but the accusing 'devotees' remind him of his wife's earnings, which, when weighed, are found to be worth so much that they cannot even be lifted off the ground (*Bhaktamāl*, pp. 451–3). The aphorism introducing Dhanā calls him the one whose crops grew in the absence of any seed (*Bhaktamāl*, p. 521). And many acts of unwonted generosity are attributed to various saints—for instance, King Caturbhuj, Sūrdās Madanmohan, and Tulsīdās (*Bhaktamāl*, pp. 708, 748, 766). A surprisingly different set of attitudes to work, wealth, and generosity on the part of a community that shares in the bhakti tradition is revealed in R. Blake Michael, 'Work as Worship in the Vīraśaiva Tradition,' *Journal of the American Academy of Religion* 50:4 (1982), pp. 605–19.

20. *Bhaktamāl*, p. 494. Along with the hagiographical sketches of Anantdās, the *Bhaktamāl* is the oldest extant text to assert that Kabīr, Ravidās, Pīpā, and Dhanā were pupils of Rāmānand (*Bhaktamāl*, p. 282). The story of Pīpā goes beyond serial affirmations of guru-to-pupil succession by having the family of 'guru-brothers' (an expression freely used in Hindi) actually travel together (*Bhaktamāl*, p. 495). For an examination of subsequent lengthenings of the Rāmānandī lineage, see Richard Burghart, 'The Founding of the Ramanandi Sect,' *Ethnohistory* 25:2 (1978), pp. 121–39. A full, critically edited text of Anantdās's treatment of Pīpā is available with an English translation in Winand M. Calleweart (in collaboration with Swapna Sharma), *The Hagiographies of Anantadās: The Bhakti Poets of North India* (Richmond, Surrey: Curzon Press, 2000), pp. 141–302, accompanied by other closely relevant materials.

21. This is substantially different from the scorn heaped on the role of renunciant in the course of praising that of the householder in the Vallabhite community, a position that can be traced all the way back to the writings of Vallabha himself. (See his 'Sannyāsanirṇaya,' in *Kṛṣṇaṣodaśagranthāḥ* [Bombay: Nirnaya Sagara Press, n.d.].) Still, the *Bhaktamāl* shows a certain bias in favor of householdership, if rightly understood. Immediately after Dhanā becomes a disciple of Rāmānand, for example, it is specified that he remained a householder (*Bhaktamāl*, p. 524). In presenting Hit Harivaṃś, who was known to have left his family behind to live in Brindavan, Nābhādās makes quite a point of the fact that his sons were married to the daughters of some of Brindavan's Brahmins even so, as if to compensate for Hit Harivaṃś's

dereliction of family responsibilities. His, then, is another life story that bridges the false dichotomy between the life of renunciation and that of the householder (*Bhaktamāl*, pp. 598–600).

22. *Bhaktamāl*, p. 502: *ghar kī... rati sāñcī.*

23. A similar pattern is followed in other episodes (*Bhaktamāl*, pp. 512–13).

24. *Bhaktamāl*, pp. 492, 50, 507, 511, 523.

25. As several notes above have already suggested, these three hagiographies—of Mīrā, Narasī, and Pīpā and Sītā—present only some of the most extended, obvious profiles of the new virtues to which a life of divine singing and service leads. The lives of other saints are often salted with the same motifs, and not only in the *Bhaktamāl*. Ravidās and his wife, for example, are presented as being no less eager to feed the saints then Pīpā and Sītā (*Bhaktamāl*, pp. 473–4, 503). Such *sādhusevā* or *sant-bhakti*, as it is called in the story of Pīpā and Sītā, is also evinced by Dhanā, Nandadās, and many others (*Bhaktamāl*, pp. 521, 696, 708, 748, 766). Sūrdās, because he accepts the same notion of God's abundance as does Narasī Mehtā, is credited in Harirāy's commentary on the *Caurāsī Vaiṣṇavan kī Vārtā* with being able to divine the location of lost coins and cattle, much as Narasī can direct pilgrims to unknown funds in Dvaraka (*Caurāsī Vaiṣṇavan kī Vārtā*, ed. Dvārikādās Parīkh [Mathura: Śrī Bajaraṅg Pustakālay, 1970], pp. 401–2). An early biography of Nānak states that he, like Pīpā, had a mysterious rapport with animals—he is able to bring a dead elephant back to life—and much is made of the monkey Hanumān in the *Bhaktamāl*'s telling of the story of Tulsīdās (W. H. McLeod, *Gurū Nānak and the Sikh Religion* [Oxford: Clarendon Press, 1968], pp. 15, 39; *Bhaktamāl*, pp. 762–3, 769–70).

26. *Bhaktamāl*, p. 474.

27. I am indebted to John B. Carman for suggesting the principal contours of what I have said in the last three paragraphs (Harvard University, 16 December 1982)

28. *Manu Smṛti* 5.146–9, trans. Georg Bühler, *The Laws of Manu* (New York: Dover, 1969 [originally 1886]), p. 195.

29. *Bhaktamāl*, pp. 470, 479–80.

30. *Ibid.*, p. 599.

31. *Ibid.*, pp. 367–7, 473, 485, 764.

32. *Ibid.*, p. 614.

33. *Ibid.*, p. 470.

34. *Ibid.*, p. 557.

35. *Ibid.*, p. 614. The quotation is from Priyādās, but similar language is used by Nābhādās on the preceding page.

36. *Ibid.*

37. *Ibid.*, p. 767.

38. *Ibid.*, p. 768.

39. Kamala Chandrakant, *Mirabai* (Bombay: India Book House, n.d.), p. 4. Lest readers forget, Mīrā is again called 'the true Hindu wife' on p. 11. The Mīrā of the comic book did not, of course, invent this bifurcation between good and bad husbands. It can be traced back at least a century before in popular mythology.

40. That the *caturāśramadharma* conception of the life-cycle applies to women in at best a secondary way has frequently been noted. (For example, Katherine Young, 'One Stage, Three Acts: The Life-Drama of a Traditional Hindu Woman,' paper presented to the American Academy of Religion, New York, November, 1979.) Even so, particularly for unusual and famous women, the *caturāśrama* model has a certain relevance.

41. *Bhaktamāl*, p. 498.

42. John B. Carman, Oral communication, 10 February 1983.

3. The *Nirguṇ/Saguṇ* Distinction

1. Paraśurām Caturvedī, ed., *Hindī Sāhitya kā Bṛhat Itihās*, vol. 4 (Varanasi: Nāgarīpracāriṇī Sabhā, VS 2025 [1968 CE]); Dīnadayāl Gupta, Devendranāth Śarmā, and Vijayendra Snātak, eds, *Hindī Sāhitya kā Bṛhat Itihās*, vol. 5 (Varanasi: Nāgarīpracāriṇī Sabhā, VS 2031 [1974 CE]).

2. Reproduced from J. S. Hawley and Mark Juergensmeyer, *Songs of the Saints of India* (New York and Delhi: Oxford University Press, 1988, 2004), p. 5.

3. E.g., Charlotte Vaudeville, *Au Cabaret de l'Amour* (Paris: Gallimard, 1959), pp. 7–9, Vaudeville, *Kabīr*, vol. 1 (Oxford: Clarendon, 1974), pp. 97–110; W. H. McLeod, *Gurū Nānak and the Sikh Religion* (Oxford: Clarendon, 1968), pp. 151–8.

4. Karine Schomer and W. H. McLeod, eds, *The Sants: Studies in a Devotional Tradition of India* (Berkeley: Berkeley Religious Studies Series; Delhi: Motilal Banarsidass, 1987). Notably, however, Kenneth E. Bryant, in another collection, has outlined a scheme that would justify the distinction between *saguṇ* and *nirguṇ* poets along rhetorical—that is, strictly literary—rather than theological lines. See Bryant, 'Sant and Vaiṣṇava Poetry: Some Observations on Method,' in Mark Juergensmeyer and N. Gerald Barrier, eds, *Sikh Studies: Comparative Perspectives on a Changing Tradition* (Berkeley: Berkeley Religious Studies Series, 1979), pp. 65–74.

5. Schomer, *The Sants*, p. 3.

6. In regard to Tulsī Sāhib's role here, see Mark Juergensmeyer, 'The Radhasoami Revival of the Sant Tradition,' in Schomer and McLeod, eds, *The Sants*, p. 337.

7. In particular, Mīrābāī is included among the 'Sants' listed as having been previously published by the Belvedere Press in its *Santbānī Pustak-mālā*

series. See [no editor named] *Santbānī Saṅgrah* (Allahabad: Belvedere Press, 1915). Mīrā is also included among the *sants* in the collection represented by the *Santbānī Saṅgrah* volume itself. Mīrā's putative initiation at the hands of Ravidās might have provided a justification for her inclusion within the *sant paramparā*. It is noteworthy that *Santbānī Saṅgrah* also contains a section where Vaishnava poets such as Sūrdās, Narasī Mehtā, and Tulsīdās are anthologized, but in that case the designation *dūsre mahātmā* ('other great souls')—as against those *mahātmās* who had actually been included in the *Santbānī Pustak-mālā* series—is introduced to explain the apparent confusion or expansion of categories (*Santbānī Saṅgrah*, p. 2).

8. Pitambar D. Barthwal, *The Nirguna School of Hindi Poetry: An Exposition of Medieval Indian Santa Mysticism* (Banaras: Indian Book Shop, 1936).

9. Cf. Wilfred Cantwell Smith, 'The Crystallization of Religious Communities in Mughal India,' in Mojtaba Minori and Ijar Afshar, eds, *Yadname-ye Irani-ye Minorsky* (Tehran: Tehran University, 1969), pp. 1–24. More recently, Vasudha Dalmia, 'Forging Community: The Guru in a Seventeenth-century Vaishnava Hagiography,' in Vasudha Dalmia, Angelika Malinar, and Martin Christof, eds, *Charisma and Canon: Essays on the Religious History of the Indian Subcontinent* (Delhi: Oxford University Press, 2001), pp. 129–54, especially pp. 147–8.

10. In particular, Rupert Snell, *The Eight-four Hymns of Hita Harivaṃśa, An Edition of the Caurāsī-pada* (Delhi: Motilal Banarsidass, 1990); W. M. Callewaert and Mukund Lath, *The Hindī Songs of Nāmdev* (Leuven: Departement Orientalistiek, 1989); Mātāprasād Gupta, *Sūr Sāgar* (Agra: K. M. Hindī tathā Bhāṣāvijñān Vidyāpīṭh, Agra University, 1979); Gopāl Nārāyaṇ Bahurā and Kenneth E. Bryant, ed., *Pad Surdās jī kā / The Padas of Surdas* (Jaipur: Maharaja Sawai Man Singh II Museum, 1982); J. S. Hawley and K. E. Bryant, *Sūr's Ocean* (New York: Oxford University Press, forthcoming); J. S. Hawley, *Sūr Dās: Poet, Singer, Saint* (Seattle: University of Washington Press; Delhi: Oxford University Press, 1984); Gurinder Singh Mann, *The Making of Sikh Scripture* (New York: Oxford University Press, 2001); Pārasnāth Tivārī, *Kabīr Granthāvalī* (Allahabad: Prayāg Viśvavidyālay, 1961); Shukdeo Singh, *Kabīr Bījak* (Allahabad: Nīlabh Prakāśan, 1972).

11. Hawley, *Sūr Dās*, pp. 121–60.

12. Here and below 'NPS' (Nāgarīpracāriṇī Sabhā) numbers are used to locate a poem of Sūr's in relation to the most widely known edition, that of the Nāgarīpracāriṇī Sabhā: *Sūrsāgar*, edited by Jagannāthdās 'Ratnākar' et al. (Benares: 1934, 1948, 1972, 1976). The actual text translated, however, which appears just below, is the one established by Kenneth Bryant for his critical edition (see Hawley and Bryant, *Sūr's Ocean*, vol. 2). The earliest dated manuscript in which this poem appears (B2) was written by a scribe in the entourage of the maharaja of Bikaner in 1624 (VS 1681); he claims to be copying from an earlier manuscript.

13. See Hawley, *Sūr Dās*, pp. 18–22, and Chapter 8 below.

14. McLeod, *Early Sikh Tradition* (Oxford: Clarendon Press, 1980).

15. Charlotte Vaudeville, 'The Govardhan Myth in Northern India,' *Indo-Iranian Journal* 22 (1980, pp. 1–45; J. S. Hawley, *Sūr Dās*, pp. 14–22, and 'The Sectarian Logic of the *Sūr Dās kī Vārtā*,' in Monika Thiel-Horstmann, ed., *Bhakti in Current Research, 1979–1982* (Berlin: Dietrich Reimer Verlag, 1983), pp. 157–69.

16. R. D. Gupta, 'Priyā Dās, Author of the *Bhaktirasabodhinī*,' *Bulletin of the School of Oriental and African Studies* 32:1 (1969), pp. 61–9; Philip Lutgendorf, 'Kṛṣṇa Caitanya and His Companions as Presented in the *Bhaktamāla* of Nābhā Jī and the *Bhaktirasabodhinī* of Priyā Dāsa,' M.A. diss., University of Chicago, 1981, pp. 25–9.

17. David Lorenzen, in collaboration with Jagdish Kumar and Uma Thukral, *Kabir Legends and Ananta-das's Kabir Parachai* (Albany: State University of New York Press, 1991), pp. 9–18. The principal problem, as I see it, has to do with the historical status of Rāmānand, who figures importantly in the *guruparamparā* of Anantdās, as apparently claimed by himself in his *Pīpā Parcaī*, though the evidence is not yet entirely clear (Lorenzen, *Kabir Legends*, p. 10n). Rāmānand's symbolic import as a conduit between later North Indian bhakti and earlier South Indian forms—and his legitimating force, therefore—is sufficiently great to make me feel uneasy about placing too great a trust in the historicity of legends and lineages associated with him. His usefulness as entrepôt between South and North, and between *sant* and Vaishnava, is simply too great, and the use to which legends associated with him are put by a hagiographer such as Priyādās makes me doubly cautious.

18. See Hawley and Juergensmeyer, *Songs of the Saints of India*, p. 24. The poem translated there is number 33 in Padam Gurcaran Siṃh, *Sant Ravidās: Vicārak aur Kavi* (Jalandur: Nav-Cintan Prakāśan, 1977).

19. Hawley and Juergensmeyer, *Songs of the Saints of India*, p. 158. The hagiographical text involved is the *Mūl Gosāīṅ Carit* (*dohās* 29–32 and the accompanying *caupāīs*) attributed to Benī Mādhavadās, as found in Kiśorīlāl Gupta, *Gosāīṅ Carit* (Varanasi: Vaṇī-Vitān Prakāśan, 1964), p. 285. In regard to the status of the text, see Philip Lutgendorf, 'The Quest for the Legendary Tulsīdās,' *Journal of Vaiṣṇava Studies* 1: 2 (1993), pp. 79–101, and—somewhat expanded—in Winand Callewaert and Rupert Snell, eds, *According to Tradition: Hagiographical Writing in India* (Wiesbaden: Otto Harrassowitz, 1994), pp. 65–85.

20. I confess that on the basis of the awkward meter used in this poem and its lack of any great poetic adornment, I wonder whether the 'real' Sūrdās—I am convinced there was one—composed this poem. Its manuscript pedigree is not the absolute best (A1, B2, B3, B4, J4, U1, U2), but it is sufficiently strong to suggest very powerfully that this poem was known in the sixteenth century. The use of the word *pragaṭ* in verse 9 raises the question as to whether an avatar

theory of saints, such as the one expressed in Mahipati's *Bhaktavijaya*, was assumed by the poet.

21. If, for a moment, we accept that distinction. To the contrary, see Hawley, *Sūr Dās*, pp. 141–8.

22. Catalogue of the Rajasthan Oriental Research Institute, Jodhpur, in reference to Hindi manuscript 30587 (VS 1788).

23. The *sphuṭkar pad* manuscript is accession no. 773/48, dated in the NPS register to VS 1757, as a *terminus ad quem*. The additional two are listed in Group 1.

24. From this point onward, in referring to manuscript anthologies, I will frequently cite only the *vikram saṃvat* (VS) dating that one finds in the manuscripts themselves. The comparable dating according to the Julian calendar can usually be determined by subtracting 57 from the VS number.

25. Rawatmal Saraswat and Dinanath Khatri, *Catalogue of the Rajasthani Manuscripts in the Anup Sanskrit Library* (Bikaner: Maharaja of Bikaner, 1947), pp. 50–71. The category *phuṭkar pad* covers poems described as being *dohās*, *soraṭhās*, *savaiyās*, and *kavitts*. The last-mentioned term is apparently used as a designation large enough to include *pads* within its span.

26. I refer to the various *Khoj Reports* of the Nāgarīpracāriṇī Sabhā and to the earlier manuscript survey coordinated by Mātāprasād Gupta.

27. This manuscript is not listed among the *pad saṅgrah* (*sphuṭ*) listed as such in Gopal Narayan Bahura, *Literary Heritage of the Rulers of Amber and Jaipur* (Jaipur: Maharaja Sawai Man Singh II Museum, 1976), p. 168.

28. Regrettably, my notes contain no information as to the number of folios.

29. The manuscript has been photographed, and awaits further examination.

30. E.g., Śyāmsundar Kīrtankār of Kota or Rādheśyām Kīrtankār of the 'second *gaddī*' in Nathdvara.

31. Vaudeville, '*Sant Mat:* Santism as the Universal Path to Sanctity,' in Schomer and McLeod, eds, *The Sants*, pp. 27–9.

32. Jaipur: Maharaja Sawai Man Singh II Museum, 1982 (actually published 1984). I am grateful to Gurinder Singh Mann for enlightening discussions about the shape of the Fatehpur manuscript.

33. At this point I omit a manuscript that would seem from its catalogue description to belong here on the list. It is accession no. 39687 in the Jodhpur branch of the Rajasthan Oriental Research Institute, entitled *guṭkā sant vāṇī saṅgrah*. The catalogue states that its date of composition in VS 1710, but the colophon page—now, at least—is missing, hence no date can reliably be assigned. It seems notable that a '*nirguṇ*' poem of Sūr's, the *sūr pacīsī*, is included, given the general *sant* designation.

34. This manuscript was photographed by Kenneth Bryant on 12 December 1980.

35. A recent statement in regard to this issue can be found in Pashaura Singh, 'The Text and Meaning of the *Ādi Granth*' (PhD diss., University of

Toronto, 1991), pp. 186–90. That, in turn, is superseded by Gurinder Singh Mann, *The Making of Sikh Scripture*, pp. 115–17.

36. Karine Schomer, 'Kabir in the *Gurū Granth Sāhib*: An Exploratory Essay,' in Juergensmeyer and Barrier, eds, *Sikh Studies*, pp. 75–86; Linda Hess [and Sukhdev Singh], *The Bījak of Kabir* (San Francisco: North Point Press, 1983), pp. 6–7.

37. David N. Lorenzen, 'The Kabir Panth: Heretics to Hindus,' D. N. Lorenzen, ed., *Religious Change and Cultural Domination* (Mexico City: E1 Colegio de México, 1981), pp. 151–71.

4. Mirabai in Manuscript

1. In Lawrence A. Babb, Varsha Joshi, and Michael Meister, eds, *Multiple Histories: Culture and Society in the Study of Rajasthan* (Jaipur: Rawat Publications), pp. 313–35; quotations from pp. 314 and 324. Worth comparing in matters of substance, but different in style and presuppositions, is Kalyāṇsiṃh Śekhāvat's *Mīrāṅ kī Prāmāṇik Jīvanī* (Jodhpur: Rājasthānī Granthāgār, 2002).

2. J. S. Hawley and Mark Juergensmeyer, *Songs of the Saints of India* (New York and Delhi: Oxford University Press, 1988 and 2004), p. 122; Nancy M. Martin, 'Mirabai in the Academy and the Politics of Identity,' in Mandakranta Bose, ed., *Faces of the Feminine from Ancient, Medieval, and Modern India* (New York: Oxford University Press, 2000), pp. 163, 170; Parita Mukta, *Upholding the Common Life: The Community of Mirabai* (Delhi: Oxford University Press, 1994), p. 26.

3. Muṅhatā Naiṇsī, *Muṅhatā Naiṇsī rī Khyāt*, vol. 1, ed. Badarīprasād Sākariyā (Jodhpur: Rājasthān Prācyavidyā Pratiṣṭhān, 1960), p. 21.

4. The Gujarati poet Dayārām (1777–1852) may serve as an example of the fluidity of historical belief before the late-nineteenth-century period when Mīrā's life became standardized. For him, Mīrā's father was Jaimal Rāṭhor, not Ratan Siṃh: *Mīrāṅ Caritra*, verse 1, as quoted by Ambāśaṃkar Nāgar, *Madhya Kālīn Hindī Sāhitya: Adhyayan aur Anveṣaṇ* (Ahmedabad: Paścimāṅcal Prakāśan, 1997), p. 177.

5. Muni Jinavijaya, ed., *Rājasthānī-Hindī Hastalikhit Granth-Sūcī*, vol. 1 (Jodhpur: Rājasthān Prācyavidyā Pratiṣṭhān, 1960), pp. 234–5; Omkārlāl Menāriyā, ed., vol. 4 (1978), pp. 38–47.

6. Philip Lutgendorf, 'The Quest of the Legendary Tulsīdās,' in Winand M. Callewaert and Rupert Snell, eds, *According to Tradition: Hagiographical Writing in India* (Wiesbaden: Harrassowitz Verlag, 1994), pp. 65–85.

7. Hukm Siṃh Bhāṭī, *Mīrāṅbāī: Aitihāsik va Sāmājik Vivecan* (Jodhpur: Rājasthān Sāhitya Saṅsthān, 1986), p. 14, cited in Taft, 'Mirabai,' p. 333, note 6.

8. Muṅhatā Naiṇsī, *Mārvāḍ rā Paraganāṅ rī Vigat*, vol. 2, ed. Badarīprasād Sākariyā (Jodhpur: Rājasthān Prācyavidyā Pratiṣṭhān, 1969), p. 471, cited in Taft, 'Mirabai,' p. 329.

9. Nābhādās et al., *Śrī Bhaktamāl*, with the *Bhaktirasabodhinī* commentary of Priyādās, ed. Sītārāmśaraṇ Bhagavānprasād Rūpakalā (Lucknow: Tejkumār Press, 1969 [originally 1910]), pp. 477–8.

10. Har Bilas Sarda, *Maharana Sāngā, the Hindupat* (Ajmer: Scottish Mission Industries Company, 1918), pp. 12–13; cf. Hawley and Juergensmeyer, *Songs of the Saints of India*, p. 177, note 18.

11. Gilbert Pollet, 'Early Evidence on Tulsīdās and his Epic,' *Orientalia Lovaniensia Periodica* 5 (1974), pp. 157–9.

12. Dvārikādās Parīkh, ed., *Caurāsī Vaiṣṇavan kī Vārtā* (Mathura: Śrī Bajaraṅg Pustakālay, 1970), pp. 713, 717, 722.

13. Devindar Siṃh Usāhaṇ, *Prem Abodh* (Patiala: Panjabi University Publication Bureau, 1989), pp. 109, 115, *caupaīs* 3, 4, 22.

14. Usāhaṇ, *Prem Abodh*, pp. 117–19, particularly *doharā* (p. 117), *chaupaīs* 32–3, and the Karmābāī *chaupaī* (p. 119).

15. Usāhaṇ, *Prem Abodh*, pp. 117–18, quoting from *chaupaī* 32 (p. 118). The motif of the avenging *sudarśan cakra* is apparently borrowed from the story of Ambarīṣ and Durvāsā. For details, see Hawley, *Sūr's Ocean*, vol. 1, §363.

16. Hawley and Juergensmeyer, *Songs of the Saints of India*, pp. 125–6.

17. Heidi R. M. Pauwels, *In Praise of Holy Men: Hagiographic Poems by and about Harirām Vyās* (Groningen: Egbert Forsten, 2002), p. 85.

18. Heidi R. M. Pauwels, 'Rāṭhauṛī Mīrā: Two Neglected Rāṭhauṛ Connections of Mīrā: Jaimal Meṛtīyo and Nāgrīdās', forthcoming in Nancy M. Martin, ed., *Mirabai: Hindu Saint for a Global World*; also 'Hagiography and Reception History: the Case of Mīrā's Padas in Nāgrīdās's Pada-prasanga-mālā,' in Monika Horstmann, ed., *Bhakti Literature in Current Research, 2001–2003* (Delhi: Manohar, forthcoming), section 2.2.

19. Dīndayāl Gupta, *Aṣṭachāp aur Vallabh Sampradāy* (Allahabad: Hindī Sāhitya Sammelan, 1970), vol. 1, pp. 129–30; Kaṇṭamaṇi Śāstrī, *Aṣṭaschāp kī Vārtā* (Kankarauli: Vidyā-Vibhāg, 1952), pp. 3–4.

20. Vrajeśvar Varmā, *Sūr-Mīmāṃsā* (New Delhi: Oriental Book Depot, n.d.), pp. 30–1; J. S. Hawley, *Sūr Dās: Poet, Singer, Saint* (Seattle: University of Washington Press and Delhi: Oxford University Press, 1984), p. 7.

21. *Vārtā*, pp. 530–1; Richard Barz, *The Bhakti Sect of Vallabhācārya* (Faridabad: Thomson Press Limited, 1976), pp. 213–14.

22. Christopher Key Chapple, 'Devotion to God in Mirabai, Jainism, and Yoga,' paper delivered to the conference 'Mirabai: Hindu Saint for a Global World,' University of California at Los Angeles, 5 October 2002.

23. Winand M. Callewaert in collaboration with Swapna Sharma, *The Hagiographies of Anantadās: The Bhakti Poets of North India* (Richmond, Surrey: Curzon Press, 2000), pp. 224, 275; the passage occurs as verse 35.16 of the *Pīpā Paracaī*.

24. Heidi R. M. Pauwels, *Kṛṣṇa's Round Dance Reconsidered: Harirām Vyās's Hindī 'Rāspañcādhyāyī'* (Richmond, Surrey: Curzon Press, 1996), pp. 4–6; *In Praise of Holy Men*, pp. 85–6, 104, 269–71.

25. Hawley and Juergensmeyer, *Songs of the Saints of India*, pp. 202–3; Winand M. Callewaert, 'The 'Earliest' Song of Mīrā (1503–1546),' *Journal of the Oriental Institute* (University of Baroda) 39 (1990), p. 376, note 17; C. L. Prabhāt, *Mīrāṅbāī (Śodh Prabandh)* (Bombay: Hindī Granth Ratnākar, 1965), p. 245, and *Mīrā: Jīvan aur Kāvya* (Jodhpur: Rājasthānī Granthāgār, 1999), pp. 462–9; Nancy M. Martin, *Mirabai* (New York: Oxford University Press, forthcoming); Pauwels, 'Rāṭhauṛī Mīrā.'

26. Prabhāt, *Mīrāṅbāī,* p. 245, and *Mīrā: Jīvan aur Kāvya*, pp. 462–9; cf. Priyabala Shah, *A Descriptive Catalogue of Sanskrit Manuscripts* [*Gujarat Vidya Sabha Collection*] (Ahmedabad: Gujarat Vidya Sabha, 1964), Vidhatri A. Vora, ed., *A Descriptive Catalog of Gujarati, Hindi, and Marathi Manuscripts of B. J. Institute Museum* (Ahmedabad: B. J. Institute of Learning and Research, 1987).

27. Prabhāt, *Mīrā: Jīvan aur Kāvya*, p. 467.

28. Bhagavāndās Tivārī, *Mīrāṅ kī Bhakti aur unkī Kāvya-Sādhanā kā Anuśīlan.* (Allahabad: Sāhitya Bhavan, 1974), p. 22.

29. Paul B. Arney, 'The Dakor and Kashi Manuscripts: Are They Genuine?' (unpublished paper, Columbia University, 1989), p. 3; cf. Tivārī, *Mīrāṅ kī Bhakti*, pp. 237–9.

30. Cf. Arney, 'The Dakor and Kashi Manuscripts,' p. 5.

31. Kalyāṇsiṃh Śekhāvat, *Mīrāṅbāī kā Jīvanvṛtt evaṃ Kāvya* (Jodhpur: Hindī Sāhitya Mandir, 1974), pp. 15, 27; Arney, 'The Dakor and Kashi Manuscripts,' pp. 9–10; Hawley and Juergensmeyer, *Songs of the Saints of India*, p. 202.

32. Callewaert, 'The 'Earliest' Song of Mīrā,' p. 369.

33. Prabhāt, *Mīrā: Jīvan aur Kāvya*, p. 462; Śekhāvat, *Mīrāṅbāī kā Jīvanvṛtt evaṃ Kāvya* , pp. 14–15.

34. Tivārī, *Mīrāṅ kī Bhakti,* pp. 24–5, and *Mīrāṅ kī Prāmāṇik Padāvalī* (Allahabad: Sāhitya Bhavan, 1974), p. 5.

35. Lalitprasād Sukul, *Mīrāṅ Smṛti Granth* (Calcutta: Bāṅgīya Hindī Pariṣad, 1949), pp. *ga—ca*, as quoted in *ibid.*, pp. 22–4.

36. Sukul, *Mīrāṅ Smṛti Granth,* quoted in *ibid.*, p. 23.

37. Sukul, *Mīrāṅ Smṛti Granth*, pp. *ca—ja*, quoted in *ibid.*, pp. 24–5.

38. Sukul, *Mīrāṅ Smṛti Granth*, quoted in *ibid.*, p. 23.

39. Martin, *Mirabai*, chapter 4; Callewaert, 'The 'Earliest' Song of Mira (1503–1546).'

40. Prabhāt, *Mīrā: Jīvan aur Kāvya*, pp. 464–5.

41. Gurinder Singh Mann, *The Making of Sikh Scripture* (New York: Oxford University Press, 2001), pp. 115–16; cf. Prabhāt, *Mīrā: Jīvan aur Kāvya*, pp. 462–5.

42. M. A. Macauliffe, 'The Legend of Mîrā Bâî, the Rajput Princess,' *Indian Antiquary* 32 (1903), p. 335, and Martin, *Mirabai*, chapter 4.

43. Callewaert, 'The 'Earliest' Song of Mira,' p. 366.

44. Pauwels, 'Rāṭhauṛī Mīrā,' forthcoming; cf. Nabhadas, *Bhaktamāl*, p. 820. On the date of the *Bhaktamāl*, see Pollet, 'Early Evidence on Tulsīdās and his Epic,' pp. 157–9.

45. Prabhāt, *Mīrā: Jīvan aur Kavya*, p. 467.

46. Rām Kṛpālu Śarmā, ed., *Granth Parijāt: Hindī Bhāṣā kā Hastalikhit Sūcī* (Jaipur: Śrī Sañjay Śarmā Sangrahālay evam Śodh Sansthān, 2001), p. 137.

47. I am grateful to Rām Kṛpālu Śarmā for discussions about this poem (Jaipur, 31 May 2004) and for permission to copy it and the colophon page of the manuscript to which it belongs. In the opening line, the word *gopī* is written just above *kātī* ('how many?'), apparently in a different hand from the body of the text. *Navrang* ('nine colors' or 'nine moods', perhaps after the nine cardinal emotions, *navaras*) is also a game played by women in the hot season, when mangoes are ripe. First, they eat the fruit, then toss the soft, pulpy skins at each other. Like Holi, a game closely associated with Krishna and his *gopīs*, this is messy fun, and it is followed by a fresh change of clothes. The final line, with its question 'How many Krishnas and Muralīs will there be?', evidently refers to the fact that Krishna—here, holding his flute—multiplies himself around the circle of the *rās līlā* so that each *gopī* feels she is holding his hand. The answer to this question, then, ought to be the same as the answer one would give to the question with which the poem begins.

48. Callewaert, 'The "Earliest" Song of Mīrā,' p. 377, note; Hawley and Juergensmeyer, *Songs of the Saints of India*, p. 202; Martin, 'Dyed in the Color of Her Lord: Multiple Representations in the Mirabai Tradition' (Ph.D. diss., Graduate Theological Union, 1995), p. 130.

49. Callewaert's act of noticing an early Mīrā poem listed as part of the Sanjay Sharma Museum (personal communication, 7 October 2002) led me to search for the poem I discuss above, and he reports having seen another in a Vrindaban collection ('The "Earliest" Song of Mira,' p. 377, note 17). Similarly Neelima Shukla-Bhatt has identified four poems attributed to Mīrābāī in manuscript 689 of the Gujarāt Vidyā Sabhā collection at the B. J. Institute, Ahmedabad, which is dated VS 1792 (1735 CE; Personal communications, 29 September 2002 and 13 April 2004).

50. I am grateful to Brajesh Kumar Singh of the Rajasthan Oriental Research Institute, Jodhpur, for guiding me through some of the fine points of financial notation on 24 March 2004.

51. Paraśurām Caturvedī, ed., *Mīrāṅbāī kī Padāvalī* (Allahabad: Hindī Sāhitya Sammelan, 1973 [originally 1932], p. 13.

5. Mirabai as Wife and Yogi

1. See Chapter 6, note 2. Also noteworthy is Philip Lutgendorf's recent study, 'The "Mira Trope" in Mainstream Hindi Cinema: Three Examples from Notable Films,' paper delivered to the international conference on Mīrābāī held

at the University of California at Los Angeles, 4 October 2002, and forthcoming in Nancy M. Martin, ed., *Mirabai: Hindu Saint for a Global World.* Lutgendorf shows that in films where Mīrā does not explicitly appear, the shadow of her legendry can still be cast over other characters. His three examples are *Jhanak jhanak payal bāje* (1955), *Kāgaz ke phūl* (1959), and *Guddī* (1971).

2. Kamala Chandrakant, *Mirabai*; Dolly Rizvi, *Kabir*; Suresh Chandra Sharma, *Tulsidas*; Pushpa Bharati, *Soordas* (all Bombay: India Book House, n.d.).

3. Nābhādās, *Śrī Bhaktamāl*, with the *Bhaktirasabodhinī* commentary of Priyādās (Lucknow: Tejkumār Press, 1969), pp. 712–13. Further on the *Bhaktamāl*, see Chapter 2, note 2.

4. Paraśurām Caturvedī, ed., *Mīrāṅbāī kī Padāvalī* (Allahabad: Hindī Sāhitya Sammelan, 1973). Hereinafter, PC.

5. Kalyāṇsiṃh Śekhāvat, ed., *Mīrāṅ-Bṛhatpadāvalī*, vol. 2 (Jodhpur: Rajasthan Oriental Research Institute, 1975); Harinārāyaṇ Śarmā, *Mīrāṅ-Bṛhatpadāvalī*, vol. 1 (Jodhpur: Rajasthan Oriental Research Institute, 1968).

6. PC 44.

7. PC 97.

8. PC 46. The phrase *giradhar nāgar* (clever Mountain-Lifter) is the standard way of naming Krishna in Mīrā's poems. It refers to the episode in which he lifted Mount Govardhan so that the inhabitants of the Braj region, his boyhood home, could take shelter from ravaging rains sent against them by the god Indra. On the formula, see Chapter 1.

9. PC 68. The phrase 'holy garments' translates *bhagavāṅ bhekh*, which means literally 'God's clothes' and presumably refers to the sort of clothing ascetics wear. The 'Dark One' is *syām*, an epithet of Krishna.

10. PC 188. Hari is a title of Krishna or Vishnu. The word *hājariyo*, here translated 'bag of beads,' refers to a sewn bag worn over the hand to conceal beads that help meditators count the number of prayers or mantras in a given sequence. It is a common Hindu belief that one's fate is written on one's forehead at birth by the god Brahmā.

11. PC 49. The word *lagan*, which occurs near the beginning of the poem, can have the sense of 'affection, love, infatuation' or the more formal meaning 'marriage.' The latter meaning is appropriate because marriages are arranged to occur at times governed by particularly auspicious astrological configurations (*lagan*). In translating, a middle course is chosen—'fortunate match'—and it is hoped that the overtones of marriage, a topic that concerns us especially here, are not lost. The phrase 'like a fish washed on shore' does not occur in the original but is implied by the general usage of the verb *talaphi talaphi* (flails) in the bhakti literature of North India.

12. PC 94. The phrase 'an antelope skin pulled up to my neck' translates two words: *gale mrigachālā.* Apparently Mīrā means that she will maintain some privacy by covering the front of her body with an antelope or deer skin,

which yogis often sit on but sometimes use as loincloths. The mention of Rām rather than Hari or Krishna is notable, but nothing out of the ordinary in poems attributed to Mīrā.

This composition presents the translator with a difficulty in that it is sometimes addressed to Krishna, sometimes to the poet's female companion (as implied by the particle *rī*; compare 'He's bound my heart,' Chapter 7). Similarly, Mīrā sometimes seems to speak of herself in the first person, sometimes in the third. These shifts of focus are easily tolerated in the original but seem to call for some clarification in English, hence the provision of a double possessive adjective ('her... my') in the final verse, where the original requires neither.

13. PC 117. The snake mentioned early in the poem is Śeṣ (Śeṣa), associated with Vishnu. The catalogue of yogic paraphernalia presented here is particularly suggestive of the Nāth Yogīs, in that allusion is made to the *mudarā* (bone earrings) characteristic of that group. Here as elsewhere—but especially in regard to the phrase 'yogi and yoginī'—it is tempting to think Mīrā may have taken the householder Nāth Yogīs as her model. Yet their largely settled lifestyle contrasts to the peregrinations Mīrā has in mind. Moreover, when the Nāth husband does set forth to wander and beg, he travels alone and only for a month at a time: there is no doubt but that he will return. In any case the drama of the poem would be diminished if Mīrā were simply patterning it on a set of practices observable in ordinary life. See Daniel Gold and Ann Grodzins Gold, 'The Fate of the Householder Nath,' *History of Religions* 24:2 (1984), pp. 113–32.

14. PC 153.

15. PC 27. In a traditional Hindu wedding, the bridegroom leads the bride around a Vedic *homa* fire built beneath a pavilion constructed in the courtyard of the bride's house. A decorative arch is often erected in front of the doorway to welcome guests—most important, the bridegroom and his party.

16. PC 51. The 'altar of pearl tears' refers to the *cauk* (altar) laid out on the floor of the bride's courtyard, beneath the pavilion, to serve as a focus of the wedding ceremony. Here various offerings and sacrifices are made into the Vedic fire, according to ancient prescriptions. The vocative *sājaṇ*, translated 'beloved,' could also be rendered 'husband'; it is appropriately used in both contexts.

17. PC 25 and 80.

18. PC 33. The *aṅgīṭhī* (stove) with which the poem concludes is a brazier into which pieces of wood or charcoal are stuffed as fuel. This is the fate to which Mīrā metaphorically assign those who criticize her actions.

19. Nābhādās, *Bhaktamāl*, pp. 712–13. The original text appears in Chapter 1.

20. Priyādās in *Bhaktamāl*, p. 717. In modern Hindi the term *sādhu* has come to refer specifically to an ascetic, a religious mendicant. Here, however, it is translated as 'saint' because the term's meaning was not restricted to ascetics

in medieval Hindi. The gloss provided by the text itself—concerning obedience to Śyām's will—also suggests this interpretation. 'The good' is another possibility.

21. Priyādās in *Bhaktamāl*, pp. 718–19.

22. *Ibid.*, p. 719.

23. *Ibid.*, p. 720.

24. *Ibid.*, p. 721.

25. *Ibid.*, p. 722.

26. In relation to this point, see Chapter 1.

27. See especially PC 55 and 71. English translations of these poems, along with all others in the Caturvedī edition, appear in A. J. Alston, *The Devotional Poems of Mirabai* (Delhi: Motilal Banarsidass, 1980).

28. For a further and somewhat more qualified consideration of this point, see Chapter 2.

29. It also makes its appearance in a number of poems attributed to Mīrā, for example, PC 39 and 41.

30. Nābhādās, *Bhaktamāl*, p. 713.

31. PC 49 and 195. For information on the general lore of the saw at Banaras, I am indebted to conversations with James C. Lochtefeld (November 1987), Krishna Chaitanya Bhatt (January 1988), and several citizens of Banaras (January 1988). Also relevant is Lochtefeld's 'Suicide in the Hindu Tradition: Varieties, Propriety and Practice,' Master's thesis, University of Washington, 1987.

32. PC 195.

33. PC 49.

34. On this general theme, see J. S. Hawley and Mark Juergensmeyer, *Songs of the Saints of India* (Delhi: Oxford University Press, 2004), pp. 6, 12–13, 21–2, 177.

35. Candrikāprasād Jijñāsu lists eight such couplets in his *Sant Pravar Raidās Sāheb* (Lucknow: Bahujan Kalyāṇ Prakāśan, 1984), p. 37. The best known of these is the third, to which S. M. Pandey makes reference in his 'Mirabai and Her Contributions to the Bhakti Movement,' *History of Religions* 5:1 (1965), pp. 57–8. To the best of my knowledge, none of these verses appears in Caturvedī's edition, where one finds only a general approbation of life with the *sants* (e.g., PC 30).

36. For the full story, see Hawley and Juergensmeyer, *Songs of the Saints of India*, p. 13. Another attempt to reconcile Jhālī and Mīrā may be found in Jijñāsu, *Sant Pravar Raidās Sāhab*, p. 36. While 'Queen Jhālī' seems to have functioned for Priyādās as if it were a personal name, Jhālī is actually a clan designation. See Chapter 4.

37. On the former topic, which is the less common of the two, see PC 140, 199, and 200, and Śekhāvat, ed., *Mīrāṅ Bṛhatpadāvalī*, vol. 2, nos. 68, 279, 351, 352. On *nirguṇ* and *saguṇ* modes in general, see Chapter 3.

38. For instance, the nomadic singers studied by Parita Mukta in *Upholding the Common Life: The Community of Mirabai* (Delhi: Oxford University Press, 1994), pp. 76–83, 105–14.

39. Lindsey Beth Harlan, 'The Ethic of Protection among Rajput Women: Religious Mediations of Caste and Gender Duties,' (PhD diss., Harvard University, 1987), pp. 273, 276.

40. James Tod, *Annals and Antiquities of Rajasthan*, vol. 1 (Delhi: Motilal Banarasidass, 1971), pp. 337–8; cf. S. S. Mehta, *A Monograph on Mirabai, the Saint of Mewad* (Bombay: author, n.d.), pp. 56, 65.

41. See Har Bilas Sarda, *Maharana Sāngā* (Ajmer: Scottish Mission Industries, 1918), pp. 95–6. The matter is reconsidered in, for example, Kalyānsiṃh Śekhāvat, *Mīrābāīṅ kā Jīvanvṛtt evaṃ Kāvya* (Jodhpur: Hindī Sāhitya Mandir, 1974, pp. 45–6.

42. For a very different construction of this history and an account of its several varieties, see Frances Taft, 'The Elusive Historical Mirabai: A Note,' in Lawrence A. Babb, Varsha Joshi, and Michael Meister, eds, *Multiple Histories: Culture and Society in the Study of Rajasthan* (Jaipur: Rawat Publications), pp. 313–35, as discussed in Chapter 4.

43. Harlan, 'Ethic of Protection,' p. 280.

44. In some versions of the Mīrā legend, this motif of *śrī* and *satī* is transposed to a point later in her life. In an elaboration of the accounts of her ascetic wanderings, it is said that Mīrā, responding to the attempts made on her life by Rāṇā Vikramājīt, deserted Chittor and returned to her native Merta. In consequence of the withdrawal of her auspicious energy from Chittor, the city suffered a series of military defeats.

45. T. L. Vaswani, *The Call of Mira Education* (Poona: Mira, n.d.). See also (anon.), *Sadhu Vaswani Mission and its Activities* (Poona: Sadhu Vaswani Mission, n.d.).

46. T. L. Vaswani, *Saint Mira* (Poona: St. Mira's English Medium School, n.d.). I am not sure at what point in the evolution of Vaswani's thought he began to use the English designation 'saint' in referring to Mīrā. His first Mīrā school, established in Hyderabad (in present-day Pakistan) in 1933, had Sindhi as its medium of instruction.

47. *Matthew* 1.19.

48. Vaswani, *Saint Mira*, pp. 36–8.

6. The Saints Subdued in *Amar Chitra Katha*

1. Numbers in parentheses after titles refer to the issue's ordinal number within the series, a number assigned and used for reference by the series itself. Where relevant the issue number is followed by a colon and the appropriate page number(s) within the issue. *Amar Chitra Katha* has also produced studies of Tukārām (68), Narasī Mehtā (94), Eknāth (123), Jñāneśvar (155), Tiruppān and Kanakadāsa (186), Rāmānuja (243), Tyāgarāja (245), Ramaṇa Mahārṣi

(290), and Cokhāmelā (292). Many other figures also qualify as exemplary but would not normally be described as saints.

2. According to a study prepared for the National Film Archive, ten films have been devoted to portraying Mīrā's life, four each for Tulsīdās and Sūrdās (whose life story has been conflated for this purpose with that of Bilvamaṅgal), and smaller numbers for Nānak, Kabīr, and Ravidās. See Kusum Gokarn, 'Popularity of Devotional Films (Hindi),' unpublished study listed as National Film Archive Project 689/5/84), Pune, 1984.

3. The original dialogue of Sadashivam's *Meera* (1947) is in Tamil, but it has been dubbed in various Indian languages; the songs are in Hindi in all versions.

4. J. S. Hawley and Mark Juergensmeyer, *Songs of the Saints of India* (New York and Delhi: Oxford University Press, 1988 and 2004), pp. 122–7.

5. Lindsey Harlan, 'The Ethic of Protection among Rajput Women: Religious Mediations of Caste and Gender Duties,' (PhD diss., Harvard University, 1987), chapter 7.

6. Madhu Kishwar and Ruth Vanita have discussed several features relating to this topic in an article that was printed after I had drafted this chapter. Their emphasis on the highlighting of Mīrā's otherworldliness in *Amar Chitra Katha* is somewhat different from mine, but other points—even specific passages—drew our common attention. Kishwar and Vanita, 'Modern Versions of Mira,' *Manushi*, 50–2 (1989), pp. 100–1. Further background on similar themes may be found in Kumkum Sangari, 'Mirabai and the Spiritual Economy of Bhakti,' *Economic and Political Weekly*, Special Articles, 7 and 14 July 1990, pp. 1474–5 and 1537–52. The reader is cautioned, however, against Sangari's acceptance of a 'vulgate' Mīrābāī, in regard to both hagiography and poetry. Sangari fails to separate out this twentieth-century Mīrābāī from earlier conceptions, and one must read her conclusions with that in mind.

7. Philip Lutgendorf, 'The Quest of the Legendary Tulsīdās,' in Winand M. Callewaert and Rupert Snell, eds, *According to Tradition: Hagiographical Writing in India* (Wiesbaden: Harrassowitz Verlag, 1994), pp. 65–85.

8. The story of Nānak falling asleep in Mecca with his feet toward the *ka'ba* is a striking example. The Sikh *janam sākhīs* represent this episode in a variety of ways; in the earlier ones, Nānak is said to sleep in a mosque outside Mecca, with his feet toward the *mehrāb*. In either case, Nānak is set upon by a *qāzī* who berates him for his irreverence, but the *ka'ba* itself (or the *mehrāb*, depending on the story) provides the response by rotating in Nānak's direction as a gesture of submission to his holy feet. Only one *janam sākhī*, the *Miharbān* (a document that represents the work of rationalizing commentators in the nineteenth century), reports the story differently, and it is this account that *Amar Chitra Katha* follows. Here neither *ka'ba* nor *mehrāb* does anything, and Nānak provides his own response. As reported by the *Miharbān Janam Sākhī*, 'Turn my shoes is that direction where the House of the Lord will not go. Place my shoes in the direction where the Ka'bah is not.' *Amar Chitra Katha* makes the

message even plainer and more generic: 'To me the whole world is the house of God. Now turn my feet to where God is not' (47:26). See W. H. McLeod *Early Sikh Tradition* (Oxford: Clarendon Press, 1980), pp. 134–5; the translation from *Miharbān* is on p. 143n.

9. Hence nineteenth-century reformers such as Rammohan Roy and Svami Dayananda were at pains to cleanse Hinduism of its miraculous element, and Sir Syed Ahmed Khan projected a similar view of Islam.

10. Other comic book publishers have not been so particular. An issue on Santoṣī Mā has been produced in a series called *Adarsh Chitra Katha* (Sukhatankar n.d.). I am grateful to H. Daniel Smith for supplying me with a copy.

11. Interestingly, Pai recalled an incident from his own childhood concerning the issue of unwanted *prasād*. The reluctant consumer was himself, and his grandmother warned him of the consequences if he cast the food aside. Pai remembers having thrown it in the gutter in disgust—not only at the *prasād* but at the idea of God that it represented.

12. Kamala Chandrakant, Interview, Bombay, 1989.

13. Even so, the staff maintained that they often fought off romantic excesses from their contributing writers. Gayatri Madan Dutt, in particular, was famous for wanting full-page illustrations in which the handsome hero chucks the heroine under the chin.

14. V. Raghavan, *The Great Integrators: The Singer-Saints of India* (New Delhi: Publications Department, Government of India, 1966), p. 15.

15. Of course this vision of Kabīr is not confined to *Amar Chitra Katha*. One sees it, for example, in the title of a study by Muhammad Hedayetullah called *Kabir: The Apostle of Hindu-Muslim Unity*, published in 1977.

16. Harirāy in Dvārikādās Parīkh, ed., *Caurāsī Vaiṣṇavan kī Vārtā* (Mathura: Śrī Bajaraṅg Pustakālay, 1970), pp. 401–3.

17. On the other hand, children within the lineage of Vallabhācārya are spared the opprobrium of having once tried to play trick on poor blind Sūrdās, as the *Vārtā* reports. The ruse is attributed instead to unnamed adults. Pushpa Bharati, *Soordas* (Bombay: India Book House Educational Trust, 1977), p. 30, and *Vārtā,* pp. 421–2.

18. *Vārtā,* p. 415, and Nābhādās, *Bhaktamāl*, p. 721.

19. The source is the *Mūl Gosāīṅ Carit* attributed to Beṇī Mādhavdās, *dohās* 29–32 and the accompanying *caupāīs*: Kiśorīlāl Gupta, *Gosāīṅ Carit* (Varanasi: Vāṇī-Vitān Prakāśan, 1964), p. 285. For further information, see Hawley and Juergensmeyer, *Songs of the Saints of India*, pp. 158, 211, and on the dating of the *Mūl Gosāīṅ Carit*, see Lutgendorf, 'The Search,' pp. 82–5.

20. For this dialogue in its earliest known form, see McLeod, *Early Sikh Tradition*, pp. 151–5.

21. Hawley and Juergensmeyer, *Songs of the Saints of India*, pp. 45–6.

22. On Ravidās, see Priyādās in Nābhādās, *Bhaktamāl*, p. 471. The Brahminizing of Kabīr apparently comes later, for both Priyādās and Anantdās

accept him as Muslim by birth. As to who might have been responsible for the change, see Charlotte Vaudeville, *Kabīr*, vol. 1 (Oxford: Clarendon Press, 1974), p. 32. I use the term Untouchable without pejorative intent. Of late, Dalit ('Oppressed') would be more acceptable speech, but both terms point to the oppression undeniably involved.

23. In the temple to Ravidās in the *camār* community at Sri Govardhanpur near Banaras, for example, there used to be a large picture of Ravidās displaying his inner sacred thread, framed and preserved under glass. Another painting in which this episode is included can also be seen today.

24. See Jijñāsu, *Sant Pravar Raidās Sāhab* (Lucknow: Bahujan Kalyāṇ Prakāśan, 1959). This work's subtitle is 'A Discriminating Biography, Written from a Buddhist Point of View.' James G. Lochtefeld has noted that the original publication date, 1956, was the year in which Ambedkar repudiated Hinduism. Lochtefeld, 'Clutching at the Elephant: Four Perspectives on the Life of Ravidas,' unpublished paper, Columbia University, 1988, p. 6.

25. Parita Mukta reports discovering in the course of fieldwork undertaken among artisans and peasants of Mewar and Marwar that the connection between Mīrā and Ravidās is taken as fact. Parita Mukta, private communication, 1989 and 'Mirabai in Rajasthan,' *Manushi* 50–2 (1989), pp. 94–9.

26. Priyādās in Nābhādās, *Bhaktamāl*, pp. 477–8.

27. 'G. D. Birla, Who Revolutionized Indian Industry,' p. 382.

28. On the association of 'primalist' (*ādi*) language with low-caste movements, see Mark Juergensmeyer, *Religion as Social Vision* (Berkeley: University of California Press, 1982), pp. 24–6, *passim*.

29. Hawley and Juergensmeyer, *Songs of the Saints of India*, pp. 10–11, 24.

30. Raghavan, *The Great Integrators*, p. 32.

31. Economics also may play a role in the success of the Malayalam version: these comic books cost less than other editions of *Amar Chitra Katha*. IBH leases the rights to an independent publisher and distributor, who sells at lower rates than IBH.

32. Kamala Chandrakant, Interview, Bombay, 1989.

33. J. S. Hawley, 'The Bharat Kala Bhavan *Sūrsāgar*,' in Alan W. Entwistle and Françoise Mallison, eds, *Studies in South Asian Devotional Literature* (Delhi: Manohar, 1994), pp. 20–34.

34. Kenneth E. Bryant, *Poems to the Child-God: Structures and Strategies in the Poetry of Sūrdās* (Berkeley: University of California Press, 1978), pp. 72–112; and Chapter 10 of the present work.

35. J. S. Hawley, 'Naming Hinduism,' *The Wilson Quarterly* 15: 3 (1991), pp. 20–34.

7. Krishna and the Gender of Longing

1. There is, of course, a huge range of interpretation concerning the 'Song of Songs', not all of which agrees in tone with that of Billings or turns to

allegory. Even within the span of Christian allegorical interpretation, not all commentators accept that the terms of reference are Christ and the Church. I am indebted to Elizabeth Castelli for discussions on these matters, and to Marcia Falk, *The Song of Songs: A New Translation and Interpretation* (San Francisco: Harper, 1990).

2. I owe these details to the work of Gurinder Singh Mann, who has examined the manuscript carefully, and I translate from his transcription. The text differs in only two instances from the one found in the so-called Banno manuscript of Kanpur, dated 1642, which is published in W. M. Callewaert, 'The 'Earliest' Song of Mira (1503–1546),' *Annali* 50:4 of the Istituto Universitario Orientale, Naples (1990), pp. 365–6; also in *Orientalia Lovaniensia Periodica* 22 (1991), p. 203. For further information and a different translation, see Nancy M. Martin (-Kershaw), 'Dyed in the Color of Her Lord: Multiple Representations in the Mirabai Tradition' (PhD diss., Graduate Theological Union, Berkeley, 1995), p. 115. Aspects of Gurinder Singh Mann's work on this poem appear in *The Making of Sikh Scripture* (New York: Oxford University Press, 2001), pp. 115–17.

3. A heading-by-heading breakdown for a manuscript of Sūrdās's poems dated 1640 is given in J. S. Hawley, *Sūr Dās: Poet, Singer, Saint* (Seattle: University of Washington Press and Delhi: Oxford University Press, 1984), p. 48. A similar pattern is manifest in poems datable to the sixteenth century itself, as will be evident in Kenneth E. Bryant's critical edition (*Sūr's Ocean*, vol. 2) and my translation of and commentary on it (*Sūr's Ocean*, vol. 1), forthcoming.

4. The Brajbhāṣā text upon which this translation is based has been established in the critical edition of Kenneth Bryant *et al.* (Bryant and Hawley, *Surdas: Poems from the Early Tradition*, §207). The poem corresponds to number 3857 in the currently standard Nāgarīpracāriṇī Sabhā *Sūrsāgar.*

5. S. K. De, *History of Sanskrit Poetics*, 2nd rev. ed. (Calcutta: K. L. Mukhopadhyaya, 1960), p. 384.

6. This history is sketched with useful brevity in Barron Holland, 'The *Satsāī* of Bihari: Hindi Poetry of the Early Riti Period' (PhD diss., University of California, Berkeley), 1969, pp. 82–7. See also Ronald Stuart Macgregor, *Hindi Literature from its Beginning to the Nineteenth Century* (Wiesbaden: Otto Harrassowitz, 1984), pp. 118–29.

7. The Brajbhāṣā original is the Bryant version (§165) that corresponds to NPS 3399.

8. A frequently cited statement on women as natural devotees in the literature of Hindu bhakti occurs at the end of A. K. Ramanujan's 'On Women Saints,' in J. S. Hawley and D. M. Wulff, eds, *The Divine Consort: Rādhā and the Goddesses of India* (Berkeley: Berkeley Religious Studies Series and Delhi: Motilal Banarsidass, 1982), p. 324. Ramanujan speaks of passivity rather than vulnerability. As to the 'natural' analogue—female incompleteness in relation to men—Cynthia Humes (Chapman University, 2 April 1998) points

out that in the classic *Nāṭyaśāstra* of Bharata only one of the eight classical temperaments assigned to a hero, *lalita guṇa* (light-heartedness), connects him intrinsically to a woman. Bharata's classification of a heroine is tellingly different. Here too Bharata employs an eightfold scheme, but in this case all eight of the 'eight states' (*avasthaḥ*), as they were later to be called, situate the heroine in relation to a man. See Rākeśagupta, *Studies in Nāyaka-Nāyikā-Bheda* (Aligarh: Granthāyan, 1967), pp. 49–51.

9. Especially *Manusmṛti* 5.147–51, 155, as in Wendy Doniger (with Brian K. Smith), trans., *The Laws of Manu* (New York: Penguin, 1991), p. 115; but see also I. Julia Leslie, *The Perfect Wife: The Orthodox Hindu Woman according to the Strīdharmapaddhati of Tryambakayajvan* (Delhi: Oxford University Press, 1989), pp. 305–17.

10. We meet this conviction in a bhakti framework in the *Subodhinī* (10.14) of Vallabhācārya, where he insists that a woman must be reborn as a man before she is fit to worship the way the *gopīs* do. On Vallabha's further struggles with this point, see Mrudula I. Marfatia, *The Philosophy of Vallabhācārya* (New Delhi: Munshiram Manoharlal, 1967), p. 222.

11. See, for example, Mary McGee, 'Desired Fruits: Motive and Intention in the Votive Rites of Hindu Women,' in Julia Leslie, ed., *Roles and Rituals for Hindu Women* (Rutherford, NJ: Fairleigh Dickinson University Press, 1991), pp. 71–88; Gloria Goodwin Raheja and Ann Grodzins Gold, *Listen to the Heron's Words: Reimagining Gender and Kinship in North India* (Berkeley: University of California Press, 1994), pp. 67–72, 121–48; and Velcheru Narayana Rao, 'A Rāmāyaṇa of Their Own: Women's Oral Tradition in Telugu,' in Paula Richman, ed., *Many Rāmāyaṇas: The Diversity of a Narrative Tradition in South Asia* (Berkeley: University of California Press, 1991), pp. 114–36.

12. I treat the theme in chapter 4 ('*Viraha*: Separation and Simple Religion') of *Sūr Dās: Poet, Singer, Saint*, pp. 93–118.

13. On the relative paucity of references to the names of individual *gopīs* (including Rādhā) in the early strata of the *Sūrsāgar*, for example, see Hawley, *Sūr Dās*, pp. 88–90.

14. D. M. Wulff, 'Rādhā's Audacity in *kīrtan* Performances and Women's Status in Greater Bengal,' in Karen King and Karen Jo Torjesen, eds, *Women and Goddess Traditions* (Minneapolis: Fortress Press, 1995), pp. 64–83.

15. See J. S. Hawley, 'Images of Gender in Poetry of Krishna,' in Caroline Walker Bynum, Stevan Harrell, and Paula Richman, eds, *Gender and Religion: On the Complexity of Symbols* (Boston: Beacon Press, 1986), pp. 231–56.

16. We may view these contrasting corpuses in Parita Mukta, *Upholding the Common Life: The Community of Mirabai* (Delhi: Oxford University Press, 1994), especially pp. 90–105, on the one hand, and in Paraśurām Caturvedī, *Mīrāṅbāī kī Padāvalī* (Allahabad: Hindī Sāhitya Sammelan, 1973), on the other. A variety of related terrains are staked out by Nancy Martin(-Kershaw) in chapter 5 of 'Dyed in the Color of Her Lord,' pp. 254–337. Martin draws

attention to a distinction between resistance and renunciation and emphasizes that sometimes '[t]he focus is not on Mira's transgression of gender roles from the perspective of upper caste men; rather the view seems to be that of a woman trying to negotiate a life of her own choosing within structures of power that subjugate her and in relation to other women who must do the same' (p. 317).

17. In a longer treatment, this sweeping generalization would require massive qualification, for *viraha* is a theme so crucial to the literature of Krishna that we meet it virtually everywhere. Yet in the sixteenth-century *Sūrsāgar*, for example, all the poems dealing specifically with the rainy season (corresponding to NPS 3918–3956) contain overtones of *viraha*, and the calendrical twelve-month (*bārahmāsā*) poems of *viraha* tend to begin with the hot or rainy season. A related genre, the four-month poem (*caumāsā*), focuses there entirely. On the latter two, see Charlotte Vaudeville, *Les Chansons des douze mois dans les littératures Indoaryennes* (Pondicherry: Institut Français d'Indologie, 1965), translated as *Bārahmāsā in Indian Literatures* (Delhi: Motilal Banarsidass, 1986). As to qualifications, for example, one would quickly admit that in Rajasthan the desert climate yields a sort of year-round 'culture of separation,' as Friedhelm Hardy has observed in his *Viraha-Bhakti* (Delhi: Oxford University Press, 1983), p. 568.

18. Lawrence A. Babb, *The Divine Hierarchy: Popular Hinduism in Central India* (New York: Columbia University Press, 1975), pp. 128–53. In regard to connections between festivals for Krishna/Vishnu and the felt hegemony of the Goddess in the rainy season and somewhat thereafter, see Charlotte Vaudeville, 'Krishna Gopāla, Rādhā, and the Great Goddess,' in Hawley and Wulff, eds, *The Divine Consort*, pp. 2–5.

19. Edward C. Dimock, Jr., 'A Theology of the Repulsive: The Myth of the Goddess Śītalā,' in Hawley and Wulff, eds, *The Divine Consort*, p. 196. Dimock notes, however (p. 184), that Jvarāsura, the fever demon who is frequently said to accompany her, is male.

20. Dorothy Dinnerstein, *The Mermaid and the Minotaur: Sexual Arrangements and the Human Malaise* (New York: Harper & Row, 1976); Nancy Chodorow, 'Family Structure and Feminine Personality,' in Michelle Zimbalist Rosaldo and Louise Lamphere, eds, *Women, Culture, and Society* (Stanford: Stanford University Press, 1974), pp. 43–66; Karen McCarthy Brown, 'Fundamentalism and the Control of Women,' in J. S. Hawley, ed., *Fundamentalism and Gender* (New York: Oxford University Press, 1994), especially pp. 180–9; Sudhir Kakar and John M. Ross, 'The Cloistered Passion of Radha and Krishna,' in Kakar and Ross, *Tales of Love, Sex and Danger* (Delhi: Oxford University Press, 1986), especially pp. 99–103; Jeffrey J. Kripal, *Kālī's Child: The Mystical and the Erotic in the Life and Teachings of Ramakrishna* (Chicago: University of Chicago Press, 1995), especially pp. 232–6; Stanley N. Kurtz, *All the Mothers are One: Hindu India and the Reshaping of Psychoanalysis* (New York: Columbia University Press, 1992), pp. 29–131.

21. I am sure this sounds reductionistic. One must recognize that whatever the narcissistic mood here—however strong the connection seems between a male self and the self projected as male in Krishna—this does not make men's worship of Krishna the same as self-worship, any more than the projection of God or Allah as male makes that deity the same as his male worshipers. In all these cases, male devotees certainly experience themselves as quite different from the gods they worship; and the general contrast between the structures of Krishna's life and the life of domestic *dharma*, so fundamental to lives of most men, underscores the point. Still, as we currently see in recent debates about ordaining women and homosexuals to the clergy in modern Western Christianity, these resonances along gender lines between worshiper and worshiped are very important. Particularly in a theological universe where the analogy between self (*jīva*) and Self (*ātman*) is the subject of direct discussion, and in which (male) adepts learn to map out the world of Krishna on their bodies through practices of meditation and visualization, the significance of these connections is not to be minimized. In a longer exposition one would also want to consider the possibility that latent homosexuality is in the air. In doing so, one would have to give due weight to the fact that same-sex attractions between men were apparently understood rather differently in sixteenth-century India than they are in the modern West or in at least some parts of urban India today. Further on this subject, see Hawley, 'The Damage of Separation: Krishna's Loves and Kali's Child,' *Journal of the American Academy of Religion* 72:2 (2004), pp. 369–93.

22. Martha Ann Selby, 'Like a Pot Brimming with Oil: The Care and Feeding of the Pregnant Body in Sanskrit Ayurvedic Texts,' Dharam Hinduja Indic Research Center, Columbia University, 12 March 1998. On problems of dating and authorship associated with the *Caraka Saṃhitā*, see Kenneth G. Zysk, *Asceticism and Healing in Ancient India* (New York: Oxford University Press, 1991), p. 33. Caraka has continued to have a major effect on Indian medical knowledge—certainly through the sixteenth century and in some settings, today as well.

23. I have been instructed by Karen Torjesen's response to Marvin Meyer's essay on 'Gender Transformation in Early Christianity,' Chapman University, 3 April 1998.

24. This is Selby's favorite example among a set of similar experiences. The Sanskrit phrase is *vimukta-bandhanatvam-iva vakṣasaḥ*, found in *Carakasaṃhitā, śarīrasthāna* 8.36. See Priyavrat Sharma, ed. and trans., *Caraka-Saṃhitā*, vol. 1 (Varanasi: Chaukhambha Orientalia, 1981), p. 476. A similar example—a Kerala text on the pains of childbirth—has been noticed by Sarah Caldwell in her 'Waves of Beauty, Rivers of Blood: Constructing the Goddess in Kerala,' in Tracy Pintchman, ed., *Seeking Mahādevī: Constructing the Identities of the Hindu Great Goddesses* (Albany: State University New York Press, 2001), p. 104, and reported in Wendy Doniger, *The Implied Spider: Poetics and*

Theology in Myth (New York: Columbia University Press, 1998), p. 114. Doniger's comment on the (un)translatability of language about women's experience from women to men (*The Implied Spider*, p. 115) is worth noting in this context, and the entire chapter in which it occurs (pp. 109–35) is an elegant exploration of 'women's voices' in relation to questions of authorship, audience, cross-gender 'gaze,' and proximate and ultimate narration.

25. Hence the title of the popular book by Elisabeth Bumiller, *May You Be the Mother of a Hundred Sons* (New York: Random House, 1990). On ritual enactments of this theme in the *puṃsāvana* and *cauk* rites, see Raj Bali Pandey, *Hindu Saṃskāras* (Delhi: Motilal Banarsidass, 1969), pp. 60–3; and Doranne Jacobson, 'Golden Handprints and Red-painted Feet: Hindu Childbirth Rituals in Central India,' in Doranne Jacobson and Susan Wadley, *Women in India: Two Perspectives*, 2nd enlarged ed. (Columbia, MO: South Asia Publications, 1992), pp. 148–53. Cf. also *Carakasaṃhitā śarīrasthāna* 8.18–19, as in Sharma, ed., *Caraka-Saṃhitā*, pp. 466–7.

26. J. M. Masson, 'The Childhood of Kṛṣṇa,' *Journal of the American Oriental Society* 94:4 (1974), pp. 454–9.

27. This is the general subject of my *Krishna, the Butter Thief* (Princeton: Princeton University Press, 1983).

28. On *rasa*, aesthetic emotion, as shared, controlled experience, especially in the context of the performing arts, see Donna M. Wulff, *Drama as a Mode of Religious Realization* (Chico, CA: Scholars Press, 1984), pp. 25–44, and David L. Haberman, *Acting as a Way of Salvation* (New York: Oxford University Press, 1988), pp. 12–39. In relation to the male poet's access to the inner world of female experience, as in the case of Sūrdās, see the theological preamble that Harirāy adds to the *Sūrdās kī Vārtā* attributed to Gokulnāth. An English translation appears in Richard Barz, *The Bhakti Sect of Vallabhācārya* (Faridabad: Thomson Press, 1976), pp. 106–7.

8. Last Seen with Akbar

1. Vincent A. Smith, *Akbar, the Great Mogul* (Delhi: S. Chand, 1958).

2. Akbar is also said to have paid visits to Svāmī Haridās and Jīv Gosvāmī, as noted in A. W. Entwistle, *Braj, Centre of Krishna Pilgrimage* (Groningen: Egbert Forsten, 1987), p. 158, note 114. In Marathi, he is pictured as having entered into a discussion-debate (*saṃvād*) with Nāmdev, despite the apparent anachronism of this connection. (For this information I am indebted to Christian Novetzke, who encountered the *saṃvād* in an eighteenth-century manuscript at Dhulia.) Other stories among the 'lives of the saints' that suggest an involvement with Akbar include Priyādās's account of the life of Sūrdās Madanmohan. Sūrdās Madanmohan is said to have become an *amīn* in the imperial administration, but to have given away all the revenue at his disposal for the feeding of *sādhus* or *sants*. When collection agents arrived from the throne, he sent a

chestful of stones rather than coins. Imprisoned on this account by Todar Mal, he composed a *dohā* that pleased Akbar, who then ordered that he be released from jail. See Nābhādās, *Bhaktamāl*, with the *Bhaktirasabodhinī* of Priyādās (Lucknow: Tejkumār Press, 1969), pp. 748–9. An English translation of the relevant section appears in Jeevan Deol, 'Sūrdās: Poet and Text in the Sikh Tradition,' *Bulletin of the School of Oriental and African Studies* 63:2 (2000), p. 171.

3. Priyādās in Nābhādās, *Bhaktamāl*, p. 721.

4. Because the terms syncretism and separation were intended by the South Asia Seminar at Texas to be suggestive rather than restrictive or precise, I have accepted them as they are. If one were to delve more seriously into issues of nomenclature, one would particularly want to consider the usages of Asim Roy, *The Islamic Syncretistic Tradition in Bengal* (Princeton: Princeton University Press, 1983), and Judith A. Berling, *The Syncretic Religion of Lin Chao-en* (New York: Columbia University Press, 1980). In regard to separation, one would need to consider the specific meaning of sectarianism.

5. See J. S. Hawley, *Sūr Dās: Poet, Singer, Saint* (Seattle: University of Washington Press and Delhi: Oxford University Press, 1984), p. 7.

6. For perspectives on the *duniyā/vilāyat* relationship as it concerns Indo-Muslim literature in Hindavī, I am greatly indebted to Aditya Behl, *Love's Subtle Magic: An Indian Islamic Literary Tradition, 1379–1545* (New York: Oxford University Press, 2012).

7. The *vārtā* of Kumbhandās, another of the *aṣṭachāp*, is rather different in this respect. Kumbhandās is more or less dragged to Akbar's court kicking and screaming. Quite a point is made of his sense that a simple farmer like him doesn't belong in a place like that, but Akbar's messengers have the power to take him along in any case. True, he is able to negotiate things so that he goes under his own steam; he walks rather than being conveyed in the palanquin Akbar has sent to transport him. So issues of independence are definitely to the fore. He gets to go in a way that suits his own sense of himself, but go he must.

8. Entwistle, *Braj*, p. 153, especially note 92 on Prabhudayāl Mītal.

9. This *farmān* is the fourth issued to Viṭṭhalnāth by Akbar, the first being in 1577. Govardhan (i.e., *gordhan*) is also mentioned indirectly in a *farmān* of 1588, but it is only in the 1593 *farmān* that Viṭṭhalnāth's building program at Govardhan is acknowledged and protected. Notably, no mention is made of the ownership of the temple itself, but only the acquisition of land for ancillary buildings. It was at this point, evidently, that Viṭṭhalnāth shifted his residence from Gokul (as in the 1577 *farmān*) to the environs of Govardhannāthjī itself. See Krishnalal Mohanlal Jhaveri, *Imperial Farmans (AD 1577 to AD 1805) granted to the Ancestors of his Holiness the Tilakayat Maharaj* (Bombay: The News Printing Press, 1928).

10. The translation is Jhaveri's (n.p.). The passages come from *farmāns* 1 and 4, the latter concerning Govardhan itself.

11. See Jhaveri, *Imperial Farmans, farmān* 1, dated 1577. However, this *farmān* says nothing about a temple *per se*, and it seems to assume that Gokulnāth was already resident there at the time of its issuance. Richard Barz says that in 1572 Akbar granted Viṭṭhalnāth a tract of land in the area, and that his residence there dates from that time, but does not report the evidence for this assertion. See Barz, *The Bhakti Sect of Vallabhācārya* (Faridabad: Thomson Press, 1976), p. 54.

12. §420 in Bryant and Hawley, *Surdas*; NPS 337.

13. Dvārikādās Parīkh, ed., *Caurāsī Vaiṣṇavan kī Vārtā* (Mathura: Śrī Bajaraṅg Pustakālay, 1970 [originally 1948]), p. 406.

14. This is not to deny that such separatism is achieved in part by appealing to a document that is pansectarian in its prestige, namely, the *Bhāgavata Purāṇa.* Such efforts at legitimation are of course a familiar motif in the construction of sectarian identities.

15. This is a judgment with which David Lorenzen does not agree. See his *Kabir Legends* (Albany: State University of New York Press, 1991), pp. 9–18.

16. I refer to the critical edition prepared by Narendra Jhā—*Bhaktamāl: Pāṭhānuśīlan evam Vivecan* (Patna: Anupam Prakāśan, 1970)—rather than the standard Tejkumār Press edition compiled by Sītārāmśaraṇ Bhagavānprasād Rūpakalā, to which I have made reference above. The latter further strengthens the Caitanyite connection by including verses attributed to Nābhādās and Priyādās on Caitanya himself. These are interposed between Raghunāth Gosāīṅ (i.e., Gosvāmī) and Sūrdās.

17. The poem was drawn to my attention by Heidi Pauwels, to whom I am extremely grateful. It appears in Pauwels, *In Praise of Holy Men: Hagiographical Poems by and about Harirām Vyās* (Groningen: Egbert Forsten, 2002), pp. 85–6.

18. For this insight I am again grateful to Heidi Pauwels, in the report she presented on recent and current research to the Eighth International Conference on Early Literature in New Indo-Aryan Languages, Leuven, 25 August 2000. See also Pauwels, 'The Early *Bhakti* Milieu as Mirrored in the Poetry of Harirām Vyās,' in Alan W. Entwistle and Françoise Mallison, eds, *Studies in South Asian Devotional Literature* (New Delhi: Manohar, and Paris: École Française d'Extrême Orient, 1994), pp. 33–40. The class of people Vyās and others call *vimukh*—those who turn their faces away from Hari—seems to overlap significantly with those called *pākhaṇḍī* in the Gauḍīya literature, and it would be interesting to know if that, in turn, is the term Marco della Tomba picked up as *pāsand* in his late-eighteenth-century soujourn in Bettiah. He apparently glosses it as 'hedonist' and contrasts those whom it represents with Vaishnavas, Rāmānandīs, Shaivas, and others. See David N. Lorenzen, 'Who Invented Hinduism?,' *Comparative Studies in Society and History* 41:4 (1999), p. 642.

19. Christian Novetzke, 'A Family Affair,' in Guy Beck, ed., *Alternative Krishnas* (Albany: State University of New York Press, 2005), pp. 120–6.

20. Richard Burghart, 'The Founding of the Ramanandi Sect,' *Ethnohistory* 25:2 (1978), pp. 121–39, and 'The History of Janakpur,' *Kailash* 6:4 (1978), pp. 257–84.

21. The translation is by Aditya Behl, *Love's Subtle Magic*. It renders folio 151a of the British Library *Afsānah-i-Shāhāṅ* (Persian manuscript add. 24409). I am extremely grateful to Aditya Behl for alerting me to the mention of Sūrdās in this passage, and to Shakeel Ahmad Khan of Aligarh Muslim University for help in determining its precise location. A printed version of the Persian text in Devanagari transliteration, together with a Hindi translation based on the rotograph copy held by Aligarh Muslim University, may be found in Parameśvarī Lāl Gupta, ed., *Kutuban kṛt Mṛgāvatī (Mūl Pāṭh, Pāṭhāntar, Ṭippaṇī evam Śodh)* (Varanasi: Viśvavidyālay Prakāśan, 1967), p. 39. Transliterations offered in the Behl text refer to standard forms of Persian words that appear somewhat differently in the original manuscript: *khośak* for *khushak*, and *galiyā* for *ghalia*.

22. Only a single couplet of Farmūlī has survived—no full collection—but from that and his depiction in other places in the *Afsānah-i-Shāhāṅ* it is clear that Muhammad Kabīr saw him as a celebrated poet of Hindi (Siddiqi, 'Shaikh Muhammad Kabir,' pp. 74–5).

23. Siddiqi, 'Shaikh Muhammad Kabir,' pp. 59–69; Askari, 'Historical Value,' pp. 184–8.

24. Siddiqi, 'Shaikh Muhammad Kabir,' pp. 74–5. Similarly Askari, 'Historical Value,' p. 188, and in regard to the passage at hand, p. 194; also Aditya Behl and Simon Weightman, with S. N. Pandey, *Mīr Sayyid Manjhan Shattārī Rājgīrī: Madhumālatī, An Indian Sufi Romance* (Oxford: Oxford University Press, 2000), pp. xii–xiii.

25. Self-promotion is not a major feature of the sort of narrative of Akbar that we get in a book such as that by Vincent Smith, who was eager to see 'the great Mogul' take his place alongside that other paradigmatically enlightened monarch of Indian history, Aśoka Maurya, as in his *Asoka, the Buddhist Emperor of India* (New Delhi: Asian Educational Resources, 1997 [originally 1901]). Other historians, however, have drawn attention to the double meaning probably attached to the affirmation *allāhū akbar* in the cult of the *dīn-i-illāhī*, e.g., Hermann Kulke and Dieter Rothermund, *A History of India* (London: Routledge, 1986), p. 203.

26. Here I am thinking especially of the story of Akbar as the sponsor of the first critical edition of the *Sūrsāgar*, a trial by water that is told in Chapter 4 of the *sūrdās kī vārtā*. A review of this episode may be found in my *Sūr Dās*, p. 10, and a translation in Barz, *Bhakti Sect*, pp. 122–3.

27. I am thinking, for example, of the integration of different personalities, positions, and even clienteles that was accomplished through the rubric of the *aṣṭachāp*.

9. The Early *Sūrsāgar* and the Growth of the Sur Tradition

1. Charlotte Vaudeville, *Étude sur les sources et la composition du Rāmāyaṇa de Tulsī Dās* (Paris: Librairie d'Amérique et d'Orient, 1955), pp. xiv–xxii.

2. His *Dasamskandh*, on which see R. S. McGregor's introduction to Nandadās, *The Round Dance of Krishna and Uddhav's Message* (London: Lauzac, 1973), p. 35.

3. Some mystery surrounds this manuscript, however. Ratnākar states that it was lent to him very briefly by its owner, Śāh Keśavdas Raīś, but makes no comment as to its organization. (*Sūrsāgar*, 1st ed., vol. 2 [*sic*: the projected vol. 1 never appeared]. Kashi: Nāgarīpracāriṇī Sabhā [NPS], 1934, p. 2.) Javāharlāl Caturvedī was the first to describe it as *skandhātmak*, but one wonders whether he had seen the manuscript itself or inferred its nature from the *skandhātmak* format of the NPS edition. (*Sūrdās: Adhyayan Sāmagrī*. Mathura: Akhil Bhāratiya Braj Sāhitya Maṇḍal, 1959, p. 7.) Kenneth E. Bryant made a search for the manuscript in 1977 but was unable to locate it. A similar uncertainty pertains to a manuscript reportedly dated VS 1740 which was in the collection of Naṭvarlāl Caturvedī of Mathura. Harbanślāl Śarmā, basing his information on that supplied by Javāharlāl Caturvedī, asserts that it is *saṃgrahātmak*, but Caturvedī then later lists it as *skandhātmak*. (Śarmā, *Sūr aur unkā Sāhitya* [Aligarh: Bhārat Prakāśan Mandir, 1965], p. 51. Caturvedī, 'Sūrsāgar kā Vikās aur uskā Rūp' in V. S. Agravāl, ed., *Kanhaiyālāl Poddār Abhinandan Granth* [Mathura: Akhil Bhāratīya Braj Sāhitya Maṇḍal, 1953], p. 128. Caturvedī, *Sūrdās: Adhyayan Sāmagrī*, p. 14.) Attempts by myself (in 1976) and Bryant (in 1977) to find this manuscript were unsuccessful. On this and related issues, see chapter 2 of my book *Sūr Dās: Poet, Singer, Saint.*

4. Two notable efforts in this direction are those of Ved Prakāś Śāstrī, *Śrīmadhāgavat aur Sūrsāgar kā Vārṇya Viṣay kā Tulnātmak Adhyayan* (Agra: Sarasvatī Pustak Sadan, 1969) and Viśvanāth Śukla, *Hindī Kṛṣṇa Bhakti Kāvya par Śrīmadbhāgavat kā Prabhāv* (Aligarh: Bhārat Prakāśan Mandir, 1966), pp. 196–216.

5. The often cited *pad* NPS 1792, which ties Sūr not only to the *Bhāgavata* but also to his 'guru' (i.e., Vallabhācārya), is an example of such a phenomenon, as are such poems as NPS 225–31, which have the *Bhāgavata* as their explicit subject.

6. For details, see the section entitled 'Intertextual Lineage and the *Bhāgavata Purāṇa*' in chapter 1 of my introduction to the forthcoming book *Sūr's Ocean*, vol. 1. Part of my purpose there is to suggest that Sūr's intertextual horizons went well beyond the *Bhāgavata.*

7. In addition to the early *Khoj Reports* of the Nāgarīpracāriṇī Sabhā (in 1902 and the years immediately following), there have been the researches of Ratnākar, Javāharlāl Caturvedī, and Mātāprasād Gupta. Published results

are contained in Ratnākar, *op. cit.*; Caturvedī, *Sūrdās: Adhyayan Sāmagrī* and *Sūr Sāgar* (Mathura: Javāharlāl Caturvedī, 1965); and Mātāprasād Gupta (posthumously, ed. by Udayśaṃkar Śāstrī), 'Sūr Sāgar kī Bhūmikā,' *Bhāratīya Sāhitya* 13:1–2 (1968), pp. 43–94; 15:1–2 (1970), pp. 145–472; 16:1–2 (1971), pp. 149–84; 17:1–2 (1972), pp. 155–96; 17:3–4 (1972), pp. 195–203; 18:1–2 (1973), pp. 145–205; 18:3–4 (1973), pp. 163–210; 19:1–2 (1974), pp. 159–208; 19:3–4 (1974), pp. 173–220; and subsequently *Sūrsāgar* (Agra: Agra University, 1979). See also Śāstrī, 'Sūrsāgar kī Sāmagrī kā Saṃkalpan aur uskā Sampādan,' *Bhāratīya Sāhitya* 17:1–2 (1972), pp. 73–103. An account of this history is provided in chapter 3 of the introduction to Hawley and Bryant, *Sūr's Ocean*, vol. 1.

8. Manuscripts of this antiquity do not occur for other works familiarly attributed to Sūrdās—the *Sūr Sārāvalī*, *Sāhitya Laharī*, and *Nal Daman*, dated AH 1110 (1698–9) and now preserved in the Prince of Wales Museum, Mumbai; *see* Viśvanāth Prasād, ed., [*Kavi Sūrdās Kṛt*] *Nal Daman* (Agra: Agra University, 1961). I therefore exclude them from consideration. Selected poems of Sūr do occur in old anthologies (*phuṭkar pad*), as we have seen—the Agra manuscript mentioned on page 80 is especially noteworthy—but aside from the middle section of J1, these too are left out of consideration.

9. These are the manuscripts reported to exist at Śergaḍh and Cīrghāṭ in Braj.

10. *Bhāratīya Sāhitya* 13:1–2 (1968), pp. 43–5.

11. An earlier review of this manuscript was formulated by Prabhu Dayāl Mītal in 'Sūr kṛt Padoṅ kī Sabse Prācīn Prati,' *Nāgarīpracāriṇī Patrikā* 67:3 1962 [VS 2013], pp. 262–7.

12. Although the colophon has been lost, this manuscript can be reliably dated because it is written in the hand of one of the favorite scribes of Maharaja Sūrya Siṃh of Bikaner. Hindi manuscript 157 and Sanskrit manuscript 209 in the same collection, dated respectively VS 1681 and 1668, are in the same hand and the quality of the paper of manuscript 156 suggested to the curator, Dīnānāth Khatrī, that it may be the oldest of the three.

13. The use of the term *mathurākṣetre* is not precise enough to determine whether the scribe hails from the region of Mathura or whether he is writing there or, as is likely, both.

14. The third digit in the date as it currently reads, 1724, is not clear and may be an alteration of an earlier 6 or 7. The latter would be too late, however, since 1774 would fall after the reign of Aurangzeb when, as the colophon states, the manuscript was transcribed.

15. The language here involves the same ambiguity as indicated in note 13.

16. Kenneth Bryant has confirmed that this last manuscript cannot be located.

17. If one is speaking instead of the general number of Sūrdās *pads* one can plausibly argue to have been in circulation in the sixteenth century, however, the number rises above 400. Such a judgment is made on the basis of dispersed evidence contained in manuscripts dating to the seventeenth century. On this

basis 433 poems are included in Bryant's forthcoming critical edition, vol. 2 of Bryant and Hawley, *Surdas: Poems from the Early Tradition.*

18. Kenneth Bryant has laid out these patterns in a series of articles: 'Toward a Critical Edition of the *Sūrasāgar*,' in Winand M. Callewaert, ed., *Early Hindī Devotional Literature in Current Research* (Delhi: Impex India, 1980), pp. 5–16; 'The Manuscript Tradition of the Sursagar: The Fatehpur Manuscript,' in Gopal Narayan Bahura and Kenneth E. Bryant, eds, *Pad Sūrdāsjī kā / The Padas of Sūrdās* (Jaipur: Maharaja Sawai Man Singh II Museum, 1982 [actually appeared 1984]), pp. vii–xx; and 'The Fatehpur Manuscript and the *Sūrsāgar* Critical Edition Project,' in Monika Thiel-Horstmann, ed., *Bhakti in Current Research, 1979–1982* (Berlin: Dietrich Reimer Verlag, 1983), pp. 37–52.

19. This is normally the pattern in U1.

20. The structure of this interesting manuscript is discussed in Chapters 3 and 15.

21. This seems likely in the case of J4, since the scribe chosen for the work was from the old Vallabhite seat at Gokul. More problematical is the case of the heads of the royal houses at Bikaner, Kota, and to a lesser extent Jaipur, who are traditionally associated with the Vallabha Sampradāy. Does the absence in these royal archives of Vallabhite hymnbooks (*sevā praṇālīs*) from this early period indicate that the sectarian affiliation came later?

22. It is the antetype of manuscript no. 10/2, which bears that date.

23. See Charlotte Vaudeville, *Pastorales par Soûr-Dâs* (Paris: Gallimard, 1971), pp. 38f; also Mahāvīr Siṃh Gahalot, 'Sūrdās kā Śṛṅgār Varṇan: Aitihāsik, Dhārmik, aur Sāhityik Pāramparik Vivecan-sahit Sūr ke Śṛṅgār-Varṇan kā Dārśanik tathā Ālaṃkarik Mūlyāṅkan' (PhD diss., Jodhpur University, 1963), pp. 275–88.

24. Contrary to what one would expect on the basis of Vaudeville's conjectures about Sūr and Viṭṭhalnāth in *ibid.*, p. 38.

25. Old versions of NPS 894, 898, 909, and 946 are samples. By 'old' I mean dating to the seventeenth century or earlier.

26. As in NPS 923, 933, and 1392, all old poems.

27. NPS 908.7–8.

28. In various ways the following poems accomplish this purpose: NPS 882, 890, 891, 906, 907, 916, 921, 939, 940, 955, and 985.

29. NPS 886.1–4.

30. NPS 4061 (1976 edition).

31. E.g., NPS 1009 or, on a smaller scale, the providential perspective which leavens such poems as NPS 960, 961, 983, and 985.

32. For instance, the refrain of the well-known poem *prathama karī hari mākhana corī*, 'It's Hari's first time stealing butter,' marks it out as the relatively late poem it is (NPS 886).

33. Cf., e.g., *sukh sindhu*, *ras sindhu*, *sukh samudra*, etc., in the *Hit Caurāsī*. These are 12.6, 18.2, and 22.4 in the text provided by Charles S. J. White,

The Caurāsī Pad of Śrī Hit Harivaṃś (Honolulu: University of Hawaii Press, 1977).

34. A good example of this locution is found in the final line of NPS 720: *sūradāsa svāmī sukha sāgara jasumati prīti baḍhāvata.* 'Sūrdās's Lord is an ocean of joy, expanding Yaśodā's love.' What is especially striking is that the portion of the line beginning with the words *sukha sāgara* constitutes an emendation made at a late date to a poem that is widely attested in the earliest manuscripts, perhaps precisely in order to include this formula.

35. E.g., NPS 2527, 2573, and the series beginning with NPS 2683.

36. NPS 2584 through 2634.

37. NPS 1362ff.

38. The refrain of the final poem in the necklace sequence, for instance, reads *parama catura vṛṣabhānu dulārī,* 'Bṛṣabhānu's daughter is exceedingly clever' (NPS 2634.1).

39. Another factor in encouraging this style of poetry may have been the example of long poems produced by figures such as Nandadās and Tulsīdās.

40. 'Sūrsāgar kī Bhūmikā,' *Bhāratīya Sāhitya* 13:1–2 (1968), p. 74.

41. In the edition of Govardhannāth Śukla (Aligarh: Bhārat Prakāśan Mandir, n.d. [1958]).

42. I am grateful to Rupert Snell for having drawn these to my attention. They are NPS 1303, 1809, 1917, 1819, 1971, and 2455.

43. See R. S. McGregor, 'Tulsīdās' Śrīkṛṣṇagītāvalī,' *Journal of the American Oriental Society* 96:4 (1976), p. 526.

10. The Verbal Icon—How Literal?

1. For a brief index of difficulties surrounding this date, see J. S. Hawley, *Sūr Dās: Poet, Singer, Saint* (Seattle: University of Washington Press and Delhi: Oxford University Press, 1984), p. 7; Alan W. Entwistle, *Braj, Centre of Krishna Pilgrimage* (Groningen: Egbert Forsten, 1987), p. 165.

2. Entwistle, *Braj*, pp. 153–4.

3. It uses the word *samarāyo*: *Caurāsī Vaiṣṇavan kī Vārtā, sūrdās kī vārtā,* ch. 1 (Mathura: Śrī Govardhan Granthamālā Kāryālay, 1970), p. 409.

4. Entwistle, *Braj*, pp. 160–1.

5. *Sūrdās kī vārtā,* ch. 6, p. 421.

6. *Ibid.*, ch. 6, p. 422. See also p. 39 in the present volume.

7. We owe the phrase 'verbal icon' to W. K. Wimsatt and Monroe C. Beardsley, *The Verbal Icon: Studies in the Meaning of Poetry* (Lexington: University Press of Kentucky, 1964). Kenneth Bryant is responsible for having brought it into the critical literature on the *Sūrsāgar*: *Poems to the Child-God* (Berkeley: University of California Press, 1978), pp. 72–112.

8. Allahabad: Śodh Sāhitya Prakāśan, 1973.

9. Entwistle, *Braj*, p. 161.

10. For numerous depictions in painting, see Amit Ambalal, *Krishna as Shrinathji* (Ahmedabad: Mapin, 1987).

11. Steven Paul Hopkins, *Singing the Body of God* (New York: Oxford University Press, 2002), pp. 93, 99-100, *passim*; Indira V. Peterson, *Poems to Śiva* (Princeton: Princeton University Press, 1989), pp. 274–6; A. K. Ramanujan, *Hymns for the Drowning* (Princeton: Princeton University Press, 1981); cf. Vasudha Narayanan, *The Way and the Goal* (Washington: Institute for Vaishnava Studies and Cambridge: Center for the Study of World Religions, Harvard University, 1987), p. 64.

12. Bryant, *Poems to the Child-God*, pp. 24–35, 79–84.

13. Or in Tamil, *ukantaruḷiṇanilaṅkal*. See Katharine Young, 'Beloved Places (*Ukantaruḷiṇanilaṅkal*): The Correlation of Topography and Theology in the Śrīvaiṣṇava Tradition of South India' (PhD diss., McGill University, 1978).

14. Ramanujan, *Hymns for the Drowning,* pp. 122–6; cf. Hopkins on Vedāntadeśika, *Singing the Body of God*, p. 103.

15. Jagannāth Dās 'Ratnākar,' Nandadulāre Vajpeyī, et al., *Sūrsāgar* (Varanasi: Kāśī Nāgarīpracāriṇī Sabhā, 1972 and 1976 [originally 1948]).

16. On the difficulties of historical musicology relating to *dhrupad* and Brajbhāṣā poetry, see Richard Widdess, 'Dhrupad as a Musical Tradition,' *Journal of Vaiṣṇava Studies* 3:1 (1994), pp. 65–70; Françoise 'Nalini' Delvoye, 'The Verbal Content of Dhrupad Songs from the Earliest Collections,' *Dhrupad Annual* 5 (1990), pp. 93–109; other essays by Delvoye listed in F. N. Delvoye, 'Dhrupad Songs Attributed to Tansen,' in Alan Entwistle and Françoise Mallison, eds, *Studies in South Asian Devotional Literature* (New Delhi: Manohar and Paris: École Française d'Extrême Orient, 1994), pp. 426–7; and Hawley, *Sūr's Ocean*, Introduction, chapter 2, 'Performance, past and present.'

17. An example is the well known poem *cakaī rī cali caraṇa sarovara jahāṅ na pema viyogu* (Bryant and Hawley, *Surdas*, §420, NPS 337), which is assigned to *rāg dhanāśarī* when it first appears in manuscript J1 (folio 4, #10) and to *rāg bilāval* when it recurs (folio 44, #16). J1 was apparently compiled from three separate pre-existing collections of poetry, in two of which this poem occurs. See G. N. Bahura and K. E. Bryant, eds, *Pad Sūrdās jī kā / The Padas of Surdas* (Jaipur: Maharaja Sawai Man Singh II Museum, 1982), pp. 7, 88, and Chapters 3 and 15 of this book.

18. For example, see Udayśaṅkar Śāstrī, 'Sūrsāgar kī Sāmagrī kā Saṅkalan aur uskā Saṃpādan,' *Bhāratīya Sāhitya* 17:1–2 (1972), p. 92, in relation to poems that cluster around the theme of stealing butter. *Kīrtankārs* in both the temple of Mathurādhīś in Kota and the *dvitīya pīṭh* in Nathdvara reported ways in which their singing of these poems varied—and in somewhat different ways—from what is now specified in the printed *sevā praṇālī*. At Kota, for example, *mākhan corī* poems are sung from *kṛṣṇajanmāṣṭamī* to the new moon (*bhādrapad kṛṣṇa*, 11–15), whereas the printed text specifies that they should

be confined to *bhādrapad kṛṣṇa* 14–15. (Interviews, 7 November 1975; 22 November 1975; 26 August 1976.)

19. NPS 1273, Bryant, *Poems to the Child-God*, pp. 95–8. Bryant worked with the Nāgarīpracāriṇī Sabhā version of this poem, which is altered in several details by his critical edition, and these encourage certain changes in translation and interpretation (see Bryant and Hawley, *Surdas*, §46). But the overriding thrust of Bryant's exegesis remains intact.

20. I mean *navanītapriya kṛṣṇa* in the general sense, not the Vallabhite *mūrti per se*. See, e.g., NPS 790, in *Krishna, the Butter Thief* (Princeton: Princeton University Press, 1983), pp. 109–12, but with an error regarding *kīḍā* on p. 111.

21. T. A. Gopinath Rao, *The Elements of Hindu Iconography* (Delhi: Motilal Banarsidass, 1985 [originally 1914]); Jitendra Nath Banerjea, *The Development of Hindu Iconography* (New Delhi: Munshiram Manoharlal, 1974 [originally 1956]).

22. Hopkins, *Singing the Body of God*, p. 162 and throughout chapter 5 (pp. 135–65).

23. Edward C. Dimock, Jr., and Tony K. Stewart, eds, *The 'Caitanya Caritāmṛta' of Kṛṣṇadāsa Kavirāja* (Cambridge: Harvard University Press, 1999), *madhya-līlā*, 19.56–84, pp. 615–16; on questions of dating, pp. 29–31.

24. Personal communication, 13 October 2003.

25. Alan Entwistle thinks it may originally have been a Rāmānandī temple, although it has now passed into Śrī Vaiṣṇava hands. See Entwistle, *Braj*, p. 314; Prabhudayāl Mītal, *Braj Dharma-Sampradāyoṅ kā Itihās* (Delhi: National Publishing House, 1968), p. 571.

26. The poem corresponds to NPS 455, but is given in the critically edited form that appears in Bryant and Hawley, *Surdas*, §433.

27. The term 'Death' translates *jam*, referring to the god Yama. I am indebted to Philip Lutgendorf (20 October 1996) for asking whether *jaman* (or *jabhan*, i.e., *yavan*), here rendered 'Greek,' should not instead be translated 'Muslim.' The word, which refers to outsiders from the west, does indeed regularly connote Muslims in the sixteenth century, but it sometimes retains the archaic flavor of its earlier usage ('Greek') at the same time. This is the sort of situation we encounter here. The parallel to the Kāpālikas, who were an ancient sect, is clear from immediate context, and it is well known that the history of Jainism stretches back millennia before the time of Sūrdās. Of course, Sūr's archaic frame of reference may have been a conscious attempt to shield from open view an anti-Mughal and perhaps anti-Muslim comment he wished to make about realities in his own time, but if so, it is to my knowledge the only occasion when poems of the early *Sūrsāgar* reveal this sort of sentiment.

28. Hopkins, *Singing the Body of God*, p. 165 (on the *Tiruvāymoḷi* in relation to *arcāvatāra*) and p. 169 (on Deśika's poetic speech as divinely given, and therefore intrinsically appealing to the Deity); on the *phalaśruti*, see 'The Poet's Telescope,' pp. 339–41.

11. Sur's Sudāmā

1. John B. Carman, *Majesty and Meekness: A Comparative Study of Contrast and Harmony in the Concept of God* (Grand Rapids: W. B. Eerdmans, 1994).

2. Anthony Grafton, *The Footnote: A Curious History* (Cambridge: Harvard University Press, 1997).

3. On early hagiographical sources relating to Sūrdās, see Nābhādās, *Śrī Bhaktamāl* (Lucknow: Tejkumār Press, 1969), p. 557; Heidi R. M. Pauwels, *In Praise of Holy Men: Hagiographic Poems by and about Harirām Vyās* (Groningen: Egbert Forster, 2003); J. S. Hawley, *Sūr Dās: Poet, Singer, Saint* (Seattle: University of Washington Press and Delhi: Oxford University Press, 1984), pp. 3–33; J. S. Hawley, *Sūr's Ocean*, introduction (forthcoming). In regard to the Fatehpur manuscript, see the fascimile edition edited by Gopal Narayan Bahura and Kenneth E. Bryant, *Pad Sūrdāsjī kā / The Padas of Surdas* (Jaipur: Maharaja Sawai Man Singh II Museum, 1982). The rationale for regarding certain poems widely represented in manuscripts dating to the seventeenth century as having been in circulation in the sixteenth is briefly stated in Kenneth E. Bryant, 'Toward a Critical Edition of the *Sūrsāgar*, in W. M. Callewaert, ed., *Early Hindī Devotional Literature in Current Research* (Delhi: Impex India, 1980), pp. 5–16, and in his introduction to Bahura and Bryant, eds, *Pad Sūrdāsjī kā*, pp. vii–xx.

4. I have discussed matters relevant to this point in Chapter 1 and at several other moments in the book. A recent unpublished paper by Christian Novetzke entitled 'Who Killed Nāmdev? The Forensics of Authorship in a South Asian Tradition' amplifies and refines many points.

5. Rupert Snell, 'Devotion Rewarded: The *Sudāmā carit* of Narottamdās,' in Christopher Shackle and Rupert Snell, eds, *The Indian Narrative: Perspectives and Patterns* (Wiesbaden: Otto Harrassowitz, 1992), pp. 175–6.

6. Rupert Snell has drawn attention to this fact ('Devotion Rewarded,' p. 192), building on the work of Manmohan Sahgal: *Panjāb meṅ Racit 'Sudāmā-Carit' Kāvya* (Delhi: Vāṇī Prakāśan, 1978). Sahgal provides examples from four different Sudāmā narratives on p. 16.

7. Françoise Mallison, 'Saint Sudāmā of Gujarāt: Should the Holy Be Wealthy?,' *Journal of the Oriental Institute, Baroda* 29:1–2 (1979), pp. 95–6. Marco Polo, *The Travels*, trans. Robert Latham (Harmondsworth: Penguin Books, 1958), p. 277.

8. Mallison, 'Saint Sudāmā,' p. 93, n. 7.

9. Françoise Mallison, 'The Cult of Sudāmā in Porbandar-Sudāmāpuri,' *Journal of the Oriental Institute, Baroda* 29:3–4 (1980), p. 217.

10. Snell, 'Devotion Rewarded,' pp. 179–80.

11. The *Nandadās Padāvalī* contains a *pad* whose opening line is *bhalau śrī vallabha-suta carana*, 'Blessings on the feet of Vallabha's son': Rūp Nārāyaṇ, *Nandadās: Vicārak, Rasik, Kalākār* (Delhi: Rādhākṛṣṇa Prakāśan, 1968), p. 256.

12. For a general look at the joys and trials of a bhakti economy as expressed in Priyādās's *Bhaktamāl* and its *Bhaktirasabodhī* commentary, see Chapter 2.

13. See Vasudha Narayanan, 'Śrī: Giver of Fortune, Bestower of Grace,' in J. S. Hawley and Donna M. Wulff, eds, *Devī: Goddesses of India* (Berkeley: University of California Press, 1996), pp. 92–4.

14. Rupert Snell has drawn attention to the role this term plays in the approximately contemporary *Sudāmācarita* of Narottamdās: 'Devotion Rewarded,' pp. 176, 183, 185. The Sanskrit word *antaryāmin* does not appear in the *Bhāgavata* itself, which has instead the phrase *sarvabhūtamano 'bhijña* (BhP 10.81.1).

15. Barbara Stoler Miller, *The Bhagavad-Gita: Krishna's Counsel in Time of War* (New York: Columbia University Press, 1986), p. 86.

16. On the centrality of Rām's meeting with Bharat (*bharat milāp*) in performances of the *Rāmcaritmānas*, see Lutgendorf, *The Life of a Text*, pp. 258–65. Rupert Snell has noticed the parallel to Narottamdās's handling of the meeting of Sudāmā and Krishna in 'Devotion Rewarded,' pp. 187–8.

17. Snell, 'Devotion Rewarded,' p. 174.

12. Creative Enumeration in Sur's *Vinaya* Poetry

1. K. E. Bryant, *Poems to the Child-God* (Berkeley: University of California Press, 1978), p. 90.

2. *Ibid.*, pp. 92, 94–105.

3. A. K. Ramanujan, *Speaking of Śiva* (Baltimore: Penguin 1973), p. 38; cf. Ramanujan, *Hymns for the Drowning* (Princeton: Princeton University Press, 1981), pp. 164–6.

4. J. S. Hawley, *Sūr Dās: Poet, Singer, Saint* (Seattle: University of Washington Press and Delhi: Oxford University Press, 1984), pp. 14–22; Hawley, 'The Sectarian Logic of the *Sūr Dās kī Vārtā*' in Monika Thiel-Horstmann, ed., *Bhakti in Current Research, 1979–1982* (Berlin: Dietrich Reimer Verlag, 1983), pp. 157–69.

5. The question whether bhakti can claim a poetics specific to itself has been raised by Ramanujan in the context of Tamil poetry. See his *Hymns for the Drowning*, pp. 161–4, in particular his first and fourth points. Also relevant to the discussion are David Shulman, 'From Author to Non-Author in Tamil Literary Legend,' *Journal of the Institute of Asian Studies* 10:2 (1993), pp. 1–23; Norman Cutler, 'Biography and Interpretation in Tamil Hinduism: *Tiruvācakam* and the *Tiruvātavūrar Purāṇam*,' paper delivered to the American Academy of Religion, Los Angeles, 1985; and Chapter 1 of this book.

6. The translations of all poems discussed in this chapter are based on critical versions prepared by Kenneth Bryant. For the Fatehpur version, see G. N. Bahura and K. E. Bryant, eds, *Pad Sūrdāsjī kā / The Padas of Surdas* (Jaipur: Maharaja Sawai Singh II Museum, 1982).

7. In certain manuscripts the line order varies, and in one version (A1, B3, V1, and therefore NPS), verse 5 differs entirely from the lemma given here, which is based on J1 and related manuscripts. In that version the names of the dramatis personae are frequently displaced from the emphatic positions to which the poet seems originally to have assigned them.

8. See C. G. Hospital, 'The Enemy Transformed: Opponents of the Lord in the *Bhāgavata Puraṇa*', *Journal of the American Academy of Religion* 46:2, Supplement, pp. 199–215.

9. Bryant, *Poems to the Child-God*, pp. 99, 102–4.

10. On the ambiguity of this phrase, see Hawley, *Sūr Dās*, p. 31.

11. Bryant, *Poems to the Child-God*, p. 95.

12. See the final lines of §402, 409, and 430 (= NPS 158, 193, 430) among poems included in J1 and parallels; also NPS 42 and 235 in other early manuscripts (trans. in Hawley, *Sūr Dās*, pp. 145, 165; cf. pp. 150–7 in general). Among J1 poems, the concluding verses of §45, 366, and 398 (= NPS 1271, 507, 133) display similar verbiage, but applied to interestingly different themes.

13. In regard to §399 (NPS 135), see Hawley, *Sūr Dās*, p. 31, and in general pp. 29–33.

14. On this theme, see *ibid.*, pp. 163–77. Peter Gaeffke has nicely compared this process with the classical 'act of truth' (*satyakriyā*)—adapted, of course, to the Kali age (Gaeffke, oral communication, Chicago, 19 April 1986).

13. Why Surdas Went Blind

1. This manuscript is housed at the Government Degree College in Datia. It bears no date, but was probably produced at some point during the nineteenth century.

2. Nābhādās, *Śrī Bhaktamāl*, with the *Bhaktirasabodhinī* commentary of Priyādās (Lucknow: Tejkumār Press, 1969), pp. 479, 713. Further, see Chapter 2.

3. Nābhādās, *Bhaktamāl*, p. 557.

4. For a lengthier consideration of this phrase and its context, see my introduction to *Sūr*'s *Ocean* (forthcoming).

5. *sūra kūra ānharau māi dvāra paryau gauṅ*, NPS 166.10.

6. *dvai locana sābita nahī teu . . . niṭhura vidhātā dīnhai jeu...sūra śyāma kau nāma sravana suni darasan nīkāi deta na veu*, NPS 2468.1, 6, 8.

7. *janama kau andhau, janama kau āndharau*, and so forth. Handy digests of such expressions from the NPS *Sūrsāgar* may be found in critical works such as those of Dvārikādās Parīkh and Prabhudayāl Mītal, *Sūr-Nirṇay* (Mathura: Sāhitya Saṁsthān, 1962), pp. 78–9; Harbanślāl Śarmā, *Sūr aur unkā Sāhitya* (Aligarh: Bhārat Prakāśan Mandir, 1971), pp. 27–9; and Vrajeśvar Varmā, *Sūr-Mimāṁsā* (New Delhi: Oriental Book Depot, n.d.), p. 27.

8. For a more detailed discussion of evidence bearing on this point, see

Hawley, *Sūr Dās*, pp. 29–32, and the end of the first chapter of my introduction to *Sūr's Ocean*, in addition to what follows here.

9. For this analysis of Dādū-Panthī manuscripts relating to the *Sūrsāgar*, I am indebted to Kenneth E. Bryant, as articulated in Bryant and Hawley, 'Poems of Sūrdās: Description of the Project' (application to the National Endowment for the Humanities, 1984), p. 15.

10. Relevant notes are given in Hawley, *Sūr Dās*, p. 181. The poem appears on folio 102a of a *Sarvāṅgī* accessioned to the Maharaja Man Singh Pustak Prakash Research Centre, Jodhpur, as Hindi manuscript no. 1359/14, *pad saṅgrah*.

11. NPS 296.3 in the version given in manuscripts J2 and J5.

12. The passage is from the eighth- or ninth-century *Paümariü* of Svayambhūdeva (3.3.8–9), and the translation closely approximates the one offered by Ram Adhar Singh, who quotes it in his *Syntax of Apabhraṁśa* (Calcutta: Simant Publications, 1980), p. 19. I am grateful to Michael C. Shapiro for calling the verse to my attention.

13. Dvārikādās Parīkh, ed., *Caurāsī Vaiṣṇavan kī Vārtā* (Mathura: Śrī Bajaraṅg Pustakālay, 1970), p. 405.

14. Two examples are translated in Hawley, *Sūr Dās*, pp. 140, 165. For further citations, *ibid*., p. 151 n. 47.

15. See Chapter 2.

16. Mark Juergensmeyer, *Radhasoami Reality: The Logic of a Modern Faith* (Princeton: Princeton University Press, 1991), p. 123.

17. *dekhe rī hari naṅgamanaṅgā*, *Vārtā*, p. 422. Full text and translation appear in Chapter 1.

18. Two examples from among a host are Śaśī Tivārī, *Sūr ke Kṛṣṇa: Ek Anuśīlan* (Hyderabad: Milind Prakāśan, 1969), pp. 48–9, and Munśīrām Śarmā, *Sūrdās kā Kāvya-Vaibhav* (Kanpur: Gratham, 1971), p. 161.

19. This critically edited version of §16 (NPS 793) has been prepared by Kenneth E. Bryant with the assistance of Mandakranta Bose and Vidyut Aklujkar.

20. An example of this genre is reproduced in Hawley, *Sūr Dās*, p. 162.

21. This is the Vallabhite gloss on a certain version of 'O *cakaī* bird, flee to those feet' (§420, NPS 337), as described in Chapter 8.

22. *Vārtā*, p. 438.

23. *Ibid.* The poem has no NPS number because it is not included in the Nāgarīpracāriṇī Sabhā edition.

14. The Received Kabir: Beginnings to Bly

1. Rabindranath Tagore assisted by Evelyn Underhill, *Songs of Kabir* (New Delhi: Cosmo Publications, 1985 [originally 1917]), p. 42; Kshitimohan Sen, *Kabīr ke Pad*, 4 vols. (Shantiniketan: Vishwa Bharati, 1910–11). Aspects

of the production of *Songs of Kabir* have been studied by Vijay C. Mishra, 'Two Truths are Told: Tagore's Kabir,' in Karine Schomer and W. H. McLeod, eds, *The Sants: Studies in a Devotional Tradition of India* (Berkeley: Graduate Theological Union and Delhi: Motilal Banarsidass, 1987), pp. 167–80; see especially pp. 173–4.

2. Robert Bly, *The Kabir Book: Forty-Four of the Ecstatic Poems of Kabir* (Boston: Beacon Press, 1971), p. 61.

3. Linda Hess has plausibly demonstrated that lyrics traveling westward from Banaras, where they may first have been heard, tended to change clothes in their framing verses. At the beginning and end, we tend to find the thickest trappings of *bhakti* to Krishna or Rām. Hess thinks this was an add-on. See Linda Hess, 'Three Kabir Collections: A Comparative Study,' in Schomer and McLeod, eds, *The Sants*, pp. 111–41.

4. Karine Schomer, 'Kabir in the *Gurū Granth Sāhib*: An Exploratory Essay,' in Mark Juergensmeyer and N. Gerald Barrier, eds, *Sikh Studies: Perspectives on a Changing Tradition* (Berkeley: Graduate Theological Union, 1979), pp. 75–86.

5. Linda Hess and Shukdeo Singh, *The Bījak of Kabir* (San Francisco: North Point Press, 1983), *passim*, and Linda Hess, 'Kabir's Rough Rhetoric,' in Schomer and McLeod, eds, *The Sants*, pp. 143–65.

6. Linda Hess, 'Three Kabir Collections,' in Schomer and McLeod, eds, *The Sants*, p. 113. It is possible that there once existed older manuscripts that aged through use and were consigned to the Ganges once a clear copy had been made (Hess and Singh, *The Bījak of Kabir*, p. 165). This explanation of the paucity of old manuscripts has been made by conservators of many scriptural traditions, however, and it is hard to know just when it might rightly apply.

7. Gurinder Singh Mann, *The Goindval Pothis: The Earliest Extant Source of the Sikh Canon* (Cambridge: Harvard University Press, 1996), pp. 1–50.

8. A facsimile edition has been published: Gopal Narayan Bahura and Kenneth E. Bryant, eds, *Pad Sūrdāsjī kā / The Padas of Surdas* (Jaipur: Maharaja Sawai Man Singh II Museum, 1982). Kabīr entries in this collection are discussed in the following chapter.

9. The most efficient access to these is provided by Winand M. Callewaert in collaboration with Swapna Sharma and Dieter Taillien, *The Millennium Kabīr Vāṇī: A Collection of Pads* (New Delhi: Manohar, 2000). They also figure in W. M. Callewaert, 'Kabīr's *Pads* in 1556,' in Monika Horstmann, ed., *Images of Kabīr* (New Delhi: Manohar, 2002), pp. 45–72. The 1614 Dādū-Panthī manuscript is housed in the Sanjay Sharma Museum in Jaipur. A great debt is owed to Rāmkripālu Śarmā, founder of the museum, for its preservation and accessibility.

10. Tagore and Underhill, *Songs of Kabir*, p. 42.

11. Dvivedī developed his views in two books: *Hindī Sāhitya kī Bhūmikā* (New Delhi: Rājkamal Prakāśan, 1991 originally 1940), pp. 92–3, and *Kabīr*

(New Delhi: Rājkamal Prakāśan, 2002 originally 1955), pp. 121–3. Monika Horstmann focuses on the profile of Rāmānand in Dvivedī's understanding of Kabīr in 'Hazārīprasād Dvivedī's Kabīr,' in Horstmann, ed., *Images of Kabīr*, pp. 115–26, and it is discussed by Hess in 'Three Kabir Collections,' in Schomer and McLeod, eds, *The Sants*, pp. 133–5.

12. Bahadur Singh, 'Problems of Authenticity in the Kabīr Texts,' in Horstmann, ed., *Images of Kabīr*, p. 197.

13. Pradeep Bandopadhyay, 'The Uses of Kabīr: Missionary Writings and Civilizational Differences,' in Horstmann, ed., *Images of Kabīr*, p. 31.

14. Tagore and Underhill, *Songs of Kabir*, pp. 11–12, 78.

15. The story of Kabīr's having 'stolen' initiation from Rāmānand apparently became known only around the turn of the eighteenth century (Priyādās, 1712), and its association with Rāmānand's bathing practices first comes to light a century later. See W. M. Callewaert, *The Hagiographies of Anantadās* (Richmond, Surrey: Curzon, 2000), pp. 47–9. Early collections of Kabīr's own utterances are entirely silent about Rāmānand, with a single possible exception. This is *Bījak śabda* 77.4 (*rāmānanda rāmarasa māte kahi kabīra hama hahi kahi thāke*), which would have to be an indirect reference to Rāmānand in any case, and appears to be absent from early dated collections (Dādū-Panthī, Sikh, Fatehpur). On *Bījak śabda* 77, see the translation by Linda Hess and Shukdev Singh on pp. 67–8 of *The Bījak of Kabir* and Hess's note in support of the rendering 'Rām's bliss' instead of 'Rāmānand' on p. 182.

16. For the other side of the argument, see David N. Lorenzen, *Kabir Legends and Ananda-das's Kabir Parachai* (Albany: State University of New York Press, 1991), pp. 9–18, 78–9.

17. Nābhādās, *Śrī Bhaktamāl*, with the *Bhaktirasabodhinī* commentary of Priyādās (Lucknow: Tejkumār Press, 1969), pp. 282, 479.

18. This reading of early Sikh history is controversial but, I think, sound. Its champion, Gurinder Singh Mann, points out that Nānak himself, though not Jaṭ by background, came from a landowning family. See *Sikhism* (Saddle River Road, NJ: Prentice-Hall, 2004), pp. 18, 96–8.

19. The first scholar to explore this connection systematically was P. D. Barthwal (*The Nirguṇa School of Hindi Poetry*, 1936), followed by others such as Hazārīprasād Dvivedī (*Kabīr*, 1955), R. K. Varmā (*Kabīr kā Rahasyavād*, 1966), and Charlotte Vaudeville (*Kabīr*, 1971; *A Weaver Named Kabir*, 1993). A recent exposition is that of Mariola Offredi, 'Kabīr and the Nāthpanth,' in Horstmann, *Images of Kabīr*, pp. 127–41.

20. Bly, *The Kabir Book*, p. 69.

21. Fatehpur, *pad* 88, in Bahura and Bryant, eds, *Pad Sūrdasjī kā*, p. 144.

22. *Gorakh Bānī, sabadi* 23, as translated by David Gordon White, *The Alchemical Body: Siddha Traditions in Medieval India* (Chicago: University of Chicago Press, 1996), p. 242.

23. The sharp contrast between Nāth Yogī perspectives and those held by

Kabīr is not accepted by many scholars and followers of Kabīr. As a case in point, Linda Hess points out that the *Gorakh Bānī* verse we have just quoted is often attributed to Kabīr himself in the impressive tradition of Kabīr performance that emerges from the Malwa region of Madhya Pradesh (Personal communication, New Delhi, 5 September 2003).

24. Pārasnāth Tivārī, *Kabīr Granthāvalī, pad* 174 (Allahabad: Allahabad University, 1961) as translated by J. S. Hawley and Mark Juergensmeyer, *Songs of the Saints of India* (New York and Delhi: Oxford University Press, 1988 and 2004), p. 50.

25. Muhammad Hedayetullah, *Kabir: The Apostle of Hindu-Muslim Unity: Interaction of Hindu-Muslim Ideas in the Formation of the Bhakti Movement with Special Reference to Kabir, the Bhakta* (Delhi: Motilal Banarsidass, 1977); Peter Gaeffke, 'Kabīr in Literature by and for Muslims,' in Horstmann, ed., *Images of Kabīr*, p. 161.

26. *Kabir by Abida* (Mumbai: Times Music India, 2003). I am grateful to David Lelyveld for making me aware of this cassette recording.

27. Bhimrao Ambedkar, 'Annihilation of Caste,' in *Dr. Babasaheb Ambedkar Writings and Speeches*, vol. 1 (Bombay: Government of Maharashtra, 1936), p. 74; quoted by Maren Bellwinkel-Schempp, 'Kabīr-panthīs in Kanpur,' in Horstmann, ed., *Images of Kabīr*, p. 216.

28. Dharmavīr, *Kabīr ke Ālocak* (New Delhi: Vāṇī Prakāśan, 1997; 2nd edition, 1998), chapter 5, pp. 73–96.

29. Rather than peppering the text with individual references as they become relevant, let me list them for the entire paragraph here. I will do so by means of a two-number set. The first—before the slash—refers to the translation of a given poem that was adopted by Tagore and Underhill (*Songs of Kabir*). The second—after the slash—cites the same poem as translated by Bly (*The Kabir Book*). Citations are by poem number, not page. As follows: 43/8, 8/5, 66/37, 14/22, 42/28.

30. For this paragraph, 72/33, 34/6, 38/9, 67/2, 39/35, 34/6.

31. For this paragraph, 53/20, 12/23.

32. Anon., *Kabīr Sāhab kā Anurāg Sāgar* (Allahabad: Belvedere Printing Works, 1918), translated as *The Ocean of Love* by Raj Kumar Bagga, Partap Singh, and Kent Bicknell (Sanbornton, NH: Sant Bani Ashram, 1982). See also Mark Juergensmeyer, 'The Radhasoami Revival of the Sant Tradition,' in Schomer and McLeod, *The Sants*, pp. 352–4.

15. Kabir in his Oldest Dated Manuscript

1. David N. Lorenzen, *Kabir Legends and Ananta-das's Kabir Parachai* (Albany: State University of New York Press, 1991), p. 18.

2. Linda Hess, 'Three Kabir Collections,' in Karine Schomer and W. H. McLeod, eds, *The Sants: A Devotional Tradition of India* (Berkeley: Graduate

Theological Union, and Delhi: Motilal Banarsidass, 1987), pp. 111–41; Karine Schomer, 'Kabir in the *Gurū Granth Sāhib*: An Exploratory Essay,' in Mark Juergensmeyer and N. Gerald Barrier, eds, *Sikh Studies: Perspectives on a Changing Tradition* (Berkeley: Graduate Theological Union, 1979), pp. 75–86.

3. Gopal Narayan Bahura and Kenneth E. Bryant, eds, *Pad Sūrdāsjī kā / The Padas of Surdas* (Jaipur: Maharaja Sawai Man Singh II Museum, 1982).

4. Gurinder Singh Mann, *The Goindval Pothis: The Earliest Extant Source of the Sikh Canon* (Cambridge: Harvard University Press, 1996), pp. 1–50.

5. It was Kedārnāth Dvivedī who drew scholarly attention to this manuscript, in his *Kabīr aur Kabīr Panth* (Allahabad: Hindī Sāhitya Sammelan, 1965), p. 3. He does not, however, report whether the manuscript was said to have been at the Nāgarīpracāriṇī Sabhā itself or elsewhere; the latter would normally have been the case for manuscripts listed in the *Khoj Reports*. David Lorenzen searched for the manuscript at the Nāgarīpracāriṇī Sabhā, but was unable to find it (*Kabir Legends*, p. 9). Moreover, it does not appear in the much later abbreviated version of the *Khoj Reports*: Kṛṣṇadev Prasād Gauḍ et al., *Hastalikhit Hindī Pustakoṅ kā Saṅkṣipt Vivaraṇ* (Varanasi: Kāśī Nāgarīpracāriṇī Sabhā), 1964, vol. 1, pp. 512–13. Given the importance of Kabīr and the unusually early date claimed for this manuscript, one would certainly have expected it to reappear in the abbreviated *Khoj Reports* if the editors had had firm information about it.

This is not the only case of purportedly early manuscripts that have proven either inauthentic or unlocatable. I can personally attest that many *Sūrsāgar* manuscripts claimed in the original Nāgarīpracāriṇī Sabhā *Khoj Reports* have been impossible to trace—at least from the 1970s onward. These reports were apparently published without the editors having the chance to authenticate all the information they collected, especially since a great deal of it was solicited by mail. The Dakor manuscript claimed to be the earliest extant source for Mīrābāī (1585 CE) would also be roughly contemporaneous with the Fatehpur manuscript if it could be authenticated, but it presents a similar set of problems (see Chapter 4).

The most recent review of the full range of early manuscripts containing poems ascribed to Kabīr—and a masterful one—is that of Winand Callewaert in collaboration with Swapna Sharma and Dieter Taillieu, *The Millennium Kabīr Vāṇī* (Delhi: Manohar, 2000), pp. 1–114.

6. Callewaert, Sharma, and Taillieu, *The Millennium Kabīr Vāṇī*, pp. 19–21.

7. Bahura, introduction to *Pad Sūrdāsjī kā*, p. v.

8. *Ibid.*, pp. iv–v, who cites Jān Kavi, *Kyām Khāṅ Rāsā*, ed. Agarchand Nahata (Jaipur: Purātattva Mandir, 1953), pp. 64–5. See also K. E. Bryant, 'The Fatehpur Manuscript and the *Sūrsāgar* Critical Edition Project,' in Monika Thiel-Horstmann, ed., *Bhakti in Current Research, 1979–1982* (Berlin: Dietrich Reimer, 1983), pp. 37–8.

9. So far as I can see, this state of affairs does not justify Vinay Dharwadker's assertions that the Fatehpur manuscript was 'prepared under royal patronage' or that its intended reader was a Kacchvāhā 'prince.' See Dharwadker, *Kabir: The Weaver's Songs* (New Delhi: Penguin, 2003), pp. 26, 28.

10. See Winand M. Callewaert, *The Sarvāṅgī of Gopāldās: A 17th Century Anthology of Bhakti Literature* (Delhi: Manohar, 1993), pp. 28–9. Recall the connection to the Sūrdās poem 'Now I am blind,' described in Chapter 13.

11. See Karine Schomer, 'Introduction' to Schomer and McLeod, eds, *The Sants*, pp. 3, 7–8.

12. 1–106; 1–181; 1–(1)27. I am considering that this third sequence includes numbers 101–27, but with the hundred digit omitted. Otherwise one would divide this set 1–100; 1–27. It is true that one of the several transitions between ragas occurs at just this point, but none of the poems listed in the 1–27 set seems to repeat any given in the 1–100 set.

13. Perhaps the *sūr pacīsī* was assigned a new number after every four couplets, once the introductory couplet was past, in an earlier manuscript. This would account for the fact that the Fatehpur scribe gives the number 49 to the *pad* preceding it and the number 56 to the *pad* that follows, while allowing the *sūr pacīsī* itself to go unnumbered—except internally, by couplet. See Bahura and Bryant, eds, *Pad Sūrdāsjī kā*, pp. 114–20. A misnumbering on p. 5 results in a calculation of the total number of *pads* as 181 rather than 183, counting 6 for the *sūr pacīsī*: 183–5=178.

14. This Kānhāṅ warrants study. He is not listed in the surveys of bhakti and *sant* literature produced by R. S. McGregor, Paraśurām Caturvedī, or Alan Entwistle: McGregor, *Hindi Literature from its Beginnings to the Nineteenth Century* (Wiesbaden: Otto Harrassowitz, 1984); Caturvedī, *Uttarī Bhārat kī Sant Paramparā* (Allahabad: Leader Press, 1972); Entwistle, *Braj, Centre of Krishna Pilgrimage* (Groningen: Egbert Forsten, 1987). Prabhudayāl Mītal refers to one Kānhār, a pupil of Harivyās Dev, in his *Braj ke Dharma-Sampradāyoṅ kā Itihās* (Delhi: National Publishing House, 1968), p. 353, and Pritam Singh was curious as to whether he could be correlated with the Kānhā of Lahore who is said to have submitted poems to Guru Arjan, for possible inclusion in the Sikh canon, but whose request was rejected (Thiel-Horstmann, ed., *Bhakti in Current Research, 1979–1982*, p. 45).

15. The poem is *merī vaha raga ragi dai cūnarī ava so raga kavahū na jāi*. In its final line, the poet claims Rāmānand to be the guru of Kabīr (*sāhava kavīra cunarī vunī gurū ṭhekā rāmānanda*), which suggests a Rāmānandī association. The story of Kabīr's having 'stolen' initiation from Rāmānand was well known in the early part of the eighteenth century—it appears in Priyādās's commentary on the *Bhaktamāl* of Nābhādās—but there is no evidence that it was in circulation earlier. (See Chapter 17, note 34.) Early collections of poetry attributed to Kabīr are silent about Rāmānand, with a single possible exception. This is *Bījak śabda* 77.4 (*rāmānanda rāmarasa māte kahi kabīra hama kahi kahi*

thāke), which would have to be an indirect reference to Rāmānand in any case, and appears to be absent from early dated collections (Dadu-Panthī, Sikh, Fatehpur). One purpose of a poem such as the one found at the beginning of the Datia *Sūrsāgar* is to establish this otherwise missing connection—a crucial one for the Rāmānand Sampradāy. On the issue of Kabīr's relation to Rāmānand, see Charlotte Vaudeville, *Kabīr* (Oxford: Clarendon Press, 1974), pp. 110–17, repeated in Vaudeville, *A Weaver Named Kabir* (Delhi: Oxford University Press, 1993), pp. 87–91; compare Callewaert, as in Chapter 17, note 34. To the contrary, Lorenzen, *Kabir Legends*, pp. 9–18, 78–9. On *Bījak śabda* 77, see the translation by Linda Hess and Shukdev Singh on pp. 67–8 of *The Bījak of Kabir* and Hess's note in support of the rendering 'Rām's bliss' instead of 'Rāmānand' on p. 182.

16. For the sake of convenience, I will refer to this as poem 15. Others are similarly numbered throughout the chapter. A conversion table enabling one to locate each poem in the facsimile edition of the Fatehpur manuscript appears as Table 15.1.

17. Instances of this expression in poems attributed to Sūrdās that were in circulation in the sixteenth century include those listed by the Nāgarīpracariṇī Sabhā [NPS] editors as 749, 1116, 1989, and 3085. The NPS text is Jagannāthdās 'Ratnākar', Nandadulāre Vājpeyī, et al., eds, *Sūr-sāgar*, 2 vols. (Varanasi: Kāśī Nāgarīpracāriṇī Sabhā), 1972 and 1976 [originally 1948].

18. I am not the first to land on the term 'catholic' in reaching for a way to describe the particular flavor of Vaishnavism in this period and region of Indian history. William Pinch precedes me in his brilliant essay, 'History, Devotion, and the Search for Nabhadas of Galta,' in Daud Ali, ed., *Invoking the Past: The Uses of History in South Asia* (Delhi: Oxford University Press, 1999), pp. 367–99. Both of us think of this catholicity in contrast to a style of Vaishnava self-identification that is associated with the institution of the *sampradāy*, which implies a particular teaching tradition transmitted by a clearly defined lineage of gurus. At that point, however, we diverge slightly. While Pinch situates the contrast in relation to celibate, ascetic lineages, as is appropriate in the case of Nabhādās, who composed his work in the monastery at Galta, I would extend the usage to lineages perpetuated by teachers who are married, as my choice of examples in this paragraph makes clear. In this general vein, but still in a Rāmānandī context, see also Monika Horstmann, 'The Rāmānandīs of Galtā,' in Lawrence A. Babb, Varsha Joshi, and Michael W. Meister, eds, *Multiple Histories: Culture and Society in the Study of Rajasthan* (Jaipur: Rawat, 2002), pp. 152–3.

19. The phrase was apparently coined by W. H. McLeod, *Gurū Nānak and the Sikh Religion* (Oxford: Clarendon, 1968), p. 152, but he based his work especially on Charlotte Vaudeville's *Au Cabaret de l'Amour* (Paris: Gallimard, 1959), pp. 7–9, and the introduction to her *Kabīr Granthāvalī (Dohā)* (Pondicherry: Institut Français d'Indologie, 1957). A more recent statement by Vaudeville is

'*Sant Mat*: Santism as the Universal Path to Sanctity,' in Schomer and McLeod, eds, *The Sants*, pp. 21–40.

20. The book is Muhammad Hedayetullah, *Kabir: The Apostle of Hindu-Muslim Unity: Interaction of Hindu-Muslim Ideas in the Formation of the Bhakti Movement with Special Reference to Kabir, the Bhakta* (Delhi: Motilal Banarsidass, 1977). The TV series, produced and directed by Anil Chaudhury, appeared on Doordarshan in 1987 in thirteen episodes. Many more episodes had originally been projected, but production difficulties forced the series to an early close. I review certain aspects of this discourse in its relation to academic scholarship in Chapter 17.

21. Poems (*pads*) of this sort are collected in Vaudeville, *Weaver*, pp. 216–19; see also Hess, *Bījak,* pp. 3, 46.

22. Nābhādās, *Śrī Bhaktamāl*, with the *Bhaktirasabodhinī* commentary of Priyādās (Lucknow: Tejkumār Press, 1969), p. 479.

23. At least as far as the Fatehpur manuscript is concerned, this necessarily puts me at loggerheads with the description of the unitary theology of 'the Kabīr poets'—if not of any historical Kabīr—that Vinay Dharwadker offers in his recent book. Dharwadker's Kabīr poets amount collectively to a sort of upanishadic sage, definitively expositing 'their nirguṇa God' (*Kabir: The Weaver's Songs,* pp. 78, 85). Dharwadker apparently finds this position enunciated with particular clarity in the Fatehpur manuscript, though he does not quote from it explicitly, since he regards it and the *Goindvāl Pothīs* as 'most likely to resemble [Kabīr's] original compositions' on account of their early date. They are therefore best able to display the 'structure in a miniature or incipent form' that was to characterize the position and tone of the Kabīr corpus as a whole (pp. 94–5). I am perfectly happy to admit that this kind of stance emerges strongly elsewhere in poetry attributed to Kabīr, but as the rest of the chapter will make clear, I don't find it at Fatehpur. And as Dharwadker says, Fatehpur is important to take into account in forming a view of the Kabīr who stands at the horizon of 'the Kabīr poets,' even if we can never glimpse him directly.

24. For a recent review, see Mariola Offredi, 'Kabīr and the Nāthpanth,' in Monika Horstmann, ed., *Images of Kabīr* (Delhi: Manohar, 2002), pp. 127–41.

25. This line presents two difficulties. First, I read *daha* ('hole, pit') as written, rather than *deha* ('body'), as in Charlotte Vaudeville's translation of another version of this poem (*Weaver*, p. 250). Second, I remain mystified by *jañjuka* in what appears to be the phrase *jañjuka ṣāi* at the end of the line. Shukdev Singh (Interview, Banaras, 12 November 2003) has suggested solving this problem by reading the phrase as *jañju kaṣāi*, with *jañju* standing in for *jañjīra* and *kaṣāi* for *kasāi* ('bound in chains'). If this was the poet's meaning, it would presumably refer to the binding of various parts of a corpse before it is lifted to the pyre, but the temporal sequence implied in the verse itself seems to be the reverse.

26. The reference to the *aṣṭamahāsiddhi* is explicit and clear. Presumably the nine jewels of Kuber are meant by the phrase *navamaḍārī*. A later hand seems to have tried to insert the syllable *ni* to yield *nava mani ḍārī* ('you threw away the nine jewels'). This doesn't fit very well with the overall diction, but it confirms the 'nine jewels' reading.

27. This reads the first word after the caesura as *anahala* ('fire'), although the final syllable does not look exactly like other occurrences of *la*. One might otherwise perhaps read *tva*, as if to align this word with *anahada*, as in *anahada nāda*, the 'unstruck sound.' One might interpret this as a reference to the 'unstruck consciousness' (*anahatva* [*sic*] *citt*, 7.1) so frequently associated with the fifth *cakra*.

28. If one read *sāvakā* after the Arabic ('long acquaintance'), an alternate translation would emerge:

I'm at war with my father and his business partner,
sticking close by Māyā's side
in hopes I'll get to be my lover's bride.

29. Modern printed versions of this poem—rather different from the text that appears here—are cited in Jayadev Siṃh and Vāsudev Siṃh, eds, *Kabīr Vāṅmay*, vol. 3 (Varanasi: Viśvavidyālay Prakāśan, 1981), pp. 90–1.

30. The poem also appears—in a substantially different version—in the 1614 *Pañcvāṇī* of the Sanjay Sharma Museum. See Callewaert, Sharma, and Taillieu, *The Millennium Kabīr Vāṇī*, p. 250.

31. In verse 4, I have read *mahāyā* along the lines of *madhuvā* ('beekeeper'), as in the edition of Śyāmsundar Dās, but this form could equally be a variant of Māyā, who is indeed the beekeeper involved, in any case. The precise identity of Gopāl, Kabīr's chosen interlocutor, is not clear.

32. The final verse appears in a completely different—and to my eye, much less distinctive—form in most printed editions. See *Kabīr Vāṅmay*, vol. 3, p. 154:

kahai kabīra nara sundara rūpa
rāma bhagati binu kucila kurūpa.

33. For a brief description of the major early recensions of Kabīr's poetry, see Chapter 14.

34. In this vein—on 'Word'—compare Hess, *The Bījak of Kabir*, p. 161, with a reference to Per Kvaerne, *An Anthology of Buddhist Tantric Songs* (Oslo: Norwegian Research Council, 1977).

35. Pārasnāth Tivārī, *Kabīr-Granthāvalī* (Allahabad: Prayāg Viśvavidyālay, 1961), *pad* 112.2 (i.e., 112.3), part 2, p. 66. For a contrasting example, see *śabda* 63 in Shukdev Singh, ed., *Kabīr-Bījak* (Allahabad: Nīlabh Prakāśan, 1972), p. 132, translated in Hess, *The Bījak of Kabir*, p. 62.

36. Poems attributed to Kabīr do sometimes characterize *viraha* as a snake (e.g., *Bījak sākhī* 99, translated in Hess, *Bījak*, p. 100), but their use of the *gāruḍī* metaphor tends to be somewhat broader (e.g., *Bījak śabda* 39,

translated in Hess, *Bījak*, p. 54). For a general comparison, see Vaudeville, *Weaver*, p. 268.

37. There is a notable overlap between the language of this verse and what appears in poem 8.2, translated above. Both verses are built on the rhyme between *vicārī* ('being mindful') and *mahatārī* ('mother'), and the sentiment is substantially the same.

38. *Sūr's Ocean* §51, 314, and 315 (NPS 1365–1367) were in circulation in the sixteenth century; a whole host were added later on. See my *Sūr Dās: Poet, Singer, Saint* (Seattle: University of Washington Press and Delhi: Oxford University Press, 1984), pp. 53, 83. On the theme in general, see Chapter 7 of the present volume.

39. *Kabīr Vāṅmay*, *pad* 245.4, p. 183:

kahai kabīra ko ko nahīṅ rakhaiṅ
rāma rasāina jini jini cākhai.

40. *rāma rāma e bhani rāma citāvani*
bhāga vaḍau pāyau (3.1).

For a selection of verses from the *Bījak* recommending the practice of repeating the name of Rām, see Hess, *Bījak*, p. 159.

41. This is apparently a somewhat different sense from the upside-down pot (*ghaṭorrdhva*) which regularly means, in the words of Helmut von Glasenapp, as translated by Agehananda Bharati, 'concentrated thought which cannot be diverted to anything.' Glasenapp, *Buddhistische Mysterien* (Stuttgart, 1940), p. 103; Bharati, *The Tantric Tradition* (New York: Anchor Books, 1970), p. 177.

42. A profusion of flower metaphors can be found in verses attributed to Kabīr. Vaudeville translates one in *Weaver*, pp. 283–4; Hess, several others, in *The Bījak of Kabir*, pp. 52, 62, 156.

43. Puṣpapāl Siṃh, *Kabīr Granthāvalī Saṭīk* (New Delhi: Aśok Prakāśan, 1972), *pad* 4.15. The verse is:

ṣodasa kaṅvala jaba cetiyā / taba mili gāe śrī banavārī re
jurumarana bhrama bhajiyā / punarapi janama nivārī re.

The entire poem structures itself around lotuses of increasing numbers of petals, on the Nāth Yogī scheme, so Puṣpapāl Siṃh is confident that the sixteen-petalled lotus refers to the *viṣuddh cakra* (*Kabīr Granthāvalī Saṭīk*, p. 290). The poem is not included—at least not under that title—in Pārasnāth Tivārī's *Kabīr Granthāvalī*. It appears in other editions, however, e.g., Bhagavatsvarūp Miśra, *Kabīr Granthāvalī* [*Sañjīvani vyākhyā sahit*] (Agra: Vinod Pustak Mandir, 1969), p. 207.

44. For example, *Kabīr Vāṅmay*, vol. 3, *pad* 311, p. 395:

kahai kabīra gura eka budhi batāī / sahaja subhāi milai rāma rāī.

45. David Gordon White, *The Alchemical Body: Siddha Traditions in Medieval India* (Chicago: University of Chicago Press, 1996), p. 242. The original is *Gorakh Bānī, śabadi* 23.

46. On this motif, see White, *The Alchemical Body*, pp. 242–4.

47. I am thinking especially of the well-known Sūrdās poem *cakaī rī cali caraṇa sarovara jahāṅ na pema viyogu* (§420, NPS 337), or the Mīrābāī poem *cālāṇ agama vā desa kāla dekhyaṅ ḍaraṅ* (PC 193). The former is translated in Chapter 8 of this book; the latter in Chapter 17.

48. Hess, *The Bījak of Kabir*, p. 147.

16. *Vinaya* Crossovers: Sur and Kabir

1. In commenting on a parallel genre in Bengali, poems of self-deprecation called *kākuvāda* or *kākukti*, Joseph T. O'Connell proposes that the act of throwing oneself at the Lord's feet has a hidden and intrinsic salvific power because it reveals the proper ontological relation of humans to the divine, namely servanthood. O'Connell, 'Gauḍīya Vaiṣṇava Symbolism of Deliverance (*uddhāra, nistāra...*) from Evil,' *Journal of Asian and African Studies* 15, nos. 1–2 (1980), pp. 126–7, 131–2.

2. E.g., Hawley, *Sūr's Ocean* vol. 1, §392.2 (=NPS 111.2), NPS 67.6 and 334.6. Attention to the last moment of life as such, however, is more a feature of later additions to the *Sūrsāgar* (e.g., NPS 80.4 and 85.4). When I speak of Sūrdās or the early *Sūrsāgar* in this chapter, I refer to poems included in the entire range of pre-1700 manuscripts listed in Chapter 9, rather than to the subset that can be shown, with more or less precision, to have been in circulation in the sixteenth century. Often I will specify which manuscript bears the reading I cite.

3. E.g., NPS 117.12 in B4, and NPS 312.12 (B4, B5: *kāla vara vyāla*; U2: *kāla bala vyāla*; cf. J2: *byāla*, B3: *jama jāla*); also NPS 326.8.

4. For an alternate translation, see Charlotte Vaudeville, *Kabīr*, vol. 2 (unpublished manuscript), *pad* 50. The line concerning the parrot and its prey presents textual difficulties, since none of the major versions actually uses the term 'silk-cotton.' In present-day editions of the *Gurū Granth Sāhib* and the *Bījak* one finds instead *nalanī* ('lotus'), and P. N. Tivārī's critically edited *Kabīr Granthāvalī*, reflecting the Rajasthani recension, reads *lalanī* ('alluring woman'). The latter is a general enough term and the former a close enough analogue, however, to indicate that the poet had the silk-cotton image in mind, as the parallel with safflower almost requires. So Vaudeville, evidently (*ibid.*, n. 4). Cf. Tivārī, *Kabīr-Granthāvalī* (Allahabad: Prayāg Viśvavidyālay, 1961), vol. 2, *pad* 97. *Sākhīs* 163–5 of the *Bījak*, each of which concerns the image of the parrot and the *semar* tree, are translated by Linda Hess in collaboration with Shukdev Singh, in *The Bījak of Kabir* (Delhi: Oxford University Press, 2002), p. 108. For the original, see Kabīr, *Bījak*, with commentary by Khemrāj Śrīkṛṣṇadās (Bombay: Venkatesvara Press, 1904 [originally 1868]), pp. 466–7. For the silk-cotton trope as it appears elsewhere in *sant* poetry, see Bahadur Singh, 'Problems of Authenticity in the Kabīr Texts,' in Monika Horstmann, ed., *Images of Kabīr* (Delhi: Manohar, 2002), pp. 193–4.

5. Charlotte Vaudeville, *Kabīr* (Oxford: Clarendon Press, 1974), vol. 1, *sākhī* 22.4, p. 272. Kabīr, *Bījak*, *sākhī* 313, p. 539.

6. Vaudeville, *Kabīr,* vol. 1, *sākhī* 24.17, p. 279. Tivārī, *Kabīr Granthāvalī, sākhī* 24.17, 2: 221.

7. Vaudeville, *Kabīr,* vol. 1, *sākhī* 1.9, pp. 153–4, Tivārī, *Kabīr Granthāvalī, sākhī* 1.9, p. 137. Cf. Vaudeville, *Kabīr*, vol. 1, *sākhī* 1.21–3, pp. 156–7.

8. The Sabhā's mention of red (*arun*) in the last line is absent in all manuscripts, but *dhām* (town) is a respectable alternative for *sindhu* (sea) in verse 5, since it is not only the Sabhā's reading but that of B1 and U1, as well. Cf. §289 = NPS 4380.5–6 and many other poems in the *bhramargīt* section on blackness.

9. Cf., e.g., W. H. McLeod, *Gurū Nānak and the Sikh Religion* (Delhi: Oxford University Press, 1976 [originally 1968]), p. 152: 'the easy path of traditional bhakti.'

10. Hess and Singh, *The Bījak of Kabir*, pp. 10–11.

11. E.g., §389 = NPS 77.8 (*saṭh*), §390 = NPS 103.8 (*mahā saṭh*, in U1, B4, J4), and *man pramodh* poems such as §420 = NPS 337, where this is the general theme.

12. Cf. also *Vinayapatrikā* 154.3, 155.5, 249.3, and 263.1.

13. *Gurū Granth Sāhib, rāg āsā*, Kabīr *pad* 28. For an alternate, annotated translation, based upon the *Kabīr Granthāvalī* edited by P. N. Tivārī, *pad* 50 (p. 29), see Vaudeville, *Kabīr*, vol. 2, *pad* 133.

14. E.g., Vaudeville, *Kabīr*, vol. 1, *sākhīs* 1.21, 14.15, and 14.31–5, pp. 157, 222, and 225–6.

15. As against later entries such as NPS 68.8 or 317.5; cf. Tulsī's *Vinayapatrikā* 83.1 and 84.2 in the same vein.

17. Bhakti, Democracy, and the Study of Religion

1. On this point, perhaps Wilfred Cantwell Smith has been the most eloquent, in his *The Meaning and End of Religion* (New York: Macmillan, 1962).

2. For further reflections on comparative and pedagogical aspects of this possibility, see J. S. Hawley, 'Who Speaks for Hinduism—and Who Against?,' *Journal of the American Academy of Religion* 68:4 (2000), pp. 711–20; and 'Comparative Religion for Undergraduates: Fraud? Failure? Frontier?,' The Wabash Center Lecture in the Arts of Pedagogy, University of Chicago Divinity School, 1 November 2002, forthcoming in *Criterion* (fall 2004) and in Thomas Idinopulis, ed., *Comparing Religions: Possibilities and Problems in Crosscultural and Intersocial Analysis* (Leiden: E. J. Brill).

3. See Wilhelm Halbfass, *India and Europe: An Essay in Understanding* (Albany: State University of New York Press, 1988), especially p. 3 (on Diogenes Laertius), p. 8 (on Eusebius), and the general discussion in chapter

1 on 'gymnosophists'. Cf. Ainslie T. Embree, *Imagining India* (Delhi: Oxford University Press, 1989), pp. 29ff.

4. Friedrich Schleiermacher, *Über die Religion: Reden an die Gebildeten unter ihrer Verächtern* (Berlin: G. Reimer, 1831).

5. Rustom Bharucha, *The Question of Faith* (New Delhi: Orient Longman, 1993), p. 92.

6. Western authors trained in other fields do, of course, figure in his thinking, for example, Nita Kumar and Sandria Frietag.

7. V. Raghavan, *The Great Integrators: The Saint-Singers of India* (New Delhi: Publications Division of the Government of India), p. 32.

8. An influential statement of this view is Ranajit Guha, 'Dominance without Hegemony and its Historiography,' *Subaltern Studies VI* (Delhi: Oxford University Press, 1989), pp. 249–64.

9. In North India, dead people's bones are sometimes referred to as flowers in religious circumstances: see Ann Grodzins Gold, *Fruitful Journeys: The Ways of Rajasthani Pilgrims* (Berkeley: University of California Press, 1988), pp. 124, 189–191. The story very nicely suggests that in the case of a person of Kabīr's stature, this figure of speech deserves to be taken literally.

10. As to whether this is the Magahar to which Kabīr's own verse refers, there is room for scholarly debate. See Charlotte Vaudeville, *Kabīr*, vol. 1 (Oxford: Clarendon Press, 1974), pp. 32–4; and David Lorenzen with Jagdish Kumar and Uma Thukral, *Kabir Legends and Anantadas's Kabir Parachai* (Albany: State University of New York Press, 1991), pp. 17, 40–2. Of the two shrines on the spot, the Muslim one, visited by both Hindus and Muslims, clearly possesses the older pedigree, presumably dating back to a Mughal grant made in AH 1110 (1698/99 CE), during the reign of Aurangzeb.

11. The full citation is: Muhammad Hedayetullah, *Kabir: The Apostle of Hindu-Muslim Unity: Interaction of Hindu-Muslim Ideas in the Formation of the Bhakti Movement with Special Reference of Kabir, the Bhakta* (Delhi: Motilal Banarsidass, 1977).

12. Dolly Rizvi, 'Kabir: The Mystic Who Tried to Bring the Hindus and the Muslims Together', *Amar Chitra Katha*, no. 55 (Bombay: India Book House Education Trust, n.d.), p. 14. See Figure 8, p. 154, in this volume.

13. I can locate a similar but partial version of this sentiment in the interrogative (which makes quite a difference), but not the full asseveration:

Hindus, Muslims—where did they come from?
Who got them started down this road?

For a translation of the poem from which this is excerpted, and the textual reference, see J. S. Hawley and Mark Juergensmeyer, *Songs of the Saints of India* (Delhi: Oxford University Press, 2004), p. 52.

14. These are poems translated from the version in which they appear in Pārasnāth Tivārī's critical edition called *Kabīr Granthāvalī* (Allahabad: Allahabad University, 1961), which is largely based upon readings given in manuscript

versions of the Dādū-Panthī *Pañcvāṇī*. These excerpts are drawn from *pads* 191 and 178. The full poems are translated in Hawley and Juergensmeyer, *Songs of the Saints of India*, pp. 51–2. The original Hindi for the portions translated is as follows:

पंडिआ कवन कुमति तुम लागे
बूड़हुगे परिवार सकल सिउं राम न जपहु अभागे

———

काजी तै कवन कतेब बखानी
पढ़त पढ़त केते दिन बीते गति एकौ नहिं जानी

15. The translation is apparently that of Hedayetullah himself, in *Kabir: The Apostle*, p. 301; a slightly different version is given on p. 206. The original is *Gurū Granth Sāhib, rāg parabhāti* 2 (*alahu eka masiti*...), which contains the following verse: *kabiru pungarā rāma alaha kā / saba gura pīra hamāre*.

16. Charlotte Vaudeville, *A Weaver Named Kabir* (Delhi: Oxford University Press, 1993), p. 218. The poem is listed by P. N. Tivārī as no. 177, and appears with apparatus in *Kabīr Granthāvalī*, p. 104. The line in question reads: *kabīra pungarā alaha rāma kā/soi gura pīra hamārā.*

17. Hedayetullah, *Kabir: The Apostle*, p. 299.

18. *Ibid.*

19. The earliest reliably dated manuscripts containing verses by Kabīr do not emerge until 1582, as we know, and 1604 (see Chapter 15). The *Pañcvāṇī* makes it first appearance in 1614. (See W. M. Callewaert and Bart Op de Beeck, *Nirguṇ-Bhakti-Sāgar: Devotional Hindī Literature*, vol. 1 (New Delhi: Manohar, 1991), pp. 23–4; cf. Tivārī, vol. 1, pp. 55–60. Also W. M. Callewaert in collaboration with Swapna Sharma and Dieter Taillieu, *The Millennium Kabīr-Vāṇī* (Delhi: Manohar, 2000), pp. 21–3. The poet himself probably lived a century earlier than 1604, although the exact time is still under dispute. On this, compare Vaudeville, *A Weaver Named Kabir*, pp. 52–5, with Lorenzen, *Kabir Legends*, pp. 9–18. Linda Hess feels that the *Sarvāṅgī* of the Dādūite Rajab deserves to be given more attention in critical decisions relating to texts of Kabīr, since his dates are reliably embraced by the period 1570–1680 and since the *Sarvāṅgī* is briefer than the *Pañcvāṇī* and is contained almost entirely within it. See Hess, 'Studies in Kabīr: Texts, Traditions, Styles and Skills' (PhD diss., University of California, Berkeley, 1980), pp. 16–17; Hess, 'Three Kabir Collections', in Karine Schomer and W. H. McLeod, eds, *The Sants: A Devotional Tradition of India* (Berkeley: Berkeley Religious Studies Series and Delhi: Motilal Banarsidass, 1987), p. 112.

20. In several studies I have tried to demonstrate this in the case of Sūrdās: see Chapter 9 and *Sūr Dās: Poet, Singer, Saint* (Seattle: University of Washington Press and Delhi; Oxford University Press, 1984), pp. 35–63.

21. Gurinder Singh Mann, *The Goindval Pothis: The Earliest Extant Source of the Sikh Canon* (Cambridge: Harvard University Press, 1996), pp. 1–50. Throughout this chapter, to avoid confusion, I use the dates of the Christian

Throughout this chapter, to avoid confusion, I use the dates of the Christian calendar, although the manuscripts themselves almost invariably give their dates *vikram saṃvat*. I apologize for any cultural insensitivity my usage may seem to imply.

22. Winand M. Callewaert, *The Sarvāṅgī of the Dādūpanthī Rajab* (Leuven: Katholieke Universiteit, 1978), p. 81; *The Sarvāṅgī of Gopāldās: A 17th Century Anthology of Bhakti Literature* (New Delhi: Manohar, 1993), p. 13; and *The Millennium Kabīr-Vāṇī* (Delhi: Manohar, 2000), pp. 21–3.

23. Callewaert and Op de Beeck, *Nirguṇ-Bhakti-Sāgar*, p. 24. Cf. W. M. Callewaert, 'Manuscripts of some Bhaktamālas, Pañcavāṇīs and Sarvāṅgīs', *IAVRI Bulletin* 3 (1976), pp. 10–12; Tivārī, *Kabīr Granthāvalī*, pp. 55–60; Hess, 'Studies in Kabir,' p. 15.

24. Hess, 'Studies in Kabir,' pp. 23–4, cf. 63–8; Shukdev Singh, *Kabīr Bījak* (Allahabad: Nīlabh Prakāśan, 1972), pp. 30–79.

25. In Mark Juergensmeyer and N. Gerald Barrier, eds, *Sikh Studies: Comparative Perspectives on a Changing Tradition* (Berkeley: Berkeley Religious Studies Series, 1970), p. 84.

26. Schomer, in 'Kabir in the *Gurū Granth Sāhib*', pp. 80–6.

27. *Śabda* 42. The name Hari appears a good bit more often, and so, of course, does Rām, but that is quite a different matter. For a somewhat tentative but very revealing tabulation of keywords relating to these matters, see Hess, 'Studies in Kabir,' pp. 38–41, and 'Three Kabir Collections,' pp. 119–23.

28. Hess, 'Studies in Kabir,' p. 23.

29. Callewaert notes that in Gopāldās's *Sarvāṅgī*, the 'signature' (*bhaṇitā, chāp*) of Kabīr is often metrically redundant in *dohās* listed under his name. (Callewaert, *Sarvāṅgī*, p. 30.) For a sampling of *dohās* popularly attributed to Kabīr but in which his signature does not occur, see the widely used collection edited by Karuṇāpati Tripāṭhī called *Kāvya Sangraḥ*, vol. 1 (Allahabad: Hindī Sāhitya Sammelan, 1966), pp. 33–7.

30. On the matter of a signature's authority, see Chapter 1.

31. Hess, 'Studies in Kabir,' p. 69; 'Three Kabir Collections', p. 141.

32. Vaudeville, *Kabīr*, vol. 1, p. 30; quoted with approval by Hess, 'Studies in Kabir,' p. 66; and 'Three Kabir Collections', p. 139.

33. Hess, 'Studies in Kabir,' pp. 45–9; 'Three Kabir Collections', pp. 123–6. The Fatehpur manuscript had not been made available to scholars at the time Hess did her study.

34. For information on Rāmānand as he appears in poetry attributed to Kabīr, see Chapter 15, note 15. The textual work that has done most to clarify the various stages at which the story of Kabīr's association with Rāmānand developed belongs to Winand Callewaert, principally as found in chapter 2 of his *The Hagiographies of Anantadās: The Bhakti Poets of North India* (Richmond, Surrey: Curzon, 2002), especially pp. 44–9. (The volume was written in

association with Swapna Sharma.) Callewaert draws attention to the first footnote attached to David Lorenzen's edition of the *Kabīr Parcaī* (*Kabir Legends*, p. 129), where Lorenzen explains that the first section of his *lemma* text does not appear in the oldest manuscripts that otherwise support it. It is in that section that the story of Kabīr's initiation appears.

35. Lorenzen, *Kabir Legends*, pp. 9–18. Cf. Vaudeville, *Kabīr*, vol. 1, pp. 36–7; Hawley and Juergensmeyer *Songs of the Saints of India*, p. 40.

36. Virulently so in the case of Gurū Nānak. W. H. McLeod's attempt to deal in a scholarly, critical manner with the *janam sākhīs* of the Sikh tradition was an important contributing factor causing him to become the target of a campaign of suspicion launched by a certain segment of that community. See McLeod, *Early Sikh Tradition: A Study of the Janam-sākhīs* (Oxford: Clarendon Press, 1980). On the controversy, see Gurinder Singh Mann and J. S. Hawley, eds, *Studying the Sikhs: Issues for North America* (Albany: State University of New York Press, 1993), pp. 14–16, 55–60, 107–10, 123–5; from a divergent perspective, see Bachittar Singh Giani, *Planned Attack on Aad Sri Guru Granth Sahib: Academics or Blasphemy* (Chandigarh: International Centre of Sikh Studies, 1994).

37. Hazārīprasād Dvivedī, *Kabīr* (New Delhi: Rājkamal Prakāśan, 1976), p. 159; see also Hess's discussion of Dvivedī's position in 'Three Kabir Collections', pp. 133–5. and that of Monika Horstmann in 'Hazārīprasād Dvivedī's Kabīr,' in Horstmann, ed., *Images of Kabīr* (Delhi: Manohar, 2002), pp. 115–26. In regard to hagiographical attempts to explain similar apparent discontinuities in poetry attributed to Sūrdās and Nāmdev by appeal to a conversion story, see J. S. Hawley, *Sūr Dās*, pp. 126–9.

38. Hedayetullah, *Kabir: The Apostle*, pp. 2–67, 282, 294–5.

39. For details, see Chapter 4, pp. 103–7.

40. Kumkum Sangari, 'Mirabai and the Spiritual Economy of *Bhakti*', *Economic and Political Weekly*, special articles (7 and 14 July 1990), pp. 1464–75, 1537–52. The quotation is from p. 1465. The desire for firm historical grounding is evident at various points. Sangari wants, for example, to compare Mīrā with 'earlier and contemporary male *bhaktas*' and to evaluate 'the historical moment in which Mira lives' (pp. 1464–65). She concedes that 'It is difficult to rescue the "real" Mirabai,' yet speaks in the preceding sentence of 'the Mira who may be gleaned from historical facts' (p. 1465). Similar criticisms of Sangari's approach are made by Parita Mukta, *Upholding the Common Life: The Community of Mirabai* (Delhi: Oxford University Press, 1994), pp. 32–4.

41. Parita Mukta, 'Upholding the Common Life: The Community of Mirabai' (PhD diss., University of Manchester, 1990) and the book of the same title based upon it; Paraśurām Caturvedī, *Mīrāṅbāī kī Padāvalī* (Allahabad: Hindī Sāhitya Sammelan, 1973). Caturvedī presents his as a critical edition, but gives no evidence of his manuscript sources or the methods he adopted in dealing

with them. On both scores, the works of Kalyāṇsiṃh Śekhāvat are much stronger: *Mīrāṅbāī kā Jīvanvṛtt evam Kāvya* (Jodhpur: Hindī Sāhitya Mandir, n.d.) and *Mīrāṅ-Bṛhatpadāvalī*, vol. 2 (Jodhpur: Rajasthan Oriental Research Institute, 1975).

42. One such community that differs greatly from those Mukta has studied is the Sindhi group responsible for the founding of St. Mira's School and College in Pune. See Hawley and Juergensmeyer, *Songs of the Saints of India*, pp. 120–1. A sense of the Gandhian perspective on Mīrā, with which this community's view is connected, emerges at various points in Mukta, *Upholding the Common Life:* for instance, p. 119.

43. Lutgendorf, *The Life of a Text: Performing the Rāmcaritmānas of Tulsidas* (Berkeley: University of California Press, 1991), especially pp. 13–29, 33–41, 53–164).

44. Bryant, *Poems to the Child-God: Structures and Strategies in the Poetry of Sūrdās* (Berkeley: University of California Press, 1978). This form of analysis runs at some points directly counter to classical *rasa* theory, which holds that an author's achievement can be measured by the degree to which s/he sustains a certain mood that author and audience hold in common: see Bryant, *Child-God*, pp. 21–39.

45. Linda Hess with Shukdev Singh, *The Bījak of Kabir* (San Francisco: North Point Press, 1983), pp. 7–24.

46. E.g., Lorenzen, 'The Kabir Panth: Heretics to Hindus', in Lorenzen, ed., *Religious Change and Cultural Domination* (Mexico City: El Colegio de México, 1981), pp. 151–71; 'Traditions of Non-caste Hinduism: The Kabir Panth', *Contributions to Indian Sociology*, n.s. 21.2 (1987), pp. 263–83; 'The Kabir-panth and Social Protest,' in Schomer and McLeod, eds, *The Sants,* pp. 281–303; and 'Politics and the Kabir Panth,' lecture delivered at the University of Washington, 13 October 1981.

47. W. C. Smith, *What is Scripture?: A Comparative Approach* (Minneapolis: Fortress Press, 1993).

48. Dharmavīr, *Kabīr ke Ālocak* (New Delhi: Vāṇī Prakāśan, 1997; 2nd edition, 1998), chapter 5, pp. 73–96, and in response Purushottam Agrawal, '*Jāt hī Pūcho Sādhu kī...':* Asmitāvādī Aticār ke sāmne Kabīr kī Kavitā,' in *Bahuvacan* 2:6 (2001), pp. 311–25.

49. Broadly on this point, see Vasudha Dalmia, Angelika Malinar, and Martin Christof, eds, *Charisma & Canon: Essays on the Religious History of the Indian Subcontinent* (Delhi: Oxford University Press, 2001).

50. Hawley and Juergensmeyer, *Songs of the Saints of India*, pp. 32, 140. The originals are to be found in Caturvedī, *Mīrāṅbāī kī Padāvalī*, p. 156 (no. 193), and in Padam Gurcaran Siṃh, *Sant Ravidās: Vicārak aur Kavi* Jalandhar: Nav-Cintan Prakāśan, 1977), p. 192 (no. 3 from the *Gurū Granth Sāhib*).

51. Rām Lakhan, Interview, Banaras, 19 August 1985.

52. C. J. Fuller, *The Camphor Flame: Popular Hinduism and Society in India* (Princeton: Princeton University Press, 1992), pp. 156–63, cf. 221–3. Cf. Milton Singer, 'The Rādhā-Krishna *Bhajanas* of Madras City,' in Singer, ed., *Krishna: Myths, Rites, and Attitudes* (Chicago: University of Chicago Press, 1971 [originally 1966]), pp. 90–138.

53. David F. Pocock, *Mind, Body, and Wealth: A Study of Belief and Practice in an Indian Village* (Oxford: Blackwell, 1973), p. 105.

54. A nice way to illustrate this in a strictly philological realm is the recent suggestion of Kenneth Bryant that the critical edition of the oldest poems in the *Sūrsāgar* should be displayed in such a way that the reader gets a more than customarily vivid sense for the variousness of the traditions of transmission associated with the Sūr corpus. He proposes a format that would present a single critical edition of a given poem with a full apparatus for variants, as is usual in a comprehensive edition of this type, but would also display a second poem, unedited, drawn from a manuscript showing a very different treatment of that poem and would be printed alongside its critically edited cousin. (K. E. Bryant, 'The Bottom of the Page: Representing Variation in an Oral Tradition', in *Studies in Early Modern Indo-Aryan Languages, Literature, and Culture*, pp. 87–100, edited by Alan W. Entwistle and Carol Salomon with Heidi Pauwels and Michael C. Shapiro. Delhi: Manohar, 1999.) At another level of inquiry, the fact that the entire manuscript base for the critical edition exists in computerized form makes the early *Sūrsāgar*, in all its diversity, available to researchers. See www.surdas.org.

55. Philip Lutgendorf speaks of similar matters under the heading 'the Brajification of Braj' in his 'Imagining Ayodhya: Notes on "Brajification" and Other Forms of Urban Renewal', paper delivered to the conference entitled 'The Continuing Creation of Vraja,' Brindavan, January, 1994, pp. 21–9.

56. I use Bharucha's vivid term: *The Question of Faith*, p. 94.

Bibliography

Agrawal, Purushottam, 'Crisis Points in the Mahabharata', lecture given at the India Habitat Centre, New Delhi, 9 September 2003.

Alston, A. J., *The Devotional Poems of Mirabai* (Delhi: Motilal Banarsidass, 1980).

Amar Chitra Katha (Bombay: India Book House [IBH]): issues on Mīrābāī (36), Kabīr (55), Tulsīdās (62), Tukārām (68), Narasī Mehtā (94), Eknāth (123), Sūrdās (137), Jñāneśvar (155), Tiruppān and Kanakadāsa (186), Rāmānuja (243), Tyāgarāja (245), Ramaṇa Mahārṣi (290), Cokhāmelā (292), and Ravidās (350).

Ambalal, Amit, *Krishna as Shrinathji* (Ahmedabad: Mapin, 1987).

Ambedkar, Bhimrao, 'Annihilation of Caste', in *Dr. Babasaheb Ambedkar Writings and Speeches*, vol. 1 (Bombay: Government of Maharashtra, 1936).

Arney, Paul B., 'The Dakor and Kashi Manuscripts: Are They Genuine?' (unpublished paper, Columbia University, 1989).

Babb, Lawrence A., *The Divine Hierarchy: Popular Hinduism in Central India* (New York: Columbia University Press, 1975).

Babb, Lawrence A., Varsha Joshi, and Michael Meister (eds), *Multiple Histories: Culture and Society in the Study of Rajasthan* (Jaipur: Rawat Publications, 2002).

Bahura, Gopal Narayan, *Literary Heritage of the Rulers of Amber and Jaipur* (Jaipur: Maharaja Sawai Man Singh II Museum, 1976).

Bahurā, Gopāl Nārāyaṇ and Kenneth E. Bryant (eds), *Pad Sūrdās jī kā / The Padas of Sūrdās* (Jaipur: Maharaja Sawai Man Singh II Museum, 1982).

Bandopadhyay, Pradeep, 'The Uses of Kabīr: Missionary Writings and Civilizational Differences', in Monika Horstmann (ed.), *Images of Kabīr* (Delhi: Manohar, 2002), pp. 9–31.

Banerjea, Jitendra Nath, *The Development of Hindu Iconography* (New Delhi: Munshiram Manoharlal, 1974 [originally 1956]).

Barthwal, Pitambar D., *The Nirguna School of Hindi Poetry: An Exposition of Medieval Indian Santa Mysticism* (Banaras: Indian Book Shop, 1936).

Barz, Richard, *The Bhakti Sect of Vallabhācārya* (Faridabad: Thomson Press, 1976).

Behl, Aditya, *Love's Subtle Magic: An Indian Islamic Literary Tradition, 1379–1545* (New York: Oxford University Press, 2012).

Behl, Aditya and Simon Weightman, with S. N. Pandey, *Mīr Sayyid Manjhan Shattārī Rājgīrī: Madhumālatī, An Indian Sufi Romance* (Oxford: Oxford University Press, 2000).

Berling, Judith A., *The Syncretic Religion of Lin Chao-en* (New York: Columbia University Press, 1980).

Bharati, Agehananda, *The Tantric Tradition* (New York: Anchor Books, 1970).

Bharati, Pushpa, *Soordas* (Bombay: India Book House Educational Trust, 1977).

Bhāṭī, Hukm Siṃh, *Mīrāṅbāī: Aitihāsik va Sāmājik Vivecan* (Jodhpur: Rājasthān Sāhitya Saṅsthān, 1986).

Bharucha, Rustom, *The Question of Faith* (New Delhi: Orient Longman, 1993).

Bly, Robert, *Kabir: Ecstatic Poems*, with an afterword by John Stratton Hawley (Boston: Beacon Press, 2004).

———, *The Kabir Book: Forty-Four of the Ecstatic Poems of Kabir* (Boston: Beacon Press, 1971).

Bly, Robert and Jane Hirshfield, *Mirabai: Ecstatic Poems*, with an afterword by John Stratton Hawley (Boston: Beacon Press, 2005).

Brown, Karen McCarthy, 'Fundamentalism and the Control of Women', in J. S. Hawley (ed.), *Fundamentalism and Gender* (New York: Oxford University Press, 1994), pp. 175–206.

Brown, Peter, 'The Saint as Exemplar in Late Antiquity', *Representations* 1:2 (1983), pp. 1–25.

Bryant, Kenneth E., 'The Bottom of the Page: Representing Variation in an Oral Tradition', in *Studies in Early Modern Indo-Aryan Languages, Literature, and Culture*, Alan W. Entwistle, Carol Salomon, Heidi Pauwels, and Michael C. Shapiro (eds) (Delhi: Manohar, 1999), pp. 87–100.

———, 'The Fatehpur Manuscript and the *Sūrsāgar* Critical Edition Project', in Monika Thiel-Horstmann (ed.), *Bhakti in Current Research, 1979–1982* (Berlin: Dietrich Reimer, 1983), pp. 37–52.

———, 'The Manuscript Tradition of the Sursagar: The Fatehpur Manuscript', in Gopal Narayan Bahura and Kenneth E. Bryant (eds), *Pad Sūrdāsjī kā / The Padas of Sūrdās* (Jaipur: Maharaja Sawai Man Singh II Museum, 1982 [actually appeared 1984]), pp. vii–xx.

———, *Poems to the Child-God: Structures and Strategies in the Poetry of Sūrdās* (Berkeley: University of California Press, 1978).

———, 'Sant and Vaiṣṇava Poetry: Some Observations on Method', in Mark Juergensmeyer and N. Gerald Barrier (eds), *Sikh Studies: Comparative Perspectives on a Changing Tradition* (Berkeley: Berkeley Religious Studies Series, 1979), pp. 65–74.

———, 'Toward a Critical Edition of the *Sūrasāgar*', in Winand M. Callewaert (ed.), *Early Hindī Devotional Literature in Current Research* (Delhi: Impex India, 1980), pp. 5–16.

Bryant, Kenneth E., and J. S. Hawley, *Surdas: Poems from the Early Tradition* (Cambridge: Harvard University Press, forthcoming).

Bumiller, Elisabeth, *May You Be the Mother of a Hundred Sons* (New York: Random House, 1990).

Burghart, Richard 'The Founding of the Ramanandi Sect', *Ethnohistory*, 25:2 (1978), pp. 121–37.

Caldwell, Sarah, 'Waves of Beauty, Rivers of Blood: Constructing the Goddess in Kerala', in Tracy Pintchman (ed.), *Seeking Mahādevī: Constructing the Identities of the Hindu Great Goddess* (Albany: State University of New York Press, 2001), pp. 93–114.

Callewaert, W. M., 'The "Earliest" Song of Mira (1503–1546),' *Annali* 50:4 of the Istituto Universitario Orientale, Naples (1990), pp. 363–78; also in *Orientalia Lovaniensia Periodica* 22 (1991).

———, 'The "Earliest" Song of Mira (1503–1546)', *Journal of the Oriental Institute, Baroda* 39 (1990), pp. 239–53.

———, 'Kabīr's *Pads* in 1556', in Monika Horstmann (ed.), *Images of Kabīr* (New Delhi: Manohar, 2002), pp. 45–72.

———, 'Manuscripts of some Bhaktamālas, Pañcavāṇīs and Sarvāṅgīs', *IAVRI Bulletin* 3 (1976), pp. 5–12.

———, *The Sarvāṅgī of the Dādūpanthī Rajab* (Leuven: Katholieke Universiteit, 1978).

———, *The Sarvāṅgī of Gopāldās: A 17th Century Anthology of Bhakti Literature* (New Delhi: Manohar, 1993).

Callewaert, W. M. and Bart Op de Beeck, *Nirguṇ-Bhakti-Sāgar: Devotional Hindī Literature*, vol. 1 (New Delhi: Manohar, 1991).

Callewaert W. M. and Mukund Laṭh, *The Hindī Songs of Nāmdev* (Leuven: Departement Orientalistiek, 1989).

Callewaert, W. M. in collaboration with Swapna Sharma, *The Hagiographies of Anantadās: The Bhakti Poets of North India* (Richmond, Surrey: Curzon Press, 2000).

Callewaert, W. M., Swapna Sharma, and Dieter Taillieu, *The Millennium Kabīr-Vāṇī* (Delhi: Manohar, 2000).

Callewaert, W. M. and Rupert Snell (eds), *According to Tradition: Hagiographical Writing in India* (Wiesbaden: Otto Harrassowitz, 1994).

Carman, John B., *Majesty and Meekness: A Comparative Study of Contrast and Harmony in the Concept of God* (Grand Rapids: W. B. Eerdmans, 1994).

———, Oral communication, 10 February 1983.

Caturvedī, Javāharlāl, *Sūrdās: Adhyayan Sāmagrī* (Akhil Bhāratīya Braj Sāhitya Maṇḍal, 1959).

———, 'Sūrsāgar kā Vikās aur uskā Rūp', in V. S. Agravāl (ed.), *Kanhaiyālāl Poddār Abhinandan Granth* (Mathura: Akhil Bhāratīya Braj Sāhitya Maṇḍal, 1953), pp. 119–32.

Caturvedī, Javāharlāl (ed.), *Sūr-Sāgar* (Calcutta: Śrīnand Mīnānī, 1965).

Caturvedī, Paraśurām, *Hindī Sāhitya kā Bṛhat Itihās*, vol. 4 (Varanasi: Nāgarīpracāriṇī Sabhā, 1968.

———, *Mīrā-Bṛhatpadāvalī* (Allahabad: Hindī Sāhitya Sammelan, 1973).

———, *Mīrāṅbāī kī Padāvalī* (Allahabad: Hindī Sāhitya Sammelan, 1973 [originally 1932]).

———, *Uttarī Bhārat kī Sant Paramparā* (Allahabad: Leader Press, 1972).

Chandrakant, Kamala, Interview, Bombay, 1989.

Chapple, Christopher Key, 'Devotion to God in Mirabai, Jainism, and Yoga', paper delivered to the conference 'Mirabai: Hindu Saint for a Global World', University of California at Los Angeles, 5 October 2002.

Chodorow, Nancy, 'Family Structure and Feminine Personality', in Michelle Zimbalist Rosaldo and Louise Lamphere (eds), *Women, Culture, and Society* (Stanford: Stanford University Press, 1974), pp. 43–66.

Cutler, Norman, 'Biography and Interpretation in Tamil Hinduism: *Tiruvācakam* and the *Tiruvātavūrar Purāṇam*', paper delivered to the American Academy of Religion, Los Angeles, 1985.

———, 'Implied Poets in the Real World: A Study of Tamil Saints', paper presented to the Wisconsin Conference on South Asia, Madison, 5 November 1983.

Dalmia, Vasudha, 'Forging Community: The Guru in a Seventeenth-century Vaishnava Hagiography', in Vasudha Dalmia, Angelika Malinar, and Martin Christof (eds), *Charisma and Canon: Essays on the Religious History of the Indian Subcontinent* (Delhi: Oxford University Press, 2001), pp. 129–54.

De, S. K., *History of Sanskrit Poetics*, 2nd rev. ed. (Calcutta: K. L. Mukhopadhyaya, 1960).

Delvoye, Françoise 'Nalini', 'Dhrupad Songs Attributed to Tansen', in Alan Entwistle and Françoise Mallison (eds), *Studies in South Asian Devotional Literature* (New Delhi: Manohar and Paris: École Française d'Extrême Orient, 1994), pp. 406–29.

———, 'The Verbal Content of Dhrupad Songs from the Earliest Collections, Part 1: The *Hazar Dhrupad* or *Sahasras*', *Dhrupad Annual* 5 (1990), pp. 93–108.

Deol, Jeevan, 'Sūrdās: Poet and Text in the Sikh Tradition', *Bulletin of the School of Oriental and African Studies* 63:2 (2000), pp. 158–86.

Devy, G. N., *After Amnesia: Tradition and Change in Indian Literary Criticism* (Bombay: Orient Longman, 1992).

Dharmavīr, *Kabīr ke Ālocak* (New Delhi: Vāṇī Prakāśaṇ, 1997).

Dharwadker, Vinay, *Kabir: The Weaver's Songs* (New Delhi: Penguin, 2003).

Dimock, Jr., Edward C., 'A Theology of the Repulsive: The Myth of the Goddess Śītalā', in J. S. Hawley and D. M. Wulff (eds), *The Divine Consort: Rādhā and the Goddesses of India* (Berkeley: Berkeley: Religious Studies Series and Delhi: Motilal Banarsidass, 1982), pp. 184–203.

Dimock, Jr., Edward C. and Tony K. Stewart (eds), *The 'Caitanya Caritāmṛta' of Kṛṣṇadāsa Kavirāja* (Cambridge: Harvard University Press, 1999).

Dinnerstein, Dorothy, *The Mermaid and the Minotaur: Sexual Arrangements and the Human Malaise* (New York: Harper & Row, 1976).

Doniger, Wendy, *The Implied Spider: Poetics and Theology in Myth* (New York: Columbia University Press, 1998).

Doniger, Wendy (with Brian K. Smith), trans., *The Laws of Manu* (New York: Penguin, 1991).

Dvivedī, Hazārīprasād, *Hindī Sāhitya kī Bhūmikā* (New Delhi: Rājkamal Prakāśan, 1991 [originally 1940).]

———, *Kabīr* (New Delhi: Rājkamal Prakāśan, 2002 [originally 1955]).

Dvivedī, Kedārnāth, *Kabīr aur Kabīr Panth* (Allahabad: Hindī Sāhitya Sammelan, 1965).

Dwyer, Rachel, *The Poetics of Devotion: The Gujarati Lyrics of Dayārām* (Richmond, Surrey: Curzon Press, 2001).

Embree, Ainslie T., *Imagining India* (Delhi: Oxford University Press, 1989)

Entwistle, A. W., *Braj, Centre of Krishna Pilgrimage* (Groningen: Egbert Forsten, 1987).

Falk, Marcia, *The Song of Songs: A New Translation and Interpretation* (San Francisco: Harper, 1990).

Feldhaus, Anne, 'Bahiṇā Bāī: Wife and Saint', *Journal of the American Academy of Religion* 50:4 (1982), pp. 87–100.

Fuller, C. J., *The Camphor Flame: Popular Hinduism and Society in India* (Princeton: Princeton University Press, 1992).

Gaeffke, Peter, 'Kabīr in Literature by and for Muslims', in Monika Horstmann (ed.), *Images of Kabīr* (Delhi: Manohar, 2002), pp. 157–63.

Gauḍ, Krishnadev Prasād et al., *Hastalikhit Hindī Pustakoṅ kā Saṅkṣipt Vivaraṇ* (Varanasi: Kāśī Nāgarīpracāriṇī Sabhā, 1964).

Gherā, B. R., Interview, New Delhi, 23 August 1983.

———, *Srī Guru Ravidās jī kā Saṃkṣipt Itihās* (n.p.: All India Adi Dharm Mission, n.d.).

Gokarn, Kusum, 'Popularity of Devotional Films (Hindi)', unpublished study, National Film Archive Project 689/5/84, Pune, 1984.

Gokulnāth [attributed], *Caurāsī Vaiṣṇavan kī Vārtā,* ed. Dvarikādās Parīkh (Mathura: Śrī Bajaraṅg Pustakālay, 1970 [originally 1948]).

———, *Sūrdās kī Vārtā,* (Mathura: Śrī Govardhan Granthamālā Kāryālay, 1970).

Gold, Ann Grodzins, *Fruitful Journeys: The Ways of Rajasthani Pilgrims* (Berkeley: University of California Press, 1988).

Gold, Ann Grodzins and Daniel Gold, 'The Fate of the Householder Nath', *History of Religions* 24:2 (1984), pp. 113–32.

Gopinath Rao, T. A., *The Elements of Hindu Iconography* (Delhi: Motilal Banarsidass, 1985 [originally 1914]).

Grafton, Anthony, *The Footnote: A Curious History* (Cambridge: Harvard University Press, 1997).

Guha, Ranajit, 'Dominance without Hegemony and its Historiography', *Subaltern Studies VI* (Delhi: Oxford University Press, 1989), pp. 210–309.

Gupta, Dīndayāl, *Aṣṭachāp aur Vallabh Sampradāy* (Allahabad: Hindī Sāhitya Sammelan, 1970).

Gupta, Dīndayāl, Devendranāth Śarmā, and Vijayendra Snātak (eds), *Hindī Sāhitya kā Bṛhat Itihās*, vol. 5 (Varanasi: Nāgarīpracāriṇī Sabhā, 1974).

Gupta, Kiśorīlāl, *Gosāīṅ Carit* (Varanasi: Vāṇī-Vitān Prakāśan, 1964).

Gupta, Mātāprasād, *Sūr Sāgar* (Agra: K. M. Hindī tathā Bhāṣāvijñān Vidyāpīṭh, Agra University, 1979).

———, 'Sūr Sāgar kī Bhūmikā', ed. Udayśaṃkar Śāstrī, *Bhāratīya Sāhitya* 13:1–2 (1968), pp. 43–94, and subsequent volumes.

Gupta, Parameśvarī Lāl (ed.), *Kutuban kṛt Mṛgāvatī (Mūl Pāṭh, Pāṭhāntar, Tippaṇī evam Śodh)* (Varanasi: Viśvavidyālay Prakāśan, 1967).

Gupta, R. D., 'Priyā Dās, Author of the *Bhaktirasabodhinī*', *Bulletin of the School of Oriental and African Studies* 32:1 (1969), pp. 57–70.

Haberman, David L., *Acting as a Way of Salvation* (New York: Oxford University Press, 1988).

Halbfass, Wilhelm, *India and Europe: An Essay in Understanding* (Albany: State University of New York Press, 1988).

Hardy, Friedhelm, 'The Tamil Veda of a *Śūdra* Saint: The Śrivaiṣṇava Interpretation of Nammāḷvār', in G. Krishna (ed.), *Contributions to South Asian Studies*, vol. 1 (Delhi: Oxford University Press, 1978), pp. 29–87.

———, *Viraha-Bhakti* (Delhi: Oxford University Press, 1983).

Harirāy, *Bhāvprakāś*, in Dvārikādās Parīkh (ed.), *Caurāsī Vaiṣṇavan kī Vārtā* (Mathura: Śrī Bajaraṅg Pustakālay, 1970).

Harlan, Lindsey, 'The Ethic of Protection among Rajput Women: Religious Mediations of Caste and Gender Duties' (PhD diss., Harvard University, 1987).

Hawley, J. S., 'The Bharat Kala Bhavan *Sūrsāgar*', in Alan W. Entwistle and Françoise Mallison (eds), *Studies in South Asian Devotional Literature* (Delhi: Manohar, 1994), pp. 480–513.

———, 'Comparative Religion for Undergraduates: Fraud? Failure? Frontier?', The Wabash Center Lecture in the Arts of Pedagogy, University of Chicago Divinity School, 1 November 2002, forthcoming in *Criterion* (Chicago: University of Chicago Divinity School, 2004) and in Thomas Idinopulis (ed.), *Comparing Religions: Possibilities and Problems in Crosscultural and Intersocial Analysis* (Leiden: E. J. Brill).

———, 'The Damage of Separation: Krishna's Loves and Kali's Child', *Journal of the American Academy of Religion* 72:2 (2004), pp. 369–93.

———, *Krishna, The Butter Thief* (Princeton: Princeton University Press, 1983).

———, 'Naming Hinduism', *The Wilson Quarterly* 15:3 (1991), pp. 20–34.

———, 'The *Sant* in Sūr Dās', in *The Sants: Studies in a Devotional Traditional of India*, Karine Schomer and W. H. McLeod (eds), (Berkeley: Berkeley Religious Studies Series; and Delhi: Motilal Banarsidass, 1987), pp. 191–211.

———, 'The Sectarian Logic of the *Sūr Dās kī Vārtā*', in Monika Thiel-Horstmann (ed.), *Bhakti in Current Research, 1979–1982* (Berlin: Dietrich Reimer Verlag, 1983). pp. 157–69.

———, *Sūr Dās: Poet, Singer, Saint* (Seattle: University of Washington Press and Delhi: Oxford University Press, 1984).

———, *Sūr's Ocean* (Cambridge: Harvard University Press, forthcoming).

———, 'Who Speaks for Hinduism—and Who Against?', *Journal of the American Academy of Religion* 68:4 (2000), pp. 711–20.

Hawley, J. S. (ed.), *Saints and Virtues* (Berkeley: University of California Press, 1987).

Hawley, J. S. and Mark Juergensmeyer, *Songs of the Saints of India* (New York and Delhi: Oxford University Press, 1988; 2nd revised edition, Delhi: Oxford University Press, 2004).

Hedayetullah, Muhammad, *Kabir: The Apostle of Hindu-Muslim Unity: Interaction of Hindu-Muslim Ideas in the Formation of the Bhakti Movement with Special Reference of Kabir, the Bhakta* (Delhi: Motilal Banarsidass, 1977).

Hess, Linda, 'Kabir's Rough Rhetoric', in Karine Schomer and W. H. McLeod (eds), *The Sants. Studies in a Devotional Tradition in India* (Berkeley: Berkeley Religious Studies Series; Delhi: Motilal Banarsidass, 1987), pp. 143–65.

———, Personal communication, New Delhi, 5 September 2003.

———, 'Studies in Kabīr: Texts, Traditions, Styles and Skills' (PhD diss., University of California, Berkeley, 1980).

———, 'Three Kabir Collections', in Karine Schomer and W. H. McLeod (eds), *The Sants: A Devotional Tradition of India* (Berkeley: Graduate Theological Union, and Delhi: Motilal Banarsidass, 1987), pp. 111–41.

Holland, Barron, 'The *Satsāī* of Bihari: Hindi Poetry of the Early Riti Period', (PhD diss., Berkeley: University of California, 1969).

Hopkins, Steven Paul, *Singing the Body of God* (New York: Oxford University Press, 2002).

Horstmann, Monika, 'The *Bhajan* Repertore of the Present-day Dādūpanth', in Monika Thiel-Horstmann (ed.), *Bhakti in Current Research, 1979–1982* (Berlin: Dietrich Reimer Verlag, 1983), pp. 385–401.

———, 'The Rāmānandīs of Galtā (Jaipur, Rajasthan)', in Lawrence A. Babb, Varsha Joshi, and Michael W. Meister (eds), *Multiple Histories: Culture and Society in the Study of Rajasthan* (Jaipur: Rawat, 2002), pp. 141–97.

——— (ed.), *Bhakti in Current Research, 1979–1982* (Berlin: Dietrich Reimer Verlag, 1983).

——— (ed.), *Images of Kabīr* (Delhi: Manohar, 2002).

——— (ed.), *Nächtliches Wachen: Eine Form indischen Gottesdienstes* (Bonn: Indica et Tibetica Verlag, 1985).

Hospital, C. G., 'The Enemy Transformed: Opponents of the Lord in the *Bhāgavata Purana*', *Journal of the American Academy of Religion* 46:2, Supplement, K (1978), pp. 199–215.

Jacobson, Doranne, 'Golden Handprints and Red-painted Feet: Hindu Childbirth Rituals in Central India', in Doranne Jacobson and Susan Wadley, *Women in India: Two Perspectives*, 2nd enlarged ed. (Columbia, MO: South Asia Publications, 1992), pp. 137–55.

Jaeger, Werner, *Paideia: The Ideals of Greek Culture*, trans. Gilbert Highet (New York: Oxford University Press, 1943–5).

Jān, Kavi, *Kyām Khāṅ Rāsā*, edited by Agarchand Nahata (Jaipur: Purātattva Mandir, 1953).

Jhā, Narendra (ed.), *Bhaktamāl: Pāṭhānuśīlan evam Vivecan* (Patna: Anupam Prakāśan, 1978).

Jhaveri, Krishnalal Mohanlal, *Imperial Farmans (AD 1577 to AD 1805) Granted to the Ancestors of His Holiness the Tilakayat Maharaj* (Bombay: The News Printing Press, 1928).

Jijñāsu, Candrikāprasād, *Sant Pravar Raidās Sāheb* (Lucknow: Bahujan Kalyāṇ Prakāśaṇ, 1984 [originally 1959]).

Jinavijaya Muni (ed.), *Rājasthānī-Hindī Hastalikhit Granth-Sūcī*, vol. 1 (Jodhpur: Rājasthān Prācyavidyā Pratiṣṭhān, 1960).

Juergensmeyer, Mark, *Radhasoami Reality: The Logic of a Modern Faith* (Princeton: Princeton University Press, 1991).

———, 'The Radhasoami Revival of the Sant Tradition', in Karine Schomer and W. H. McLeod (eds), *The Sants: Studies in a Devotional Tradition in India* (Berkeley: Berkeley Religious Studies Series, Delhi: Motilal Banarsidass, 1987), pp. 329–55.

———, *Religion as Social Vision: The Movement against Untouchability in Twentieth-Century Punjab* (Berkeley: University of California Press, 1982).

Juergensmeyer, Mark and N. Gerald Barrier (eds), *Sikh Studies: Comparative Perspectives on a Changing Tradition* (Berkeley: Berkeley Religious Studies Series, 1979).

Kabīr [attributed], *Anurāg Sāgar* (Allahabad: Belvedere Printing Works, 1918), translated by Raj Kumar Bhagge, Partap Singh, and Kent Bicknell as *The Ocean of Love* (Sanfornton, NH: Sant Bani Ashram, 1982).

Kabir by Abida (Mumbai: Times Music India, 2003).

Kakar, Sudhir and John M. Ross, 'The Cloistered Passion of Radha and Krishna', in Sudhir Kakar and J. M. Ross, *Tales of Love, Sex and Danger* (Delhi: Oxford University Press, 1986), pp. 74–103.

Kane, P. V., *History of Dharmaśāstra*, 5 vols. (Poona: Bhandarkar Oriental Research Institute, 1930–46).

Khare, R. S., *The Untouchable as Himself* (Cambridge: Cambridge University Press, 1984).

Khemrāj, *Śrīkṛṣṇadās* (Bombay: Venkatesvara Press, 1904 [originally 1868]).

Kishwar, Madhu and Ruth Vanita, 'Modern Versions of Mira', *Manushi*, 50–52 (1989), pp. 100–1.

Kripal, Jeffrey J., *Kālī's Child: The Mystical and the Erotic in the Life and Teachings of Ramakrishna* (Chicago: University of Chicago Press, 1995; 2nd revised ed., 1998).

Kulke, Hermann and Dieter Rothermund, *A History of India* (London: Routledge, 1986).

Kunjunni Raja, K., *Indian Theories of Meaning* (Madras: Vedanta Press, 1963).

———, 'Akāṅkṣā: The Main Basis of Syntactic Unity', *Adyar Library Bulletin* 21: 3–4 (1957), pp. 282–95

Kurtz, N. Stanley, *All the Mothers are One: Hindu India and the Reshaping of Psychoanalysis* (New York: Columbia University Press, 1992).

Kvaerne, Per, *An Anthology of Buddhist Tantric Songs* (Oslo: Norwegian Research Council, 1977).

Lath, Mukund, *Half a Tale: A Study in the Interrelationship between Autobiography and History* (Jaipur: Rajasthan Prakrit Bharati Sansthan, 1981).

Leslie, Julia, *The Perfect Wife: The Orthodox Hindu Woman according to the Strīdharmapaddhati of Tryambakayajvan* (Delhi: Oxford University Press, 1989).

Lindsey, Beth Harlan, 'The Ethic of Protection among Rajput Women: Religious Mediations of Caste and Gender Duties' (PhD diss., Harvard University, 1987).

Lingat, Robert, *The Classical Law of India*, trans. J. Duncan M. Derrett (Berkeley: University of California Press, 1973).

Lochtefeld, C. James, 'Clutching at the Elephant: Four Perspectives on the Life of Ravidas', unpublished paper, Columbia University, 1988.

———, 'Suicide in the Hindu Tradition: Varieties, Propriety and Practice', Master's thesis, University of Washington, 1987.

Lorenzen, David N., *Kabir Legends and Ananta-das's Kabir Parachai* (Albany: State University of New York Press, 1991).

———, 'The Kabir-panth and Social Protest', in Karine Schomer and W. H. McLeod (eds), *The Sants: Studies in a Devotional Tradition of India*

(Berkeley: Berkeley Religious Studies Series, Delhi: Motilal Banarsidass, 1987), pp. 281–303.
———, 'The Kabīr Panth: Heretics to Hindus', in D. N. Lorenzen (ed.), *Religious Change and Cultural Domination* (Mexico City: El Colegio de México, 1981), pp. 151–69.
———, 'Politics and the Kabir Panth', lecture delivered at the University of Washington, 13 October 1981.
———, 'Traditions of Non-caste Hinduism: The Kabir Panth', *Contributions to Indian Sociology*, n.s. 21 (February 1987), pp. 263–83.
———, 'Who Invented Hinduism?', *Comparative Studies in Society and History* 41:4 (1999), pp. 630–59.
Lutgendorf, Philip, 'Imagining Ayodhya: Notes on "Brajification" and Other Forms of Urban Renewal', paper delivered to the conference entitled 'The Continuing Creation of Vraja', Brindavan, January 1994.
———, 'Kṛṣṇa Caitanya and His Companions as Presented in the *Bhaktamāla* of Nābhā Jī and the *Bhaktirasabodhinī* of Priyā Dāsa' (Master's essay, University of Chicago, 1981).
———, *The Life of a Text: Performing the Rāmcaritmānas of Tulsidas* (Berkeley: University of California Press, 1991).
———, Private communication, 7 April 1987.
———, 'The Quest for the Legendary Tulsīdās', *Journal of Vaiṣṇava Studies* 1:2 (1993), pp. 79–101.
———, 'The Quest of the Legendary Tulsīdās', in Winand M. Callewaert and Rupert Snell (eds), *According to Tradition: Hagiographical Writing in India* (Wiesbaden: Harrassowitz Verlag, 1994), pp. 65–85.
Macauliffe, M. A., 'The Legend of Mîrā Bâî, the Rajput Princess', *Indian Antiquary* 32 (1903), pp. 329–35.
Mallison, Françoise, 'Saint Sudāmā of Gujarāt: Should the Holy Be Wealthy?', *Journal of the Oriental Institute, Baroda* 29:1–2 (1979), pp. 90–9.
———, 'The Cult of Sudāmā in Porbandar-Sudāmāpuri', *Journal of the Oriental Institute, Baroda* 29:3–4 (1980), pp. 216–23.
Mann, Gurinder Singh, *The Goindval Pothis: The Earliest Extant Source of the Sikh Canon* (Cambridge: Harvard University Press, 1996).
———, *The Making of Sikh Scripture* (New York: Oxford University Press, 2001).
Mann, Gurinder Singh and J. S. Hawley (eds), *Studying the Sikhs: Issues for North America* (Albany: State University of New York Press, 1993).
Marfatia, Mrudula I., *The Philosophy of Vallabhācārya* (New Delhi: Munshiram Manoharlal, 1967).
Martin, Nancy M., 'Dyed in the Color of Her Lord: Multiple Representations in the Mirabai Tradition' (PhD diss., Graduate Theological Union, 1995).
———, *Mirabai* (New York: Oxford University Press, forthcoming).
———, 'Mirabai in the Academy and the Politics of Identity', in Mandakranta

Bose (ed.), *Faces of the Feminine from Ancient, Medieval, and Modern India* (New York: Oxford University Press, 2000), pp. 162–82.
———, (ed.), *Mirabai: Hindu Saint for a Global World* (forthcoming).
Masson, J. M., 'The Childhood of Kṛṣṇa: Some Psychoanalytic Observations', *Journal of the American Oriental Society* 94:4 (1974), p. 454–9.
McGee, Mary, 'Desired Fruits: Motive and Intention in the Votive Rites of Hindu Women', in Julia Leslie (ed.), *Roles and Rituals for Hindu Women* (Rutherford, NJ: Fairleigh Dickinson University Press, 1991), pp. 71–88.
McGregor, R. S., *Hindi Literature from its Beginnings to the Nineteenth Century* (Wiesbaden: Otto Harrassowitz, 1984).
———, *Nanddas: The Round Dance of Krishna and Uddhav's Message* (London: Lauzac, 1973).
———, 'Tulsīdās' Śrīkṛṣṇagītāvalī', *Journal of the American Oriental Society* 96:4 (1976), pp. 520–7.
McLeod, W. H. , *Early Sikh Tradition: A Study of the Janam-sākhīs* (Oxford: Clarendon Press, 1980).
———, *The Evolution of the Sikh Tradition* (Delhi: Oxford University Press, 1975).
———, *Gurū Nānak and the Sikh Religion* (Delhi: Oxford University Press, 1976 [originally 1968]).
Mehta, S. S., *A Monograph on Mirabai, the Saint of Mewad* (Bombay: author, n.d.).
Meyer, Marvin, 'Gender Transformation in Early Christianity', presentation to the conference on 'Love and Gender in the World Religions', Chapman University, 3 April 1998.
Michael, R. Blake, 'Aṣṭāvaraṇa in the *Śūnyasaṃpādane*' (PhD diss., Harvard University, 1979).
———, 'The Housewife as Saint: Tales from the *Śūnyasaṃpādane*', paper delivered to the American Academy of Religion, New York, 1979.
———, 'Work as Worship in the Vīraśaiva Tradition', *Journal of the American Academy of Religion* 50:4 (1982), pp. 605–19.
Miller, Barbara Stoler, *The Bhagavad-Gita: Krishna's Counsel in Time of War* (New York: Columbia University Press, 1986).
Mīrābāī [attributed], *Mīrāṅ-Bṛhatpadāvalī,* vol. 2, ed. Kalyāṇsiṃh Śekhāvat (Jodhpur: Rajasthan Oriental Research Institute, 1975).
Mishra, Vijay C., 'Two Truths are Told: Tagore's Kabir', in Karine Schomer and W. H. McLeod (eds), *The Sants: Studies in a Devotional Tradition of India* (Berkeley: Graduate Theological Union and Delhi: Motilal Banarsidass, 1987), pp. 167–80.
Miśra, Bhagavatsvarūp, *Kabīr Granthāvalī* [*Sañjīvani vyākhyā sahit*] (Agra: Vinod Pustak Mandir, 1969).
Mītal, Prabhu Dayāl, *Braj ke Dharma-Sampradāyoṅ kā Itihās* (Delhi: National Publishing House, 1968).

Mukta, Parita, 'Mirabai in Rajasthan', *Manushi* 50–52 (1989), pp. 94–9.

———, *Upholding the Common Life: The Community of Mirabai* (Delhi: Oxford University Press, 1984).

Nābhādās et al., *Śrī Bhaktamāl*, with the *Bhaktirasabodhinī* commentary of Priyādās, edited by Sītārāmśaraṇ Bhagavānprasād Rūpakalā (Lucknow: Tejkumār Press, 1969 [originally 1910]).

Nāgar, Ambāśaṃkar, *Madhya Kālīn Hindī Sāhitya: Adhyayan aur Anveṣaṇ* (Ahmedabad: Paścimāñcal Prakāśan, 1997).

Naiṇsī, Muṅhatā, *Mārvāḍ rā Paraganāṅ rī Vigat*, vol. 2, edited by Badarīprasād Sākariyā (Jodhpur: Rājashthān Prācyavidyā Pratiṣṭhān, 1960).

Nārāyaṇ, Rūp, *Nandadās: Vicārak, Rasik, Kalākār* (Delhi: Rādhākṛṣṇa Prakāśan, 1968).

Narayanan, Vasudha, 'Śrī: Giver of Fortune, Bestower of Grace', in J. S. Hawley and Donna M. Wulff (eds), *Devī: Goddesses of India* (Berkeley: University of California Press, 1996), pp. 87–108.

———, *The Way and the Goal* (Washington: Institute for Vaishnava Studies and Cambridge: Center for the Study of World Religions, Harvard University, 1987).

Narayana Rao, Velcheru, 'A Rāmāyaṇa of Their Own: Women's Oral Tradition in Telugu', in Paula Richman (ed.), *Many Rāmāyaṇas: The Diversity of a Narrative Tradition in South Asia* (Berkeley: University of California Press, 1991), pp. 114–36.

Narayana Rao, Velcheru, David Shulman, and Sanjay Subrahmanyam, *Textures of Time: Writing History in South India 1600–1800* (New Delhi: Permanent Black, 2001).

Novetzke, Christian, 'A Family Affair', in Guy Beck (ed.), *Alternative Krishnas* (Albany: State University of New York Press, 2005), pp. 113–38.

———, 'Who Killed Nāmdev? The Forensics of Authorship in a South Asian Tradition', unpublished paper.

O'Connell, Joseph T., 'Gauḍīya Vaiṣṇava Symbolism of Deliverance (*uddhāra, nistāra*...) from Evil', *Journal of Asian and African Studies* 15:1–2 (1980), pp. 124–35.

Offredi, Mariola, 'Kabīr and the Nāthpanth', in Monika Horstmann (ed.), *Images of Kabīr* (Delhi: Manohar, 2002), pp. 127–41.

Padam, Gurcaran Siṃh, *Sant Ravidās: Vicārak aur Ḳavi* (Jalandhar: Nav-Cintan Prakāśan, 1977).

Pandey, Raj Bali, *Hindu Saṃskāras* (Delhi: Motilal Banarsidass, 1969).

Pandey, S. M., 'Mīrabāī and Her Contributions to the Bhakti Movement', *History of Religions* 5:1 (1965), pp. 54–73.

Pangarkar, L. R., *Marāṭhī Vāṇmayācā Itihās* (Pune: Vidarbh Marāṭhavāḍā Book Company, 1972 [originally 1935]).

Parīkh, Dvārikādās (ed.), *Caurāsī Vaiṣṇavan kī Vārtā* (Mathura: Śrī Bajaraṅg Pustakālay, 1970 [originally 1948]).

Parīkh, Dvārikādās and Prabhudayāl Mītal, *Sūr-Nirṇay* (Mathura: Sāhitya Saṁsthān, 1962).

Pauwels, Heidi R. M., 'The Early *Bhakti* Milieu as Mirrored in the Poetry of Harirām Vyās', in Alan W. Entwistle and Françoise Mallison (eds), *Studies in South Asian Devotional Literature* (New Delhi: Manohar, and Paris: École Française d'Extrême Orient, 1994), pp. 24–50.

———, 'Hagiography and Recension History: The Case of Mīrā's Padas in Nāgrīdās's Pada-prasanga-mālā', in Monika Horstmann (ed.), *Bhakti Literature in Current Research, 2001–2003* (Delhi: Manohar, forthcoming).

———, *In Praise of Holy Men: Hagiographic Poems by and about Harirām Vyās* (Groningen: Egbert Forsten, 2002).

———, *Kṛṣṇa's Round Dance Reconsidered: Harirām Vyās's Hindī 'Rāspañcādhyāyī'* (Richmond, Surrey: Curzon Press, 1996).

———, 'Rāṭhauṛī Mīrā: Two Neglected Rāṭhauṛ Connections of Mīrā: Jaimal Meṛtīyo and Nāgrīdās', in Nancy M. Martin (ed.), *Mirabai: Hindu Saint for a Global World,* forthcoming.

Peterson, Indira V., *Poems to Śiva* (Princeton: Princeton University Press, 1989).

Pinch, William R., 'History, Devotion, and the Search for Nabhadas of Galta', in Daud Ali (ed.), *Invoking the Past: The Uses of History in South Asia* (Delhi: Oxford University Press, 1999), pp. 367–99.

Pollet, Gilbert, 'Early Evidence on Tulsīdās and His Epic', *Orientalia Lovaniensia Periodica* 5 (1974), pp. 153–62.

———, 'Eight Manuscripts of the Hindī *Bhaktamāla* in England', *Orientalia Lovaniensia Periodica* 1 (1970), pp. 203–22.

———, 'The Mediaeval Vaiṣṇava Miracles as Recorded in the Hindi "Bhakta Māla"', *Le Muséon* 80 (1976), pp. 475–87.

Polo, Marco, *The Travels*, trans. Robert Latham (Harmondsworth: Penguin Books, 1958).

Prabhāt, C. L., *Mīrā: Jīvan aur Kāvya* (Jodhpur: Rājasthānī Granthāgār, 1999).

———, *Mīrāṅbāī (Śodh Prabandh)* (Bombay: Hindī Granth Ratnākar, 1965).

Priyādās, *Bhaktirasabodhinī*, See Nābhādās.

Rākeśagupta, *Studies in Nāyaka-Nāyikā-Bheda* (Aligarh: Granthāyan, 1967).

Raghavan, V., *The Great Integrators: The Singer-Saints of India* (New Delhi: Publications Department, Government of India, 1966).

Raheja, Gloria Goodwin and Ann Grodzins Gold, *Listen to the Heron's Words: Reimagining Gender and Kinship in North India* (Berkeley: University of California Press, 1994).

Ram Lakhan, Interview, Banaras, 19 August 1985.

Ramanujan, A. K., *Hymns for the Drowning: Poems for Viṣṇu by Nammāḻvār* (Princeton: Princeton University Press, 1981).

———, 'On Women Saints', in J. S. Hawley and D. M. Wulff (eds), *The Divine Consort: Rādhā and the Goddesses of India* (Berkeley: Berkeley Religious Studies Series and Delhi: Motilal Banarsidass, 1982), pp. 316–24.

———, *Speaking of Śiva* (Baltimore: Penguin Books, 1973).

'Ratnākar', Jagannāth Dās, Nandadulāre Vājpeyī et al., *Sūrsāgar* (Varanasi: Kāśī Nāgarīpracāriṇī Sabhā, 1972 and 1976 [originally 1948]).

Rizvi, Dolly, 'Kabir: The Mystic Who Tried to Bring the Hindus and the Muslims Together', *Amar Chitra Katha*, no. 55 (Bombay: India Book House Education Trust, n.d.).

Roy, Asim, *The Islamic Syncretistic Tradition in Bengal* (Princeton: Princeton University Press, 1983).

(anon.), *Sadhu Vaswani Mission and its Activities* (Poona: Sadhu Vaswani Mission, n.d.).

Sahgal, Manmohan, Commentary on the *Japjī* in *Śrī Gurū Granth Sāhib* (Lucknow: Bhuvan Bāṇī Trust, 1978).

———, *Panjāb meṅ Racit 'Sudāmā-Carit' Kāvya* (Delhi: Vāṇī Prakāśan, 1978).

Sangari, Kumkum, 'Mirabai and the Spiritual Economy of *Bhakti*', *Economic and Political Weekly*, special articles (7 and 14 July 1990), pp. 1464–75 and 1537–52.

Santbānī Saṅgrah (Allahabad: Belvedere Press, 1915).

Saraswat, Rawatmal and Dinanath Khatri, *Catalogue of the Rajasthani Manuscripts in the Anup Sanskrit Library* (Bikaner: Maharaja of Bikaner, 1947).

Sarda, Har Bilas, *Maharana Sāngā, the Hindupat* (Ajmer: Scottish Mission Industries Company, 1918).

Śarmā, Harbanślāl, *Sūr aur unkā Sāhitya* (Aligarh: Bhārat Prakāśan Mandir, 1971).

Śarmā, Harinārāyaṇ, *Mīrā Bṛhatpadāvalī*, vol. 1 (Jodhpur: Rajasthan Oriental Research Institute, 1968).

Śarmā, Kailāś Candra, *Bhaktamāl aur Hindī Kāvya meṅ unkī Paramparā* (Rohtak: Manthan Publication, 1983).

Śarmā, Munśīrām, *Sūrdās kā Kāvya-Vaibhav* (Kanpur: Gratham, 1971).

Śāstrī, Kaṇṭhamaṇi, *Aṣṭaschāp kī Vārtā* (Kankarauli: Vidyā-Vibhāg, 1952).

Śāstrī, Udayśāṃkar, 'Sūrsāgar kī Sāmagrī kā Saṅkalan aur uskā Saṃpādan', *Bhāratīya Sāhitya* 17:1–2 (1972), pp. 73–101

Śāstrī, Ved Prakāś, *Srīmadhāgavat aur Sūrsāgar kā Vārṇya Viṣay kā Tulnātmak Adhyayan* (Agra: Sarasvatī Pustak Sadan, 1969).

Schleiermacher, Friedrich, *Über die Religion: Reden an die Gebildeten unter ihrer Verächtern* (Berlin: G. Reimer, 1831).

Schomer, Karine, 'Kabir in the *Gurū Granth Sāhib*: An Exploratory Essay', in Mark Juergensmeyer and N. Gerald Barrier (eds), *Sikh Studies: Perspectives on a Changing Tradition* (Berkeley: Graduate Theological Union, 1979), pp. 75–86.

Schomer, Karine and W. H. McLeod (eds), *The Sants: Studies in a Devotional Tradition of India* (Berkeley: Berkeley Religious Studies Series; Delhi: Motilal Banarsidass, 1987).

Śekhāvat, Kalyāṇsiṁh, *Mīrāṅ-Bṛhatpadāvalī* (Jodhpur: Rajasthan Oriental Research Institute, 1975).

———, *Mīrāṅbāī kā Jīvanvṛtt evaṃ Kāvya* (Jodhpur: Hindī Sāhitya Mandir, 1974).

Selby, Martha Ann, 'Like a Pot Brimming with Oil: The Care and Feeding of the Pregnant Body in Sanskrit Ayurvedic Texts', Dharam Hinduja Indic Research Center, Columbia University, 12 March 1998.

Sen, Kshitimohan, *Kabīr ke Pad*, 4 vols. (Shantiniketan: Vishwa Bharati, 1910–11).

Sen, Sukumar, *A History of Bengali Literature* (New Delhi: Sahitya Academy, 1971).

Shah, Priyabala, *A Descriptive Catalogue of Sanskrit Manuscripts* [*Gujarat Vidya Sabha Collection*] (Ahmedabad: Gujarat Vidya Sabha, 1964).

Sharma, Priyavrat (ed. and trans.), *Caraka-Saṃhitā*, vol. 1 (Varanasi: Chaukhambha Orientalia, 1981).

Shulman, David, 'From Author to Non-Author in Tamil Literary Legend', *Journal of the Institute of Asian Studies* 10:2 (1993), pp. 1–23.

Siṃh, Jayadev and Vasudev Siṃh, *Kabīr Vāṅmay*, vol. 3: *Śabad* (Varanasi: Viśvavidyālay Prakāśan, 1981).

Singer, Milton, 'The Rādhā-Krishna *Bhajanas* of Madras City', in Milton Singer (ed.), *Krishna: Myths, Rites, and Attitudes* (Chicago: University of Chicago Press, 1971 [originally, 1966]), pp. 90–138.

Singh, Adhar, *Syntax of Apabhraṁśa* (Calcutta: Simant Publications, 1980).

Singh, Giani Bachittar, *Planned Attack on Aad Sri Guru Granth Sahib: Academics or Blasphemy* (Chandigarh: International Centre of Sikh Studies, 1994).

Singh, Bahadur, 'Problems of Authenticity in the Kabīr Texts', in Monika Horstmann (ed.), *Images of Kabīr* (Delhi: Manohar, 2002), pp. 191–8.

Singh, Pashaura, 'The Text and Meaning of the *Adi Granth*' (PhD diss., University of Toronto, 1991).

Singh, Pritam, 'Bhāī Banno's Copy of the Sikh Scripture', in Monika Thiel-Horstmann (ed.), *Bhakti in Current Research 1979–1982* (Berlin: Dietrich Reiner Verlag, 1983).

Singh, Shukdev, Interview, Banaras, 12 November 2003.

Smith, Vincent A., *Akbar, the Great Mogul* (Delhi: S. Chand, 1958).

———, *Asoka, the Buddhist Emperor of India* (New Delhi: Asian Educational Resources, 1997 [originally 1901]).

Smith, Wilfred Cantwell, 'The Crystallization of Religious Communities in Mughal India', in Mojtaba Minori and Ijar Afshar (eds), *Yadname-ye Irani-ye Minorsky* (Tehran: Tehran University, 1969), pp. 1–24.

———, 'A Human View of Truth', *SR: Sciences Religieuses / Studies in Religion*, 1 (1971), pp. 6–24.

———, *The Meaning and End of Religion* (New York: Macmillan, 1962).

———, *What is Scripture?: A Comparative Approach* (Minneapolis: Fortress Press, 1993).

Snell, Rupert, 'Devotion Rewarded: The *Sudāmā-carit* of Narottamdās', in Christopher Shackle and Rupert Snell (eds), *The Indian Narrative: Perspectives and Patterns* (Wiesbaden: Otto Harrassowitz, 1992), pp. 173–94.

———, *The Eight-four Hymns of Hita Harivaṃśa, An Edition of the Caurāsī-pada* (Delhi: Motilal Banarsidass, 1990).

Śukla, Rāmcandra, *Hindī Sāhitya kā Itihās: Saṃśodhit evam Pravardhit Saṃskaraṇ* (Allahabad: A to Zed Publishing, 2001 [originally Benares, 1929]).

Śukla, Viśvanāth, *Hindī Kṛṣṇa Bhakti Kāvya par Śrīmadbhāgavat kā Prabhāv* (Aligarh: Bhārat Prakāśan Mandir 1966).

Sukul, Lalitprasād, *Mīrāṅ Smṛti Granth* (Calcutta: Bāṅgīya Hindī Pariṣad, 1949).

Taft, Frances, 'The Elusive Historical Mirabai: A Note', in Lawrence A. Babb, Varsha Joshi, and Michael Meister (eds), *Multiple Histories: Culture and Society in the Study of Rajasthan* (Jaipur: Rawat Publications, 2002), pp. 313–35.

Tagore, Rabindranath, assisted by Evelyn Underhill, *Songs of Kabir* (New Delhi: Cosmo Publications, 1985 [originally 1917]).

Thiel-Horstmann, Monika. See Horstmann, Monika.

Tivārī, Bhagavāndās, *Mīrāṅ kī Bhakti aur unkī Kāvya-Sadhanā kā Anuśīlan.* (Allahabad: Sāhitya Bhavan, 1974).

Tivārī, Bhagavāndās (ed.), *Mīrāṅ kī Prāmāṇik Padāvalī* (Allahabad: Sāhitya Bhavan, 1974).

Tivārī, Pārasnāth, *Kabīr Granthāvalī* (Allahabad: Allahabad University, 1961).

Tivārī, Śaśi, *Sūr ke Kṛṣṇa: Ek Anuśīlan* (Hyderabad: Milind Prakāśan, 1969).

Tod, James, *Annals and Antiquities of Rajasthan*, (Delhi: Motilal Banarasidass, 1971 [originally 1829, 1832]).

Tripāthī, Karuṇāpati (ed.), *Kāvya Saṅgrah*, vol. 1 (Allahabad: Hindī Sāhitya Sammelan, 1966).

Tulpule, S. G., *Classical Marāṭhī Literature from the Beginning to A.D. 1818* (Wiesbaden: Otto Harrassowitz, 1979).

Upadhyaya, K. N., *Guru Ravidas: Life and Teachings* (Beas, Punjab: Radha Soami Satsang, Beas, 1982).

Usāḥaṇ, Devindar Siṃh, *Prem Ambodh* (Patiala: Panjabi University Publication Bureau, 1989).

Vallabhācārya, 'Sannyāsanirṇaya', in *Kṛṣṇaṣodaśagranthāḥ* (Bombay: Nirnaya Sagara Press, n.d.).

Varmā, Dhīrendra, *Sūrsāgar-Sār Saṭīk* (Allahabad: Sāhitya Bhavan, 1972).

Varmā, Vrajeśvar, *Sūr-Mimāṁsā* (New Delhi: Oriental Book Depot, n.d.).
Vaswani, T. L., *The Call of Mira Education* (Poona: Mira, n.d.).
———, *Saint Mira* (Poona: St. Mira's English Medium School, n.d.).
Vaudeville, Charlotte, *Au Cabaret de l'Amour* (Paris: Gallimard, 1959).
———, *Les Chansons des douze mois dans les littératures Indoaryennes* (Pondicherry: Institut Français d'Indologie, 1965), translated by C. Vaudeville as *Bārahmāsā in Indian Literatures* (Delhi: Motilal Banarsidass, 1986).
———, *Étude sur les sources et la composition du Rāmāyaṇa de Tulsī Dās* (Paris: Librairie d'Amérique et d'Orient, 1955).
———, 'The Govardhan Myth in Northern India', *Indo-lranian Journal* 22 (1980), pp. 1–45.
———, *Kabīr* (Oxford: Clarendon Press, 1974).
———, *Kabīr Granthāvalī (Dohā)* (Pondicherry: Institut Français d'Indologie, 1957).
———, 'Krishna Gopāla, Rādhā, and the Great Goddess', in J. S. Hawley and D. M. Wulff (eds), *The Divine Consort: Rādhā and the Goddesses of India* (Berkeley: Berkeley Religious Studies Series and Delhi: Motilal Banarsidass, 1982).
———, *Pastorales par Soûr-Dâs* (Paris: Gallimard, 1971).
———, '*Sant Mat*: Santism as the Universal Path to Sanctity', in Karine Schomer and W. H. McLeod (eds), *The Sants: Studies in a Devotional Tradition in India* (Berkeley: Berkeley Religious Studies Series; Delhi: Motilal Banarsidass, 1987), pp. 21–40.
———, *A Weaver Named Kabir* (Delhi: Oxford University Press, 1993).
Vora, Vidhatri A. (ed.), *A Descriptive Catalog of Gujarati, Hindi, and Marathi Manuscripts of B.J. Institute Museum* (Ahmedabad: B.J. Institute of Learning and Research, 1987).
White, Charles S. J., *The Caurāsī Pad of Śrī Hit Harivaṃś* (Honolulu: University of Hawaii Press, 1977).
White, David Gordon, *The Alchemical Body: Siddha Traditions in Medieval India* (Chicago: University of Chicago Press, 1996).
Widdess, Richard, 'Dhrupad as a Musical Tradition', *Journal of Vaiṣṇava Studies* 3:1 (1994), pp. 61–82.
Wimsatt, W. K. and Monroe C. Beardsley, *The Verbal Icon: Studies in the Meaning of Poetry* (Lexington: University Press of Kentucky, 1964).
Womack, Julie, 'Ravidas and the Chamars of Banaras', undergraduate essay, University of Wisconsin, 1983.
Wulff, Donna M., *Drama as a Mode of Religious Realization* (Chico, CA: Scholars Press, 1984).
———, 'Rādhā's Audacity in *kīrtan* Performances and Women's Status in Greater Bengal', in Karen King and Karen Jo Torjesen (eds), *Women and Goddess Traditions* (Minneapolis: Fortress Press, 1995), pp. 64–83.

Young, Katherine, 'Beloved Places (*Ukantaruḷiṉanilaṅkal*): The Correlation of Topography and Theology in the Śrīvaiṣṇava Tradition of South India' (PhD diss., McGill University, 1978).

———, 'One Stage, Three Acts: The Life-Drama of a Traditional Hindu Woman', paper presented to the American Academy of Religion, New York, November, 1979.

Zvabilel, Dusan, *Bengali Literature* (Wiesbaden: Otto Harrassowitz, 1976).

Zvelebil, Kamil, *Tamil Literature* (Wiesbaden: Otto Harrassowitz, 1974).

Zysk, Kenneth G., *Asceticism and Healing in Ancient India* (New York: Oxford University Press, 1991).

Index